IMPORTANT

HERE IS YOUR REGISTRATION CO
YOUR PREMIUM McGRAW-HILL O

GW01019465

For key premium online resources you need THIS CODE to gain access. Once the code is entered, you will be able to use the Web resources for the length of your course.

If your course is using **WebCT** or **Blackboard**, you'll be able to use this code to access the McGraw-Hill content within your instructor's online course.

Access is provided if you have purchased a new book. If the registration code is missing from this book, the registration screen on our Website, and within your WebCT or Blackboard course, will tell you how to obtain your new code.

Registering for McGraw-Hill Online Resources

To gain access to your McGraw-Hill web resources simply follow the steps below:

1. USE YOUR WEB BROWSER TO GO TO: **www.mhhe.com/cohoon**
2. CLICK ON **FIRST TIME USER**.
3. ENTER THE REGISTRATION CODE* PRINTED ON THE TEAR-OFF BOOKMARK ON THE RIGHT.
4. AFTER YOU HAVE ENTERED YOUR REGISTRATION CODE, CLICK **REGISTER**.
5. FOLLOW THE INSTRUCTIONS TO SET-UP YOUR PERSONAL UserID AND PASSWORD.
6. WRITE YOUR UserID AND PASSWORD DOWN FOR FUTURE REFERENCE. KEEP IT IN A SAFE PLACE.

TO GAIN ACCESS to the McGraw-Hill content in your instructor's **WebCT** or **Blackboard** course simply log in to the course with the UserID and Password provided by your instructor. Enter the registration code exactly as it appears in the box to the right when prompted by the system. You will only need to use the code the first time you click on McGraw-Hill content.

Thank you, and welcome to your McGraw-Hill online Resources!

REGISTRATION CODE

reiterated-56738586

* YOUR REGISTRATION CODE CAN BE USED ONLY ONCE TO ESTABLISH ACCESS. IT IS NOT TRANSFERABLE.

0-07-292008-4 T/A COHOON: JAVA PROGRAM DESIGN

Java
Program
Design

James P. Cohoon
University of Virginia

Jack W. Davidson
University of Virginia

Mc Graw Hill **Higher Education**

Boston   Burr Ridge, IL   Dubuque, IA   Madison, WI   New York   San Francisco   St. Louis
Bangkok   Bogotá   Caracas   Kuala Lumpur   Lisbon   London   Madrid   Mexico City
Milan   Montreal   New Delhi   Santiago   Seoul   Singapore   Sydney   Taipei   Toronto

Higher Education

JAVA PROGRAM DESIGN

Published by McGraw-Hill, a business unit of The McGraw-Hill Companies, Inc., 1221 Avenue of the Americas, New York, NY 10020. Copyright © 2004 by The McGraw-Hill Companies, Inc. All rights reserved. No part of this publication may be reproduced or distributed in any form or by any means, or stored in a database or retrieval system, without the prior written consent of The McGraw-Hill Companies, Inc., including, but not limited to, in any network or other electronic storage or transmission, or broadcast for distance learning.

Some ancillaries, including electronic and print components, may not be available to customers outside the United States.

This book is printed on acid-free paper.

International   1 2 3 4 5 6 7 8 9 0 VNH/VNH 0 9 8 7 6 5 4 3
Domestic   1 2 3 4 5 6 7 8 9 0 VNH/VNH 0 9 8 7 6 5 4 3

ISBN 0–07–235447–X
ISBN 0–07–119255–7 (ISE)

Publisher: *Elizabeth A. Jones*
Sponsoring editor: *Kelly Lowery*
Developmental editor: *Melinda Dougharty*
Marketing manager: *Dawn R. Bercier*
Senior project manager: *Kay J. Brimeyer*
Senior production supervisor: *Laura Fuller*
Senior media project manager: *Stacy A. Patch*
Senior media technology producer: *Phillip Meek*
Senior designer: *David W. Hash*
Cover/interior designer: *Rokusek Design*
Lead photo research coordinator: *Carrie K. Burger*
Photo research: *Mary Reeg*
Supplement producer: *Brenda A. Ernzen*
Typeface: *10/13 Times Roman*
Printer: *Von Hoffmann Corporation*

Library of Congress Cataloging-in-Publication Data

Cohoon, James P.
    Java program design / James P. Cohoon, Jack W. Davidson. — 1st ed.
        p.   cm.
    Includes index.
    ISBN 0–07–235447–X — ISBN 0–07–119255–7 (ISE)
    1. Java (Computer program language). I. Davidson, Jack W. (Jack Winfred). II. Title.

    QA76.73.J38C656   2004
    005.13′3—dc21   2003053975
                                                            CIP

INTERNATIONAL EDITION ISBN 0–07–119255–7
Copyright © 2004. Exclusive rights by The McGraw-Hill Companies, Inc., for manufacture and export. This book cannot be re-exported from the country to which it is sold by McGraw-Hill. The International Edition is not available in North America.

www.mhhe.com

To Audrey and Joanne; Emily, Genevieve, Hannah, JJ, and Zachary; Kathleen, Nina, and Terry; James and Patricia; Thomas and Lavaughn, Eleanor; James and Gertrude

Preface

Java is now a very appropriate choice for introductory programming courses. The reasons are many. The use of the Internet continues its explosive growth. Web-ready application programs are becoming the dominant software model, and Java is *the* programming language for the Internet. Java also offers maturing software development tools, numerous packages for application programming of all types including multi-threaded, advanced graphical user interfaces, and portability with its architecture-neutral design. The importance of security and robustness has taken on new meaning in recent years, and Java's support of these concerns is integral throughout its design. Being object-oriented, makes Java a good pedagogical vehicle for modern software engineering and programming concepts.

CONTEXT

Since the early 1990s, with the strong support of the National Science Foundation, our department has developed, refined, and extended a new computer science curriculum. In the examination of our curriculum and those of peer schools, several strategic principles regularly arise.

- Use a programming language with broad acceptance outside the classroom.
- Use modern software development tools.
- Encourage teamwork.
- Develop systems according to software engineering principles.
- Encourage the reuse of existing libraries and tools.
- Build software with graphical user interfaces to do input and output.
- Use a pedagogy and examples that appeal to a diverse audience.

The development of this text and its supplementary materials has been designed to provide support for the advancement of these principles.

Most of the important concepts and problems in computer science cannot be appreciated unless one has a good understanding of what a program is and how to write one. Unfortunately, learning to program is difficult. Like writing well, programming well takes years of practice. Teaching programming is very similar in many respects to teaching writing.

Students are taught writing by reading examples of good prose and by repeated writing exercises where they learn how to organize their ideas so they can be presented most effectively. As students develop their skills, they progress from writing and editing a paragraph or two, to creating larger pieces of prose, such as essays, short stories, and reports.

Our approach to teaching program design is similar to teaching writing. Throughout the text, we present and discuss many examples of both good and bad programming. Self-check and programming exercises give students the opportunity to practice designing, organizing, and writing code. In addition, we offer examples that facilitate learning the practical skill of modifying existing code. This introduction is done through the use of code that is specifically designed to be modified by the student.

We have found this approach to be effective because it compels students to be active participants—they must read and understand the provided code. To support this effort, the code used in this text is available electronically at our website.

GOALS OF THE TEXT

This book is targeted for a first programming course, and it has been designed to be appropriate for people from all disciplines. We assume no prior programming skills and use mathematics and science at a level appropriate to first-year college students.

The primary goals of the text are to

- Introduce students to the Java programming language;
- Present and encourage the use of the object-oriented paradigm;
- Demonstrate effective problem-solving techniques;
- Engage the student with real-world examples;
- Teach students software-engineering design concepts;
- Introduce students to Java's core and graphical libraries;
- Give students practice organizing and writing code;
- Teach students the practical skill of modifying existing code;
- Offer instructive examples of good and bad programming;
- Provide effective coverage of testing and debugging.

WHAT IS DIFFERENT AND WHY

The text provides in-depth coverage of all materials that an introductory course would need, introduces much of the remaining material generally covered in follow-on courses, and gives pointers to the rest. The breadth and the arrangement of chapters provides flexibility for the instructor in what and when topics are introduced. The chapter coverage and extensive appendices enable advanced learners to go further, and makes the book valuable as a reference source.

Some of the things that distinguish our book include the following:

- *Gentle introduction to objects*: The book implements what we call the "objects right" approach. Teaching the object-oriented paradigm in introductory courses for the last ten-plus years has shown us that Java can be successfully introduced to beginning programmers. We know that delaying user-defined classes to the end of a course inhibits the ability of students to integrate the central pillar of the object-oriented programming paradigm and forces superficial coverage of other important object-oriented programming principles. Therefore, our presentation introduces objects early— or as we prefer, right. Students begin using objects from standard packages right from the beginning. They quickly develop meaningful programs for interesting problems. Using this solid introduction, we then present the *basics* of class and object-oriented design. After exploring control structures, we present a deeper look at methods, classes, and object-oriented design.

- *Focus on problem solving*: One of the biggest obstacles faced by many beginning students is not knowing basic problem-solving techniques. The text addresses this issue by introducing basic problem-solving skills in Chapter 1 and then applying the new concepts in each chapter to problems selected for their appeal to a variety of audiences. Students are first walked through examples that illustrate effective problem solving, and then they are given a chance to tackle similar problems on their own.

- *Introduction to software-engineering design concepts*: Software-engineering design concepts are introduced via problem studies and software projects. Besides numerous small examples, each chapter considers one or more problems in detail. As appropriate, there are object-oriented analysis and design, and algorithm development to realize the design.

- *Coverage of testing and debugging*: An important skill for programmers is how to test and debug the programs they design and implement. Chapter 13 introduces important software engineering concepts and practices with regard to testing and debugging. The chapter discusses testing techniques such as unit testing, integration testing, and code inspections. The sections on debugging focus on teaching students how to use the scientific method to find errors. The chapter also discusses common errors of beginning programmers and how to recognize them. After control structures have been introduced, this chapter material can be taught whenever an instructor deems it appropriate.

- *Engaging and inclusive examples*: Students learn from interesting situations they might encounter in real life. Diverse case studies and programming projects are drawn from topics as varied as physical fitness, spam, medical diagnosis, statistical analysis, psychological typing, data visualization, graphs, entertainment, and animation. By offering this variety of examples, the text demonstrates how programmers can participate and contribute to our daily lives.

- *Exclusive use of standard Java classes*: The text uses only standard Java classes in introducing Java programming concepts. In particular, there are no author-written classes for acquiring input. Instead standard classes and techniques are presented in a way that makes sense to beginning programmers.

- *Lab manual*: A printed lab manual accompanies the text for schools that use laboratories in their introductory courses. The lab material offers a hands-on experience that reinforces Java programming concepts and skills.

- *Programming and style tips*: Besides explaining Java and object-oriented programming, the text also provides advice on how to be a better and more knowledgeable programmer and designer. There are important tips on such topics as avoiding common programming errors, writing readable code, and following software engineering practices.

- *Self-test, exercises, and software projects*: Every chapter provides a self-test exercise section with answers to enable students to evaluate their skills on important concepts. The text also provide several hundred exercises with solutions are available to instructors through the publisher. Once the basics of Java are introduced in Chapter 2, that chapter and all successive chapters supply a programming project that exercises chapter concepts.

- *Reference appendices*: Appendices C, D, and E provide nearly two hundred pages of description of the standard Java APIs. The coverage makes the text a handy reference manual well after the course completes.

CHAPTER OVERVIEW AND FEATURES

Introduction

Each chapter begins with a brief introduction designed to focus the student's attention and prepare them for the material to be covered. We emphasize both the immediate significance of the topic as well as its place in the broader programming context.

Objectives

A list of chapter objectives follows the introduction and provides a set of specific learning goals for the student. This list enables students to measure their progress as they move through chapter material and lets them evaluate their level of comprehension at the end. It also serves as a guide for instructors to use when preparing tests and quizzes.

Icons and aside boxes

Icons and shaded boxes indicate warnings, style tips, advanced material, and information pertaining to the Java language itself.

Indicates a warning about programming. Often these are tips on how to avoid common programming errors.

Indicates that the associated material is related to programming style.

Indicates that the associated material is concerned with the Java programming language itself.

Indicates programming tips or material that presents a more detailed discussion or a sidebar to the current topic.

Full-color design

An inviting, full-color design highlights related material, indicates section breaks, calls out special features, and makes key information easy to reference.

(a) Chapter text

(b) Case study

(c) End of chapter material   (d) Reference appendix

Code formatting

Specially formatted code listings make sections of code easy to find and reference. Each complete listing is numbered according to its place in the chapter, separated from related material by coloring and line numbering. Partial sections of code are clearly set off from surrounding text and are generously annotated with easy-to-spot author comments.

UML diagrams

The use of UML diagrams helps clarify relationships between classes while at the same time familiarizing students with this widely used system of notation.

Case studies

Each chapter includes multiple case studies designed to teach effective problem-solving skills and to reinforce object-oriented programming and software engineering design concepts. The specific learning objective is highlighted at the beginning of each case study, and problem-solving steps are highlighted with special icons. The case studies are colored to distinguish them from other chapter material. Coverage of the case studies is optional; they apply chapter concepts rather than introducing new concepts.

End-of-chapter reviews

Each chapter ends with a thorough, point-by-point summary of the chapter's major ideas. The end of chapter materials are color highlighted for easy access.

Self-tests

Each chapter includes a self-test with answers supplied at the end of the chapter. These self-check sections are designed to help students evaluate whether they have mastered the chapter objectives and to reinforce the key ideas of the chapter.

Programming projects

Except for Chapter 1, which provides background material, each chapter has at least one interesting programming case study presented in a manner that makes it suitable for use as a class assignment. Programming case studies include determining your exercise training zone; harvesting e-mail addresses; medical diagnosis; automobile loan calculator; and an aquarium simulation.

Exercises

An exercise section at the end of each chapter offers a variety of problems requiring a range of efforts levels.

CHAPTER SUMMARIES

- *Chapter 1: Background*—computer organization; software; software engineering principles; object-oriented software development; problem solving.
- *Chapter 2: Java basics*—program organization; method `main()`; commenting and whitespace; classes, keywords, identifiers, and naming conventions; methods; program execution; SDK; constants; variables; operations; primitive types; operators; precedence; interactive programs; primitive variable assignment.
- *Chapter 3: Using objects*—`String`; reference variables; `null`; inserting, extracting, and concatenating strings; reference assignment; `String` methods.
- *Chapter 4: Being classy*—introduces user-defined classes; instance variables; constructors; instance methods; inspectors; mutators; facilitators; simple graphics.
- *Chapter 5: Decisions*—boolean algebra and truth tables; logical expressions; **boolean** type; Boolean equality and ordering operators; testing floating-point values for equality; operator precedence; short-circuit evaluation; **if** statement; **if-else** statement; string and character testing; sorting; **switch** statement.
- *Chapter 6: Iteration*—**while** statement; simple string and character processing; **for** statement; index variable scope; **do-while** statement.
- *Graphics Interlude: GUI–based programming*—graphical user interfaces; `swing`; `awt`; and event-based programming
- *Chapter 7: Programming with methods and classes*—parameter passing; invocation and flow of control; class variables; scope; local scope; name reuse; overloading; overriding; `equals()`; `toString()`; `clone()`.
- *Chapter 8: Arrays and collections*—one-dimensional arrays; definitions; element access and manipulation; explicit initialization; constant arrays; members; array processing; methods; program parameters; sorting; searching; multidimensional arrays; matrices; collections framework; `ArrayList`; collections algorithms.
- *Chapter 9: Inheritance and polymorphism*—object-oriented design; reuse; base class; derived class; single inheritance; **super**; is-a, has-a, and uses-a relationships; controlling inheritance; default, **protected**, and **private** members; polymorphism; abstract base class; **interface** hierarchies.
- *Graphics Interlude: GUI-based programming*—case studies in the design and implementation of graphical user interfaces for personality typing and the smiley guessing game.

- *Chapter 10: Exceptions*—abnormal event; exceptions; throwing; trying; catching; exception handlers; **finally**; stream specialization.

- *Chapter 11: Recursive problem solving*—recursive functions, sorting, searching, visualization.

- *Chapter 12: Threads*—multiple independent flows of control; processes; threads; scheduling and repeating threads; `Timer`; `TimerTask`; `Thread`; `Date`; `Calendar`; `JOptionPane`; sleeping; animation; systems software.

- *Chapter 13: Testing and debugging*—software development; code reviews; black-box and white-box testing; inspections; test harness; statement coverage; unit, integration testing, and system testing; regression testing; boundary conditions; path coverage; debugging.

- *Appendix A: Tables and operators*—Unicode character set; reserved words; operators and precedence.

- *Appendix B: Number representation*—binary numbers; decimal numbers; two's compliment; conversions.

- *Appendix C: Applets*—applet programming.

- *Appendix D: Standard Java packages*—`java.io`; `java.lang`; `java.math`; `java.net`; `java.text`; `java.util`.

- *Appendix E: Standard Java graphical packages*—`java.applet`, `java.awt`, and `javax.swing`.

GRAPHICS INTERLUDES

From personal observations and from conversations and communications with colleagues, we recognize that not all introductory programming courses are able to introduce graphical user interfaces (GUIs). The time may not be available to introduce the `swing` API and event-driven programming. Therefore, we have coalesced this material into two *Graphical Interludes*, and their coverage is optional. However, for instructors who want to stress this material, the GUI coverage can be introduced after the class concepts of Chapter 4 are presented.

We do distinguish between graphical user interfaces and creating graphical images. The Java standard APIs make it quite simple to display rectangles, lines, circles, ovals, triangles, and polygons. Their display is almost as easy as displaying text to a console window. Examples in other chapters make independent use of these Java features. These examples are also for the most part optional. However, it is our experience that students enjoy creating graphical imagery and that the concepts of object-oriented programming are easier to understand when examples have a visual nature.

USING THIS BOOK

This text has more material than can be covered in a single course. The extra coverage was deliberate—it enables instructors to select their topics on programming and software development.

The book has been designed for teaching flexibility. For example, if instructors desire to delay the introduction of classes, they first can cover most of the control structure materials (Sections 5.1–5.9 and Sections 6.1–6.5). Similarly, if an instructor desires to introduce arrays before classes, the fundamental array material (Sections 8.1–8.3 and Section 8.7) can proceed the discussion of classes. Also except for the example in Section 9.2, the discussion of inheritance can precede the coverage of arrays.

The testing and debugging material of Chapter 13 can be covered anytime after classes and arrays have been introduced.

We use the following layout for our course.

Week	Topic	Readings
1	Computing and object-oriented design	Chapter 1
2	Programming fundamentals	Chapter 2
3	Object manipulation	Chapter 3 (Sections 3.1–3.5)
4	Class basics	Chapter 4
4–5	Conditional statements	Chapter 5 (Sections 5.1–5.7, 5.10)
5–6	Iteration statements	Chapter 6 (Sections 6.1–6.5)
7	Graphical user interfaces	Graphics Interlude: I
8–9	Classes	Chapter 7
10–11	Arrays and lists	Chapter 8
12–13	Inheritance and polymorphism	Chapter 9
13	Exceptions	Chapter 10 (Section 10.1)
14	Testing and debugging	Chapter 13 (Sections 13.1–13.2)

SUPPLEMENTARY MATERIALS

The publisher website at www.javaprogramprogramdesign.com offers the source code and data files for all listings in the text. Other materials include a complete set of slides, which are available in PowerPoint and PDF formats, and introductions to the various Java programming IDEs. Other educational supplements are available at our class web site http://www.cs.virginia.edu/javaprogramdesign.

THE AUTHORS

Jim Cohoon is a professor in the computer science department at the University of Virginia and is a former member of the technical staff at AT&T Bell Laboratories. He joined the faculty after receiving his Ph.D. from the University of Minnesota. He has been nominated twice by his department for the university's best-teaching award. In 1994, Professor Cohoon was awarded a Fulbright Fellowship to Germany, where he lectured on object-oriented programming and software engineering. Professor Cohoon's research interests include algorithms, computer-aided design of electronic systems, optimization strategies, and computer science education. He is the author of more than 70 papers in these fields. He is a member of the Association of Computing Machinery (ACM), the ACM Special Interest Group on Design Automation (SIGDA), the ACM Special Interest Group on Computer Science Education (SIGCSE), the Institute of Electrical and Electronics Engineers (IEEE), and the IEEE Circuits and Systems Society. He is a member of ACM Council, SIG Governing Board Executive Committee, former member of ACM Publications Board, and is past chair of SIGDA. He can be reached at cohoon@virginia.edu. His Web home page is http://www.cs.virginia.edu/cohoon.

Jack Davidson is also a professor in the computer science department at the University of Virginia. He joined the faculty after receiving his Ph.D. from the University of Arizona. Professor Davidson has received NCR's Faculty Innovation Award for innovation in teaching. Professor Davidson's research interests include compilers, computer architecture, systems software, and computer science education. He is the author of more than 80 papers in these fields. He is a member of the ACM, the ACM Special Interest Group on Programming Languages (SIGPLAN), the ACM Special Interest Group on Computer Architecture (SIGARCH), SIGCSE, the IEEE, and the IEEE Computer Society. He served as an associate editor of *Transactions on Programming Languages and Systems*, ACM's flagship journal on programming languages and systems, from 1994 to 2000. He was chair of the 1998 Programming Language Design and Implementation Conference (PLDI '98) and program co-chair of the 2000 SIGPLAN Workshop on Languages, Compilers, and Tools for Embedded Systems (LCTES 2000). He can be reached at jwd@virginia.edu. His Web home page is http://www.cs.virginia.edu/~jwd.

DELVING FURTHER

The following are primary references on the Java language.

- Ken Arnold, James Gosling, and David Holmes, *The Java Programming Language*, Third Edition, Addison-Wesley Pub Co; ISBN: 0201704331, June 2000.
- Bill Joy (Editor), Guy Steele, James Gosling, and Gilad Bracha, *The Java Language Specification,* Second Edition, Addison-Wesley, ISBN: 0201310082, June 2000.

The following are good sources on the standard libraries and more-advanced object-oriented design, and program development.

- David M. Geary, *Graphic Java 1.2, Mastering the JFC: AWT,* Volume 1, Prentice Hall, ISBN: 0130796662; September 1998.
- David M. Geary, *Graphic Java 2,* Volume 2, *Swing*, Prentice Hall, ISBN: 0130796670, March 1999.
- Joshua Engel, *Programming for the Java Virtual Machine*, Addison-Wesley, ISBN: 0201309726, June 1999.

- Cay S. Horstmann and Gary Cornell, *Core Java 2,* Volume I, *Fundamentals*, Prentice Hall PTR, ISBN: 0130894680, December 2000.

- Cay S. Horstmann and Gary Cornell, *Core Java 2:* Volume II, *Advanced Features*, Prentice Hall, ISBN: 0130927384, December 2001.

- Matthew Robinson and Pavel A. Vorobiev, *Swing*, Manning Publications Company; ISBN: 1884777848, December 1999.

- Stephen A. Stelting and Olav Maassen, *Applied Java Patterns*, Prentice Hall; ISBN: 0130935387, December 2001.

- Sun Microsystems, *Java Look and Feel Design Guidelines: Advanced Topics,* Addison Wesley Professional; ISBN: 0201775824, December 2001.

- Al Vermeulen (Editor), Scott W. Ambler, Greg Bumgardner, Eldon Metz, Alan Vermeulen, Trevor Misfeldt, Jim Shur, and Patrick Thompson, *The Elements of Java Style*, Cambridge University Press; ISBN: 0521777682, January 2000.

- John Zukowski, *Java Collections*, APress; ISBN: 1893115925, April 2001.

ACKNOWLEDGMENTS

We thank the University of Virginia for providing an environment that made this book possible. In particular, we thank Jack Stankovic for his tireless efforts in leading the computer science department to national prominence. We also thank Jenna Cohoon, Joanne Cohoon, and Tom Horton for their comments. We thank Hannah Cohoon for her fish artwork and JJ Cohoon for his icon artwork.

We thank all of the people at McGraw-Hill for their efforts in making this edition a reality. In particular, we thank Betsy Jones, for her support and encouragement; Tom Cason for sage advice; Kay Brimeyer, for her behind-the-scenes product-management skills; David Hash, for leading the art and cover-design team; Pat Steele, for copyediting. and Dawn Bercier for her creative marketing ideas. Special thanks go to Kelly Lowery, our editor, for support, direction, and focus throughout this project; Melinda Dougharty, our developmental editor, for managing and synthesizing the reviewing process; and Mary Cahall for her organizational ability.

We thank the following testers, readers, and reviewers for their valuable comments and suggestions on this text:
A. Arokiasamy, Multimedia University of Malaysia
David Aspinall, University of Edinburgh
Ivan Bajic, San Diego State University
Dwight Barnett, Virginia Tech
David Bethelmy, Embry-Riddle Aeronautical University
Robert Biddle, Victoria University of Wellington
Elizabeth Boese, Colorado State University
Gene Boggess, Mississippi State University
Mike Buckley, University at Buffalo
Robert Burton, Brigham Young University
Judith Challinger, California State University, Chico

Errol Chopping, Charles Sturt University

Ilyas Cicekli, University of Central Florida

Charles Daly, Dublin City University

J. Greggory Dobbins, University of South Carolina

Stephen Fickas, University of Oregon

Jeffrey Forbes, Duke University

Gerald Gordon, DePaul University

Heng Aik Koan, National University of Singapore

Michael Huhns, University of South Carolina

Norm Jacobson, University of California, Irvine

Cerian Jones, Montana Tech

Cathy Key, University of Texas, San Antonio

Barry Lawson, University of Richmond

Evelyn Lulis, DePaul University

Blayne Mayfield, Oklahoma State University

Jim McElroy, California State University, Chico

Hugh McGuire, University of California, Santa Barbara

Keitha Murray, Iona College

Faye Navabi, Arizona State University

Richard Pattis, Carnegie Mellon

Hal Perkins, University of Washington

Pete Petersen, Texas A&M University

Vera Proulx, Northeastern University

Graham Roberts, Flinders University

Celia Schahczenski, Montana Tech

Carolyn Schauble, Colorado State University

Carol Scheftic, California Polytechnic State University, San Luis Obispo

Eric Schwabe, DePaul University

Mike Scott, University of Texas

Barbara Ann Sherman, University of Buffalo

Barry Soroka, California Polytechnic State University, Pomona

David Vineyard, Kettering University

We thank our spouses, Audrey and Joanne, and our children for their efforts, cooperation, and sacrifices in making this book happen.

Finally, we thank the users of this book. We welcome your comments, suggestions, and ideas for improving this material. Please write in care of the publisher, McGraw-Hill, or send electronic mail to cohoon@virginia.edu or jwd@virginia.edu.

J. P. C
J. W. D

Detailed table of contents

1 BACKGROUND

The Internet and computing revolution will provide excellent career opportunities and interesting challenges for years to come. The opportunities run the gamut from designing hardware and software to entrepreneurial activities such as marketing emerging technologies. The challenges include developing software capable of running on many different types of computers and developing programs with hundreds of thousands of lines of code whose correctness is critical (e.g., radiation therapy and online auction systems). To cope with such challenges—both big and small—most computing practitioners now use object-oriented design techniques.

In this chapter, we introduce basic computing and network terminology and the concepts behind object-oriented design. We also introduce Java, an object-oriented programming language that has played a fundamental role in the growth of the Internet. For example, with Java, you can develop interactive Web-based applications offering dynamic graphics and secure communication. Java provides an extensive collection of portable programming resources that enable the rapid development of many different types of applications (e.g., multimedia, e-commerce, and telecommunication). We end the chapter with a discussion of problem solving to help with your development of software solutions.

OBJECTIVES

- Introduce hardware and software terminology.
- Introduce high-level programming languages.
- Introduce Java programming, compilation, and execution.
- Introduce the basics of object-oriented design.
- Present useful problem-solving strategies.

1.1 INTRODUCTION

Traditionally programming texts begin with a program that displays the message "Hello, world." They do so because the features of such a program are simple enough to be explained readily and functional enough to make the discussion worthwhile. Our first Java program is different.

```java
// Authors: J. P. Cohoon and J. W. Davidson
// Purpose: display a quotation in a console window

public class DisplayForecast {

    // main(): application entry point
    public static void main(String[] args) {
        System.out.print("I think there is a world market for");
        System.out.println(" maybe five computers.");
        System.out.println("  Thomas Watson, IBM, 1943.");
    }
}
```

Instead of displaying the functional "Hello, world." our program displays a now humorous forecast by a former chairperson of IBM. The output of the program is

```
I think there is a world market for maybe five computers.
   Thomas Watson, IBM, 1943.
```

The differences between this book and the typical Java text come about because our goal is more ambitious than just introducing you to the Java language. *We want to teach you how to program effectively, and we want do so in an interesting manner.* Learning tends to be easier when the proper motivation is given. Our examples have been designed for their relevance and appeal to a wide variety of people. In fact, a caution raised by one reviewer was that the examples sometimes bordered on being too interesting.

So let's begin.

Programming effectively requires a variety of skills and a general understanding of computing.

- Because a program is a set of instructions for how a computer is to behave, a basic understanding of computer organization is important. By having a mental model of the way a computer carries out its instructions, you'll be able to visualize better both how existing software operates and which resources are needed in the design of new software.

- Web-enabled software is fast becoming the dominant software paradigm. Therefore, a familiarity with networking basics is necessary.

- When developing software, standard engineering principles usually are followed. The primary way that these principles are applied is with the object-oriented programming methodology. This important methodology promotes thinking about software in a manner that models how we think about and interact with the physical world.

- Last, but perhaps most important, you must be able to problem solve. Program design, implementation, and testing is problem solving through the use of a computer system. You cannot make a computer do something if you do not know how to do it yourself.

Thus, to be an effective software designer you need to understand the basics of computer organization, software, networking, engineering practices, and problem solving. Therefore, before we analyze any programs, we use this chapter to introduce each of these concepts. In the following chapters, we will expand on them as we present, demonstrate, and explain program design and development using the Java programming language.

1.2 COMPUTER ORGANIZATION

Most computers have four major parts—a central processing unit, memory, input devices, and output devices. The *central processing unit* (CPU) is the brain of the computer. It is where computations are performed and decisions are made. *Memory* is where the data

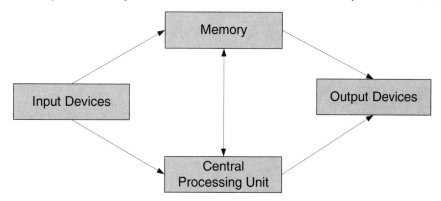

and software are kept while being processed by the CPU. It is essentially a workspace and scratch pad for the CPU. The CPU both *fetches* information from and temporarily *stores* information in the memory. More memory typically means that a computer can run larger software applications and do certain tasks faster. In general, *input devices* and *output devices* communicate information between the computer and its users or between itself and other computers. For example, keyboards and mice are input devices that enable a user to issue requests, while monitors and printers are output devices that enable information to be displayed.

Digital computers use the binary number system, rather than the decimal number system, to represent numbers. The binary number system has only two digits, 0 and 1. A binary digit is referred to as a *bit*. The binary number system is used because the fundamental building block of a computer is a switch, much like the familiar on/off switch for an electric light. The state of the switch indicates whether the value of the associated digit is 0 or 1. In early computers, these switches were built from mechanical relays. The resulting machines were huge. They occupied an entire room, and they required special

Figure 1.1   **Intel Pentium 4 microprocessor.**

power and cooling. In today's machines, the switches are made from ultrasmall transistors. Consequently, an entire computer can fit on a single silicon *chip*. Because the entire
computer fits on a chip, these chips are referred to as *microprocessors*. Intel's Pentium 4®
microprocessor contains about 55 million transistors in an area a little over 1 square inch
(see Figure 1.1).

The principles behind the binary number system are the same as those used in the
decimal number system. Both the decimal and binary number systems are *positional
number systems*; that is, the position of a digit indicates its relative value. For example, in
the decimal number 4,506, the 5 is in the 100's place and thus indicates a value of 500.
Reading the number from the right, each digit represents an increasing power of 10. Thus,
the value of the 4,506 can be expressed as

$$4 \times 10^3 + 5 \times 10^2 + 0 \times 10^1 + 6 \times 10^0$$

The binary number system works the same way
except that we use increasing powers of 2. For example,
the binary number 1101 represents the decimal 13.

A discussion of the binary
number system appears in
Appendix B

$$1 \times 2^3 + 1 \times 2^2 + 0 \times 2^1 + 1 \times 2^0$$

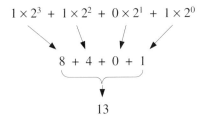

$$8 + 4 + 0 + 1$$

13

When talking about computer storage, its size is reported in *bytes*, where a byte is 8
bits.

We now discuss the other terminology scientists use to describe the speed and storage
capacity of a computer. Using that terminology, we then continue our introduction to
computer organization by analyzing an advertisement for a personal computer (see
Figure 1.2 on page 6).

1.2.1	**COMPUTING UNITS OF MEASURE**

When specifying the speed of a computer, computer manufacturers sometimes report how long it takes the machine to perform a basic operation. In these cases, the units of measure are thousandths, millionths, billionths, and trillionths of a second (see Table 1.1 for the most frequently used measures). Computers currently do most arithmetic operations in picoseconds, but it is expected in the near future that computers will operate in femtoseconds.

Table 1.1   Commonly used powers of 2 and their abbreviations.

Fraction of a Second	Value	Abbreviation
10^{-3}	$\dfrac{1}{1,000}$	millisecond (ms)
10^{-6}	$\dfrac{1}{1,000,000}$	microsecond (µs)
10^{-9}	$\dfrac{1}{1,000,000,000}$	nanosecond (ns)
10^{-12}	$\dfrac{1}{1,000,000,000,000}$	picosecond (ps)
10^{-15}	$\dfrac{1}{1,000,000,000,000,000}$	femtosecond (fs)

Computer manufacturers will also report the speed of a computer using its *clock rate*. Clock rate is an indication of how many operations the computer can perform in a second and typically is expressed as *hertz* (cycles per second). For example, a computer with a clock rate of 2 billion hertz can perform an operation every 500 ps (i.e., 1 ÷ 2 billion seconds). When expressing hertz values, scientists use the prefixes in Table 1.2. For our previous example, we would write 2 GHz (spoken as "2 gigahertz") as the computer speed. In general, the higher the clock rate, the faster the computer.

Table 1.2   Commonly used powers of 10 and their abbreviations.

Value	Abbreviation
1,000	kilo (K)
1,000,000	mega (M)
1,000,000,000	giga (G)
1,000,000,000,000	tera (T)

In terms of measures of capacity or size, computer scientists prefer to count things using powers of two. This system is convenient because digital computers use the binary number system. Table 1.3 shows the powers of 2 that are most often used. As the table

---

Table 1.3 **Commonly used powers of 2 and their abbreviations.**

Power of 2	Value	Abbreviation
2^{10}	1,024	kilo (K)
2^{20}	1,048,576	mega (M)
2^{30}	1,073,741,824	giga (G)
2^{40}	1,099,511,627,776	tera (T)

shows, the abbreviation for 2^{10} is K, where the K comes from the stem "kilo." The prefix *kilo* is used because 1,024 is closest to 1,000. Similarly, the prefix *mega* is used for 2^{20} because its value (1,048,576) is closest to 1,000,000. When these units are used to specify the storage capacity of a machine, we really do mean the exact power of 2. For example, a machine that has 128 megabytes of memory has 128×2^{20} bytes, or 134,217,728 bytes of memory. The use of these prefixes to mean different things can sometimes be confusing. However, context normally tells us whether the binary or decimal system is being used.

1.2.2 BUYING A PERSONAL COMPUTER

Now we are ready to examine a typical advertisement for a personal computer. Most advertisements will list the specifications of the major components of the computer. Figure 1.2 contains a typical personal computer advertisement specification.

Figure 1.2 **A typical personal computer advertisement.**

- Intel® Pentium 4 Processor at 3.06GHz with 512K cache
- 512MB DDR SDRAM
- 200GB ATA-100 Hard Drive (7200 RPM, 9.0 ms seek time)
- 17" LCD Monitor
- 64MB NVIDIA GeForce4 MX Graphics Card®
- 16x Max DVD-ROM Drive
- 48x/24x/48x CD-RW Drive
- 56K PCI Telephony Modem
- Windows XP Home Edition®
- 10/100 Fast Ethernet Network Card

The first line of the advertisement describes the microprocessor in the computer. The computer comes with an Intel Pentium 4® processor running at 3.06 GHz. The advertisement tells us the processor performs 3.06 billion operations per second (i.e., each operation takes about 327 picoseconds). The microprocessor comes with a 512-kilobyte cache. A cache is a very high speed memory used by a microprocessor to store both recently used and soon to be used information and instructions.

The second line of the ad tells us how much and the type of main memory the machine has. Main memory is where data and software reside when they are being executed by the CPU. This machine has 512 megabytes of main memory, which is a very good amount for running the Windows operating system. More memory is generally better, but having more than 1 GB is not cost effective for the typical user.

This particular machine comes with DDR SDRAM memory. The DDR is an acronym for double data rate. What this characteristics means is that data stored in DDR memory can be supplied to the CPU twice as fast as non-DDR memory. The double data rate is achieved in a manner that is analogous to how the jump rope game "double dutch" is played. Instead of a single clock signal (i.e., one rope), there are two clock signals (i.e., two ropes) that double the rate data can be delivered (i.e., the jumper must jump twice as fast).

The acronym SDRAM stands for synchronous dynamic random access memory. The DRAM portion of SDRAM indicates the type of technology used to store the binary information. In DRAM memory, the 1 or 0 for a bit is stored in a capacitor, where a capacitor is a device that holds an electrical charge. If the device is charged up, then it represents a binary 1; if the device has no charge it represents a 0. The synchronous in SDRAM indicates that the memory is designed to work in lockstep with the clock speed for which the CPU is optimized. Be aware there are many other types of memory—some faster and some slower.

The next line of the advertisement gives the specification of the hard disk drive of the machine (see Figure 1.3 for a photograph of a hard disk drive). The hard disk is where data files and software reside. So the larger your hard disk, the more software you can install and the more data you can store (e.g., pictures and music). The advertisement tells us that the capacity of the disk is 200 GB and that the disk is attached to the system using the UATA-100 interface (ultra-advanced technology attachment). This interface defines how fast data can be moved from the disk to the CPU and vice versa. UATA-100 supports transfer rates of 100 MB/second.

The other parameters of the hard disk give some additional indication of the performance of the disk. The rotational speed (7,200 RPM) tells us how fast the disk platters spin. Because we must wait for the data to pass under a *read/write head* before it can be scanned, the speed of rotation affects how long it takes to read data. A faster rotational speed translates to a smaller delay. Less expensive disk drives spin at 5,400 RPM and more expensive disks spin at 10,000 RPM.

Data is written on the disk by a set of read/write heads that move across the disk. The data is written in concentric rings called *tracks*. Another important disk parameter is the seek time. The seek time is the average time to move the heads to a particular track. The advertisement tells us that it takes 9.0 ms to move the heads to a particular track. The seek time is enormous with respect to the time to read or write main memory. Therefore, we can deduce from this fact that reading or writing to a hard disk is much slower than reading or writing to main memory.

Figure 1.3   **The internals of a hard disk drive.**

The advertised machine comes with a 17-inch liquid crystal display (LCD). This type of display often is referred to as a flat panel display (see Figure 1.4). These displays show an image using the same technology found in some watches and calculators. The other type of display technology uses a CRT (cathode ray tube). CRT technology is used in most televisions. Compared to CRT displays, LCD panels are very lightweight and take up much less space. LCDs are more expensive currently than CRTs. However, the prices of LCD monitors are dropping as factories convert from production of CRTs to LCDs.

Figure 1.4   **Digital LCD monitor (Photo courtesy of Hewlett-Packard).**

The two most important characteristics of a monitor are the size of its screen and its resolution. The viewing area of a typical monitor ranges in size from 14 inch to 24 inch. The resolution is how many dots per inch can be displayed across and down the screen. A dot in this context often is referred to as a *pixel*, which stands for "picture element." The higher the resolution, the sharper the image on the screen. Most monitors support a resolution of 1,024 by 768. High-end monitors may support higher resolutions such as 1,280 by 1,024 and 1,920 by 1,200.

The image to display is sent from the computer to the monitor through a device called a *graphics card*. Because displaying high-resolution images requires significant computation resources, graphics cards contain a microprocessor designed specifically for displaying images. These microprocessors often are referred to as GPUs (graphic processing units) to differentiate them from CPUs. Our advertised machine contains a GPU called the GeForce4 from a company called NVIDIA. Some of the other more popular graphics cards are made by ATI Technologies and Matrox. A key characteristic of a graphics card is how much memory it has. The amount of memory on the graphics card determines the resolution of the image that can be displayed, the number of colors that can be displayed, and the speed at which the monitor can be updated. Low-end graphics cards have 16 to 32 MB of memory, while the high-end graphics cards have 128 MB of memory. The listed graphics card has 64 MB of memory, which should perform well for most applications, including graphics intensive games.

The advertised machine includes both a DVD drive and a CD-RW drive. A DVD drive enables the playing of DVD movies on the computer. This DVD drive does not support creating DVDs, but such drives are commonly available for the consumer market. A key parameter for DVD and CD-RW drives is the speed at which data can be read or written. Speeds for DVD and CD-RW drives are given in multiples of the speed of the first available drives. The specified DVD drive has a speed rating of 16x, which means it can read at 16 times the speed of the first DVD drives.

The RW in CD-RW indicates the drive can both read and write CDs. These drives are very popular because they enable consumers to create their own music CDs. They are also a good way to back up files. A CD can hold 650 MB of data or several hours of music. The specification for a CD-RW is given in sets of three—the listed drive has the specification 48x/24x/48x. This specification indicates that the drive can write to CD-R media at 48 speed, can write to CD-RW media speed at 24 and can read discs at 48 speed. (CD-R media can be written only once and CD-RW media can be rewritten).

The machine comes with a 56K modem. A modem (short for modulator/demodulator) enables the computer to connect to the Internet over the telephone line. The 56K indicates the speed at which the modem can send data. A 56K modem can transmit 56 kilobits per second. However, most 56K modems rarely achieve this maximum rate. First, most telephone networks limit the top speed to 53 kilobits per second. Second, the actual rate depends on several factors including the telephone line conditions (e.g., the presence of static or interference) and the distance to the central telephone company equipment.

The advertisement also gives the operating system that comes installed on the machine. This machine comes with a version of Microsoft Windows—Windows XP. There are a two major variants of Windows XP: the home edition and the professional edition. The professional edition includes additional features: the ability to encrypt the file system to protect valuable data, a remote desktop so that you can access the machine over the Internet, and offline files and folders, which is useful for a mobile machine that sometimes is connected to a file server.

The last detail of the advertisement specifies a high-speed network card. A high-speed network card is useful if you want to create your own local area network in your home, or if you have a broadband connection to the Internet. A *broadband* connection is a

Operating systems

There are other operating systems available for machines. An increasingly popular operating system is Linux. Linux frequently is used by researchers and in computing systems dedicated to high-end applications such as Web servers, network gateways, and file servers. One major reason for Linux's popularity is that the source code for Linux is available freely. By having access to the source code, Linux can be modified to suit the particular needs of the application. There are several different versions of Linux available with Red Hat Linux being the one used most widely. Before downloading a version of Linux over the Internet, make sure you have a fast connection. Linux is quite large and can take several hours to download over a broadband connection.

high-speed connection via either a cable modem or via digital subscriber line (DSL) service from the telephone company. Unlike the slow speed of a telephone modem connection, cable modems and DSL service offer transmission speeds of several megabytes per second.

This particular network card can send and receive data at either 10 MB/second or 100 MB/second. Either speed is more than enough for home networking speeds. The faster transfer rate would be desirable if the machine is to be used to provide services to other machines on the network (e.g., file storage and backup).

Because computer networks and especially the Internet are so important, we now turn our attention to them.

1.3   INTERNET COMPUTING

The birth and growth of the Internet has changed society fundamentally. It is not unreasonable to compare the impact of the Internet to the impact of Gutenburg's printing press.

The printing press made the dissemination of information much more affordable. Consequently, information became available to a much larger group of people. As a result, restricting access to information was harder for those in power. The widespread access to information fomented a fundamental shift in existing social structures.

The Internet is having a similar effect. It has made vast amounts of information available cheaply to a huge and still growing group of people. Similarly, the Internet makes it difficult for those in power to control what information is available and who can access it.

On a societal basis, many experts believe this quantum leap in information availability has again initiated a major shift in our existing social structures.

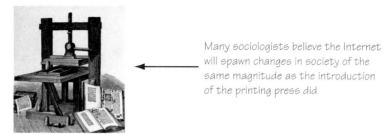

Many sociologists believe the Internet will spawn changes in society of the same magnitude as the introduction of the printing press did

So, what is the Internet and how did it develop? The Internet is a vast infrastructure that supports the rapid transmission of information between computers. The Internet consists of thousands of local, regional, national, and international networks connected together. It is a network of networks. Because the Internet spans national boundaries, no one entity really controls the entire Internet. However, there are organizations responsible for developing technical aspects of the Internet and setting standards.

The beginning of the Internet dates back to the early 1960s and a U.S. government agency called the Advanced Research Projects Agency (ARPA). ARPA's mission was to ensure that the United States kept pace technologically. In the 1960s, ARPA was funding research at both industrial and university laboratories throughout the United States. ARPA decided that research productivity would be improved if the scientists at the laboratories could share computational resources by networking the computers at the various ARPA-supported laboratories. After several years of development, the ARPAnet became operational in 1969. The first network interconnected machines at four universities—three in California and one in Utah.

Over the years, the ARPAnet grew both in number of sites connected and in the number of supported applications. The first ARPAnet e-mail application was developed in 1971. Numerous utilities also were developed for transferring files between machines and for allowing researchers to run software applications remotely at other sites. Realizing the value of networking machines together, the National Science Foundation established NSFNet in 1986. (The National Science Foundation is a U.S. government agency funding basic scientific research.) NSFNet was a high-speed, coast-to-coast transmission line that enabled educational institutions and research laboratories to connect machines together. NSFNet eventually interconnected many existing networks and the term Internet crept into our vocabulary. Then in 1990, Tim Berners-Lee developed the World Wide Web. At this time the size and use of the Internet began to grow exponentially.

1.3.1 NETWORKS

A network consists of a method of connecting machines together, and a set of rules that enable the machines to exchange information. The method of connection can be a stan-

Figure 1.5 **A home network connected to the Internet.**

dard telephone line using a 56K modem, a DSL connection, or a connection using a network card. Figure 1.5 shows a home network with two computers.

Because the Internet is a network of networks, there must be some mechanism for
connecting networks together. The connections are accomplished by using special computers called *routers* that connect a local or regional network to a high-speed transmission
line called a *backbone*. You can think of backbones as a highway system that enables traf-
fic to move speedily from one region to another (up to 10 gigabits per second). Figure 1.6
depicts a backbone map for the United States for a generic Internet service provider.

The job of a router is to direct Internet messages to their proper destinations. Think of
a router like a railway yard switch. The switch determines on which track (the particular
network) a train (a packet of messages) should be sent to reach its destination. Because of
the huge number of messages they must handle, routers usually contain specialized computers designed specifically to handle Internet messages.

In order for machines to communicate over the Internet, there must be a set of rules
that govern how data is sent. Without an agreement on the set of rules, the machines cannot communicate efficiently. For example, when people talk over two-way radios, after
one person finishes speaking he or she says "Over." The "Over" signals that it is the other
person's turn to speak. When a speaker wants to end the conversation, the speaker says
"Over and out." The rules that govern communication are called *communication protocols*.

An important part in the growth of the Internet was the development of efficient protocols. The most important Internet protocol is the TCP/IP (Transmission Control Proto-
col/ Internet Protocol). It governs how packets of information are sent across the Internet.
The TCP specifies both how a message is to be split into the packets and how the packets
are to be assembled to reproduce the original message. The IP handles the address part of
a packet so that it gets to the right destination.

Figure 1.6 **Representative U.S. backbone.**

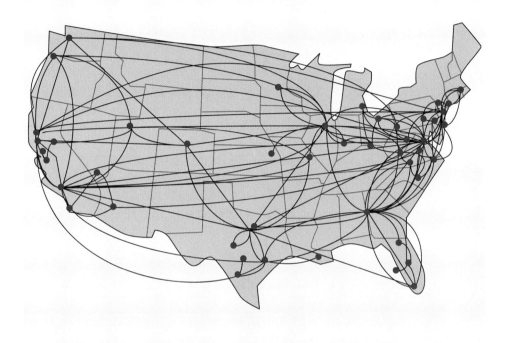

There are other specialized protocols. Most of these protocols are implemented using TCP/IP. Some other common protocols used on the Internet include:

■ The *File Transfer Protocol* (FTP) specifies how to exchange files between computers.

■ The *Simple Mail Transfer Protocol* (SMTP) specifies how e-mail is moved across the Internet.

■ The *Post Office Protocol 3* (POP3) governs how electronic mail (e-mail) is exchanged between your mail reader (e.g., Outlook and Netscape Communicator) and your Internet Service Provider (ISP). Another protocol for communicating e-mail between your local machine and your Internet service provider is IMAP (Internet Message Access Protocol).

■ The *Hypertext Transfer Protocol* (HTTP) is the set of rules for exchanging files (text, graphic images, sound, video, and other multimedia files) over the World Wide Web (WWW). It specifies the actions that are taken when you click on a link within a document.

■ The *Secure Sockets Layer* (SSL) is a protocol that specifies how information is encrypted before being sent over the Internet. It is used widely in electronic commerce. You can tell if a Web page is using SSL by noting whether its WWW address begins with https instead of http.

We now turn our attention to the software components of a computing system and why Java is so important to future software development.

1.4   SOFTWARE AND JAVA

One of the important things to realize about the Internet is that there are many different types of machines connected to it. Personal computers, personal digital assistants, cell phones, workstations, and larger computers referred to as mainframes all are connected to it. This situation creates a very interesting problem. How can we develop software that can run on any machine connected to the Internet regardless of its machine type? Solving this problem was one of the key design goals of the Java programming language. To understand this problem and the importance of Java for Internet computing, this section examines how a Java program is executed on a machine connected to the Internet.

1.4.1   PROGRAMMING LANGUAGES

By itself, a computer will not do anything useful. There must be a program that directs the computer to perform some specific task. A *program* is a sequence of instructions that tells the computer what to do. When the program instructions are carried out by the computer, we say the program is *executed*.

Program instructions are written in a language that is designed specifically for giving commands to a computer. We call these languages, *programming languages*.

The most primitive type of programming language is a *machine language*. A machine language program or *object code* is a program to which a computer can respond directly. Each object code instruction corresponds to a fundamental operation of the machine.

The instruction set for a machine is a set of binary codes that are unique to its CPU type. Consequently, different computers use different machine languages. The machine language understood by Intel's Pentium processor is quite different from the machine language understood by IBM's PowerPC® processor.

A major problem with machine language programming is that it is very tedious and error prone to write directly in binary codes. Slightly less tedious is *assembly language* programming. An assembly language is a symbolic language for coding machine language instructions. Like machine language programmers, assembly language programmers must have a complete understanding of basic operations of the machine. Furthermore, because the corresponding machine operations are so primitive, for even very simple tasks, assembly language programs can be quite long and complicated.

Over the years, computer scientists have put much effort into developing programming languages that permit people to write programs in a way that is more natural. Such programming languages are referred to as *high-level programming languages*. The adjective high-level indicates that the programming language is at a higher level than assembly language.

A distinguishing characteristic of a high-level programming language is that detailed knowledge of the machine being programmed is not required. Another characteristic is that a high-level programming language uses a vocabulary and structure that is close to the type of problem being solved. For example, the programming language FORTRAN, which is used to solve scientific and engineering problems, uses a notation that is mathematical. Indeed, the name FORTRAN is derived from the phrase *formula translation*. Because of the close coupling of a programming language to types of problems, there are literally hundreds of high-level programming languages.

The commands in a high-level language program are not executed directly by a computer. A high-level language program has to be translated first. The conversion is accomplished by a specialized program called a *translator*. A translator accepts a program written in a one language and translates it to an equivalent program in another language. The input to the translator is the *source program* and the output of the translator is the *target program*. Most translators convert a high-level language program to a machine language program. For high-level languages, a translator normally is referred to as a *compiler*.

A particular type of translator of interest to Java programmers is an *interpreter*. An interpreter is a translator that both translates and executes the source program.

1.4.2 RUNNING A JAVA PROGRAM

To understand the steps of translating and executing a high-level program, let's discuss how a simple Java program is translated and executed. We will use the forecast program that started this chapter. The program performs the straightforward task of printing a quotation to a *console window* (i.e., a window that allows commands to be entered at a prompt). The program file is named DisplayForecast.java. That is, the program is stored in a file whose name is DisplayForecast.java. A copy of DisplayForecast.java is given in the Listing 1.1.

Listing 1.1   DisplayForecast.java

```
1.  // Authors: J. P. Cohoon and J. W. Davidson
2.  // Purpose: display a quotation in a console window
3.
4.  public class DisplayForecast {
5.
6.      // method main(): application entry point
7.      public static void main(String[] args) {
8.          System.out.print("I think there is a world market for");
9.          System.out.println(" maybe five computers.");
10.         System.out.println("   Thomas Watson, IBM, 1943.");
11.     }
12. }
```

At this time, we are unconcerned with the details of the program—we leave it to Chapter 2 to explain the various components of this program. For our purposes, the important part of the program is the three *statements* that display the message (lines 8–10). These are the high-level language statements that will be executed when the program is executed.

Normally, there are two steps required to execute a Java program. The first step is to translate the Java source program to a target machine program. The target program produced by a Java compiler is called a *class file*.

There are many different Java software development environments (i.e., Java translation and execution systems) available. For this textbook, we sometimes used the Java translator from Sun Microsystems®. Sun Microsystems is the company that developed the Java programming language and they make available a free Java software development kit (SDK) that can be downloaded from www.javasoft.com.

Figure 1.7 contains a screen snapshot showing the compilation of program Dis-playForecast. The command to invoke the SDK compiler is javac and it takes a single argument that is the name of the file that contains the source program. Because there are no error messages from the compiler, the source program was translated successfully to a target program that can now be executed.

Figure 1.7   Compiling DisplayForecast.java.

To execute the target program, we use a Java interpreter. A Java interpreter reads the target program created by a Java compiler and executes it. The SDK Java interpreter is invoked with the command java and the name of the program. Figure 1.8 contains a screen snapshot showing the execution of the Java program DisplayForecast and the *output* (display) that it produces. When invoking an interpreter to execute a Java program, do not give a file extension, give only the name of the program—DisplayForecast.

At the beginning of this section, we mentioned that one of the key features of Java is that a Java program can run on a variety of different types of machines. This feature makes Java ideal for developing Internet applications where there are many different

Figure 1.8   **Executing DisplayForecast.java.**

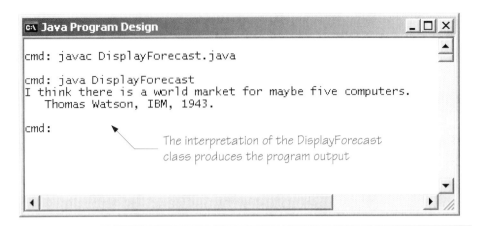

types of machines connected to the network. It is the Java interpreter that makes this happen.

When we compile a Java program, the Java compiler does not produce a machine language program for a particular computer like the compilers for other programming languages such as C, C++, or FORTRAN do. Rather the Java compiler produces a program for an interpreter called the *Java Virtual Machine* (JVM). Essentially, the JVM is a program that mimics the operation of a real machine. The JVM reads the program produced by the Java compiler and executes the Java machine language instructions produced by the Java compiler. The Java machine language instructions are called Java *bytecodes* and can be viewed as architecturally neutral object code. The bytecodes are stored in a file with an extension of `.class`. For program `DisplayForecast.java`, a Java compiler produces a bytecode file named `DisplayForecast.class`.

Now here's the key idea—we can execute a Java class file on any machine that has a copy of a JVM on it. Figure 1.9 illustrates this process. Suppose, you want to send the program to some friends so that they can run it on their machine, where your machine is a PC, and your friends have an Apple. You first compile `DisplayForecast.java` to produce `DisplayForecast.class`. You then send the file `DisplayForecast.class` to the friends over the Internet (e.g., via email or FTP). Using a JVM that is running on the your friends's Apple machine, your friends can interpret the program you sent.

You might wonder what's the big deal. Why not just send the source program and let your friend compile it and run it? There are several potential problems with this approach.

First, application source programs are sometimes quite large. Sending a source program over the network can take significant time—especially if the connection from the Internet to the friend's home computer is a slow modem connection. The Java bytecodes were designed to be small and compact and thus sending a class file is much more efficient than sending a machine-language program or a Java source program.

Second, while you might not care if your friend saw your source program, most companies do not want to send source programs over the Internet as they may contain impor-

Figure 1.9   **Java and the Internet.**

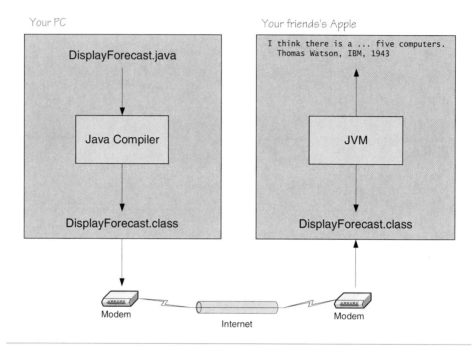

tant information such as formulas that they do not wish to disclose. Sending a `class` file offers some protection for proprietary information.

Third and most important, some devices may not have the necessary computation resources (e.g., memory or CPU speed) to run the Java compiler. For example, many technologists believe that soon household appliances will be connected to the Internet. A refrigerator connected to the Internet might be capable of running a Java application that tracks your food consumption. When you are running low on eggs or milk, the Java application will send an order over the Internet to your grocery store for more eggs and milk. To keep costs reasonable, a refrigerator will contain a low-cost CPU that is unlikely to have the necessary resources to compile a Java application.

We now turn our attention to the practice of designing and developing software.

1.5   ENGINEERING SOFTWARE

As computers have become faster, cheaper, and more powerful, they have become indispensable tools in our everyday lives. They are in appliances such as televisions, DVD players, and microwave ovens. Furthermore, whenever we use a telephone or an automated teller machine, we are accessing a network of computers.

However, faster, cheaper, more powerful computers only are part of the equation. A computer system has *both* hardware and software components. While there have been tremendous advances in hardware technology, the advances in software design have been more modest. Part of the problem is that the expectations for software have grown considerably. Figure 1.10 illustrates the *complexity paradox*—the complexity of a system grows as attempts are made to make it easier to use.

Figure 1.10   Ease of use versus internal complexity.

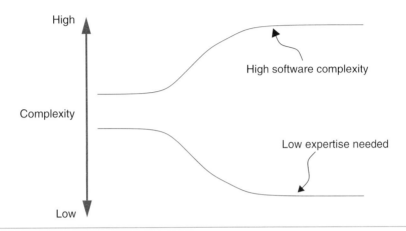

For example, early systems for graphing data required users to specify in detail how the graph should look by supplying information such as the coordinates of the graphical elements, the scale, and how and where the graph should be labeled. Essentially, the user had to do most of the work. However, modern spreadsheet tools contain "wizards," which analyze the data and produce a graph automatically. Such automatic graphing systems are much easier to use, but this ease of use comes at a price—increased software complexity.

Several factors account for the increased complexity. First, to do more, the software is larger. It is not unusual for application programs, such as spreadsheets, word processors, and drawing programs, to consist of millions of lines of code. Another factor that increases complexity is the interaction between components. For example, a word processor may contain one component for spell checking and correction, and another component that provides the services of a thesaurus.

Let's consider the spell-checking component. When a possible spelling error is detected, the spelling checker must report the possible error to the user. Thus the spelling checker must interact with the component of the application that creates a window or a dialog box so that the possible error can be displayed and the user queried about what action, if any, to take. If the user agrees it is a spelling error, the checker can correct the misspelling. To make the correction, the checker must interact with the component of the word processor responsible for replacing text in the document. Obviously, as the number of components grows, the number of interactions between components can grow rapidly.

Software engineering is the area of computer science that is concerned with how to build software systems. The goal of a software engineer is to produce a software system that is *effective, reliable, understandable, cost effective, adaptable,* and *reusable.* Let's examine these properties.

A software application should be effective and reliable. That is, it should work correctly and not fail. Imagine that you have spent several hours writing an important paper with a word processor. Then while doing a pasting operation, the word processor quits unexpectedly and you lose all your work. This ineffective, unreliable action would undoubtedly make you upset, and rightfully so.

One step to making a software system reliable is to make it understandable. The design and operation of the system must be clear to other software professionals. Understandability is important because large software systems are constructed by many people working in teams. The software construction is smoother if everyone working on it understands the overall operation of the system and its components.

Understandability is also important because of the long lifetime of software. A software product usually evolves over time. Software engineers who had nothing to do with its original development often make enhancements and fix *bugs* (errors). This process is called *software maintenance.* As a measure of the difficulty of maintaining software, experts estimate that two-thirds of the cost of developing software is devoted to maintenance. This cost can be reduced when the design and operation of a system are comprehensible.

A software system should be cost effective. That is, the cost to develop and maintain a software system should not exceed the expected profit from selling the system. Many software companies have gone bankrupt because they have underestimated either the cost of developing a system or the time to design, build, and maintain the software.

Because of its potentially long lifetime, software should be adaptable. It often is difficult to predict which features and capabilities eventually will be added to a software product. By designing software so that additional features and capabilities can be added easily, maintenance costs can be reduced.

Because of high development costs, software should be reusable. If many millions of dollars are spent to develop some software, it makes sense to make its components flexible so they can be reused when developing other software. This strategy is common practice in other businesses—the automotive engineer does not design a new car from scratch. Rather, the engineer borrows from the design and components of existing cars.

We now consider some engineering principles whose application encourage the development and maintenance of cost-effective quality software.

1.5.1 SOFTWARE ENGINEERING PRINCIPLES

Software engineers have developed a number of design principles that help realize the goals in the previous section by managing the complexity of a large software system. Four of the more important principles are abstraction, encapsulation, modularity, and hierarchy.

Abstraction is the process of determining the relevant properties and features of an object while ignoring nonessential details. The relevant properties are defined by how the object is to be used and manipulated. For example, an auto salesperson views a car from the standpoint of its selling features, while a mechanic views the car from the standpoint of the systems that require maintenance. If you are concerned with developing a help system to assist car owners who do their own repairs, you need to be sure that the mechanic's view is considered. [1]

A salesperson views a car in terms of its selling features; a mechanic views a car in terms of its maintenance systems

By focusing programming efforts on the relevant properties and ignoring irrelevant details, the complexity of dealing with an object is reduced. Consider the task of finding a file on a disk and reading its contents. If we had to handle the low-level disk-access details, accomplishing the task would be quite difficult. We would have to understand how data is stored on the disk and the machine language commands that control the operation of the disk drive. Instead, the operating system provides a view that lets us access a file simply by supplying the name of the file. The file system handles the low-level details of reading the data on the disk drive and returning it to the program.

Encapsulation or *information hiding* is the process of separating the component of an object into external and internal aspects. The external aspects of an object need to be visible to other objects in the system. The internal aspects are details that should not affect other parts of the system. Hiding the internal aspects of an object means that they can be changed without requiring changes to other system parts.

Consider a car radio. The external aspects are the controls and the types of connectors needed to hook the radio to the electrical system, the speakers, and the antenna. The internal aspects are the details of how the radio works. To install and use a radio in a car, we do not need to know anything about electrical engineering. The radio can be viewed as a box with buttons and cables. Another big benefit of encapsulation is that it simplifies making changes. The radio in a car can be replaced with one that includes an MP3 player without affecting other components of the car.

Because automobile manufacturers follow the encapsulation principle, it is simple to replace a standard car radio with an MP3 player

When applied to the design of a software system, encapsulation enables the internal operation of a software component to be changed without affecting other aspects of the system. For example, if an automated voice-mail system has been encapsulated correctly, we should be able to change the component that handles message storing without affect-

---

1   2001 PT Cruiser Photo/Courtesy of DaimlerChrysler Corporation.

Figure 1.11   A partial organization chart of a company.

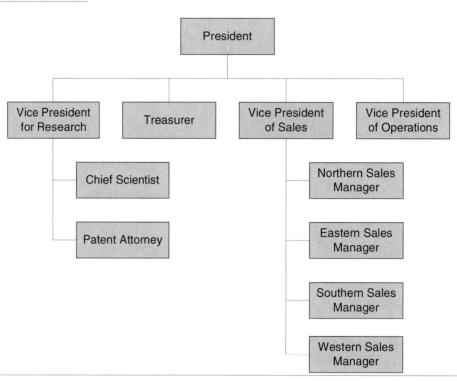

ing other parts of the system. Increasing the number of messages that a user can store, should not affect how users access the voice-mail system to retrieve messages.

Most complex systems are *modular*. They are constructed by combining simpler working components or packages. Proper modularization of a complex system also helps manage complexity. Breaking things down into smaller, easier to understand pieces makes the larger system easier to understand. For example, an automobile can be decomposed into subsystems. Automobile subsystems include a cooling system, an ignition system, and an exhaust system. By thinking about an automobile in terms of its subsystems, we can grasp more readily the car's overall structure and operation.

A ranking or ordering of objects based on some relationship between them is a *hierarchy*. Hierarchies can help us understand complex organizations and systems. Figure 1.11 contains a partial organizational chart for the management of a company. The chart shows the management hierarchy based on the relationship of who reports to whom. The hierarchy helps employees understand the structure of their company.

A useful way of ordering abstractions is from most general to least general. A hierarchical ordering based on natural relationships is called a *taxonomy*. Such a hierarchy makes all the abstractions easier to understand because it exposes the relationship of the characteristics and behaviors they have in common. For example, consider a taxonomy of musical instruments that organizes instruments by how they produce their sound.

■ Idiophones: Solid instruments that are intrinsically sonorous, e.g., bell and cymbal.

- Membranophones: Instruments with taut membranes, e.g., drum and tambourine.

- Aerophones: Instruments that enclose and free masses of air, e.g., trumpet and saxophone.

- Chordophones: Instruments with stretched strings, e.g., lyre and violin.

- Electrophones: Instruments with oscillating electric circuits, e.g., synthesizer and electric piano.

Knowing that a violin is a chordophone enables us to understand its similarity to a lyre in spite of their different outward appearances

We next consider object-oriented design. This methodology provides an approach that supports the software engineering principles of abstraction, encapsulation, modularity, and hierarchy.

1.6 OBJECT-ORIENTED DESIGN

The object-oriented design and programming methodology has been notably successful in helping software developers achieve the goals of reliability, cost-effectiveness, adaptability, understandability, and reusability.

Object-oriented software design promotes thinking about software in a way that closely models the way we think about and interact with the real world. At an early age, we learn about objects and how to manipulate them. Babies learn that if they shake a rattle, it will make noise. Later as we develop our cognitive skills, we realize that objects have properties, and we begin to be able to think about them abstractly. A growing baby soon realizes that noise making is a property of all rattles.

To illustrate how viewing the world as objects with properties helps us manage complexity, consider the following activity. You are getting ready for bed and you remember that you must get up early in the morning. You reach over to your clock radio and set the alarm switch to on and push the hour and minutes alarm buttons to indicate the wake-up time. You go to sleep and the next morning the radio comes on at the desired time.

Now let's analyze this activity. First, you recognized the need for action—having to get up early and deciding that the clock radio could help meet that need. So you go over to the clock radio, which is a physical object. This object has properties like weight and size, and it also can do something. For one it can play music at an indicated time. It's not necessary for you to know entirely how the clock radio works. You need to know only which switches and buttons to use. The switches and buttons are the *interface* to the clock radio. If you understand the interface to an object, you can use it to perform some tasks without understanding how the object works internally. Moving the appropriate switches and pushing the appropriate buttons are signals to the clock radio to modify its behavior.

A clock radio is an object with attributes and behaviors. Its interface provides buttons and switches that signal the clock radio to perform different actions

Such interactions are so routine that it is easy to overlook how amazing this activity is. You were able to make an object perform a complex activity without understanding the internal operation of the object. You were able to do so because you had an appropriate abstraction of the object. Indeed your mental abstraction of a clock radio means that when you travel and stay at a hotel room, you are able to set its clock radio even though it is a different clark radio. Similar objects often exhibit similar behavior.

This way of dealing with the complex world around us also can be applied to software design and programming. A key step in developing a complex system using object-oriented design is to determine the objects that constitute the system. By carefully creating appropriate abstractions of these objects and separating their internal implementation from their external behavior, we can manage the complexity of a large software system.

So what exactly do we mean by an object? Physical things are certainly objects. A ball, a file cabinet, an address book, a tree, and a computer all are objects. What about things like a word, a bank account, or a musical note? These things are not physical objects, but they are objects—in the sense that they have attributes and properties, and we can perform actions on them. A word has a length and meaning, and if we are talking in regard to a word processor, a word can be inserted or deleted from a document. A bank account has a balance to which funds can be deposited or debited. A musical note has pitch, duration, and loudness and can be played. For the most part, something is an object if it has a *name*, *properties associated with it*, and *behaviors such as message handling*.

Typically, when an object receives a message, the message causes the object either to take some action or to change one of its properties. Continuing with our clock radio example, when you push the "music on" button, the current broadcast is played.

If we are going to take an object-oriented approach to developing software, it makes sense to use a programming language such as Java that supports thinking and implementing solutions in terms of objects. A language with features that support thinking about and implementing solutions in terms of objects is an *object-oriented programming language*.

Using an object-oriented programming language to implement an object-oriented design is called *object-oriented programming*. Notice we were very careful to include the phrase "implement an object-oriented design." As you will see later, you can use an object-oriented language, but not think in terms of objects.

Programming languages generally give programmers the ability to specify the *types* of objects to be used in their programs, where a type is a collection of values and the operations that can be performed on those values. An example of a type would be the set of integers and the arithmetic operations that can be performed on them.

Object-oriented languages provide programmers the ability to create a type known as a *class* for representing the properties and message-handling behaviors of a type of object. Classes normally are organized so that the manipulation of a property is handled via a message to the object. Thus, the class encapsulation process is similar in nature to the process of designing a car radio, which has interfaces for both its user and to the electrical system. Programmers use a class to create *instances* of it. An instance is an object with a particular value for each property and attribute of the class.

In practical terms, a class can be thought of as a model or template for an object. From the class, objects with specific properties can be created, or *instantiated*. An object is an instance of exactly one class. As another example, consider a star-shaped cookie cutter. When it is pressed into dough, a cookie is formed. The cutter corresponds to a class—it is a cookie mold. An individual cookie is an object—it is constructed using the cookie cutter.

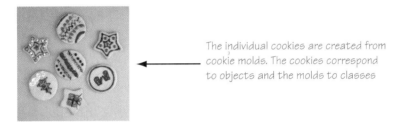

The individual cookies are created from cookie molds. The cookies correspond to objects and the molds to classes

The difference between a class and an object is subtle but important. Whereas a class is a concept, an object is a concrete entity, it is a specific instance of a class. For example, the concept of a car corresponds to a class, but the particular SUVs you may see driving down a street are objects. Similarly, the notion of a bank account corresponds to a class, but your savings account is an object.

We can use a class type to represent playing cards. The properties of a card would be its rank and suit. Card message handling would include *methods* that queried an object regarding its rank value and suit value. The queen of clubs and the nine of diamonds would be playing card instances or objects.

Another important feature of object-oriented languages is that they let programmers exploit the similarity of objects to *derive* new types of objects from existing types of objects. In this situation, we call the old type, the *superclass* and the new class a *subclass*. The subclass both *extends* or *specializes* the functionality of the superclass and *inherits* the properties and behaviors of the superclass.

Specialization is something we see all the time. For example, a poem, novel, biography, and office memo are all types of writing with specialized attributes. An example in Java is the graphical superclass for representing the attributes and behaviors expected of any component that can be placed in a window. The superclass is used as the basis for deriving specialized components such as buttons, menus, scroll bars, labels, and text entry areas. As another example, an aquarium simulation is developed in Chapter 12. The superclass for the simulator is a standard Java class rendering (drawing) images. A snapshot of the application is given in Figure 1.12.

We next turn our attention to a more basic aspect of software development—problem solving.

Figure 1.12   Snapshot of aquarium program of Chapter 12.

1.7   **PROBLEM SOLVING**

Developing a program with its classes and objects for some particular problem is more than just writing code—it is a creative process. While many programmers liken software creation to the construction of a formal piece of logic, other programmers consider software creation to be an artistic endeavour more like the painting of a large detailed canvas.

No matter which approach you take, we recommend the following steps when developing a computer program for some problem.

- *Analysis*: Determine the inputs, outputs, and components of the problem. Their description should be sufficiently specific to enable you to solve the problem.

- *Design*: Describe the required information and methods for solving your problem. If necessary, reanalyze the problem to gain a better understanding so that a relatively straightforward and flexible design can be implemented.

- *Implementation*: Write the code that implements the various information structures and their associated methods, and write the code that manages the overall process. If necessary, reanalyze and redesign so that clear code can be produced.

- *Testing*: Test the various code components individually and collectively. If the problem is not solved correctly or satisfactorily, then reanalyze, redesign, reimplement, and retest as appropriate.

These steps provide a framework to help ensure that your problem is solved correctly. You definitely want to make sure that your efforts are geared in the right direction—a clever solution for the wrong problem is not a solution at all.

Each of the steps is important. Analysis emphasizes what needs to be done; design emphasizes how it is to be done; implementation emphasizes the doing; and testing emphasizes whether it was done correctly.

Be aware that the four steps are not performed necessarily just once. Problem solving often is an iterative process. In doing the design, you might realize more analysis is needed. And in doing the implementation, you might find that more design or analysis is needed. Similarly, in doing the testing you might find that more design, analysis, or implementation is needed.

A pictorial representation of the four basic problem-solving steps is given in Figure 1.13. Because of the importance of these steps in producing solid software, this text does not just present code in isolation. For many problems, we trace through the development process.

How you go about the problem-solving process will depend somewhat on your own way of thinking and acting (see Figure 1.14). For example, some people use a *bricolage* approach where the various features and aspects of the problems are tried and manipulated repeatedly according to the programmers's personal ways of organizing information. For these people, a mistake is not an error in calculation, but a correction waiting to be made in the natural course of solving the problem.

In contrast, many other people take a *planned* approach, using logic and formalism coupled with a structured methodology. Our recommendation is to use an approach that is natural for you. However, be aware that the planned approach is by far the dominant method taught. The structure that the planned approach offers often makes it easier to verify that the software meets all problem specifications. Also be aware that some experts believe that object-oriented design encompasses aspects of both the bricolage and planned approaches. A well-designed object requires both concrete and abstract thinking.

To assist your own design and development efforts, in Sections 1.7.1 through 1.7.4 we present basic problem solving tips. By applying them, you may be inspired on how to solve your own assigned problems.

Figure 1.13 **Problem-solving steps when computer programming.**

Figure 1.14 **Programming approaches—bricolage versus planned.**

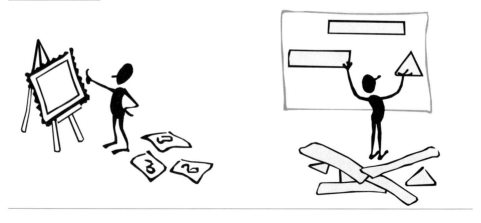

1.7.1   ASK QUESTIONS AS NEEDED

Suppose some clients ask you to give them a method for performing temperature conversion. If you think briefly about it, you should realize that the request has some ambiguities—there is insufficient information for you to solve the problem (e.g., what type of conversion is needed). Therefore, the best thing for you to do is to ask the clients some clarifying questions—you want as much as information as possible about the problem so that you can know what truly is being asked. Some obvious first questions are

- What kind of input temperatures must be dealt with?
- What range of input temperatures must be dealt with?
- What level of precision is required?
- What kind of conversion is wanted?
- Who will use the conversion?
- Under what conditions will the conversion be used?

If the clients then tell you that it will be used by a normal person under normal conditions where the input temperature is always a Celsius temperature and that its Fahrenheit equivalent is what is wanted, you might then ask the clients

- What is meant by normal?

Suppose the answer is temperatures that you might experience in your local area. You might then ask the person

- Are you aware of a formula for this conversion?

Here the answer is most likely no—the clients are asking you because they do not know the formula.

Other obvious questions are

- What type of solution is wanted?
- How should the conversion be expressed?

Suppose the answers indicate that a pen-and-paper procedure is fine. At this point you probably believe that the questions have given you the *inputs*, *outputs*, and *components* of the problem. Together this information forms the *problem requirements* or *problem statement*. Having a problem statement that you understand is an absolute necessity.

A good thing to do when you believe you understand the problem requirements is to write them down in a straightforward manner and to show to them to the person who posed the problem. For your problem, a possible statement could be

> Give a method for converting a requested Celsius temperature to its Fahrenheit equivalent. The requested Celsius temperature comes from the range –50° to 50° and is accurate to one degree.

If you find out that your problem statement is incorrect, then ask additional questions to determine which parts require clarification.

Once you have a problem statement, you typically then attempt to find out what is known about the problem. In general, it is important to know both what attempts have succeeded and what attempts have failed. With respect to the problem at hand, at this point you might excuse yourself to go do a little research. The purpose of the research is to find out what is known about Celsius to Fahrenheit conversion.

An examination of almost any encyclopedia or major dictionary reveals that the following formula holds always for a Celsius to Fahrenheit conversion.

$$Fahrenheit = \frac{9}{5}Celsius + 32$$

To be sure that you understand the formula, you might try some known Celsius to Fahrenheit correspondents — 0°C and 32°F, 100°C and 212°F, and –40°C and –40°F. Because this formula solves what you believe to be the problem, you can go report back your finding. If the client indicates that the formula is satisfactory, then the problem has been solved and you are done. If the formula is not satisfactory, then additional questions are necessary to modify the problem statement because some miscommunication has occurred.

Your research often can require significant time and also cause you to pose additional questions with the client to *refine* the problem statement. These efforts are worthwhile because the result is a better understanding of the problem. A true understanding of the problem makes it easier to solve and produce a satisfactory solution.

Refinement can also be used in developing a solution. First sketch a solution and then repeatedly refine the components of the solution until the entire process is specified completely. This process is known as *top-down design*.

1.7.3   BREAK COMPLEX PROBLEMS INTO SUBPROBLEMS

Suppose you and your friends have been given a huge collection of postcards and you are asked to determine whether there is a postcard that has a picture of grazing sheep One way to solve the problem is for you individually to look at the cards one by one. If your scan finds a postcard with the grazing sheep then you can stop and report yes. If you scan all the postcards and do not find such a picture then you report no.

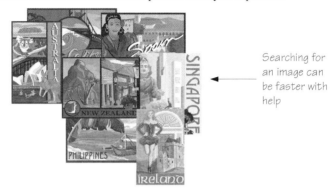

Searching for an image can be faster with help

If your friends will cooperate, a method that generally completes faster than the individual approach is to divide the cards in a roughly even manner among the people present and for each person to scan a separate pile. If someone finds a picture of grazing sheep then you can all stop and report yes. If everyone completes their scan and the desired picture is not found then you report no. Here we have divided the problem into subproblems and defined both how to solve the subproblems and how to combine the solutions to the subproblems into a solution for the overall problem. The name for this method of problem solving is *divide-and-conquer*.

Divide-and-conquer is typically easiest to apply when the subproblems are similar in nature to the original problem. Such similarity occurred in our postcard searching decomposition. The goal of the original problem is to determine whether a postcard collection includes a postcard with grazing sheep and the goal of each of the subproblems is to determine whether a subset of a postcard collection includes a postcard with grazing sheep.

Computer science needs you

Developing software is definitely not just for "geeks." Software projects need individuals with disparate skills. Being an analyst requires communication skills and the ability to perceive and understand a user's needs. Having a strong creative streak is a plus for a designer. An implementer requires detailed knowledge of a program language, clarity of thought and expression, and the ability to pay attention to detail. A tester with good imagination and analytic skills can make sure that software is checked out in all the ways a client might use it.

Divide-and-conquer is also a good technique when you encounter a very complex problem. Such problems may appear overwhelming at first. However, by dividing the problem into its constituent tasks and examining each in turn, you can develop eventually a solution to the entire problem. Be aware that for truly complex problems, it may even be useful to apply the divide-and-conquer technique even to the subproblems.

We next turn our attention to some important problem-solving practices—make use of what has come before and prepare now for the future.

I.7.4   REUSE AND EXPECT FUTURE REUSE

If someone were to ask you to build a wooden box, our guess is that you would not first plant an acorn to grow an oak tree for the wood nor would you build a forge to create hammers, nails, and a saw blade.

Starting with an acorn is not the preferred way to begin building a wooden box

Instead you might reuse materials and tools from a previous project or acquire them from an appropriate place such as a lumber or hardware store. You do so because you know there is an available infrastructure that makes this component of the task simple to complete.

Similarly, when developing software for some problem you should also consider *reuse*. Many software libraries have been developed that contain what is called *Application Programmer Interfaces* (*APIs*). An API is a collection of programmer resources for developing software for a particular type of application. There are hundreds of APIs available for Java programmers. For example, there are APIs for developing file exchanges, cryptography, telephony, and speech recognition programs. We shall further discuss APIs in the next several chapters. But for now, realize that there might be available software components that can *directly* solve either your entire problem or a component of it. Experienced programmers welcome software reuse because the borrowed software often has been analyzed already and proven to be effective.

For example, suppose a client asked us to produce a program that examines their customer accounts to determine which customer has the largest outstanding balance and which customer has the largest unfilled order. We could make use of an API that contained searching methods. Such methods have been well understood for many years. For both of the client's tasks we can make use of a method that searches a list of numbers for the largest value.

Besides the direct use of previously developed materials, you also should be open to the *indirect* use of the materials. By indirect use we mean that we adapt for the problem at hand some previously developed information structure or method that solved an analo-

Figure 1.15 **Finding the largest value is independent of the measure.**

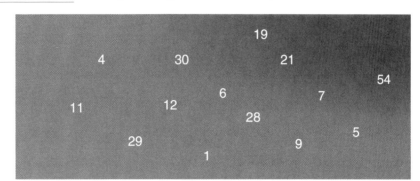

gous problem. For example, suppose you already have developed a process that reported the weight of the largest crystal in a list of crystal weights from some chemical annealing experiment. The procedure that determined the largest weight probably could be used to find the number of copies sold by the most popular book from a list of book sales. Numbers are numbers. When you are finding the largest number in a list all that matters is the size of the number. It does not matter what units the numbers are measuring (see Figure 1.15).

Because you want to reuse previously developed materials, it makes sense that you develop a solution process with as few assumptions as possible. That way, you increase your chances of being able to reuse those materials.

1.7.5 FURTHER READING

There are many ways to problem solve and to program. An interesting sociological examination of different styles can be found in

- Sherry Turkle and Seymour Papert, Epistemological Pluralism: Styles and Voices Within the Computer Culture, *Signs: A Journal of Women in Culture and Society*, pp. 128–157, Autumn, 1990.

This work inspired some of the remarks in this section.

For the interested reader there are many fine books on problem solving with perhaps the most famous one being

- George Polya, *How to Solve It; A New Aspect of Mathematical Method*, Princeton Press, 1988 (reissue edition).

Two others to consider are

- Wayne A. Wickelgren, *How to Solve Mathematical Problems*, Dover Publications, 1995.
- Paul Zeitz, *The Art and Craft of Problem Solving*, John Wiley & Sons, 1999.

1.8   REVIEW

- Information is encoded in a computer using the binary number system. A binary digit is called a bit.
- The basic unit of storage in a computer is a byte or 8 bits.
- The central processing unit, or CPU, is the brain of a computer. It is where computations are performed and decisions are made.
- A microprocessor is computer on a single chip.
- Performing the action specified by an instruction is known as executing the instruction.
- A program is a sequence of instructions that performs some task.
- A network enables computers to share resources and to transmit data among the computers.
- An operating system is system software that controls and manages the computing resources such as the memory, the input and output devices, and the CPU.
- A programming language is a language for giving commands or instructions to a computer.
- A translator translates a program from one language to another.
- A machine language consists of primitive operations that a computer can perform directly.
- A compiler is a type of translator that typically translates a program written in one language to another language. The typical compiler translates a high-level language program to a low-level language program (e.g., into object codes or bytecodes).
- An interpreter is a translator that both translates and executes the source program.
- A Java compiler translates a Java program into bytecodes. Bytecodes are similar to object codes in that they are low-level instructions. The advantage of a bytecode is that it is machine neutral.
- A Java bytecode interpreter is known as a Java Virtual Machine.
- Abstraction is the process of isolating the essential, inherent aspects of an object while ignoring nonessential or irrelevant details.
- Encapsulation or information hiding is the process of separating the external aspects of an object, which can be viewed or accessed by other objects, from the internal implementation details, which should be hidden from other objects.
- Modularity is the process of dividing an object into smaller pieces so each small object or module can be dealt with individually.
- Object-oriented languages provide a way of forming an abstraction by organizing the properties and messages into a single concept. In particular, abstractions are organized normally so that properties are encapsulated—the accessing and modifying of the properties is done via messages.
- A type is a collection of values and the operations that can be performed on those values.
- A class is a type where the values of the associated objects are viewed as properties and the operations on the objects include message handling.

- In practical terms, a class can be thought of as a model or template for an object. From the class, objects with specific properties can be created, or instantiated.
- When doing problem solving, the recommended steps are
  - *Analysis*: Determine the inputs, outputs, and components of the problem.
  - *Design*: Describe the necessary information and the necessary methods to manipulate that information to solve your problem.
  - *Implementation*: Write the code that implements the various information structures and their associated methods, and write the code that manages the overall process.
  - *Testing*: Test the various code components individually and collectively.

1.9 SELF-TEST

S1.1 What information must the CPU supply to a memory controller to update an attribute of an object?

S1.2 How many of bits of memory are there in a machine with 64 megawords of memory where a *word* is 4 bytes?

S1.3 Give the decimal value of the following numbers:
  a) 01001_2 b) 11111100_2
  c) 0110100_2 d) 1111111110_2
  e) 10100011001011111_2 f) 11111111_2

S1.4 Suppose we have a machine with three words of memory, w_1, w_2, and w_3 with currently w_1 and w_2 in use. Give a sequence of instructions that interchanges the value stored in w_1 and w_2.

S1.5 What kind of program translator in an interpreter?

S1.6 What is a type in the context of a programming language?

S1.7 What is a class?

S1.8 What is a bytecode?

1.10 EXERCISES

1.1 Why is the CPU the brain of the computer?

1.2 How do we measure the power of a CPU?

1.3 How many bytes are there in 10 gigabytes?

1.4 What is the difference in uses for main memory and disk space?

1.5 A computer has 64 megabytes of memory. Exactly how many bits of memory does it have?

1.6 Convert the following numbers to decimal representation.
  a) 111111_2 b) 1001011_2
  c) 1010010011_2 d) 1001111_2
  e) 10000001_2 f) 1010110_2

1.7   What are the differences between assembly and machine language programs?

1.8   What are the differences between assembly and high-level language programs?

1.9   How does Java translation differ from most other high-level program translation?

1.10   What is a Java Virtual Machine?

1.11   Find out all you can about one of the machines in a computer laboratory at your school. At a minimum, you should obtain the following information:

   a) The name of the company that manufactured the microprocessor in the machine.

   b) The clock speed of the processor.

   c) The amount of RAM in the machine.

   d) The size of the hard disk.

   e) The resolution of the graphics display.

   f) The name and version of the operating system.

1.12   Find an advertisement for one of the mail-order companies that sell computers. Find out what the acronyms and terms in the advertisement mean. Some of the terms and acronyms you might see are cache, PnP, SCSI, EIDE, burst mode, EPP, USB, and Firewire.

1.13   The capacity of hard disk drives doubles approximately every 18 months with cost remaining constant. Current hard drives have a capacity of approximately 200 gigabytes and cost about $300 How much can we expect to pay per gigabyte in six years?

1.14   For the operating system you are using, name the commands that manipulate files. In particular, name the command that performs the following actions:

   a) Delete a file.   b) Rename a file.
   c) Copy a file.   d) Move a file.
   e) Create a directory.   f) Delete a directory.

1.15   Interview a computer scientist at your institution. Write a one-page summary of the interview. Here are some questions you might ask the interviewee:

   a) Why did you choose to become a computer scientist?

   b) What are your areas of research expertise?

   c) What are the most important research problems in your research area?

   d) What are the most important research problems in the field of computer science?

   e) Do you work with industry in your research? Which companies are your industrial partners? What are the advantages/disadvantages of working on research with industrial partners?

1.16   What is software engineering? What are its goals. Elaborate.

1.17   Define abstraction, encapsulation, modularity, and hierarchy in your own terms.

1.18   Describe the differences between a class and a object

1.19   Consider an automated teller machine (ATM) at a bank. What are the relevant properties of an ATM for the following people?

   a) ATM user   b) ATM repair person

c) Bank teller   d) Bank president

1.20 Give an example of encapsulation at work in a telephone-answering machine.

1.21 Most organizations have a hierarchical structure. Pick an organization to which you belong and produce a diagram that illustrates its hierarchy.

1.22 Are the following objects? Justify your answer.
   a) Beauty   b) Time
   c) Jealousy   d) Tree
   e) Forest   f) Quantum mechanics

1.23 Most electronic devices are designed using the principle of modularity, which makes the devices easier to manufacture and repair. Name the major components or modules of the following devices:
   a) Television   b) VCR
   c) Microwave oven   d) Boom box
   e) Radio   f) Telephone

1.24 In an object-oriented inheritance hierarchy, the objects at each level are more specialized than the objects at the higher levels. Give three real-world examples of a hierarchy with this property.

1.25 Suppose you have been assigned the job of developing software for the following activities. Formulate a list of relevant questions to ask of your client.

   a) Calendar scheduler

   b) Spell checker

   c) Contacts organizer

1.26 Suppose you have been asked to test software that has been developed for the following applications. Suggest possible test instances and explain their purpose.
   a) Rational number calculator (e.g., $\frac{1}{3} + \frac{5}{8}$)
   b) Two-dimensional point plotter
   c) Loan calculator

1.27 Sketch the object-oriented design of the card game blackjack. What are the key objects? What are the properties and behaviors of these objects? How do the objects interact?

1.28 Sketch the object-oriented design of a system to control a soda-dispensing machine. What are the key objects? What are the properties and behaviors of these objects? How do the objects interact?

1.29 Give an abstraction for rational numbers (e.g, 6/21, 4/30).

1.30 Give an abstraction for a two-dimensional coordinate.

1.31 Give an abstraction for a pixel.

1.32 A traveler with three animals needs to cross the river in a rowboat that can fit at most the traveler and two of the animals at a time. An animal left temporarily by itself is okay. However, if two animals are left alone together even temporarily, they will attack each other. Give a solution for getting the traveler and all three animals safely across the river.

1.33   The Tower of Hanoi puzzle starts with 3 pegs and a stack of 64 rings on the left-most peg. The stack of rings are arranged in order of increasing diameter from top to bottom. The goal of the puzzle is to end up with the stack of 64 rings on the rightmost peg. You are allowed to move only one ring at a time and it must go from one peg directly to another peg. In addition, you can never place a ring of greater diameter on top of a ring of lesser diameter. Give a divide-and-conquer solution for the puzzle.

| 1.11 | **SELF-TEST ANSWERS** |

S1.1   To update the value of an object's attribute the CPU must specify to the memory controller the address of that attribute and the value that is to be stored in that address.

S1.2   A machine with 64 megawords has 64×4 megabytes. Because a byte consists of 8 bits, there are a total of $64 \times 4 \times 8$ megabits = 2048 megabits = 2 gigabits.

S1.3   The decimal conversions are
    a) $01001_2 = 9$ b) $11111100_2 = 252$
    c) $0110100_2 = = 52$ d) $1111111110_2 = 1{,}022$
    e) $1010001100101111_2 = 41{,}744$ f) $11111111_2 = 255$

S1.4   To swap w_1 and w_2, we first use w_3 as a temporary holder of w_1's original value. We then update w_1 with w_2's value. We then update w_2 with w_3's value. That is,

w_3 is assigned the value of w_1
w_1 is assigned the value of w_2
w_2 is assigned the value of w_3

S1.5   A type is a collection of values and the operations that can be performed on those values.

S1.6   An interpreter is a translator that both translates and executes the source program.

S1.7   A class is a type where the values of the associated objects are viewed as properties and the operations on the objects include message handling.

S1.8   Bytecodes are machine-neutral, low-level instructions similar in purpose to object codes.

2 JAVA BASICS

This chapter introduces the basics of Java program design. It presents a series of programs that interact with their users through text-based outputs and inputs. The chapter also introduces the Java primitive types. These types and their associated operators enable programs to create and manipulate integer, floating-point, and character values and variables. The chapter provides detailed coverage of the assignment operator and getting input values. The assignment operator enables variables to be modified. Understanding its behavior is a key concept that all programmers must master. Of equal importance is understanding how to input data values—for most programs to be useful, they must be able to react to user requests.

OBJECTIVES

- Introduce basic program structures using interesting examples.
- Demonstrate how to trace through programs to understand their execution.
- Demonstrate the importance of good programming style.
- Describe how to produce character and numeric output.
- Introduce operators, expressions, and the primitive integer, floating-point, and character types.
- Explain the roles of variables and constants in a program.
- Use BufferedReader objects as a means of getting input values to a program.
- Introduce method invocation and parameter passing.
- Present the assignment operation and demonstrate its importance in performing computations.

2.1 A FIRST PROGRAM

As part of the computing introduction of Chapter 1, we listed program `DisplayFore-cast.java`. Because the program performs a straightforward task with a minimal amount of language mechanics, we use it to give a sense of basic program structure. The task of program `DisplayForecast.java` is to display an alleged forecast by Thomas Watson. The two-line quotation is *output* (displayed) to a *console window* (i.e., a window that enables commands to be entered at a prompt). The message output by the program is

```
I think there is a world market for maybe five computers.
    Thomas Watson, IBM, 1943.
```

A copy of `DisplayForecast.java` file is given in Listing 2.1. A run of the program is given in Figure 2.1.

Listing 2.1   DisplayForecast.java

```
1.  // Authors: J. P. Cohoon and J. W. Davidson
2.  // Purpose: display a quotation in a console window
3.
4.  public class DisplayForecast {
5.
6.      // method main(): application entry point
7.      public static void main(String[] args) {
8.          System.out.print("I think there is a world market for");
9.          System.out.println(" maybe five computers.");
10.         System.out.println("   Thomas Watson, IBM, 1943.");
11.     }
12. }
```

The heart of the program is the three *statements* that display our message (lines 8–10). Each of the statements is an instruction to be executed. Together, they cause the forecast and its attribution to be displayed.

The statements are part of a method named `main()` (lines 7–11). A *method* is the Java term for a *named* unit of code that performs some action or implements some behavior. Some programming languages use the terms *function* or *procedure* or *subroutine* instead of method.

Method `main()` is part of the class `DisplayForecast` (lines 4–12). A *class* defines an object form—think of it as a model or template for an object. Besides having methods that implement behaviors, objects also can have attributes (*data fields* or *data values*).

The other parts of program `DisplayForecast.java` are *comments* that document the authors, purpose, and parts of the program (lines 1, 2, and 6) and *whitespace*, which is used to make the various elements of the program more distinct (lines 3 and 5).

We now discuss in more detail the form and meaning of the twelve lines of code that make up program `DisplayForecast.java`. The discussion begins with how and why commenting is done. We then discuss the basics of class definitions, statement formation, method definitions, and displaying output.

Figure 2.1   Executing DisplayForecast.java.

Resources

All programs and classes defined in this text are available at our website at www.jav-aprogramdesign.com.

2.1.1   COMMENTING AND WHITESPACE

A fact that is sometimes difficult for beginning programmers to appreciate fully is that the typical program is read frequently by many other people. A program must be composed of legal Java (i.e., be understandable to the compiler). However, we also want other programmers to understand the program.

Thousands of programmers often work on large commercial software systems. Some programmers might add new features, while others fix *bugs*, the programming term for errors. To accomplish their tasks, programmers must be able to understand how their assigned programs work. Thus, it is important to write and document programs so that other people can understand what they do and if necessary *debug* them (remove errors).

Even when we write programs for our personal use, modification often is necessary. Although we understood how the program worked when we wrote it, as months or years pass, we may forget important details.

Comments are the mechanism that enables us to include notes in a program. These notes are *not* processed by the compiler. Their purpose is to help explain and document how the program works and who its authors are.

Keeping in mind the importance of commenting, program `DisplayForecast.java` begins on lines 1–2 with two *single-line program heading comments*. The double slash delimiter `//` indicates that the rest of the line is a comment to be ignored by the compiler.

Comment that identifies the authors of the program

```
// Authors: J. P. Cohoon and J. W. Davidson
// Purpose: display a quotation in a console window
```

Consecutive double slashes indicate that the remainder of the line is a comment

Comment that explains the purpose of the program

These header comments help readers of the program by indicating both a point of contact for asking questions and the program's purpose.

Line 6 of `DisplayForecast.java` is another single-line comment. The comment describes an important fact about the method that follows—the method is the one where our program starts its execution.

```
method main(): application entry point
```

Observe that the comment on line 6 is indented with respect to line 4. When coding, programmers use *indentation* to indicate that the indented material is a component of the material that preceded it. The comment of line 6 and the method that follows are indented because together they make up the definition of class `DisplayForecast`.

When a program component itself is made up of parts, those parts are indented further. For example, because lines 8–10 make up the actions of method `main()`, they are indented with respect to line 7. Each level of indentation is normally three or four characters wide.

The comment and method are indented because they are elements of class DisplayForecast

```
public class DisplayForecast {

   // method main(): application entry point
   public static void main(String[] args) {
      System.out.print("I think there is a world market for");
      System.out.println(" maybe five computers.");
      System.out.println("   Thomas Watson, IBM, 1943.");
   }
}
```

The statements are indented further because they are elements of method main()

Lines 3 and 5 of our program are blank lines. Blank lines can be as important as comments. They enable the various sections of a program to be visually distinct, making the program easier to read and understand. *Whitespace* characters (i.e., blanks, tabs, etc.) between the various elements of a program are ignored during translation, so they can be inserted as deemed appropriate.

Attention to detail

The single-line comment delimiter // must be typed with no whitespace between the slashes when entering the delimiter into your program file. The presence of whitespace would alter the meaning. For example, whitespace between the slashes would mean that a malformed arithmetic expression was being entered, rather than a comment.

2.1.2   CLASSES, KEYWORDS, AND IDENTIFIERS

The fourth line of program `DisplayForecast.java` begins the definition of the class `DisplayForecast`. All Java programs consist of at least one class definition.

The class definition for program `DisplayForecast.java` begins with the two *keywords* **public** and **class**. Keywords are words that are reserved by the Java language for particular purposes. Because keywords have special meanings, they cannot be changed by the programmer and they cannot be used by the programmer to name things. Keywords are case sensitive and consist of only lowercase letters. Thus the strings

    PUBLIC   Public

are not keywords. Instead they are valid Java names, or in programming parlance, *identifiers*. Using them as identifiers is not recommended, because readers of your code might not notice the case differences and become confused. A complete list of keywords appears in Appendix A.2. In this text, keywords are displayed in a bold-face monospaced font.

The keyword **class** on line 4 indicates that a class definition is being initiated. Java permits *modifiers* to be placed in front of the keyword **class**. These modifiers can place restrictions on the nature of the class being defined. Modifier **public** indicates that Java classes in other files are permitted to create and use objects of the class in question. A file is allowed to contain at most one **public** class.

The name of the class being defined comes next. Java requires that the name of a public class have the same name as its program file. Therefore, the name of this class is `DisplayForecast`.

Following the name of the class is a left brace {. Java uses braces {} to *delimit* the statements that make up the definition of a class. For class `DisplayForecast`, the right brace on line 12 is the matching brace for the left brace on line 4. Therefore, lines 4–12 contain the definition of `DisplayForecast`.

The rule for forming a valid name is that it must be a valid Java identifier and cannot clash with the keywords. Java's rules for a valid identifier are as follows:

- An identifier must begin with an alphabetic letter, underscore (_), or a dollar sign ($);

- Subsequent characters in a identifier (if any) must be either alphabetic, digits, underscores, or dollar signs;

- Whitespace cannot be embedded among the characters that form an identifier.

- An identifier cannot be composed of more than 65,535 characters.

    Examples of valid Java identifiers are

    `height    firstValue    LIGHT_YEAR    $amount    München    π`

The identifiers `München` and π might seem surprising. Because Java is an international language, rather than using the customary ASCII character set, it uses the Unicode character set, an international standard. This character set is sufficiently rich to write the major world languages. In particular, the German ü and the Greek π are available with Unicode.

Besides `DisplayForecast`, the other identifier names in `DisplayForecast.java` are `main`, `String`, `args`, `System`, `out`, `print`, and `println`. Identifier `main` is the name of the method where program execution begins; `String` and `System` are the names of Java classes; `args` and `out` are variables that enable us to reference some program resources; and `print` and `println` are the names of methods that enable messages to be sent to the console.

Naming

Besides being a legal identifier, a name should be descriptive of its purpose. For example, use `height` rather than the ambiguous `h` or `ht`. We will discuss naming conventions as we introduce different program elements. The conventions used in this text are based on the standard Java code conventions. Sun Microsystems provides an easy-to-read document that discusses standard code conventions at its website `www.javasoft.com/docs/codeconv`.

2.1.3 METHODS

The *entry point* (starting point) of execution for a Java application program is in a method `main()`. (As indicated previously, a method is a named piece of code.) The style convention for this text when referring to a method is to include a pair of parentheses after its name. The parentheses are a visual cue that we are referring to a method.

In general, a Java method definition may have the following elements in the specified order with the italicized elements being optional.

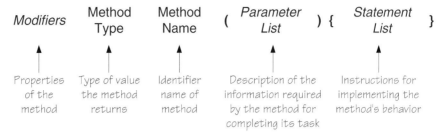

Modifiers	Method Type	Method Name	(	*Parameter List*	) {	*Statement List*	}
Properties of the method	Type of value the method returns	Identifier name of method		Description of the information required by the method for completing its task		Instructions for implementing the method's behavior	

For `DisplayForecast`'s method `main()`, modifiers **public** and **static** are used. Method modifier **public** indicates that the method can be used by other Java classes. These other classes can be defined either in the same file or in other files. Modifier **static** indicates that `main()` is to be a service provided by the class that does not require association with a particular class object. In the object-oriented programming methodology, such methods are known as *class* methods.

Some methods *return* (produce) values that can be used by the part of the program that *invoked* (started up) the methods to be *executed* or *run* (carried out). For example, a square root method returns the square root of its *parameter*, where a parameter is a value given to the method so that it can perform its task. A square root method when invoked with the parameter 64, returns the value 8, and when invoked with the parameter 144, returns the value 12.

Some methods accomplish their task without returning values. Such methods, like method `main()`, are labeled **void** to indicate that no value is returned.

In giving its definition, a pair of left and right parentheses follows the name of a method. The parentheses can contain optionally a *formal parameter list*. The formal parameters describe the types of information that are given to the method when it is invoked. For example, a square root method would expect a number for its parameter.

> Chapters 3 and 4 discuss the basics of parameter passing. Chapter 7 considers parameter passing in detail

In the case of the method `main()` of an application program, Java requires a single parameter of type `String[]`, where type `String[]` is a representation for a list of strings. The meaning behind this particular parameter is deferred to Chapter 8.

Naming

By convention, the parameter to method `main()` has the name `args`. So all of the application programs that we develop have a method `main()` with a formal parameter list `String[] args`.

A pair of matching braces follows the parenthesis that marks the end of the formal parameter list. These braces group the statement list that makes up the method's action.

For method `main()` of `DisplayForecast.java`, the statement list is the statements of lines 8–10.

```
System.out.print("I think there is a world market for");
System.out.println(" maybe five computers.");
System.out.println("   Thomas Watson, IBM, 1943.");
```

In Java, a single statement can span multiple lines so there must be some delimiter that indicates that the statement is finished. The semicolon (`;`) serves this purpose—much as a period serves to end this sentence.

When a Java interpreter starts to run a Java application program, the *flow of control* is given to the application's method `main()`. This action causes the statements of the method `main()` to be executed in order. Therefore, when program `DisplayForecast.java` runs, the statement in line 8 is executed first, then the statements in lines 9 and 10 are executed.

2.1.4   SELECTING METHODS PRINT() AND PRINTLN()

As noted previously, the statement list that specifies the behavior of method `main()` is

```
System.out.print("I think there is a world market for");
System.out.println(" maybe five computers.");
System.out.println("   Thomas Watson, IBM, 1943.");
```

The statements cause our quotation to be displayed in the window in which the program is executed (see Figure 2.1). The quotation is displayed because of the capabilities of the class `System`, which is one of the *standard* (official) Java classes. In particular, `System` is part of a package named `java.lang`, where *package* is the Java term for a software library.

Program `DisplayForecast.java` needs access to a *member* (component) `out` of `System`. To access `System` member `out`, the program *selects* it from `System` using the period (`.`), which is Java's *selector* mechanism.

Member `out` is a *variable*, which means it has a value. With that value, the program has access to an object for displaying text to the console window running the application. This object is known as an *output stream*, where a stream is a programming term for an object representing an output device such as a monitor or an input device such as a keyboard or a file. The methods associated with a stream object enable a programmer to interact with the device without being concerned with low-level details of the device's operation.

Because of its association with the console window, the `System.out` output stream is known as the *standard output stream*. Java uses its standard class `PrintStream` to represent the standard output stream. Figure 2.2 provides a representation of `System.out` and its relation to `PrintStream`.

Figure 2.2   **System.out representation.**

Figure 2.3   **Member selection.**

The standard output stream has *member methods* named `print()` and `println()` that the program invokes to print the forecast. Member methods are the means by which objects have behaviors.

The `print()` and `println()` methods are invoked through additional applications of the period selector. Figure 2.3 demonstrates the selection process for the invocation in line 8.

When invoked, the behavior performed by method `print()` is to display the value of its parameter to the associated output stream. In this case, the output stream is the console window running the program and the parameter is the *literal character string* `"I think there is a world market for"`, where a literal character string is a sequence of characters delimited on both sides by the double quote character (`"`).

A literal character string is *not* allowed to span multiple lines in your program. Therefore, the following statement is illegal in Java.

```
System.out.print("I think there is a world
market for ");
```

Illegal a literal character
cannot span multiple lines

When a method is invoked, the action associated with the method is executed. For method `print()`, its action causes its character string argument to be displayed in the console window at the point where the *window cursor* is located currently. A cursor is a special window symbol. It is typically a blinking rectangle or underscore.

After displaying the argument, the cursor is located immediately after the last character that was displayed. In the following depiction of the `print()` output, the ■ is our representation for the cursor.

```
I think there is a world market ■
```

After executing the first print()
statement, the cursor is located
immediately after the "t" in market

Method `println()` differs from `print()` in that after displaying its parameter, it moves the cursor to the start of the next line in the window. Therefore, after the executing the first `println()` statement, program output looks like

```
I think there is a world market for maybe five computers.
■
```

After executing the first println()
statement, the cursor is located at
the start of the next line

The execution of the second `println()` statement completes the program output.

```
I think there is a world market for maybe five computers.
   Thomas Watson, IBM, 1943.
```

Experiment

The next several programs are similar to `DisplayForecast.java` in that they output textual information. A way to view them is as experiments with the `print()` and `println()` methods. You are encouraged strongly to take the code and make further modifications. Observing how modifications affect program behavior is often an effective way to start making sense of programming constructs.

Suppose instead of displaying a quotation, we wanted to display the following reminders.

> Jan 1: send card to mom.
> May 9: send card to dad.
> May 15: send card to parents.
> Sep 20: send card to in-laws.

With an understanding of `DisplayForecast.java`, such a program should now be easy to write. We call the program displaying the four reminders `CalendarDisplay.java`. The program is presented in Listing 2.2. Notice that we left out the author portion of our header commentary. We continue this policy throughout the remainder of the text. We do so because the authors are obvious within a textbook.

Each of the four `println()` statements in `CalendarDisplay.java`'s method `main()` causes a new output line to be displayed.

```
Jan 1: send card to mom.
May 9: send card to dad.
May 15: send card to parents.
Sep 20: send card to in-law.
```

Listing 2.2   CalendarDisplay.Java

```
1.  // Purpose: display a series of four reminders
2.
3.  public class CalendarDisplay {
4.
5.      // main(): application entry point
6.      public static void main(String[] args) {
7.          System.out.println("Jan 1: send card to mom.");
8.          System.out.println("May 9: send card to dad.");
9.          System.out.println("May 15: send card to parents.");
10.         System.out.println("Sep 20: send card to in-laws.");
11.     }
12. }
```

2.1.5   ESCAPE SEQUENCES

Now suppose that we want a program that displays the following quotation of Daniel Hillis from *The Pattern on the Stone* (1999):

> "The difference between the right program and almost the right program is like the difference between lightning and a lightning bug. The difference is just a bug."

The following `print()` and `println()` statements correctly display the text.

```
System.out.print("The difference between the right ");
System.out.println("program and almost the right");
System.out.print("program is like the difference between ");
System.out.println("lightning and a lightning");
System.out.println("bug. The difference is just a bug.");
```

The display produced is the following.

```
The difference between the right program and almost the right
program is like the difference between lightning and a lightning
bug. The difference is just a bug.
```

However, suppose we wanted quotation marks to also be displayed at the start and end of the quotation. A program for this task is given in Listing 2.3. The program is called QuotationDisplay.java.

Listing 2.3   QuotationDisplay.java

```
1.  // Purpose: display a quoted quotation
2.
3.  public class QuotationDisplay {
4.
5.     // main(): application entry point
6.     public static void main(String[] args) {
7.        System.out.print("\"The difference between the right ");
8.        System.out.println("program and almost the right");
9.        System.out.print("program is like the difference between ");
10.       System.out.println("lightning and a lightning ");
11.       System.out.println("bug. The difference is just a bug.\"");
12.    }
13. }
```

The program uses *escape sequences* to produce the quotation marks. An escape sequence is a special two-character sequence representing another character. Without escape sequences it would not be possible to have a literal character string containing a double quote.

Java uses the backslash character \ as the starting character in an escape sequence. The escape sequence for a double quote is \". Thus, to display quotation marks around our quotation, we modify the actions of method main() from QuotationDis-play.java as follows.

```
System.out.print("\"The difference between the right ");
System.out.println("program and almost the right");
System.out.print("program is like the difference between ");
System.out.println("lightning and a lightning");
System.out.println("bug. The difference is just a bug.\"");
```

In the first statement, we added the double quote escape sequence at the start of the literal character string and in the last statement we added the double quote escape sequence at the end of the literal character string. The output of the program is now

```
"The difference between the right program and almost the right
program is like the difference between lightning and a lightning
bug. The difference is just a bug."
```

Java defines several escape sequences. For example, \t is the escape sequence for a tab character, \n is the escape sequence for a newline character, and \\ is the escape sequence for a backslash. The complete list is given in Table 2.1.

The newline escape sequence gives us the ability to move the cursor to the start of the next line in the midst of an output operation. For example, program PetDisplay.java of Listing 2.4 uses the single statement

```
System.out.println("Nilla\nBuffer\nDarby\nGalen");
```

Table 2.1	**Java escape sequences.**

Escape Sequence	Meaning
\b	backspace
\n	newline
\t	tab
\r	carriage return
\\	backslash
\"	double quote
\'	single quote

Listing 2.4 **PetDisplay.java**

```
1. // Purpose: display pet names
2.
3. public class PetDisplay {
4.
5.     // main(): application entry point
6.     public static void main(String[] args) {
7.         System.out.println("Nilla\nBuffer\nDarby\nGalen");
8.     }
9. }
```

to display four lines to standard output—the names of past and present family pets.

```
Nilla
Buffer
Darby
Galen
```

Program `TabularDisplay.java` of Listing 2.5 uses the tab escape sequence to produce tabular output. The output of the program is

```
Person  Height  Shoe size
=========================
Hannah  5'1"    8
Jenna   5'10"   9
JJ      6'1"    14
Joanne  5'5"    8.5
Jim     6'4"    15
```

Programmers normally use the tab escape sequence rather than a tab character in literal strings because it explicitly tells the reader that a tab is being used rather than what might appear to be an arbitrary number of spaces.

We now turn our attention to programs that make use of some of the numeric types provided by Java. We use these types and their associated operators to create and manipulate values and variables. Understanding how to manipulate values and variables is a crucial programming skill.

Listing 2.5   **TabularDisplay.java**

```
1. // Purpose: display a quoted quotation
2.
3. public class TabularDisplay {
4.
5.     // main(): application entry point
6.     public static void main(String[] args) {
7.         System.out.println("Person\tHeight\tShoe size");
8.         System.out.println("=========================");
9.         System.out.println("Hannah\t5'1\"\t8");
10.        System.out.println("Jenna\t5'10\"\t9");
11.        System.out.println("JJ\t6'1\"\t14");
12.        System.out.println("Joanne\t5'5\"\t8.5");
13.        System.out.println("Jim\t6'4\"\t15");
14.    }
15. }
```

Syntax errors

When an invalid Java program is translated, the compiler produces a list of *syntax errors*. A syntax error is a violation of the rules for defining a valid program. For example, suppose the definition of class `DisplayForecast` had contained incorrectly

    public class `DisplayForecast` (

The Java compiler will display an error message indicating that the left parenthesis was not expected.

When a compiler indicates a syntax error has been found on a particular line, the adjacent lines often need to be examined also. For example, a common mistake in entering a program is to forget a semicolon. This syntax error often is associated with the line after the statement that had the missing semicolon. The mistake is reported there because the error does not occur until that code is considered—it is the starting element of what was intended to be a new statement that is unexpected.

2.2   **SIMPLE COMPUTATIONS**

Good programmers often write short programs that compute useful things. For example, a value of interest to many people is their *body mass index* (BMI), which is a metric measure of fitness and health. According to the U.S. National Center for Chronic Disease Prevention and Health Promotion Nutrition and Physical Activity at `www.cdc.gov`, people with scores less than 18.5 may be underweight for their height; people with scores 25 or greater may be overweight for their height; and people with in between scores may be considered normal.

Computing a BMI is a straightforward calculation—it is the ratio of the person's weight in kilograms to the square of the person's height in meters. Thus, in developing a program to compute a particular BMI, two values of interest are the person's metric weight and height. With these two values, the BMI value can be calculated.

Listing 2.6   BMI.java

```
1.  // Purpose: Compute body mass index for given weight and height
2.
3.  public class BMI {
4.
5.      // main(): application entry point
6.      public static void main(String[] args) {
7.          // define constants
8.          final double KILOGRAMS_PER_POUND = 0.454;
9.          final double METERS_PER_FOOT = 0.3046;
10.
11.         // set up person's characteristics
12.         double weightInPounds = 75.5;  // our person's weight
13.         double heightInFeet = 4.5;      // our person's height
14.
15.         // convert to metric equivalents
16.         double metricWeight = weightInPounds * KILOGRAMS_PER_POUND;
17.         double metricHeight = heightInFeet * METERS_PER_FOOT;
18.
19.         // perform bmi calculation
20.         double bmi = metricWeight / (metricHeight * metricHeight);
21.
22.         // display result
23.         System.out.println("A person with");
24.         System.out.println("   weight " + weightInPounds + " lbs");
25.         System.out.println("   height " + heightInFeet + " feet");
26.         System.out.println("has a BMI of " + Math.round(bmi));
27.     }
28. }
```

The authors live in the United States, and in the United States, weights and heights are expressed normally in the English system of pounds and feet. Therefore, in producing a BMI calculator of general use here, four other values are of interest. Two of these values are the particular person's weight in pounds and height in feet. The other two values are the constants 0.454 and 0.3046, which are respectively the number of kilograms per pound and the number of meters per foot. With these four values, the person's metric weight and height can be calculated, which in turn enables the BMI value to be calculated.

Program `BMI.java` of Listing 2.6 defines and manipulates these seven values to compute and display the BMI for a person of particular weight and height (75.5 lbs and 4.5 feet tall).

The output of the program is

```
A person with
   weight 75.5 lbs
   height 4.5 feet
has a BMI of 18
```

One difference between this program and our previous programs is the introduction of comments within method `main()`. The internal comments serve to highlight and explain the major activities of the method.

```
// define constants ...
// set up person's characteristics ...
// convert to metric equivalents ...
// perform bmi calculation ...
// display result ...
```

In the following discussion, the other differences between this program and previous programs are highlighted. These differences represent important new program elements.

2.2.1 CONSTANTS

One important difference of `BMI.java` from previous programs is its use of *primitive constants* and *variables* of *type* **double**. A type is essentially a set of values along with the operators that can manipulate and create values from that set.

A Java type is classified as either a *primitive* or *reference type*. The primitive types support the manipulation of numeric, character, and logical values. The type **double** is a numeric primitive type for *floating-point* values; that is, decimal values such as 75.5 and 4.5. Reference types are used to represent values that are more complex in nature such as an output stream, bank record, or a graphical user interface. These more complex values are called objects as they have generally both attributes and behaviors.

> The primitive types are discussed in Section 2.3

A *constant* is the symbolic name for a memory location whose value cannot be changed once the program has initialized the location. Its name must be a valid Java identifier.

Before we can use a constant in a calculation, we must first define and initialize the constant. A constant definition normally takes the following form.

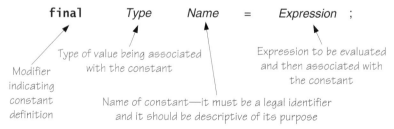

In particular, line 8 of method `main()` statement makes KILOGRAMS_PER_POUND a **double** constant.

```
final double KILOGRAMS_PER_POUND = 0.454;
```

The statement associates KILOGRAMS_PER_POUND with a memory location containing the *literal* **double** floating-point value 0.454, where a literal numeric value is a number. The effect of the definition is depicted in the diagram that follows. (In this and subsequent depictions, a lock indicates that the value cannot be changed.)

KILOGRAMS_PER_FOOT [🔒 0.4545]

The contents of the location is fixed during program execution because of the use the modifier keyword **final**. The keyword **double** indicates that the constant being defined is associated with a **double** value. The semicolon after the definition indicates that no more **double** constants are being defined in this statement. From this point on in method main(), KILOGRAMS_PER_POUND is synonymous with the **double** value 0.454.

Similarly, the statement

final double METERS_PER_FOOT = 0.3046;

makes METERS_PER_FOOT synonymous with the **double** value 0.3046.

METERS_PER_FOOT [🔒 0.3046]

Java allows several constants to be defined in a single statement by separating the definitions with commas. For example, the following statement defines DOOR_WIDTH and DOOR_HEIGHT as **double** constants.

final double DOOR_HEIGHT = 2.00, DOOR_WIDTH = 0.75;

Because of concerns of program readability this style of constant definition is discouraged—the definitions do not stand out as much as in individual statements and combining definitions inhibits commenting.

```
final double DOOR_HEIGHT = 2.00;    // meters
final double DOOR_WIDTH = 0.75;     // meters
```

The definitions of constants DOOR_WIDTH and DOOR_HEIGHT have inline comments. As indicated previously, the // indicates the remainder of the line is a comment. There is no requirement that the entire line be a comment.

Constants

Good programmers prefer the systematic use of symbolic names over literal values—so-called "magic" numbers—because the names provide meaning and their use reduces the potential introduction of errant values through incorrect keyboarding.

It is a Java programming convention that the identifier name of a constant be composed of uppercase letters with underscores separating the various words that make up a name. Thus, the use of KILOGRAMS_PER_POUND in BMI.java rather than kilogramsPerPound.

| 2.2.2 | **VARIABLES** |

Besides making use of constants, program BMI.java makes use of variables of type **double**. A *variable* is the symbolic name for a memory location whose contents *can* be modified during program execution. A basic variable definition normally takes the following form.

Type | Name | = | Expression | ;

Type of value associated with the variable | Name of variable—it must be a legal identifier and it should be descriptive of its purpose | Expression to be evaluated and initially associated with the constant

The definition begins with the type of value in which we are interested. The symbolic name comes next, which must be a valid Java identifier. The definition concludes with an equal sign followed by an expression whose value initializes the memory location being associated with the symbolic name.

In our program, weightInPounds, heightInFeet, metricWeight, metricHeight, and bmi are all local primitive variables of type **double**. They are variables because of the lack of the modifier **final** in their definitions. They are *local* variables because their use is limited to the method that defines them. They are *primitive* variables, because the type **double** is one of Java's primitive types.

> Local versus nonlocal is explored in Chapters 4 and 7

Before we can use a local variable in a calculation, we must first define and initialize the variable. For example, the definition of weightInPounds in line 12

```
double weightInPounds = 75.5;   // our person's weight
```

initializes the variable to the **double** value 75.5, where the semicolon indicates that no more **double** variables are being defined in this statement.

The effect of the weightInPounds definition is

weightInPounds | 75.5

Because the value of weightInPounds is allowed to change, there is no lock used in its depiction.

Similarly, the statement

```
double heightInFeet = 4.5;      // our person's height
```

makes heightInFeet a **double** variable whose memory location is initialized to the **double** value 4.5. The effect of the definition is

heightInFeet | 4.5

Together the definitions of weightInPounds and heightInFeet define the characteristics of the person to be processed.

Java does not require that a variable definition include initialization. For example, consider the following code segment defining local variables `sampleWeight` and `currentTemperature`.

```
double sampleWeight;
double currentTemperature;
```

Local variables are left uninitialized if no initialization value is specified. Our representation of such variables is

sampleWeight	–
currentTemperature	–

where the "–" indicates an uninitialized value.

Although variables can be defined without initialization, Java compilers require that variables be initialized before their values are used.

Multiple variables can be defined in a single statement by separating the definitions by commas. The following statement uses this style to define and initialize **double** variables `currentReading` and `maximumReading`.

```
double currentReading = 6.21, maximumReading = 19.54;
```

As with defining constants, this style of variable definition is discouraged because of program readability. The preferred style has one definition per statement.

```
char currentReading =  6.21;   // meters per second
char maximumReading = 19.54;   // meters per second
```

Naming variables

It is a Java coding style convention that the identifier name of a variable be descriptive of the represented value and that it begin with a lowercase letter. If a variable name is composed of a single word, then the entire name is in lowercase. If a variable name is composed of multiple words, then the words are concatenated together and all letters are lowercase except for the letters that start successive words. Thus, the coding style calls for `bodyTemperature` rather than the nondescriptive `bt` or the underscore using `body_temperature`.

2.2.3   OPERATIONS

The next section of method `main()` from `BMI.java` converts the person's characteristics into their metric equivalents.

```
// convert to metric equivalents
double metricWeight = weightInPounds * KILOGRAMS_PER_POUND;
double metricHeight = heightInFeet * METERS_PER_FOOT;
```

Assignment statement

Section 2.6, discusses the assignment statement, which can assign a value to an uninitialized variable or constant.

The definition of variable `metricWeight` does not initialize the variable with a literal numeric value. Instead, `metricWeight` is initialized with the value of the expression

```
weightInPounds * KILOGRAMS_PER_POUND
```

The expression uses the **double** multiplication operator `*` to form the product of the current value of variable `weightInPounds` times the constant `KILOGRAMS_PER_POUND`. The product represents the metric equivalent of the weight in pounds. Similarly, the definition

```
double metricHeight = heightInFeet * METERS_PER_FOOT;
```

initializes `metricHeight` with the product of the current value of variable `heightIn-Feet` times the constant `METERS_PER_FOOT`. Thus, `metricHeight` represents the metric equivalent of the height in feet. The effects of the definition are[1]

metric Weight	34.2770
metric Height	1.3706

Together the two definitions form the conversion section of our program.

At this point, we are ready to compute the BMI of our person. As we stated at the beginning of this section, BMI is the ratio of the person's metric weight to the square of the person's metric height. The program defines a variable `bmi` to store that value.

```
// perform bmi calculation
double bmi = metricWeight / (metricHeight * metricHeight);
```

Variable `bmi` is initialized to the value of the expression

```
metricWeight / (metricHeight * metricHeight)
```

The expression uses the **double** division operator `/`, **double** multiplication operator `*`, and the parentheses grouping operators `(` and `)`. The parentheses cause the subexpression

```
metricHeight * metricHeight
```

to be evaluated as a unit. The value of the subexpression is the square of the current value of variable `metricHeight`. The subexpression value then is divided into `metric-Weight`. The result of that division is used to initialize variable `bmi`.

bmi	18.2439

---

1   When we depict **double** values, the values may be sometimes truncated (e.g., the actual value represented by `metricHeight` is 1.3706999999999998).

In general, floating-point division is an approximation of real division. The result is approximate, because Java uses only 8 bytes of memory for each **double** value, which limits the number of digits that can be represented.

The next section of our program displays the BMI information to the user. The section is made up of four `println()` invocations.

```
// display result
System.out.println("A person with");
System.out.println("  weight " + weightInPounds + " lbs");
System.out.println("  height " + heightInFeet + " feet");
System.out.println("has a BMI of " + Math.round(bmi));
```

The first invocation of `println()` is similar to previous `println()` invocations—it gives the method a literal character string for displaying.

```
System.out.println("A person with");
```

After method `println()` completes, the output produced so far is

```
A person with
```

The next invocation of `println()`

```
System.out.println("  weight " + weightInPounds + " lbs");
```

supplies the value of the *expression* "   weight " + weightInPounds + " lbs" to `println()`. Our use of the term expression is deliberate. "   weight " + weightInPounds + " lbs" requires operator evaluation. The expression is composed of two `String` concatenation operations.

A Java compiler can tell by context that the + operators in this expression calls for `String` concatenation
rather than addition. Operator + performs addition when
both of its operands are numeric; the operator performs `String` concatenation when at least one of the operands is a `String`.

The String class is discussed in detail in Chapter 3

The evaluation of the String concatenation expression occurs in the following manner. First, "   weight " and weightInPounds is evaluated. Because the value of weightInPounds is 75.5, the concatenation produces a string with value "   weight 75.5". This string then is concatenated with the literal string " lbs". The resulting string has value "   weight 75.5 lbs" and is used as the actual parameter in the `println()` invocation. A pictorial examination of the expression evaluation is given in Figure 2.4.

After executing the statement, the program output to this point is

```
A person with
   weight 75.5 lbs
```

Using similar analysis, after the next `println()` invocation

```
System.out.println("  height " + heightInFeet + " feet");
```

Figure 2.4   **Evaluation of " weight " + weightInPounds + " lbs".**

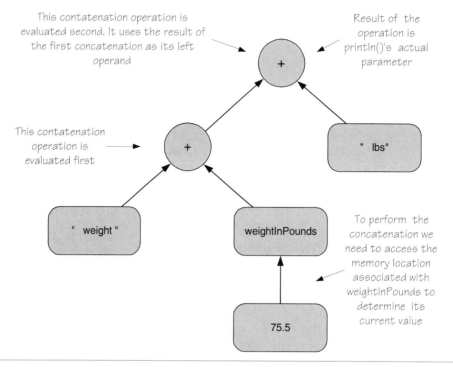

This contatenation operation is evaluated second. It uses the result of the first concatenation as its left operand

Result of the operation is println()'s actual parameter

This contatenation operation is evaluated first

" lbs"

" weight "

weightInPounds

To perform the concatenation we need to access the memory location associated with weightInPounds to determine its current value

75.5

the program output is now

```
A person with
   weight 75.5 lbs
   height 4.5 feet
```

The last `println()` statement requires analysis.

```
System.out.println("has a BMI of " + Math.round(bmi));
```

The program does not display merely the value of variable `bmi`, as in the statement

```
System.out.println("has a BMI of " + bmi);
```

With such a statement the program output would be

```
A person with
   weight 75.5 lbs
   height 4.5 feet
has a BMI of 18.24391242817714
```

The 14 digits displayed after the decimal are distracting and serve no real purpose. Therefore, rather than displaying `bmi`, our statement displays `Math.round(bmi)`.

```
System.out.println("has a BMI of " + Math.round(bmi));
```

Method `Math.round()` is a class method of standard Java class `java.lang.Math`. As it is a class method, the method is a service provided by the class that does not require association with a particular class object. The method takes a **double** floating-point value as its parameter and returns the nearest integer value. Thus, the program outputs

```
A person with
    weight 75.5 lbs
    height 4.5 feet
has a BMI of 18
```

Program BMI.java has shown the usefulness of constants, variables, and operators. We now introduce all of the primitive types.

2.3   PRIMITIVE TYPES

Java has seven primitive types besides **double**. There are five primitive integer types **byte**, **short**, **int**, **long**, and **char** (**char** is also the character type); another primitive floating-point type **float**; and a logical type **boolean**. The names of the primitive types are all keywords.

The different primitive types have different representation capabilities. For example, the **short** uses 2 bytes to represent an integer value and an **int** uses 4 bytes. As a result, a **short** variable can store integer values only in the range –32,768 … 32,767, and an **int** variable can store integer values only in the range –2,147,483,648 … 2,147,483,647.

As another example of representation capabilities, the **float** type uses 4 bytes to represent a floating-point number and the **double** type uses 8 bytes to represent a floating-point number. As a consequence, a **float** variable has typically only 6 places of accuracy and a **double** value has typically only 15 places of accuracy.

Java's motivation for having multiple numeric types is to give programmers full access to all the types supported by typical and specialized computer hardware (e.g, PCs, mobile telephones, PDAs). In the applications in this text, we generally use the primary primitive types **int**, **char**, and **double**.

Representation

A complete specification of the values associated with the primitive types is given in Appendix A.3.

2.3.1   INT TYPE

Most programming languages have a basic type for storing and manipulating integer variables and values. In Java this type is **int**.

Java provides the usual integer arithmetic *binary* operators such as addition +, subtraction –, multiplication *, and quotient /, where the term binary indicates that the oper-

---

Listing 2.7   **CelsiusToFahrenheit.java**

```
 1. // Purpose: Convert a Celsius temperature to Fahrenheit
 2.
 3. public class CelsiusToFahrenheit {
 4.
 5.     // main(): application entry point
 6.     public static void main(String[] args) {
 7.         // set Celsius temperature of interest
 8.         int celsius = 28;
 9.
10.         // convert to Fahrenheit equivalent
11.         int fahrenheit = 32 + ((9 * celsius) / 5);
12.
13.         // display result
14.         System.out.println("Celsius temperature");
15.         System.out.println("    " + celsius);
16.         System.out.println("equals Fahrenheit temperature");
17.         System.out.println("    " + fahrenheit);
18.     }
19. }
```

---

ator is applied to two operands. The addition, subtraction, and multiplication operators work as expected. For example, $1 + 2$ is 3, $18 - 11$ is 7, and $3 * 21$ is 63.

Integer division sometimes confuses beginning programmers. When given integer operands, the quotient operator produces the integer quotient result (i.e., there is no remainder). For example, $20 / 6$ is 3, $19 / 11$ is 1, $4 / 5$ is 0, and $8 / -3$ is -2.

Java also provides a *modulus* operator (%). The modulus operator % produces the remainder associated with an integer division. For example, $18 \% 3$ is 0, $17 \% 2$ is 1, $12 \% 16$ is 12, $7 \% -3$ is 1 and $-7 \% 3$ is -1. A complete list of integer operators is given in Appendix A.3. Java does not have an exponentiation operator. However, standard class `java.lang.Math` does provide methods for performing exponentiation.

Listing 2.7 presents a program `CelsiusToFahrenheit.java` using several **int** operators that converts an integer Celsius temperature of interest to its integer Fahrenheit equivalent. The conversion uses the formula

$$Fahrenheit = 32 + \frac{9}{5}Celsius$$

The output of the program is

```
Celsius temperature
    28
equals Fahrenheit temperature
    82
```

In the program, variable `celsius` holds the value of our temperature of interest.

```
int celsius = 28;
```

In writing the definition of **int** variable `fahrenheit`, we were cognizant of the fact that an **int** initialization expression is being evaluated.

```
int fahrenheit = 32 + ((9 * celsius) / 5);   // correct
```

For example, we did not express the definition in the manner:

```
int fahrenheit = 32 + ((9 / 5) * celsius);    // incorrect
```

Because of its integer operands, the term 9 / 5 from this errant statement evaluates to 1, which makes the definition equivalent to

```
int fahrenheit = 32 + celsius;                // incorrect
```

The correct implementation reorders and regroups the expression terms 9 and cel-sius so that their product is divided by 5.

2.3.2   CHAR TYPE

Closely related to numeric types is the character type **char**. In Java, characters are encoded in 2 bytes using the Unicode character set encoding.

Normally, programmers do not use a literal numeric representation of a character. Instead they represent the character within single quotes. The compiler will translate automatically the character representation into the Unicode encoding. For example, programmers use 'a' when they need to refer explicitly to character *a* rather than its Unicode value of 97. Because the underlying representation of **char** is integer, the operators defined on the integer types are defined on **char** variables and values as well.

The Unicode character set encoding guarantees that

```
'0' < '1' < '2' < ... < '9'
'a' < 'b' < 'c' < ... < 'z'
'A' < 'B' < 'C' < ... < 'Z'
```

These relationships are useful, because they enable values that are made up of sequences of characters to be sorted into *lexicographic* (alphabetic) order.

Additionally, with the Unicode character set we know that

```
'2' + 1
```

yields an integer that is the encoding for the character '3'. In fact, for any digit *d* except for 9, the expression '*d*' + 1 yields the next sequential character digit. Thus,

- '0' + 1 evaluates to '1';
- '1' + 1 evaluates to '2';

   ...

- '8' + 1 evaluates to '9'.

yields the next sequential character digit.

The following relationship exists with regard to the lower case Latin letters.

- 'a' + 1 evaluates to 'b';
- 'b' + 1 evaluates to 'c';

   ...

- 'y' + 1 evaluates to 'z'.

Listing 2.8 **LowerToUpper.java**

```
1.  // Purpose: Demonstrate char arithmetic
2.
3.  public class LowerToUpper {
4.
5.      // main(): application entry point
6.      public static void main(String[] args) {
7.          // set lower case character of interest
8.          char lowerCaseLetter = 'c';
9.
10.         // convert to uppercase equivalent
11.         int upperCaseLetter = 'A' + (lowerCaseLetter - 'a');
12.
13.         // display result
14.         System.out.println("Uppercase equivalent of");
15.         System.out.println("    " + lowerCaseLetter);
16.         System.out.println("is");
17.         System.out.println("    " + upperCaseLetter);
18.     }
19. }
```

In addition, the following relationship exists with regard to the upper case Latin letters.

- 'A' + 1 evaluates to 'B';

- 'B' + 1 evaluates to 'C';

  …

- 'Y' + 1 evaluates to 'Z'.

These relationships are all useful, as they enable a character to be classified efficiently as to whether it represents a lowercase character, an uppercase character, or a digit.

Listing 2.8 of LowerToUpper.java provides an example of **char** arithmetic. The program converts a lower case letter to its upper case equivalent. The character of interest is represented in the program by **char** variable lowerCaseLetter.

```
char lowerCaseLetter = 'c';
```

The uppercase equivalent is stored in upperCaseLetter.

```
char upperCaseLetter = 'A' + (lowerCaseLetter - 'a');
```

The term (lowerCaseLetter - 'a') evaluates to the difference in the Unicode encodings of the characters represented by lowerCaseLetter and 'a'. In this case, the difference is 99 – 97 or 2, which indicates the character represented by lowerCaseLetter has an encoding 2 beyond that of the encoding of 'a' encoding. In general, the difference of any lower case letter and 'a' represents that character's offset from the encoding of 'a'. Because the upper case letters also have consecutive encodings, adding such an offset to 'A' produces the uppercase equivalent.

The output of the program is

```
Uppercase equivalent of
    c
is
    C
```

Literal character versus literal character string

A common beginning programmer mistake is to confuse character values and string values. A literal character is an encoding for exactly one character within *single* quotes. Thus, 'a', 'H', '=', and '\n' are all valid literal character values. The expressions "a" and 'abc' are not legal literal characters: "a" is not a literal character because the a is not in single quotes; and 'abc' is not a literal character because abc is not an encoding for a single character.

A literal character string is an encoding for zero or more characters within *double* quotes. Thus, "abc", "", and "a" are all valid literal character strings. Expressions 'a' and 'abc' are not legal literal character strings because of their use of single quotes.

Class Character

Because converting characters from one case to another is a common programming activity, standard Java class java.lang.Character provides in part class methods:

char Character.toLowercase(**char** ch)
> Returns the lowercase equivalent of ch, if it exists; otherwise, the method returns ch.

char Character.toUppercase(**char** ch)
> Returns the uppercase equivalent of ch, if it exists; otherwise, the method returns ch.

2.3.3   DOUBLE TYPE

The type **double** uses 8 bytes to represent a floating-point value. Java provides the usual arithmetic operators, except for an exponentiation operator. A complete list of floating-point operators is given in Appendix A.3.

Listing 2.9 of KilometersToMiles.java converts a **double** distance in kilometers to its mile equivalent. The program makes use of conversion

$$Miles = 0.621371 \times Kilometers$$

The output of the program is

```
3.2 kilometers = 1.9883872 miles
```

As lines 14–15 illustrate, sometimes statements do not fit conveniently on a single line. This situation is not a problem because Java ignores the whitespace between program elements. Therefore, even though the initialization expression for distanceIn-Miles is expressed over two lines, its evaluation is unaffected. The standard convention

---

Listing 2.9 **KilometersToMiles.java**

```
1.  // Purpose: Convert kilometers to miles
2.
3.  public class KilometersToMiles {
4.
5.      // main(): application entry point
6.      public static void main(String[] args) {
7.          // define constant of interest
8.          final double MILES_PER_KILOMETER = 0.621371;
9.
10.         // set mile of interest
11.         double distanceInKilometers = 3.2;
12.
13.         // convert to metric equivalent
14.         double distanceInMiles = distanceInKilometers
15.                                     * MILES_PER_KILOMETER;
16.
17.         // display result
18.         System.out.println(distanceInKilometers + " kilometers = "
19.                             + distanceInMiles + " miles");
20.     }
21. }
```

Infinity and beyond

Java provides several predefined constants for programming convenience. The constants are members of the classes `Integer`, `Double`, and `Float`. These classes are part of standard package `java.lang`.

`Integer.MAX_VALUE`
> The largest positive value of type **int**.

`Integer.MIN_VALUE`
> The smallest negative value of type **int**.

`Double.MAX_VALUE`
> The largest positive value of type **double**.

`Double.MIN_VALUE`
> The smallest positive value of type **double**.

`Double.POSITIVE_INFINITY`
> The positive infinity value of type **double**. A value bigger than any valid finite **double** value.

`Double.NEGATIVE_INFINITY`
> The negative infinity value of type **double**. A value smaller than any valid finite **double** value.

`Double.NaN`
> The not-a-number value of type **double**. A **double** value that does not correspond to a numeric value. `Double.NaN` is not comparable to any other **double** value including itself. For example, because division by zero is undefined, `1.0 / 0.0` evaluates to `Double.NaN`.

The class `Float` defines an analogous set of constants for the **float** type as `Double` does for the **double** type.

for breaking a long expression into a multiline expression is that the continuation line should begin with an operator and if it is reasonable, the continuation line should be indented to place the trailing part of the expression underneath the leading part of the expression. Both measures signal the reader that the line is a continuation of the expression from the previous line.

Decimal and scientific notation

Java provides two basic ways to write floating-point literals—in *decimal* or *scientific notation*. A number in decimal notation consists a whole-number part and a fractional part separated by a period. One of the whole-number part or fractional part can be empty. If present, the whole-number part and fraction parts are decimal numerals. For example, `123.456`, `0.0`, `.9`, and `1.` are all in decimal notation.

Java also provides the ability to express floating-point numeral using *scientific notation*. A number in scientific notation consists of a number in decimal notation concatenated with either an e or E followed by an exponent. The exponent is an integer decimal literal. For example, `1.23e10`, `0.23E-4`, `-45.e+23`, and `23.68E12` are all floating-point literals in scientific notation. These numbers are equivalent respectively to 1.23×10^{10}, 0.23×10^{-4}, -45×10^{23}, and 23.68×10^{12}.

2.4	**EXPRESSIONS**

Our examples have been chosen carefully so that the *expressions* in them would have obvious evaluations. For example, consider the definition of variable `fahrenheit` in program `CelsiusToFahrenheit.java`.

```
int fahrenheit = 32 + ((9 * celsius)/5);
```

Our use of parentheses was deliberate—with the parentheses being present there is clearly one legitimate way to evaluate the expression.

Consider the initialization of variable `expr` in the following code segment

```
int expr = 4 + 2 * 5;
```

It seems that there are two possible values for `expr`. If the addition is performed first, then `expr` is initialized to 30; if instead, the multiplication is performed first, then `expr` is initialized to 14. Now consider the code segment

```
System.out.println(5 / 2.0);
```

What value is displayed? The answer depends on whether integer or floating-point division is performed in evaluating `5 / 2.0`.

In fact, the evaluations of `4 + 2 * 5` and `5 / 2.0` are unambiguous in Java. In this section, we discuss Java's rules for evaluating expressions. These rules ensure that the evaluation of *any* Java expression is unambiguous. In particular, the Java rules for evaluating expressions call for `expr` to be initialized to 14 and for 2.5 to be displayed.

2.4.1   UNARY AND BINARY OPERATORS

Expressions are Java's mechanism for applying operations to values and variables. They are the means by which we calculate new values from old ones. The values and variables being operated on are called the *operands*. The process of applying the operation to the operands is referred to as *evaluating the expression*. The evaluation of an expression yields a result that has a value *and* a Java type. The notion that an expression yields *both* a value and type is very important.

The simplest form of a Java expression is a literal or variable with no explicit operation being applied. Suppose `sampleSize` is an **int** variable with definition

```
int sampleSize = 20;
```

Then the result of evaluating the expression

```
sampleSize
```

is the **int** value 20. In a real sense, an operation is being applied to the `sampleSize`. The operation being applied is one that fetches the value in the memory location associated with `sampleSize`.

The – operator in expressions

```
-23
-n
```

is a unary operator, where the term *unary* means that the operator is applied to a single operand. Java has several unary operators. In these expressions, we are using the *unary negation operator* for negating a value. Obviously, the first result is the **int** value −23. Suppose n is a **double** variable with the value 10.5

```
double n = 10.5;
```

Then the expression -n evaluates to the **double** value −10.5.

The *unary plus operator* is included for symmetry with the unary minus operator. The expression

```
+244
```

yields the **int** value 244.

As demonstrated in our introduction to the primitive types, Java has many binary operators. For example, the expressions

```
6 * 21
29 / 11
6.9 + 19.82
1.1 - 2.8
```

yield respectively the values **int** value 126, **int** value 2, **double** value 26.72, and **double** value -1.7.

Although it does not make a difference when doing arithmetic with literal and variable operands, Java specifies for a binary operation that the left operand be evaluated before the right operand.

Multiplication must be explicit

The equation for a line is written normally as $y = mx + b$. In the formula, it is understood implicitly that m and x are being multiplied. In Java, there is no implicit multiplication. The expression mx + b uses the plus operation on variables mx and b.

2.4.2   PRECEDENCE

Like many programming languages, Java allows programmers to write expressions composed of multiple binary and unary operators. For example, consider the statement

```
int result = 3 * 5 / 2;
```

Depending on whether the multiplication is performed first or second, the value of the variable `result` is either 7 or 6.

To evaluate an expression in general, we need a set of *precedence rules* and *associativity rules* that tell us the order in which to apply the operators.

Let's begin by discussing precedence. Each operator is assigned a precedence level. Operators with higher precedence are applied before operators with lower precedence are applied.

Arithmetic expressions are evaluated just as we learned in grade school. The grouping operators () have the highest precedence. The unary operators – and + have higher precedence than the multiplicative operators of multiplication *, division /, and modulus %. The multiplicative operators have higher precedence than addition and subtraction.

Table 2.2 specifies in part the precedence level of the arithmetic and grouping operators. A complete operator table is given in Appendix A.3.

Table 2.2   **Basic operator precedence and associativity**

Precedence	Operator	Associativity
17	()	Nonassociative
13	unary + and –	Right associative
12	* / %	Left associative
11	+ –	Left associative

Thus, in the definition

```
int expr = 4 + 2 * 5;
```

variable `expr` is initialized to 14 rather than 30. It is initialized in this manner because multiplication has higher precedence than addition.

As other examples, consider the following expressions:

```
2 / 3 + 5        // division takes precedence over addition
-8 * 4           // negation takes precedence over multiplication
8 + 7 % 2        // modulus takes precedence over addition
```

In the first expression, because the division operator has higher precedence than the addition operator, the division is performed first. The result is 0, which is added to 5 to yield an overall expression value of **int** value 5. In the second example, the unary minus operator is applied to 8, and the resulting value –8 is multiplied by 4 to yield an overall expression value of **int** value –32. In the third expression, the modulus operation is performed first and yields the value 1. This value is added to 8 to yield an overall expression value of **int** value 9.

We can use parentheses to override the order of evaluation. Suppose we wanted to compute the average of three **double** variables a, b, and c. The following code segment is *not* correct.

```
double average = a + b + c / 3.0;    // incorrect average
```

Because the division operator has the highest
precedence, it is calculated first. The expression is
equivalent to a + b + (c / 3.0)

Because of its precedence, the division c / 3.0 is calculated first. The sum of a + b then is calculated. The two intermediary results then are summed. By using parentheses, we can rewrite the definition to achieve the desired result.

```
double average = (a + b + c) / 3.0;  // correct average
```

The parentheses group the terms whose sum is the
left operand of the division

Parenthesized expressions can be *nested*. In other words, a parenthesized expression can contain other parenthesized expressions. In such cases, the innermost parenthesized expressions are evaluated first. Consider the following expression:

```
(2 + (3 + 2) * 5) / (4 - 2)
```

Because the parenthesized subexpression (3 + 2) is nested within another parenthesized expression, it is evaluated first. Afterward, the expressions contained in the outer sets of parentheses can be evaluated. The resulting value is the **int** value 13.

In addition to precedence rules, associativity rules are also needed. It is the associativity rules that indicate how to evaluate expressions with operators of the same precedence. Such is the case for the initialization expression in the definition of variable result that started this section.

```
int result = 3 * 5 / 2;
```

As indicated in Table 2.2, multiplication and division are *left associative*. This associativity causes the compiler to evaluate the operands from left to right. Therefore, in the initialization expression for result, operand 5 associates with the operator on its left, and the correct value of the expression is the **int** value 7. (Remember, integer division truncates.)

Use of parentheses

Although it is important to know the rules of precedence, we often use parentheses to make the order of evaluation explicit even in cases where they are not needed. This technique helps readers understand the code more readily—such comprehension is important if they are modifying your code. For example, the expression

```
a * b + c / d - 3.0
```

and the parenthesized expression

```
(a * b) + (c / d) - 3.0
```

both perform the same computation, but the meaning of the latter one is clear.

2.4.3   WIDENING AND NARROWING OPERAND CONVERSION

Up to this point, we have considered numeric expressions where all the operands are of same type. But what if one operand of an addition is of type **int** and the other is of type **char**? Or what if one operand of a multiplication is of type **int** and the other is of type **double**? In total, there are 49 possible operand combinations per numeric binary operator. Rather than having different arithmetic operations for each possible operand combination, Java applies *unary conversion rules* to the operands before any operations are performed. One of these rules governs whether integer or floating-point arithmetic is performed.

- If either of the operands are floating point, then floating-point arithmetic is performed. Otherwise, integer arithmetic is performed.

Other rules ensure that operands are converted to the same type of value. One such rule is

- If either of the operands are of type **double**, then any non-**double** operand is *widened* automatically (i.e., converted) to **double**.

For example, suppose the following definitions are in effect.

```
int    i = 4;
int    j = 30;
double d = 6.21;
double e = 19.54;
```

Then, the following expressions are all integer expressions

```
1 + 2
i * 3
i / j
```

and the following expressions are all floating-point expressions

```
6.9 + 11.28
11.29 * d
e * d
```

Loss of information

While integer widening does not introduce any loss of information about a value, narrowing can introduce a loss of information (e.g., converting an **int** to a **short**. Narrowing is accomplished by discarding the high-order bits. Thus, it is possible a change in a sign can occur with narrowing. For example, the value of expression **(short)** 32768 is -32768.

Floating-point widening from a **float** value to a **double** value does not introduce any loss of information about a value. However, the widening of an integer to a **float** or **double** value can introduce a loss of precision depending on the number. Narrowing a floating-point value also can introduce a loss of information.

In the following floating-point expressions, the integer operands are widened to **double** before expression evaluation.

```
11.29 + 1991
i / d
```

If the result of an integer initialization expression is for a variable of a different type from the value of the expression, then the value is converted to the variable's type by widening or narrowing. For example, in the following code segment, the value of the **int** expression 5 * 5 is widened to **double** in the first definition and narrowed to **char** in the second definition.

```
double a = 5 * 5;
char b = 5 * 5;
```

For detailed information on arithmetic conversion rules, the reader is directed to a Java reference manual such as *The Java Language Specification*, J. Gosling, B. Joy, G. Steele, and, G. Bracha, Addison-Wesley, New York, 2000. An online version of the text is available on the Web at www.javasoft.com.

For operator + there are subtleties besides the unary conversion rules. If at least one of its operands is a String, then concatenation is performed; otherwise addition is performed.

Consider the following code segment. What output does it produce? In determining your answer, use the fact that + is left associative.

```
String s = 1 + 2 + "3";
String t = "1" + 2 + 3;
System.out.println(s);
System.out.println(t);
```

The output is

```
33
123
```

Because + is left associative the additive term 1 + 2 is evaluated first in the initialization expression 1 + 2 + "3". Therefore, s is initialized with the value of the concatenation 3 + "3".

For the same reason, concatenation "1" + 2 is evaluated first in the initialization expression "1" + 2 + 3. Therefore, t is initialized with the value of the concatenation "12" + 3.

OVERFLOW, UNDERFLOW, AND EXCEPTIONS

Arithmetic operators have the potential to produce a value that is larger or smaller than the integer types can handle. These situations are called respectively *overflow* and *underflow*. There is no signal to a program by a Java interpreter that indicates whether an overflow or underflow has occurred. For example, the following code segment

```
int biggestInt = Integer.MAX_VALUE;
int overflowInt = biggestInt * biggestInt;
System.out.println(biggestInt + " * " + biggestInt
                + " evaluates to " + overflowInt + " in Java");
```

displays as its output

```
2147483647 * 2147483647 evaluates to 1 in Java
```

So take care when dealing with very big and very small numbers.

Java does signal a program automatically when division by 0 is attempted. Consider the following code segment, which attempts a divide by 0. (Because factor is defined to be 1, the expression (factor - 1) evaluates to 0.)

```
int factor = 1;
int result = 2 / (factor - 1);
System.out.println("Divide by zero was completed.");
```

The code segment never executes the println() statement. Attempting a divide by zero is unexpected by Java. As such, it is known as an *exception*. The signaling process is known as *throwing* an exception. If a program does not have code that *catches* (processes) the exception, then the program is terminated.

Chapter 10 examines exception handling

We next turn our attention to developing a program that interacts with its user through the use of statements performing input and output.

INTERACTIVE PROGRAMS

A major deficiency of BMI.java is that the weight and height of the person is fixed. Unless you know somebody with a weight of 75.5 pounds and a height of 4.5 feet, the program is not that interesting. For the program to be useful, generally it must have interactive input and output (I/O) with its user. What we want is an BMI calculator with the ability to compute the BMI for the weight and height of the user's choosing. We can create such a program by modifying `BMI.java` of Listing 2.6 to make use of an input stream object that is capable of *extracting* (getting) the values a user enters with the keyboard.

```
BMI Calculator

Enter weight (lbs): 130.0
Enter height (feet): 5.75

A person with
     weight 130 lbs
     height 5.75 feet
has a BMI of 19
```

In the preceding sample run of such a program, the bold text was entered by the user in response to the requests for a weight and height. We use this type convention throughout the text. The output was produced by `BMICalculator.java` of Listing 2.10.

Program `BMICalculator.java` begins with an **import** statement.

```
import java.io.*;
```

An **import** statement indicates that the program requires access to other Java resources. In creating and accessing the input stream object for getting input values, the program uses classes that are defined in standard Java software library `java.io`. In Java parlance, a software library is known as a *package* or *application programming interface* (*API*). Because only classes defined in package `java.lang` are available implicitly to a program, it is necessary to import the needed classes from the `io` API.

There are hundreds of APIs available for Java programmers. For example, there are APIs for developing multimedia, cryptography, telephony, and speech recognition programs. In Java, the resources supplied by an API are primarily classes. The classes and other elements of an API generally are organized in a hierarchical manner to form a package.

Documentation of the major APIs is included in an appendix. For a reference on all of the standard APIs see www.javasoft.com

The * in the **import** statement is a special character indicating that all resources of `java.io` are to be made available to the program. For this reason, it is sometimes called the *wildcard* character.

Rather than using the * shorthand for gaining access to all `io` resources, the program could have imported individually the particular class resources by *fully specifying* their names.

```
import java.io.BufferedReader;
import java.io.InputStreamReader;
import java.io.IOException;
```

We defer the discussion of these classes until we examine the statements that extract the input values.

The definition of method `main()` begins on line 8. The definition indicates that the method possibly can throw an exception.

```
public static void main(String[] args) throws IOException {
```

Listing 2.10 **BMICalculator.java**

```
 1. // Purpose: Compute BMI for user-specified weight and height
 2.
 3. import java.io.*;
 4.
 5. public class BMICalculator {
 6.
 7.     // main(): application entry point
 8.     public static void main(String[] args) throws IOException {
 9.         // defining constants
10.         final double KILOGRAMS_PER_POUND = 0.454;
11.         final double METERS_PER_FOOT = 0.3046;
12.
13.         // displaying legend
14.         System.out.println("BMI Calculator\n");
15.
16.         // set up input stream
17.         BufferedReader stdin = new BufferedReader(
18.                 new InputStreamReader(System.in));
19.
20.         // get person's characteristics
21.         System.out.print("Enter weight (lbs): ");
22.         double weight = Double.parseDouble(stdin.readLine());
23.
24.         System.out.print("Enter height (feet): ");
25.         double height = Double.parseDouble(stdin.readLine());
26.
27.         // convert to metric equivalents
28.         double metricWeight = weight * KILOGRAMS_PER_POUND;
29.         double metricHeight = height * METERS_PER_FOOT;
30.
31.         // perform bmi calculation
32.         double bmi = metricWeight
33.                             / (metricHeight * metricHeight);
34.
35.         // display result
36.         System.out.println("A person with");
37.         System.out.println("    weight " + weight + " (lbs)");
38.         System.out.println("    height " + height + " (feet)");
39.         System.out.println("has a BMI of " + bmi);
40.     }
41. }
```

In calculating the BMI, the program requires that the user provide numeric values for the weight and height in question. If the user does not supply two numeric values, variables `weight` and `height` cannot be initialized correctly. In this case, Java signals the program that an exception (error) has occurred. Ideally, the program's processing of the inputs should take this possibility into account. However, until additional language features are introduced, all our programs ignore any exceptions that arise. As a result, if an exception does arise, Java terminates the program.

Method `main()`'s starts in a straightforward manner by defining conversion constants and by displaying a legend.

```
// defining constants
final double KILOGRAMS_PER_POUND = 0.454;
final double METERS_PER_FOOT = 0.3046;

// displaying legend
System.out.println("BMI Calculator\n");
```

In the next section, the program becomes interesting. There, method `main()` defines and initializes a variable `stdin` of type `BufferedReader`.

```
BufferedReader stdin = new BufferedReader(
        new InputStreamReader(System.in));
```

With this variable the program has access to a `BufferedReader` object, which is an input stream. `BufferedReader` objects have a method `readLine()` that can extract character strings from an input stream.

The `BufferedReader` object created in lines 17–18 can extract strings from the input stream `System.in`. By default, `System.in` is associated with the keyboard.

Chapters 3 and 4 focus on the use of objects and reference variables. For now, we limit our use of objects to a single `BufferedReader`.

Because `BufferedReader` is a class, its variables are not primitive type variables—they are *reference type (object) variables*. The syntax for defining and initializing a reference type variable such as `stdin` is different than the defining a primitive type variable. The `stdin` variable initialization process has two parts. First, the **new** expression *constructs* a new `BufferedReader` object.

```
new BufferedReader(new InputStreamReader(System.in))
```

A new operation constructs a new object. The value of the operation is a reference to the new object. This new operation constructs a BufferedReader object out of a new InputStreamReader object that was built using the object representing the standard input stream

The value of that **new** expression is a *reference* (pointer) to the memory location that holds the new `BufferedReader` object. Thus, the value of an object variable is *not* an object but a *reference* to an object.

Therefore, the definition in lines 17–18 sets aside a memory location for variable `stdin`. The value of this memory location is a reference to a memory location that holds a new `BufferedReader` object. The new `BufferedReader` referenced by `stdin` is built out of a new `InputStreamReader`, which is in turn built out of the standard input stream represented by `System.in`.

Figure 2.5   Variable stdin references a BufferedReader.

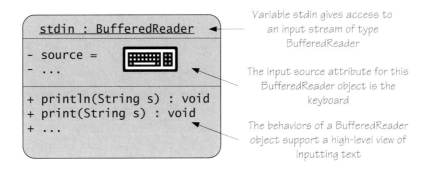

The program constructs the BufferedReader because the input methods associated with System.in are too low level (e.g., they extract input data on a byte-by-byte basis). Figure 2.5, depicts the representation of memory associated with stdin.

The next section of main() first *prompts* the user to supply the weight and then extracts the entered input value. The section then prompts and extracts the height value.

```
// get person's characteristics
System.out.print("Enter weight (lbs): ");
double weight = Double.parseDouble(stdin.readLine());

System.out.print("Enter height (feet): ");
double height = Double.parseDouble(stdin.readLine());
```

A prompt is issued by invoking method System.out.print(). A prompt cues the user to enter the value that we need. For prompts, print() is preferred over println(). Leaving the cursor near the prompt string rather than on the next line makes it more obvious that input is wanted from the user.

To extract the weight of the person, the program needs a place to store the input value. Line 22 defines and initializes the variable weight with the associated input value.

```
double weight = Double.parseDouble(stdin.readLine());
```

A **double** variable is used because we want to be able to enter the value as a decimal number.

The initialization expression for variable weight is the result of the invocation

```
Double.parseDouble(stdin.readLine())
```

The initialization expression has two parts that should be examined.

The subexpression

```
stdin.readLine()
```

invokes the readLine() method of the BufferedReader object referenced by stdin, The invocation produces the parameter value supplied to Double.parseDouble().

More to come

The nuances of classes in general and the particulars of BufferedReader are deferred until later chapters. For now only enough background is supplied so that you can make similar uses of the particular classes that BMICalculator.java employs.

Interactive input and output

It is important that programs tell the users what is expected of them. For example, BMI-Calculator.java tells the user to input the weight in pounds and the height in feet. These prompts may seem unnecessary: we know that two numbers are needed because we wrote the program. However in general, a user runs a program without seeing the source code, so it is important for a program to tell to the user what is expected. That is why the weight prompt of BMICalculator.java displays

```
Enter weight (lbs):
```
rather than displaying just
```
Enter weight:
```
The latter is insufficient—the user would not know what type of weight is wanted (e.g., carats, ounces, pounds, grams, kilograms, etc.)

In addition to telling the user what form the input should take, another general principle is to echo the input supplied by the user whenever it is practical. This practice gives the user some assurance that the input was received and interpreted correctly. For example, in BMICalculator.java, the weight and height are displayed along with the BMI. Thus, the user can see whether the program correctly interpreted the input.

Method readLine() waits for a line to be entered completely by the user. Once the line is entered, the whole line—whitespace and all except for the terminating newline character—is converted to string format and returned.

For this application, the user should enter a single number in reaction to the prompt. Therefore, the invocation stdin.readLine() should return a string that consists of a single number in floating-point form.

The class Double besides providing such constants as Double.MAX_VALUE and Double.MIN_VALUE (see page 66), provides a class method parseDouble() that takes a numeric string as an actual parameter and returns the **double** value with that representation. For example, the expression

```
Double.parseDouble("3.14159")
```

returns the **double** value 3.14159.

Similarly, the expression

```
Double.parseDouble(stdin.readLine())
```

returns the **double** representation of the current input line.

To extract the height of the person, a process is performed similar to extracting the weight of the person. First, a prompt is issued to tell the user what value we require.

```
System.out.print("Enter height (feet): ");
```

A **double** variable then is defined to store the extracted value.

```
double height = Double.parseDouble(stdin.readLine());
```

The remainder of the program performs metric conversions and displays the results in the same way that BMI.java of Listing 2.6 does and warrants no further discussion.

We next turn our attention to the assignment operator. This important operator enables a program to update the value of a variable.

2.6   PRIMITIVE VARIABLE ASSIGNMENT

Besides signaling in a variable definition that the variable is to be initialized, the symbol = is also the Java *assignment operator*. The assignment operator takes two operands. The left operand is the *target* variable; the right operand is the *modifying expression*. When evaluated, the assignment operator updates the value in the memory location associated with a *target* variable based on the modifying expression.

For example, the code segment

```
int j = 6;
j = 1982;
```

first defines an **int** variable j that is initialized to 6. The result of this action is depicted next.

```
j   6
```

An assignment statement then updates target j with the **int** value 1982.

```
j = 1982;
```

The result of this action would be

```
j   1982
```

The assignment operator works in the following manner. First, the left operand is evaluated to make sure that its value can be modified (e.g., a non-**final** variable). The right operand then is evaluated and its value is used to update the memory location associated with the left operand. For our particular assignment, the memory location associated with variable j is reset to the **int** value 1982. The assignment expression is read as "j gets 1982" or "j is assigned 1982."

Some people find it convenient to think of memory locations as mailboxes. An assignment operator places information in a mailbox. The variable name acts like the address. However, the analogy is not perfect—while a mailbox can hold several pieces of mail at one time, a memory location holds a *single* value. A new value assigned to a memory location *replaces* the existing value.

To better see what the assignment operator does, let's examine the following code segment.

```
int a = 1;
int aSquared = a * a;
a = 5;
aSquared = a * a;
```

The first two lines of the code segment define **int** variables a and aSquared. Each variable has a memory location allocated to it that is initialized to 1. Upon initialization, the memory for the variables has depiction

When the first assignment statement is evaluated

```
a = 5;
```

variable a is set to 5 and the value of aSquared is unchanged. Memory now has depiction

After the second assignment is evaluated

```
aSquared = a * a;
```

the value of variable aSquared is set to 25 and the value of variable a remains at 5. Memory now has this depiction

Now consider the following code segment

```
int i = 0;
i = i + 1;
```

This code segment first defines an **int** variable i with an value of 0. The memory for the variable has depiction

The assignment may not make sense at first glance.

```
i = i + 1;
```

But you must remember that the = operator is the assignment operator rather than the equality operator. The target of the assignment is the variable i. Variable i is to be reset to the value of the modifying expression i + 1, which equals 0 + 1, which is 1. Thus, i is reset to 1.

i `1`

The assignment statement is used sometimes to give an initial value to a variable. Although the following example is contrived, it does demonstrates this ability.

```
int asaRating;
asaRating = 400;
```

The first statement in the example, defines but does not initialize variable asaRating. Upon its definition, memory for the variable has depiction

asaRating `-`

where character "–" is again our indicator of an uninitialized value. Next, the assignment statement initializes variable asaRating to **int** value 400.

asaRating `400`

2.6.1 SWAPPING

A common programming *pattern* (task) is to *swap* or exchange the values of two variables. For example, let's suppose that variables x and y are defined and initialized and we want to swap their values.

```
double x = 5.12;
double y = 19.28;
```

Thus, the starting memory depiction for the variables is

x `5.12`

y `19.28`

We want to copy the value of x into y and copy the value of y into x. It is tempting to write the following assignment statements to accomplish the task.

```
x = y;    // Copy y into x
y = x;    // Copy x into y
```

However, this code would result in both x and y having the original value of y, which is 19.28. To see this outcome, let's trace through the code.

```
x = y;    // Copy y into x
```

After the first assignment, the value of y, which is 19.28, is copied into the memory location for x. This assignment results in the depiction

x | 19.28 |

y | 19.28 |

After the second assignment, the value of x, which is now 19.28, is copied into the memory location for y.

```
y = x;    // Copy x into y
```

Although y is reset, it is reset with the same value. Thus, this assignment also yields the depiction

x | 19.28 |

y | 19.28 |

The problem was that the first assignment statement overwrote the value of x that we needed to remember in order to reset y. To perform the task correctly, we use another variable to copy the value of one of the variables it is changed. In the following code segment, **double** variable named rememberX serves this purpose.

```
double x = 5.12;
double y = 19.28;
double rememberX = x;    // Make copy of original value of x
x = y;                   // Copy y into x
y = rememberX;           // Copy original value of x into y
```

After the three definitions in the segment are performed, memory has the depiction

x | 5.12 |

y | 19.28 |

rememberX | 5.12 |

The first assignment

```
x = y;                   // Copy y into x
```

updates x so memory now has depiction

x | 19.28 |

y | 19.28 |

rememberX | 5.12 |

And after the second assignment

```
y = rememberX;           // Copy original value of x into y
```

memory has depiction

```
      x |  19.28  |

      y |   5.12  |

remberX |   5.12  |
```

Thus, accomplishing our task of swapping variables x and y.

| 2.6.2 | ASSIGNMENT PRECEDENCE AND ASSOCIATIVITY |

Like other operators, the assignment operator produces a value. The value of an assignment operation is the new value of the left operand. Assuming j and k have been declared to be **int** variables, the statement

```
j = 5 * 3;
```

both stores a 15 in the variable j and evaluates to the **int** value 15.

Because assignment produces a value, we can write expressions such as

```
k = j = 5 * 3;
```

So what does the preceding assignment expression mean? The answer lies in knowing the precedence and associativity of the assignment operator. The natural and correct interpretation is that first 5 and 3 are multiplied together. Thus, the precedence of = is lower than that of *. Therefore, the interpretation of the previous expression is

```
k = j = (5 * 3);
```

Continuing with this example, observe that j is surrounded on both sides by the assignment operator =. In this situation, the associativity of = determines whether j binds with the = on the right or the = on the left. Unlike the arithmetic operators, the assignment operator is right associative. Therefore, the correct interpretation of the expression is

```
k = (j = (5 * 3));
```

which says that the result of the assignment of the product of 5 * 3 to j is assigned to k. Again this interpretation is natural because if assignments were left associative, the interpretation would be

```
(k = j) = (5 * 3);
```

which makes no sense.

Compound assignment

Java has several special operators for performing commonly occurring operations. One can think of these operators as language shorthands. For example, a common operation is to apply an operator to a variable and then store the result back into the same variable. As an example, consider adding 5 to a variable i. In many programming languages, this operation might be written as

```
i = i + 5;
```

However, Java has a compound additive assignment operator that accomplishes the same thing. In Java, the above expression is written usually as

```
i += 5;
```

Some of the other compound assignment operators are *=, -=, and /=. They respectively scale, reduce, and divide the target variable. For example,

```
i *= expression; // i's new value is i * (expression)
i -= expression; // i's new value is i - (expression)
i /= expression; // i's new value is i / (expression)
```

Assignment conversions and casting

If the target and modifying expression do not have the same type, it is necessary to convert the modifying expression to the type of the target. If the assignment conversion is a widening conversion, then Java will perform the conversion automatically.

For example, suppose the following definitions are in effect.

```
int i = 1;
double d = 2.0;
```

Then the following assignment is legal.

```
d = 1;  // legal: compiler widens int 1 to double 1.0
```

The **int** value 1 is widened automatically to the **double** value 1.0.

Java does not perform automatically narrowing conversions. Therefore, the following statement does not compile.

```
i = d;  // illegal: no implicit narrowing of double to int
```

Java does allow a program to request explicitly a narrowing through *casting*. A cast converts a value of one type to a value of another type. The form of a cast is

(Type) expression

The type to which the
expression is to be converted

Through casting the following statement accomplishes what the preceding illegal assignment could not do.

```
i = (int) d;    // legal: explicitly narrows double to int
```

A cast of a floating point value to an integer value always truncates. Therefore, the value assigned to i in the following statement is 6.

```
i = (int) 6.9;  // truncation of 6.9 to integer 6_
```

2.6.3   INCREMENT AND DECREMENT

Java has special operators for incrementing or decrementing a numeric variable. The operator ++ is the increment operator, and the operator -- is the decrement operator. When applied to the primitive variables, these operators respectively add or subtract 1 from the value of the variable. For example, the following code segment

```
int i = 4;
++i;
System.out.println("i is " + i);
```

results in the output

```
i is 5
```

For all intents and purposes, the expression

```
++i
```

is equivalent to assignment

```
i = i + 1;      // also i += 1
```

Interestingly, there are two forms of the increment and decrement operators—*prefix* and *postfix*. The term prefix means the operator appears before the operand; and the term postfix means the operator appears after the operand. The expressions ++i and i++ are respectively prefix and postfix examples. The earlier code segment could have been

```
int i = 4;
i++;
System.out.println("i is " + i);
```

which would produce exactly the same output. So what is the difference between the prefix and postfix versions of the increment operator? The difference becomes apparent when the operation is used as part of a larger expression. Consider this code fragment:

```
int i = 4;
int j = 4;
System.out.println("i is " + ++i);   // increment is first
System.out.println("j is " + j++);   // concatenation is first
System.out.println("i is " + i);
System.out.println("j is " + j);
```

Are the concatenation operations performed before or after i and j are incremented? In the case of the ++ prefix operator, i is incremented first and then the display is performed. The output is therefore

```
i is 5
j is 4
i is 5
j is 5
```

Thus, the prefix increment returns the value of the variable after it has been incremented; whereas, the postfix increment returns the value of the variable before it is incremented.

> ### *Be kind to your program readers*
>
> Some programmers, in an attempt to be clever, write a single statement that would be better understood if written using several statements. Such coding malpractices often involve the increment and decrement operators. As an example, consider the following statement that defines and initializes a variable k using previously defined **int** variables i and j.
>
> ```java
> int k = 5 + i++ * ++j;
> ```
>
> The following segment is equivalent and far easier to understand.
>
> ```java
> ++j;
> int k = 5 + (i * j);
> ++i;
> ```

The decrement operator is similar to the increment operator except that it subtracts 1. Examples are

```java
i--;
--i;
```

2.7 | CASE STUDY — AVERAGING FIVE NUMBERS

We next develop a program `AverageFive.java` that computes the average of five integer inputs.

> The objective of this case study is to show the use of the assignment statements and input extraction when problem solving

ANALYSIS AND DESIGN

So what constants, variables, and objects are needed to accomplish this task? And how do these data structures interact?

One needed constant is the integer list size, which is 5. Another needed value is an integer variable representing the sum of the input values. With these two values the average can be computed. The average is also an integer value.

The integer sum of input values can be built up in a straightforward manner by extracting the input values one by one and adding the current input value to the running total. Therefore, an integer variable representing the current input value is also appropriate. This summing process also indicates that the variable representing the running total should be initialized to 0—when the program starts, no values have been processed.

To extract the current input value, a `BufferedReader` object associated with `System.in` is appropriate.

Implementation

Based on the preceding analysis, the following constants and variables should be used by program `AverageFive.java`:

- `LIST_SIZE`: **int** constant representing the number of input values (5);
- `currentInput`: **int** variable representing the current extracted input value;
- `runningTotal`: **int** variable representing the sum of the extracted input values (initially 0);
- `stdin`: references `BufferedReader` representation of the standard input stream given by `System.in`;
- `average`: **int** variable representing the average of the input values.

Program `AverageFive.java` is given in Listing 2.11. Its method `main()` consists of four sections corresponding to the following steps.

Step 1. Define necessary data structures.
Step 2. Process inputs to determine input total.
Step 3. Compute average.
Step 4. Display average.

The first section of method `main()` defines the variables that the program needs to compute the average.

```
// define necessary data structures (Step 1)
final int LIST_SIZE = 5;      // list size
int currentInput;             // current input value
int runningTotal = 0;         // running total of processed inputs
BufferedReader stdin =        // standard input stream
    new BufferedReader(new InputStreamReader(System.in));
```

Listing 2.11 **AverageFive.java**

```java
1.  // Purpose: Average five user integer inputs
2.
3.  import java.io.*;
4.
5.  public class AverageFive{
6.
7.      // main(): application entry point
8.      public static void main(String[] args) throws IOException {
9.          // define necessary data structures (Step 1)
10.         final int LIST_SIZE = 5;     // number of inputs to process
11.         int currentInput;            // current input value
12.         int runningTotal = 0;        // sum of inputs processed so far
13.         BufferedReader stdin =       // input stream
14.             new BufferedReader(new InputStreamReader(System.in));
15.
16.         // process inputs to determine input total (Step 2)
17.         System.out.print("Enter an integer number: ");
18.         currentInput = Integer.parseInt(stdin.readLine());
19.         runningTotal += currentInput;
20.
21.         System.out.print("Enter an integer number: ");
22.         currentInput = Integer.parseInt(stdin.readLine());
23.         runningTotal += currentInput;
24.
25.         System.out.print("Enter an integer number: ");
26.         currentInput = Integer.parseInt(stdin.readLine());
27.         runningTotal += currentInput;
28.
29.         System.out.print("Enter an integer number: ");
30.         currentInput = Integer.parseInt(stdin.readLine());
31.         runningTotal += currentInput;
32.
33.         System.out.print("Enter an integer number: ");
34.         currentInput = Integer.parseInt(stdin.readLine());
35.         runningTotal += currentInput;
36.
37.         // compute average (Step 3)
38.         int average = runningTotal / LIST_SIZE;
39.
40.         // display average (Step 4)
41.         System.out.println("The input average is " + average);
42.     }
43. }
```

The second section individually extracts and processes the five inputs. For each of the inputs, the same tasks are performed: a prompt is issued to supply an input; the input is extracted; and the input is added to the running total of the inputs.

```java
System.out.print("Enter a integer number: ");
currentInput = Integer.parseInt(stdin.readLine());
runningSum += currentInput;
```

The currentInput assignment uses the class method parseInt() of class Integer. The method takes an integer string (e.g, "12") as a parameter and returns the **int** value represented by that string. The method is similar in nature to the `Double` class method `parseDouble()`. Once the integer has been extracted, its value is used to increment `runningSum` through the use of the compound assignment operator +=.

The final two program sections compute and display the average in a straightforward manner.

```
// compute average (Step 3)
int average = runningSum / LIST_SIZE;

// display result (Step 4)
System.out.println("The input average is " + average);
```

Our implementation calculated the average as an integer. An alternative would be to calculate a floating-point average.

```
double average = ((double) runningSum) / LIST_SIZE;
```

For floating-point division to be performed at least one of the operands needs to be floating point. By casting `runningSum` to a **double** value, floating division is performed.

This example completes our introduction to the basics of Java program design and the manipulation of numeric values and variables. Chapter 3 considers the manipulation of objects and their variables.

2.8   REVIEW

- Comments enable us to provide notes to readers of a program. Comments are not processed by the compiler. The single-line comment form uses a double slash // to indicate that the rest of the line is a comment.

- Blank lines can be as important as comments. They enable the various sections of program to be distinct visually.

- Keywords are words that are a reserved part of the language with special meanings. Because keywords have special meanings, they cannot be changed by the programmer and they cannot be used by the programmer to name things. Keywords are case sensitive and consist of only lowercase letters.

- An identifier is a name defined by and given meaning to by the programmer. Java requires that the names of all program elements be valid identifiers. The rule for forming a valid Java name is that it must be an identifier and cannot clash with the keywords. The rules for a valid identifier are as follows: an identifier must begin with either an alphabetic letter, an underscore, or a dollar sign; subsequent characters in a identifier (if any) must be either alphabetic, numeric, underscores, or dollar signs; no spaces can be embedded among the characters that form an identifier; and an identifier cannot be composed of more than 65,535 characters.

- A class is a description of a type of object. A class description specifies the attributes of an object and the methods for implementing its behaviors.

- A bug is the programming term for an error. To debug a program is to remove its errors.

- The keyword **class** indicates that a class definition is being initiated. Java permits modifiers to be placed in front of the keyword **class**. Modifier **public** indicates that the class in question can be used by Java classes that are defined in other files.

- A method in Java may have the following elements in the order with the italicized elements being optional.

| *Modifiers* | Method Type | Method Name | (| *Parameter List* |) { | *Statement List* | } |

- When a method is invoked, the actions associated with the method are executed.

- A class method is a service provided by a class. The method does not require association with a particular class object. The Java method modifier for indicating a class method is **static**.

- Member methods are the means by which objects have behaviors. A member method is invoked in conjunction with an object.

- If a method does not return a value, then the return type of the method is **void**.

- Programmers use indentation to indicate that the indented material is an element of the material that preceded it. Indenting provides visual cues to a reader about the structure of a program. It is normal practice to indent by three to four spaces.

■ The entry point of execution for a Java application program is a **void** method named main(). Java requires that the parameter list for the method main() consist of exactly one formal parameter of type String[].

■ Braces {} are used by Java to group statements. The left brace { is the opening delimiter and a right brace } is the closing delimiter.

■ A single statement can span multiple lines so there must be some delimiter that indicates that the statement is finished. The semicolon (;) serves this purpose.

■ A literal character string is a string of characters delimited on both sides by the double quote character ("). A literal character string is not allowed to span multiple lines.

■ System is a standard Java class that has a member named out. Member out gives access to the standard output stream, which is associated automatically with the console window running the application.

■ The period is used for selection. We use it when we want to reference a particular member of a class or object.

■ An escape sequence is a special two character sequence representing another character. Java uses the backslash character \ as the starting character in an escape sequence. The complete list is given in Table 2.1.

■ A syntax error is a violation of the rules for defining a valid Java program. If the source file is not valid Java, then the compiler produces a list of syntax errors.

■ There are five primitive integer types **byte**, **short**, **int**, **long**, and **char** (**char** is also the character type); two primitive floating-point type **float** and **double**; and a logical type **boolean**. The names of the primitive types are keywords.

■ A constant is the symbolic name for a memory location whose value cannot be changed during program execution once the program has initialized that memory location. To indicate that the contents of the location are to be fixed use keyword **final**.

■ The systematic use of symbolic names is preferred over literal values because the names provide meaning and because their use reduces the potential introduction of errant values through incorrect keyboarding.

■ A variable is the symbolic name for a memory location whose contents can be modified by the program during program execution.

■ The identifier names of variables and constants should be descriptive of their purposes.

■ A variable is a local variable if it is defined within a method.

■ By default, local variables are undefined initially. Java requires that an undefined variable be assigned a value before its value is accessed.

■ The String concatenation operator + concatenates its left and right operands to produce a string.

■ For the numeric types, Java provides the usual arithmetic operators: addition +, subtraction -, multiplication *, and division /. Java also provides the modulus operator % that computes remainders.

■ Java provides two basic ways to express floating-point literals—in decimal or scientific notation.

- An expression is Java's mechanism for producing new values by applying operations to values and variables. The process of applying the operation to the operands is referred to as evaluating the expression. The evaluation of an expression yields a result that has a value and a type.

- A binary operator requires two operands. The left operand is evaluated first.

- When an expression throws an exception it is signaling that an unexpected behavior has occurred.

- Arithmetic operators have the potential to produce overflow or underflow, i.e., a value that is larger or smaller than the memory location properly can represent. No exception is thrown to indicate that overflow has occurred.

- A unary operator is applied to a single operand.

- Java has unary conversion rules that are applied before any operations are performed. The application of these rules ensures that the operands have the same type.

- For consistent expression evaluation Java uses a set of associativity and precedence rules that tell the order in which to apply operators. The unary operators have higher precedence than the multiplication, division, and remainder operators, which in turn, have higher precedence than addition and subtraction.

- `System.in` references a representation of the standard input stream. The extraction methods of this representation are limited to reading **byte** values.

- The class reference type `BufferedReader` has a member method `readLine()` that can extract strings from an input stream.

- To define a new value of a reference type, a **new** operation is performed.

- The `Double` class has a class method `parseDouble()` that takes a numeric string as its parameter and returns the **double** number associated with that string.

- The `Integer` class has a class method `parseInt()` that takes a numeric string as its parameter and returns the **int** number associated with that string.

- The = is the Java assignment operator. The assignment operator updates the value in the memory location associated with a target variable (left operand) with the value of the right operand. The assignment operator, besides storing a value in memory, also produces a result (the new value of the left operand).

- Java allows a program to request explicitly a narrowing through casting. A cast converts a value of one type to a value of another type.

- Java has compound assignment operators for all of the binary arithmetic operators.

- Java has operators ++ and -- for incrementing or decrementing a primitive numeric variable value by 1.

2.9   SELF-TEST

S2.1   What does the following program output?

```
public class DisplayMotto {

    // main(): application entry point
    public static void main (String[] args) {
        System.out.println("We will not suffer\nalone.");
    }
}
```

S2.2   What does the method return type **void** indicate?

S2.3   Provide a single `println()` invocation that displays the following output.

```
JJ
Jenna
Hannah
```

S2.4   Which of the following lines are not valid Java identifiers? Explain.

```
java.awt.Graphics
x-ray
2BeOrNot2Be
Mary'sLostLamb
Spiro Zambini
```

S2.5   What is the length of the literal character string `"1\t2\t3"`?

S2.6   How do methods `System.out.print()` and `System.out.println()` differ?

S2.7   Define a Java constant equal to 2.9979×10^{8} that approximates the speed of light in meters per second.

S2.8   Define a **double** variable `area` that is initialized to the area of a circle with radius 3.5. You may find it useful to use the constant `Math.PI`, which is the **double** value closest to π.

S2.9   Evaluate the following Java operations. Your answer should include both the value and its type.

a) `13 % 3`
b) `5 / 4`
c) `5.0 / 4.0`
d) `100 / 2*5`

S2.10 Add parentheses to indicate explicitly how the following expressions are evaluated.

a) `1.5 * 3.0 + 8 + 2 / 8`
b) `8 + 5 * 6 / 4 - 2`

S2.11 Write a Java expression for the following mathematical expression.

$$a^{3}(a+1)(a-7)$$

S2.12 Write a Java expression for the following mathematical expression.

$$\frac{1}{1+x^{2}}$$

S2.13 Suppose water costs 0.021 cents per 100 gallons. Write a single statement that defines a floating-point value `total` that is initialized to the cost of buying n gallons of water.

S2.14 What is the output of the following code segment?

```
int t1 = 17;
int t2 = 3;
int t3 = 7;
System.out.println("value = " + (t1 % t2 * 5 / t3));
System.out.println("value = " + (t3 * (-5 / 2) + t2));
System.out.println("value = " + (t3 + t1 * 4 + t1));
```

S2.15 What is the output of the following code segment?

```
System.out.println(1 + 1 + "1");
System.out.println("1" + 1 + 1);
```

2.10   EXERCISES

2.1   Why do programmers comment?

2.2   What is the purpose of indentation?

2.3   Separately identify the keywords, variables, classes, methods, and parameters in the following definition.

```
import java.io.*;

public class Test {
    public static void main(String[] args) {
        BufferedReader stdin = new BufferedReader(
            new InputStreamReader(System.in));
        System.out.print("Number: ");
        double n = Double.parseDouble(stdin.readLine());
        System.out.println(n + " * " + n + " = " + n * n);
    }
}
```

2.4   What does the modifier **public** indicate for a class?

2.5   Which of the following are valid Java identifiers?

a) lowScore	j) lifeGuard	s) Not!
b) lowScore_	k) $Cost	t) _123
c) low_Score	l) co$st	u) extends
d) _lowScore	m) Cost$	v) main
e) void	n) x.y.z	w) applet
f) VOID	o) returnValue	x) java
g) Main	p) A	y) Java
h) 2BaseHit	q) C:\Temp	z) JApplet
i) Score2	r) 1	

2.6 Indicate whether the following names conform to the Java naming convention. For those that follow the convention indicate what a reader would expect them to be (e.g, method, class, variable). Explain.

a)	issquare	i)	Temperature	q)	setBoundary
b)	IsSquare	j)	getToken	r)	sendMessage
c)	is_square	k)	get_Token	s)	ThisColor
d)	Square	l)	_getToken	t)	planetType
e)	mySquare	m)	gettoken	u)	PlanetValue
f)	BigSquare	n)	Token	v)	planet
g)	fillSquare	o)	walking	w)	CurrentTime
h)	temperature	p)	Drawing	x)	MyName

2.7 Suppose line 8 of `DisplayForecast.java` was replaced with the following?
`// System.out.print("I think there is a world market for");`

What would the output of the program then be and why?

2.8 Is `System.out.println()` necessary? Explain.

2.9 Write a program to display the greeting "Hi-dee-ho daddy-o."

2.10 Write a program to display the family motto "We are even loonier than you think."

2.11 Write a program to produce the following output.

```
Shape                Number of Sides
==================================
Diamond                    4
Rhombus                    4
Square                     4
Triangle                   3
```

2.12 Write a program to produce the following output.

```
Pitter-patter
 .  .   .   . .
  .  Goes the rain
 .  .   .   .   . .
  .  .  On the steps
```

2.13 Write a program that displays a tic-tac-toe board. The board should have an "O" preplaced in the center location of the board.

2.14 What is the result of the following expressions? Express your answer as a value and a type.

a)	5 % 3	g)	27 / 2.0 / 3	m)	28 + 3 * 5
b)	5 / 3	h)	27 / 2 / 3	n)	(14 / 3) + 4
c)	5.0 / 3.0	i)	22.1 + 1.0	o)	2
d)	7.0 / 0.0	j)	31 % 3	p)	-23 + 7 * 2
e)	25 / 7	k)	30 % 5	q)	12 % 5 % 3
f)	21 / 3	l)	7 - 2	r)	12 % 3 % 5

2.15 Assume the following declarations:

```
double d1 = 3.1;
double d2 = 1.0;
int i1 = 5;
int i2 = 10;
int i3 = 7;
char c1 = '0';
```

What is the result of the following expressions? Express your answer as a value and a type.

a) d2 + d1
b) i1 + d1
c) i1 + i2 * i3
d) i2 % i3
e) i3 / i2 + i1 * 5
f) d2 - i3

g) d1 / i2 + d1
h) i2 + i3 + 3.0
i) i2 * d2 + 4
j) i1 / i3
k) c1 + 5
l) 'x' + 2

2.16 Indicate the decimal equivalents of the following values.

a) 3.1234e-5
b) 3.1234e+5
c) 1234.0e-5
d) 0.1234e+5

2.17 Add parentheses to demonstrate explicitly how the following expressions are evaluated.

a) 9 / 2 * 8 + 5 * 3 - 7 % 4
b) 7 * 3 - 5 / 2 * 6 + 12
c) 5 % 2 + 3 % 2 - 4 / 3

2.18 If necessary, add parentheses to the following expressions so that the term 4 + 7 is multiplied by the term 3 – 8.

a) 7 * 4 + 7 * 3 - 8 * 2
b) 12 - 4 + 7 * 3 - 8 - 5
c) 4 + 7 * (3 - 8) - 12

2.19 Define constants or variables for the following pieces of information.

a) The side of a square whose length is 4.5.

b) One thousand meters.

c) Avogadro's number.

d) One-sixtieth of a minute.

e) The number of wheels on a tricycle.

f) An exclamation point.

g) The square root of 2.

h) The character corresponding to the digit 0.

2.20 Suppose the following definitions are in effect.

```
int a = 10;
int b = 20;
double u = 55.5;
double v = 22.2;
```

Identify which of the following definitions are valid. If the definition is invalid, indicate why. If the definition is valid, your answer should specify its initialization value.

a) `int i = b + u;`
b) `double x = b + u;`
c) `int j = b / 2;`
d) `double y = a + b;`
e) `double z = v / 2;`

2.21 Write a Java statement that implements the following equation.

$$q = \left(\frac{T_1 \times T_2}{D - k}\right) + T_2$$

Your assignment statement should use the following variables.

```
double q;               // result
double k = 1.35;        // constant of irritation
double D = 9.2;         // duration
double T1 = 98.4;       // start time
double T2 = 101.12;     // end time
```

2.22 Write Java expressions that are equivalent to the following mathematical formulas:

a) $a^2 + 5a - 4$

b) $3a + 7 / 4a - 2$

c) $a^3(c + 1)(a + b)$

d) $b^2 + 4ac$

e) $a + \dfrac{b}{c} + d$

f) $\dfrac{4}{3}\pi r^2$

g) $-(a^2 - b^3)$

h) $a\left(\dfrac{b}{c}\right)$

i) $(a + b)(c + d)(e + f)$

2.23 Write a single assignment statement that causes **int** variable n to have the whole number part of **double** variable x. For example, if x had the value 123.45, then n's value should become 123.

2.24 Write a single assignment statement that causes **double** variable y to have the fractional part of **double** object x. Assume that there is an **int** variable n containing the whole number part of x.

2.25 Write a code segment that *circularly shifts* the values of **int** variable a, b, c, and d. For example, if the variable values are initially 10, 20, 30, and 40 respectively, then the final values are 40, 10, 20, and 30 respectively. It may be convenient to introduce a temporary variable to accomplish this task.

2.26 What is the output of the following code segment?

```
int a = 1;
int b = 2;
int c = 3;
int d = 3;
a = c + (c = 5);
```

```
b = (d = 5) + d;
System.out.println("a = " + a);
System.out.println("b = " + b);
```

2.27 Correct the following statements.

```
int 5 = a;
int b 7;
int c = 9.2;
```

2.28 Suppose x and y are variables of type **double**. Does the following code always successfully swap the values of x and y?

```
double rmbr = x;
x = y;
y = rmbr;
```

2.29 Write a program that computes the volume of an object. The program should ask the user to input the object mass and density. The mass will be given in grams; the density will be in grams per cubic centimeter. The relationship of mass, density, and volume of a variable is given by

$$Density = \frac{Mass}{Volume}$$

Your program should output the volume in cubic centimeters.

2.30 Redo LowerToUpper.java of Listing 2.8 so that it is an interactive program that prompts and extracts the lowercase character of interest.

2.31 Write a program to compute the mass of a block of aluminum. The program should input the dimensions of the block (i.e., length, width, and height) in centimeters. The density of aluminum is 2.7 g/cm^3.

2.32 Write a program that prompts and extracts the distance a train travels in miles and the time it takes to travel that distance. The program should compute and display the average speed of the train for that journey.

2.33 Write a program that prompts for and reads a floating-point number and evaluates the polynomial

$$3x^4 - 10x^3 + 13$$

The program should display both the number read and the result of evaluating the polynomial.

2.34 Write a program that prompts for and reads your age in years and outputs your age in days. Assume that there are 365 days in a year.

2.35 Write a program that computes the number of minutes it takes for light to reach the Earth from the Sun.

2.36 Write a program that prompts for a person's age and heart rate. The program computes and displays the number of heart beats since the person was born. Assume that there are 365 days in a year.

2.37 Suppose there was a numeric type longish that used 6 bytes to represent an integer. What would be the range of integer numbers that could be represented?

2.38 Rewrite BMICalculator.java so that the user supplies the height in feet and inches.

2.39 Interest on credit card accounts can be quite high. Most credit card companies compute interest on an average daily balance. Here is an algorithm for computing the average daily balance and the monthly interest charge on a credit card.

Step 1. Multiply the net balance shown on the statement by the number of days in the billing cycle.

Step 2. Multiply the net payment received by the number of days the payment was received before the statement date.

Step 3. Subtract the result of the calculation in step 2 from the result of the calculation in step 1.

Step 4. Divide the result of step 3 by the number of days in the billing cycle. This value is the average daily balance.

Step 5. Compute the interest charge for the billing period by multiplying the average daily balance by the monthly interest rate.

Here is an example to illustrate the algorithm. Suppose a credit card statement showed a previous balance of $850. Eleven days before the end of the billing cycle, a payment of $400 is made. The billing cycle for the month is 31 days, and the monthly interest rate is 1.32%. The calculation of the interest charge is as follows:

Step 1. $850 \times 31 = \$26,350$

Step 2. $400 \times 11 = \$4,400$

Step 3. $26,350 - \$4,400 = \$21,950$

Step 4. $21,950 \div 31 = \$708.06$

Step 5. $708.06 \times 0.0132 = \$9.34$

Write a program that computes the monthly interest charge on a credit card account. Your program should acquire as input the previous balance, the payment amount, the number of days in the billing cycle, the day of the billing cycle the payment was made, and the monthly interest rate.

2.40 Suppose a, b, and c are **int** variables initialized respectively to 1, 2, and 3. What values are assigned to e, f, and g?

a) `int e = ++a;`

b) `int f = b++;`

c) `int g = ++c + c++;`

2.41 Write a code segment that defines a BufferedReader variable stdin that is to be built of out of an InputStreamReader associated with System.in. The code segment should then define two **int** variables a and b such that they are initialized with the next two input values from the standard input stream.

2.11   PROGRAMMING PROJECT — YOU

Developing software can be a rewarding experience—it is a chance to be both creative and analytical. People of all sorts report high levels of satisfaction in completing a programming task and demonstrating its capabilities. The goal of this introductory problem-solving case study and our other case studies is for you to experience such satisfaction as you learn to program and problem solve in Java.

> The objective of this case study is to practice the display of information using methods `print()` and `println()`

At the end of the main body of each chapter, we present a problem or two for you to consider. The problems have been selected for their relevance to the concepts being discussed, as well as being appropriately complex and interesting to a broad range of people. We provide background and problem-solving guidance on how to go about designing and implementing solutions.

The first case study is a personal one—design and produce a display giving a short autobiography that could be used as part of an application for a club membership. The information you supply and how you present it is your choice. However, at a minimum you must supply contact information such as your name and e-mail address. To get you started, you may consider describing some of your personal favorites (e.g, author, artist, music, activities) and plans (e.g., career, travel).

ANALYSIS AND DESIGN

So what tasks must be accomplished to produce a Java program that creates the desired display? For one, you must determine what personal information is to be displayed. For another, you must determine how the information is to be displayed. After making these decisions, you can create a preliminary design of the information and its layout. You might want to get feedback from friends. They can make suggestions on the information to make sure it is sufficiently interesting.

Snapshots of our own personal efforts are given in Figure 2.6 and Figure 2.7.

Implementation

Name the program `MeDisplay.java`. To implement and run the program, you will need access to Java tools. Some versions of this text are bundled with a CDROM supplying a Java IDE for you to use. In addition, our website `www.javaprogramdesign.com` contains links to some freely available tools such as the SDK.

For this case study, you will develop a class `MeDisplay` that consists of a single method `main()`. The class should be documented and laid out appropriately. For example, the code should make use of program header and method comments, whitespace and a consistent indentation scheme.

For your information, our programs produced each line of text using individual statements.

Figure 2.6　　**A MeDisplay compilation and run.**

TESTING

Just as you should seek the comments of others to evaluate your preliminary design, you should also demonstrate your working program to others to get advice on how the presentation might be improved.

Figure 2.7 **A MeDisplay compilation and run.**

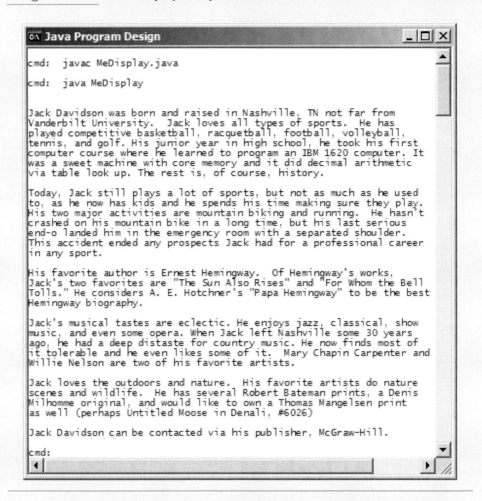

```
cmd:  javac MeDisplay.java

cmd:  java MeDisplay


Jack Davidson was born and raised in Nashville, TN not far from
Vanderbilt University.  Jack loves all types of sports.  He has
played competitive basketball, racquetball, football, volleyball,
tennis, and golf. His junior year in high school, he took his first
computer course where he learned to program an IBM 1620 computer. It
was a sweet machine with core memory and it did decimal arithmetic
via table look up. The rest is, of course, history.

Today, Jack still plays a lot of sports, but not as much as he used
to, as he now has kids and he spends his time making sure they play.
His two major activities are mountain biking and running.  He hasn't
crashed on his mountain bike in a long time, but his last serious
end-o landed him in the emergency room with a separated shoulder.
This accident ended any prospects Jack had for a professional career
in any sport.

His favorite author is Ernest Hemingway.  Of Hemingway's works,
Jack's two favorites are "The Sun Also Rises" and "For Whom the Bell
Tolls." He considers A. E. Hotchner's "Papa Hemingway" to be the best
Hemingway biography.

Jack's musical tastes are eclectic. He enjoys jazz, classical, show
music, and even some opera. When Jack left Nashville some 30 years
ago, he had a deep distaste for country music. He now finds most of
it tolerable and he even likes some of it.  Mary Chapin Carpenter and
Willie Nelson are two of his favorite artists.

Jack loves the outdoors and nature.  His favorite artists do nature
scenes and wildlife.  He has several Robert Bateman prints, a Denis
Milhomme original, and would like to own a Thomas Mangelsen print
as well (perhaps Untitled Moose in Denali, #6026)

Jack Davidson can be contacted via his publisher, McGraw-Hill.

cmd:
```

2.12   PROGRAMMING PROJECT — TRAINING ZONE

There are two kinds of exercise—aerobic and anaerobic exercise. Normally, sustained activities such as bicycling, running or swimming are aerobic exercises. While activities requiring bursts of actions such as weight lifting and tennis are anaerobic exercises. Both types of exercise have their advantages. For example, anaerobic exercise can stimulate muscle growth and aerobic exercise can raise your metabolism by stimulating the production of fat-burning enzymes.

> The objective of this case study is to practice interactive programming in the context of problem solving

For a sustained activity to be an aerobic exercise there needs to be an elevation in the heart rate. However, the elevation cannot be extreme. If the elevation is extreme, then muscles are oxygen deprived and they burn sugars rather than fat. Research indicates that there is a heart beat rate training zone that should be kept in order to get the maximum aerobic effect from an exercise. The actual training zone for a person is based on many factors, such as the individual's normal heart rate, fitness, health, weight, etc. However, there are formulas indicating reasonable training zones for the majority of fit people with normal heart rates. The formula used in this section comes from `HealthCentral.com`. The formula work as follows: subtract the age of interest from 220; 65% of that value is the low end of the training zone range and 80% of that value is the high end of the training zone range.

The goal of this case study is to develop a program that computes a training zone according to the following problem statement.

> *Provide an interactive training zone calculator that prompts a user for her or his age. The calculator program then computes and displays the training zone for that age. The low end of the training zone is 65% of the difference between 220 and the specified age. The high end of the training zone is 80% of the difference between 220 and the specified age.*

ANALYSIS AND DESIGN

Before determining the necessary information structures and algorithm, you should depict a sample input/output behavior. A depiction should help clarify what information is being provided and what information is to be computed. Furthermore, if the software is being developed for a client, then it also aids you in verifying with the client that the proper problem is being solved. An example of a possible input/output behavior for the training zone calculator is given in Figure 2.8.

Figure 2.8 **A possible training zone calculator console window display.**

An analysis of the problem statement indicates one piece of information that must be gotten from the user—the age of interest. From that information and the training zone formula you derive the lower and upper heart beat rates for the training zone associated with that age of interest. An analysis of the problem also indicates that in developing an algorithm three integer variables are appropriate: *ageOfInterest*, *lowBeatRate*, and *high-BeatRate*. In addition, three constants are appropriate: *BASE_RATE* with value 220, *LOW_ZONE_MULTIPLIER* with value 65%, and *HIGH_ZONE_MULTIPLIER* with value 80%.

From the preceding discussion, an algorithm for solving the problem is relatively easy.

Step 1. Provide a suitable legend for the calculator.

Step 2. Prompt the user for the age for which they desire a suggested training zone.

Step 3. Extract the user-specified age and assign it to variable *ageOfInterest*.

Step 4. Compute the low heart beat rate by assigning *lowBeatRate* the value of the expression *LOW_ZONE_MULTIPLIER* × (*BASE_RATE* – *ageOfInterest*).

Step 5. Compute the high heart beat rate by assigning *highBeatRate* the value of the expression *HIGH_ZONE_MULTIPLIER* × (*BASE_RATE* – *ageOfInterest*).

Step 6. Display the training zone information as defined by *ageOfInterest*, *lowBeatRate*, and *highBeatRate*.

Implementation

Producing a Java program `TrainingZone.java` from the suggested algorithm can be done nicely with a single class `TrainingZone`. The class should be documented and laid out appropriately. For example, the code should make use of program header and method comments, whitespace, and a consistent indentation scheme.

TESTING

One way to test a program informally is to do a hand-check—compute by hand what the output should be for several different ages. Then run the program using those same ages and compare the results. Determine for any discrepancies whether the program or hand calculation is incorrect. If the program is incorrect, review the formulas already given and your implementation of them. Also consider adding temporarily statements displaying intermediary results in an effort to determine where your program's correctness breaks down. (Such statements are called *debugging statements*.) Testing and debugging is examined in detail in Chapter 13.

2.13   SELF-TEST ANSWERS

S2.1   The program outputs

```
We will not suffer
alone.
```

S2.2   The return type **void** indicates that the method does not a produce a return value.

S2.3   The invocation should be

```
System.out.println("JJ\nJenna\nHannah");
```

S2.4   None of the lines are valid identifiers. The first line is composed of three identifiers separated by periods. The second line is not a valid name as a hyphen is not a valid character in composing a name. The third line is not a valid name because it begins with a digit. The fourth line is not a valid name as an apostrophe is not a valid character in composing a name. The fifth line is not a valid name as it contains embedded whitespace.

S2.5   The literal character string "1\t2\t3" has length 5. The three digits each count for 1 and each occurrence of the tab character escape sequence \t counts for 1.

S2.6   System.out.print() differs from System.out.println() in that it allows additional output to be sent to the current line after its invocation. System.out.println() moves the cursor to the start of the next line.

S2.7   **final** double LIGHT_SPEED = 2.9979e8;

S2.8   **double** area = 3.5 * 3.5 * Math.PI;

S2.9

   (a) The **int** value 1.

   (b) The **int** value 1.

   (c) The **double** value 1.25.

   (d) The **int** value 250. The whitespace does not influence the evaluation.

S2.10

   (a) ((1.5 * 3) + 8) + (2 / 8)

   (b) (8 + ((5 * 6) / 4)) - 2

S2.11 Expression: (a * a * a) * (a + 1) * (a - 7)

S2.12 Expression: 1 / (1 + x*x)

S2.13 Statement: **double** total = 0.021 * n / 100;

S2.14 The output is

```
value = 1
value = -11
value = 92
```

S2.15 The output is

```
21
111
```

3

USING OBJECTS

We now explore how to create and manipulate a variety of objects using standard Java classes. Our exploration begins with the `String` class. The `String` class is Java's principal mechanism for encapsulating a sequence of zero or more characters. Like the values of all Java class types, a `String` value is an object. An object is very different from a primitive type value. An object has attributes and behaviors. An attribute is a characteristic. For example, a rectangle object has length and width. An object behavior may be as simple as changing a width attribute or as intricate as drawing its representation on a window screen. Because objects are more complex than primitive values, their variables are treated differently than primitive type variables. The memory location of an object variable stores a reference to a memory location that holds an object rather than holding the object itself.

OBJECTIVES

- Develop a mental model of an object and a reference.
- Describe how to define and use object type constants and variables.
- Explain the roles of constructors, member methods, and class methods.
- Present object assignment.
- Introduce the String class and its methods for creating, examining, searching, evaluating, and manipulating substrings and characters.

3.1 CLASSES

The use of objects in Chapter 2 was limited to input and output operations (e.g., an input stream using variable `stdin` and an output stream using variable `System.out` in AverageFive.java). Starting in this chapter and in successive chapters, we create and manipulate objects from many of the other classes that Java provides (e.g, classes `String`, `Rectangle`, `Color`, and `JFrame`).

The Java standard classes are very important in their own right. For example, some provide text processing capabilities and others support the design and development of graphical interfaces. In addition, your exposure to and use of these well-designed classes will give you a firmer foundation in the principles of the object-oriented programming and should make it easier for you to design and implement your own classes in a thoughtful manner. In fact, starting with Chapter 4, we show you how to design and develop your own classes!

The first of the standard classes that we consider is the `String` class. The `String` class is ubiquitous in Java programming because it is Java's principal mechanism for encapsulating a sequence of characters into an object with attributes and behaviors. For example, Java internally treats a literal character string as a `String` constant. The `String` class is part of package `java.lang`.

```
public class PersonalComputerForecast {

    // method main(): application entry point
    public static void main(String[] args) {
        System.out.print("There is no reason anyone would want");
        System.out.println(" a computer in their home.");
        System.out.println("  Ken Olson, DEC Chairman, 1977.");
    }
}
```

Literal character strings are represented in Java as String objects

The `String` class provides a variety of methods to implement the behaviors you would expect with strings. For example, there are methods for creating strings; examining, searching, and accessing individual characters; and producing substrings. However, there are *no* methods to modify a `String`—once a `String` object has been created, it is *immutable*. Java provides `java.lang.StringBuffer` for applications requiring the ability to modify an existing sequence of characters

We begin our examination of Java objects and classes with object variables. We begin here because an object typically is used and manipulated through an object variable.

3.2 OBJECTS AND VARIABLES

As discussed in Chapter 2, a primitive variable is a symbolic name for a memory location. The type of value stored in that location corresponds to the type of the primitive variable being used; e.g., an **int** variable is associated with a memory location storing an **int** value and a **double** variable is associated with memory location storing a **double** value.

Java treats object variables differently. Although an object variable is the symbolic name for a memory location being used by the program, the memory location for an object variable does *not* store a value of that object type. Instead the value in the memory location tells the program where to find a value (object) of that type.

We say that an object variable *references* or *points to* an object of the object type. Thus, a **String** variable references a memory location that holds a value of type **String**. Similarly, a **BufferedReader** variable references a memory location holding a **BufferedReader** value.

Figure 3.1   **Primitive type and object type variable values.**

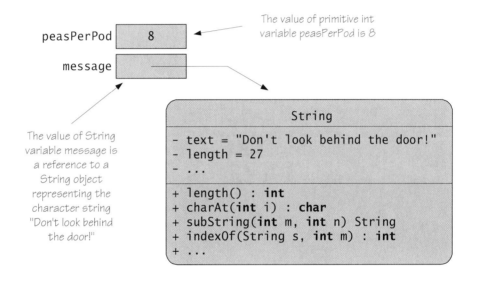

Figure 3.1 illustrates the difference between a primitive and object variable. In the figure, peasPerPod is variable of type **int** with value 8 and message is a variable of type **String** that refers to a **String** object representing the character string "Don't look behind the door!". As the illustration indicates, the memory location associated with **int** variable peasPerPod contains the 8, but the memory location for **String** variable message contains a reference to a memory location containing the **String** representation of "Don't look behind the door". Our subsequent representations of **String** variables will be more concise. For example, our shorthand representation of message is

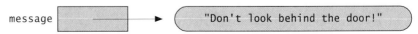

In this representation, we are giving only the crucial attribute—the text associated with the **String** object. We do not list the other attributes as they can be inferred from the

text, and we do not list the methods implementing the `String` behaviors as they are the same for every `String` object.

INITIALIZATION

The syntax for object variable definitions is similar to that of primitive variable definitions. There are two forms—definitions that do and do not specify initial values.

The following code segment defines three `String` variables `prompt`, `errorMsg`, and `fileType`. All three definitions specify initial values for the variables.

```
String prompt = "Enter a new number: ";
String errorMsg = "Number must be positive.";
String fileType = "html";
```

The initial values are given through the use of literal character strings, which Java considers to be `String` constants. In particular, the value associated with a literal character string is a reference to a `String` representation of the associated character string.

A `String` variable cannot be initialized with a **char** variable or a literal **char** value. Therefore, the following definition is illegal.

```
String s = '!';    // illegal
```

The rules of the Java require the use double quotes even for strings of length one.

```
String s = "!";    // legal
```

We can initialize a `String` variable using another `String` variable. The following code segment first defines and initializes a `String` variable a. Variable a is then used to initialize `String` variable b.

```
String a = "excellence";
String b = a;                 // b references the same object as a
```

The definitions result in both variables being associated with the same value—the memory location associated with the `String` representation of the literal character string `"excellence"`. Thus, the two definitions have representation

In Chapter 2, we used the class `BufferedReader` to encapsulate an input stream.

```
BufferedReader stdin = new BufferedReader(
    new InputStreamReader(System.in));
```

In this definition, variable `stdin` references a newly *constructed* (created) `Buffered-Reader` *instance* (object). The instance is built out of a newly constructed `Input-StreamReader`, which in turn is built out of the standard input stream. By viewing the input stream as a `BufferedReader` object, we have access to `BufferedReader` methods that produce `String` representations of user-entered data.

The following figure depicts succinctly that `stdin` references a `BufferedReader` associated with the standard input stream.

The next code segment defines a variable `r` that references a newly constructed `Rectangle` with width 5 and height 2, which is situated with its top-left corner at coordinate (3, 4).

```
int x = 3;
int y = 4;
int width = 5;
int height = 2;
Rectangle r = new Rectangle(x, y, width, height);
```

The first two parameters of the Rectangle constructor specify the position of the upper-left-hand corner of the new Rectangle

The third and fourth parameters of the Rectangle constructor specify the dimensions of the new Rectangle

```
int x = 3;
int y = 4;
int width = 5;
int height = 2;
Rectangle r = new Rectangle(x, y, width, height);
```

The `Rectangle` class is part of the `java.awt` package. A `Rectangle` represents a rectangular area whose attributes of interest are its top-left corner location, width, and height. The representation of the variables defined in the previous code segment is

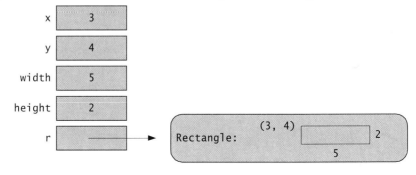

3.2.2 NULL AND UNINITIALIZED REFERENCES

The next code segment defines three local variables `dayOfWeek`, `inStream`, and `frame` without specifying initial values for these variables.

```
String dayOfWeek;
BufferedReader inStream;
Rectangle frame;
```

Like other local variable definitions that do not specify initial values, the values of these variables are undefined. The representation of these variables would be

where "–" indicates an uninitialized value. Although Java allows local object type variables to be defined in this manner, it requires that the variables be initialized before their values are used.

Besides assigning object references to an object variable, a program can also assign the **null** reference. Conceptually, a **null** reference corresponds to the empty address. The value indicates that the variable is not referencing an object. In the code segment

```
String fontName = null;
BufferedReader fileStream = null;
Rectangle boundingBox = null;
```

variables `fontName`, `fileStream`, and `boundingBox` are all initialized to the **null** reference. A pictorial representation of these definitions would be

It is important to realize that a variable with value **null** is different than an uninitialized variable. Although neither of them references an object, a variable with value **null** can be assigned to another variable.

```
String s1 = null;
String s2;
String s3 = s1;      // legal: s1 has the value null
String s4 = s2;      // illegal: s3 does not have a value
```

The **null** value indicates that no information is being represented by the variable.

ASSIGNMENT

Like primitive variables, one object variable can be assigned to another. The assignment results in both variables referring to the *same* object.

Suppose `String` values `word1` and `word2` that have been initialized as follows.

```
String word1 = "luminous";
String word2 = "graceful";
```

Thus, the two variables have representation

If a code segment assigns `word2` to `word1` as in the following statement

```
word1 = word2;
```

then `word1` now references the same object as `word2`.

Variable `word1` is now an *alias* for the object referenced by `word2`.

Because the `String` representation of the character string `"luminous"` is no longer needed, the memory for that `String` object is reclaimed *automatically* by Java so that it can be reused by other parts of the program. This recycling is known as *garbage collection* and is an important feature of Java.

An assignment statement also can be used to give a value to an uninitialized object variable. For example, the following code segment first defines a local `Rectangle` variable `inset` and then assigns `inset` a newly constructed `Rectangle` value.

```
Rectangle inset;
inset = new Rectangle(1, 1, 6, 2);
```

From its definition, `inset` has representation

With the assignment, `inset` references a 6 × 2 rectangle located at (1, 1).

Now consider the following code segment.

```
String a = "alpha";
String b = a;
a = "beta";
```

The segment begins by defining a `String` variable a. After that definition, variable a has depiction

The segment then defines a `String` variable b. The definition causes variables a and b to reference the same `String`.

The code segment then assigns a new value to variable a—variable a now references a `String` whose value is `"beta"`. Even though a and b were both referencing previously the same `String`, the assignment to variable a does not affect variable b's reference.

Variable b remains a reference to the string `"alpha"`. It does so because variables a and b had their own independent references to the representation of `"alpha"`. Therefore, a change to variable a does not affect variable b and vice-versa.

3.4 FINAL VARIABLES

In Chapter 2 we used modifier **final** to define primitive type constants. We can also use this modifier to define object constants. However, when an object constant is defined—be it `String` or any other object type—we are specifying *only* that the reference cannot be changed. That is, the constant must always refer to the same memory location.

The following code segment defines two `String` constants.

```
final String POEM_TITLE = "The Appearance of Brown";
final String WARNING = "The weather ball is black";
```

We are not allowed to make changes to what these variables reference. Our representation for these definitions is

The locks indicate the memory locations holds constants

Thus, the following statement would not compile as it attempts to change what variable WARNING references.

```
WARNING = "The weather ball is green";  // illegal for constant
```

Although an object constant must always refer to the same memory location, it does not mean necessarily that the value stored at that location cannot be modified through its member methods.

For example, because of its definition `Rectangle` constant `BLOCK` must reference a particular `Rectangle` memory location throughout its existence. Initially, that memory location references a 4×2 rectangle situated at $(6, 9)$.

```
final Rectangle BLOCK = new Rectangle(6, 9, 4, 2);
```

The depiction of constant `BLOCK` would be

However, we can change the `Rectangle` object that `BLOCK` references, For example, the following code segment resituated the `Rectangle` so that its top-left corner is at $(1, 4)$ and that its dimensions are 8×3.

```
BLOCK.setLocation(1, 4);
BLOCK.resize(8, 3);
```

After the code segment completes, the depiction of memory would be

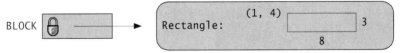

The `String` class does not provide any methods to modify an existing `String`. Therefore, it is always the case that the object to which a `String` constant references is itself unchanging. (i.e., a `String` is immutable). Thus, for `String` constant `LANGUAGE` defined next

```
String LANGUAGE = "Java";
```

the following representation occurs.

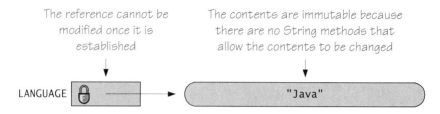

The reference cannot be modified once it is established

The contents are immutable because there are no String methods that allow the contents to be changed

LANGUAGE → "Java"

| 3.5 | **STRING OPERATIONS AND METHODS** |

To display a `String`, a program can make use of the `print()` and `println()` methods of `System.out`. For example, the following code segment displays the value referenced by `String` variable `adage` to standard output.

```
String adage = "Every day can be a good day!";
System.out.println(adage);
```

The first statement defines `adage` to be a `String` variable that is initialized to a reference a memory location containing a `String` representation of the character string `"Every day can be a good day!"`.

adage → "Every day can be a good day!"

The second statement invokes `System.out.println()` to display the character sequence associated with `String` variable `greeting`. The invocation produces output

```
Every day can be a good day!
```

The next code segment shows how to use a `BufferedReader` to extract a user-supplied string from standard input and assign it to a `String` variable.

```
BufferedReader stdin = new BufferedReader(
    new InputStreamReader(System.in));

System.out.print("Enter your account name: ");
String response = stdin.readLine();
```

First, variable `stdin` is initialized to reference a `BufferedReader` view of standard input.

stdin → BufferedReader:

As in the interactive console programs of Chapter 2, the code segment then uses a `print()` statement to display the prompt message. After executing the `print()` statement, standard output looks like

```
Enter your account name:
```

The character string that the user supplies in reaction to the prompt is extracted by Buff-eredReader method readLine() and a reference to that string is returned by the method. The value of that reference is used to initialize variable response. For example, if the user entered *artiste*.

```
Enter your account name: artiste
```

then the variable response defined in the last statement of the segment would reference a String representation of "artiste".

The next code segment extracts the first and middle names of a person and then ech-oes them back.

```
BufferedReader stdin = new BufferedReader(
    new InputStreamReader(System.in));

System.out.print("Enter your first name: ");
String firstName = stdin.readLine();

System.out.print("Enter your middle name: ");
String middleName = stdin.readLine();

System.out.println("Your name is " + firstName + " "
    + middleName + ".");
```

Like the previous code segment, this code segment begins with the definition of a variable stdin that is initialized to reference a BufferedReader representation of standard input. A prompt then indicates that the user should enter a first name. Suppose the user's response to the prompt was to enter *Joanne*.

```
Enter your first name: Joanne
```

The next statement in the code segment defines a String variable firstName. The variable is initialized with the value returned by the invocation of stdin.readLine(). Given the user's response, variable firstName has representation.

Suppose the user's response to the second prompt has depiction

```
Enter your middle name: Audrey
```

The second readLine() invocation results in middleName being assigned a reference to a String object representing the character string "Audrey". Therefore, variables firstName and middleName have representation

The next statement of the code segment

```
System.out.println("Your name is " + firstName + " "
    + middleName + ".");
```

echoes the extracted values back to the user to complete the code segment. The parameter
`"Your name is " + firstName + middleName + "."` to `println()` makes multiple
uses of the `String` concatenation operator `+` for combining strings. The result is a
`String` object whose value represents the character string `"Your name is Joanne
Audrey."`. Therefore, the display would now show

```
Enter your first name: Joanne
Enter your middle name: Audrey
Your name is Joanne Audrey.
```

The concatenation operator also can be used to combine numbers or **char** values
with literal character strings or `String` objects. The result is a `String` with the natural
interpretation. For example, the definitions

```
String s1 = 1000 + " grams to a kilogram.";
String s2 = "Pi is less than " + 3.1416 + '.';
```

result in variables with the following representations.

Java also provides the `String` append assignment operator, `+=`. The append assignment causes its left operand to be assigned a reference to a *new* `String` object representing the concatenation of the left operand's value before the assignment with the value of
the right operand. Like concatenation, the append assignment operation's right operand
can be a number, character, or string. The following code segment makes multiple uses of
the `+=` operator.

```
String s = "Jeepers";
s += '-';
s += "creepers";
s += '!';
System.out.println(s);
```

The segment results in output

```
Jeepers-creepers!
```

Because the right operand of the `+=` operator can be an expression, the following
code segment results in the same output.

```
String s = "Jeepers";
s += '-' + "creepers" + '!';
System.out.println(s);
```

The preceding code segments give the illusion it is the `String` object to which s references that undergoes change. However, what really changes in the code segments is the

---

Listing 3.1   WordLength.java

```
1.  // Purpose: Display the length of a user-specified word
2.
3.  import java.io.*;
4.
5.  public class WordLength {
6.
7.      // main(): application entry point
8.      public static void main(String[] args) throws IOException {
9.          // set input stream
10.         BufferedReader stdin = new BufferedReader(
11.             new InputStreamReader(System.in));
12.
13.         // get desired word
14.         System.out.print("Enter a word: ");
15.         String word = stdin.readLine();
16.
17.         // compute length of word
18.         int wordLength = word.length();
19.
20.         // display result
21.         System.out.println("Word " + word + " has length "
22.             + wordLength + ".");
23.     }
24. }
```

---

value of variable s. Each append assignment operation causes variable s to reference a different String.

Besides working with the concatenation and assignment operators, a String can be directed through its member methods to perform a variety of behaviors. At this point, we mention only some of the most useful String member methods. In subsequent chapters, we introduce others. As a reminder, member methods are the means by which an object Java implements a behavior, and class methods are services provided by the class.

String member method length() enables a String object to communicate the number of characters that make up the string that *it* represents. When invoked, the method does not take any parameters. The absence of parameters is typical of most member methods that return an attribute of their associated object.

Program WordLength.java of Listing 3.1 uses the method to help display the number of characters in a user-specified word. A sample run of the program is demonstrated below.

```
Enter a word: tarantism
Word tarantism has length 9.
```

Like previous console programs, WordLength.java consists of a single method named main(). Method main() begins with the definition of BufferedReader variable stdin that is associated with the standard input stream. A section of code then both prompts the user for a word and extracts the user's response.

```
System.out.print("Enter a word: ");
String word = stdin.readLine();
```

The program then determines the length of the user-specified word in line 18.

```
int length = word.length();
```

Invocation word.length() causes Java to initialize the **int** variable wordLength to the length of the word entered by the user.

The program completes its job by displaying the result of its calculation.

```
System.out.println("Word " + word + " has length "
    + wordLength + ".");
```

Another useful String member method is charAt(). This method expects a single index as its parameter and returns the value of the character at that position in its String. While such behavior seems *relatively* natural given the method name and its parameter, what is not natural is that in Java, as in several other programming languages, *the first character of a String is located at index 0.*

Consider the following definition of String variable alphabet.

```
String alphabet = "abcdefghijklmnopqrstuvwxyz";
```

Our customary representation for this variable while convenient is misleading.

The representation does not show that each character in the string is stored in its own memory location. A representation that captures this important notion is

In this depiction each letter in the string is boxed individually. The letter 'a' is in the first box, which has index 0; the letter 'b' is in the second box, which has index 1; and so on.

Keeping this representation of variable alphabet in mind, the values of the **char** variables c1, c2, and c3 defined in the following code segment can be determined readily.

```
char c1 = alphabet.charAt(9);
char c2 = alphabet.charAt(15);
char c3 = alphabet.charAt(2);
```

The variables are initialized respectively to the values 'j', 'p', and 'c'.

Yet another useful String processing capability is being able to obtain a substring of a string. Class String provides this capability in part with a member method sub-string() that takes two integer parameters. The first parameter specifies the index of

the starting position in the string to be copied and the second parameter specifies the index of the position that is one *beyond* the last character to be copied. Method `substring()` returns a new `String` representing the portion of its string specified by the two indices.

The following code segment initializes variable `month` so that it references a `String` object whose representation is the first six characters referenced by `weddingDate`. The `substring()` invocation is `weddingDate.substring(0,6)`. Observe that the difference 6 – 0 is 6, which is the length of the substring to be returned.

```
String weddingDate = "August 21, 1976";
String month = weddingDate.substring(0, 6);
System.out.println("Month is " + month + ".");
```

The segment displays

```
Month is August.
```

The class `String` also has a member method `substring()` that takes a single **int** parameter. The method returns a new `String` that is a substring of the `String` to be copied. The substring starts with the character whose index is specified by the parameter and continues to the end of the string. The next code segment uses the method to determine the last four characters of the `String` referenced by `firstDate`.

```
String firstDate = "January 9, 1974";
int n = firstDate.length();
String year = firstDate.substring(n-4);
System.out.println("Year is " + year + ".");
```

The segment displays

```
Year is 1974.
```

Yet another useful `String` member method is `trim()`. Method `trim()` returns a newly created string that represents the portion of its `String` excluding any leading and trailing whitespace. For example, the code segment

```
String t1 = "    world    is turning   ";
String t2 = t1.trim();
```

produces `String` variables `t1` and `t2` with representation

Observe that method `trim()` did not affect the spacing between the words—it removed only the leading and trailing spaces.

The class `String` also includes member methods to search for a substring within a `String`. One of these methods is the method `indexOf()` requiring two parameters. The first parameter is the substring to be found and the second parameter is the index from which to start the search of the `String` object. If the substring can be found, then the method returns the starting position of the first such occurrence. Otherwise, the method returns –1.

Consider the following code segment.

```
String fruit = "banana";
String searchString = "an";

System.out.println("Looking for \"" + searchString + "\" in \""
        + fruit + "\"");

int n1 = fruit.indexOf(searchString, 0);
int n2 = fruit.indexOf(searchString, n1 + 1);
int n3 = fruit.indexOf(searchString, n2 + 1);

System.out.println("   First search result: " + n1);
System.out.println("   Second search result: " + n2);
System.out.println("   Third search result: " + n3);
```

It produces the output

```
Looking for "an" in "banana"
    First search result: 1
    Second search result: 3
    Third search result: -1
```

The two `String` variables defined in the segment have the following "boxed" representations

The first search for substring `"an"` in the `String` referenced by variable `fruit` begins at index 0. Because this search first finds the substring at index 1, variable `n1` is initialized to 1.

The second search for `"an"` in the string referenced by variable `fruit` begins at index 2 (i.e., `n1 + 1`). This search first finds the substring at index 3. Therefore, variable `n2` is initialized to 3.

The third search for `"an"` in the string referenced by variable `fruit` begins at index 4 (i.e., `n2 + 1`). Because this search is unsuccessful, variable `n3` is initialized to –1.

The `String` class also provides a collection of class methods all with the name `valueOf()`. Because they are class methods, they are providing services. In particular, they provide services related to strings.

For each of the types **bool**, **char**, **int**, **long**, **float**, and **double** there is a `valueOf()` class method, which takes a single parameter of that type. A `valueOf()` method returns a reference to a newly created `String` representing the value of its parameter in character string form. The `valueOf()` methods are defined to be class methods rather than member methods because their tasks do not involve accessing or manipulating existing strings.

```
int v1 = -12;
bool v2 = true;
double v3 = 3.14;
char v4 = 'a';
String s1 = String.valueof(v1);
```

```
String s2 = String.valueof(v2);
String s3 = String.valueof(v3);
String s4 = String.valueof(v4);
```

defines variables s1, s2, s3, and s4 with representation

Last occurrence

The String class also provides member methods for searching for the last occurrence of a string. For example, there is a method lastIndexOf() that takes two parameters—the substring of interest and a maximal index value to be used in searching for the substring. If the substring can be found in the String starting at some index not greater than the index parameter, then the method returns the starting position of the last such occurrence within the String object. If the substring cannot be found under these conditions, lastIndexOf() returns –1.

Consider the following code segment that searches for "iss" in "Mississippi".

```
String state = "Mississippi";
String searchString = "iss";
System.out.println("Looking for \"" + searchString
        + "\" in \""+ state + "\"");
int n1 = state.indexOf(searchString, 0);
int n2 = state.lastIndexOf(searchString, state.length()-1);
System.out.println("   First search result: " + n1);
System.out.println("   Second search result: " + n2)
```

The segment produces output

```
Looking for "iss" in "Mississippi"
   First search result: 1
   Second search result: 4
```

3.6   CASE STUDY — DATE TRANSLATION

To gain additional experience with the String library and problem solving, we next develop a program that converts a date from American format to standard format.

> The objective of this case study is to show the use of the String library for manipulating information when problem solving

A date expressed in American format consists of a month followed by whitespace followed by a particular day of that month followed by a comma followed by whitespace followed by a year. For example, April 13, 1743, and January 15, 1929, are both dates in the American format.

A date expressed in international format consists of the year followed by a hyphen followed by month followed by a hyphen followed by the particular day of a month. For example, 1874-November-30 and 1918-July-18 are both dates in the standard format.

PROBLEM STATEMENT

Provide a console-based interactive program that converts a user-specified date in American format (e.g., July 4, 1776) to international format (e.g., 1776-July-4).

SAMPLE OUTPUT

```
Date format translator
   Converts a date from American format (e.g., July 4, 1776)
   to standard format (e.g., 1776-July-4).

Enter date in American format: January 1, 2000

The translation of
   January 1, 2000
to standard format is
   2000-January-1
```

ANALYSIS AND DESIGN

An analysis of the problem indicates an input date must be acquired and manipulated. An appropriate object representation for the date is a String. From that String, three objects can be created representing the input date's month substring, the day substring, and the year substring. The three substrings can then be concatenated in the proper order to produce a String object representing the date in standard format.

Thus, in solving the problem the following variables and their associated objects are created, used, and manipulated:

- stdin: BufferedReader representing the standard input stream;
- buffer: String representing the input date in American format;
- month: String representing the month;
- day: String representing the day of the month;
- year: String representing the year;
- standardDate: String representing the date in standard format.

In addition, although its availability is taken generally for granted, the standard output stream is also needed.

■ System.out: PrintStream representing the standard output stream;

With these variables, *pseudocode* (algorithm) can be written that describes the object interactions and manipulations for solving the problem.

Step 1.   Display a suitable legend describing the program's purpose to the standard output.

Step 2.   Issue a prompt to the standard output that requests the user to enter a date in American format.

Step 3.   Get a String representation of the date of interest from the standard input and assign it to variable buffer.

Step 4.   Echo buffer's date representation to the standard output.

Step 5.   Examine buffer's date representation and extract a String representation of the input month. Assign the representation to variable month.

Step 6.   Examine buffer's date representation and extract a String representation of the input day. Assign the representation to variable day.

Step 7.   Examine buffer's date representation and extract a String representation of the input year. Assign the representation to variable year.

Step 8.   Assign to variable standardDate the String concatenation of year, month, and day with appropriate separating hyphens.

Step 9.   Display standardDate's date representation to the standard output.

We next discuss how to implement the pseudocode in Java.

IMPLEMENTATION

The legend display is implemented easily using method System.out.println().

```
// produce a legend (Step 1)
System.out.println("Date format translator");
System.out.println("   Converts a date from American"
    + " format (e.g., July 4, 1776)");
System.out.println("   to standard format (e.g.,"
    + " 1776-July-4).");
System.out.println();
```

Similarly, displaying a prompt is straightforward with method System.out.print().

```
// prompt the user for a date in American format (Step 2)
System.out.print("Enter a date in American format: ");
```

Using BufferedReader method readLine(), the date of interest can be extracted from the standard input stream to initialize the variable buffer.

```
// acquire the input entered by the user (Step 3)
BufferedReader stdin = new BufferedReader(
    new InputStreamReader(System.in));
String buffer = stdin.readLine();
```

Before manipulating the input string represented by buffer, the string is echoed back to indicate its intended purpose.

```
// echo the input back (Step 4)
System.out.println("The translation of");
System.out.println("   " + buffer);
```

For example, suppose `buffer` represented " February 29, 1904 " with depiction

The output of this segment would then be

```
The translation of
    February 29, 1904
```

The month portion of the input string is determined by first trimming any leading or trailing whitespace that surrounds the input date.

```
// get month entered by the user (Step 5)
buffer = buffer.trim();
int m = buffer.indexOf(" ");
String month = buffer.substring(0, m);
buffer = buffer.substring(m+1).trim();
```

The trimming results in `Buffer` being assigned a newly created `String` that represents the input string without any leading or trailing whitespace (i.e., two initial blanks and one trailing blank was removed).

As a result of the trimming, the month substring consists of the characters preceding the first blank in the string now referenced by `buffer`. To search for the index m of that blank, `String` member method `indexOf()` is used. In particular, the method `indexOf()` that takes a single parameter of type `String` is invoked. The invocation returns the starting index of the first occurrence of the search string.

```
int m = buffer.indexOf(" ");
```

To create the `String` representation of the month, a `String` member method `substring()` is used.

```
String month = buffer.substring(0, m);
```

The method's two parameters are 0 and m, which specify respectively the index of the starting position in the string to be copied and the index of the position that is one beyond the last character to be copied. The method creates and returns a `String` copy of the specified characters.

Once the month substring is created, `buffer` is updated to reference the trimmed portion of the user input that follows the month.

```
buffer = buffer.substring(m+1).trim();
```

The update assigns `buffer` the evaluation of the expression `buffer.substring(m+1).trim()`. The evaluation of this expression begins by creating a `String` copy of the characters starting at index m+1 and continuing to end of the string. From that copy, a `String` is then created that represents the trimmed version of the copy.

buffer "29, 1904"

The day portion now begins with what is left of the input. In particular, the day portion is the substring preceding the comma. Thus, the task of the sixth step is similar to the that of the fifth step. However, instead of searching for a blank, the search in this step is for a comma.

```
// get day entered by the user (Step 6)
int n = s.indexOf(",");
String day = buffer.substring(0, n);
buffer = buffer.substring(n+1).trim();
```

The code reflects the similarity of the tasks. A variable n is assigned the index of the comma. Using that index, a String representation of the day is created. Variable buffer is then updated so that it references a representation of the trimmed portion of the input following the comma.

After the update, buffer now references a String representation of the year portion of the input. By using that fact, the seventh step is straightforward, Variable year is initialized with the value of buffer.

```
// get year entered by the user (Step 7)
String year = buffer;
```

With variables month, day, and year appropriately set, a standard format version of the input date can be created through concatenation and assigned to variable standard-Date. Doing so, completes the eighth step.

```
// create standard format version of input (Step 8)
String standardDate = year + "-" + month + "-" + day;
```

The implementation of the last step is straightforward—display the transformed date.

```
// display the translation (Step 9)
System.out.println("to standard format is");
System.out.printlh("   " + standardDate);
```

To develop a program, the code needs to be assembled in a method main() within an appropriately named class. We named the class DateTranslation and provide the complete solution for the problem in DateTranslation.java of Listing 3.2.

TESTING

Although the preceding analysis demonstrated the correctness of the code, it is possible that the analysis was incomplete or did not take some input cases into account. It is also possible that the implementation of the design introduced errors (e.g., a mistyped index). Therefore, testing of the program is appropriate.

Although testing the program with every possible input date is impossible, it is possible to test the program with each possible input date form. The basic input form has the following elements:

- month whitespace day comma year.

However, whitespace can precede or follow the year. There can also be whitespace preceding the month. Therefore, the other possible input forms are

- month whitespace day comma year whitespace;
- month whitespace day comma whitespace year;
- month whitespace day comma whitespace year whitespace;
- whitespace month whitespace day comma year;
- whitespace month whitespace day comma year whitespace;
- whitespace month whitespace day comma whitespace year whitespace.

The exercises test `DateTranslation.java` using each of the input forms.

Listing 3.2 DateTranslation.java

```java
1.  // Convert user-specified date from American to standard
2.  // format
3.
4.  import java.io.*;
5.
6.  class DateTranslation {
7.
8.      // main(): application entry point
9.      static public void main(String args[]) throws IOException {
10.         // produce a legend (Step 1)
11.         System.out.println("Date format translator");
12.         System.out.println("   Converts a date from an American"
13.             + " format (e.g., July 4, 1776)");
14.         System.out.println("   to standard format (e.g.,"
15.             + " 1776-July-4).");
16.         System.out.println();
17.
18.         // prompt the user for a date in American format (Step 2)
19.         System.out.print("Enter a date in American format: ");
20.
21.         // acquire the input entered by the user (Step 3)
22.         BufferedReader stdin = new BufferedReader(
23.            new InputStreamReader(System.in) );
24.         String buffer = stdin.readLine().trim();
25.
26.         // echo the input back (Step 4)
27.         System.out.println("The translation of");
28.         System.out.println("   " + buffer);
29.
30.         // get month entered by the user (Step 5)
31.         int m = buffer.indexOf(" ");
32.         String month = buffer.substring(0, m);
33.         buffer = buffer.substring(m+1).trim();
34.
35.         // get day entered by the user (Step 6)
36.         int n = buffer.indexOf(",");
37.         String day = buffer.substring(0, n);
38.         buffer = buffer.substring(n+1).trim();
39.
40.         // get year entered by the user (Step 7)
41.         String year = buffer;
42.
43.         // create standard format version of input (Step 8)
44.         String standardDate = year + "-" + month + "-" + day;
45.
46.         // display the translation (Step 9)
47.         System.out.println("to standard format is");
48.         System.out.println("   " + standardDate);
49.     }
50. }
```

REVIEW

- The value of an object variable is a reference to a location that holds an object of its object type.
- The **null** reference corresponds to the empty address.
- The memory for unreferenced objects is reclaimed automatically so that it can be reused as needed. This recycling is called garbage collection.
- Once initialized, an object type constant cannot change the object to which it refers.
- A String is an encapsulation of a sequence of characters.
- The String method length() returns the number of characters that make up its string.
- The String += operator performs an append assignment.
- The first character of a String object has index 0.
- String provides several substring() member methods that return a new String object representing a portion of the associated string.
- String provides several indexOf() member methods that provide the ability to find the first occurrence of substring subject to some conditions.
- String provides several lastIndexOf() member methods that provide the ability to find the last occurrence of a substring subject to some conditions.
- String member method charAt() expects a single index as its parameter and returns the value of the character at that position in its String.
- String member method trim() returns a newly created string that represents its string except for any leading and trailing whitespace.
- The String class provides a collection of class methods each named valueOf(). For each of the types **bool**, **char**, **int**, **long**, **float**, and **double** there is a valueOf() method that expects a single parameter of that fundamental type. A valueOf() method returns a reference to a newly created String representing the value of its parameter in character form.
- There are no methods to modify a String—once a String object has been created, it is immutable.
- The Java awt API provides in part the class Rectangle. A Rectangle represents a rectangular area in coordinate space.
- There is a Rectangle constructor that expects as its parameters: the x-coordinate of the top-left corner, the y-coordinate of the top-left corner, the width, and the height.
- Rectangle member method setLocation() uses its parameters to reset the x- and y-coordinates of its rectangle.
- Rectangle member method resize() uses its parameters to resize the width and height of its rectangle.
- The creation of a class type object is accomplished by invoking a member constructor method that creates and initializes the attributes of the object.

| 3.8 | **SELF-TEST** |

S3.1 Give a depiction of memory after the following code segment is executed

```
int i = 1;
String s = "string1";
String t = s;
```

S3.2 Does the following code segment make sense? Explain.

```
String s = "string1";
String t;
s = t;
```

S3.3 What is the output of the following code segment? Explain.

```
String s = "abcdefghij";
System.out.println(s.indexOf("i"));
```

S3.4 True or false: The empty string and **null** are equivalent in concept. Explain.

| 3.9 | **EXERCISES** |

3.1 Define and initialize appropriately named `String` variables and constants for the following concepts. Justify your choice of variable or constant definition.

a) The response given by a user when queried for a color.

b) A message to a user asking for the current temperature.

c) A response to a user indicating that the input entry was invalid.

d) The response given by a user when queried for a first name.

e) The third month of the year.

f) The English language vowels.

3.2 Give a depiction of memory after the following code segment is executed.

```
int i = 10;
int j = i;
String s = "string1";
String t = s;
s = "string2";
```

3.3 Give a depiction of memory after the following code segment is executed.

```
String s = "string1";
String t = "string2";
String u;
u = s;
s = t;
t = u;
```

3.4 How are primitive and object variables different. Explain.

3.5 What is held constant in an object type constant? Explain.

3.6 What is automatic garbage collection? Why might it be important?

3.7 Why is the `String` class available to our program without the use of an **import** statement? Explain.

3.8 What is the value of the following expressions?

a) `1 + 2 + " buckle my shoe"`

b) `"one-" + "two"+ " buckle my shoe"`

c) `"" + 1 + 2 + " buckle my shoe"`

d) `'1' + 2 + " buckle my shoe"`

e) `1 + "-2" + " buckle my shoe"`

3.9 Draw a picture of memory after the following code segment completes.

```
String s;
String t = null;
String u = "";
```

3.10 Does the following code segment make sense? Explain.

```
String s = "string1";
String t = null;
s = t;
```

3.11 What is the output of the following code segment? Explain.

```
String s = "abcdefghij";
System.out.println(s.length());
```

3.12 Correct the following code segment. Explain your changes.

```
String s = "1234567890";
int i = s.length;
int j = s.indexOf('5');
int k = s;
```

3.13 What is the output of the following code segment? Explain.

```
String s = "perseverance";
String t = s.substring(4,6);
String u = s.substring(3,8);
String v = s.substring(0,9);
System.out.println(t);
System.out.println(u);
System.out.println(v);
```

3.14 What is the output of the following code segment? Explain.

```
String s = "telephone directory";
String t = s.substring(5,9);
String u = s.substring(1,1);
String v = s.substring(12,16);
System.out.println(t);
System.out.println(u);
System.out.println(v);
```

3.15 What is the output of the following code segment? Explain.

```
String s = "abracadabra";
```

```
int n1 = s.indexOf("ra");
int n2 = s.indexOf("ra", 2);
int n3 = s.indexOf("ra", 5);
int n4 = s.indexOf("ra", 10);
System.out.println(n1);
System.out.println(n2);
System.out.println(n3);
System.out.println(n4);
```

3.16 What is the output of the following code segment? Explain.

```
String s = "deadheaded";
int n1 = s.indexOf("ead");
int n2 = s.indexOf("dh", 2);
int n3 = s.indexOf("d", 5);
int n4 = s.indexOf("d", 10);
System.out.println(n1);
System.out.println(n2);
System.out.println(n3);
System.out.println(n4);
```

3.17 What is the output of the following code segment? Explain.

```
String alphabet = "qwertyuiopasdfghjklzxcvbnm";
char c1 = alphabet.charAt(0);
char c2 = alphabet.charAt(9);
char c3 = alphabet.charAt(25);
System.out.println(c1);
System.out.println(c2);
System.out.println(c3);
```

3.18 What is the output of the following code segment? Explain.

```
String alphabet = "qazwsxedcrfvtgbyhnujmikolp";
char c1 = alphabet.charAt(2);
char c2 = alphabet.charAt(10);
char c3 = alphabet.charAt(24);
System.out.println(c1);
System.out.println(c2);
System.out.println(c3);
```

3.19 What is the output of the following code segment? Explain.

```
int v1 = 3;
boolean v2 = false;
double v3 = 1.414;
char v4 = 'c';
String s1 = String.valueof(v1);
String s2 = String.valueof(v2);
String s3 = String.valueof(v3);
String s4 = String.valueof(v4);
```

3.20 What is the output of the following code segment? Explain.

```
char v1 = 'j';
int v2 = false;
boolean v3 = true;
double v4 = 6.21;
String s1 = String.valueof(v1);
```

```
String s2 = String.valueof(v2);
String s3 = String.valueof(v3);
String s4 = String.valueof(v4);
```

3.21 What is the output of the following code segment? Explain.

```
String s = "abcd      ";
String t = "    abcd    ";
String u = "  ab   cd  ";
System.out.println( s.trim() );
System.out.println( t.trim() );
System.out.println( u.trim() );
```

3.22 What is the output of the following code segment? Explain.

```
String s = "a b c d e f";
String t = " a    b     ";
String u = "         abc";
System.out.println( s.trim() );
System.out.println( t.trim() );
System.out.println( u.trim() );
```

3.23 After the following code segment is executed, is it safe for Java to reclaim the memory to which s referred upon initialization? Explain.

```
BufferedReader stdin = new BufferedReader(
    new InputStreamReader(System.in));
String s = stdin.readLine();
String t = s;
s = "aardvark";
t = "weasel";
```

3.24 Define a String variable s that represents the concatenation of the values referenced by String variables u and v and the character '!'.

3.25 Write a program that prompts for and accepts a telephone number in the form *ddd–ddd–dddd*, where *d* is a digit, and prints it out in the following format: (*ddd*) *ddd–dddd*.

3.26 The string @ @ @ is a valid address according to the problem statement for the e-mail address case study of Section 3.10. Why was this allowed? What program abilities are required to handle such cases? What program abilities are required to handle the finding of all e-mail addresses in some text of interest?

3.27 Develop and test an input suite for DateTranslation.java of Listing 3.2. The suite should consider the following possibilities.

- month whitespace day comma year whitespace;

- month whitespace day comma whitespace year;

- month whitespace day comma whitespace year whitespace;

- whitespace month whitespace day comma year;

- whitespace month whitespace day comma year whitespace;

- whitespace month whitespace day comma whitespace year whitespace.

3.10   PROGRAMMING PROJECT — HARVESTER

Have you ever wondered how unsolicited e-mail or as it commonly is called, *spam*, comes from mass-marketing companies that you have never heard of? Mass-marketers use a variety of techniques, one of which is *e-mail harvesting*. An e-mail harvester is a program that searches the Web for files containing e-mail addresses.

> The objective of this case study is to practice using the String library for manipulating information in the context of problem solving

For example, there are websites such as `http://www.ibiblio.org/` that maintain the archives of postings to electronic news groups such as `comp.lang.java`. Within these archives are tens of thousands of e-mail addresses from the various posters of news group articles. Although we are definitely not encouraging spam, the purpose of this case study is to design and document a program `EmailSearch.java` that searches a user-provided string to see if contains an e-mail address.

PROBLEM STATEMENT

Provide an interactive program that prompts a user for the text of interest. The program then displays the first e-mail address contained in that text. For our purposes an e-mail address is composed of an "@" and the two maximal-length strings with no embedded whitespace surrounding that "@". If there is no e-mail address in the text, then the program displays an "@".

In developing your solution `EmailAddress.java`, use only the parts of the Java programming language that we have already introduced. The case study has been designed so that it exercises your use of the material presented in this chapter.

SAMPLE OUTPUT

```
Java Program Design                              _ □ ×

cmd:  javac EmailAddress.java

cmd:  java EmailAddress

Email Address Harvester

Input line: Write us at javaprogramdesign@mhhe.com some day.

Extracted email address: javaprogramdesign@mhhe.com

cmd:
```

ANALYSIS AND DESIGN

So how do we search for an e-mail address? According to our definition, an e-mail address is a maximal string of characters that contains an "@" but does not contain whitespace. For example, consider the input text "there is no-one@home.org.moon today, try again tomorrow says nobody@nobody at home."

- "there" is not an e-mail address according to our definition—it does not contain an embedded "@".

- "is no-one@home.org.moon" and "no-one@home.org.moon today" are not e-mail addresses according to our definition—both strings contain whitespace

- "one@home.org" is not an e-mail address according to our definition—the string is not maximally nonwhitespace with respect to the input text; i.e., in the input text there are nonwhitespace characters immediately preceding and following the string "one@home.org"

- "nobody@nobody" is an e-mail address according to our definition—the string is a maximal-length nonblank string containing an "@". However, because "nobody@nobody" is not the first e-mail address within the supplied text, it is not the solution to our problem.

- "no-one@home.org.moon" is a valid e-mail address according to our definition—the string is a maximal-length nonblank string containing a "@". Because it is the first e-mail address in the supplied text, the address is the solution to our problem.

We express one caveat as we design a solution to our problem. At this point in the text we have not yet introduced how to execute actions selectively based on some test for conditions. Our programs have what is known as *straight-line* behavior—they perform the same tasks every time they are run. Because of this restriction, we must be especially thoughtful in how we process the user-supplied text so that we always produce a correct solution to our problem regardless of whether the user's entry contains an e-mail address.

It is clear that knowing the position of the first "@" in the text message is important. Suppose we know that the first "@" in the text is the *j*-th character there; i.e., its *index* is j. We are then interested in determining indices *i* and *k*, where *i* is the minimal index into the text such that all characters in positions *i* through *j* are nonblank and *k* is the maximal index into the text such that all characters in positions *j* through *k* are nonblank. The solution to our problem is then the string composed of the characters from index *i* to index *k* of the input text.

Input line: Write us at javaprogramdesign@mhhe.com some day.

Index i   Index j   Index k

IMPLEMENTATION

Our analysis suggests the following algorithm.

Step 1.	Prompt for an input text message.
Step 2.	Get input text *message*.
Step 3.	Set *j* to the index of the first "@" in *message*.
Step 4.	Set *i* to the minimal index in *message* such that all characters in positions *i* through *j* are nonblank.
Step 5.	Set *k* to the maximal index in *message* such that all characters in positions *j* through *k* are nonblank.
Step 6.	Set *address* to the substring of *message* with indices *i* through *k*.

Step 7. Display *address.*

So how can we can implement such an algorithm? The first step is not difficult, we already have the ability to acquire `String` input via a console program.

The second statement is straightforward with the `String`. Member method `indexOf()` can be used to determine index *j*. But how do we find the indices *i* and *k* of the next two steps of the algorithm? What we can do is search for the indices of the last blank in *message* that precedes index *j* and the first blank in *message* that follows index *j*. These indices can be found respectively using `String` member methods `lastIndexOf()` and `indexOf()`.

With indices *i* and *k* we can use the `String substring()` method to determine *address.* But what if there are no blanks before or after the e-mail address or what if there is no e-mail address? In these cases, the values of *i* and *k* do not make sense for specifying the answer string.

So how can we ensure success? We can handle the special case of missing blanks by searching

" " + *message* + " "

rather than searching *message.* The surrounding blanks ensure that if the e-mail address is present, then there are definitely blanks surrounding the message. When problem solving be open to modifying the input. It often can simplify the problem handling. However, be sure the modification does not affect whether the correct solution is calculated.

If a further alteration is made to the string to be searched, all cases can be handle readily. This alteration is left to you.

TESTING

Start the verification of your program with our example string "there is no-one@home.org.moon today, try again tomorrow says nobody@nobody at home". However, this string does not test exhaustively your program. For example, input strings with no blanks should also be considered. As part of your documentation, list your test set and explain how it considers all important cases. (For an example of what is expected, see the date translation test case analysis beginning on page 127.)

| 3.11 | **SELF-TEST ANSWERS** |

S3.1 The memory has the following depiction.

This depiction occurs because `i` is a primitive integer variable with value 1 and because `s` and `t` are `String` variables referencing the same location.

S3.2 The code segment does not make sense. Variable t is uninitialized and therefore it cannot be assigned to s. We can however assign s to t.

S3.3 The output is 8. An 8 is displayed because String positions are numbered starting at 0 and the first position in character sequence represented by s is in the eighth position.

S3.4 False: The empty string and the **null** address are not equivalent in concept. The empty string corresponds to a character sequence of length 0. The **null** address corresponds to the empty address, which is more like the absence of a string.

4 BEING CLASSY

We now introduce how to create and manipulate simple objects with attributes and behaviors that *you* can specify. We do so through the use of classes. The class is Java's principal mechanism for supporting object-oriented design. A class enables objects to be created with attributes and behaviors. In Java, an attribute is represented using a data field and a behavior is implemented with a method. By using classes to represent the various types of information being examined and manipulated, *each information type is designed and implemented only once and then reused as often as needed without having to reanalyze and rejustify the representation.*

OBJECTIVES

- Introduce Java's primary object-oriented design mechanism—the class.
- Explore the use of instance variables and class constants.
- Consider class construction using default and nondefault constructors.
- Explore the use of member methods for accessing and mutating the attributes of an object.
- Explore the use of member methods for manipulating an object.
- Demonstrate the value of encapsulation and information hiding,
- Introduce the basics of window creation and graphical rendering.

4.1   PREPARATION

After this chapter, your programming skills will be very different. Thus far, our introduction to effective Java programming has given you experience with computing systems and problem solving, variables, types, input and output, expressions, assignments, objects, and standard classes and their methods. That material was background for what Java is really about—*the ability to design and implement your own objects*. With that ability you can model, create, and manipulate the attributes and behaviors of any information item or physical world object.

This chapter *introduces* you to the *basics* of designing and implementing your own objects by using Java's principal mechanism for specifying a new type of object—the class.

In a very real sense, this entire chapter is a case study. It is a case study that focuses on using classes and object-oriented design to problem solve. Chapters 1 and 9 will extend this introduction to consider the intricacies of methods, classes, object-oriented design, and inheritance. The intervening chapters will consider other important Java programming mechanisms.

The importance of classes to object-oriented design cannot be overrated. A class enables an information type to be *designed and implemented only once* and then *reused as often as needed* without having to reanalyze and rejustify the representation.

Before starting our introduction to class creation, we present a short program Two-Windows.java in Listing 4.1 that displays two empty graphical windows. One of the windows is titled "Bigger" and the other window is titled "Smaller".

We examine the program TwoWindows.java because our first class will be manipulating a window. By becoming familiar now with the Java window class, its use later on will not be a distraction to our exploration of classes.

Method main() of program TwoWindows.java begins by defining and initializing JFrame variables w1 and w2.

```
JFrame w1 = new JFrame("Bigger");
JFrame w2 = new JFrame("Smaller");
```

A JFrame is the principal way in Java to represent a titled, bordered graphical window. Class JFrame is part of the standard package swing. The swing package is one of several APIs (application programmer interfaces) that comprise the *Java Foundations Classes* (*JFC*). Although now part of the Java standard, the Java Foundation Classes are

---

Listing 4.1   TwoWindows.java

```
1.  // Purpose: Displays two different windows.
2.
3.  import javax.swing.*;
4.
5.  public class TwoWindows {
6.      // main(): application entry point
7.      public static void main(String[] args) {
8.          JFrame w1 = new JFrame("Bigger");
9.          JFrame w2 = new JFrame("Smaller");
10.
11.         w1.setSize(200, 125);
12.         w2.setSize(150, 100);
13.
14.         w1.setVisible(true);
15.         w2.setVisible(true);
16.     }
17. }
```

---

extensions of the original Java specification. Because it is an extension, the swing package is found at javax.swing.

The JFrame constructor used in the definitions of w1 and w2 takes a single String parameter that specifies the title of the window.

Method main() then sizes the windows. The resizing is accomplished through JFrame member method setSize(). The parameters of method setSize() specify the desired width and height in pixels. (*Pixel* stands for picture element and it is the size of the smallest dot that can be drawn on the monitor.)

```
w1.setSize(200, 125);
w2.setSize(150, 100);
```

As a result of these invocations, the window referenced by w1 has a width of 200 pixels and a height of 125 pixels and the window referenced by w2 has a width of 150 pixels and a height of 100 pixels.

Now that the windows are configured properly, method main() makes them visible using JFrame member method setVisible().

```
w1.setVisible(true);
w2.setVisible(true);
```

The invocations must be made because a JFrame is invisible by default. A parameter with value **true** indicates that the JFrame is to be visible; and a parameter with value **false** indicates that the JFrame is not to be visible.

Now that you have seen how to represent and display graphical windows, we are ready to start our introduction to creating your own classes.

Because understanding and learning is easier when you are able to visualize what is going on, the introductory class examples in this chapter involve the representation and drawing of colored rectangles. Later chapters will consider many other class representations including ones for clocks, calculators, aquariums, and instant messengers.

<table>
<tr><td>4.2</td><td></td></tr>
</table>

4.2   A VERY SIMPLE CLASS

Our class representation of a colored rectangle will be called ColoredRectangle and its initial definition is given in Listing 4.2. This first version is for objects that support the display of a square window containing a blue filled-in rectangle, where the window has a side length of 200 pixels and the rectangle is 40 pixels wide and 20 pixels high. This lack of flexibility is a temporary condition accepted to enable a simpler introduction to the class concept.

Classes exist to be used and the first use of class ColoredRectangle will be by the program BoxFun.java of Listing 4.3. A look at program BoxFun.java should help you understand class ColoredRectangle—the program is an illustration of the capabilities of ColoredRectangle.

The following screen capture depicts the windows produced by program Box-Fun.java.

That the two windows are the same is the result of the ColoredRectangle's simplicity—the attributes of the ColoredRectangle objects are fixed (e.g, size, location, and color). In Section 4.3, we consider a second version of class ColoredRectangle that support objects with different attributes and with several behaviors. The result is a more realistic representation of a colored rectangle.

Listing 4.2 **ColoredRectangle.java — version I**

```
1.  // Purpose: Displays a colored rectangle within a window.
2.
3.  import javax.swing.*;
4.  import java.awt.*;
5.
6.  public class ColoredRectangle {
7.     // instance variables to describe object attributes
8.     private int width;        // rectangle width
9.     private int height;       // rectangle height
10.    private int x;            // rectangle x-coordinate position
11.    private int y;            // rectangle y-coordinate position
12.    private JFrame window;    // window displaying rectangle
13.    private Color color;      // color of rectangle
14.
15.    // ColoredRectangle(): default constructor
16.    public ColoredRectangle() {
17.       window = new JFrame("Box Fun");
18.       window.setSize(200, 200);
19.
20.       width = 40;
21.       height = 20;
22.       x = 80;
23.       y = 90;
24.
25.       color = Color.BLUE;
26.
27.       window.setVisible(true);
28.    }
29.
30.    // paint(): display the rectangle in its window
31.    public void paint() {
32.       Graphics g = window.getGraphics();
33.       g.setColor(color);
34.       g.fillRect(x, y, width, height);
35.    }
36. }
```

As the listing of BoxFun.java suggests, with class ColoredRectangle we can make use of the same object-oriented programming features as we do with standard classes. In particular, we can create instances of class ColoredRectangle

```
ColoredRectangle r1 = new ColoredRectangle();
ColoredRectangle r2 = new ColoredRectangle();
```

and initiate behaviors through method invocations.

```
r1.paint();  // draw the window associated with r1
r2.paint();  // draw the window associated with r2
```

As with objects of the standard classes, a ColoredRectangle member method invocation sends a message to the object targeted by its invocation. For example, the Box-Fun.java invocation r1.paint() instructs the ColoredRectangle referenced by variable r1 to display itself; and the invocation r2.paint() instructs the Colored-

---

Listing 4.3 **BoxFun.java**

```
1.  // Purpose: Create two windows containing colored rectangles.
2.  import java.io.*;
3.
4.  public class BoxFun {
5.      // main(): application entry point
6.      public static void main(String[] args) throws IOException {
7.          ColoredRectangle r1 = new ColoredRectangle();
8.          ColoredRectangle r2 = new ColoredRectangle();
9.
10.         System.out.println("Enter when ready");
11.         System.in.read();
12.
13.         r1.paint();  // draw the window associated with r1
14.         r2.paint();  // draw the window associated with r2
15.     }
16. }
```

Rectangle referenced by variable r2 to display itself.

We now turn out attention to the definition of ColoredRectangle itself. The class definition has three major sections each of which are introduced with a comment. The first section lists the attributes of a ColoredRectangle object; the second section defines a ColoredRectangle constructor; and the third section defines member method paint().

4.2.1 INSTANCE VARIABLES AND ATTRIBUTES

In Java, an object attribute commonly is referred to as a *data field* with the variable representing a data field known as an *instance variable*. In particular, each ColoredRectangle object has the following instance variables.

    private int width
        Represents the width of the rectangle to be displayed.
    private int height
        Represents the height of the rectangle to be displayed.
    private int x
        Represents the x-coordinate of the upper-left-hand corner of the rectangle to be displayed.
    private int y
        Represents the y-coordinate of the upper-left-hand corner of the rectangle to be displayed.

```
private JFrame window
```
Represents the window containing the rectangle drawing.
```
private Color color
```
Represents the color of the rectangle to be drawn. Class `Color` is part of `awt` API. The `awt` was Java's original graphical library. It is used now primarily for color and font representation, and drawing.

The definitions of the six `ColoredRectangle` instance variables in Listing 4.2 use the simplest available form,

```
private int width;      // rectangle width
private int height;     // rectangle height
private int x;          // rectangle x-coordinate position
private int y;          // rectangle y-coordinate position
private JFrame window;  // window displaying rectangle
private Color color;    // color of rectangle
```

Each instance variable is defined without specifying an initial value. Therefore, whenever a new `ColoredRectangle` object is to be constructed, Java first initializes the new instance variables to default values. By default, numeric instance variables are initialized to 0, **boolean** instance variables are initialized to **false**, and reference-type instance variables are initialized to **null**.

Thus, *every* time a new `ColoredRectangle` object is to undergo construction, *new* `width`, `height`, `x`, `y`, `window`, and `color` instance variables are created and default initialized for the new object. The numeric attributes `width`, `height`, `x`, and `y` are initialized to zero and the class-type attributes `window` and `color` are initialized to **null**.

The instance variable definitions specify each of the variable to be **private**. This modifier indicates that direct access to the instance variables is limited to the class itself. Thus, class `ColoredRectangle` practices *information hiding* by *encapsulating* its attributes.

> Chapters 7 and 9 discuss the nuances of instance variables. Remember, our intent is to keep this introduction as simple as possible

Defining instance variables to be **private** is a standard practice. When attributes are **private**, other classes are forced to use the class's interface methods to manipulate its attributes. Those interface methods normally are programmed to ensure that the requested manipulations are valid. Because the initial definition of class `ColoredRectangle` does not provide any methods to give access to the attributes, once a `ColoredRectangle` is constructed it is immutable. In Section 4.3, we introduce several `ColoredRectangle` methods for accessing and modifying the attributes of a `ColoredRectangle` object.

4.2.2   A DEFAULT CONSTRUCTOR

The second section of Listing 4.2 defines a default constructor for class `ColoredRectangle`. A *constructor* is a special type of Java method. When a constructor is used, Java automatically creates a new object with all the attributes of its class. It is the job of the constructor to assign those attributes sensibly. A *default constructor* configures the new instance of the class without any external guidance.

```
public ColoredRectangle()
```

> Constructs an object representing a 40 × 20 blue rectangle centered in a new 200 × 200 window.

Unlike other methods (e.g., method `main()` of program `BoxFun.java`), a constructor does not have a return type. A return type for a constructor is considered superfluous—a constructor always returns a reference to the newly built object of its class. Furthermore, the name of a constructor is always the same as the name of the class. Therefore, `ColoredRectangle()` indicates a constructor for class `ColoredRectangle`.

```
public class ColoredRectangle {
   // instance variables to describe object attributes
   ...

   // ColoredRectangle(): default constructor
   public ColoredRectangle() {

      ...                    The name of a constructor always matches the
                             name of its class
   }
      ...                    A constructor does not list its return type.  A constructor
                             always returns a reference to a new object of its class
}
```

The statement list or *body* of the `ColoredRectangle` constructor begins with an assignment to the `window` instance variable for the `ColoredRectangle` object under construction. As a result of the assignment, `window` references a new `JFrame`. The `JFrame` constructor creating that window object titles the window using its `String` parameter `"Box Fun"`.

```
window = new JFrame("Box Fun");
```

The `ColoredRectangle` constructor then sizes the window to the desired dimensions. For this purpose, the `ColoredRectangle` constructor signals the window through `JFrame` member method `setSize()`. Method `setSize()` expects two parameters giving the new width and height of the window in pixels.

```
window.setSize(200, 200);
```

In this invocation, both parameters have value 200.

The `ColoredRectangle` constructor then initializes the width, height, and coordinate position of the rectangle to be displayed.

```
width = 40;
height = 20;
x = 80;
y = 90;
```

Table 4.1	Color constants.	
Color.BLACK	Color.GREEN	Color.PINK
Color.BLUE	Color.LIGHT_GRAY	Color.RED
Color.CYAN	Color.MAGENTA	Color.WHITE
Color.DARK_GRAY	Color.ORANGE	Color.YELLOW
Color.GRAY		

The object under construction then has its instance variable `color` set to `Color.BLUE`.

```
color = Color.BLUE;
```

`Color.BLUE` is a `Color` class constant of awt class `Color` representing the color blue. The other `Color` class constants are listed in Table 4.1.

To complete the construction of the colored rectangle, its window is made visible.

```
window.setVisible(true);
```

By using the `ColoredRectangle` default constructor in a **new** expression, a new `ColoredRectangle` object is created by Java. The attributes of this new object then are configured by executing the statement list that makes up the body of the `ColoredRectangle` constructor.

For example, the following statement defines and initializes a `ColoredRectangle` variable `rectangle`.

```
ColoredRectangle rectangle = new ColoredRectangle();
```

The statement causes variable `rectangle` to be initialized with a reference to a new `ColoredRectangle` object with attributes that represent a `Color.Blue` rectangle that is 40 pixels wide and 20 pixels high. The rectangle is associated with a new `JFrame` window that has a side length of 200 pixels with the `String` title of "Box Fun". A depiction of the memory for variable `rectangle` is given in Figure 4.1.

We now turn are ready to our attention the `ColoredRectangle` method `paint()`.

4.2.3   AN INSTANCE METHOD

The third section of Listing 4.2 defines an instance method `paint()` that displays its `ColoredRectangle` object. Method `paint()` is known as a *member method* or *instance method* because it must be invoked in conjunction with an instance of a `ColoredRectangle` (i.e., a `ColoredRectangle` object).

```
public void paint()
```
    Draws a rectangle of appropriate size and position in the window associated with the rectangle.

Instance methods are similar to constructors in that they are associated with a particular object when they are invoked. Different invocations can associate an instance method with different objects. (In `BoxFun.java`, `ColoredRectangle` member method

Figure 4.1 **Depiction of memory associated with variable rectangle.**

rectangle

The value of a
ColoredRectangle
variable is a
reference to a
ColoredRectangle
object

ColorRectangle
- width = 40
- height = 20
- x = 80
- y = 90
- window =
- color =

+ paint() : **void**

String
- text = "Box Fun"
- ...

+ length() : **int**
+ ...

Color
- color =
- ...

+ brighter() : Color
+ ...

JFrame
- width = 200
- height = 200
- title =
- ...

+ setVisible(**boolean** status) : **void**
+ ...

paint() is invoked twice. Once for the ColoredRectangle referenced by variable r1 and once for the ColoredRectangle referenced by variable r2.)

A *member method definition* includes both a *header*, which describes its invocation interface, and a *body*, which comprises the method's actions. The actions are given as a statement list nested within matching braces. A method header always must supply the return type, method name, and a specification of its parameters. Supplying an access right is optional (e.g., **public**, **private**)

Optional modifier   Type of value that   Identifier name
indicating access rights   the method returns   of method

Modifier ReturnType MethodName (ParameterList)

A description of the form the parameters are to take. The parameter
declarations (if any) are comma separated. A parameter declaration
consists of the parameter's type and name

Nondefault initialization

Instead of defining the ColoredRectangle attributes to be initialized with default values, we could have defined them to have explicit values.

```
// instance variable alternative definitions
int width = 40;          // rectangle width
int height = 20;         // rectangle height
int x = 80;              // rectangle x-coordinate position
int y = 90;              // rectangle y-coordinate position
JFrame window = new JFrame("Box Fun");// window displaying
                                      // rectangle
Color color = Color.BLUE; // color of rectangle
```

With these definitions, the body of the default constructor could be shorter—it would need only to size the window and make it visible.

```
// ColoredRectangle(): alternative definition
public ColoredRectangle() {
    window.setSize(200, 200);
    window.setVisible(true);
}
```

We chose to implement the default constructor for better reader understanding. The default constructor describes completely what a new ColoredRectangle object looks like.

The method name and the types of its parameters form the *signature* of a method. Java requires that all methods of a class have distinct signatures.

From Listing 4.2, we see that paint() has the following definition.

```
public static void paint() {
    Graphics g = window.getGraphics();
    g.setColor(color);
    g.fillRect(x, y, width, height);
}
```

The definition shows that paint() has a return type of **void** and an empty parameter list. The method signature is therefore paint().

A method header can be preceded with *modifiers* that indicate access rights and other characteristics of the method. The modifier **public** for paint() indicates that other classes are allowed to invoke method areaRectangle().

The method body of areaRectangle() consists of the statements

```
Graphics g = window.getGraphics();
g.setColor(color);
g.fillRect(x, y, width, height);
```

By using the rectangle and window attributes of the associated object, an appropriate rectangle can be drawn (*rendered* or *painted* in computer graphics parlance).

The rendering is accomplished by first accessing the *graphical context* in which the drawing commands are to be issued. A graphical context is of type `java.awt.Graphics`.

A `Graphics` object provides all the necessary information for carrying out a rendering request (e.g., color, component on which the rendering is to occur, font, etc.). Besides encapsulating such information, `Graphics` objects have a variety of methods for drawing rectangles, lines, polygons, arcs, ovals, and strings.

Access to the graphical context of the window is obtained through `JFrame` instance method `getGraphics()`,

```
Graphics g = window.getGraphics();
```

Variable `g` is a variable whose *scope* of use is *local* to method `paint()`. Such a limitation is not imposed on instance variables. Their scope of use is the entire class.

Chapter 7 discusses the nuances of scope

The access to the window's graphic context through local variable g, enables the rendering color to be set with `Graphics` method `setColor()`.

```
g.setColor(color);
```

The actual display within the window is accomplished by using the position and size attributes of the associated object as parameters in the invocation of `Graphics` method `fillRect()`.

```
g.fillRect(x, y, width, height);
```

Method `fillRect()` renders a filled-in rectangle. The method expects four parameters. The first two parameters specify respectively the locations of the x- and y-coordinates for the upper left corner of the rectangle to be drawn. The rendering origin is the upper left hand corner of the window's container. The next two parameters specify respectively the width and height of the rectangle to be filled. (See Figure 4.2 for a depiction of the Java coordinate system properties.) All four values are given in pixels. The rectangle is rendered using the current color.

If we desired to draw only the perimeter of the rectangle, we would have used method `drawRect()`.

In a rendering request, the location of the rendering is specified relative to the *upper left-hand* corner of the object on which the drawing commands are performed. The direction of the x-axis is rightward. Therefore, increasing an x-coordinate value means moving rightward. The direction of the y-axis is downward. Therefore, increasing a y-coordinate value means moving downward.

Figure 4.2   Java coordinate system properties.

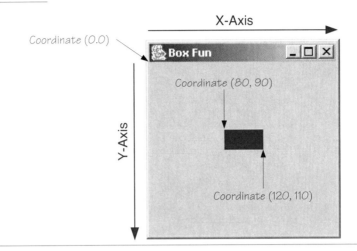

| 4.2.4 | **USAGE** |

Now that we have presented all of class ColoredRectangle, let's revisit program Box-Fun in Listing 4.3.

```
public class BoxFun {
    // main(): application entry point
    public static void main(String[] args) throws IOException {
        ColoredRectangle r1 = new ColoredRectangle();
        ColoredRectangle r2 = new ColoredRectangle();

        System.out.println("Enter when ready");
        System.in.read();

        r1.paint();  // draw the window associated with r1
        r2.paint();  // draw the window associated with r2
    }
}
```

Its method main() begins with the definitions of variables r1 and r2. These definitions are similar in form to object variables definitions in the previous chapters—the variables are initialized with references to newly constructed objects. *Each of these new ColoredRectangle objects has its own instances variables for maintaining its particular attributes.*

Except for the values of their window instance variables, the ColoredRectangle objects referenced by variables r1 and r2 have like instance variables values. The window instance variables are different because the default constructor always assigns the window instance variable a reference to a new JFrame. (See Figure 4.3 for a depiction of r1 and r2.)

Figure 4.3   **Depiction of the memory associated with variables r1 and r2.**

CLASSPATH

Our implementations of ColoredRectangle.java and BoxFun.java have them in the same folder. The compiled versions of those files are also in that same folder. Therefore, when an interpreter executes program BoxFun.java, the interpreter automatically finds the .class file for class ColoredRectangle. If the .class file for Colored-Rectangle was kept in a different folder, then the operating system variable CLASS-PATH would need to have that folder included in its folder list.

The next two next statements enable users to configure the "Box Fun" windows prior to the rectangle rendering.

```
System.out.print("Enter when ready");
System.in.read();
```

The prompt tells the user that an input is expected in order for the program to proceed. Until some input is given, the program waits.

If your computing system is like our system, the two windows produced during the ColoredRectangle construction are placed one on the top of other. Before providing some input in reaction to the prompt, we arrange the windows so that they can both be seen. After doing so, the Enter key is typed. Its value is extracted by System.in method read() and the program continues with the invocations of the paint() method.[†]

Because r1 and r2 reference different ColoredRectangle objects with different window attributes, the paint() invocations modify two windows.

```
r1.paint();  // display the window associated with r1
r2.paint();  // display the window associated with r2
```

The first invocation renders a rectangle in the window of the ColoredRectangle referenced by r1. The second invocation renders a rectangle in the window of the ColoredRectangle object referenced by r2.

Thus, when an instance method is being executed, the attributes of the object associated with the invocation are accessed and manipulated. This property of instance methods is of paramount importance in the object-oriented programming paradigm. It is what enables objects to have behaviors. Therefore, it is crucial when examining code that you understand what object is being manipulated.

```
public class ColoredRectangle {
   // instance variables to describe object attributes
   ...

   // paint(): display the rectangle in its window
   public void paint() {
      window.setVisible(true);  ◄───────────────────┐
      Graphics g = window.getGraphics();             │
      g.setColor(color);
      g.fillRect(x, y, width, height);
   }
   ...

}
```

Instance variable window references the JFrame attribute of the object that caused the invocation. That is, the invocation r1.paint() causes the window attribute of the ColoredRectangle referenced by r1 to be accessed. Similarly, the invocation r2.paint() causes the window attribute of the ColoredRectangle referenced by r2 to be accessed.

The values of these instance variables are also from the ColoredRectangle object that invoked method paint().

[†]   If during the rendering, one window is on top of the other, the bottom window will not show its rectangle after the top window is moved—the reason being the code displays the rectangle only once. Chapter 9 considers how to have an image rerendered automatically on an *exposure* event.

When analyzing code, we encourage you to first diagram each of your objects, and you then use the appropriate diagram to supply the values for the code being analyzed.

This discussion completes our basic introduction to classes. We now develop a more realistic version of class `ColoredRectangle`. This new definition has an additional constructor and several methods for accessing and modifying the attributes of a `Colored-Rectangle` object.

Program termination

The closing of a `JFrame` does not terminate its program automatically. One way to terminate the program is to type the operating system break sequence `Ctrl+c` in the console window.

Another way is to configure the `JFrame` to do the termination through its member method `setDefaultCloseOperation()`. If the following code segment is added to `TwoWindows.java` of Listing 4.1 at line 10, the program will terminate automatically when either of its windows is closed.

```
w1.setDefaultCloseOperation(JFrame.EXIT_ON_CLOSE)
w2.setDefaultCloseOperation(JFrame.EXIT_ON_CLOSE)
```

4.3   METHODS WITH PARAMETERS AND RETURN VALUES

When designing a class, always consider its possible uses. The intended usage of an object determines what behaviors are appropriate, and what attributes are needed to implement those behaviors.

Before reading on, list what you would expect of a `ColoredRectangle`. You are encouraged to perform this activity every time our text introduces a new class—to become an effective programmer you should practice design whenever possible.

ANALYSIS AND DESIGN

If you think about it you will agree that a new `ColoredRectangle` object should be able to have any color; be positioned anywhere within its window; and have no restrictions on its width and height. Furthermore, the attributes of a `ColoredRectangle` object should be accessible and updateable.

This analysis indicates there should be several additions to class `ColoredRectangle`. One of these additions should be the following construction behavior:

- *Specific construction*: construct a rectangle representation using supplied values for its attributes.

A reasonable class design almost always calls for encapsulating the attributes of its objects (i.e., protecting the attributes from direct modification by nonclass code). By providing both *accessor methods* that supply the values of the attributes and *mutator methods* that manage requests for changing attributes, a class can ensure that its objects always have sensible values. Our new `ColoredRectangle` design will follow this important software engineering practice. In particular, the following behaviors should be added to `ColoredRectangle` in support of *information hiding*.

- *Accessors:* provide the width, height, x-coordinate position, y-coordinate position, color, or window of the associated rectangle.

- *Mutators:* set the width, height, x-coordinate position, y-coordinate position, color, or window of the associated rectangle to a given value.

We next implement the methods that carry out these behaviors.

IMPLEMENTATION

The definition of the new `ColoredRectangle` class is given in Listing 4.4. The new accessors, mutators, and constructor start on line 36 after the unchanged definitions of default constructor `ColoredRectangle()` and method `paint()`. Methods such as `paint()` are sometimes referred to as *facilitators* because they support an expected use of the object.

The first of the new definitions is that of mutator `setWidth()`.

```
// setWidth(): width mutator
public void setWidth(int w) {
    width = w;
}
```

By invoking mutator `setWidth()` of a `ColoredRectangle` object, the object is signaled to change its width attribute. The mutator requires that the invoking expression *pass* (supply) a single parameter value to it. The passed information is referred to as the *actual parameter* or *actual argument*. The parameter provides information that is otherwise unavailable to `setWidth()`. In particular, the parameter supplies the desired value for the width attribute of the associated `ColoredRectangle`. For example, the following code segment first defines a variable s that references a new `ColoredRectangle` object, which initially has the default width attribute of length 40. The mutator for that object then is invoked to reset the width to 80.

```
ColoredRectangle s = new ColoredRectangle();
s.setWidth(80);
```

A depiction of the memory associated with the code segment is given in Figure 4.4.

Listing 4.4   ColoredRectangle.java — version 2

```
1.  // Purpose: Support the manipulation of a rectangle in a window.
2.
3.  import javax.swing.*;
4.  import java.awt.*;
5.
6.  public class ColoredRectangle {
7.      // instance variables to describe object attributes
8.      private int width;        // rectangle width
9.      private int height;       // rectangle height
10.     private int x;            // rectangle x-coordinate position
11.     private int y;            // rectangle y-coordinate position
12.     private JFrame window;    // window displaying rectangle
13.     private Color color;      // color of rectangle
14.
15.     // ColoredRectangle(): default constructor
16.     public ColoredRectangle() {
17.         window = new JFrame("Box Fun");
18.         window.setSize(200, 200);
19.
20.         width = 40;
21.         height = 20;
22.         x = 80;
23.         y = 90;
24.         color = Color.BLUE;
25.
26.         window.setVisible(true);
27.     }
28.
29.     // paint(): display the rectangle in its window
30.     public void paint() {
31.         Graphics g = window.getGraphics();
32.         g.setColor(color);
33.         g.fillRect(x, y, width, height);
34.     }
35.
36.     // setWidth(): width mutator
37.     public void setWidth(int w) {
38.         width = w;
39.     }
40.
41.     // setHeight(): height mutator
42.     public void setHeight(int h) {
43.         height = h;
44.     }
45.
46.     // setX(): x mutator
47.     public void setX(int ulx) {
48.         x = ulx;
49.     }
50.
51.     // setY(): y mutator
52.     public void setY(int uly) {
53.         y = uly;
54.     }
```

Listing 4.4   **ColoredRectangle.java — version 2 (Continued)**

```
55.
56.      // setWindow(): window mutator
57.      public void setWindow(JFrame f) {
58.         window = f;
59.      }
60.
61.      // setColor(): color mutator
62.      public void setColor(Color c) {
63.         color = c;
64.      }
65.
66.      // getWidth(): width accessor
67.      public int getWidth() {
68.            return width;
69.      }
70.
71.      // getHeight(): height accessor
72.      public int getHeight() {
73.         return height;
74.      }
75.
76.      // getX(): x accessor
77.      public int getX() {
78.         return x;
79.      }
80.
81.      // getY(): y accessor
82.      public int getY() {
83.         return y;
84.      }
85.
86.      // getWindow(): window accessor
87.      public JFrame getWindow() {
88.         return window;
89.      }
90.
91.      // getColor(): color accessor
92.      public Color getColor() {
93.         return color;
94.      }
95.
96.      // ColoredRectangle(): specific constructor
97.      public ColoredRectangle(int w, int h, int ulx, int uly,
98.                              JFrame f, Color c) {
99.         setWidth(w);
100.        setHeight(h);
101.        setX(ulx);
102.        setY(uly);
103.        setWindow(f);
104.        setColor(c);
105.     }
106. }
```

Figure 4.4   **Depiction of memory associated with variable s.**

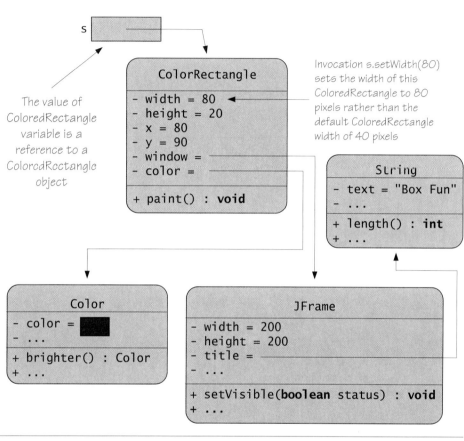

The value of ColoredRectangle variable is a reference to a ColoredRectangle object

Invocation s.setWidth(80) sets the width of this ColoredRectangle to 80 pixels rather than the default ColoredRectangle width of 40 pixels

Whenever a method is invoked, Java executes the statement list that makes up the invoked method's definition. In particular, the next statement to be executed is the first statement in the invoked method's statement list. We say that *flow of control* is *transferred* temporarily to that method. The actual parameters in the invocation are used to initialize the *formal parameters* in the method's definition. For *each* method invocation, Java individually sets aside memory for that *particular* invocation to store the values of the formal parameters. This memory is known commonly as an *activation record*.

Actual Parameters $\xrightarrow{\text{Initialize}}$ Formal parameters

Once the actual parameters have been used to initialize the formal parameters, the actual parameters and the formal parameters are independent of each other. The method then begins executing its statement body. If during its execution, a method updates the value of a formal parameter, the change does not affect the actual parameter. The change is limited to the activation record containing the value of the formal parameter. This type of correspondence between the actual and formal parameters is known as *value parameter passing*. In general, the first actual parameter initializes the first formal parameter, the second actual parameter initializes the second formal parameter, and so on. Thus, to invoke a method, the number of actual parameters and formal parameters must be the same.

Because the definition of mutator `setWidth()` specifies the name of its formal parameter to be w, the invocation `s.setWidth(80)` causes method `setWidth()` to be executed with formal parameter w initialized to 80.

Formal parameters are essentially variables that are *local* to their method. The formal parameters are created with the invocation of their method, their values are accessible only within the method, and they are destroyed when their method completes. The only difference between the formal parameters and the other variables defined by a method is that the formal parameters are initialized using the values of the actual parameters.

Therefore, if `setWidth()` were to update the value of formal parameter w (which it does not), the change would be visible only within `setWidth()`—the actual parameter would remain unchanged.

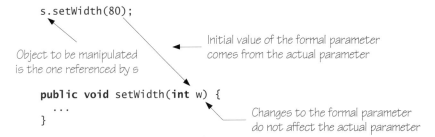

In a transfer of control to method `setWidth()`, its single statement method body is executed. The statement assigns the value of formal parameter w to instance variable width. The particular instance variable that is updated, is the one belonging to the `ColoredRectangle` object initiating the invocation. After executing the statement body, Java transfers the flow of control back to the code segment that invoked the method. A depiction of an invocation process is given in Figure 4.5.

There is a subtlety to recognize about the `ColoredRectangle` mutator `setWidth()`. While the mutator updates the width attribute of its `ColoredRectangle` object, the mutator does not invoke method `paint()` to reflect that change in its window. Therefore, the rendering of a `ColoredRectangle` is unaffected by a `setWidth()` invocation. A `ColoredRectangle` object must be *repainted* for the update to be visible in the window.

```
ColoredRectangle r = new ColoredRectangle();
r.paint();       // a default colored rectangle is rendered
r.setWidth(100); // rectangle has mutated, but not its rendering
r.paint();       // rendering reflects the rectangle mutation
```

Figure 4.5   Evaluation of the invocation s.setWidth(80).

```
ColoredRectangle s = new ColoredRectangle();
s.setWidth(80);
```

The invocation sends a message to the ColoredRectangle referenced by s to modify its width attribute. To do so, there is a temporary transfer of flow of control to setWidth(). The value of the actual parameter is 80

```
public class ColoredRectangle {
   ...
   // setWidth(): width mutator
   public void setWidth(int  w) {
      width = w;
   }

   ...
}
```

For this invocation of method setWidth(), w is initialized to 80. The object being referenced within the method body is the object referenced by s

Method setWidth() sets the instance variable width of its ColoredRectangle. For this invocation, width is set to 80 and the ColoredRectangle is the one referenced by s

Method setWidth() is completed. Control is transferred back to the statement that invoked setWidth()

The other `ColoredRectangle` mutators perform tasks comparable to `setWidth()` for the other attributes.

```
// setHeight(): height mutator
public void setHeight(int h) {
   height = h;
}

// setX(): x mutator
public void setX(int ulx) {
   x = ulx;
}

// setY(): y mutator
public void setY(int uly) {
      y = uly;
}

// setWindow(): window mutator
public void setWindow(JFrame f) {
   window = f;
}

// setColor(): color mutator
public void setColor(Color c) {
   color = c;
}
```

The use of these mutators is demonstrated in the following code segment that defines and manipulates two `ColoredRectangle` variables u and v.

```java
ColoredRectangle u = new ColoredRectangle();
ColoredRectangle v = new ColoredRectangle();
u.setHeight(100);
u.setColor(Color.PINK);
v.setX(25);
v.setY(50);
JFrame display =
    new JFrame("Fun");
v.setWindow(display);
```

Sends a message to u's ColoredRectangle to modify its height attribute to 100

Sends a message to u's ColoredRectangle to modify its color attribute to pink

Sends a message to v's ColoredRectangle to modify its x-axis position to 25

Sends a message to v's ColoredRectangle to modify its y-axis position to 50

Sends a message to v's ColoredRectangle to modify its window attribute to display's JFrame

The six `ColoredRectangle` accessor methods do not require parameters. When invoked, these methods each signal the object associated with the invocation to supply the value of a particular attribute.

```java
// getWidth(): width accessor
public int getWidth() {
   return width;
}

   // getHeight(): height accessor
public int getHeight() {
   return height;
}

// getX(): x accessor
public int getX() {
   return x;
}

// getY(): y accessor
public int getY() {
   return y;
}

// getWindow(): window accessor
public JFrame getWindow() {
   return window;
}

// getColor(): color accessor
public Color getColor() {
   return color;
}
```

Because the accessors do not take parameters, when they are invoked there is an immediate temporary transfer of the flow of control to their method bodies. For example, in the following code segment, the invocation t.getWidth() causes the body of accessor getWidth() to be executed.

```
ColoredRectangle t = new ColoredRectangle();
int w = t.getWidth();
System.out.println(w);
```

Like the bodies of the other accessors, the body of the getWidth() accessor consists of a single statement. The statement is a **return** statement. A **return** statement is an explicit indication that the flow of control is transferred back to the invoking statement. For non-**void** methods, the **return** statement supplies the value associated with the invocation. A **return** statement has the form

$$\text{\textbf{return} } \textit{ReturnExpression} \text{ ;}$$

For non-void methods, this value is returned to the invoking method; for void methods no value is supplied. Execution continues at the statement that did the method invocation

where *ReturnExpression* evaluates to a value of the method's return type.

We call the value produced by an invocation, the *return value*. The type of the return value is the method's *return type*. The return type of getWidth() is **int**.

The method return type precedes the name of the method in the method definition

```
public int getWidth() {
  return width;
}
```

For method getWidth(), the return value is the value of the width attribute for the ColoredRectangle associated with the invocation. In invocation t.getWidth(), the return value is the value of the instance variable width for the ColoredRectangle referenced by t

The return value is used as the value of the invocation. Because the ColoredRectangle object referenced by t was constructed using the default constructor, the value used to initialize **int** variable w is 40.

Figure 4.6 depicts the flow of control process for our t.getWidth() invocation.

The other new method defined in Listing 4.4 is a specific constructor for ColoredRectangle.

```
// ColoredRectangle(): specific constructor
public ColoredRectangle(int w, int h, int ulx, int uly,
                        JFrame f, Color c) {
  setWidth(w);
  setHeight(h);
  setX(ulx);
  setY(uly);
  setWindow(f);
  setColor(c);
}
```

Figure 4.6 **Evaluation of the invocation t.getWidth().**

```
ColoredRectangle t = new ColoredRectangle();
int w = t.getWidth();
```

The invocation sends a message to the ColoredRectangle referenced by t to return the value of its width attribute. To do so, there is a temporary transfer of flow of control to getWidth()

```
public class ColoredRectangle {
    ...
    // getWidth(): width accessor
    public int getWidth() {
        return width;
    }
    ...
}
```

Method getWidth() starts executing. For this invocation, the object being referenced within its body is the object referenced by t

The return expression evaluates to 40 (the width attribute of the ColoredRectangle object referenced by t)

Method getWidth() completes by supplying its return value (40) to the statement that invoked it. Also, the invoking statement regains the flow of control. From there variable w is initialized with the return value of the invocation (i.e., w is initialized to 40)

This constructor requires that an invoking expression pass six actual parameter values to it. These values are used by the constructor in setting the attributes for the Colored-Rectangle object under construction. For example, the following code segment results in variable w being initialized with reference to a new ColoredRectangle object.

```
JFrame display = new JFrame("Even more fun");
display.setSize(400, 400);
ColoredRectangle w = new ColoredRectangle(60, 80, 20, 20,
                          display, Color.YELLOW);
```

The new ColoredRectangle represents a yellow rectangle with a width of 60 pixels and a height of 80 pixels. In addition, when rendered, the rectangle is to be drawn with its upper-left hand corner positioned at coordinate (20, 20) in the JFrame represented by variable display.

The definition of ColoredRectangle() specific constructor has the names of its formal parameters being w, h, ulx, uly, f, and c. Therefore, the invocation Colored-Rectangle(60, 80, 20, 20, display, Color.YELLOW) causes ColoredRectangle() to be executed with its formal parameters w, h, ulx, uly, f, and c initialized respectively to the values of 60, 80, 20, 20, display, and Color.YELLOW.

Observe that rather than directly setting the instance variables representing the attributes, specific constructor ColoredRectangle() uses the mutators. There are three major benefits to using the mutators. First, the code is more readable. The mutator names indicate explicitly how the formal parameters are being used. Second, errors in representation are less likely with consistent use of mutators and accessors. By limiting direct access of instance variables to mutators and accessors, it is easier to ensure that an object represents a reasonable instance of its class. Third, enhancements and changes to a class are generally simpler to make when direct access to the instance variables is controlled. By limiting the direct access, fewer methods typically need to be considered when analyzing for bugs or improvements.

Using accessors to get attribute values have similar benefits. Therefore, the use of accessors is also encouraged.

Because of the preference for use of the public interface over direct access to attributes, the self-test section considers a reimplementation of the `ColoredRectangle` default constructor and instance method `paint()`.

We conclude our introduction to programmer-defined classes with one more example using `ColoredRectangle`. The example is program `SeeingDouble.java` and a copy of the program is given in Listing 4.5.

Listing 4.5   SeeingDouble.java

```
1.  // Purpose: demonstrate a nuance of graphical programming
2.
3.  import java.io.*;
4.  import java.awt.*;
5.
6.  public class SeeingDouble {
7.      // main(): application entry point
8.      public static void main(String[] args) throws IOException {
9.          ColoredRectangle r = new ColoredRectangle();
10.
11.         System.out.println("Enter when ready");
12.         System.in.read();
13.
14.         r.paint();
15.
16.         r.setY(50);
17.         r.setColor(Color.RED);
18.         r.paint();
19.     }
20. }
```

The program first creates a `ColoredRectangle` object and then pauses for the window to be rendered.

```
ColoredRectangle r = new ColoredRectangle();

System.out.print("Enter when ready");
System.in.read();
```

The program then renders the colored rectangle for the first time.

```
r.paint();
```

The program then modifies the y-coordinate position and color of the `ColoredRectangle` object. The modified colored rectangle is then repainted.

```
r.setY(50);
r.setColor(Color.RED);
r.paint();
```

The result is the display given in Figure 4.7.

Figure 4.7   **The display associated with ColoredRectangleDemo.**

Observe in the figure that there are two rectangle renderings. It is not a bug that both rectangles are visible—when method `paint()` is invoked it just displays a rectangle using the current values of its object's instance variables. It has not been designed to erase a previous rendering. If such behavior is wanted, an `erase()` method should be introduced to the class and invoked prior to the method `paint()` invocation. (An `erase()` method is considered in the exercises.)

4.4 SUMMARY

Although our focus in this chapter has been the design and development of a representation for a colored rectangle, the Java class mechanism enables you to represent any object. Constructors enable you to create new objects and configure them; instance variables enable you represent the attributes of an object; and methods enable you to describe the behaviors of an object.

We encourage you to consider the programming case study of Section 4.8 to try out your new object-oriented programming skills.

4.5 REVIEW

- The value of an object variable is a reference to a location that holds an object of its type.
- The creation of a class type object is accomplished by invoking a member constructor method that creates and initializes the attributes of the object.
- An instance variable is Java's mechanism for defining an object attribute. Every object of a class has its own copy of the instance variables for representing its particular attributes. An instance variable also is known as a data field.
- Object behaviors are implemented using member methods. Member methods can access the instance variables of the associated object. This capability enables a constructor to configure the instance variables of the object being created and it enables a member method to manipulate the attributes of its associated object.
- Information is passed to a method via parameters. The result of a method's computation is brought back as the return value. The type of value brought back by a method is the return type.
- A **return** statement supplies a value from the invoked method to the invoking method.
- A method that does not return a value has a return type of **void**.
- A statement block is a list of statements within braces.
- To define a method, a programmer must specify completely its interface and actions. The actions occur within the method body. The method body is a statement block.
- The parameters in the invocation are called the actual parameters. The actual parameters are represented in the invoked method by its formal parameters.
- Every method invocation creates an activation record. The values of the formal parameters and other objects defined in the method are kept in the activation record.
- When a method is invoked, flow of control is transferred from the invoking method to the invoked method. When the invoked method completes, control is transferred back to the invoking method. If the invoked method returns a value, then that value essentially is substituted for the invocation.
- Java uses the pass-by-value parameter-passing style. When an actual parameter is passed in this style, the formal parameter is called a value parameter because it is initialized to the value of the actual parameter. Subsequent changes to the formal parameter do not affect the actual parameter.
- By practicing information hiding in a data abstraction, client programs are generally immune from changes in the implementation of the abstraction.
- Constructors initialize objects of a class type. It is standard practice to ensure that every class object has all of its data fields sensibly initialized.
- A constructor has the same name as its class.
- A default constructor is a constructor that requires no parameters.
- An accessor method returns the value of an attribute of an object. Accessor names often begin with "get".

- A mutator method provides the means to modify an attribute of an object. Mutator names often begin with "set".

- A facilitator method performs a task that depends in part on the attributes of an object.

- An instance variable is a data field for which each object has its own copy of the data.

- Whenever a new object is to be constructed Java first initializes the new instance variables. By default, numeric instance variables are initialized to 0, **boolean** instance variables are initialized to **false**, and reference-type instance variables are initialized to **null**.

- Instance methods are similar to constructors in that they are associated with a particular object when they are invoked. Different invocations can have the method associated with different objects.

- When designing your own classes, keep in mind that instance variables normally are declared to be **private**. This information hiding helps ensure the integrity of the variables.

- The programmer interface to a class is made up of the **public** members.

- The **private** members of a class can be used only by other members of the class.

- JFrame is the swing class for representing a window. A JFrame is similar in form to the other windows on your desktop and can be manipulated like those other windows.

- A JFrame constructor takes a single string as its parameter, which is displayed as the window title.

- A JFrame can be displayed by invoking its member method setVisible(); it can be resized by invoking its member method setSize().

- Rendering is accomplished by first accessing the graphical context in which the drawing commands are to be issued. The graphical context is of type awt class Graphics. A Graphics object provides all the information necessary for carrying out a rendering request (e.g., color, the component on which the rendering is to occur, font, etc.). Besides encapsulating such information, Graphics objects have a variety of methods for drawing rectangles, lines, polygons, arcs, ovals, and strings.

- Access to the graphical context of a JFrame is obtained through member method getGraphics().

- The current rendering color can be set using Graphics method setColor().

- Graphics method fillRect() renders a filled-in rectangle. The method expects four parameters. The first two parameters specify respectively the locations of the x- and y-coordinates for the upper left corner of the rectangle to be drawn. The next two parameters specify respectively the width and height of the rectangle to be filled. All four values are given in pixels. The rectangle is rendered using the current color. To draw only the perimeter of a rectangle use Graphics method drawRect().

- In a rendering request, the location of the rendering is specified relative to the upper left-hand corner of the object on which the drawing commands are performed. The direction of the x-axis is rightward. The direction of the y-axis is downward. Both x- and y-coordinates are given in pixels.

4.6   SELF-TEST

S4.1   Implement **public** methods getArea() and getPerimeter() for class ColoredRectangle. The perimeter of a rectangle is the sum of its side lengths and the area of a rectangle is the product of its width and length.

S4.2   Define an instance method doubleSize() that doubles the size of a ColoredRectangle.

S4.3   Define an instance method rotateClockwise() that rotates the shape of a ColoredRectangle object by 90°.

S4.4   Implement a class Name for representing names. Each Name object should have three attributes—a first, middle, and family name. There should be a default and specific constructor. The class should support encapsulation and information hiding by providing accessors and mutators for the three Name attributes. The class should also provide a method toString() that supplies the entire name.

S4.5   Why might an instance method be defined to be **private**?

S4.6   Reimplement the ColoredRectangle default constructor and facilitator paint() to use mutators and accessors to achieve their purposes.

4.7   EXERCISES

4.1   Describe what happens during a method invocation.

4.2   What is an actual parameter?

4.3   What is a formal parameter?

4.4   Discuss flow of control.

4.5   What are the differences between a data field and a method?

4.6   What are the differences between a mutator and an accessor method?

4.7   Whose purpose is to configure initially the values of instance variables?

4.8   What type of method is responsible generally for setting the value of an instance variable?

4.9   What type of method is responsible generally for providing the value of an instance variable?

4.10   What are the differences in using **public** and **private** access modifiers?

4.11   Why is it unnecessary (inappropriate) for constructors to have return types?

4.12   How many parameters does a default constructor require? Why?

4.13   Why are data fields typically defined in a nonpublic section?

4.14   Does a non-**void** method necessarily contain a **return** statement? Explain.

The definition of the following class C is in effect for Exercises 4.15–4.22.

```
public class C {
    private int counter;
```

```
    public C() {
        counter = 0;
    }

    public C(int n) {
        counter = n;
    }

    public void increment() {
        ++counter;
    }

    public void decrement() {
        --counter;
    }

    public int getCount() {
        return counter;
    }

    public void display() {
        System.out.println(getCount());
    }
}
```

4.15 How many constructors does class C have? List them.

4.16 How many accessors does class C have? List them.

4.17 How many mutators does class C have? List them.

4.18 How many facilitators does class C have? List them.

4.19 What is the output of the following code segment?
```
C c1 = new C();
c1.increment();
C c2 = new C();
c2.increment();
c1.increment();
c2.decrement();
c2.increment();
c1.display();
c2.display();
```

4.20 What is the output of the following code segment?
```
C c1 = new C();
c1.increment();
C c2 = new C();
c2.increment();
c1.increment();
c2.decrement();
c2.increment();
int counter = 0;
c1.display();
c2.display();
```

4.21 What is the output of the following code segment?
```
C c1 = new C();
c1.increment();
```

```
C c2 = new C();
c2.increment();
c1.increment();
c2.decrement();
c2.increment();
int c1_counter = 0;
int c2_counter = 0;
c1.display();
c2.display();
```

4.22 Which statements in the following code segment are legal? Explain.

```
C c1 = new C();
C c2 = new C(c1.getCount());
C c3 = new C(5);
c1.increment(5);
c2.decrement() = 5;
c1.counter = 5;
c2.counter = 5;
C c4 = new C(c2.counter);
```

4.23 Implement a method `erase()` for `ColoredRectangle`.

4.24 Develop and implement a class `Account` that represents a savings account. An `Account` object should have three attributes: the name of the account, the owner of the account, and the current balance. The class should provide the following constructors behaviors.

- `Name()`: configures a new account with name "name", owner "owner", and balance 0.

- `Name(String s, String t, double n)`: configures a new account with name s, owner t, and balance n.

- `void deposit(double n)`: adds amount n to the current balance of the associated account.

- `void withdraw(double n)`: subtracts amount n from the current balance of the associated account.

- `void close()`: zeroes out the account balance, sets the owner to "".

- `String getAccountName()`: returns the name of the associated account.

- `String getOwner()`: returns the owner of the associated account.

- `double getBalance()`: returns the balance of the associated account.

- `void setName(String s)`: sets the name of the associated account to s.

- `void setOwner(String s)`: sets the owner of the associated account to s.

- `String toString()`: returns a textual representation of the attributes of the associated account.

4.25 Develop and implement a class `Date` to represent a date. A `Date` object should have three attributes: the day of the month, the month, and the year. The class should provide the following constructors behaviors.

- `Date()`: configures a new account to represent the date 1 January 2000.

- `Date(int d, int m, int y)`: configures a new date with day d, month m, and year y.

- `int getDay()`: returns the day of the associated date.

- **int** getMonth(): returns the month of the associated date.
- **int** getYear(): returns the year of the associated date.
- **void** setDay(**int** d): sets the day of the associated date to d.
- **void** setMonth(**int** m): sets the month of the associated date to m.
- **void** setYear(**int** y): sets the year of the associated date to y.
- String toString(): returns a textual representation of the associated date.

4.8   PROGRAMMING PROJECT — RATIONALITY

The purpose of this case study is to design and implement the class Rational as a representation for manipulating rational numbers. To begin, we remind you about rational number basics.

> The objective of this case study is to practice object-oriented design and development when problem solving

A rational number is the ratio of two integers and is represented typically in the manner *a/b*. We call *a* the *numerator* and *b* the *denominator*. The denominator is suppose to be nonzero.[†] The basic operations have the following definitions:

- Addition:
$$\frac{a}{b} + \frac{c}{d} = \frac{ad + bc}{bd}$$

- Subtraction: $\dfrac{a}{b} - \dfrac{c}{d} = \dfrac{ad - bc}{bd}$

- Multiplication: $\dfrac{a}{b} \times \dfrac{c}{d} = \dfrac{ac}{bd}$

- Division: $\dfrac{a}{b} \div \dfrac{c}{d} = \dfrac{ad}{bc}$

ANALYSIS AND DESIGN

To represent a rational number, you need to represent its numerator and denominator. This necessity implies that a class representing rational numbers needs at least two instance variables—one variable to represent the particular numerator and the other variable to represent the particular denominator of the object.

    private int numerator
        Numerator of the associated rational number.
    private int denominator
        Denominator of the associated rational number.

Previous experience with rational numbers and other Java APIs tells us that the Rational abstraction should provide methods to initialize and manipulate a rational number object in at least the following ways:

[†]   In Chapter 5, we consider the **if** statement that allows us to determine whether a value is valid.

Figure 4.8　**A possible interaction with RationalDemo.java.**

```
Java Program Design

cmd: javac Rational.java

cmd: javac RationalDemo.java

cmd: java RationalDemo

Enter numerator of a rational number: 1
Enter denominator of a rational number: 2

Enter numerator of a rational number: 1
Enter denominator of a rational number: 3

For r = 1/2 and s = 1/3

    r + s = 5/6
    r - s = 1/6
    r * s = 1/6
    r / s = 3/2

cmd:
```

- Construct a rational number by default or from a numerator and denominator specification.

- Compute the rational result of adding, subtracting, multiplying, and dividing two rational numbers.

- Produce a String representation of a rational number suitable for displaying to the standard output stream.

To support both these client activities and information hiding, methods implementing the following activities should also be present:

- Access the values of the numerator and denominator.

- Set the values of the numerator and denominator.

You may find it convenient to define other methods. We also leave it to you consider what documentation is necessary for the other methods.

To aid you in your design of the necessary information structures and algorithms, we provide the Rational client program RationalDemo.java of Listing 4.6. This program illustrates the look and feel that we want in the various components of the class Rational. We depict a sample input/output behavior of the program in Figure 4.8.

IMPLEMENTATION

Produce the rational number abstraction Rational.java and a client Java program MyDemo.java that thoroughly tests your rational implementation.

Listing 4.6   RationalDemo.java

```
1.  // Demonstrate Rational data abstraction
2.
3.  import java.io.*;
4.
5.  public class RationalDemo {
6.      // main(): application entry point
7.      public static void main(String[] args) throws IOException {
8.          BufferedReader stdin = new BufferedReader(
9.              new InputStreamReader(System.in));
10.         System.out.println();
11.
12.         // extract values for rationals r and s
13.         Rational r = new Rational();
14.         System.out.print("Enter numerator of a rational number: ");
15.         int a = Integer.parseInt(stdin.readLine());
16.         System.out.print("Enter denominator of a rational number: ");
17.         int b = Integer.parseInt(stdin.readLine());
18.         r.setNumerator(a);
19.         r.setDenominator(b);
20.         System.out.println();
21.         System.out.println();
22.
23.         Rational s = new Rational();
24.         System.out.print("Enter numerator of a rational number: ");
25.         int c = Integer.parseInt(stdin.readLine());
26.         System.out.print("Enter denominator of a rational number: ");
27.         int d = Integer.parseInt(stdin.readLine());
28.         s.setNumerator(c);
29.         s.setDenominator(d);
30.
31.         // operate on r and s
32.         Rational sum = r.add(s);
33.         Rational difference = r.subtract(s);
34.         Rational product = r.multiply(s);
35.         Rational quotient = r.divide(s);
36.
37.
38.         // display operation results
39.         System.out.println("For r = " + r.toString() + " and s = "
40.             + s.toString());
41.         System.out.println("    r + s = " + sum.toString());
42.         System.out.println("    r - s = " + difference.toString());
43.         System.out.println("    r * s = " + product.toString());
44.         System.out.println("    r / s = " + quotient.toString());
45.         System.out.println();
46.
47.         System.out.println();
48.     }
49. }
```

TESTING AND DOCUMENTATION

While our program `RationalDemo.java` illustrates and tests much of the behavior, it is not complete. Expand upon this program in `MyDemo.java` to provide more explicit evidence regarding the correctness of all your methods.

You should document both your design and implementation. In documenting your design, justify the access specification of all members. You should justify your approach and explain the behaviors and nuances of your methods. For example, when discussing the default constructor, you should state what is the default representation and why it was selected.

4.9   SELF-TEST ANSWERS

S4.1 Definitions of methods for computing the area and perimeter would be

```java
public int getArea() {
    int w = getWidth();
    int h = getHeight();
    return w * h;
}

public int getPerimeter() {
    int w = getWidth();
    int h = getHeight();
    return 2*w + 2*h;
}
```

S4.2 A definition for method `doubleSize()` would be

```java
public void doubleSize() {
    int w = getWidth();
    int h = getHeight();
    setWidth(2*w):
    setHeight(2*h);
}
```

S4.3 A definition for method `rotateClockwise()` would be

```java
public void rotateClockwise() {
    int w = getWidth();
    int h = getHeight();
    setWidth(h):
    setHeight(w);
}
```

S4.4 A class definition would be

```java
public class Name {
    // instance variables
    String firstName;
    String middleName;
    String familyName;

    // Name(): default constructor
    public Name() {
        firstName = middleName = familyName = "";
```

```
        }

        // Name(): specific constructor
        public Name(String first, String middle, String family) {
            setFirstName(first);
            setMiddleName(middle);
            setFamilyName(family);
        }

        // getFirstName(): first name accessor
        public String getFirstName() {
            return firstName;
        }

        // getMiddleName(): middle name accessor
        public String getMiddleName() {
            return middleName;
        }

        // getFamilyName(): family name accessor
        public String getFamilyName() {
            return familyName;
        }

        // setFirstName(): first name mutator
        public String setFirstName(String s) {
            firstName = s;
        }

        // setMiddleName(): middle name mutator
        public String setMiddleName(String s) {
            middleName = s;
        }

        // setFamilyName(): family name mutator
        public String setFamilyName(String s) {
            familyName = s;
        }

        // toString(): whole name supplier
        public String toString() {
            return getFirstName() + " " + getMiddleName()
                              + " " + getFamilyName();
        }
    }
```

S4.5 An instance method might be declared **private** if it was used to assist in implementing some behavior, or if accessing the method would be inappropriate.

S4.6 A reimplementation of the class members would be

```
        // ColoredRectangle(): default constructor
        public ColoredRectangle() {
            JFrame w = new JFrame("Box Fun");
            w.setSize(200, 200);
            setWindow(w);

            setWidth(40);
            setHeight(20);
```

```
        setX(80);
        setY(90);
        setColor(Color.BLUE);
}

// paint(): display the rectangle in its window
public void paint() {
    int w = getWidth();
    int h = getHeight();
    int ulx = getX():
    int uly = getY();
    Color c = getColor();
    JFrame w = getWindow();

    w.setVisible(true);

    Graphics g = w.getGraphics();
    g.setColor(c);
    g.fillRect(ulx, uly, w, h);
}
```

Up to this point, our programs have had the *straight-line* property that each time they are run, the same sequence of statements is executed. This form of programming is adequate for solving simple problems. However, for general problem solving we need the ability to control which statements are executed and how often. In this chapter, we consider both the **if** and **switch** *conditional constructs* that control whether a statement list is executed. (In Chapter 6, we consider Java's iterative constructs.) Because the **if** constructs use logical expressions to determine their course of action, we begin with logical expressions.

OBJECTIVES

- Present the logical type **boolean** and its associated operators.
- Explain how to construct truth tables.
- Explore the nuances of the **if**, **if-else**, and **if-else-if** statements.
- Introduce the **switch** statement.
- Demonstrate the differences in integral equality testing, floating-point equality testing, reference equality testing, and **equals()** testing.
- Strengthen program design skills.

| 5.1 | **BOOLEAN ALGEBRA AND TRUTH TABLES** |

A *logical expression* is an expression whose value is either the logical value *true* or the logical value *false*. For example, two logical expressions are

- A square is an equilateral rectangle (true).

- The year 2007 is a leap year (false).

The three primary logical operators for combining logic values into logical expressions are *and*, *or*, and *not*. The operators are used in the following examples:

- Jim is smiling *and* Patricia is puzzled.

- Gertrude is going to the musical *or* Jim is going for a walk to buy a newspaper.

- Joanne is *not* watching television.

In normal conversation, there may be some mild confusion over the meaning of a logical operator. For example, if Gertrude is going to the musical or Jim is going for a walk to buy a newspaper, can it be the case that they are both going out? However, unlike normal conversation, there is no mathematical ambiguity—each operator has a well-defined specification for the value of its operation given the values of the operands.

A *truth table* is an easy way of indicating the conditions that make a logical operation true and the conditions that make it false. A truth table lists all possible combinations of operand values and the result of the operation for each combination.

The truth table for the binary logical operator *and* is given in Table 5.1(a). In this and successive truth tables, we use p and q as placeholders to represent the left and right operands of the binary logical operator being discussed. We also use p in the discussion of the unary logical operator *not*.

Binary logical operators have four possible operand value combinations and therefore four entries in their truth tables. Unary logic operators have two table entries.

The logical *and* truth table, Table 5.1(a), shows that the operation is true only if both of its operands are true; otherwise, the operation is false. For example, the second entry of the truth table indicates that when p is false and q is true, the *and* operation evaluates to false. In the fourth entry where both p and q are true, the *and* operation evaluates to true.

Table 5.1(b) gives the truth table for the logical *or* operator. This truth table indicates that the *or* operation evaluates to true if at least one of its operands is true; otherwise, the operation evaluates to false.

Table 5.1(c) gives the truth tale for the unary logical *not* operator. The *not* operation evaluates to true if its operand is false, and to false if its operand is true.

| Table 5.1 | **Truth table for the fundamental logic operators.** |

p	*q*	*p and q*
false	false	false
false	true	false
true	false	false
true	true	true

(a) Logical *and*

p	*q*	*p or q*
false	false	false
false	true	true
true	false	true
true	true	true

(b) Logical *or*

p	*not p*
false	true
true	false

(c) Logical *not*

5.1.1   LOGICAL EXPRESSIONS

We can form *compound* expressions by combining logical operations. For example, the following expression is true when both *p* and *q* are false; otherwise, the expression is false.

    not (p or q).

When *p* and *q* are both false, subexpression (*p or q*) is false and the negation of subexpression (*p or q*) is true, making the overall expression *not (p or q)* true. Any other combination of values for *p* and *q* makes subexpression (*p or q*) true, and the negation of that subexpression false, making the overall expression *not (p or q)* false.

The truth table in Table 5.2 shows the evaluation of *not(p or q)* in tabular form. To do so, the table has entries for the subexpression (*p or q*) and the expression *not (p or q)*.

| Table 5.2 | **Truth table for not(p or q).** |

p	*q*	*p or q*	*not (p or q)*
false	false	false	true
false	true	true	false
true	false	true	false
true	true	true	false

Table 5.3 **Truth table for (not p) and (not q).**

p	q	*not p*	*not q*	*(not p) and (not q)*
false	false	true	true	true
false	true	true	false	false
true	false	false	true	false
true	true	false	false	false

Another truth table is given in Table 5.3. This truth table shows the evaluation of the expression *(not p) and (not q)*. To do so, the table has entries for subexpression *(not p)*, subexpression *(not q)*, and expression *(not p) and (not q)*.

It is interesting to compare the values of the expressions *not (p or q)* and *(not p) and (not q)* for each operand combination, By doing so, you can see that the two expressions are *equivalent* to each other. That is, when given the same operands, they produce the same values. This equivalence is famous and is known as a DeMorgan's equivalence. There is another DeMorgan equivalence — *not (p and q)* equals *(not p) or (not q)*. The proof of this equivalence is left to the exercises. Together the two equivalences are known as DeMorgan's law. The equivalences are sometimes useful in simplifying logical expressions.

5.2	**BOOLEAN TYPE**

The Java logical type is named **boolean** after the 19th-century British mathematician George Boole who formalized the study of logical values. The type **boolean** has two symbolic literal constants **true** and **false** that correspond to logical true and false respectively.

Like other local Java primitive variables, **boolean** variables are uninitialized by default. Thus, the following code segment defines two uninitialized variables.

```
boolean isWhitespace;
boolean haveFoundMissingLink;
```

Recalling that we use an "–" to indicate an unknown value, the depiction of these variables would be

Observe that the variables have names indicating conditions. Such a naming style is a standard Java programming practice for **boolean** variables. The reason for using this naming style is that **boolean** variables normally are used in testing whether some program or data property is true.

The preferred definition of a **boolean** variable includes an explicit initialization value. The following code segment defines two variables with initialization values.

```
boolean canProceed = true;
boolean completedSecretMission = false;
```

Our representation of these variables would be

canProceed	true
completedSecretMission	false

5.2.1 BOOLEAN EQUALITY AND ORDERING OPERATORS

There are three **boolean** logical operators: &&, ||, and !. Operator && performs an *and* operation, operator || performs an *or* operation, and operator ! performs a *not* operation.

In addition, there are other operators such as the *equality* operators == and !=. The == operator, when given **boolean** operands, evaluates to **true** if both operand expressions have the same value, and it evaluates to **false** otherwise. Operator !=, when given **boolean** operands, evaluates to **true** if the two operand expressions have different values, and it evaluates to **false** otherwise.

Suppose the following definitions are in effect.

```
boolean p = true;
boolean q = false;
boolean r = true;
boolean s = false;
```

The following expressions evaluate to **true**.

```
p         // p has value true
p && r    // logical and is true when both operands are true
p || q    // logical or is true when at least one of the operands
          // is true
!s        // logical not is true when its operand is false
p == r    // equality is true when the operands have the same
          // value
q != r    // inequality is true when the operands have different
          // values
```

And the following expressions evaluate to **false**.

```
q         // q has value false
p && s    // logical and is false when at least one of the
          // operands is false
q || s    // logical or is false when both operands are false
!r        // logical not is false when the operand is true
r == s    // equality is false when the operands have different
          // values
q != s    // inequality is false when the operands have the same
          // value
```

The equality operators can also be applied using other primitive type values as operands. The operators work generally as expected. (Later, we discuss the pitfalls of testing floating-point values for equality and the appropriateness of the equality operator with reference variable operands.)

Suppose the following integer and character variables definitions are in effect.

```
int i = 1;
int j = 2;
int k = 2;
char c = '#';
char d = '%';
char e = '#';
```

The following expressions evaluate to **true**.

```
j == k    // equality is true when the operands have the same
          // value
i != k    // inequality is true when the operands have different
          // values
c == e    // equality is true when the operands have the same
          // value
d != e    // inequality is true when the operands have different
          // values
```

And the following expressions evaluate to **false**.

```
i == j    // equality is false when the operands have different
          // values
j != k    // inequality is false when the operands have the same
          // value
c == d    // equality is false when the operands have different
          // values
c != e    // inequality is false when the operands have the same
          // value
```

Java also provides *ordering* operators for the primitive types. They are used to determine the relative size of two values. There are four Java ordering operators, <, >, <=, and >=. These operators correspond respectively to the mathematical operators of $<$, $>$, $\leq$, and $\geq$. Together the equality operators and ordering operators are known as the *relational* operators.

For **boolean** comparison purposes, **false** is less than **true**.

For character comparison purposes, orderings are based on the Unicode character representation. For example, because the Unicode encoding of character 'e' is 101, the Unicode encoding of character 'j' is 106, and the Unicode encoding of character '=' is 51, character 'e' is both less than character 'j' and greater than character '='.

The Unicode character set has the following properties.

- Character digits '0', '1', …, '9' are arranged in the expected comparison order. In particular, digit character '0' has the encoding 48, character '1' has the encoding 49, and so on.

A partial listing of the Unicode character set is given in Appendix A.

- Upper case Latin letters 'A', 'B', ..., 'Z' are arranged in the expected comparison order. In particular, character 'A' has the encoding 65, character 'B' has the encoding 66, and so on.

- Lower case Latin letters 'a', 'b', ..., 'z' are arranged in the expected comparison order. In particular, character 'a' has the encoding 97, character 'b' has the encoding 98, and so on.

Thus, with the Unicode encodings the lower case character digits are less than the upper case Latin letters, which are less than the lower case Latin letters

We now consider some examples using the ordering operators. Suppose the following definitions are in effect.

```
int i = 1;
int j = 2;
int k = 2;
char c = '2';
char d = '3';
char d = '3';
char f = 'c';
char g = 'D';
```

The following expressions are then **true**.

```
i < j    // < is true when the value of the left operand is
         // less than the value of the right operand
d > e    // > is true when the value of the left operand is
         // greater than the value of the right operand
i <= k   // <= is true when the value of the left operand is
         // less than or equal to the value of the right operand
j >= k   // >= is true when the value of the left operand is
         // greater than or equal to the value of the right
         // operand
g < f    // >= is true when the value of the left operand is
         // greater than or equal to the value of the right
         // (the Unicode values for uppercase Latin letters are
         // (smaller than values for lowercase Latin letters)
```

And the following expressions are **false**.

```
j < k    // < is false when the value of the left operand is
         // not less than the value of the right operand
c > e    // > is false when the value of the left operand is
         // not greater than the value of the right operand
d <= c   // <= is false when the value of left operand is
         // greater than the value of the right operand
i >= k   // >= is false when the value of the left operand is
         // less than the value of the right operand
```

Short-circuit evaluation

When evaluating a logical expression, the value of the expression is sometimes known before all the operands have been considered. For example, if an operand of an **&&** operation is known to be **false**, then the value of the **&&** operation must be **false**. Similarly, if an operand of an || operation is known to be **true**, then the value of the || operation must be **true**. Java uses these properties to make the evaluation of logical operations more efficient.

When evaluating a logical operation, Java evaluates the left operand before it evaluates the right operand. If the value of the operation can be determined from the left operand, then the right operand is not evaluated. This kind of evaluation is known as *short-circuit evaluation*.

Short-circuit evaluation is useful when some property must be true for some other expression to be evaluated. For example, suppose you are interested in knowing whether scoreSum divided by nbrScores is greater than the value expectation. This condition can be evaluated only if nbrScores is nonzero. The following expression correctly represents the condition.

    (nbrScores != 0) && ((scoreSum / nbrScores) > expectation)

Because the left operand of the **&&** is evaluated first, we know that if the right operand of the **&&** is evaluated, nbrScores cannot be 0 and therefore dividing by nbrScores makes sense. Without short-circuit evaluation, the right operand of the **&&** could be evaluated with nbrScores being 0, causing an illegal divide-by-zero to occur.

5.2.2 OPERATOR PRECEDENCE REVISITED

More complicated expressions can be built by using multiple operators in the same expression. To evaluate such expressions, the precedence of the relational and logical operators must be known with respect to the other operators.

The not operator ! has the same high precedence as other unary operators. Among the binary operators, the relational and logical operators have lower precedence than the arithmetic operators and higher precedence than the assignment operators. Relational operators have greater precedence than the logical operators. Among the relational operators, the ordering operators have higher precedence than the equality operators. Among the logical operators, **&&** has higher greater precedence than ||. Because of operator precedence, the following two expressions are equivalent.

- depth + delta < prevDepth * 1.1 && isOn || !rising
- (((depth + delta) < (prevDepth * 1.1)) && isOn) || (! rising)

And the next two expressions are also equivalent.

- prevCheckIsOk != rpm < d || isWarm && isRunning
- (prevCheckIsOk != (rpm < d)) || (isWarm && isRunning)

To ensure readability and understanding, we continue to stress the use of parentheses.

Table 5.4 **Precedence and associativity of selected operators.**

Operation	Precedence	Associativity
Grouping operator: ()	17	None
Unary operators: +, -, !	13	Right
Multiplicative arithmetic: *, /, %	12	Left
Additive arithmetic: +, -	11	Left
Relational ordering:<, >, <=, >=	10	Left
Relational equality: ==, !=	9	Left
Logical and: &&	4	Left
Logic or: ||	3	Left
Assignment: =, +=, -=, *=, /=, %=	1	Right

The precedence and associativity of the arithmetic, relational, ordering, logical operators, and assignment operators are summarized in Table 5.4. A complete specification of the operator precedence is given in Appendix A.

Given this introduction to logical expressions, we are now ready to use them in control constructs. The first control construct that we consider is the **if** statement.

5.3 IF STATEMENT

The **if** statement has two forms. The simpler of the two forms has syntax

When an **if** statement is reached within a program, the parenthetic expression *TestExpression* is evaluated. If *TestExpression* evaluates to **true**, *Action* is executed; otherwise, *Action* is not executed. Either way, program execution continues with the next statement in the program.

The preceding description of an **if** statement execution process is its *semantic* definition. The semantics are demonstrated in the *flowchart* diagram in Figure 5.1.

Figure 5.1   Representation of basic if statement semantics.

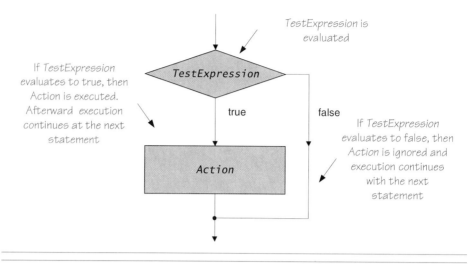

Figure 5.2   Semantics of updating measure if it is negative.

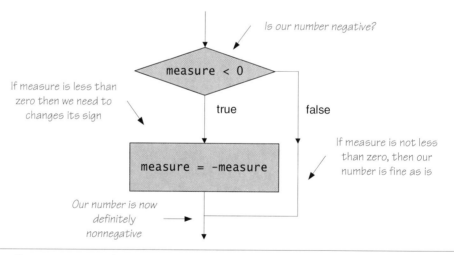

Suppose `measure` is a variable that has been defined previously, and we now need to make sure it is positive. The following code segment accomplishes this task.

```
if (measure < 0)          // is measure less than 0?
    measure = - measure;   // it is, so change its sign
```

The segment uses an **if** statement. If the test expression (`measure < 0`) evaluates to **true**, then `measure` is negative and assigning it with its additive inverse changes `measure` to the equivalent positive number. If instead the test expression (`measure < 0`) is **false**, then `measure` must be nonnegative and no action needs to be performed. The action associated with the code segment is given pictorially in Figure 5.2.

Figure 5.3   **Semantics of swapping based on variable values.**

Often, several statements need to be executed based on the value of an expression. To indicate that a group of statements is to be executed, the statements in the group are surrounded by left and right braces. The various statements in the group are separated by semicolons. The semicolons are necessary so that the individual statements can be distinguished.

An **if** statement with a statement-list action is demonstrated in the following code segment, which swaps the values of variables value1 and value2, if value2 is less than value1. The action associated with the code segment is depicted in Figure 5.3.

```
if (value2 < value1) {     // values are not in sorted order
    // swapping puts them in order
    int rememberValue1 = value1;
    value1 = value2;
    value2 = rememberValue1;
}
```

In this segment, the expression (value2 < value1) tests whether value2 is less than value1. If the expression (value2 < value1) evaluates to **true**, then those two variables have their values interchanged in the associated action.

```
int rememberValue1 = value1;
value1 = value2;
value2 = rememberValue1;
```

This interchange swaps the two values so that the value in value2 is at least as large as the value in value1. It is important to note that variable rememberValue1 exists only

---

Listing 5.1   SortTwo.java

```
1.  // displays two user-specified values in sorted order
2.
3.  import java.io.*;
4.
5.  public class SortTwo {
6.     // main(): application entry point
7.     public static void main(String[] args) throws IOException {
8.        // set input stream
9.        BufferedReader stdin = new BufferedReader(
10.               new InputStreamReader(System.in));
11.
12.        // get numbers
13.        System.out.print("Enter an integer number: ");
14.        int value1 = Integer.parseInt(stdin.readLine());
15.        System.out.print("Enter another integer number: ");
16.        int value2 = Integer.parseInt(stdin.readLine());
17.
18.        // rearrange numbers if necessary
19.        if (value2 < value1) {     // values are not in sorted order
20.           // swapping puts them in order
21.           int rememberValue1 = value1;
22.           value1 = value2;
23.           value2 = rememberValue1;
24.        }
25.
26.        // display values
27.        System.out.println("The numbers in sorted order are "
28.              + value1 + " and then " + value2);
29.     }
30.  }
```

---

within the action associated with the **if** statement. The braces of that action delimit its *scope*. (We consider the notion of scope in detail in Chapter 7.)

If instead the test expression (value2 < value1) is **false**, then it is already the case that value2 is at least as large as value1. In this case, nothing needs to be done with the two values.

A complete program SortTwo.java for sorting two numbers is given in Listing 5.1 One run of the program had the following input/output behavior.

```
Enter an integer number: 21
Enter another integer number: 6
The numbers in sorted order are 6 and then 21
```

And another program run had the following input/output behavior.

```
Enter an integer number: 4
Enter another integer number: 30
The numbers in sorted order are 4 and then 30
```

Because the only interesting code in the program is the **if** statement, we do not discuss the program further.

Before discussing the **if-else** statement, we first turn our attention to two safe programming practices.

| 5.3.1 | **AVOIDING GOTCHAS** |

When developing programs with **if** statements, there are two practices that you should follow generally.

- Use braces to surround the actions;
- Do not compare floating-point values using the equality operators.

We *strongly* recommend the use of braces to surround the action of an **if** statement regardless of whether the action is composed of single or multiple statements. Software often is modified—sometimes to correct errors and other times to extend its functionality. These changes can cause the action of an **if** statement to change from simple to complex. By having the braces already in place, it is easier to avoid introducing logic errors when making changes.

By using braces consistently, errors such as the following can be avoided.

Displayed when p and q are different

```
if (p != q)
   System.out.println("The != test indicates");
   System.out.println("p is different from q");
```

Because there are no braces to indicate the if action is composed of two statements, the output of the second println() is displayed always

The underlying reason that programs generally should not test floating-point values for equality is the finite precision of the floating-point types. Finite precision coupled with expression evaluation can lead to anomalies. For example, the following expression, while mathematically true, does not evaluate to **true** within a Java program.

```
1 == 0.1 + 0.1 + 0.1 + 0.1 + 0.1 + 0.1 + 0.1 + 0.1 + 0.1 + 0.1
```

It does not evaluate to **true**, because the right operand of the == operator sums to the **double** value 0.9999999999999999.

Rather than directly testing for floating-point equivalence, programs test whether the values of interest are sufficiently close to each other to be considered the same. This testing is done by using a tolerance constant. Two values are considered equivalent if the absolute value of their difference is less than the value of the tolerance constant. For example, suppose the tolerance is specified through a Java constant EPSILON.

```
final double EPSILON = 0.000001;
```

The following expression would then indicate whether variables x and y are sufficiently close to be considered equivalent.

```
Math.abs(x-y) <= EPSILON
```

The expression makes use of the Math class method Math.abs() that returns the absolute value of its floating-point parameter. Thus, the expression evaluates to **true** when x and y are sufficiently close to each other to be considered equivalent and **false** other-wise.

<table>
<tr><td>5.4</td><td></td></tr>
</table>

IF-ELSE STATEMENT

The second form of the **if** statement deals with situations where different actions are to be taken based on the value of a logical expression. This form of the **if** statement has syntax

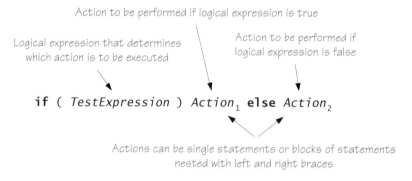

where $Action_1$ and $Action_2$ can each be either a single statement with a terminating semi-colon (;) or a block of statements enclosed in left and right braces. When the **if-else** statement is executed, *TestExpression* is evaluated. If *TestExpression* evaluates to **true**, $Action_1$ is executed; otherwise, $Action_2$ is executed. Figure 5.4 demonstrates the seman-tics of the **if-else** statement.

In the following code segment, two input values are extracted, and the maximum of the two values is displayed.

```
BufferedReader stdin = new BufferedReader(
       new InputStreamReader(System.in));

System.out.print("Enter an integer number: ");
int value1 = Integer.parseInt(stdin.readLine());
System.out.print("Enter another integer number: ");
int value2 = Integer.parseInt(stdin.readLine());

int maximum;
if (value1 < value2) {   // is value2 larger?
   maximum = value2;      // yes: value2 is larger
}
else { // (value1 >= value2)
   maximum = value1;      // no: value2 is not larger
}
System.out.println("The maximum of " + value1 + " and "
       + value2 + " is " + maximum);
```

Figure 5.4   **Semantic representation of an if-else statement.**

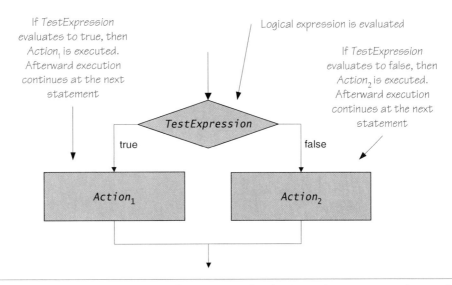

If *TestExpression* evaluates to true, then *Action₁* is executed. Afterward execution continues at the next statement

Logical expression is evaluated

If *TestExpression* evaluates to false, then *Action₂* is executed. Afterward execution continues at the next statement

TestExpression

true

false

Action₁

Action₂

After determining the inputs `value1` and `value2`, the code segment evaluates the expression (`value1 < value2`) in the **if-else** statement.

```
if (value1 < value2) {    // is value2 larger?
    maximum = value2;     // yes: value2 is larger
}
else { // (value1 >= value2)
    maximum = value1;     // no: value2 is not larger
}
```

If the test expression evaluates to **true**, `value2` is the maximum of the two inputs and it is used to set variable `maximum`. Observe that the right brace signals the end of the action taken if the test expression evaluates to **true**.

If instead the test expression (`value1 < value2`) evaluates to **false**, `value1` is at least as large as `value2`. Therefore, in the **else** part, `value1` is used to set `maximum`. Figure 5.5 demonstrates the semantics of this statement.

Thus our analysis shows that when this **if-else** statement is completed, `maximum` is appropriately set and can be used as needed.

A complete program `Maximum.java` for finding the larger of two numbers is given in Listing 5.2. One sample run of the program had the following input/output behavior

```
Enter an integer number: 9
Enter another integer number: 23
The maximum of 9 and 23 is 23
```

And another program run had the following input/output behavior

```
Enter an integer number: 16
Enter another integer number: 3
The maximum of 16 and 3 is 16
```

Figure 5.5   Finding the maximum of two values.

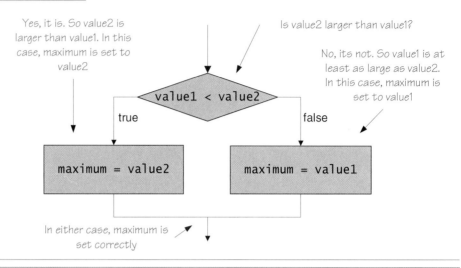

Listing 5.2   Maximum.java

```
1.  // displays two user-specified values in sorted order
2.  import java.io.*;
3.
4.  public class Maximum {
5.      // main(): application entry point
6.      public static void main(String[] args) throws IOException {
7.          // set input stream
8.          BufferedReader stdin = new BufferedReader(
9.              new InputStreamReader(System.in));
10.
11.         // get numbers
12.         System.out.print("Enter an integer number: ");
13.         int value1 = Integer.parseInt(stdin.readLine());
14.         System.out.print("Enter another integer number: ");
15.         int value2 = Integer.parseInt(stdin.readLine());
16.
17.         // determine maximum
18.         int maximum;
19.         if (value1 < value2) {    // is value2 larger?
20.             maximum = value2;      // yes: value2 is larger
21.         }
22.         else { // (value1 >= value2)
23.             maximum = value1;      // no: value2 is not larger
24.         }
25.
26.         // display maximum
27.         System.out.println("The maximum of " + value1 + " and "
28.             + value2 + " is " + maximum);
29.     }
30. }
```

Because the only interesting code in program Maximum.java is its **if** statement, we do not discuss the program further.

Consistent indentation and brace location

In the programs for this chapter, we always indent the *Action* statements associated with the **if** statements. The indentation is a clue to the reader that the execution of an *Action* statement depends on the less-indented **if** statement expression. A consistent indentation scheme is necessary for program readability. Most programmers typically use three or four blanks per level of indentation.

The placement of the braces that group the statement list is a matter of personal taste. Our method for brace placement is the following:

- Include the opening left brace on the initial line of the **if** statement to conserve line space;
- Place the closing brace on its own line at the same indentation level as the associated **if** statement as a visual clue that subsequent statements in the program are not associated with this **if** statement.

To get a sense of how hard it can be to understand a poorly indented program, consider the following nonindented, noncommented version of SortTwo.java from Listing 5.1.

```java
import java.io.*;
public class SortTwo {
public static void main(String[] args) throws IOException {
BufferedReader stdin = new BufferedReader(
new InputStreamReader(System.in));
System.out.print("Enter an integer number: ");
int value1 = Integer.parseInt(stdin.readLine());
System.out.print("Enter another integer number: ");
int value2 = Integer.parseInt(stdin.readLine());
if (value2 < value1) {
int rememberValue1 = value1;
value1 = value2;
value2 = rememberValue1;
}
System.out.println("The numbers in sorted order are "
+ value1 + " and then " + value2);
return;
}
}
```

5.5   NESTED CONSTRUCTS

As stated in the discussion of the **if** and **if-else** statements, the associated actions can be any Java statement or any list of statements with braces. Therefore, the actions can contain other **if** and **if-else** statements!

The following code segment uses a nested **if** statements to control the navigation of a robot when it encounters a door. (In the segment, assume `isDoorUnlocked` and `isLightOff` are previously defined **boolean** variables.)

```java
if (isDoorUnlocked) {
   System.out.println("Open the door");
   if (isLightOff) {
      System.out.println("Turn on the light");
   }
   System.out.println("Enter the room");
}
else {
   System.out.println("Turn around and leave");
}
```

The code segment has the robot enter the room if the door is unlocked. However, before entering, the robot ensures that the light is on in the room. If the door is locked, then the code segment has the robot turn and around and leave.

The indentation pattern of the code segment indicates that the described actions are what we intend. But how does the Java compiler—which ignores indentation—know to match the **else** action with the outer **if** statement rather than the nested **if** statement?

The compiler can tell which **if** statement to match an **else** action based on the Java requirement that only either a single statement or a list of statements enclosed within braces separate an **else** action from its associated **if**. For our code segment, this requirement necessitates that the turn around and leave command be associated with the status of door being locked.

As another example, consider the following code segment that makes use of some previously defined **boolean** variables p and q. The segments differ in what **if** statement is matched with the **else** action,

```java
if (p) {                              // p is true
   if (q) {                           // p is true, q is true
      System.out.println("A");        // p is true, q is true
   }                                  // p is true, q is true
   else {                             // p is true, q is false
      System.out.println("B");        // p is true, q is false
   }                                  // p is true, q is false
}                                     // p is true
```

In this segment, the **else** and its statement are associated with the **if** statement that evaluates q. For the string "B" to be displayed, expression p must be true and expression q must be **false**. In the next code segment using variables p and q, braces surround the inner **if** statement:

```java
if (p) {                              // p is true
   if (q) {                           // p is true, q is true
      System.out.println("A");        // p is true, q is true
   }                                  // p is true, q is true
}                                     // p is true
else {                                // p is false
   System.out.println("B");           // p is false
}                                     // p is false
```

Objects and == and !=

The values of reference variables (e.g., `String` variables) generally are not tested using the == and != operators. The reasons why are discussed in Section 5.7 where we discuss the `equals()` method for objects.

Following convention

Avoid writing expressions such as (a == **true**) or ((a < b) == **true**). Instead, write respectively the equivalent expressions, (a) and (a < b), which are easier to understand.

Similarly, avoid expressions such as (a == **false**) or ((a < b) == **false**). Instead, write respectively the following equivalent expressions, (!a) and (a >= b), which are easier to understand.

If you do not follow this advice, realize that explicitly testing whether a **boolean** expression equals a particular **boolean** value is viewed disdainfully by many programmers—they consider it a sign of programming immaturity.

Because of these braces, the **else** is matched to the first **if** statement. Therefore, string "B" is displayed whenever p evaluates to **false**, regardless of the value of q.

In the next turn section, we turn our attention to a specialized form of nested **if-else** statements—the **if-else-if** construct.

5.6   IF-ELSE-IF CONSTRUCT

Consider the following simple task: report whether a user-specified input integer value is zero, positive, or negative. An algorithm for this task is straightforward.

Step 1.   Prompt and extract a user-supplied value.
Step 2.   If the value is zero, then report that the value is zero
Step 3.   If instead the value is positive, then report that the value is positive
Step 4.   Otherwise, report that the value is negative.

Now consider the following code segment using a nested **if-else** structure to implement the algorithm.

```
BufferedReader stdin = new BufferedReader(
        new InputStreamReader(System.in));

System.out.print("Enter an integer: ");
int number = Integer.parseInt(stdin.readLine());

if (number == 0) {
    System.out.println(number + " is zero");
}
else {
    if (number > 0) {
        System.out.println(number + " is positive");
    }
```

```
    else {
        System.out.println(number + " is negative");
    }
}
```

We would argue that this code segment is correct, but its indentation style does not communicate sufficiently that one of three possible conditions is being determined and reported. We can rewrite this code segment in the following manner to better communicate the situation.

```
BufferedReader stdin = new BufferedReader(
        new InputStreamReader(System.in));

System.out.print("Enter an integer: ");
int number = Integer.parseInt(stdin.readLine());

if (number == 0) {
    System.out.println(number + " is zero");
}
else if (number > 0) {
    System.out.println(number + " is positive");
}
else {
    System.out.println(number + " is negative");
}
```

In the new code segment, the second **if** statement is placed on the same line as the first **else** and the trailing code is reduced by one level of indentation.

```
if (number > 0) {
    System.out.println(number + " is positive");
}
else {
    System.out.println(number + " is negative");
}
```

The **if** statement is still the action associated with the first **else**. However, the overall appearance of the code segment indicates that one of three conditions is being determined and reported. This code segment is an example of the **if-else-if** idiom. The **if-else-if** idiom is built by combing multiple **if-else** statements.

Our next example is SortThree.java of Listing 5.3. The program uses the **if-else-if** idiom to assist in the sorting of three numbers. In particular, the program extracts three user-specified values n1, n2, and n3 and displays those values in sorted order, that is, nondecreasing order. We use the term *nondecreasing* rather than "ascending" because the input values may contain duplicates.

For three numbers, there are only six possible number orderings:

- $n1 \le n2 \le n3$
- $n1 \le n3 \le n2$
- $n2 \le n1 \le n3$
- $n2 \le n3 \le n1$
- $n3 \le n1 \le n2$

Listing 5.3 SortThree.java

```
1.   // Sorts three user-specified numbers
2.
3.   import java.io.*;
4.
5.   public class SortThree {
6.       // main(): application entry point
7.       public static void main(String[] args) throws IOException {
8.           // set input stream
9.           BufferedReader stdin = new BufferedReader(
10.              new InputStreamReader(System.in));
11.
12.          // extract inputs
13.          System.out.println("Enter three integers one per line:");
14.          String s1 = stdin.readLine();
15.          String s2 = stdin.readLine();
16.          String s3 = stdin.readLine();
17.
18.          // did we get three inputs
19.          if ((s1 == null) || (s2 == null) || (s3 == null)) {
20.              System.out.println("Cannot sort without three inputs");
21.              System.exit(1);
22.          }
23.
24.          // convert the inputs into numeric form
25.          int n1 = Integer.parseInt(s1);
26.          int n2 = Integer.parseInt(s2);
27.          int n3 = Integer.parseInt(s3);
28.
29.          // define outputs
30.          int o1;
31.          int o2;
32.          int o3;
33.
34.          // determine which of the six orderings is applicable
35.          if ((n1 <= n2) && (n2 <= n3)) {   // n1 <= n2 <= n2
36.              o1 = n1;
37.              o2 = n2;
38.              o3 = n3;
39.          }
40.          else if ((n1 <= n3) && (n3 <= n2)) { // n1 <= n3 <= n2
41.              o1 = n1;
42.              o2 = n3;
43.              o3 = n2;
44.          }
45.          else if ((n2 <= n1) && (n1 <= n3)) { // n2 <= n1 <= n3
46.              o1 = n2;
47.              o2 = n1;
48.              o3 = n3;
49.          }
50.          else if ((n2 <= n3) && (n3 <= n1)) { // n2 <= n3 <= n1
51.              o1 = n2;
52.              o2 = n3;
53.              o3 = n1;
54.          }
```

Listing 5.3 **SortThree.java (Continued)**

```
55.        else if ((n3 <= n1) && (n1 <= n2)) { // n3 <= n1 <= n2
56.            o1 = n3;
57.            o2 = n1;
58.            o3 = n2;
59.        }
60.        else { // n3 <= n2 <= n1
61.            o1 = n3;
62.            o2 = n2;
63.            o3 = n1;
64.        }
65.
66.        // display results
67.        System.out.println("\n" + n1 + " " + n2 + " " + n3
68.            + " in sorted order is " + o1 + " " + o2 + " " + o3);
69.    }
70. }
```

- n3 ≤ n2 ≤ n1

The program first defines and extracts the input values using `String` variables `s1`, `s2`, and `s3`.

```
BufferedReader stdin = new BufferedReader(
        new InputStreamReader(System.in));

// extract inputs
System.out.println("Enter three integers one per line:");
String s1 = stdin.readLine();
String s2 = stdin.readLine();
String s3 = stdin.readLine();
```

A test then determines whether any of the `String` variables are **null**. Method `readLine()` returns a **null** value when the user indicates through an operating system-dependent escape sequence that no more values are being supplied. This escape sequence is `Ctrl+z` in Windows-based systems and `Ctrl+d` in Unix and OS X-based systems.

```
// did we get three inputs
if ((s1 == null) || (s2 == null) || (s3 == null)) {
    System.out.println("Cannot sort without three inputs");
    System.exit(1);
}
```

If the user does not supply three values, then a usage message is printed and the program is terminated using `System` class method `exit()`. Whenever method `exit()` is invoked, it terminates the program that invoked the method. The parameter to `exit()` is a program termination status signal for the operating system. For most operating systems, a nonzero program termination status value indicates that the program was unsuccessful in accomplishing its task.

Because `exit()` terminates program `SortThree.java` if the user does not supply three inputs, it must be the case when the flow of control reaches line 23 of the program that there are three inputs to process. This condition removes the need for the program to have those remaining statements made into an **else** action for the **if** statement.

The ? : operator

The operator ? : can sometimes be used in place of a conditional statement. The operator has the following form:

    TestExpression ? *Expression*$_1$: *Expression*$_2$

When executed, *TestExpression* is evaluated first. If *TestExpression* evaluates to **true**, then the value of the operation is *Expression*$_1$; otherwise, the value of the operation is *Expression*$_2$. A colon separates the two expressions.

Suppose `value1` and `value2` are **int** variables that have been initialized already. The following statement uses operator ? : in defining a variable **min** that is the lesser of those two values.

```
int min = (input1 <= input2) ? input1 : input2;
```

Without the use of the operator, the definition and initialization would take several statements.

```
int min;
if (input1 <= input2) {
    min = input1;
}
else {
    min = input2;
}
```

The program next produces the **int** representations n1, n2, and n3 of the inputs and defines variables o1, o2, and o3 for recording the sorted ordering.

```
// convert the inputs into numeric form
int n1 = Integer.parseInt(s1);
int n2 = Integer.parseInt(s2);
int n3 = Integer.parseInt(s3);

// define outputs
int o1;
int o2;
int o3;
```

The program then proceeds to determine what is the sorted ordering of the input. The first of these tests checks whether the inputs n1, n2, and n3 are sorted already.

```
if ((n1 <= n2) && (n2 <= n3)) {   // n1 <= n2 <= n2
    o1 = n1;
    o2 = n2;
    o3 = n3;
}
```

If the input values are sorted, then they are copied respectively to o1, o2, and o3. Observe that the test expression is

```
(n1 <= n2) && (n2 <= n3)
```

and not

```
(n1 <= n2 <= n3)      // illegal
```

This alternative expression has the right mathematical look but is not a syntactically correct Java expression. Because of operator associativity, the alternative expression is equivalent to

```
(n1 <= n2) <= n3
```

which compares a logical value (the result of comparing n1 to n2) to n3. Such an expression is invalid Java and cannot be used.

If the three input values are not in sorted order, then a test is made to determine whether n1 is the smallest, n3 is the middle value, and n2 is the largest value. If this test evaluates to **true**, then n1 is copied to o1, n3 is copied to o2, and n2 is copied to o3.

```
else if ((n1 <= n3) && (n3 <= n2)) { // n1 <= n3 <= n2
    o1 = n1;
    o2 = n3;
    o3 = n2;
}
```

If instead this test evaluates to **false**, another ordering is considered.

The testing process continues until five different orderings have been considered and rejected. At that point, there is only one untried ordering (i.e., n3 ≤ n2 ≤ n1), and it must represent the sorted ordering. For this case, n3 is copied to o1, n2 is copied to o2, and n1 is copied to o3.

```
else { // n3 <= n2 <= n1
    o1 = n3;
    o2 = n2;
    o3 = n1;
}
```

We now turn our attention on how to test whether two objects (i.e., non-primitive values) are equivalent.

5.7 TESTING OBJECTS FOR EQUALITY

In the next series of examples, the following definition of BufferedReader variable stdin is in effect.

```
BufferedReader stdin = new BufferedReader(
        new InputStreamReader(System.in));
```

The first example determines whether two user-specified **int** values n1 and n2 are the same.

```
System.out.print("Enter an integer number: ");
int n1 = Integer.parseInt(stdin.readLine());
System.out.print("Enter another integer number: ");
int n2 = Integer.parseInt(stdin.readLine());
```

```
if (n1 == n2) {
   System.out.println(n1 + " and " + n2 + " are the same");
}
else {
   System.out.println(n1 + " and " + n2 + " differ");
}
```

The code is straightforward. It first defines and initializes two variables n1 and n2 with user-specified values. It then tests whether the values are the same by evaluating the **boolean** expression n1 == n2.

If we wanted a code segment that reports whether two user-specified **char** values are the same, we would use comparable code for the testing.

```
System.out.print("Enter a character: ");
char c1 = (char) stdin.readLine().charAt(0);
System.out.print("Enter another character: ");
char c2 = (char) stdin.readLine().charAt(0);

if (c1 == c2) {
   System.out.println(c1 + " and " + c2 + " are the same");
}
else {
   System.out.println(c1 + " and " + c2 + " differ");
}
```

This segment defines **char** variables c1 and c2 and uses the expression c1 == c2 to test whether the values are the same.

Similarly, if we wanted a code segment that reports whether two user-supplied character strings are the same, we would be tempted to use comparable code.

```
System.out.print("Enter a string: ");
String s1 = stdin.readLine();
System.out.println("Enter another string: ");
String s2 = stdin.readLine();                     Tests whether s1 and s2
                                                  reference the same String
if (s1 == s2) {  ◄──────────────
   System.out.println(s1 + " and " + s2 + " are the same");
}
else {
   System.out.println(s1 + " and " + s2 + " differ");
}
```

However, this code segment does not do what is intended. Yes, String variables s1 and s2 are initialized to be references to the input values. But the **boolean** expression s1 == s2 does not test whether these input values are equivalent, instead this expression tests whether s1 and s2 are referencing the same memory location, which for this code segment is never **true**.

To understand why the code segment behaves so, suppose the user in reaction to both prompts enters the string "pastel".

```
Enter a string: pastel
Enter another string: pastel
```

The definitions of variables s1 and s2 cause them to reference separate String objects. These two String objects both have values that correspond to "pastel".

The expression s1 == s2 tests whether *variables s1 and s2 have the same value*; that is, it tests whether s1 and s2 both reference the same location. And because they do not, the expression is **false**.

To instead test whether the *strings referenced by s1 and s2 have the same representation*, we use the String member method equals().

Tests whether s1 and s2 represent
the same character sequence

```
if (s1.equals(s2)) {
    System.out.println(s1 + " and " + s2 + " are the same");
}
else {
    System.out.println(s1 + " and " + s2 + " differ");
}
```

String method equals() returns **true** only when its parameter corresponds to the same character string as the character string represented by the invoking string.

Listing 5.4 uses the code segment in the complete program StringTest.java to report whether two user-specified input strings are the same.

Listing 5.4   StringTest.java

```
1.  // determines whether user-specified strings are the same.
2.
3.  import java.io.*;
4.
5.  public class StringTest {
6.      // main(): application entry point
7.      public static void main(String[] args) throws IOException {
8.          // set input stream
9.          BufferedReader stdin = new BufferedReader(
10.             new InputStreamReader(System.in));
11.
12.         // get strings of interest
13.         System.out.println("Enter a string: ");
14.         String s1 = stdin.readLine();
15.         System.out.println("Enter another string: ");
16.         String s2 = stdin.readLine();
17.
18.         // are the strings equivalent
19.         if (s1.equals(s2)) {
20.             System.out.println(s1 + " and " + s2 + " are the same");
21.         }
22.         else {
23.             System.out.println(s1 + " and " + s2 + " differ");
24.         }
25.     }
26. }
```

The awt class `Rectangle` also provides a member method `equals()`. Two Rectangle objects are equal if and only if they have the same width, height, and top-left corner. Its use is demonstrated in the following code segment.

```
Rectangle r1 = new Rectangle(0, 0, 5, 3);
Rectangle r2 = new Rectangle(0, 0, 5, 3);
Rectangle r3 = r1;

if (r1 == r2) {
   System.out.println("r1 and r2 refer to the same object\n");
}
else if (r1.equals(r2)) {
   System.out.println("r1 and r2 refer to different objects "
      + "representing the same\nrectangle\n");
}
else {
   System.out.println("r1 and r2 refer to different objects "
      + "representing different\nrectangles\n");
}

if (r1 == r3) {
   System.out.println("r1 and r3 refer to the same "
      + "rectangle");
}
else if (r1.equals(r3)) {
   System.out.println("r1 and r3 refer to different objects "
      + "representing the same\nrectangle");
}
else {
   System.out.println("r1 and r3 refer to different objects "
      + "representing different\nrectangles");
}
```

In the segment, `Rectangle` variables r1, r2, and r3 all refer to a 5×3 rectangle with a top-left corner situated at the origin $(0, 0)$. The `Rectangle` objects referenced by r1 and r2 were constructed individually. The `Rectangle` object referenced by r3 is the same `Rectangle` object referenced by r1. The output of the program reflects this initialization.

```
r1 and r2 refer to different objects representing the same
rectangle

r1 and r3 refer to the same object
```

All objects have a method `equals()`. However, the implementation of the method is type specific. For many classes, its implementation is analogous to the implementations of the `equals()` for `String` and `Rectangle`—the method determines whether the two references have equivalent representations. However, some classes report merely whether the references are the same. You should make it a practice to read the documentation associated with a class so that you understand its various behaviors.

In Section 5.8, we turn our attention to the other Java conditional statement, the **switch** statement.

Literal string constants

Consider the following definitions for `String` variables `s` and `t`.

```
String s = "abc";
String t = "abc";
```

It is clear that `s.equals(t)` evaluates to **true**, but is `s == t` also **true**? The answer is yes. Java represents a literal character string internally as a `String` constant. If the same literal character string appears more than once in a class, then all occurrences reference the same `String` constant. Therefore, the variables `s` and `t` from our example are assigned the same `String` reference. As a result, `s == t` evaluates to **true**.

Character processing

Programmers who are doing string processing often are interested in determining whether characters have some particular property. For this purpose, Java provides a collection of class methods as part of the standard package `java.lang.Character`. For example, method `Character.isWhitespace()` tests whether its parameter is a space, tab, formfeed, or newline character; and method `Character.isDigit()` tests whether its parameter is a decimal digit. The following list includes some of the more frequently used `Character` class methods for testing properties of characters.

- `isDigit()`: Tests whether character is numeric.
- `isLetter()`: Tests whether character is alphabetic.
- `isLowerCase()`: Tests whether character is lowercase alphabetic.
- `isWhiteSpace()`: Tests whether character is one of the space, tab, formfeed, or newline characters.
- `isUpperCase()`: Tests whether character is uppercase alphabetic.

Two other `Character` class methods of frequent interest are

- `toLowerCase()`: If the character is alphabetic, then the lowercase equivalent of the character is returned; otherwise, the character is returned.
- `toUpperCase()`: If the character is alphabetic, then the uppercase equivalent of the character is returned; otherwise, the character is returned.

5.8   SWITCH STATEMENT

A software engineer is confronted sometimes with a programming task where the action to be executed depends on the value of a specific integral expression. The **if-else-if** construct can be used to solve such tasks by separately comparing the desired expression to a particular value and, if the expression and value are equal, then executing the appropriate action.

For example, suppose we are developing a program with a graphical display where the location of a graphical element named `sprite` is to be updated based on the value of

char variable cmd ('u', 'd', 'l', 'r' for up, down, left, and right respectively). Using **if** statements, the code might look like the following:

```
if (cmd == 'u') {
    sprite.moveUp();
}
else if (cmd == 'd') {
    sprite.moveDown();
}
else if (cmd == 'l') {
    sprite.moveLeft();
}
else if (cmd == 'r') {
    sprite.moveRight();
}
else {
    System.out.println("Unexpected request: " + cmd);
    System.exit(1);
}
```

Because such programming tasks occur frequently, Java includes a **switch** statement. The command character reporting task can be done in a more readable manner using that statement.

```
switch (cmd) {
    case 'u':
        sprite.moveUp();
        break;
    case 'd':
        sprite.moveDown();
        break;
    case 'l':
        sprite.moveLeft();
        break;
    case 'r':
        sprite.moveRight();
        break;
    default:
        System.out.println("Unexpected request: " + cmd);
        System.exit(1);
}
```

Switch statements and floating point values

Because of the requirement that both the *SwitchExpression* and the individual *CaseExpressions* be integral, the **switch** statement cannot be used to determine actions based on the value of a floating-point object. Such processing requires **if-else-if** statements.

As our example suggests, a basic **switch** statement has the following syntax:

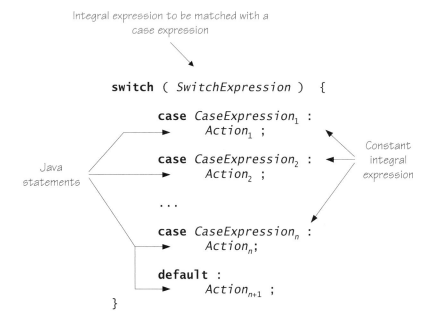

Integral expression to be matched with a
case expression

switch (*SwitchExpression*)   {

case *CaseExpression*₁ :
   *Action*₁ ;

Java statements

Constant integral expression

case *CaseExpression*₂ :
   *Action*₂ ;

. . .

case *CaseExpression*ₙ :
   *Action*ₙ;

default :
   *Action*ₙ₊₁ ;
}

The *Action* associated with a *case* expression is either a single statement or a group of statements. Even if the *Action* is a group of statements, no surrounding braces are required.

When a **switch** statement is executed, its *SwitchExpression* is evaluated; if the value of that expression equals the value of a *CaseExpression* in that **switch** statement, then flow of control is transferred to the $Action_i$ associated with the matching $CaseExpression_i$.

If no *CaseExpression* equals the value of the *SwitchExpression* and if a **default** case is supplied, then the **default** $Action_{n+1}$ code is executed. In the command character example, the **default** case issues an error message and terminates the program if an invalid command is received.

If no *CaseExpression* equals the value of the *SwitchExpression* and no **default** case is supplied, then none of the *Actions* are executed. In practice, most **switch** statements include a **default** *Action* that handles unexpected conditions.

What happens after the selected *Action* is executed depends on the statements that make up *Action*. Normally, the last statement in an *Action* is a **break** statement. The **break** statement indicates that the **switch** statement has completed its task and that the flow of control should continue with the statement after the **switch** statement. If no **break** statement is supplied, then control continues with the next statement within the **switch** statement itself.

In the following code segment, no **break** statements are used within the **switch** statement.

```
switch (i) {
   case 3:
      System.out.println("Hello, friend");
   case 2:
      System.out.println("Hello, friend");
   default: {
      System.out.println("Hello, friend");
}
```

If the value of i is 3, then the segment displays "Hello, friend" three times.

```
Hello, friend
Hello, friend
Hello, friend
```

The message is displayed three times, as the value of i matches the first case. Therefore, each of the three actions in the **switch** statement are executed because there are no **break** statements that stop the *fall-through* behavior.

If the value of i is 2, then the string "Hello, friend" is displayed two times.

```
Hello, friend
Hello, friend
```

The message is displayed two times, as the value of i matches the second case. Therefore, each of the two subsequent actions in the **switch** statement are executed because there are no **break** statements that stop the fall-through behavior.

If the value of i is neither 2 nor 3, then the **default** action is executed and the string is displayed just once.

```
Hello, friend
```

Normally, one should avoid using the "fall-through" behavior of the **switch** statement to achieve a desired effect. The *Action* of a case should almost always end with a **break** statement. However, there is one situation where using the fall-through behavior makes sense.

What if we would like the same *Action* to be performed for different values of the *SwitchExpression*? For example, suppose we wanted to allow a movement command character to be entered in either lower or upper case. In this situation, we can use the fall-through behavior to write clearer code. For example, to handle upper and lower case 'u', the **case** statements would be:

```
case 'u':
case 'U':
   sprite.moveUp();
   break;
```

The *Action* for the **case** 'u' is empty, and control flows into the **case** 'U' and its *Action* is executed. The following code fragment uses this fall-through technique to allow movement commands to be entered in either lower or upper case. It follows the common practice of placing the cases for identical code on a single line.

```
switch (cmd) {
    case 'u': case 'U':
        sprite.moveUp();
        break;
    case 'd': case 'D':
        sprite.moveDown();
        break;
    case 'l': case 'L':
        sprite.moveLeft();
        break;
    case 'r': case 'R':
        sprite.moveRight();
        break;
    default:
        System.out.println("Unexpected graphic request: " + cmd);
        System.exit(1);
}
```

Another use of a **switch** statement is demonstrated in program DaysIn-Month.java of Listing 5.5. The program prompts a user for a year and month and then reports the number of days in that month.

Method main() of DaysInMonth.java begins by defining constants that enable the program to use names rather than numeric literals for the 12 months in a year. Method main() also defines a constant CALENDAR_START with the value 1582, which was the year that the current international calendar system—the Gregorian calendar—was first adopted. The program also defines a BufferedReader variable stdin for extracting values from standard input.

After extracting the input values, the program first determines whether the input represents a valid request.

```
if ((year < CALENDAR_START) || (month < 1) || (month > 12)) {
    System.out.println("Bad request: " + year + " "
        + month);
    System.exit(1);
}
```

A request is valid if both the year and month are sensible. If they are not, the program displays an error message to standard output and terminates the program. Because of the exit() statement, the statements that follow the **if** statement are executed only if the input request was valid.

The program next determines whether the year of interest is a leap year. In the Gregorian calendar system, years not evenly divisible by 4 are not leap years. All years evenly divisible by 4 are leap years except for years evenly divisible by 100 that are not also evenly divisible by 400. For example,

- 2000 is a leap year (evenly divisible by 4, 100 and 400);
- 2004 is a leap year (evenly divisible by 4 and not evenly divisible by 100);
- 2007 is not a leap year (not evenly divisible by 4);

Listing 5.5 DaysInMonth.java

```java
1.  // Compute the number of days in a user-specified month
2.
3.  import java.io.*;
4.
5.  public class DaysInMonth {
6.      // main(): application entry point
7.      public static void main(String[] args) throws IOException {
8.          final int JANUARY = 1;      final int JULY = 7;
9.          final int FEBRUARY = 2;     final int AUGUST = 8;
10.         final int MARCH = 3;        final int SEPTEMBER = 9;
11.         final int APRIL = 4;        final int OCTOBER = 10;
12.         final int MAY = 5;          final int NOVEMBER = 11;
13.         final int JUNE = 6;         final int DECEMBER = 12;
14.
15.         final int CALENDAR_START = 1582;
16.
17.         // get an input reader
18.         BufferedReader stdin = new BufferedReader(
19.             new InputStreamReader(System.in));
20.
21.         // get date information of interest
22.         System.out.println("");
23.         System.out.print("Enter year: ");
24.         int year = Integer.parseInt(stdin.readLine());
25.         System.out.print("Enter month: ");
26.         int month = Integer.parseInt(stdin.readLine());
27.
28.         // validate input
29.         if ((year < CALENDAR_START) || (month < 1) || (month > 12)) {
30.             System.out.println("Bad request: " + year + " "
31.                 + month);
32.             System.exit(1);
33.         }
34.
35.         // determine whether year is a leap year
36.         boolean isDivisibleBy4 = (year % 4) == 0;
37.         boolean isDivisibleBy100 = (year % 100) == 0;
38.         boolean isDivisibleBy400 = (year % 400) == 0;
39.
40.         boolean isLeapYear = isDivisibleBy4
41.             && ((! isDivisibleBy100) || isDivisibleBy400);
42.
43.     // use month and year information to determine number of days
44.     int days;
45.     switch (month) {
46.         case JANUARY: case MARCH: case MAY: case JULY: case AUGUST:
47.         case OCTOBER: case DECEMBER:
48.             days = 31;
49.             break;
50.         case APRIL: case JUNE: case SEPTEMBER: case NOVEMBER:
51.             days = 30;
52.             break;
53.         case FEBRUARY:
54.             days = isLeapYear ? 29 : 28;
```

Listing 5.5   **DaysInMonth.java (Continued)**

```
55.            break;
56.          default:
57.             days = 0;
58.       }
59.
60.       System.out.println("");
61.       System.out.println("Month " + month + " in year " + year
62.                           + " has " + days + " days");
63.    }
64. }
```

Figure 5.6   **Diagram capturing leap year specification.**

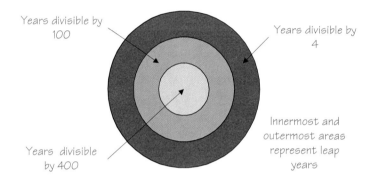

- 2100 is not a leap year (evenly divisible by 4 and 100, not evenly divisible by 400).

The leap year rules are captured in the Venn diagram of Figure 5.6.

Thus, to determine whether the year is a leap year, the program determines the status of three conditions: is the year divisible by 4, is the year divisible by 100, and is the year the divisible by 400. To determine these conditions, the Java modulus operator % is used to check whether the factors of interest divide the value of variable year evenly.

```
boolean isDivisibleBy4 = (year % 4) == 0;
boolean isDivisibleBy100 = (year % 100) == 0;
boolean isDivisibleBy400 = (year % 400) == 0;
```

For example, the term (year % 4) produces the remainder of year when divided by 4. Therefore, the expression (year % 4) == 0 evaluates to **true** when year is a multiple of 4, and **false** otherwise.

The three conditions are used in the initialization of **boolean** variable isLeapYear that indicates whether the year is a leap year.

```
boolean isLeapYear = isDivisibleBy4
    && ((! isDivisibleBy100) || isDivisibleBy400);
```

The number of days in the input month can then be calculated by determining to which group the input month belongs: months with 31 days, months with 30 days, or Feb-

Using the switch statement effectively

Appropriate use of the `switch` statement makes programs easier to understand and can result in more efficient programs. Here are some guidelines for effective use of the `switch` statement.

- Keep the *Action* code short. This helps make the structure of the `switch` statement clear. A lengthy piece of *Action* code obscures the structure of the code.
- Always provide a `default` case. Failing to provide a `default` case can lead to undetected errors.
- Avoid fall-through cases. They make the code harder to understand and more difficult to maintain. The only time a fall-through case is appropriate is when the cases have identical *Action* statements.
- Order the cases in some meaningful way. Depending on the situation, it may make sense to order the cases alphabetically or according to frequency of occurrence (i.e., put the case that occurs most often at the beginning).

ruary. Although an `if-else-if` construct would work, a `switch` statement yields a more readable code segment.

```
// use month and year information to determine number of days
int days;
switch (month) {
   case JANUARY: case MARCH: case MAY: case JULY: case AUGUST:
   case OCTOBER: case DECEMBER:
      days = 31;
      break;
   case APRIL: case JUNE: case SEPTEMBER: case NOVEMBER:
      days = 30;
      break;
   case FEBRUARY:
      days = isLeapYear ? 29 : 28;
      break;
   default:
      days = 0;
}
```

The cases in the `switch` statement use the previously defined constants for representing the months. The named constants contribute to program readability. If the input month is a valid month, the `switch` statement correctly assigns variable days. An invalid month is processed by the `default` case of the `switch` statement, causing variable days to be set to 0. Although this `default` case is not necessary because of the earlier validation of the date, it is prudent to include it.

The action for assigning the number of days in the month of February uses the previously mentioned ternary operator ?. If isLeapYear evaluates to **true**, then days is assigned 29; otherwise days is assigned 28.

With variable days set properly, the program completes its task by displaying the result of its calculation.

```
System.out.println("");
System.out.println("Month " + month + " in year " + year
```

```
                                      + " has " + days + " days");
```

This discussion completes the analysis of DaysInMonth.java. We next turn our attention to two case studies that make use of conditional statements in their implementations. The first application is concerned with recognizing a valid code number; the second application is concerned with developing a representation for triangles.

5.9   CASE STUDY — CHECKSUM VALIDATION

A common requirement for software applications supporting inventory management is to validate the items being manipulated. For example, suppose the manager of a store wants to add a new item to the store's inventory database. To do so, the manager would need to

> The objective of this case study is to practice using the **if-else** statement when problem solving

insert a new entry into the database that gives the name and price of the item along with its code number. Correctly entering all three pieces of information is very important; e.g., a wrong price could affect greatly the store's profitability, and an improperly entered code would make it impossible for price scanners to recognize the item.

One way to increase the likelihood of correct data entry is to ask users to verify that the values were entered correctly. With regard to name and price there is not much more that can be done except to follow the standard practice of echoing input values. However, various *checksum* schemes have been created for code numbers so that software can verify whether a number is legal. Checksum software tests whether the digits of a potential code number have some particular property.

For example, there is a verification scheme for the Universal Product Code© numbers that most manufactured items now have. Figure 5.7 shows a sample UPC number in a form that is scannable by a bar code reader.

Figure 5.7   A Universal Product Code number in bar code form.

A valid Universal Product Code (UPC) number is a 12-digit value that meets the following criteria.

- Let m be the sum of the 2nd, 4th, 6th, 8th, and 10th digits. (The numbering of the digits is from left to right.)
- Let n be the sum of the 1st, 3rd, 5th, 7th, 9th, and 11th digits.
- Let $r = 10 - ((m + 3 \cdot n) \bmod 10)$.
- A number meets the UPC encoding criteria if its 12th digit equals r.

  Consider 780070121354. For this number,
  $$m = 8 + 0 + 0 + 2 + 3 = 13$$
  $$n = 7 + 0 + 7 + 1 + 1 + 5 = 21$$
  $$r = 10 - ((13 + 3 \cdot 21) \bmod 10) = 10 - (76 \bmod 10) = 10 - 6 = 4$$

Because r equals 4, the number corresponds to a possible UPC code. Now consider the number 123456789011. For this number,
$$m = 2 + 4 + 6 + 8 + 0 = 20$$

$$n = 1 + 3 + 5 + 7 + 9 + 1 = 26$$
$$r = 10 - ((20 + 3 \cdot 26) \bmod 10) = 10 - (98 \bmod 10) = 10 - 8 = 2$$

Because r does not equal 1, the number is not a valid UPC code.

ANALYSIS AND DESIGN

The values to be manipulated by an algorithm for computing a UPC are obvious. Three essential values are m, n, and r. In addition, the input string s is needed and its numeric representation *number*. With *number*, the 12 components digits *d1. d2. .... d12* can be determined for initializing m, n, and r.

We use the UPC encoding criteria and the preceding values in the following algorithm for checking whether a number is a possible UPC code.

```
Prompt user to supply a twelve-digit number.
Extract the input and assign it to s.
Convert s into a numeric representation number.
If number is negative or has more than twelve digits
    Report number is not a UPC code
Else
    Assign the least significant (twelfth) digit of number to
        d12.
    Assign the eleventh digit of number to d11.
    Assign the tenth digit of number to d10.
    Assign the ninth digit of number to d9.
    Assign the eighth digit of number to d8.
    Assign the seventh digit of number to d7.
    Assign the sixth digit of number to d6.
    Assign the fifth digit of number to d5.
    Assign the fourth digit of number to d4.
    Assign the third digit of number to d3.
    Assign the second digit of number to d2.
    Assign the first digit of number to d1.
    Assign m the value d2 + d4 + d6 + d8 + d10.
    Assign n the value d1 + d3 + d5 + d7 + d9 + d11.
    Assign r the 10 - ((m + 3·n) mod 10).
    If r equals d12 then
        Report number is a feasible UPC code
    Else
        Report number is not a UPC code
```

IMPLEMENTATION

The key insights into translating this algorithm into a valid Java program are knowing how to represent the input, how to organize the program to test for necessary properties, and how to extract the digits from the input number.

Our implementation of the algorithm is UPC.java of Listing 5.6. The program represent the input number using **long** variable number. It does so, because feasible UPC codes are too large to be represented using an **int**—the maximum **int** value is only ten digits long. For the same reason, constant MAX_POSSIBLE_UPC_CODE is defined to be a **long** value.

```
final long MAX_POSSIBLE_UPC_CODE = 999999999999L;
```

In its definition, the "L" in 999999999999L indicates that the numerical literal is a **long** value.

Listing 5.6 UPC.java

```java
1.  // Checks whether a user-specified value meets the UPC criteria
2.
3.  import java.io.*;
4.
5.  public class UPC {
6.      // main(): application entry point
7.      public static void main(String[] args) throws IOException {
8.          final long MAX_POSSIBLE_UPC_CODE = 999999999999L;
9.
10.         // set input stream and get number
11.         BufferedReader stdin = new BufferedReader(
12.             new InputStreamReader(System.in));
13.
14.         System.out.print("Enter a 12-digit whole number: ");
15.         String s = stdin.readLine();
16.
17.         long number = Long.parseLong(s);
18.
19.         // determine whether number is a possible upc code
20.         if ((number < 0) || (number > MAX_POSSIBLE_UPC_CODE)) {
21.             // not a upc code
22.             System.out.println(s + " is an invalid UPC code");
23.         }
24.         else {
25.             // might be a upc code
26.
27.             // determine individual digits
28.             int d12 = (int) (number % 10);
29.             number /= 10;
30.             int d11 = (int) (number % 10);
31.             number /= 10;
32.             int d10 = (int) (number % 10);
33.             number /= 10;
34.             int d9 = (int) (number % 10);
35.             number /= 10;
36.             int d8 = (int) (number % 10);
37.             number /= 10;
38.             int d7 = (int) (number % 10);
39.             number /= 10;
40.             int d6 = (int) (number % 10);
41.             number /= 10;
42.             int d5 = (int) (number % 10);
43.             number /= 10;
44.             int d4 = (int) (number % 10);
45.             number /= 10;
46.             int d3 = (int) (number % 10);
47.             number /= 10;
48.             int d2 = (int) (number % 10);
49.             number /= 10;
50.             int d1 = (int) (number % 10);
51.             number /= 10;
52.
53.             // compute sums of first 5 even digits and the odd digits
54.             int m = d2 + d4 + d6 + d8 + d10;
```

Listing 5.6 **UPC.java (Continued)**

```
55.            int n = d1 + d3 + d5 + d7 + d9 + d11;
56.
57.            // use UPC formula to determine required value for d12
58.            int r = 10 - ((m + 3*n) % 10);
59.
60.            // based on r, can test whether number is a UPC code
61.            if (r == d12) {
62.               // is a upc code
63.               System.out.println(s + " is a feasible UPC code");
64.            }
65.            else {
66.               // not a upc code
67.               System.out.println(s + " is an invalid UPC code");
68.            }
69.         }
70.      }
71. }
```

An examination of UPC.java shows that its organization mirrors the organization of the previously supplied algorithm.

```
// set input stream and get number ...

// determine whether number is a possible upc code
if ((number < 0) || (number > MAX_POSSIBLE_UPC_CODE)) {
   // not a upc code ...
}
else {
   // might be a upc code

   // determine individual digits ...

   // compute sums of first 5 even digits and the odd digits ...

   // use UPC formula to determine required value r for d12 ...

   if (r == d12) {
      // is a upc code ...
   }
   else {
      // not a upc code ...
   }
}
```

Once the program extracts the input, it tests whether the number lies outside the legal range for UPC codes. If it does, then the program reports that the number is not a UPC code. Otherwise, the individual digits of the number are determined. A test is then made to see whether the digits form a valid UPC code.

Determining the least significant digit d12 is simple with the Java modulus operator %. The expression number % 10 evaluates to remainder of number divided by 10, which is the value of the least significant digit of number.

```
int d12 = (int) (number % 10);
```

The **int** cast is necessary because the expression number % 10 is a **long** expression.

By updating number by dividing it by 10,

```
number /= 10;
```

the next leastmost significant digit can be determined by taking the new value of number modulus 10.

```
int d11 = (int) (number % 10);
```

This process can be repeated to determine the other digits of the number.[†]

Once the individual digits have been determined, the variables m, n, and r from the UPC formula can be defined.

```
int m = d2 + d4 + d6 + d8 + d10;
int n = d1 + d3 + d5 + d7 + d9 + d11;
int r = 10 - ((m + 3*n) % 10);
```

Finally, a test comparing the values of r and d12 determines whether the number is a feasible UPC code.

```
if (r == d12) {
    System.out.println(number + " is a feasible UPC code");
}
else {
    System.out.println(number + " is an invalid UPC code");
}
```

We now our attention to the development of a representation for triangles.

5.10   CASE STUDY — TRIANGLES

Triangles are an important shape in the world of computer graphics. In particular, when computer animations are created, scenes are decomposed typically into a collection of triangles. Figure 5.8 shows such a decomposition.

The objective of this case study is to practice using the conditional statements in the context of the design and

Let's suppose that we have been assigned the task of developing and implementing a representation ColoredTriangle for a triangle. Clearly, we need to represent the three endpoints that denote the position of the triangle and we also need to know its color. So what constructors and behaviors should be present and what information, if any, must be maintained to implement the behaviors?

ANALYSIS AND DESIGN

With our experiences from designing and implementing class ColoredRectangle of Chapter 4 and using standard classes, we recognize the importance of at least two ColoredTriangle constructors—a default constructor and a constructor that enables a specific triangle to be constructed.

---

† Chapter 6 considers iteration. By using an iteration construct lines 28–55 can be simplified substantially.

Figure 5.8 **Preliminary triangular decomposition and rendering.**

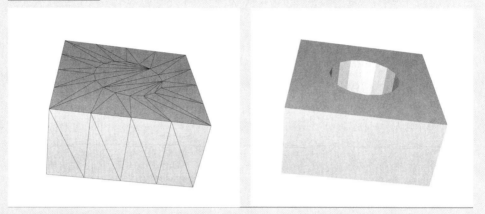

- *Default construction*: construct a reasonable triangle representation even though no explicit attributes values are given.

- *Specific construction*: construct a triangle representation from explicitly given attributes values.

We also recognize the importance of accessors and mutators.

- *Accessors*: provide the color or a requested endpoint of the associated triangle.

- *Mutators*: set the color or a specified endpoint of the associated triangle to a given value.

For drawing purposes, we recognize the importance of the following behavior.

- *Render*: draw the associated triangle in a given graphical context.

In designing the rendering behavior, we have a decision to make. Should there be a `ColoredTriangle` attribute that represents the graphical target for the drawing (e.,g., a `JFrame` as there was for `ColoredRectangle` of Chapter 4)? Or should the graphical target be specified as a parameter to the rendering method?

If our intention was to add `ColoredTriangle` to a library already containing `ColoredRectangle`, then consistency with `ColoredRectangle` would dictate the form of `ColoredRectangle`.

However, our initial design of `ColoredRectangle` stressed simplicity over functionality—it did not recognize the tension between these two properties. Our `ColoredTriangle` design takes a more balanced view and gives a `ColoredTriangle` object the ability to render itself to different graphical targets (e.g., different windows). This decision is similar to the rendering philosophy of the standard Java graphical packages `awt` and `swing`.

IMPLEMENTATION

To implement our triangle representation, we use an instance variable of type `java.awt.Color` to represent the color of a triangle.

```
private Color color
```

Color of the associated triangle.

To represent the three triangle endpoints we have a choice. We could use six **int** data fields x1, y1, x2, y2, x3, and y3, or we could make three uses of the awt class Point, which provides a representation of a location in integer coordinate space. For our implementation, we chose to use class Point. We did so because Point directly captures the notion of location.

> private Point p1
>> References the first point of the associated triangle.
>
> private Point p2
>> References the second point of the associated triangle.
>
> private Point p3
>> References the third point of the associated triangle.

The following constructors and methods are used to implement the behaviors discussed in the analysis section. (Implementations of some other possible methods are considered in the self-test questions and exercises.)

> public ColoredTriangle()
>> Constructs a default triangle representation. The default representation is a black triangle with points at coordinates (1, 1), (2, 2), and (3, 3).
>
> public ColoredTriangle(Point v1, Point v2, Point v3, Color c)
>> Constructs a triangle using color c whose endpoints are equivalent to the points referenced by p1, p2, and p3.
>
> public Point getPoint(int i)
>> Returns the ith point of the associated triangle.
>
> public void setPoint(int i, Point v)
>> Sets the ith point of the associated triangle so that its value is equivalent to the point referenced by v.
>
> public Color getColor()
>> Returns the color of the associated triangle.
>
> public void setColor(Color c)
>> Sets the color of the associated triangle to c.
>
> public void paint(Graphics g)
>> Renders the triangle to graphic context g.

An implementation of the data fields and methods of ColoredTriangle.java is given in Listing 5.7. Because most of the methods have straightforward definitions, we limit our discussion to only some of them.

The purpose of the ColoredTriangle default constructor is to configure a new ColoredTriangle object to represent a black triangle with endpoints at coordinates (1, 1), (2, 2), and (3, 3).

```
// ColoredTriangle(): default constructor
public ColoredTriangle() {
    Point a = new Point(1, 1);
    Point b = new Point(2, 2);       Create endpoint values
    Point c = new Point(3, 3);
    setPoint(1, a);
    setPoint(2, b);                  Copy desired endpoint values to data fields
    setPoint(3, c);
    setColor(Color.BLACK);    Copy desired color to data fields
}
```

Listing 5.7   ColoredTriangle.java

```
1.  // Representation of a triangle in colored coordinate space
2.
3.  import java.awt.*;
4.
5.  public class ColoredTriangle {
6.      // instance variables
7.      private Point p1;     // first endpoint
8.      private Point p2;     // second endpoint
9.      private Point p3;     // third endpoint
10.     private Color color; // triangle color
11.
12.     // ColoredTriangle(): default constructor
13.     public ColoredTriangle() {
14.         Point a = new Point(1, 1);
15.         Point b = new Point(2, 2);
16.         Point c = new Point(3, 3);
17.         setPoint(1, a);
18.         setPoint(2, b);
19.         setPoint(3, c);
20.         setColor(Color.BLACK);
21.     }
22.
23.     // ColoredTriangle(): specific constructor
24.     public ColoredTriangle(Point a, Point b, Point c, Color d) {
25.         setPoint(1, a);
26.         setPoint(2, b);
27.         setPoint(3, c);
28.         setColor(d);
29.     }
30.
31.     // getPoint(): endpoint accessor
32.     public Point getPoint(int i) {
33.         if (i == 1) {
34.             return p1;
35.         }
36.         else if (i == 2) {
37.             return p2;
38.         }
39.         else if (i == 3) {
40.             return p3;
41.         }
42.         else {
43.             System.out.println("Unexpected endpoint access: " + i);
44.             System.exit(i);
45.             return null;
46.         }
47.     }
48.
49.     // setPoint(): endpoint mutator
50.     public void setPoint(int i, Point v) {
51.         if (i == 1) {
52.             p1 = new Point(v.x, v.y);
53.         }
54.         else if (i == 2) {
```

Listing 5.7 **ColoredTriangle.java (Continued)**

```
55.          p2 = new Point(v.x, v.y);
56.        }
57.        else if (i == 3) {
58.          p3 = new Point(v.x, v.y);
59.        }
60.        else {
61.          System.out.println("Unexpected endpoint access: " + i);
62.          System.exit(i);
63.        }
64.    }
65.
66.    // getColor(): color accessor
67.    public Color getColor() {
68.      return color;
69.    }
70.
71.    // setColor(): color mutator
72.    public void setColor(Color c) {
73.      color = c;
74.    }
75.
76.    // paint(): render facilitator
77.    public void paint(Graphics g) {
78.      Point v1 = getPoint(1);
79.      Point v2 = getPoint(2);
80.      Point v3 = getPoint(3);
81.      Color c = getColor();
82.
83.      g.setColor(c);
84.
85.      Polygon t = new Polygon();
86.      t.addPoint(v1.x, v1.y);
87.      t.addPoint(v2.x, v2.y);
88.      t.addPoint(v3.x, v3.y);
89.
90.      g.fillPolygon(t);
91.    }
92. }
```

To configure the object, the ColoredTriangle constructor first makes use of a Point constructor to initialize three Point variables a, b, and c so that they reference the desired endpoint values. The ColoredTriangle constructor then uses those values to set the endpoints of the new triangle. The endpoints of the new triangle are set using mutator setPoint(). The constructor uses the mutator rather than direct assignment to the instance variables. It does so for purposes of encapsulation and information hiding. The resulting code is more readable, less likely to introduce errors in representation, and simpler to manipulate when introducing enhancements.

The endpoint accessor and mutator methods getPoint() and setPoint() are quite similar in structure. We begin their analysis with method getPoint().

```
// getPoint(): endpoint accessor
public Point getPoint(int i) {
```

```java
   if (i == 1) {
      return p1;
   }
   else if (i == 2) {
      return p2;
   }
   else if (i == 3) {
      return p3;
   }
   else {
      System.out.println("Unexpected endpoint access: " + i);
      System.exit(i);
      return null;
   }
}
```

Method `getPoint()` uses case analysis to determine which endpoint is desired. The case analysis uses the **if-else-if** construct. If `i` has the value of 1, 2, or 3, then the appropriate endpoint is returned. Otherwise, some error handling code is executed.

The error handling code for method `getPoint()` first displays an error message to tell the user what has occurred and then invokes method `System.exit()` to terminate the program. Thus, the **return** statement that follows the `exit()` invocation is never executed. However, most Java compilers (e.g., `javac`) will not compile successfully the class without the **return** statement. The reason most compilers require a **return** statement is because every execution path in this method is supposed to produce a return value of type `Point`. The compilers do not recognize what happens in method `exit()` to make this particular **return** statement unnecessary—to most compilers, the `exit()` invocation is just viewed as another Java statement.

Method `setPoint()` uses similar case analysis to determine which instance variable should be updated based on the value of its parameter `v`.

```java
// setPoint(): endpoint mutator
public void setPoint(int i, Point v) {
   if (i == 1) {
      p1 = new Point(v.x, v.y);
   }
   else if (i == 2) {
      p2 = new Point(v.x, v.y);
   }
   else if (i == 3) {
      p3 = new Point(v.x, v.y);
   }
   else {
      System.out.println("Unexpected endpoint access: " + i);
      System.exit(i);
   }
}
```

When updating an instance variable, the mutator does not assign directly the value of parameter `v`. Instead, it assigns the instance variable a reference to a new `Point` object.

The new `Point` is a duplicate of the object referenced by `v`. For example, the following assignment shows the update for instance variable `p1`.

```
p1 = new Point(v.x, v.y);
```

The duplicate is assigned so that the `ColoredTriangle` can maintain its representation, regardless whether the `Point` referenced by `v` is updated subsequently. Because class `Point` allows **public** access to its data fields, accessors are not needed for getting the x- and y-coordinates associated with a `Point` object.[†]

The last method that we consider is method `paint()`. This method renders a triangle to the graphics context indicated by its parameter `g`.

```
// paint(): render facilitator
public void paint(Graphics g) {
    Point v1 = getPoint(1);
    Point v2 = getPoint(2);
    Point v3 = getPoint(3);
    Color c = getColor();

    g.setColor(c);

    Polygon t = new Polygon();
    t.addPoint(v1.x, v1.y);
    t.addPoint(v2.x, v2.y);
    t.addPoint(v3.x, v3.y);

    g.fillPolygon(t);
}
```

The simplest way to render a triangle is to use `Graphics` method `fillPolygon()`. Method `fillPolygon()` takes a single parameter of type `Polygon`. Class `Polygon` is part of the awt package. Its default constructor creates a representation of an empty polygon. A polygon representing our triangle can then be constructed by using `Polygon` method `addPoint()`. Method `addPoint()` takes two **int** parameters specifying the x- and y-coordinates of a new polygon endpoint. Therefore, the following code suffices for adding the three points to the new `Polygon`,

```
t.addPoint(v1.x, v1.y);
t.addPoint(v2.x, v2.y);
t.addPoint(v3.x, v3.y);
```

We demonstrate a use of the method in program `TriangularCat.java` of Listing 5.8. The program creates and draws a collection of triangles to render a picture that vaguely resembles a cat. A depiction of the cat drawing is given in Figure 5.9. When you finish appreciating this postmodern cat drawing, our introduction to the conditional statements of Java is complete.

---

†   Chapter 7 considers the `clone()` method that returns a duplicate of an object.

Listing 5.8   TriangularCat.java

```
1.  // Draw a cat
2.
3.  import java.awt.*;
4.  import javax.swing.*;
5.  import java.io.*;
6.
7.  public class TriangularCat {
8.      // main(): application entry point
9.      public static void main(String[] args) throws IOException {
10.         ColoredTriangle body = new ColoredTriangle(
11.             new Point(20, 110), new Point(190, 150),
12.             new Point(190, 65), Color.BLACK);
13.
14.         ColoredTriangle head = new ColoredTriangle(
15.             new Point(190, 90), new Point(270, 90),
16.             new Point(230, 30), Color.YELLOW);
17.
18.         ColoredTriangle leftEye = new ColoredTriangle(
19.             new Point(220, 50), new Point(215, 60),
20.             new Point(225, 60), Color.BLUE);
21.
22.         ColoredTriangle rightEye = new ColoredTriangle(
23.             new Point(240, 50), new Point(235, 60),
24.             new Point(245, 60), Color.BLUE);
25.
26.         ColoredTriangle mouth = new ColoredTriangle(
27.             new Point(215, 75), new Point(245, 80),
28.             new Point(245, 70), Color.BLUE);
29.
30.         ColoredTriangle backLegs = new ColoredTriangle(
31.             new Point(20, 110), new Point(25, 160),
32.             new Point(15, 160), Color.GRAY);
33.
34.         ColoredTriangle frontLegs = new ColoredTriangle(
35.             new Point(190, 150), new Point(195, 200),
36.             new Point(185, 200), Color.GRAY);
37.
38.         JFrame window = new JFrame("Triangular cat");
39.         window.setSize(285, 250);
40.         window.setVisible(true);
41.         Graphics g = window.getGraphics();
42.
43.         System.out.print("Enter any key when ready");
44.         System.in.read();
45.
46.         body.paint(g);
47.         head.paint(g);
48.         mouth.paint(g);
49.         leftEye.paint(g);
50.         rightEye.paint(g);
51.         backLegs.paint(g);
52.         frontLegs.paint(g);
53.     }
54. }
```

Figure 5.9   **Triangular cat.**

5.11   REVIEW

- A logical expression is an expression whose value is either the logical value true or the logical value false.
- There are three primary logical operators that we use to combine logic values into logical expressions. These logical operators are *and*, *or*, and *not*.
- A truth table is an easy way of indicating the conditions that make a logical operation true and which conditions make it false. A truth table lists all possible combinations of operand values and the result of the operation for each combination.
- The logical *and* operation is true only if both of its operands are true; otherwise, the operation is false.
- The logical *or* operation is true if at least one of its operands is true; otherwise, the operation is false.
- The logical *not* operation is true if its operand is false, and the operation is false if its operand is true.
- The Java logical type **boolean** has two symbolic literal constants **true** and **false** that correspond to logical true and false respectively. Although technically not keywords, **true** and **false** are reserved identifier literals.
- There are three **boolean** logical operators: &&, ||, and !. Operator && is used to perform an *and* operation, operator || is used to perform an *or* operation, and operator ! is used to perform a *not* operation.
- There are two equality operators == and !=. The == operator evaluates to **true** if both operand expressions have the same value, and it evaluates to **false** otherwise. Operator != evaluates to **true** if the two operand expressions have different values, and it evaluates to **false** otherwise.
- Java provides ordering operators for the primitive types. They are used to determine the relative size of two values. There are four ordering operators, <, >, <=, and >=. They correspond to the mathematical operators of $<$, $>$, $\leq$, and $\geq$. Together the equality and ordering operators are known as the relational operators.
- The not operator ! has the same high precedence as other unary operators. Among the binary operators, the relational and logical operators have lower precedence than the arithmetic operators and greater precedence than the assignment operators. Relational operators have greater precedence than the logical operators. Among the relational operators, the ordering operators have greater precedence than the equality operators. Among the logical operators, && has greater precedence than ||.
- When evaluating a logical operation, Java always evaluates the left operand before it evaluates the right operand. If the value of the operation can be determined from the left operand, then the right operand is not evaluated. This kind of evaluation is known as short-circuit evaluation.
- For **boolean** comparison purposes, the value of the constant **false** is less than the value of the constant **true**.
- For character comparison purposes, orderings are based on Unicode character representation.

- Programs generally should not test floating-point values for equality. Instead programs should test whether the values of interest are sufficiently close to each other to be considered the same. The underlying reason for this behavior is the finite precision of the floating-point types.

- The **if** statement has two forms. The simpler of the two forms has syntax

  if (*TestExpression*) *Action*

  When an **if** statement is reached within a program, the parenthetic expression *TestExpression* is evaluated. If *TestExpression* evaluates to **true**, *Action* is executed; otherwise, *Action* is not executed. Either way, program execution continues with the next statement in the program.

- The second form of the **if** statement deals with programming situations where one of two different actions is to be taken based on the value of a logical expression. This form of the **if** statement has syntax

  if (*TestExpression*) *Action*$_1$ **else** *Action*$_2$

  where *Action*$_1$ and *Action*$_2$ can each be either a single statement with a terminating semicolon (;) or a block of statements nested with left and right braces. When the **if-else** statement is executed, *TestExpression* is evaluated. If *TestExpression* evaluates to **true**, *Action*$_1$ is executed; otherwise, *Action*$_2$ is executed.

- A consistent indentation scheme makes the logic of a program more understandable to a reader, but it does not affect the translation of the program. Language syntax and semantics rules determine precisely how a program is to be translated.

- The == operator when applied to reference variables tests whether the variables refer to the same memory location.

- To test whether two objects have the same representation, use member method `equals()`.

- The **if-else-if** idiom is used to solve tasks requiring one of several actions to be executed depending on which **boolean** condition evaluates to **true**.

- When a **switch** statement is executed, its *SwitchExpression* is evaluated; if the value of that expression equals the value of a *CaseExpression* in that **switch** statement, then flow of control is transferred to the *Action*$_i$ associated with the matching *CaseExpression*$_i$. If no *CaseExpression* equals the value of the *SwitchExpression* and if a **default** case is supplied, then the **default** *Action*$_{n+1}$ code is executed. The last statement in an *Action* is normally a **break** statement. The **break** statement indicates that the **switch** statement has completed its task and that the flow of control should continue with the statement after the **switch** statement. If a **break** statement is not supplied, then the flow of control continues with the next statement within the **switch** statement itself.

SELF-TEST

S5.1　Produce a truth table for the logical operator *nand*. Operator *nand* is true if at least one of its operands is false.

S5.2　Consider the following code segment:

```java
if (i == j) {
    System.out.println("A");
}
else if ((i % j) < 3) {
    System.out.println("B");
}
else if (i < (j - 1)) {
    System.out.println("C");
}
else {
    System.out.println("D");
}
```

a) If i is 9 and j is 4, what is the output?

b) If i is 4 and j is 9, what is the output?

c) If i is 5 and j is 6, what is the output?

d) If i is 5 and j is 9, what is the output?

S5.3　What is output of the following code segment?

```java
int i = 5;
int j = 7;
int k = 6;
if ((i < j) || (k < 5)) {
    System.out.println("yes");
}
else {
    System.out.println("no");
}
if ((i < j) && (k < 5)) {
    System.out.println("yes");
}
else {
    System.out.println("no");
}
```

S5.4　Consider the following code fragment whose output is based on the values of **boolean** variables a, b, c, and d.

```java
if (a && b) {
    if (!c && !d) {
        System.out.println(1);
    }
    else if (!d) {
        System.out.println(2);
    }
    else {
        System.out.println(3);
    }
```

```
      }
      else if (c == d) {
         System.out.println(4);
      }
      else if (c) {
         System.out.println(5);
      }
      else {
         System.out.println(6);
      }
```

a) Give values for a, b, c, and d that cause the code fragment to display 1 to the standard output stream.

b) Give values for a, b, c, and d that cause the code fragment to display 2 to the standard output stream.

c) Give values for a, b, c, and d that cause the code fragment to display 3 to the standard output stream.

d) Give values for a, b, c, and d that cause the code fragment to display 4 to the standard output stream.

e) Give values for a, b, c, and d that cause the code fragment to display 5 to the standard output stream.

f) Give values for a, b, c, and d that cause the code fragment to display 6 to the standard output stream.

S5.5 Write a code segment that sets integer k to 3 if the integer m is less than 5 and j is less than 0; otherwise, k should be changed to 1 if m is not less than k.

S5.6 Convert the following code into a **switch** statement, where i, k, and n are **int** variables.

```
      if (i == 3) {
         n = 1;
         k = 5;
      }
      else if (i == 4) {
         n = 5;
      }
      else if (i == 6) {
         n = 6;
      }
      else {
         n = 0;
      }
```

S5.7 Implement a code segment that determines the relationship between the intervals b1 ... e1 and b2 ... e2 (i.e, are the intervals are the same, do they overlap, does one interval proceed the other).

S5.8 Implement a member method getPerimeter() for ColoredRectangle. The method returns the perimeter of the triangle. In your implementation you may find it convenient to use Point method distance(). For Point variables p and q, p.distance(q) returns the Euclidean distance between the Point objects referenced by p and q.

| 5.13 | **EXERCISES** |

5.1   Suppose the following definitions are in effect.

```
boolean p = true;
boolean q = false;
boolean r = false;
String s = "b";
String t = "b";
String u = t;
int i = 10;
int j = 0;
```

Evaluate the following expressions.

a) !p == q

b) s != t

c) t != u

d) s == u

e) t == u

f) s.equals(u)

g) t.equals(u)

h) r == (p && q)

i) q && (p || r)

j) q || (p && !r)

k) p && !q && !r || (p == !q)

l) s < t

m) s + t < t

n) i * j

5.2   Suppose the following definitions are in effect.

```
boolean p = false;
boolean q = true;
boolean r = true;
int i = 1;
int j = 0;
```

Evaluate the following expressions:

a) p && q || !p && !q

b) p || q && !p || !q

c) q == 1 || 0 < 1

d) 0 == 1 == true

e) p && (q || r)

f) ! ! p

g) false < true

h) j = i

5.3   Using the operator precedence rules, parenthesize the following expressions.

a) `1 + 2 == 3 * 4`

b) `1 + 2 == 3 * 4 && 5 / 6 == 7`

c) `p == q <= r`

d) `p < q == r`

e) `p == q || r`

f) `p == q && r`

g) `p || q && r || s`

In Exercise 5.4–5.11, i, j, k, m, and n are **int** variables.

5.4   Define an expression that evaluates to **true** when i equals j.

5.5   Define an expression that evaluates to **true** when i lies in the interval 6 … 9.

5.6   Define an expression that evaluates to **true** only when i is even and j is odd, or when i is odd and j is even.

5.7   Define an expression that evaluates to **true** only if the following conditions are all met: i is greater than 11, j is at most 28, and m and n have different values.

5.8   Define an expression that evaluates to **true** only if none of the following conditions are met: i plus j equals 30, i is less than 4, and i times j is greater than 54.

5.9   Define an expression that evaluates to **true** if any of the following conditions are met: i is twice the value of j, j is smaller than k but larger than n, or m is negative.

5.10 Write code segments that implement the following actions:

a) If i divided by j is 4, then i is set to 100.

b) If i times j is 8, then i is set to 50; otherwise, j is set to 60.

c) If i is less than j, then j is doubled; if instead i is even, then i is doubled; otherwise, both i and j are incremented by 1.

d) If both i and j are 0, then i is set 1 and j is set to 2; if instead only i is 0, then i is set to 5 and j is set to 10; if instead only j is 0, then i is set to 10 and j is set to 5; otherwise, both i and j are set to 4.

5.11 Consider the following **if** statement:

```
if ((i == 3) || (j == 4)) {
    System.out.println("yes");
}
else {
    System.out.println("no");
}
```

Are there values for i and j that cause the display of both "yes" and "no"? Why?

5.12 Assume the following definitions are in effect:

```
boolean p = false;
boolean q = true;
boolean r = true;
```

Consider the following expressions. Determine whether they have short-circuit evaluations and, if so, where.

a) `q && p && r`

b) `q && p || r`

c) `!q || (i != j)`

d) `(p || q && r) && (3 <= 4)`

e) `r || (p || !q || !r && (4 > 3))`

5.13 Consider the following code segment using **boolean** objects a, b, c, and d.

```
if (!c || d)
    if (a && c)
        System.out.println(1);
    else if (b)
        System.out.println(2);
    else
        System.out.println(3);
else if (!c == d)
    System.out.println(4);
else if (c)
    System.out.println(5);
else
    System.out.println(6);
```

a) Give values for a, b, c, and d that cause the code segment to display 1 to the standard output stream.

b) Give values for a, b, c, and d that cause the code segment to display 2 to the standard output stream.

c) Give values for a, b, c, and d that cause the code segment to display 3 to the standard output stream.

d) Give values for a, b, c, and d that cause the code segment to display 4 to the standard output stream.

e) Give values for a, b, c, and d that cause the code segment to display 5 to the standard output stream.

f) Give values for a, b, c, and d that cause the code segment to display 6 to the standard output stream.

5.14 Write the truth table that the following code segment computes.

```
if (p)
    operation = true;
else if (q)
    operation = false;
else
    operation = true;
```

5.15 Write the truth table that the following code segment computes.

```
if (p)
    if (q)
        operation = true;
    else
        operation = false;
else
    operation = false;
```

5.16 Write the truth table for the logical binary operation of isomorphism (*iso*). The operation evaluates to true if the operands evaluate to the same value; otherwise, *iso* evaluates to false. Is there a Java operator that computes *iso*? Explain.

5.17 Write the truth table for the logical binary operation of exclusive-or (*xor*). The operation evaluates to true if exactly one of its operands evaluates to true; otherwise, *xor* evaluates to false. Write a code segment that tests whether p *xor* q evaluates to **true**, where p and q are **boolean** variables.

5.18 Prove using truth tables the DeMorgan equivalence *not (p and q)* equals *(not p) or (not q)*

5.19 Provide the truth table for the following logical expressions:

a) *(not p) and q*

b) *p and ((not p) or q)*

5.20 If i is 4, what is the output of the following code segment?

```
switch (i) {
    case 1: case 2: case 3: {
        System.out.println("yes");
        break;
    }
    case 5: case 6:
        System.out.println("no");
        break;
    }
    case 10: case 11:
        System.out.println("maybe");
        break;
    }
    default:
        System.out.println("sometimes");
    }
}
```

5.21 If i is 7, what is the output of the following code segment?

```
switch (i) {
    case 1: case 2: case 3: {
        System.out.println("yes");
    }
    case 5: case 6: {
        System.out.println("no");
    }
    case 10: case 11: {
        System.out.println("maybe");
        break;
    }
    default: {
        System.out.println("sometimes");
    }
}
```

5.22 Develop a boolean expression that evaluates to **true** when a year is a leap year that does not use the unary operator !.

5.23 Search the Web to find the formula for validating a potential ISBN number, where an ISBN number is a book product code. Develop a program that reports when a user-specified value is a potential ISBN number.

5.24 Design and implement a program that extracts a user-specified line slope and intercept. The program should report whether the line is vertical.

5.25 Design and implement a program that extracts two user-specified line slopes and intercepts. The program should report whether the lines are orthogonal to each other.

5.26 Design and implement a program that extracts two user-specified x- and y-coordinates. The program should report the slope and y-intercept of the associated lines.

5.27 Design and implement a program that extracts the coefficients for a quadratic equation. The program should report the number of real and imaginary roots.

5.28 Design and implement a program that extracts two integer values as input. The program should display whether the inputs are both positive, both negative, or one positive and one negative.

5.29 Design and implement a program that extracts two floating-point values as input. The program should determine whether the difference in the two values is at most `Epsilon`, where `Epsilon` is a program-defined constant equal to 0.00001.

5.30 Suppose we want to sort four numbers. How many different orderings can there be?

5.31 Design and implement a program that sorts four input values.

5.32 Provide a code segment that prompts a user for an extracted value in the interval 0 ... 99. The segment then displays the value in words. For example, if the input value is 21, then twenty-one is displayed.

5.33 Design and implement a program that displays the absolute value of its input.

5.34 Design and implement a program that accepts a date as input. The program should display the date's position in that year. For example, if the date is 12 29 2006, then the displayed number is 363.

5.35 Design and implement a program `DateValidator.java` that reports whether a user-specified date is a valid date.

5.36 Reimplement the `ColoredRectangle` method `paint()` so that it resembles the `ColoredTriangle` method `paint()`. Your new implementation should make make the target a parameter to `paint()` and you should use `fillPolygon()` rather than `fillRect()`.

When solving Exercises 5.37–5.43, you may find it convenient to use `Point` method `distance()`. For `Point` variables p and q, `p.distance(q)` returns the Euclidean distance between the `Point` objects referenced by p and q.

5.37 Implement a **double** member method `getArea()` for `ColoredTriangle`. The method returns the area of its triangle. The area a of a triangle can be computed using Heron's formula: $a = \sqrt{s(s-a)(s-b)(s-c)}$, where s is one-half of the perimeter of the triangle and a, b, and c are the lengths of the three sides of the triangle.

5.38 Implement a **boolean** member method isEquilateral() for ColoredTriangle that returns whether its triangle is an equilateral triangle. A triangle is an equilateral triangle if all three sides of the triangle have the same length.

5.39 Implement a **boolean** member method isIsosceles() for ColoredTriangle that returns whether its triangle is an isosceles triangle. A triangle is isosceles if at least two sides of the triangle have the same length.

5.40 Implement a **boolean** member method isScalene() for ColoredTriangle that returns whether its triangle is a scalene triangle. A triangle is scalene if sides of the triangle are all of different lengths.

5.41 Implement a **boolean** member method isRight() for ColoredTriangle that returns whether its triangle is a right triangle. A triangle is right if there are two side lengths where the sum of their squares is equal to the square of the other side length.

5.42 Implement a **boolean** member method isObtuse() for ColoredTriangle that returns whether its triangle is an obtuse triangle. A triangle is obtuse if there are two side lengths where the sum of the their squares is less than the square of the other side length.

5.43 Implement a **boolean** member method isAcute() for ColoredTriangle that returns whether its triangle is an acute triangle. A triangle is acute if it is neither right nor obtuse.

5.14   PROGRAMMING PROJECT — MEDICAL ASSISTANT

In this programming case study you develop a very basic tool for medical diagnosis. Diagnostic tools are examples of *expert systems*. An expert system is a program that behaves like a human expert for a particular application domain. The application domain in this case study contains the likely causes of a fever.

> The objective of this case study is to practice using the **if** and **if-else** statements when problem solving

Expert systems are typically *rule-based*, where a rule has two components. The first component is the conditions under which the rule is applicable; the second component is the recommended action under those conditions.

A rule-based system performs a series of queries to determine the situation at hand so that it can determine which of its rules apply. The queries are done in a manner that uses the responses from previous queries to determine future queries. Such a process enables the program to determine quickly the specifics of the situation.

Because the tool that you are developing is concerned only with suggesting the possible cause of a fever, the first rule to consider is

No fever $\Rightarrow$ *no recommendation* (i.e., no fever implies no recommendation).

where $\Rightarrow$ is the mathematical symbol for implication. If the response to the initial query indicates the user does not have a fever, then the tool should announce no recommendation can be made. If the initial query indicates that the user does have a fever, then a follow-up query is asked. Based on the response to that query, other queries are made.

As a matter of professional ethics before going further, we make the disclaimer that the program you are asked to develop is intended solely for pedagogical purposes. The design and development of a true diagnostic tool requires interaction with medical personnel, testing in controlled environments to determine the validity of the program, and official certification. For information on the professional code for computer scientists, visit the ACM website `www.acm.org`. The ACM is the major professional society of computer scientists.

PROBLEM STATEMENT

The tool you design and produce should be based on the diagram in Figure 5.10. This diagram is a simplification of the American Medical Association's (AMA) diagram/procedure for dealing with fevers in their reference The American Medical Association Family Medical Guide: Third Edition, C.B. Clayman (medical editor), Random House, ISBN 0-679-41290-5, 1994.

SAMPLE OUTPUT

A sample program run is depicted in Figure 5.11.

IMPLEMENTATION

Your program's name should be `FeverDiagnosis.java`. The program should start by displaying a legend that provides introductory information on its use and limitations. In particular, your tool should indicate that the program performs no true diagnostic activity, no decisions should be made based on the tool's analysis and that if the user really has a fever, the user should contact her or his doctor.

After displaying the legend, the tool should then begin a querying process that determines the user's situation. Upon making a determination, the diagnostic analysis should be displayed. As part of this display, list the symptoms that caused that recommendation to be displayed. For example, suppose the user had responded yes to fever, no to coughing, yes to headache, and yes to at least one of the following: pain when bending your head forward, nausea or vomiting, bright light hurting your eyes, drowsiness, or confusion. It is these symptoms that indicate the possibility of meningitis. In this situation, an output similar to the one depicted in Figure 5.11 should occur.

TESTING

Because there is a very limited number of scenarios that your program must handle, you should test your program completely to verify that it correctly implements the process in Figure 5.10. To make sure that your testing is complete, individually list and test the response sequence associated with each possible program outcome. For example, the response sequence (yes, yes, yes,) indicating yes to fever, yes to coughing, and yes to shortness of breath or wheezing or coughing phlegm should cause your program to indicate the possibilities of pneumonia or infection to airways. And the response sequence (yes, yes, no, yes) indicating yes to fever, yes to coughing, no to shortness of breath or wheezing or coughing phlegm, and yes to headache should cause your program to indicate the possibility of a viral infection.

Figure 5.10 Procedure to diagnose the cause of a fever.

Figure 5.11   **Sample run of FeverDiagnosis,java**

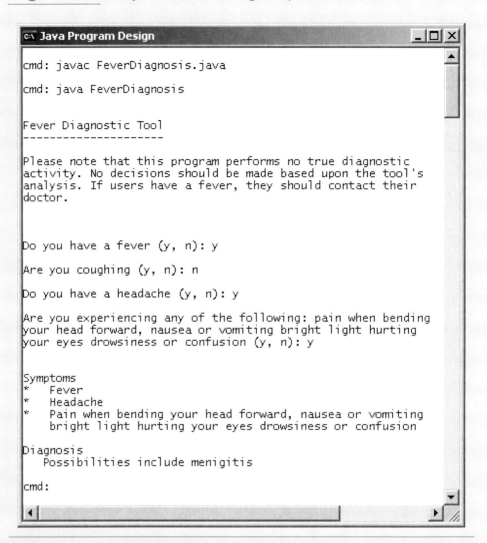

```
cmd: javac FeverDiagnosis.java

cmd: java FeverDiagnosis


Fever Diagnostic Tool
---------------------

Please note that this program performs no true diagnostic
activity. No decisions should be made based upon the tool's
analysis. If users have a fever, they should contact their
doctor.


Do you have a fever (y, n): y

Are you coughing (y, n): n

Do you have a headache (y, n): y

Are you experiencing any of the following: pain when bending
your head forward, nausea or vomiting bright light hurting
your eyes drowsiness or confusion (y, n): y


Symptoms
*    Fever
*    Headache
*    Pain when bending your head forward, nausea or vomiting
     bright light hurting your eyes drowsiness or confusion

Diagnosis
     Possibilities include menigitis

cmd:
```

REFERENCES

For information on expert systems in general see

- *Introduction to Expert Systems*, P. Jackson, Addison-Wesley Longman, ISBN: 0-201-87686-8, 1998.

For information on medical expert systems, see

- *Rationalizing Medical Work: Decision-support Techniques and Medical Practices*, M. Berg, MIT Press, ISBN: 0-262-02417-9, 1997.

5.15 **SELF-TEST ANSWERS**

S5.1 A truth table for the logical operator *nand*.

p	q	p nand q
false	false	true
false	true	true
true	false	true
true	true	false

S5.2 For the code segment,

    a) If i is 9 and j is 4, the output is B.

    b) If i is 4 and j is 9, the output is C.

    c) If i is 5 and j is 6, the output is D.

    d) If i is 5 and j is 9, the output is C.

S5.3 The output of the code segment is

```
yes
no
```

S5.4

    a) With a = **true**, b = **true**; c = **false**; and d = **false** the segment outputs 1.

    b) With a = **true**, b = **true**; c = **true**; and d = **false** the segment outputs 2.

    c) With a = **true**, b = **true**; c = **false**; d = **true** the segment outputs 3.
       With a = **true**, b = **true**; c = **true**; d = **true** the segment outputs 3.

    d) With a = **true**, b = **false**; c = **false**; and d = **false** the segment outputs 4.
       With a = **true**, b = **false**; c = **true**; and d = **true** the segment outputs 4.
       With a = **false**, b = **false**; c = **false**; and d = **false** the segment outputs 4.
       With a = **false**, b = **false**; c = **true**; and d = **true** the segment outputs 4.
       With a = **false**, b = **true**; c = **false**; and d = **false** the segment outputs 4.
       With a = **false**, b = **true**; c = **true**; and d = **true** the segment outputs 4.

    e) With a = **true**, b = **false**; c = **true**; and d = **false** the segment outputs 5.
       With a = **false**, b = **false**; c = **true**; and d = **false** the segment outputs 5.
       With a = **false**, b = **true**; c = **true**; and d = **false** the segment outputs 5.

    f) With a = **true**, b = **false**; c = **false**; and d = **true** the segment outputs 6.
       With a = **false**, b = **false**; c = **false**; and d = **true** the segment outputs 6.
       With a = **false**, b = **true**; c = **false**; and d = **true** the segment outputs 6.

S5.5 The code segment could be

```
if ((m < 5) && (j < 0)) {
    k = 3;
}
else if (! (m < k)) {
    k = 1;
}
```

S5.6 An equivalent **switch** statement would be

```
switch (i) {
   case 3: {
      n = 1;
      k = 5;
      break;
   }
   case 4: {
      n = 5;
      break;
   }
   case 6: {
      n = 6;
      break;
   }
   default: {
      n = 0;
   }
}
```

S5.7 A code segment could be

```
String i1 = "Interval " + b1 + " ... " + e1;
String i1 = "Interval " + b2 + " ... " + e2;
if (e1 < b2) {
   System.out.println(i1 + " precedes " + i2);
}
else if (e2 < b1) {
   System.out.println(i2 + " precedes " + i1);
}
else if ((b1 == b2) && (e1 == e2)) {
   System.out.println(i1 + " equals " + i2);
}
else {
   System.out.println(i1 + " intersects " + i2);
}
```

S5.8 An implementation of getPerimeter() could be

```
// getPerimeter(): perimeter facilitator
public double getPerimeter() {
   Point v1 = getPoint(1);
   Point v2 = getPoint(2);
   Point v3 = getPoint(3);

   double a = v1.distance(v2);
   double b = v2.distance(v3);
   double c = v3.distance(v1);

   return a + b + c;
}
```

6 ITERATION

Thus far, our programs have had the property that each statement in the program is run at most once. In this chapter, we consider the **while**, **for**, and **do-while** *looping constructs* that control how many times a statement list is *iterated* (executed). Loops make programs much more powerful and capable of solving significant problems. Mastering the design and implementation of loops is an important part of a programmer's education.

OBJECTIVES

- Introduce the **while** loop.
  - Introduce the **for** loop.
  - Introduce the **do-while** loop.
  - Demonstrate the importance of looping constructs in problem solving.
  - Encourage a systematic approach to loop design.
- Provide the means for doing simple file processing.

6.1   WHILE STATEMENT

Consider the following problem statement.

> *Prompt a user to supply a list of positive numbers, one per line. The end of the list is to be indicated with a negative number. Report the average of the positive numbers.*

This straightforward task cannot be solved using the Java statements that we have already introduced. The reason is that the list size is unknown.

If we know the size of the list, we can supply sufficient code to extract and sum all of inputs (e.g., Program `AverageFive.java` of Listing 2.11 determines the average of a list with five values).

However, without knowing the size of the list, we cannot guarantee there would be sufficient code to extract and sum all of the inputs. To process a list of unknown size, we need an iterative construct that enables the execution of statements to occur multiple times.

Java provides several iterative constructs. Our examination begins with the **while** statement.

Program `NumberAverage.java` of Listing 6.1 uses a **while** statement to solve our list processing problem. Its solution form or algorithmic *pattern* is one that you often see in programming.

```
Prepare for processing
Get the first input
While there is an input to process, repeatedly do {
   Process current input
   Get the next input
}
Perform final processing
```

For `NumberAverage.java`, an input is processed both by adding its value to a variable `valueSum` that maintains a running total of the previously processed values and by incrementing a variable `valuesProcessed` that records the number of processed inputs. The iteration ends when a newly extracted input is determined to be a negative number.

A sample run of program `NumberAverage.java` follows.

```
Enter positive numbers one per line.  Indicate the end of the
list with a negative number.
4.5
0.5
1.1
-1
Average: 2.1
```

To understand how the **while** statement works, let's trace through the actions of program `NumberAverage.java` as it produced this sample run.

Listing 6.1 *NumberAverage.java*

```
1.  // Compute average of a list of positive numbers
2.
3.  import java.io.*;
4.
5.  public class NumberAverage {
6.     // main(): application entry point
7.     public static void main(String[] args) throws IOException {
8.        // set up the list processing
9.        BufferedReader stdin = new BufferedReader(
10.            new InputStreamReader( System.in ) );
11.
12.        int valuesProcessed = 0;   // no values processed so far
13.        double valueSum = 0;        // running total
14.
15.        // prompt user for values
16.        System.out.println("Enter positive numbers one per line.  "
17.           + "Indicate the end of the\nlist with a negative number.");
18.
19.        // get first value
20.        double value = Double.parseDouble(stdin.readLine());
21.
22.        // process values one-by-one
23.        while (value >= 0) {
24.           // add value to running total
25.           valueSum += value;
26.           // processed another value
27.           ++valuesProcessed;
28.           // prepare for next iteration --- get next value
29.           value = Double.parseDouble(stdin.readLine());
30.        }
31.
32.        // display result
33.        if (valuesProcessed > 0) {
34.           // compute and display average
35.           double average = valueSum / valuesProcessed;
36.           System.out.println("Average: " + average);
37.        }
38.        else {
39.           System.out.println("No list to average");
40.        }
41.     }
42.  }
```

Method main() begins by defining a BufferedReader variable stdin to represent the standard input stream.

```
// set up the list processing
BufferedReader stdin = new BufferedReader(
    new InputStreamReader( System.in ) );
```

It also defines the variables valuesProcessed and valueSum that are used in the processing of an input.

```
int valuesProcessed = 0;   // no values processed so far
double valueSum = 0;        // running total
```

The role of `valuesProcessed` is to indicate how many values have been processed. Because no values have been processed yet, `valuesProcessed` is initialized to 0. Variable `valueSum` maintains the running total of the input values processed so far. Therefore, it is initialized to 0.

By properly updating variables `valuesProcessed` and `valueSum` whenever an input value is extracted, the average of the inputs can be computed. The average will be equal to `valueSum / valuesProcessed`.

The program next issues a prompt that tells the user both how to supply the values *and* how to indicate that there are no more values to consider.

```
// prompt user for values
System.out.println("Enter positive numbers one per line. "
   + "Indicate the end of the\nlist with a negative number.");
```

In particular, the user is told that positive numbers are to be entered, one per line. The user is also told that a negative number means that the list is complete. In programming parlance, this end of list value is called a *sentinel*.

The extraction of the values and their processing then can proceed. The first value is extracted before the loop.

```
// get the first value   ←——————— First value acquired before the loop starts
double value = Double.parseDouble(stdin.readLine());
```

The value is extracted before the **while** loop because the statements that make up the action of a loop have been designed to process a list value. They are not intended for dealing with the sentinel.

In general, a **while** loop has the following form

When a **while** statement is executed, its test expression is evaluated first. If the expression evaluates **true**, its *body* is executed, where the body is the action of the **while** statement. The evaluation process then is repeated. If the expression reevaluates to **true**, the body is executed again. This process is called *looping*, and it continues until the test expression evaluates to **false**. At that point, execution continues with the next statement in the program.

The test expression for the **while** loop of program NumberAverage.java is (value >= 0). It will be the case for each iteration of the loop that if the test expression is **true**, then there is a value that needs to be included in the average.

```
// process values one-by-one
while (value >= 0) {
    // add value to running total
    valueSum += value;
    // processed another value
    ++valuesProcessed;
    // prepare to iterate -- get the next input
    value = Double.parseDouble(stdin.readLine());
}
```

Test expression is evaluated at the start of each iteration of the loop. Its value indicates whether there is a number to process

If test expression is true, these statements are executed. Afterward, the test expression is reevaluated and the process repeats

For this program run, variable value is initially 4.5. Therefore, the test expression evaluates to **true** and the body of the loop is executed. Because the processing of a value requires several statements, the **while** loop body is surrounded by braces. However, even if the action was a single statement, our programming style is to use braces *always*.

As the **while** loop body begins its execution, variables valuesProcessed, value-Sum, and value have representation

valuesProcessed	0
valueSum	0.0
value	4.5

The first statement in the **while** loop body increments valueSum by value.

```
// add value to running total
valueSum += value;
```

Because this addition completes the processing of the current input, variable values-Processed is incremented.

```
// processed another value
++valuesProcessed;
```

Variables valuesProcessed, valueSum, and value now have representation

valuesProcessed	1
valueSum	4.5
value	4.5

Figure 6.1   Semantic representation of a while statement.

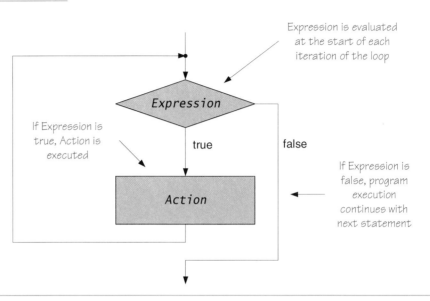

Although the processing of the current list value is completed, the **while** loop needs to perform one more action—it must update value with the next input. The update ensures that the **while** loop is ready for another evaluation of its test expression.

```
// prepare for next iteration --- get next value
value = Double.parseDouble(stdin.readLine());
```

Update value to prepare for next evaluation of the test expression

For the program run, the input extraction results in variable value being assigned 0.5. With the assignment, variables valuesProcessed, valueSum, and value now have representation

valuesProcessed	1
valueSum	4.5
value	0.5

The **while** loop is now ready to repeat, the repetition causes the **while** loop test expression (value >= 0) to be reevaluated. Because the expression evaluates to **true** (0.5 is greater than or equal to 0), the **while** loop body iterates. (See Figure 6.1 for a depiction of the execution of a **while** loop in general.)

The first statement in the body of loop again increments valueSum by value.

```
// add value to running total
valueSum += value;
```

Because this addition completes the processing of the current input, variable values-Processed is incremented.

```
// processed another value
++valuesProcessed;
```

Variables valuesProcessed, valueSum, and value now have representation

valuesProcessed	2
valueSum	5.0
value	0.5

Variable value then is updated with the next input value. The update again ensures that the **while** loop is ready for another evaluation of the test expression.

```
// prepare for next iteration --- get next value
value = Double.parseDouble(stdin.readLine());
```

For the program run, the input extraction results in variable value being assigned 1.3. With the assignment, variables valuesProcessed, valueSum, and value now have representation

valuesProcessed	2
valueSum	5.0
value	1.3

The **while** loop test expression (value >= 0) then is reevaluated. Because the expression still evaluates to **true** (1.3 is greater than or equal to 0), the **while** loop body iterates.

The first statement in loop again increments valueSum by value

```
// add value to running total
valueSum += value;
```

and the next statement increments variable valuesProcessed.

```
// processed another value
++valuesProcessed;
```

The assignments cause valuesProcessed, valueSum, and value to have representation

valuesProcessed	3
valueSum	6.3
value	1.3

Variable value then is updated with the next input value. For the program run, the input extraction value results in variable value being assigned –1.

```
// prepare for next iteration --- get next value
value = Double.parseDouble(stdin.readLine());
```

Hand-checking

The tracing of the execution of a method by hand is an important program debugging technique. Hand-checking code can give insight into how a method works.

With this assignment, variables `valuesProcessed`, `valueSum`, and `value` now have representation

valuesProcessed	3
valueSum	6.3
value	-1

The **while** loop test expression (`value >= 0`) then is reevaluated. Because –1 is not greater than or equal to 0, the expression evaluates to **false** and the loop is ended.

The list values have now all been processed and the average can be computed and displayed.

```
// display result
if (valuesProcessed > 0) {
   // compute and display average
   double average = valueSum / valuesProcessed;
   System.out.println("Average: " + average);
}
else {
   System.out.println("No list to average");
}
```

Although the sample run processed a list with three values, program `NumberAverage` works for lists of any size. You are encouraged to hand-check the program with other inputs.

We now turn our attention to another task whose solution makes use of a **while** statement. The task is to convert user-supplied text entered into lower case.

Our solution to this text conversion problem is program `LowerCaseDisplay.java` of Listing 6.2. The input/output behavior of a sample program run is shown in Figure 6.2.

Program `LowerCaseDisplay.java` follows the same algorithmic form as `NumberAverage.java`. What differs between the programs is how the processing proceeds.

```
Prepare for processing
Get the first input
While there is an input to process, repeatedly do {
   Process current input
   Get the next input
}
Perform final processing
```

To prepare for its input processing, program `LowerCaseDisplay.java` defines a String variable `converted`.

```
String converted = "";
```

Listing 6.2   **LowerCaseDisplay.java**

```
1.  // Echo input back in lowercase
2.
3.  import java.io.*;
4.
5.  public class LowerCaseDisplay {
6.      public static void main(String[] args) throws IOException {
7.          // prepare for conversion
8.          BufferedReader stdin = new BufferedReader(
9.              new InputStreamReader(System.in));
10.
11.         System.out.println("Enter input to be converted:");
12.
13.         String converted = "";
14.
15.         // get the first input
16.         String currentLine = stdin.readLine();
17.
18.         // process lines one-by-one
19.         while (currentLine != null) {
20.             // process current line
21.             String currentConversion = currentLine.toLowerCase();
22.             converted += (currentConversion + "\n");
23.
24.             // prepare for next iteration -- get next input line
25.             currentLine = stdin.readLine();
26.         }
27.
28.         // display result
29.         System.out.println("\nThe conversion is:\n" + converted);
30.     }
31. }
```

Variable `converted` maintains the input text that has already been converted. Because no text has been converted initially, the variable references initially a string of length 0 (i.e., an *empty string*).

The processing of input values begins with the definition of `String` variable `currentLine` in line 16.

```
// get the first input
String currentLine = stdin.readLine();
```

If the user provides text, then `currentLine` is initialized with the first line from the standard input stream. If instead, the user indicates that they are not providing an input, then `currentLine` is initialized with the value **null**.

As Figure 6.2 shows, an empty line is not an indication that no text is being provided. Instead, an empty line corresponds to an empty string. To indicate that no more text is being provided, the user must enter an operating system-dependent escape sequence (sentinel). The Windows sentinel value is `Ctrl+z` and for most other operating systems it is `Ctrl+d`. For historic reasons regarding earlier programming languages, software developers commonly refer to the sentinel value as *end-of-file*.

Figure 6.2   **Sample run of LowerCaseDisplay.java.**

An empty line
was entered

A Ctrl+z was
entered. It is the
Windows escape
sequence for
indicating
end-of-file

With the initialization of `currentLine`, the **while** loop processing begins.

```
// process lines one-by-one
while (currentLine != null) {
    // process current line
    String currentConversion = currentLine.toLowerCase();
    converted += (currentConversion + "\n");

    // prepare for next iteration -- get next input line
    currentLine = stdin.readLine();
}
```

```
// display result
System.out.println("\nThe conversion is:\n" + converted);
```

The **while** test expression evaluates the value of `currentLine`.

```
while (currentLine != null) { // process current value
```

If test expression (`currentLine != null`) evaluates to **true**, then `currentLine` references a string in need of processing. If the test expression evaluates to **false**, then end-of-file has been reached. Thus, the **while** loop iterates only if there is a nonempty text line to process.

The processing of the current line requires that variable `converted` be updated. Its representation must be appended with the lower case conversion of the current line.

The conversion is produced by `String` member method `toLowerCase()`.

```
String currentConversion = currentLine.toLowerCase();
```

The conversion result initializes a `String` variable `currentConversion`.

The String append assignment operator += then uses that value in an update of variable converted.

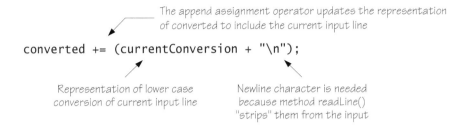

The append assignment operator updates the representation of converted to include the current input line

```
converted += (currentConversion + "\n");
```

Representation of lower case conversion of current input line

Newline character is needed because method readLine() "strips" them from the input

The append assignment completes the processing of the current line. To prepare for the next iteration of the loop, another input stream extraction is attempted.

```
// prepare for next iteration -- get next input line
currentLine = stdin.readLine();
```

If the extraction is successful, variable currentLine references the next input value; otherwise, its value is **null** indicating end-of-file.

The **while** test expression then is reevaluated. If the extraction was successful, then the test expression evaluates to **true** and the loop body iterates to process the next input line. However, if end-of-file was indicated, then the test expression evaluates to **false** and the loop terminates.

When the loop is finished, the program displays the converted text.

```
// display result
System.out.println("\nThe conversion is:\n" + converted);
```

Although the **while** statement has sufficient flexibility to handle all iteration needs, Java provides two other iterative statements—the **for** and **do-while**. Programmers tend to use the three iterative statements for different types of tasks.

Loop design

It is especially important when you design a loop that you understand its purpose and its effects on other parts of the programs. Some good questions to consider in your design and analysis are the following.

- What initialization is necessary for the loop's test expression?
- What initialization is necessary for the loop's processing?
- What causes the loop to terminate?
- What actions should the loop perform?
- What actions are necessary to prepare for the next iteration of the loop?
- What conditions are true and what conditions are false when the loop is terminated?
- When the loop completes what actions are need to prepare for subsequent program processing?

The **while** statement tends to be used when the number of necessary iterations is unknown. The **for** statement tends to be used when the number of iterations is known.

The **do-while** tends to be used when at least one iteration is necessary but the number of additional iterations is unknown. We next consider the **for** statement.

6.2 FOR STATEMENT

The following annotated code segment demonstrates a **for** statement in use. The segment displays the value of 2^i for i in the interval 0 … 4. That is, the segment displays the values 1, 2, 4, 8, 16.

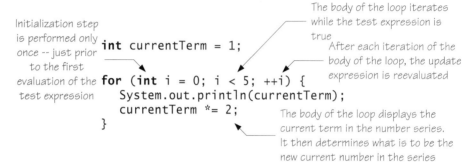

The code segment begins by defining an **int** variable currentTerm, which represents the current term to be displayed in the number series.

```
int currentTerm = 1;
```

The execution of the **for** loop then begins. There are four parts to a **for** loop, the first three of which occur within the parentheses that follow the keyword **for**. In order, these parts are the *initialization step*, the *test expression*, and the *update step*. The fourth part is the *body of the loop* and it occurs immediately after the parentheses.

The initialization step is performed only once—at the start of the execution of the loop.

Next, the test expression is evaluated. If the test expression is initially **false**, then execution immediately continues with the next statement in the program. If the expression is **true**, the body of the loop is executed and then the update step is performed. The update step is permitted to be an assignment, method invocation, or omitted.

Figure 6.3   **Semantic representation of a for statement.**

Every part has a purpose

Programmers tend to use the initialization step to do the work that is required to make sensible the first evaluation of the test expression and tend to use the update step to make sensible the next evaluation of the test expression.

The test expression then is reevaluated. If the expression is again **true**, the execution of the loop body and update step is iterated. This process continues until the test expression evaluates to **false**. Execution then continues with the next statement in the program.

To better under the **for** loop, let's trace through the execution of the **for** loop from our example. (Its semantics are depicted in Figure 6.3.)

```
for (int i = 0; i < 5; ++i) {
   System.out.println(currentTerm);
   currentTerm *= 2;
}
```

The initialization step of the **for** loop defines and initializes an **int** variable i. In traditional programming terminology, i is known as the *index variable*—its value changes with each iteration. The value of i reflects the index of the current term in the number series. Because i is initialized to 0, variables currentTerm and i have representation

The test expression i < 5 determines if there are terms in the number series still needing to be displayed. If i is less than 5, then i is indexing a term that needs displaying. Because 0 is less than 5, the test expression evaluates initially to **true**.

The body of **for** loop displays currentTerm and then scales currentTerm by 2. The scaling causes currentTerm to represent the next term in the number series.

```
System.out.println(currentTerm);
currentTerm *= 2;
```

The output produced thus far is

```
1
```

The upstate step then is executed, causing index i to be incremented by 1. Variables currentTerm and i now have representation

The loop then reevaluates the test expression i < 5. Because 1 is less than 5, the **for** loop body is iterated. In the loop body, currentTerm is redisplayed and rescaled by 2. The result is that currentTerm has value 4. The output produced thus far is

```
1
2
```

The update step ++i then is performed, causing index i to be incremented by 1. Variables currentTerm and i now have representation.

The loop then reevaluates the expression i < 5. Because 2 is less than 5, the **for** loop body is iterated. In the body, currentTerm is redisplayed and rescaled. The result is that currentTerm has value 8. The output produced thus far is

```
1
2
4
```

The update step ++i then is performed, causing index i to be incremented by 1. Variables currentTerm and i now have representation.

currentTerm	8
i	3

The loop then reevaluates the expression i < 5. Because 3 is less than 5, the **for** loop body iterates again. The body of the loop redisplays and rescales currentTerm. The new value of currentTerm is 16. The output produced thus far is

```
1
2
4
8
```

The update step ++i then is performed, causing index i to be incremented by 1. Variables currentTerm and i now have representation

currentTerm	16
i	4

The loop then reevaluates the expression i < 5. Because 4 is less than 5, the **for** loop body iterates again. The body of the loop redisplays and rescales currentTerm. The new value of currentTerm is 32. The output produced thus far is

```
1
2
4
8
16
```

The update step ++i then is performed, causing index i to be incremented by 1. Variables currentTerm and i now have representation

currentTerm	32
i	5

The loop then reevaluates the expression i < 5. Because 5 is not less than 5, the test expression evaluates to **false** and the loop is completed.

Infinite loops

All of the loop examples in this chapter include some action that causes the iteration statement to complete eventually. Without such an occurrence, the programs would have what is known as an *infinite loop*—they would continue to execute until some operating system command eventually terminated them. To avoid such a problem in your programs, make sure that you understand what is going on in your iteration statements. In particular, make sure that your iteration statements are designed to terminate.

6.2.1   INDEX VARIABLE SCOPE

Suppose we modified our code segment to display the value of i after the **for** loop has executed. What value gets displayed?

```
int currentTerm = 2;

for (int i = 0; i < 5; ++i) {
    System.out.println(currentTerm);
    currentTerm *= 2;
}

System.out.println("i is " + i);
```

This question is a trick. The code segment does not compile. The *scope* of the index variable is limited to the **for** loop. Conceptually, i is a variable that is local only to the loop. We consider the notion of scope in more detail in Chapter 7.

6.2.2   COMPUTING THE NUMBER OF COMBINATIONS

Our next **for** loop example makes use of the products of nonnegative integers called *factorials*. Let *n* be a nonnegative integer, then the product of the integers 1 through *n* is denoted as *n*! (pronounced "en-factorial"). Mathematically, *n*! has definition

$$n! = \begin{cases} 1 & \text{if } n = 0 \\ 1 \times 2 \times \ldots \times n & \text{if } n \geq 1 \end{cases}$$

The computing of *n*! is straightforward with a **for** loop.

```
int nFactorial = 1;
for (int i = 2; i <= n; ++i) {
    nFactorial *= i;
}
```

In the preceding code segment, variable nFactorial is used to store the solution. An initial value of 1 ensures that nFactorial is set correctly for n equal to 0 or 1.

The **for** loop initialization step defines an index variable i that represents the next factor by which nFactorial needs to be multiplied. Index i is initialized to 2—the first factor required in a factorial computation.

The test expression i <= n determines whether i is part of n!. If it is, then the factor is used to scale nFactorial. Thus, the **for** loop considers in turn each of the factors 2, 3, ..., and n. When the loop is finished, nFactorial is set to the desired value.

Several factorial computations are performed by program Combination.java of Listing 6.3. Program Combination.java uses those computations to determine the number of different combinations that can be made by choosing n objects from a set of m objects. For example, with a standard deck of 52 playing cards there are 2,598,960 different possible poker hands that can be constructed by choosing 5 of the 52 cards.

Listing 6.3   **Combination.java**

```
1.  // Compute C(m,n) for user-specified m and n
2.
3.  import java.io.*;
4.
5.  public class Combination{
6.      // main(): application entry point
7.      public static void main(String[] args) throws IOException {
8.          // set input stream
9.          BufferedReader stdin = new BufferedReader(
10.             new InputStreamReader( System.in ) );
11.
12.         // prompt and extract user inputs
13.         System.out.print("Enter number of distinct objects");
14.         int m = Integer.parseInt( stdin.readLine() );
15.         System.out.print("Enter desired subset size");
16.         int n = Integer.parseInt( stdin.readLine() );
17.
18.         // compute the three needed factorials
19.         int mFactorial = 1;
20.         for (int i = 2; i <= m; ++i) {
21.             mFactorial *= i;
22.         }
23.
24.         int nFactorial = 1;
25.         for (int i = 2; i <= n; ++i) {
26.             nFactorial *= i;
27.         }
28.
29.         int mDiffNFactorial = 1;
30.         for (int i = 2; i <= m - n; ++i) {
31.             mDiffNFactorial *= i;
32.         }
33.
34.         // compute and displays combinations
35.         int combinations = mFactorial
36.             / (nFactorial * mDiffNFactorial);
37.
38.         System.out.println("We can make " + combinations
39.             + " different combinations when choosing " + n
40.             + " objects from " + m + " different objects");
41.     }
42. }
```

The number of different combinations that can be made by choosing *n* objects from a set of *m* objects is written mathematically as $C(m, n)$. The formula for $C(m, n)$ is

$$C(m, n) = \frac{m!}{(m - n)!n!}$$

The first **for** loop in program Combination.java computes m!.

```
int mFactorial = 1;
for (int i = 2; i <= m; ++i) {
    mFactorial *= i;
}
```

and the second loop computes n!.

```
int nFactorial = 1;
for (int i = 2; i <= n; ++i) {
   nFactorial *= i;
}
```

and the third loop computes (m-n)!.

```
int mDiffNFactorial = 1;
for (int i = 2; i <= m - n; ++i) {
    mDiffNFactorial *= i;
}
```

The same but different

Although each of the **for** loops in Listing 6.3 uses an index variable i, they are different variables with the same name. The scope of a **for** loop index variable is limited to the loop.

Using the values mFactorial, nFactorial, and mDiffNFactorial we can compute and display the number of combinations.

```
int combinations = mFactorial
  / (nFactorial * mDiffNFactorial);

System.out.println("We can make " + combinations
   + " different combinations when choosing " + n
   + " objects from " + m + " different objects");
```

We now consider the remaining Java iterative statement—the **do-while** statement.

| 6.3 | DO-WHILE STATEMENT |

In some situations an action needs to be done at least once and possibly multiple times. For such situations, a program can use the **do-while** statement. The statement has the form

A **do-while** loop *begins* by executing the body of its loop. *Afterward*, the test expression is evaluated. If the test expression evaluates to **true**, then the body is repeated. This process continues until test expression evaluates to **false**. The **do-while** semantics are demonstrated in Figure 6.4.

Figure 6.4 **Semantic representation of a do-while statement.**

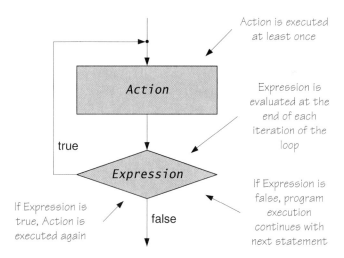

In the first example of this section, a **do-while** loop is used to display individually the digits of an **int** variable number. For pedagogic purposes, assume number has the value 141932.

```
do {
    int digit = number % 10;
    System.out.println(digit);
    number = number / 10;
} while (number != 0);
```

The current digit is acquired using the modulus operator %. After displaying the digit, number is divided by 10 to remove that digit from further consideration. Once number has value 0, all digits have been displayed. The following output is a sample run of the code segment.

```
2
3
9
1
4
1
```

Some programmers would be tempted to use a **while** loop rather than a **do-while** loop for this task. However, the **while** loop implementation that those programmers probably would consider first does not work.

```
while (n != 0) {
    int digit = n % 10;
    System.out.println(digit);
    n = n / 10;
}
```

While versus do-while

Use a **while** loop when the action can occur zero or more times; use a **do-while** loop when the action can occur one or more times.

This loop does not always produce the correct output. In particular, it does not handle correctly the case when n is 0. For this case, the **while** loop does not produce any output. However, the correct output is a single line displaying a 0.

The **do-while** is useful particularly in the processing of a user reply to a prompt. For example, the following code segment repeatedly issues a prompt and then expects a single character reply indicating yes or no. If a reply is not given, the code segment assumes no. If an incorrect response is given, it is ignored and the process is repeated.

```java
BufferedReader stdin = new BufferedReader(
    new InputStreamReader( System.in ) );

char reply = 'n';

boolean stillDeciding = true;

do {
    System.out.print("Decision (y, n): ");
    String response = stdin.readLine();
    if (response == null) {
        stillDeciding = false;
    }
    else if (response.length() == 1) {
        reply = response.charAt(0);
        reply = Character.toLowerCase(reply);
        if ((reply == 'y') || (reply == 'n')) {
            stillDeciding = false;
        }
    }
} while (stillDeciding);
```

The code segment defines a **char** variable reply to indicate whether the user's reply indicated yes or no. Variable reply is initialized to 'n' (i.e., no is the assumed response). A **boolean** variable stillDeciding is defined also. The variable indicates whether the user has yet to make a decision. Its initialize value is **true**, because the decision has not yet been determined.

```java
char reply = 'n';
boolean stillDeciding = true;
```

The body of the **do-while** begins with an issuing of a prompt and the extraction of the response.

```java
System.out.print("Decision (y, n): ");
String response = stdin.readLine();
```

A test then determines whether the end-of-file sentinel was supplied. (Java sets variable response to **null** only if no input could be extracted.)

```java
if (response == null) {
```

```
        stillDeciding = false;
    }
```

If the user signaled end-of-file, then no is assumed and the decision is made implicitly.

If instead, the user provided a response, the loop body tests whether the response has the expected length of 1. If it does, processing the response makes sense.

```
else if (response.length() == 1) {
    reply = response.charAt(0);
    reply = Character.toLowerCase(reply);
    if ((reply == 'y') || (reply == 'n') {
        stillDeciding = false;
    }
}
```

To process the response, the code first grabs the character that makes up the string. To simplify the testing, the character is converted to its lowercase equivalent using `Charac-ter` class method `toLowerCase()`. If the character is a 'y' or an 'n', a decision has been made. If the character is something different, no explicit action needs to be taken—variable `stillDeciding` remains **true**, causing the loop test expression to evaluate to **true** and the loop to iterate.

If instead, the user provides a response that is greater than length 1, then the response is ignored. Because `stillDeciding` remains **true**, the loop test expression evaluates to **true** and the loop iterates.

The following output is a sample run of the code segment

```
Decision (y, n): not sure
Decision (y, n):
Decision (y, n): thinking
Decision (y, n): yeah
Decision (y, n): Y
```

Scope

The scope of variables defined in the statement body of a **do-while** loop is limited to that statement body. Therefore, variables defined in the body *cannot* be used in the loop's test expression. For example, the following code segment does not compile because j is undefined in the test expression j != 6211954.

```
do {
    int j = Integer.parseInt(stdin.readLine());
while (j != 6211954);  // j is undefined at this point
```

Our next series of examples nest one loop within another loop.

Looping pitfalls

Some common pitfalls in writing loops are

- Loop not executing because the initialization work is incorrect.
- *Off-by-one* errors where the index variable for the loop is either not initialized properly (e.g., starting with a value of 1 when a value of 0 is needed) or where the test expression allows the body of the loop to iterate one time too many (e.g., using a test expression i <= n rather than i < n) or where the test expression allows the action of the loop to be executed one time too few (e.g., using i < n rather than i <= n).

6.4   NESTED LOOPS

Consider the following code segment

```java
int m = 2;
int n = 3;
for (int i = 0; i < n; ++i) {
   System.out.println("i is " + i);
   for (int j = 0; j < m; ++j) {
      System.out.println("   j is " + j);
   }
}
```

Why does it produce this output?

```
i is 0
   j is 0
   j is 1
i is 1
   j is 0
   j is 1
i is 2
   j is 0
   j is 1
```

The statement

```java
System.out.println("i is " + i);
```

is part of the action associated with the **for** loop that begins on the third line of the segment. We say that this loop is the *outer* loop. The expression i < n that controls the iteration of the loop evaluates to **true** three times with i taking on in turn the values 0, 1, and 2. Thus, there are three lines of output that begin with "i is ". Each time there is such a display, the **for** loop beginning on the fifth line of the segment is executed. We say this loop is an *inner* or *nested* loop.

It is important to realize that an inner loop starts up once per iteration of its outer loop. For our example, each time the inner loop is executed, the expression j < m evaluates to **true** two times with j taking on in turn the values 0 and 1. Thus, causing the output

```
j is 0
j is 1
```

to be displayed each time there is an output line beginning with "i is ".

Nesting one loop in another loop produces a multiplicative effect in terms of the number of statements that are executed. For our example, the outer **for** loop action is executed n times. Each one of those times, the inner **for** loop action is executed m times. As a result, the inner **for** loop action is performed a total of m × n times.

`MultiplicationTable.java` of Listing 6.4 uses nested loops to produce a standard multiplication table The output of the program is

```
* |  0   1   2   3   4   5   6   7   8   9  10  11  12
-----------------------------------------------------
 0 |  0   0   0   0   0   0   0   0   0   0   0   0   0
 1 |  0   1   2   3   4   5   6   7   8   9  10  11  12
 2 |  0   2   4   6   8  10  12  14  16  18  20  22  24
 3 |  0   3   6   9  12  15  18  21  24  27  30  33  36
 4 |  0   4   8  12  16  20  24  28  32  36  40  44  48
 5 |  0   5  10  15  20  25  30  35  40  45  50  55  60
 6 |  0   6  12  18  24  30  36  42  48  54  60  66  72
 7 |  0   7  14  21  28  35  42  49  56  63  70  77  84
 8 |  0   8  16  24  32  40  48  56  64  72  80  88  96
 9 |  0   9  18  27  36  45  54  63  72  81  90  99 108
10 |  0  10  20  30  40  50  60  70  80  90 100 110 120
11 |  0  11  22  33  44  55  66  77  88  99 110 121 132
12 |  0  12  24  36  48  60  72  84  96 108 120 132 144
```

Method `main()` of `MultiplicationTable.java` has two sections. The first section produces the header for the table.

```
// display table header
System.out.print(" * |");
for (int i = 0; i <= MAX_FACTOR; ++i) {
   if (i < 10) {
      System.out.print("   " + i);
   }
   else {
      System.out.print("  " + i);
   }
}
System.out.println();
for (int i = 0; i <= MAX_FACTOR+1; ++i) {
   System.out.print("----");
}
System.out.println();
```

The second section displays the various products that make up the multiplication table. Nested **for** loops display the products. The outer **for** loop manages index variable i, which represents the left operand for the current product of interest. The values of interest are 0 ... MAX_FACTOR, where MAX_FACTOR has value 12. The inner **for** manages

Listing 6.4   **MultiplicationTable.java**

```java
1.  // Produces standard times table
2.
3.  public class MultiplicationTable {
4.      // main(): application entry point
5.      public static void main(String[] args) {
6.          final int MAX_FACTOR = 12;
7.
8.          // display table header
9.          System.out.print(" * |");
10.         for (int i = 0; i <= MAX_FACTOR; ++i) {
11.             if (i < 10) {
12.                 System.out.print("   " + i);
13.             }
14.             else {
15.                 System.out.print("  " + i);
16.             }
17.         }
18.         System.out.println();
19.         for (int i = 0; i <= MAX_FACTOR+1; ++i) {
20.             System.out.print("----");
21.         }
22.         System.out.println();
23.
24.         // display table
25.         for (int i = 0; i <= MAX_FACTOR; ++i) {
26.             // display row label
27.             if (i < 10) {
28.                 System.out.print(" " + i + " |");
29.             }
30.             else {
31.                 System.out.print(i + " |");
32.             }
33.
34.             // display row entries
35.             for (int j = 0; j <= MAX_FACTOR; ++j) {
36.                 // compute entry
37.                 int product = i * j;
38.
39.                 // pretty-print entry
40.                 if (product < 10) {
41.                     System.out.print("   " + product);
42.                 }
43.                 else if (product < 100) {
44.                     System.out.print("  " + product);
45.                 }
46.                 else {
47.                     System.out.print(" " + product);
48.                 }
49.             }
50.
51.             System.out.println();
52.         }
53.     }
54. }
```

index variable j, which represents the right operand for the current product of interest. The values of interest are again 0 … MAX_FACTOR.

```
for (int i = 0; i <= MAX_FACTOR; ++i) { ...
   for (int j = 0; j <= MAX_FACTOR; ++j) { ...
   }
   ...
}
```

For each value of i, the program must display a row of the table. To do so, three actions must be performed: display the row label, display the row of products using left operand i, and display a newline character to end the row.

To ensure that the various row labels are aligned correctly, an **if** statement evaluates whether i is less than 10. If so, the basic label composed by concatenating i with " |" is preceded by a blank (" "). Otherwise, only the basic label is displayed.

```
// display row label
if (i < 10) {
   System.out.print(" " + i + " |");
}
else {
   System.out.print(i + " |");
}
```

After displaying the label, the inner **for** loop iterates for each value j of interest.

```
// display row entries
for (int j = 0; j <= MAX_FACTOR; ++j) {
   // compute entry
   int product = i * j;

   // pretty-print entry
   if (product < 10) {
      System.out.print("    " + product);
   }
   else if (product < 100) {
      System.out.print("   " + product);
   }
   else {
      System.out.print(" " + product);
   }
}
```

With i and j both being set, the product can be computed and displayed. To ensure that the table entries are aligned, an **if-else-if** construct determines the number of digits in the product.

To complete the processing of a row, a newline character is displayed. This action is accomplished with a println() statement.

```
// finish up row
System.out.println();
```

6.5 SIMPLE FILE PROCESSING

Java I/O libraries provide an interface between the program and the hardware devices that make up the computer system. The interface spans two levels of abstraction. At the lower level, the abstraction is a file. In this context, a *file* is a logical concept that represents a particular hardware device like a monitor, modem, or keyboard or represents a particular portion of a hardware device like a disk file on a hard disk or on a DVD. At the higher level, the abstraction is a stream. The *stream* is a hardware-independent view of the device. The data coming from or going to the hardware device is just a sequence of bytes.

The stream and file views are both important. The stream view enables a program to make I/O requests while being unconcerned how the requests are carried out. The file view captures the important physical characteristics of the device. The I/O requests of the stream view are translated automatically by the compiler into file-level specific actions that accomplish the desired requests.

While you may not have paid much attention to it, you have already seen and used three different input stream representations. In fact, we use three of them whenever we define a `BufferedReader` variable `stdin` for processing data from the standard input stream (e.g., `BMICalculator.java` of Listing 2.10).

BufferedReader is an input stream that uses a buffer to store character inputs for efficiency purposes

System.in is an InputStream variable. InputStream is the superclass of Java's input streams

```
BufferedReader stdin
    = new BufferedReader(new InputStreamReader(System.in));
```

InputStreamReader provides a character view of the bytes that make up an input stream

Besides using these input streams, our console programs also have used the output stream variable `System.out`. `System.out` references a `PrintStream` that converts the characters generated by `print()` and `println()` methods into a stream sequence of bytes.

The `System` class also provides the output stream variable `System.err` for sending error or status messages. Like `System.out`, `System.err` print requests are directed by default to the console window. Several example error messages are given below:

```
System.err.println("System being rebooted in 2 minutes");
System.err.println("Zero balance: withdrawal ignored");
System.err.println("Modem is not online, no call possible");
```

`System.err` is preferred over `System.out` for such messages, because operating systems often provide a way for specifying that a program's standard output commands go to a file rather than the console window.

> The > is a command-line operator in Windows, Linux, and OS X. It instructs the operating system to send the program's standard output requests to the file specified by its right operand (Output.txt)

```
cmd: java DisplayForecast > Output.txt
cmd: type Output.txt
I think there is a world market for maybe five computers.
   Thomas Watson, IBM Chairman, 1943.
cmd:
```

Because the viewing of error or system status messages should not be delayed until the user gets around to looking at the output file, `System.err` is preferred over `System.out` for warnings.

Java also provides stream representations for files. `FileReader` is a subclass of `InputStreamReader` that provides an input view of a file. `FileWriter` is a subclass of `OutputStreamWriter` that provides an output view of a file. For now, our concern is `FileReader`. There is one `FileReader` constructor of particular interest.

`FileReader(String s)`

> Opens the file with name `s` so that values can be extracted. The name can be either an absolute pathname or a pathname relative to the current working folder. If the file cannot be opened, a `FileNotFoundException` is thrown.

With a `FileReader`, we can create a `BufferedReader` that is associated with the file of interest. For example, the following code segment displays the first line from the file `blurb.txt`.

```
FileReader reader = new FileReader("blurb.txt");
BufferedReader fileIn = new BufferedReader(reader);
String currentLine = fileIn.readLine();
System.out.println(currentLine);
```

In the code segment, variable `fileIn` is a reference to a `BufferedReader` providing a stream view of the file `blurb.txt`. The `BufferedReader` is constructed using variable `reader`, which references a `FileReader` view of the file `blurb.txt`.

Because `fileIn` references a `BufferedReader`, the segment can use `BufferedReader` method `readLine()` to extract a line of text from the file. Program `FileLister.java` of Listing 6.5 expands upon this example to display the entire contents of a user-specified file.

Program `FileLister.java` begins by defining a `BufferedReader` variable `stdin` that is a reference to the standard input stream. The reference is needed as the name of the file comes from the standard input stream.

```
// set up standard input stream
BufferedReader stdin = new BufferedReader(
    new InputStreamReader( System.in ) );
```

The program then prompts and extracts the filename.

```
// determine filename
System.out.print("Filename: ");
String filename = stdin.readLine();
```

With the filename, the program can define a `FileReader` variable `reader` that references the associated file.

```
// open file stream for text processing
FileReader reader = new FileReader(filename);
```

The `FileReader` is used to initialize a `BufferedReader` variable `fileIn` that is a reference to the file stream of interest.

```
BufferedReader fileIn = new BufferedReader(
    new FileReader( filename ) );
```

Listing 6.5   **FileLister.java**

```
1.  // Lists contents of a user-specified file
2.
3.  import java.io.*;
4.
5.  public class FileLister {
6.
7.      // main(): application entry point
8.      public static void main(String [] args) throws IOException {
9.          // set up standard input stream
10.         BufferedReader stdin = new BufferedReader(
11.             new InputStreamReader( System.in ) );
12.
13.         // determine filename
14.         System.out.print("Filename: ");
15.         String filename = stdin.readLine();
16.
17.         // set up file stream
18.         BufferedReader fileIn = new BufferedReader(
19.             new FileReader( filename ) );
20.
21.         // process lines one by one
22.         String currentLine = fileIn.readLine();  // get first line
23.
24.         while (currentLine != null) {
25.             // display current line
26.             System.out.println(currentLine);
27.
28.             // get next line
29.             currentLine = fileIn.readLine();
30.         }
31.
32.         // close the file stream
33.         fileIn.close();
34.     }
35. }
```

The program attempts to read the first value before the loop.

```
// process lines one by one
String currentLine = fileIn.readLine(); // get first line
```

If there is a value, then the **while** test expression `currentLine != ` **null** will be **true** and the value will be processed. If there is no value, the test expression will be **false** indicating that the file is empty.

```
while (currentLine != null) {          // did we get value
```

For the case of an input being present, the loop body displays the line and attempts to extract the next input to prepare for the next iteration of the loop.

```
// display current line
System.out.println(currentLine);

// prepare for next iteration
currentLine = fileIn.readLine();
```

Once an extraction fails, the test expression `currentLine != ` **null** evaluates to **false** and the loop terminates.

Because the program no longer needs access to the file, `BufferedReader` member method `close()` is invoked to release the program's control of the file back to the operating system.

```
// close the file stream
fileIn.close();
```

Suppose the file `blurb.txt` contains the opening sentence from "Paul Clifford" by Edward George Bulwer-Lytton (1830). If the user indicated that file, program `FileReader.java` would have the following input/output behavior.

```
Filename: blurb.txt
It was a dark and stormy night; the rain fell in torrents--
except at occasional intervals, when it was checked by a violent
gust of wind which swept up the streets (for it is in London that
our scene lies), rattling along the housetops, and fiercely
agitating the scanty flame of the lamps that struggled against
the darkness.
```

As another example of file processing, program `FileAverage.java` of Listing 6.6 revisits the average problem considered by `NumberAverage.java` of Listing 6.1. This console program produces the average of the numeric inputs from a user-specified file.

Suppose the file `numbers.txt` contains the following values: 1, 4, 32, 5, 12, 28, 6, 21, 54, 4, 30, 54, 6, 9, 82, 11, 29, 85, 11, 28, 91, 1, 1, 1. Then when using that file, our program has the following input/output behavior.

```
Filename: numbers.txt
Average file data value: 25.25
```

Program `FileAverage.java` begins in the same manner as `FileLister.java`. The program first defines a `BufferedReader` variable `stdin` that is a reference to the standard input stream. It then prompts and extracts the filename. With the filename, the program defines a `FileReader` variable `reader` that references the associated file. The

---

Listing 6.6 FileAverage.java

```java
1.  // Compute the average of a user-specified file of data values
2.
3.  import java.io.*;
4.
5.  public class FileAverage {
6.      // main(): application entry point
7.      public static void main(String[] args) throws IOException {
8.          // set up standard input stream
9.          BufferedReader stdin = new BufferedReader(
10.             new InputStreamReader(System.in));
11.
12.         // determine filename
13.         System.out.print("Filename: ");
14.         String filename = stdin.readLine();
15.
16.         // open file stream for text processing
17.         FileReader reader = new FileReader(filename);
18.         BufferedReader fileIn = new BufferedReader(reader);
19.
20.         // initially no values have been processed
21.         int valuesProcessed = 0;
22.         double valueSum = 0;
23.
24.         // process values one by one
25.         String currentLine = fileIn.readLine(); // get first value
26.
27.         while (currentLine != null) {           // did we get it
28.             // convert string to numeric value
29.             double value = Double.parseDouble(currentLine);
30.             // add value to running total
31.             valueSum += value;
32.             // processed another total
33.             ++valuesProcessed;
34.             // prepare for next iteration
35.             currentLine = fileIn.readLine();
36.         }
37.
38.         // close up file
39.         fileIn.close();
40.
41.         // ready to compute average
42.         if (valuesProcessed > 0) {
43.             double average = valueSum / valuesProcessed;
44.             System.out.println("Average file data value: " + average);
45.         }
46.         else {
47.             System.err.println(filename + ": no values to average");
48.         }
49.     }
50. }
```

FileReader is used to initialize a BufferedReader variable fileIn that references the file stream of interest.

From this point `FileAverage.java`'s behavior is analogous to `Average.java` of Listing 6.1. However, rather than processing the values from the standard input stream referenced by `stdin`, the program processes the values from the file input stream referenced by `fileIn`. In addition, `FileAverage.java`'s does not make use of a negative number sentinel—the operating system automatically provides an end-of-file sentinel.

Prior to any reading of the values, the number of values processed is 0 and the running total is 0.

```
// initially no values have been processed
int valuesProcessed = 0;
double valueSum = 0;
```

The program attempts to read the first value before the loop.

```
// process values one by one
String currentLine = fileIn.readLine(); // get first value
```

If there is a value, then test expression `currentLine != ` **null** will be **true** and the value will be processed. If there is no value, the test expression will be **false**, indicating that the file is empty. (The **if** statement after the **while** loop correctly accounts for this condition.)

For the case of a value being present, the program converts the input value to a **double** representation; adds the value to running total; increments the number of values processed; and attempts to extract the next input to prepare for the next iteration of the loop.

```
// process values one by one
String currentLine = fileIn.readLine(); // get first value

while (currentLine != null) {            // did we get it
    // convert string to numeric value
    double value = Double.parseDouble(currentLine);
    // add value to running total
    valueSum += value;
    // processed another total
    ++valuesProcessed;
    // prepare for next iteration
    currentLine = fileIn.readLine();
}
```

Once an extraction fails, the test expression `currentLine != ` **null** evaluates to **false** and the loop terminates. With the termination of the loop, access to the file stream no longer is needed. Therefore, the stream is closed.

```
// close up file
fileIn.close();
```

The **if** statement then determines whether an average can be computed. If the number of values processed is nonzero, then there is an average to calculate.

```
double average = valueSum / valuesProcessed;
System.out.println("Average file data value: " + average);
```

If there were no values to process, then a message is displayed to the standard error stream indicating the problem.

```
System.err.println(filename + ": no values to average");
```

This completes our analysis of `FileAverage.java`. We next turn our attention to the development of a simple API for keeping track of important characteristics of a data set.

6.6 CASE STUDY — DATA SET ANALYSIS

In analyzing a data set there are often four values of particular interest: the minimum, the maximum. the mean, and the standard deviation. Together the minimum and maximum let us know the range of the values; the mean is the average data set value, which often gives insight on what is a typical value; and the standard deviation gives insight on how clustered the data set values are around the average. (Our implementation of a data set representation DataSet.java leaves the computing of a standard deviation to the exercises.)

> The objective of this case study is to practice using conditional and iterative statements in the context of the design and implementation of a class

Table 6.1 lists an example data set for the number of Internet users per 100 people of population for 189 of the political entities recognized by the United Nations. The data set is for the year 2000 and comes from the United Nation's Department of Economic and Social Affairs. The mean value is approximately 8.28 and the standard deviation is approximately 13.01. The minimal value is 0.1 (Democratic Republic of the Congo, Myanmar, and Somalia) and the maximum value is 73.4 (Falkland Islands).

Table 6.1   Internet use per 100 people of population for 189 entities.

0.09	0.16	8.97	0.23	6.52	6.75	1.42	13.65	34.45	25.86
0.16	4.32	5.84	0.08	3.74	1.78	22.89	6.24	0.25	0.22
1.44	1.01	1.54	2.94	9.14	5.28	0.08	0.07	0.05	0.27
41.30	1.84	0.04	0.04	16.58	1.74	38.64	13.70	2.07	0.22
5.67	0.27	5.59	0.54	17.88	9.71	0.01	36.59	0.22	7.78
1.86	1.42	0.71	0.80	0.15	0.13	27.21	73.40	1.47	37.23
14.43	6.43	1.22	0.92	0.42	29.18	0.15	9.47	4.36	1.75
0.70	0.10	0.25	6.04	0.25	0.62	7.15	59.79	0.54	0.94
0.39	20.70	20.26	23.04	3.11	29.31	2.53	0.62	0.65	1.80
40.25	7.84	1.06	0.11	6.19	8.58	0.19	0.02	0.18	6.09
22.66	0.19	0.15	15.90	2.23	0.17	13.08	1.17	0.19	7.29
2.74	39.71	1.26	0.71	0.06	0.01	1.71	0.22	24.39	11.15
21.67	0.99	0.04	0.18	49.05	25.05	3.55	0.09	1.10	3.17
2.81	0.73	9.74	2.01	7.25	24.94	10.22	5.01	1.20	18.60
3.57	0.06	4.79	3.09	0.56	48.70	4.36	0.93	0.42	7.40
0.10	29.87	12.03	15.08	0.46	0.01	5.49	13.43	0.64	0.10
2.70	0.99	45.58	29.62	0.19	28.10	0.05	3.79	2.47	0.86
7.73	2.61	3.06	0.13	0.18	0.69	28.20	30.12	0.33	45.07
11.09	0.49	2.03	3.93	0.25	0.08	3.76	0.19	0.37	

Suppose x is a list of n values $x_1, x_2, \ldots x_n$, then its mean is written as $\bar{x}$, where the overline character "¯" is the statistical mean symbol. Mean $\bar{x}$ has following definition.

$$\bar{x} = (x_1 + x_2 + \ldots + x_n)/n$$

As an example, the following data set represents the birth months of nine people familiar to authors.

4, 6, 6, 11, 11, 2, 3, 3, 12

The mean value is $(4 + 6 + 6 + 11 + 11 + 2 + 3 + 3 + 12)/9$, which is approximately 6.444.

ANALYSIS AND DESIGN

In developing a representation `DataSet` for a data set it is clear that four methods are certainly necessary.

`public double getMinimum()`

Returns the minimum value in the data set. If the data set is empty, then `Double.NaN` is returned, where `Double.NaN` is the Java **double** value representing the status *not-a-number*.

`public double getMaximum()`

Returns the maximum value in the data set. If the data set is empty, then `Double.NaN` is returned.

`public double getAverage()`

Returns the average value in the data set. If the data set is empty, then `Double.NaN` is returned.

`public double getStandardDeviation()`

Returns the standard deviation value of the data set. If the data set is empty, then `Double.NaN` is returned.

But what constructors and what other behaviors should a data set representation have? Before reading on, determine your own answer to this question.

With regard to constructors, we believe two constructors are appropriate—a default constructor that represents a data set with no values and a constructor that represents a data set whose characteristics are determined from a file of values.

`public DataSet()`

Initializes a representation of an empty data set.

`public DataSet(String s)`

Initializes the data set using the values from the file with name `s`.

In terms of member methods, we believe methods are appropriate for indicating the number of values in the data set, adding values to the data set being represented, clearing the values represented by the data set; and adding values from a file to the data set being represented.

`public int getSize()`

Returns the number of values in the data set being represented.

`public void addValue(double x)`

Adds the value `x` to the data set being represented.

`public void clear()`

Sets the representation to that of an empty data set.

`public void load(String s)`

Adds the vales from the file with name `s` to the data set being represented.

To implement these behaviors, the following instance variables suffice.

`private int n`

Number of values in the data set being represented

`private double minimumValue`

Minimum value in the data set being represented.

`private double maximumValue`

Maximum value in the data set being represented.

`private double xSum`

The sum of values in the data set being represented

Program `DataSetTester.java` of Listing 6.7 demonstrates some uses of class `DataSet`. The program displays results regarding four data sets: `age.txt`, which contains the ages of 2,208 different women; `stature.txt`, which contains the height in centimeters of those same women; `foot-length.txt`, which contains the foot length in centimeters of those same; and an empty data set. The original source for the first three data sets is a 1987 survey by the United States government. For each survey participant over 100 separate measurements were taken. The survey results are known as MIL-STD-1472D. The output produced by the program is given in Figure 6.5.

Figure 6.5   **Snapshot of a run of DataSetTester.java.**

Listing 6.7 DataSetTester.java

```java
1.  import java.io.*;
2.
3.  public class DataSetTester {
4.      public static void main(String[] args) throws IOException {
5.          DataSet dataset = new DataSet("age.txt");
6.          System.out.println();
7.          System.out.println("Minimum: " + dataset.getMinimum());
8.          System.out.println("Maximum: " + dataset.getMaximum());
9.          System.out.println("Mean: " + dataset.getAverage());
10.         System.out.println("Size: " + dataset.getSize());
11.         System.out.println();
12.         dataset.clear();
13.         dataset.load("stature.txt");
14.         System.out.println("Minimum: " + dataset.getMinimum());
15.         System.out.println("Maximum: " + dataset.getMaximum());
16.         System.out.println("Mean: " + dataset.getAverage());
17.         System.out.println("Size: " + dataset.getSize());
18.         System.out.println();
19.         dataset.clear();
20.         dataset.load("foot-length.txt");
21.         System.out.println("Minimum: " + dataset.getMinimum());
22.         System.out.println("Maximum: " + dataset.getMaximum());
23.         System.out.println("Mean: " + dataset.getAverage());
24.         System.out.println("Size: " + dataset.getSize());
25.         System.out.println();
26.         dataset.clear();
27.         System.out.println("Minimum: " + dataset.getMinimum());
28.         System.out.println("Maximum: " + dataset.getMaximum());
29.         System.out.println("Mean: " + dataset.getAverage());
30.         System.out.println("Size: " + dataset.getSize());
31.         System.out.println();
32.     }
33. }
```

IMPLEMENTATION

A straightforward implementation of DataSet is given in Listing 6.8. For example, the default and specific constructors can each be implemented respectively by invoking methods clear() and load().

```java
// DataSet(): default constructor
public DataSet() {
    clear();
}

// DataSet(): specific constructor
public DataSet(String s) throws IOException {
    load(s);
}
```

Method clear() has the task of setting the representation to that of an empty data set. The task is accomplished by setting all of the instance variables to appropriate values. In particular, the size n of the data set is to 0. Because there are no associated values for the data set, the sum of the values xSum is set to 0. Lastly, minimumValue and maxi-

Listing 6.8   *DataSet.java*

```
1.   // Data set summary representation
2.   import java.io.*;
3.
4.   public class DataSet {
5.       // instance variables
6.       private int n;
7.       private double xSum;
8.       private double minimumValue;
9.       private double maximumValue;
10.
11.      // DataSet(): default constructor
12.      public DataSet() {
13.          clear();
14.      }
15.
16.      // DataSet(): specific constructor
17.      public DataSet(String s) throws IOException {
18.          load(s);
19.      }
20.
21.      // clear(): empties the data set
22.      public void clear() {
23.          n = 0;
24.          xSum = 0;
25.          minimumValue = Double.NaN;
26.          maximumValue = Double.NaN;
27.      }
28.
29.      // add(): adds the value to the set
30.      public void addValue(double x) {
31.          xSum += x;
32.          ++n;
33.          if (n == 1) {
34.              minimumValue = maximumValue = x;
35.          }
36.          else if (x < minimumValue) {
37.              minimumValue = x;
38.          }
39.          else if (x > maximumValue) {
40.              maximumValue = x;
41.          }
42.      }
43.
44.      // load(): adds the values from the file to set
45.      public void load(String s) throws IOException {
46.          // get a reader for the file
47.          BufferedReader fileIn = new BufferedReader(
48.              new FileReader(s));
49.
50.          // add values one by one
51.          String currentLine = fileIn.readLine();
52.          while (currentLine != null) {
53.              double x = Double.parseDouble(currentLine);
54.              addValue(x);
```

Listing 6.8 *DataSet.java (Continued)*

```
55.          currentLine = fileIn.readLine();
56.       }
57.
58.       // close up file
59.       fileIn.close();
60.    }
61.
62.    // getAverage(): compute data set average
63.    public double getAverage() {
64.       if (n == 0) {
65.          return Double.NaN;
66.       }
67.       else {
68.          return xSum / n;
69.       }
70.    }
71.
72.    // getMinimum(): produce minimum data set value
73.    public double getMinimum() {
74.       return minimumValue;
75.    }
76.
77.    // maximum(): produce maximum data set value
78.    public double getMaximum() {
79.       return maximumValue;
80.    }
81.
82.    // getSize(): produce data set size
83.    public int getSize() {
84.       return n;
85.    }
86. }
```

---

mumValue are set to `Double.NaN` because there is no minimum or maximum value associated with an empty data set. (See Section 2.4 for a discussion of class `Double` class constants).

```
// clear(): empties the data set
public void clear() {
   n = 0;
   xSum = 0;
   minimumValue = Double.NaN;
   maximumValue = Double.NaN;
}
```

Method `load()` uses its parameter `s` to create a `BufferedReader` associated with the file whose name is `s`. The values in that file are extracted one at a time with each value in turn being added to the data set.

```
// load(): adds the values from the file to set
public void load(String s) throws IOException {
   // get a reader for the file
   BufferedReader fileIn = new BufferedReader(
      new FileReader(s));
```

```
        // add values one by one
        String currentLine = fileIn.readLine();

        while (currentLine != null) {
            double x = Double.parseDouble(currentLine);
            addValue(x);
            currentLine = fileIn.readLine();
        }

        // close up file
        fileIn.close();
    }
```

The values are added using method `addValue()`. After all the values have been processed, the file stream is closed. Thus, this processing is very similar to the processing by `FileLister.java` of Listing 6.5 and `FileAverage.java` of Listing 6.6.

Method `addValue()` processes a new value x to be associated with the data set,

```
    // add(): adds the value to the set
    public void addValue(double x) {
        xSum += x;
        ++n;
        if (n == 1) {
            minimumValue = maximumValue = x;
        }
        else if (x < minimumValue) {
            minimumValue = x;
        }
        else if (x > maximumValue) {
            maximumValue = x;
        }
    }
```

First, the new value is added to the sum variable xSum. In addition, the size n of the data set is incremented by 1.

Case analysis determines whether `minimumValue` or `maximumValue` require updating. If the data set consists currently of a single value, then that value is both the minimum and the maximum value of the data set.

```
    if (n == 1) {
        minimumValue = maximumValue = x;
    }
```

Otherwise, the data set has more than one value and the new value may be smaller than the minimum. If it is smaller than the minimum, its value is now the minimum value of the data set.

```
    else if (x < minimumValue) {
        minimumValue = x;
    }
```

If it is not smaller than the minimum, it may be larger than the maximum. If it is larger than the maximum, its value is now the maximum value of the data set.

```
    else if (x > maximumValue) {
```

```
        maximumValue = x;
}
```

Otherwise, there is no change in the minimum or maximum values of the data set.

The remaining member methods are sufficiently simple to warrant no further analysis.

TESTING

By comparing the results produced by program `DataSetTester.java` of Listing 6.7 to the published results for those three standard data sets, we develop confidence in the correctness of class `DataSet`. To further increase the level of confidence, additional data sets should be constructed and their results analyzed. These data sets should ensure that every statement is executed.

This discussion completes our introduction to iteration. In Chapter 7 we consider many of the nuances of method and class design in Java.

6.7 REVIEW

- The **while** statement has form

  while (*Expression*) *Action*

  When a **while** statement is executed, its test expression is evaluated first. If the expression evaluates **true**, its body is executed, where the body is the action of the **while** statement. The evaluation process then is repeated. If the expression reevaluates to **true**, the body is executed again. This process is called looping, and it continues until the test expression evaluates to **false**. At that point, execution continues with the next statement in the program.

- If a **while** test expression initially evaluates to false, then its **while** body is never executed.

- The **for** statement has form

  for (*ForInit* ; *ForExpression* ; *ForUpdate*) *Action*

  The **for** initialization step is performed only once—at the start of the execution of the loop. Next, the test expression is evaluated. If the test expression is initially **false**, then execution immediately continues with the next statement in the program. If the expression is **true**, the body of the loop is executed and then the update step is performed. The update step is permitted to be an assignment, method invocation, or omitted. The test expression then is reevaluated. If the expression is again **true**, the execution of the loop body and update step is iterated. This process continues until the test expression evaluates to **false**. Execution then continues with the next statement in the program.

- The **do-while** has form

  do *Action* ; **while** (*Expression*)

  A **do-while** loop begins by executing the body of its loop. Afterward, the test expression is evaluated. If the test expression evaluates to **true**, then the body is repeated. This process continues until test expression evaluates to **false**.

- The System class provides output stream System.err. Programs use this stream to display messages regarding abnormal situations.

- I/O libraries provide an interface between the program and the hardware devices that make up the computer system. The interface spans two levels of abstraction. At the lower level, the abstraction is a file. A file is a logical concept that represents either a particular hardware device or a particular portion of a hardware device At the higher level, the abstraction is a stream. A stream is a hardware-independent view of an device.

- A stream view enables a program to issue generic I/O requests on flows of data while being unconcerned about how the requests are to be carried out.

- A file view captures the important physical characteristics of the device. The input/output requests of the stream view are translated automatically by the compiler into file-level specific actions that accomplish the desired requests.

- Java provides stream representations for file streams. `FileReader` is a subclass of `InputStreamReader` for providing an input view of a file.
- `FileReader` constructor `FileReader(String s)` opens the file with name `s` so that values can be extracted. The name can be either an absolute pathname or a pathname relative to the current working folder. If the file cannot be opened, a `FileNotFoundException` is thrown.

6.8 SELF-TEST

S6.1 Implement a program that produces the first n numbers in the Fibonacci sequence, where n is a user-specified integer value. The sequence starts with the following numbers: 1, 1, 2, 3, 5, 8, 13, 21. After the initial two 1s, each number in the sequence is the sum of the two previous numbers. For example, $1 + 1 = 2, 1 + 2 = 3$, $2 + 3 = 5, 3 + 5 = 8$, and so on.

S6.2 What is the output of the following code segment?

```
int counter1 = 0;
int counter2 = 0;
int counter3 = 0;
int counter4 = 0;
int counter5 = 0;
for (int i = 0; i < 5; ++i) {
    ++counter1;
    for (int j = 0; j < 10; ++j) {
        ++counter2;
        for (int k = 0; k < 2; ++k) {
            ++counter3;
        }
        ++counter4;
    }
    ++counter5;
}
System.out.println(counter1);
System.out.println(counter2);
System.out.println(counter3);
System.out.println(counter4);
System.out.println(counter5);
```

S6.3 What is the output of the following code segment?

```
int n = 10;
int i;
for (i = 0; i < n; ) {
    ++n;
    i += 3;
}
System.out.println(i);
```

S6.4 What is the output of the following code segment?

```
int n = 3;
```

```
while (n > 0) {
    System.out.println(n);
    --n;
}
int m = 3;
do {
    System.out.println(m);
    --m;
} while (m > 0);
```

EXERCISES

6.1 Redo `Combination.java` using the following equivalent form of $C(m, n)$.

$$C(m, n) = \frac{m \times (m - 1) \times (m - 2) \times \ldots \times (n + 1)}{(m - n)!}$$

6.2 Geneticists uses the symbols A, G, T, and C in writing a DNA sequence. Develop a program that extracts a user-specified DNA sequence and reports whether the sequence is composed of valid symbols.

6.3 Stirling's approximation for $n!$ is

$$n! \approx \sqrt{2\pi n} \left(\frac{n}{e}\right)^n$$

Develop a program that produces a table with m entries for a user-specified value of m. For each value n in the range $1 \ldots m$, the program should report the difference between $n!$ and Stirling's approximation. To calculate a square root use class method `Math.sqrt()`. To calculate a power use class method `Math.pow()`. To approximate π use double constant `Math.PI`. To approximate e use double constant `Math.E`.

6.4 Display prime numbers in the range $1 \ldots n$, where n is a user-specified value. A number i is prime if its only factors are 1 and itself.

6.5 Display perfect numbers in the range $1 \ldots n$, where n is a user-specified value. A number i is perfect if the sum of its factors is i.

6.6 Rearrange the following code segment so that it is indented properly.

```
if ((n > 0) && (m > 0)) { for (int i = 0; i < n;
++i) { for (int j = 0; j < m; ++j) { if (i ! =
j) { System.out.println("0"); } else {
System.out.println ("1"); } } } } else {
System.out.println("2"); }
```

6.7 Provide a code segment that prompts a user for an extracted positive integer value less than 10 million. The segment then displays the value in words. For example, if the input value is 21, then twenty-one is displayed.

6.8 What is wrong with the following code segment that is suppose to count the number of times a specified key value occurs in a list of numbers? How can it be corrected?

```
BufferedReader stdin = new BufferedReader(
   new InputStreamReader( System.in ) );
System.out.print("Enter key value: ");
int key = Integer.parseInt(stdin.readLine());
System.out.println("Enter list of numbers: ");
String s = stdin.readLine();
int value = Integer.parseInt(s);
int counter = 0;
for (int i = 0; s != null ; ++i) {
   if (key == value) {
      ++counter;
   }
}
System.out.println(counter + " of the " + i
   + " values equal " + key);
```

6.9 What is the output of the following code segment?

```
int counter1 = 0;
int counter2 = 0;
int counter3 = 0;
int counter4 = 0;
int counter5 = 0;
for (int i = 0; i < 10; ++i) {
   ++counter1;
   for (int j = 0; j < 10; ++j) {
      ++counter2;
      if (i == j) {
         ++counter3;
      }
      else {
         ++counter4;
      }
   }
   ++counter5;
}
System.out.println(counter1 + " " + counter2 + " "
   + counter3 + " " + counter4 + " " + counter5);
```

6.10 Correct the following code segment so that it displays the number of inputs that are bigger than the first input.

```
BufferedReader stdin = new BufferedReader(
   new InputStreamReader( System.in ) );
int firstValue = Integer.parseInt(stdin.readLine());
String s = stdin.readLine();
int sum = 1;
while (s != null) {
   int currentValue = Integer.parseInt(s);
   if (firstValue == currentValue) {
      ++sum;
   }
}
```

```
System.out.println(sum);
```

6.11 Provide a code segment displays the sum of odd integers from 1 to n.

6.12 Provide a code segment that iteratively extracts *n* pairs of integers. For each
      extracted pair of integers *a* and *b*, the program displays the product $a \times a+1 \times \ldots b$.

6.13 Provide a code segment that displays the sum of integers from a to b.

6.14 Provide a code segment using nested loops that displays a daily calendar of form.

```
 9:00
 9:15
 9:30
 9:45
10:00
10:15
10:30
10:45
  ...
 5:00
```

6.15 Consider the following code segment:

```
int i = 1;
while (i <= n) {
    if ((i % n) == 0) {
        ++i;
    }
}
System.out.println(i);
```

a) What is the output if n is 0?

b) What is the output if n is 1?

c) What is the output if n is 3?

6.16 Consider the following code segment:

```
for (i = 0; i < n; ++i) {
    --n;
}
System.out.println(i);
```

a) What is the output if n is 0?

b) What is the output if n is 1?

c) What is the output if n is 3?

d) What is the output if n is 4?

6.17 Design and implement a program that counts the number of its inputs from the
      standard input stream in each of the categories positive, negative, and zero.

6.18 Design and implement a program that extracts values from the standard input
      stream and then displays the smallest and largest of those values to the standard
      output stream. The program should display appropriate messages for special cases
      where there are no inputs and only one input.

6.19 A sequence of numbers is monotonic increasing if the values are in sorted order.
      For example, 1, 1, 3, 4, 9 is a monotonic sequence, but 1, 3, 2, 4, 9 is not a mono-

tonic sequence because 3 is greater than 2. Design and implement a program that determines whether its input sequence is in monotonic increasing order.

6.20 Design and implement a program that prompts its user for a nonnegative value n. The program then displays as its output:

```
1 2 3 ... n-1 n
1 2 3 ... n-1
...
1 2 3
1 2
1
```

6.21 A character is whitespace if it is a blank (' '), a tab ('\t'), a newline character ('\n'), or a formfeed ('\f'). Design and implement a program that counts the number of whitespace characters in standard input.

6.22 Design and implement a program that extracts lines from standard input and then reports the average line length.

6.23 Design and implement a program that prompts a user for a filename. The program verifies that each line in that file starts with a valid telephone number. For example, in the United States, a valid telephone number has syntax:

$$D \ D \ D \ '\text{-}' \ D \ D \ D \ '\text{-}' \ D \ D \ D \ D$$

where the first D cannot be a zero. For each invalid telephone number, the program should display the corresponding line to the standard error stream.

6.24 Design and implement a program that prompts a user for a filename and string. The program then counts the numbers of occurrences of that string in the specified file.

6.25 Design and implement a program that prompts a user for a filename. The program then displays the number of lines and characters in the file.

6.26 Modify `DataSet.java` so that the class also provides a method for computing the standard deviation of the data set. The formula for the standard deviation s of a data set with mean $\bar{x}$ and values $x_1, x_2, \ldots x_n$, is

$$s = \sqrt{\frac{(x_1 - \bar{x})^2 + (x_2 - \bar{x})^2 + \ldots + (x_n - \bar{x})^2}{n-1}}$$

It can be shown mathematically that s also equals

$$s = \sqrt{\frac{(x_1 \cdot x_1 + x_2 \cdot x_2 + \ldots + x_n \cdot x_n) - n\bar{x} \cdot \bar{x}}{n-1}}$$

The second formulation is preferred because it means that the standard deviation can be computed knowing only the sum of the values.

$$x_1 + x_2 + \ldots + x_n$$

and the sum of the squares of the values

$$x_1 \cdot x_1 + x_2 \cdot x_2 + \ldots + x_n \cdot x_n$$

| 6.10 | **PROGRAMMING PROJECT — FOUR HOBO PROBLEM** |

The following riddle dates back to the late 19th century. (Its revival is credited to Will Shortz, crossword puzzle editor of the *New York Times*.)

> The objective of this case study is to practice using iteration with nested loops in the context of problem solving

PROBLEM STATEMENT

There were once four hoboes traveling across the country. During their journey they ran short on funds, so they stopped at a farm to look for some work. The farmer said there were

200 hours of work that could be done over the next several weeks. The farmer went on to say that how they divided up the work was up to them. The hoboes agreed to start the next day. The following morning, one of the hoboes—who was markedly smarter and lazier than the other three—said there was no reason for them all to do the same amount of work. This hobo went on to suggest the following scheme: The hoboes would all draw straws. A straw would be marked with a number. The number would indicate both the number of days the drawer must work and the number of hours to be worked on each of those days. For example, if the straw was marked with a 3, the hobo who drew it would work 3 hours a day for 3 days. It goes without saying that the lazy hobo convinced the others to agree to this scheme and that through sleight of hand, the lazy hobo drew the best straw. The riddle is to determine the possible ways to divide up the work according to the preceding scheme.

ANALYSIS AND DESIGN

So what tasks must be accomplished to produce a Java program that solves the four hobo problem? The first task is to recognize what it means to be a possible solution to the problem. Knowing the solution form can give insight on how to generate possible solutions.

A solution to the riddle consists of four positive integer numbers a, b, c, and d such that $a^2 + b^2 + c^2 + d^2 = 200$. The necessity of having four numbers and examining the sum of the squares are *explicit constraints* of the problem.

So what does knowing the solution form tell us? Most importantly, it tells us some limits on the possible values involved in a solution. For one, the values of a, b, c, and d are each at least 1. For another, the values of a, b, c, and d can be at most 200; otherwise, the sum of their squares cannot be equal to 200. In fact, a, b, c, and d can be at most $\lfloor \sqrt{200} \rfloor$; that is, a, b, c, and d can be no bigger than the largest integer whose square is at most 200. That integer is 14. Thus, we know $1 \le a, b, c, d \le 14$. These conditions on a, b, c, and d are *implicit constraints*.

IMPLEMENTATION

You should name your program `FourHobo.java`. The class should be appropriately documented and laid out. For example, the code should make use of program header and method comments, whitespace, and a consistent indentation scheme.

Together the explicit and implicit constraints imply a way to solve the problem: systematically generate all combinations of four numbers, where each of the numbers is from the inclusive interval 1 … 14, and check for each combination whether it has the property that the squares of the numbers sum to 200. Because there are only $14 \times 14 \times 14 \times 14 = 38,416$ such combinations to consider, this task is not too onerous—nested loops to generate the various values for a, b, c, and d with the innermost loop performing the test.

Nested loops, rather than consecutive loops, are the way to go, because for each value of a, we need to consider a collection of possibilities for b, c, and d. And for each subcombination value of a and b, we need to consider a collection of possibilities for c and d. And for each subcombination value of a, b, and c, we need to consider a collection of values for d.

As we stated before 38,416 combinations is not an excessive number of combinations to consider. However, among the 38,416 combinations there are effectively many duplicates. For example, the combination ($a = 1$, $b = 1$, $c = 2$, $d = 2$) is equivalent to combinations (1, 2, 1, 2), (1, 2, 2, 1), (2, 1, 1, 2), (2, 1, 2, 1), and (2, 2, 1, 1). They all represent incorrect solutions of two straws of length 1 and two straws of length 2.

There are, in fact, 1,214 unique combinations. This number is significantly less than 38,416, so it is worthwhile to generate only the unique combinations. An easy way to ensure no duplications is to generate the combinations in ascending order. As a result, each generated combination will have the property that $a \le b \le c \le d$.

TESTING

Testing for this problem can be rather complete. It should be possible to verify that all 1,214 unique combinations are generated. Furthermore, among puzzle solvers it is well known that there are only two unique combinations where $a^2 + b^2 + c^2 + d^2 = 200$. And if we assume the lazy hobo is both smart and dishonest, then one solution is preferred.

6.11   **SELF-TEST ANSWERS**

S6.1 `Fibonacci.java`

```
import java.io.*;

public class Fibonacci {
    public static void main(String[] args)
            throws IOException {
```

```
            BufferedReader stdin = new BufferedReader(
              new InputStreamReader( System.in ) );

            System.out.print("Number of Fibonacci values: ");
            int n = Integer.parseInt( stdin.readLine() );

            if ( n < 1 ) {
                System.out.println(n + ": illegal size");
            }
            else if ( n == 1 ) {
                System.out.println("1    1");
            }
            else {
                System.out.println("1    1");
                System.out.println("2    1");

                int prev1 = 1;
                int prev2 = 1;

                for (int i = 3; i <= n; ++i) {
                    int curr = prev1 + prev2;
                    System.out.println(i + "    " + curr);
                    prev2 = prev1;
                    prev1 = curr;
                }
            }
        }
    }
```

S6.2 The output is

```
5
50
100
50
5
```

S6.3 The output is

```
15
```

S6.4 The output is

```
3
2
1
3
2
1
```

GUI–BASED PROGRAMMING

Graphical user interface–based programming is the dominant model in real-world programming. Its importance makes it imperative that all programmers have a basic familiarity with its concepts. This chapter provides a gentle introduction to graphical user interfaces (GUIs) by exploring the design and development of a windchill calculator. The program makes uses many of the major graphical elements of the Java packages awt and swing.

OBJECTIVES

- To introduce the awt and swing packages.
    - To introduce graphical user interfaces and event-driven programming.
    - To manipulate containers and components to build effective interfaces.
    - To demonstrate the purpose of a layout manager for organizing the placement of GUI components within a container.
- To build containers similar in form to desktop windows.
- To gain practice manipulating and configuring labels and entry areas.
- To develop action listeners and performers for GUI events like button clicking.

GUI AND EVENT-DRIVEN PROGRAMMING

Users prefer graphical user interface–based programs over console-based programs. Studies indicate that users find graphical user interfaces (GUIs) easier to manipulate and more forgiving when misused. The GUI ease of functionality comes at a programming price—GUI-based programs are more complex in their structure than console-based programs. This trade-off is illustrated in Figure I.1.

Figure G.I.I   **The trade-off between ease of use and software complexity.**

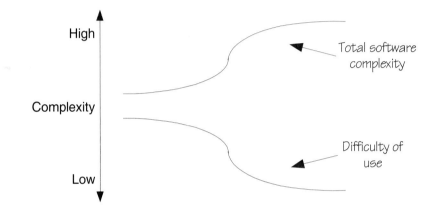

Despite the complexity of GUI programming, its dominance in real-world software development makes it imperative that GUI programming be considered even in an introductory text.

Our first example of a GUI is a program that calculates the *windchill* temperature for a user-specified temperature and windspeed. Windchill temperature is the temperature perceived by a person when taking into account the actual temperature and the speed of the wind.

In terms of calculation complexity, a windchill GUI program is equivalent to the body mass index program BMICalculator.java of Listing 2.10. However, a windchill GUI program has other complexities. In addition to the values for performing the computation, there are also the objects that comprise the GUI. The preceding windchill GUI has nine major graphical components: a window, a legend, three data labels, three data areas, and a run button. For a console-based windchill calculator, none of these components are present.

Besides having more objects to consider, a GUI program also has to deal with the interactions of its graphical components. For example, *whenever* a user clicks the windchill calculator run button, the button *dispatches* a signal. The GUI must have a *listener* for that signal that causes the current temperature and windspeed data entry values to be obtained, the windchill temperature to be calculated, and the result of that computation to be assigned to the windchill temperature entry area.

Java GUI-based programming typically makes use of the `swing` API. The `swing` API provides over 40 different types of graphical components and 250 classes to support the use of these components.

> Definitions of many swing components are available in Appendix E. For complete documentation see www.javasoft.com

In creating a GUI, the following `swing` classes are particularly useful:

`JFrame`
  Represents a titled, bordered window.
`JTextArea`
  Represents an editable multiline text entry component.
`JLabel`
  Represents a display area suitable for one or both of a single-line text or image.
`JTextField`
  Represents an editable single-line text entry component.
`JButton`
  Represents a push button.

Figure I.2 illustrates the use of these classes in the windchill calculator GUI. A detailed discussion of these classes occurs in the next sections.

Besides having a different look and feel from console-based programs, GUI-based programs follow a different program execution paradigm—*event-driven programming*.

A comparison of the *flow of control* (program execution) of a console-based program to a GUI-based program shows similarities and differences. A console program begins and ends in its method `main()`. To solve the intended problem, the method `main()` statements are executed in order. After the last statement in `main()` executes, the program terminates.

The execution of a GUI-based program also begins in its method `main()`. However, method `main()` is responsible normally only for creating an *instance* (object) of the GUI. After creating the GUI, the flow of control goes from method `main()` to an *event-dispatching loop* that checks repeatedly for user interactions with the GUI (i.e., *action events*). When an action event occurs, an *action performer* method is invoked for each *listener* of that event. The performer then processes the interaction. After the performer *handles* the event, flow of control is given again to the event-dispatching loop to watch for future user interactions. This process continues until an action performer signals that the program has completed its task. The execution process is illustrated in Figure I.3.

GUI-based programs typically have at least three methods. One method is the class method `main()` that defines an instance of the GUI. The creation of that object is accomplished by invoking a constructor that creates and initializes the components of the GUI.

Figure G.I.2   GUI annotated with swing components use.

Title bar of JFrame instance. The JFrame contains eight GUI elements

These two lines are a single JTextArea instance

These three lines all contain a JLabel and a JTextField instance

JButton instance

The constructor also registers any event listeners that handle any program-specific responses to user interactions.

The third method is an action performer instance method that processes the events of interest. For many GUIs there is a separate listener-performer object for each of the major components of the GUI. An action performer is always a **public** instance method with name actionPerformed().

GUI-based programs also have instance variables for representing the graphical components and the values necessary for its task. Thus, a GUI is a true object. Once constructed, a GUI has attributes and behaviors. The attributes are the graphical component instance variables and the behaviors are the actions taken by the GUI when events occur.

We now proceed with the development of windchill calculator program Windchill.java.

G.I.2	**WINDCHILL CALCULATOR**

There are several formulas for calculating the windchill temperature t_{wc}. The one used by program Windchill.java is provided by U.S. National Weather Service and is applicable for a windspeed greater than four miles per hour.

$$t_{wc} = 0.081(t - 91.4)(3.71\sqrt{v} + 5.81 - 0.25v) + 91.4$$

In this formula, variable t is the Fahrenheit temperature and variable v is the windspeed in miles per hour.

Figure G.I.3   GUI and console-based execution process.

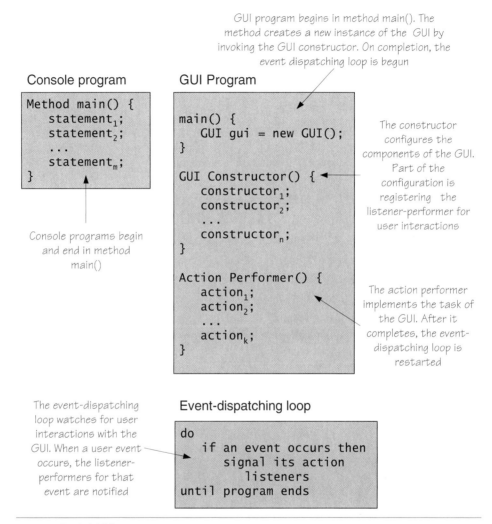

GUI program begins in method main(). The method creates a new instance of the GUI by invoking the GUI constructor. On completion, the event dispatching loop is begun

Console program

```
Method main() {
    statement₁;
    statement₂;
    ...
    statementₘ;
}
```

Console programs begin and end in method main()

GUI Program

```
main() {
    GUI gui = new GUI();
}

GUI Constructor() {
    constructor₁;
    constructor₂;
    ...
    constructorₙ;
}

Action Performer() {
    action₁;
    action₂;
    ...
    actionₖ;
}
```

The constructor configures the components of the GUI. Part of the configuration is registering the listener-performer for user interactions

The action performer implements the task of the GUI. After it completes, the event-dispatching loop is restarted

The event-dispatching loop watches for user interactions with the GUI. When a user event occurs, the listener-performers for that event are notified

Event-dispatching loop

```
do
    if an event occurs then
        signal its action
            listeners
until program ends
```

A `Windchill` GUI object has nine attributes and therefore nine instance variables. These variables are

- `window`: references a `JFrame` representing the window containing the other components of the GUI;

- `legendArea`: references a `JTextArea` representing the multiline program legend;

- `fahrTag`: references a `JLabel` representing the label for the data entry area supplying the temperature;

- `fahrText`: references a `JTextField` representing the data entry area supplying the temperature;

- `windTag`: references a `JLabel` representing the label for the data entry area supplying the windspeed;

- `windText`: references a `JTextField` representing the data entry area supplying the windspeed;
- `chillTag`: references a `JLabel` representing the label for the entry area giving the windchill;
- `chillText`: references a `JTextField` representing the entry area giving the windchill;
- `runButton`: references a `JButton` representing the button that signals a windchill calculation request.

In addition to these instance variables, the `Wind-chill` class also defines the following *class constants*. Class constants are common values to which all objects of the class *share* access.

Class constants are considered in detail in Chapter 7.

- `WINDOW_WIDTH`: an **int** value giving the initial width of a GUI;
- `WINDOW_HEIGHT`: an **int** value giving the initial height of a GUI;
- `AREA_WIDTH`: an **int** value giving the width of a program legend;
- `FIELD_WIDTH`: an **int** value giving the width of a data entry area;
- `LEGEND`: reference to the `String` representation of a program legend;
- `LAYOUT_STYLE`: reference to a `FlowLayout` that manages the layout of the GUI components within the window. In particular, a `FlowLayout` manager arranges the GUI components in a top-to-bottom, left-to-right manner in the order that they are added to the window.

The definition of program `Windchill.java` in Listing I.1 is markedly different from our previous program definitions. The differences are apparent from the start of the `Windchill` class definition (line 7).

public class Windchill **implements** ActionListener {

The keyword indicates that the class will implement some interface specifications

ActionListener requires a method actionPerformed() be implemented for handling GUI action events

Keyword **implements** indicates that the class definition satisfies the specifications of the *interfaces* that follow the keyword. Informally, an interface is a template describing features of a class. Java requires that action performers for GUI events implement the `ActionListener` interface.

Interfaces are discussed in Chapter 9

Most events are handled directly by the GUI component with which the user interacted (e.g., a `JTextField` object handles the entering and editing of data in its text box). However, an application-specific response is needed for a run-button event—the event must initiate the computing and displaying of the windchill. To define its response for that event, class `Windchill` implements the **ActionListener** interface. Figure I.4 illustrates the `Windchill` event-handling process.

Listing G.1.1 Windchill.java

```
1.   // Windchill GUI
2.
3.   import javax.swing.*;
4.   import java.awt.*;
5.   import java.awt.event.*;
6.
7.   public class Windchill implements ActionListener {
8.      // class constants
9.      private static final int WINDOW_WIDTH = 350;    // pixels
10.     private static final int WINDOW_HEIGHT = 185;   // pixels
11.     private static final int FIELD_WIDTH = 20;      // characters
12.     private static final int AREA_WIDTH = 40;       // characters
13.
14.     private static final FlowLayout LAYOUT_STYLE =
15.        new FlowLayout();
16.
17.     private static final String LEGEND = "This windchill "
18.        + "calculator is intended for velocities greater than 4 mph.";
19.
20.     // instance variables
21.
22.     // window for GUI
23.     private JFrame window = new JFrame("Windchill Calculator");
24.
25.     // legend
26.     private JTextArea legendArea = new JTextArea(LEGEND, 2,
27.        AREA_WIDTH);
28.
29.     // user entry area for temperature
30.     private JLabel fahrTag = new JLabel("Fahrenheit temperature");
31.     private JTextField fahrText = new JTextField(FIELD_WIDTH);
32.
33.     // user entry area for windspeed
34.     private JLabel windTag = new JLabel("         Windspeed (mph)");
35.     private JTextField windText = new JTextField(FIELD_WIDTH);
36.
37.     // entry area for windchill result
38.     private JLabel chillTag = new JLabel(" Windchill temperature");
39.     private JTextField chillText = new JTextField(FIELD_WIDTH);
40.
41.     // run button
42.     private JButton runButton = new JButton("Run");
43.
44.     // Windchill(): constructor
45.     public Windchill() {
46.        // configure GUI
47.        window.setSize(WINDOW_WIDTH, WINDOW_HEIGHT);
48.        window.setDefaultCloseOperation(JFrame.EXIT_ON_CLOSE);
49.
50.        legendArea.setEditable(false);
51.        legendArea.setLineWrap(true);
52.        legendArea.setWrapStyleWord(true);
53.        legendArea.setBackground(window.getBackground());
54.
```

Listing G.1.1 **Windchill.java** **(Continued)**

```
55.            chillText.setEditable(false);
56.            chillText.setBackground(Color.WHITE);
57.
58.            // register event listener
59.            runButton.addActionListener(this);
60.
61.            // add components to container
62.            Container c = window.getContentPane();
63.            c.setLayout(LAYOUT_STYLE);
64.
65.            c.add(legendArea);
66.            c.add(fahrTag);
67.            c.add(fahrText);
68.            c.add(windTag);
69.            c.add(windText);
70.            c.add(chillTag);
71.            c.add(chillText);
72.            c.add(runButton);
73.
74.            // display GUI
75.            window.show();
76.        }
77.
78.        // actionPerformed(): run button action event handler
79.        public void actionPerformed(ActionEvent e) {
80.            // get user's responses
81.            String response1 = fahrText.getText();
82.            double t = Double.parseDouble(response1);
83.            String response2 = windText.getText();
84.            double v = Double.parseDouble(response2);
85.
86.            // compute windchill
87.            double windchillTemperature = 0.081 * (t - 91.4)
88.                    * (3.71*Math.sqrt(v) + 5.81 - 0.25*v) + 91.4;
89.
90.            int perceivedTemperature =
91.                    (int) Math.round(windchillTemperature);
92.
93.            // display windchill
94.            String output = String.valueOf(perceivedTemperature);
95.            chillText.setText(output);
96.        }
97.
98.        // main(): application entry point
99.        public static void main(String[] args) {
100.           Windchill gui = new Windchill();
101.       }
102.   }
```

The Windchill class definition has four sections. The first section, lines 8–42, specifies a collection of **private** class constants and instance variables that are used elsewhere in the definition.

Figure G.I.4 **Run button action-event processing.**

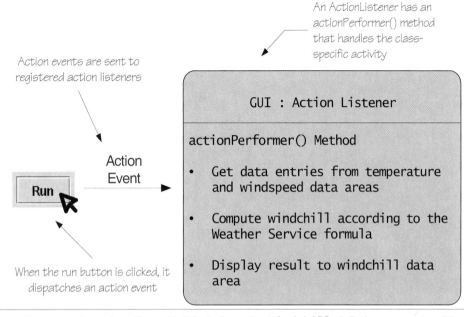

The second section, lines 44–76, defines the Windchill default constructor. The constructor configures the instance variable GUI components so that they are ready to perform the windchill computation upon user request.

The third section, lines 78–96, defines the event handler method actionPerformed(). Implementing this event handling method is the only requirement of the ActionListener interface. The interface requires the method have the form

public void actionPerformed(ActionEvent e)

where class ActionEvent is part of standard package java.awt.event. The Action-Event class is the basis for representing all swing windowing events.

The fourth section, lines 98–101, defines method main(), the application program's entry point. With GUI-based programs, method main() often is trivial to implement. For example, in this program it defines only a new instance of the class's GUI.

Windchill gui = **new** Windchill();

We now discuss each of the four sections in turn.

G.I.2.I CLASS CONSTANTS AND INSTANCE VARIABLES

The class constants and instance variables section begins with the definitions of six constants. The constants are used in configuring the various components of the windchill

GUI. The indication that the six definitions are specifying class constants is their use of modifiers **final** and **static**. Modifier **final** indicates a constant is being defined; modifier **static** indicates that the element is common to the entire class rather than to just an individual object.

Constants WINDOW_WIDTH and WINDOW_HEIGHT are the initial dimensions of the GUI. Constant FIELD_WIDTH is the width of the text boxes for the inputs and output of the windchill computation. Constant AREA_WIDTH is the width of the text box for displaying the windchill legend.

```
// class constants
private static final int WINDOW_WIDTH = 350;    // pixels
private static final int WINDOW_HEIGHT = 185;   // pixels
private static final int FIELD_WIDTH = 20;      // characters
private static final int AREA_WIDTH = 40;       // characters
```

FlowLayout constant LAYOUT_STYLE describes how the components of the GUI are to be arranged in the window. In particular, a FlowLayout manager arranges GUI components in a top-to-bottom, left-to-right manner in the order that they are added to the window.

```
private static final FlowLayout LAYOUT_STYLE =
    FlowLayout();
```

Figure I.5 shows that if the width of the JFrame is increased, the GUI components flow upward to fill the available space.

Figure G.I.5   **Increased window width causes component rearrangement.**

If a window does not specify a layout manager, then the last component added to the window occupies the entire window. Figure I.6 demonstrates how the windchill GUI would look if no layout manager is specified.

The last constant definition is for String constant LEGEND representing the text of the program legend.

```
private static final String LEGEND = "This windchill "
    + " calculator is intended for velocities greater than 4 mph."
```

Figure G.I.6 **Windchill GUI in the absence of a layout manager.**

Following the class constants come the instance variables definitions. The definitions initialize the instance variables of each new `Windchill` GUI object. Each `Windchill` GUI object has its own copy of the instance variables.

The first instance variable is the `JFrame` variable `window`. A `JFrame` acts as a *container* that holds the components of the GUI. A `JFrame` is similar in form to the other windows on your desktop (e.g, it has a frame and title bar) and can be manipulated like other windows (e.g., minimized, maximized, and moved).

Variable `window` references a new `JFrame` window object. The `JFrame` constructor titles the new window using its `String` parameter `"Windchill Calculator"`.

```
// window for GUI
private JFrame window = new JFrame("Windchill Calculator");
```

The second instance variable is `legendArea`. It references a new `JTextArea` object that acts as a multiline text box. The `JTextArea` constructor creating the object takes three parameters.

```
// legend
private JTextArea legendArea = new JTextArea(LEGEND, 2,
    AREA_WIDTH);
```

The first parameter is the string to be displayed in its text box, which in this case is the `String` referenced by `LEGEND`. The second and third parameters are the dimensions of the new text box—the number of lines and the numbers of characters per line. For `legendArea`, its `JTextArea` is a two-line text box that displays `AREA_WIDTH` characters per line.

There is a pair of instance variables associated with each of the following: the input temperature, the input windspeed, and the windchill output. Each pair defines two new objects—a `JLabel` and a `JTextField`. The label clues the user on what information is needed or supplied, and the text entry area serves as the conduit between the user and the program.

For example, variable `fahrTag` references a new `JLabel` object whose label signals the user to supply the temperature of interest and variable `fahrText` references a new `JTextField` object that provides the text box in which the user enters that temperature.

```
// user entry area for temperature
private JLabel fahrTag = new JLabel("Fahrenheit temperature");
private JTextField fahrText = new JTextField(FIELD_WIDTH);
```

The label is produced using a `JLabel` constructor. The constructor uses its `String` parameter `"Fahrenheit temperature"` to set the text of its new label. The text entry area is produced using a `JTextField` constructor. This constructor uses its **int** parameter `FIELD_WIDTH` for the width of its new text box.

The text that makes up a `JLabel` is noneditable by the program user. However, the text fields of a `JTextArea` or `JTextField` are user-editable by default.

A JLabel is noneditable by the user

By default the text field of a JTextField is editable by the user

The objects referenced by variables `windTag` and `windText` enable the user to supply the windspeed of interest. The objects referenced by variables `chillTag` and `chillText` provide the means for displaying the result of a windchill request.

```
// user entry area for windspeed
private JLabel windTag = new JLabel("          Windspeed (mph)");
private JTextField windText = new JTextField(FIELD_WIDTH);

// entry area for windchill result
private JLabel chillTag = new JLabel(" Windchill temperature");
private JTextField chillText = new JTextField(FIELD_WIDTH);
```

In order to align the three label and text entry pairs one after the other in the window, blanks are used to make the windspeed and windchill labels the same length as the temperature label.

On our system, the default label and entry area font is a monospaced font (i.e., all characters have the same width). However, the default font on most computer systems is nonmonospaced. On such systems determining the number of blanks to align labels can be a trial-and-error process.

The last of the instance variables is `runButton`.

```
// run button
private JButton runButton = new JButton("Run");
```

Variable `runButton` references a new `JButton` object. The `JButton` constructor creating the object expects a single parameter that specifies the button's label. In this case, the new button has the label `"Run"`.

With these class constants and instance variables, the `Windchill` default constructor configures and displays the GUI so that whenever its run button is clicked, the `action-`

Performed() method first accesses the entry areas that are referenced by fahrText and windText so that it can compute the associated windchill. Method actionPer-formed() then displays the windchill in the entry area referenced by chillText.

We now turn our attention to Windchill default constructor Windchill().

G.I.2.2   GUI CONSTRUCTION

When a constructor begins execution, it configures, as necessary, the newly initialized copies of the instance variables for the object under construction. For the Windchill GUI, all nine instance variables require manipulation.

The Windchill constructor begins by sizing the window that will hold the GUI. For this purpose, the Windchill constructor signals the window through JFrame instance method setSize(). Method setSize() expects two parameters giving the width and height of the new window in pixels.

```
window.setSize(WINDOW_WIDTH, WINDOW_HEIGHT);
```

The constructor then configures the program to terminate when the window closes. It does so by invoking JFrame instance method setDefaultCloseOperation().

```
window.setDefaultCloseOperation(JFrame.EXIT_ON_CLOSE);
```

The parameter JFrame.EXIT_ON_CLOSE is a JFrame class constant whose value indicates that the program is to be terminated when this JFrame is closed.

The legend for the GUI then is configured. Variable legendArea is associated with the JTextArea object that holds the program's legend. Because the user should not be allowed to alter the warning, the JTextArea object is signaled through its instance method setEditable() to make its text field *noneditable*.

```
legendArea.setEditable(false);
```

Method setEditable() expects a single **boolean** value as its parameter. The **boolean** value **false** indicates that the text field of the JTextArea is noneditable; a **boolean** value of **true** indicates that the text field is editable. Figure I.7 illustrates why a legend should be made noneditable.

The other configuring done with legendArea ensures that the legend is displayed properly within its entry area. By default, a JTextArea object does not wrap its text. To signal that wrapping is desired, its method setLineWrap() is invoked.

```
legendArea.setLineWrap(true);
```

Method setLineWrap() expects a single **boolean** value as its parameter. The value **false** indicates that its text is not to be wrapped; a value of **true** indicates that its text is to be wrapped.

Simply requesting line wrapping is insufficient. The default line wrapping style is to break up text only when a text-field line is completely full. This style can cause a word to

Figure G.I.7 **Dangers of an editable legend.**

Figure G.I.8 **Bad line wrapping.**

split over two lines (see Figure I.8). To ensure line wrapping only at word boundaries, a JTextArea object is signaled through its method setWrapStyleWord().

```
legendArea.setWrapStyleWord(true);
```

Method setWrapStyleWord() expects a single **boolean** value as its parameter. The value **true** indicates that its text is to be wrapped at word boundaries; the value **false** indicates that its text is to wrapped when a text-field line is full.

The background color of the legend area can be altered to match the background color of the window (the default background color of a JTextArea is white). To signal a JTextArea background color change, its method setBackground() is invoked with a parameter specifying the desired color.

```
legendArea.setBackground(window.getBackground());
```

To match the two background colors, the color of the JFrame is obtained using its instance method getBackground().

Abstract Window Toolkit

The package `java.awt` (*Abstract Window Toolkit*) was a solid first attempt at providing a portable graphics library for user interfaces. Because `awt` components generally require more work by the operating system than their `javax.swing` counterparts require, Java programmers tend to look to `swing` for graphical components. However, the `awt` is used by programmers and by `swing` for such things as color and font representation and drawing.

Definitions of many awt classes are available in Appendix E. For complete documentation go to www.javasoft.com

The `JTextField` associated with `chillText` should be made noneditable—it is the program that supplies the value, not the user.

```
chillText.setEditable(false);
```

The prohibition regarding the editing of the text field applies only to the user and not to the object itself.

Making it noneditable, causes Java to change its background color from the standard `JTextField` background color. To override the color change, `JTextField` method `setBackground()` is invoked.

```
chillText.setBackground(Color.WHITE);
```

`Color.WHITE` is a class constant of class `java.awt.Color` representing the color white.

The action performer for a `JButton` then is specified using `JButton` instance method `addActionListener()`.

```
runButton.addActionListener(this);
```

The parameter to `addActionListener()` specifies the object whose method `action-Performed()` processes the clicking of the run button. The object in question is the GUI under construction; that is, it is the object currently being configured by the `Windchill` default constructor method. The parameter to `addActionListener()` is **this**. Keyword **this** is the Java mechanism for referencing the object being manipulated by a constructor or an instance method.

It may seem confusing, but the GUI components are not added directly to the `JFrame`. Instead they are added to the container inside that frame. As its name indicates, a `JFrame` is a frame. The frame includes the title bar and border edging that can be manipulated like other windows under the operating system. Inside the perimeter of the frame is a *content pane*. The content pane is the container that directly holds the other components of the GUI. The type of the content pane is `awt` class `Container`.

To gain access to the content pane, the `Windchill` constructor uses `JFrame` method `getContentPane()` to initialize `Container` variable c.

```
Container c = window.getContentPane();
```

With variable c, the layout manager can be set for the content pane using `Container` method `setLayout()`.

```
c.setLayout(LAYOUT_STYLE);
```

To complete the configuration of the GUI, the eight GUI components are added to the content pane using `Container` method `add()`.

```
c.add(legendArea);
c.add(fahrTag);
c.add(fahrText);
c.add(windTag);
c.add(windText);
c.add(chillTag);
c.add(chillText);
c.add(runButton);
```

Once the configuration is complete, it is appropriate to make the window *visible*. Up until this point, the `Windchill` constructor has set up the graphical components that make up its interface, but it has not displayed them. To do so, the constructor uses `JFrame` method `setVisible()`.

```
window.setVisible(true);
```

By default, `JTextArea`, `JLabel`, `JTextField`, and `JButton` instances are visible once the window in which they have been placed is made visible. Therefore, setting their visibility individually is not necessary. The display completes the construction of the GUI, so the `Windchill` default constructor is done.

G.I.2.3   EVENT HANDLING AND ACTIONPERFORMED()

Implementing the button action performer method `actionPerformed()` is relatively straightforward. When invoked in response to the user selecting the run button, the performer first gets the user inputs from the text fields associated with `JTextField` variables `fahrText` and `windText`. Method `actionPerformed()` uses the two values to compute the associated windchill. The windchill value then is used to set the text field associated with variable `chillText`.

A `JTextField` has a method `getText()` that returns a copy of the text in its text field in `String` form. The `String` representation can be converted to a numeric representation using `Double` class method `parseDouble()`. Thus, to initialize a **double** variable t representing the temperature of interest, the `Windchill` action performer uses code segment

```
// compute windchill
String response1 = fahrText.getText();
double t = Double.parseDouble(response1);
```

For the GUI depicted in Figure I.9, variable t is initialized to the **double** value 21.

Figure G.I.9   **Depiction of a sample run of Windchill.java**

The action performer uses a similar segment to initialize a **double** variable v representing the windspeed of interest.

```
String response2 = windText.getText();
double v = Double.parseDouble(response2);
```

For the GUI depicted in Figure I.9, variable v is initialized to the value 6.

Given v and t, a **double** variable windchillTemperature can be defined and properly initialized. To translate the windchill formula

$$t_{wc} = 0.081(t - 91.4)(3.71\sqrt{v} + 5.81 - 0.25v) + 91.4$$

into a valid Java expression, a square root is needed. API Math provides a class method sqrt() for calculating square root values. With that method, the translation of the windchill formula can be accomplished.

```
// compute windchill
double windchillTemperature = 0.081 * (t - 91.4)
          * (3.71*Math.sqrt(v) + 5.81 - 0.25*v) + 91.4;
```

Because variable windchillTemperature is a **double** variable, its value can have a significant number of digits after the decimal point. These digits are uninteresting to most users. Therefore, the action performer uses Math class method round() to produce the integer value closest to windchillTemperature.

```
int perceivedTemperature =
     (int) Math.round(windchillTemperature);
```

As method round() returns a **long** value, the cast (**int**) converts that value to an **int** value. The cast is necessary because Java does not implicitly narrow a **long** value to an **int** value.

To display the windchill, the action performer converts the **int** value to a String representation using the String class method valueOf(). The method expects a single **int** value as its parameter and returns a String version of the number.

```
// display windchill
String output = String.valueOf(perceivedTemperature);
```

The action performer uses that string value as a parameter to JTextField method set-Text(). The method updates the text box associated with variable chillText. In particular, by invoking

```
chillText.setText(output);
```

the correct windchill output is displayed (e.g., see Figure I.9).

The displaying of the windchill computation finishes the event handling for the button-clicking event. The program then continues with the event-dispatching loop until another action event occurs or the program is ended.

G.I.2.4   METHOD MAIN()

Method main() of the Windchill program is trivial to implement. The method just defines a new instance of Windchill.

```
public static void main(String[] args) {
    Windchill gui = new Windchill();
}
```

No other work is needed, because the constructor handles the building and display of the GUI and the actionPerformed() method handles the user interaction.

If desired, method main() can be modified to create multiple Windchill GUIs. Each of the windchill calculators would be displayed simultaneously.

```
public static void main(String[] args) {
    Windchill gui1 = new Windchill();
    Windchill gui2 = new Windchill();
}
```

This scenario is depicted in Figure I.10.

This discussion completes our introduction to GUIs.

FigureG.I.10 Two instances of the windchill calculator.

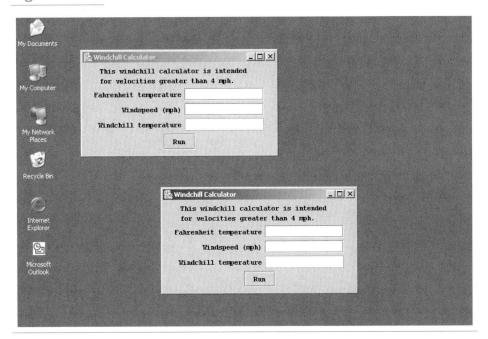

REVIEW

- The execution of GUI-based program begins in its method `main()`. Method `main()` is responsible normally only for creating an instance (object) of the GUI. After creating the GUI, the flow of control goes from method `main()` to an event-dispatching loop that checks repeatedly for user interactions with the GUI (action events). When an action event occurs, an action performer method is invoked for each listener of that event. The performer then processes the interaction. After the performer handles the event, flow of control is again given to the event-dispatching loop to watch for future user interactions. The process continues until an action performer signals that the program has completed its task.

- A container is a GUI component that can hold other GUI components.

- A layout manager organizes the placement of GUI components within a container.

- The `awt` class `FlowLayout` arranges the GUI components of a container in a top-to-bottom left-to-right manner in the order that they were added to the container.

- `JFrame` is the `swing` class for representing a window. A `JFrame` is similar in form to the other windows on your desktop and can be manipulated like those other windows.

- A `JFrame` constructor takes a single string as its parameter, which is displayed as the window title.

- A `JFrame` can be displayed by invoking its instance method `setvisible()` with the **boolean** value **true** as its parameter.

- Most `swing` components have a instance method `setBackground()` that expects a `Color` value as its parameter. The value is used to set the background color of the component.

- `JLabel` is the `swing` class for representing a single-line label in a noneditable form.

- One `JLabel` constructor takes a `String` parameter that specifies the text to be displayed. By default, a `JLabel` object is visible once the container in which it has been placed is visible.

- `JTextField` is the `swing` class for representing a single-line text box by which the user can provide input information to the program.

- One `JTextField` constructor takes an **int** parameter that specifies the width of the text box in characters. By default a `JTextField` object is visible once the container in which it has been placed is visible.

- A `JTextArea` is the `swing` class for representing a multiline text box by which the user can provide input information to the program.

- One `JTextArea` constructor takes two **int** parameters. The first parameter is the number of rows of characters for the text box; the second parameter is the width of the text box in characters. By default a `JTextArea` object is visible once the container in which it has been placed is visible.

- `JTextField` and `JTextArea` both have an instance method `setEditable()`. Method `setEditable()` expects a single **boolean** value as its parameter. The value **false** indicates that the text is currently noneditable; a value of **true** indicates that the text is currently editable. By default, the text boxes of a `JTextField` and a `JTextArea` are editable.

- `JButton` is a the `swing` class for representing a push button.

- One `JButton` constructor takes a `String` parameter that specifies the button label.

- A `JButton` has an instance method `addActionListener()` for specifying which object is responsible for implementing the action associated with the button. A button click generates an event that causes the indicated object's method `actionPerformed()` to be executed.

- An interface specifies what methods a class must define.

- The `ActionListener` interface requires the implementation of a method `actionPerformed()`. The method takes a parameter of class type `ActionEvent`.

- Objects that handle a button event must implement the `ActionListener` interface.

- `JTextField`, `JLabel`, and `JTextArea` all have an instance method `getText()`. The method returns a `String` that represents the associated object's text.

- `JTextField`, `JLabel`, and `JTextArea` all have an instance method `setText()`. The method expects a single `String` value as a parameter. The value is used to update the associated object's text.

G.I.4 SELF-TEST

SI.1 Give a code segment that creates a new `JFrame` with dimensions 200 by 225. When this `JFrame` closes, it should terminate its program.

SI.2   Give a code segment that defines a new `JTextArea` that uses two lines to display the text "Ring around the rosey, a pocketful of posies." The `JTextArea` should not allow line wrapping that breaks up a word.

SI.3 Give a code segment that defines a window with the title `"By any other name"`. The window should contain a label `"Rose"`.

SI.4 Design and implement a program `TemperatureConverter.java` that implements the following GUI.

G.I.5   EXERCISES

I.1   Design and implement a program that produces the following window.

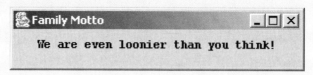

I.2   Design and implement a program that computes the average of three numbers. Your program should use a GUI similar to the following.

I.3   Design and implement a program that inputs the weight of an object in pounds and outputs the weight of the object in kilograms. Your program should use a GUI similar to the following.

I.4   Design and implement a GUI program that computes the volume of a requested object described in terms of its mass and density. The mass will be given in grams; the density will be in grams per cubic centimeter. The relationship of mass, density, and volume of a variable is given by

$$Density = \frac{Mass}{Volume}$$

I.5   Design and implement a GUI program that gets from its user the distance a train travels in miles and the time it takes to travel that distance. The program should compute and display the average speed of the train for that journey.

I.6   Design and implement a GUI program that gets from its user a person's age and heart rate. The program computes and displays the number of heart beats since the person was born. Assume that there are 365 days in a year.

I.7   Design and implement a GUI program that computes the monthly interest charge on a credit card account. The program should acquire the previous balance, the payment amount, the number of days in the billing cycle, the day of the billing cycle the payment was made, and the monthly interest rate. For a formula on credit card interest see Exercise 2.39.

I.8   Design and implement a GUI program that processes a user-supplied date. The program should display the date's position in that year. For example, if the date is 12 29 2006, then the displayed number is 363.

I.9   Design and implement a GUI program that processes a value in the interval 0 … 99. The program displays the value in words. For example, if the input value is 21, then twenty-one is displayed.

I.10   Design and implement a GUI program that process two user-specified x- and y-coordinates. The program reports the slope and y-intercept of the associated lines.

I.11   Design and implement a GUI program that processes two integer values as input. The program displays whether the inputs are both positive, both negative, or one positive and one negative.

I.12   Design and implement a GUI program that processes a user-specified filename and string. The program displays the numbers of occurrences of that string in the specified file.

I.13   Design and implement a program that processes a user-specified filename. The program displays the number of lines and characters in the file.

G.I.6   PROGRAMMING PROJECT — TRAINING ZONES

There are two kinds of exercise—aerobic and anaerobic exercise. Normally, sustained activities such as bicycling, running, or swimming are aerobic exercises. While activities requiring bursts of activity such as weight lifting and tennis are anaerobic exercises. Both types of exercise have their advantages. For example, anaerobic exercise can stimulate muscle growth and aerobic exercise can raise your metabolism by stimulating the production of fat-burning enzymes.

> The object of this programming project is to design and implement a GUI-based program

For a sustained activity to be an aerobic exercise there needs to be an elevation in the heart rate. However, the elevation cannot be extreme. If the elevation is extreme then muscles are oxygen deprived and they burn sugars rather than fat. Research indicates that there is a heart beat rate training zone that should be kept in order to get the maximum aerobic effect from an exercise. The actual training zone for a person is based on many factors, such as the individual's normal heart rate, fitness, health, weight, etc. However, there are formulas indicating reasonable training zones for the majority of fit people with normal heart rates. The formula we use in this section comes from the USA President's Council on Fitness and Sports (www.fitness.gov). The formula works as follows: subtract the age of interest from 220; 65% of that value is the low end of the training zone range and 80% of that value is the high end of the training zone range.

The problem goal is a program that computes a training zone according to the following problem statement.

> *Provide a GUI-based training zone calculator that acquires an age of interest. The calculator then computes and displays the training zone for that age. The low end of the training zone is 65% of the difference between 220 and the specified age. The high end of the training zone is 80% of the difference between 220 and the specified age.*

ANALYSIS AND DESIGN

Before designing the necessary information structures and algorithm, you should depict a sample input/output behavior. A depiction should helps clarify what information is being provided and what information is to be computed. Furthermore, if the software is being developed for a client, then it also aids you in verifying with the client that the proper problem is being solved. An example of a possible interface for the training zone calculator is given in Figure I.11.

Figure G.I.11 **A possible training zone calculator GUI.**

An analysis of the problem statement indicates that you need to acquire one piece of information from the user—the age of interest. From that information and the training zone formula you derive the lower and upper heart beat rates for the training zone associated with that age of interest. An analysis of the problem also indicates that in developing an algorithm three integer variables are appropriate: *ageOfInterest*, *lowBeatRate*, and *highBeatRate*. Also, three constants are appropriate: *BASE_RATE* with value 220, *LOW_ZONE_MULTIPLER* with value 65%, and *HIGH_ZONE_MULTIPLIER* with value 80%.

These calculation variables and constants are in addition to the GUI component variables that you decide to use. For the interface displayed in Figure I.11, variables were used for the window, legend, labels, text fields, and run button.

IMPLEMENTATION

Producing a Java program `TrainingZone.java` from the problem statement can be done nicely with a single class `TrainingZone`. The class should be documented and laid out appropriately. For example, the code should make use of program header and method comments, whitespace, and a consistent indentation scheme.

TESTING

One way to test a program informally is to do a *hand-check*—compute by hand what the output should be for several different ages. Then run your program using those same ages and compare the results. If there are any discrepancies, determine whether your program or hand calculation is incorrect. If the program is incorrect, review the formulas given above and your implementation of them. You may also consider adding some debugging statements or using a debugger to display intermediary results in an effort to determine where your program's correctness breaks down.

G.I.7   SELF-TEST ANSWERS

S.I.1 A possible code segment is

```
JFrame window = new JFrame("Window");
window.setSize(WINDOW_WIDTH, WINDOW_HEIGHT);
window.setDefaultCloseOperation(JFrame.EXIT_ON_CLOSE);
```

S.I.2 A possible code segment is

```
JTextArea saying = new JTextArea("Ring around the rosey, "
    + "a pocketful of posies.", 2, 25);
saying.setLineWrap(true);
saying.setWrapStyleWord(true);
```

S.I.3 A possible code segment is

```
JFrame window = new JFrame("By any other name");
JLabel roseLabel = new JLabel("Rose");

Container c = window.getContentPane();
c.setLayout(new FlowLayout())
c.add(roseLabel);
```

S.I.4 A possible program is

```
import javax.swing.*;
import java.awt.*;
import java.awt.event.*;

public class TemperatureConverter implements
                                ActionListener {
```

```
       private static final int FIELD_WIDTH = 20;

       private JFrame window
          = new JFrame("Temperature converter");
       private JLabel fahrLabel = new JLabel("Fahrenheit");
       private JLabel celsiusLabel = new JLabel("  Celsius");
       private JTextField fahrField
          = new JTextField(FIELD_WIDTH);
       private JTextField celsiusField
          = new JTextField(FIELD_WIDTH);

       private JButton runButton = new JButton("Run");

       public TemperatureConverter () {
          window.setDefaultCloseOperation(
            JFrame.EXIT_ON_CLOSE);

          runButton.addActionListener(this);
          celsiusField.setEditable(false);
          celsiusField.setBackground(Color.WHITE);

          Container c = window.getContentPane();
          c.setLayout(new FlowLayout());

          c.add(fahrLabel);
          c.add(fahrField);
          c.add(celsiusLabel);
          c.add(celsiusField);
          c.add(runButton);

          window.setVisible(true);
       }

       public void actionPerformed(ActionEvent e) {
          int fahrenheit
            = Integer.parseInt(fahrField.getText());
          double celsius = 5 * (fahrenheit-32) / 9;

          celsiusField.setText(String.valueOf(celsius));
       }

       public static void main(String[] args) {
          TemperatureConverter gui
            = new TemperatureConverter();
       }
    }
```

7 PROGRAMMING WITH METHODS AND CLASSES

To assist in the object-oriented design and implementation of software systems, Java provides many different class and method mechanisms. When properly applied, these mechanisms enable designers to produce effective data representations that enable information to be expressed and manipulated in an intuitive manner. This chapter explores Java mechanisms that support the manipulation and calculation of values through method invocations; the use of class and instance variables; and the implementation of constructors, accessors, mutators, and facilitators. The examination begins with the method invocation process.

OBJECTIVES

- Explain the method invocation process.
- Introduce the concepts of locality, scope, and nesting.
- Consider the nuances of method overloading and overriding.
- Explore the use of class methods and class constants and variables through the use of the static modifier.
- Explore the use of instance methods for accessing and manipulating object attributes.

7.1 MODIFIER STATIC

There are two types of methods in Java—instance methods and class methods. An instance method operates on a object (i.e., an *instance* of the class) and a class method is a service provided by a class and it is not associated with a particular object.

Both instance and class methods are used in the following code segment.

```
String s = new String("Help every cow reach its potential!");
int n = s.length();    ◄───────────────── Invoking instance method length()
String t = String.valueOf(n);  ◄───
                                      ◄──── Invoking class method valueOf()
```

In the code segment, instance method `length()` is invoked with respect to the `String` object referenced by variable s. Therefore, when this invocation executes, it is the attributes of the `String` object referenced by s that are being examined. Because the length of that `String` is 35, **int** variable n is initialized to 35.

In the same code segment, method `valueOf()` is invoked. Because the invocation expression `String.valueOf(n)` starts with the class name rather than an object, it is clear that `valueOf()` is a class method. `String` class method `valueOf()` provides the service of returning a reference to a `String` representation of its actual parameter. As a result, `String` variable t references a `String` object representing "35".

Besides supporting class methods, Java also supports class variables and class constants. Each class variable or class constant is a common value to which all objects of the class share access. Class variables and class constants represent collective information that is not specific to individual objects of the class. For example, a particular rectangle has its own specific width and height, but all rectangles have four sides. The value associated with a class variable or class constant is often referred to as a class *data field*.

Many of the standard Java classes make use of class variables and class constants. Examples include the predefined colors of class `Color` and the mathematical constants of class `Math`.

```
Color favoriteColor = Color.MAGENTA;  ◄───  Accessing Color class
                                             constant MAGENTA
double favoriteNumber = Math.PI - Math.E;  ◄───
                                             Accessing Math class
                                             constants PI and E
```

Because the `Color` and `Math` class constants are **public**, access to those constants is not limited to the respective classes.

In Java, class methods, variables, and constants are specified through the use of the modifier **static**. Examples of class methods and class constants are provided in class Conversion of Listing 7.1. We previously gave examples of class methods whenever we defined the method main() of an application program.

Class Conversion supports conversion between English and metric values. It provides several **public** class methods and **private** class constants that support standard conversions. The class make uses of the following equivalencies.

- *d* degrees Fahrenheit = (*d* – 32)/1.8 degrees Celsius

- 1 mile = 1.609344 kilometers

- 1 gallon = 3.785411784 liters

- 1 ounce (avdp) = 28.349523125 grams

- 1 acre = 0.0015625 square miles = 0.40468564 hectares

Using the provided formula for Fahrenheit to Celsius makes it straightforward to define a temperature conversion method

Modifier public indicates other classes can use the method

Modifier static indicates the method is a class method

```
public static double fahrenheitToCelsius(double fahrenheit) {
    return (fahrenheit - 32) / 1.8;
}
```

Observe there is no reference in the method to an attribute of an implicit Conversion object (i.e., a "this" object). This absence is a class method requirement. Class methods are invoked without respect to any particular object

and a complementary temperature conversion method.

```
public static double celsiusToFahrenheit(double celsius) {
    return 1.8 * celsius + 32;
}
```

To perform the other conversions, class Conversion makes use of several constants that it represents as class constants.

```
private static final double KILOMETERS_PER_MILE = 1.609344;
private static final double LITERS_PER_GALLON = 3.785411784;
private static final double GRAMS_PER_OUNCE = 28.349523125;
private static final double HECTARES_PER_ACRE = 0.40468564;
```

Java allows all methods of a class to use its class constants and class variables. Furthermore, if the class constants and class variables are **public**, classes elsewhere can use them. Because the Conversion class constants are **private**, only Conversion methods are permitted to use them.

Listing 7.1   Conversion.java

```java
1.  // Conversion methods
2.
3.  public class Conversion {
4.      // conversion equivalencies
5.      private static final double KILOMETERS_PER_MILE = 1.609344;
6.      private static final double LITERS_PER_GALLON = 3.785411784;
7.      private static final double GRAMS_PER_OUNCE = 28.349523125;
8.      private static final double HECTARES_PER_ACRE = 0.40468564;
9.
10.     // temperature conversions methods
11.     public static double fahrenheitToCelsius(double fahrenheit) {
12.         return (fahrenheit - 32) / 1.8;
13.     }
14.
15.     public static double celsiusToFahrenheit(double celsius) {
16.         return 1.8 * celsius + 32;
17.     }
18.
19.     // length conversions methods
20.     public static double kilometersToMiles(double kilometers) {
21.         return kilometers / KILOMETERS_PER_MILE;
22.     }
23.
24.     public static double milesToKilometers(double miles) {
25.         return miles * KILOMETERS_PER_MILE;
26.     }
27.
28.     // mass conversions methods
29.     public static double litersToGallons(double liters) {
30.         return liters / LITERS_PER_GALLON;
31.     }
32.
33.     public static double gallonsToLiters(double gallons) {
34.         return gallons * LITERS_PER_GALLON;
35.     }
36.
37.     public static double gramsToOunces(double grams) {
38.         return grams / GRAMS_PER_OUNCE;
39.     }
40.
41.     public static double ouncesToGrams(double ounces) {
42.         return ounces * GRAMS_PER_OUNCE;
43.     }
44.
45.     // area conversions methods
46.     public static double hectaresToAcres(double hectares) {
47.         return hectares / HECTARES_PER_ACRE;
48.     }
49.
50.     public static double acresToHectares(double acres) {
51.         return acres * HECTARES_PER_ACRE;
52.     }
53. }
```

With constant `KILOMETERS_PER_MILE`, it is straightforward to define length conversion methods.

```
// length conversions methods
public static double kilometersToMiles(double kilometers) {
   return kilometers / KILOMETERS_PER_MILE);
}

public static double milesToKilometers(double miles) {
   return miles * KILOMETERS_PER_MILE;
}
```

When a Java compiler translates one of these methods and encounters an identifier (e.g., `KILOMETERS_PER_MILE`), it first determines whether the identifier has been defined in that method. If so, that definition is used. If there is no such definition in effect, the compiler then determines whether the identifier is the name of a class or instance variable. If so, then that definition is used. Otherwise the identifier must be defined in one of the packages that the source file has imported.

With class constants `LITERS_PER_GALLON` and `GRAMS_PER_OUNCE`, it is straightforward to define the mass conversion methods.

```
// mass conversions methods
public static double litersToGallons(double liters) {
   return liters / LITERS_PER_GALLON;
}

public static double gallonsToLiters(double gallons) {
   return gallons * LITERS_PER_GALLON;
}

public static double gramsToOunces(double grams) {
   return grams/ GRAMS_PER_OUNCE;
}

   public static double ouncesToGrams(double ounces) {
      return ounces * GRAMS_PER_OUNCE;
}
```

Similarly, with class constant `HECTARES_PER_ACRE`, the area conversion methods have straightforward definitions.

```
// area conversions methods
public static double hectaresToAcres(double hectares) {
   return hectares / HECTARES_PER_ACRE;
}

public static double acresToHectares(double acres) {
   return acres * HECTARES_PER_ACRE;
}
```

A use of class `Conversion` is demonstrated in program `Converter.java` of Listing 7.2. The program prompts a user for metric values and produces the English equivalents. A sample run of the program is displayed in Figure 7.1.

Listing 7.2   Converter.java

```
1.  // Demonstrates some uses of class Conversion
2.
3.  import java.io.*;
4.  import java.text.*;
5.
6.  public class Converter {
7.      // main(): application entry point
8.      public static void main(String[] args) throws IOException {
9.          BufferedReader stdin = new BufferedReader(
10.             new InputStreamReader(System.in));
11.
12.         System.out.println();
13.         System.out.print("Enter a length in kilometers: ");
14.         double kilometers = Double.parseDouble(stdin.readLine());
15.
16.         System.out.println();
17.         System.out.print("Enter a mass in liters: ");
18.         double liters = Double.parseDouble(stdin.readLine());
19.
20.         System.out.println();
21.         System.out.print("Enter a mass in grams: ");
22.         double grams = Double.parseDouble(stdin.readLine());
23.
24.         System.out.println();
25.         System.out.print("Enter an area in hectares: ");
26.         double hectares = Double.parseDouble(stdin.readLine());
27.
28.         double miles = Conversion.kilometersToMiles(kilometers);
29.         double gallons = Conversion.litersToGallons(liters);
30.         double ounces = Conversion.gramsToOunces(grams);
31.         double acres = Conversion.hectaresToAcres(hectares);
32.
33.         NumberFormat style = NumberFormat.getNumberInstance();
34.         style.setMaximumFractionDigits(2);
35.         style.setMinimumFractionDigits(2);
36.
37.         System.out.println();
38.         System.out.println(kilometers + " kilometers = "
39.                 + style.format(miles) + " miles ");
40.         System.out.println(liters + " liters = "
41.                 + style.format(gallons) + " gallons");
42.         System.out.println(grams + " grams = "
43.                 + style.format(ounces) + " ounces");
44.         System.out.println(hectares + " hectares = "
45.                 + style.format(acres) + " acres");
46.         System.out.println();
47.     }
48. }
```

The conversion invocations occur in lines 28-31, where the values of actual parameters kilometers, liters, grams, and hectares are the user-supplied values.

```
double miles = Conversion.kilometersToMiles(kilometers);
double gallons = Conversion.litersToGallons(liters);
double ounces = Conversion.gramsToOunces(grams);
```

```
double acres = Conversion.hectaresToAcres(hectares);
```

If variables miles, gallons, ounces, and acres were displayed directly, then the conversion output would resemble the following rather than the display of Figure 7.1.

```
2.0 kilometers = 1.242742384474668 miles
3.0 liters = 0.7925161570744452 gallons
4.0 grams = 0.14109584779832166 ounces
5.0 hectares = 12.355269141746666 acres
```

To avoid the display of uninteresting digits, a NumberFormat object is created. Class NumberFormat is part of standard package java.text. The class provides in part methods for formatting and parsing numbers. The NumberFormat object is referenced by variable style.

```
NumberFormat style = NumberFormat.getNumberInstance();
```

Converter.java uses the NumberFormat object to control the number of fractional digits that appear in the formatting of a floating-point value. The digit display is controlled through NumberFormat instance methods setMinimumFractionDigits() and setMaximumFractionDigits().

```
style.setMaximumFractionDigits(2);
style.setMaximumFractionDigits(2);
```

Together the invocations cause NumberFormat method format() to return a representation with two digits after the decimal pint.

Figure 7.1 **Sample conversions.**

To produce a formatted version of a floating-point value, `NumberFormat` method `format()` is used. This instance method returns a `String` representation of its actual parameter. `Converter.java` invokes method `format()` four times—once for each of the conversion values.

```
System.out.println(kilometers + " kilometers = "
        + style.format(miles) + " miles ");
System.out.println(liters + " liters = "
        + style.format(gallons) + " gallons");
System.out.println(grams + " grams = "
        + style.format(ounces) + " ounces");
System.out.println(hectares + " hectares = "
        + style.format(acres) + " acres");
```

Although class `Converter` made use of only class constants, Java also allows class variables. For example, program `Demonstration.java` of Listing 7.3 uses a class variable `count` to maintain the number of class constructions that the program has performed.

Listing 7.3 **Demonstration.java**

```
 1.  public class Demonstration {
 2.     static private int counter = 0;
 3.     public Demonstration() {
 4.        ++counter;  // another construction has been performed
 5.     }
 6.     // main(): application entry point
 7.     public static void main(String[] args) {
 8.        Demonstration d1 = new Demonstration();
 9.        Demonstration d2 = new Demonstration();
10.        Demonstration d3 = new Demonstration();
11.        System.out.println(Demonstration.counter);
12.     }
13.  }
```

Because there are three invocations of the `Demonstration` constructor within the program, its output is

```
3
```

This analysis completes our discussion of modifier **static** and its effect on methods, constants, and variables. We now turn our attention to examining the nuances of parameter passing.

Class NumberFormat

Class `NumberFormat` also provides methods for controlling the integer part of a number.

void `setMaximumIntegerDigits(int n)`

Sets to n the maximum number of digits used in formatting the integer part of a number by this `NumberFormat`.

void `setMinimumIntegerDigits(int n)`

Sets to n the minimum number of digits used in formatting the integer part of a number by this `NumberFormat`.

A complete discussion of class `NumberFormat` appears in Appendix D.

Class methods and instance variables

Because a class method is associated with its class and not a particular object, any use of an instance variable within it must indicate explicitly the associated object. The following class StaticDemo illustrates this requirement.

```java
public class StaticDemo {
    private int number;
        public StaticDemo(int n) {
        number = n;
    }
    static void print1(StaticDemo v) {
        System.out.println(v.number);  // display v's attribute
    }
    void print2() {
        System.out.println(number);  // display attribute of
    }                                //  invoking object
}
```

Class StaticDemo has methods print1() and print2() for printing the number attribute of a StaticDemo. Because method print1() is a class method, it requires a StaticDemo as a parameter to indicate which number attribute should be displayed. Because method print2() is an instance method, there is automatically a StaticDemo object associated with its code—the StaticDemo that invoked the method.

7.2   PARAMETER PASSING

We start our discussion of parameter passing with a review of what happens during a method invocation. In this example, we make use of class methods add(), multiply(), and main() from program Demo.java of Listing 7.4. Method add() computes a sum and multiply() computes a product. The two methods are invoked by method main() to compute the sum and product of 8 and 11.

In method main(), variable sum is initialized through the invocation add(a,b) and variable product is initialized through the invocation multiply(a, b). In both invocations, the actual parameters a and b have values 8 and 11.

Actual parameters provide information that is otherwise unavailable to a method. For methods add() and multiply(), the two parameters supply the operands of interest. Without them, add() would not know what to sum and multiply() would not know what to multiply.

Whenever a method is invoked, flow of control is transferred temporarily to that method. The actual parameters in the invocation are used to initialize the formal parameters in the method's definition. For *each* method invocation, Java sets aside memory—known as the *activation record*—for that *particular* invocation. The activation record stores, among other things, the values of the formal parameters.

Listing 7.4 **Demo.java**

```
1.  // Parameter passing demonstration
2.
3.  public class Demo {
4.     // add(): returns the sum of its parameters
5.     public static double add(double x, double y) {
6.        double result = x + y;
7.        return result;
8.     }
9.
10.    // multiply(): returns the product of its parameters
11.    public static double multiply(double x, double y) {
12.       x = x * y;
13.       return x;
14.    }
15.
16.    // main(): application entry point
17.    public static void main(String[] args) {
18.       System.out.println();
19.       double a = 8;
20.       double b = 11;
21.
22.       double sum = add(a, b);
23.       System.out.println(a + " + " + b + " = " + sum);
24.
25.       double product = multiply(a, b);
26.       System.out.println(a + " * " + b + " = " + product);
27.    }
28. }
```

Figure 7.2 **Program Demo output.**

Java uses value parameter passing in an invocation. Once the actual parameters have been used to initialize the formal parameters, the actual parameters and formal parameters are independent of each other. If a method updates the value of a formal parameter, the change does not affect the actual parameter. The change is limited to the activation record containing the value of the formal parameter. As an example, we trace through a run of program Demo.java. The output of the program is displayed in Figure 7.2.

The definition of method add() specifies the names of its formal parameters to be x and y. Therefore, the invocation add(a, b) causes add() to be executed with its formal parameters x and y initialized respectively to the values of a and b.

```
                     double sum = add(a, b);
```

Initial values of formal parameters
come from the actual parameters ⟶

```
public static double add(double x, double y) { ...
```

Immediately prior to the add() invocation, the activation record for method main() would have depiction

With the invocation, a new activation record is created for method add() and the flow of control is transferred to the method. In creating this activation record, formal parameter x is initialized to the value of the actual parameter a, which in this case is the value 8.0, and formal parameter y is initialized to the value of the actual parameter b, which in this case is the value 11.0.

Therefore, if add() updates the value of its formal parameters, the change is visible only within add()—the actual parameters are left unchanged.

Formal parameters x and y are used in the initialization of variable result.

```
double result = x + y;
```

After the definition of result, the activation record for add() has depiction

Placement of declarations

In older style programs, the convention was to place all declarations at the beginning of the method. Java permits declarations to appear almost anywhere in a method. As with any stylistic issue, there are pros and cons to both approaches.

Placing a declaration at the point of the first use of the variable has the advantage that you don't have to look back at the beginning of the method to determine the type of the variable. In addition, because Java allows variable definitions to occur at the point they are first needed, variables can be initialized normally in their definition. Furthermore, if you change the code, so that the variable is no longer needed, you are much more likely to delete the now unnecessary declaration. We have encountered older style code that, after several years of maintenance, contains many useless declarations.

On the other hand, having all the declarations in a central location has some advantages. You know right where to look for the declaration. With the advent of integrated development environments and browsing tools, this advantage seems less significant. In our code, we place a declaration at or near the point of its first use.

The **return** statement for add()

```
return result;
```

then is evaluated. The return value is the value of result, which is the **double** value 19.0.

The method's completion causes the memory associated with its activation record to be released. The flow of control is returned to method main(), where the add() return value is used to initialize sum. The activation record associated with main() now has depiction

A println() invocation then displays the first line of program output.

```
8.0 + 11.0 = 19.0
```

Method multiply() is invoked to initialize variable product.

```
double product = multiply(a, b);
```

This invocation causes a transfer of the flow of control to multiply() with its formal parameters x and y initialized respectively to the values a and b. Because of the transfer, an activation record is created for method `multiply()`. The new activation record has depiction

Parameters x and y are used in an assignment to x.

```
x = x * y;
```

After the assignment, the current activation records have depiction

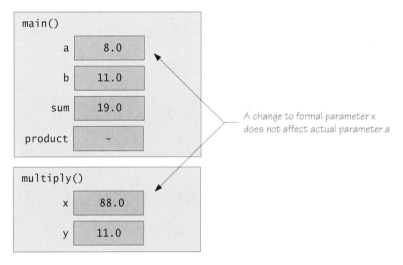

Because a formal parameter is essentially a variable local to its method, a change to formal parameter does not affect the corresponding actual parameter. The assignment to formal parameter x of `multiply()` did not affect actual parameter a of `main()`.

Formal parameters are created with the invocation of their method, their values are accessible only within the method, and they are destroyed when their method completes. The only difference between the formal parameters and the other variables defined by a method is that the formal parameters are initialized using the values of the actual parameters.

```
            double product = multiply(a, b);
```
Initial values of formal parameters
come from the actual parameters
```
public static double multiply(double x, double y) {
    x = x * y;
    return x;
}
```
Changes to formal parameters do
not affect the actual parameters

The **return** statement for `multiply()` is evaluated then.

```
return x;
```

The return value is the value of the expression x, which is 88.0. The method's completion causes the memory associated with its activation record to be released. The flow of control is returned to method `main()`, where the `multiply()` return value is used to initialize `product`. The activation record associated with `main()` now has depiction

The last statement in method `main()` then is executed. This statement displays the result of the `multiply()` invocation.

```
System.out.println(a + " * " + b + " = " + product);
```

The output of the statement verifies our statement regarding the independence of actual and formal parameters—the display of variable a shows that it has the same value after the invocation as it had before the invocation.

```
8.0 * 11.0 = 88.0
```

Regardless, of the type of parameter, Java uses the value parameter passing style. Therefore, no matter whether the parameters are primitive values or references, the value of an actual parameter does not change. This property is demonstrated in `PassingReferences.java` of Listing 7.5. The output of program is depicted in Figure 7.3.

The program consists of three class methods: `f()`, `g()`, and `main()`.

- Method `f()` has a single formal parameter v. The method assigns to v a reference to a new `Point` representing (0, 0).

- Method `g()` also has a single formal parameter v. However, this method does not make an assignment to its parameter v. Instead, `g()` changes the object to which v refers. In particular, that object has its location attribute set to (0, 0).

- Method `main()` invokes methods `f()` and `g()`.

Listing 7.5 **PassingReferences.java**

```
1.  // Parameter passing demonstration
2.
3.  import java.awt.*;
4.
5.  public class PassingReferences {
6.     // f(): set the value of the formal parameter
7.     public static void f(Point v) {
8.        v = new Point(0, 0);
9.     }
10.
11.    // g(): modifies the contents of the referred to object
12.    public static void g(Point v) {
13.       v.setLocation(0, 0);
14.    }
15.
16.    // main(): application entry point
17.    public static void main(String[] args) {
18.       Point p = new Point(10, 10);
19.       System.out.println(p);
20.
21.       f(p);
22.       System.out.println(p);
23.
24.       g(p);
25.       System.out.println(p);
26.    }
27. }
```

Figure 7.3 **Program PassingReferences output.**

By analyzing the results of the method main() invocations, a deeper understanding of the possible effects of passing references can be obtained.

Method main() begins by initializing, and displaying a Point variable p. Variable p references an object referencing the location (10. 10).

```
Point p = new Point(10, 10);
System.out.println(p);
```

Every class has a constructor

If a class does not define at least one constructor, then Java will create a default constructor for the class. The provided default constructor will invoke the default constructor of the *superclass* (parent class) for the new class. If the class does not define explicitly a superclass, then the superclass is class `Object`. Chapter 9 considers the nuances of deriving classes from a class other than `Object`.

The output produced by the first `println()` invocation is

```
java.awt.Point[x=10,y=10]
```

After completing the initial segment, the activation record for method `main()` has depiction

Observe that although variable p is part of the activation record for method `main()`, the memory for the `Point` to which it refers is not part of the activation record. Java divides the memory allocated to a program into two portions—the *stack* and the *heap*. Activation records are maintained in the stack and the space for objects comes from the heap.

Method `f()` then is invoked with p as the actual parameter.

```
f(p);
```

With its invocation, an activation record is created and flow of control is transferred to it. The depiction of the activation records is now

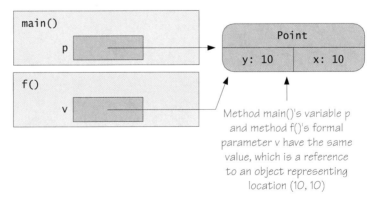

Method main()'s variable p and method f()'s formal parameter v have the same value, which is a reference to an object representing location (10, 10)

Because Java performs value parameter passing, the actual and formal parameters p and v have the same value, that is, they reference the same `Point` object.

The assignment statement in method `f()` is executed then.

```
v = new Point(0, 0);
```

The assignment gives f() formal parameter v a new value, that is, v now references a new Point object representing the location (0, 0). This assignment does not modify method main() variable p because variable p has its own memory where it stores its value.

The depiction of the activation records is now

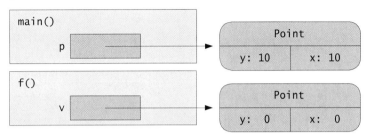

The activation record for f() then is released and the flow of control is transferred back to method main() where the println() statement is executed.

```
System.out.println(p);
```

The activation records now have depiction

An examination of the output produced by the second println() invocation confirms our analysis—there has been no change in p.

```
java.awt.Point[x=10,y=10]
```

Method g() then is invoked with p as the actual parameter.

```
g(p);
```

With its invocation, an activation record is created and flow of control is transferred to it. The depiction of the activation records is now

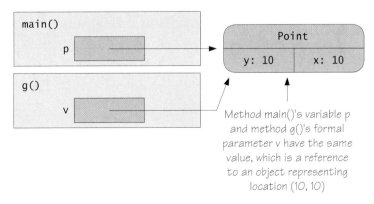

Method main()'s variable p and method g()'s formal parameter v have the same value, which is a reference to an object representing location (10, 10)

The actual and formal parameters p and v have the same value, that is, they reference the same Point object.

The Point instance method invocation is executed then.

```
v.setLocation(0, 0);
```

This invocation causes an update to the Point object to which parameter v references. The update changes the representation to that of (0, 0).

Observe that this update changed neither actual parameter p nor formal parameter v. However, the object to which they both refer has been updated and its change is visible through them. The activation records now have depiction

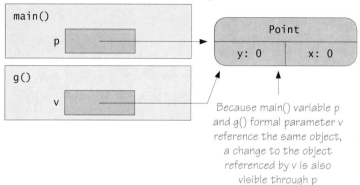

Because main() variable p and g() formal parameter v reference the same object, a change to the object referenced by v is also visible through p

With the update in location, flow of control is transferred then back to method main() and the println() statement is executed.

```
System.out.println(p);
```

An examination of the output produced by the final println() invocation confirms our analysis—the Point object which p references has undergone change.

```
java.awt.Point[x=0,y=0]
```

In summary, the value of an actual parameter does not change with method invocation. However, if the actual parameter is a reference, then the object to which the actual parameter refers can be modified in a method invocation.

We now turn our attention to the use of the keyword **this** and some methods that should be present in almost any class implementation. In the accompanying discussion, a class Triple is used to illustrate these programming concepts.

7.3   THIS

Class Triple of Listing 7.6. supports the representation of objects with three numeric attributes. The class defines a default and specific constructor; an accessor getValue(); mutator setValue(); and facilitators toString(), clone(), and equals().

```
public Triple()
```
Constructs a default Triple value representing three zeros.

Listing 7.6   Triple.java

```java
1.  // Purpose: Support the representation of a three-tuple.
2.
3.  public class Triple {
4.     // instance variables for the three attributes
5.     private int x1;      // first value
6.     private int x2;      // second value
7.     private int x3;      // third value
8.
9.     // Triple(): default constructor
10.    public Triple() {
11.       this(0, 0, 0);
12.    }
13.
14.    // Triple(): specific constructor
15.    public Triple(int a, int b, int c) {
16.       setValue(1, a);
17.       setValue(2, b);
18.       setValue(3, c);
19.    }
20.
21.    // getValue(): attribute accessor
22.    public int getValue(int i) {
23.       switch (i) {
24.          case 1: return x1;
25.          case 2: return x2;
26.          case 3: return x3;
27.          default:
28.             System.err.println("Triple: bad get: " + i);
29.             System.exit(i);
30.             return i;
31.       }
32.    }
33.
34.    // setValue(): attribute mutator
35.    public void setValue(int i, int value) {
36.       switch (i) {
37.          case 1: x1 = value; return;
38.          case 2: x2 = value; return;
39.          case 3: x3 = value; return;
40.          default:
41.             System.err.println("Triple: bad set: " + i);
42.             System.exit(i);
43.       }
44.    }
45.
46.    // toString(): string representation facilitator
47.    public String toString() {
48.       int a = getValue(1);
49.       int b = getValue(2);
50.       int c = getValue(3);
51.
52.       return "Triple[" + a + ", " + b + ", " + c + "]";
53.    }
54.
```

Listing 7.6 **Triple.java (Continued)**

```
55.     // clone(): duplicate facilitator
56.     public Object clone() {
57.        int a = getValue(1);
58.        int b = getValue(2);
59.        int c = getValue(3);
60.
61.        return new Triple(a, b, c);
62.     }
63.
64.     // equals(): equal facilitator
65.     public boolean equals(Object v) {
66.        if (v instanceof Triple) {
67.           int a1 = getValue(1);
68.           int b1 = getValue(2);
69.           int c1 = getValue(3);
70.
71.           Triple t = (Triple) v;
72.           int a2 = t.getValue(1);
73.           int b2 = t.getValue(2);
74.           int c2 = t.getValue(3);
75.
76.           return (a1 == a2) && (b1 == b2) && (c1 == c2);
77.        }
78.        else {
79.           return false;
80.        }
81.     }
82. }
```

```
public Triple(int a, int b, int c)
```
Constructs a representation of the values a, b, and c.
```
public int getValue(int i)
```
Returns the ith element of the associated Triple.
```
public void setValue(int i, int value)
```
Sets the ith element of the associated Triple to value.
```
public String toString()
```
Returns a textual representation of the associated Triple.
```
public Object clone()
```
Returns a new Triple whose representation is the same as the associated Triple.
```
public boolean equals(Object v)
```
Returns whether v is equivalent to the associated Triple.

The default constructor for class Triple is syntactically interesting—it uses the specific constructor to initialize a new Triple object.

```
// Triple(): default constructor
public Triple() {
   this(0, 0, 0);
}
```

The new Triple object (the this object) is constructed by invoking the Triple constructor expecting three int values as actual parameters

Keyword **this** is a reference to the object being acted upon. It provides a notation for an object to refer to itself. In a constructor, **this** references the object under construction; in an instance method, **this** references the object being manipulated. Thus, for the Triple class, **this** is a reference to the Triple object being acted upon by one of its constructors or methods.

Our use of **this** in the Triple default constructor signifies that the object under construction is to be configured with zeros for its attribute values. The configuration is performed by invoking the Triple constructor whose signature matches the invocation (i.e., the Triple specific constructor expecting three **int** values as parameters).

This type of construction is common in defining Java constructors. Typically, one constructor has a detailed initialization process. The other constructors then use that definition by invoking it with appropriate values. By using that single detailed initialization process, it is less likely that some aspect of object configuration is omitted.

If another constructor of the class assists the initialization, Java requires that the **this**() invocation be at the beginning of the statement body. Therefore, the following constructor definition is illegal.

```
public Triple() {
       int a = 0;
       int b = 0;
       int c = 0;
       this(a, b, c);   ◄───── Illegal this() invocation. A this() invocation
}                              must begin its statement body
```

The Triple specific constructor of Listing 7.6 uses its three actual parameters to initialize the attributes of the Triple object under construction. It does so, through the use of the Triple mutators.

```
// Triple(): specific constructor
public Triple(int a, int b, int c) {
   setValue(1, a);
   setValue(2, b);
   setValue(3, c);
}
```

The Triple specific constructor could have used explicit **this** references to indicate that it is the object under construction whose setValues() mutators are being invoked.

```
// Triple(): specific constructor - alternative definition
public Triple(int a, int b, int c) {
   this.setValue(1, a);
   this.setValue(2, b);
   this.setValue(3, c);
}
```

However, in practice Java programmers tend generally to omit explicit **this** references. It is understood implicitly that the methods being invoked are acting upon the object under consideration.

7.4   INHERITED METHODS AND OVERRIDING

Class `Triple` like every other Java class is automatically an *extension* of the standard class `Object`; that is, class `Object` specifies some basic behaviors common

Chapter 9 considers inheritance in detail

to all objects. In object-oriented programming terminology these behaviors are said to be *inherited*. One of the methods that `Triple` inherits from `Object` is method `toString()`.

It generally is recommended that every class *override* the `toString()` definition provided by `Object` (i.e., provide a different implementation). By doing so, `System.out.println()` can display a meaningful representation of all of the attributes of the object rather than just its `Object` attributes.

```
System.out.println(p);    // displays string version of object p
System.out.println(q);    // displays string version of object q
```

This capability can be quite useful when debugging a program.

For a `Triple` object, a reasonable `String` representation would be a listing of its three attributes. The class `Triple` implementation is

```
// toString(): string representation facilitator
public String toString() {
   int a = getValue(1);
   int b = getValue(2);
   int c = getValue(3);

   return "Triple[" + a + ", " + b + ", " + c+ "]");
}
```

With this method, code segment

```
Triple t1 = new Triple(10, 20, 30);
System.out.println(t1);

Triple t2 = new Triple(8, 88, 888);
System.out.println(t2);
```

produces as its output

```
Triple[10, 20, 30]
Triple[8, 88, 888]
```

Observe that the name of the class was displayed as part of the representation. This practice is quite common if the expected use of `toString()` is to provide debugging information.

Forgetting to override toString()

If a class does not override `toString()`, then the inherited method is used to produce its string representations. `Object` method `toString()` returns a string consisting of the class name appended with character `'@'` and the hash code of the object. Such information is not particularly useful in most programming contexts.

The other `Triple` methods of interest are `clone()` and `equals()`. Like method `toString()`, methods `clone()` and `equals()` are overrides of methods inherited method from class `Object`.

Method `clone()` returns a new `Triple` object that is a duplicate of the current object.

```
// clone(): duplicate facilitator
public Object clone() {
    int a = getValue(1);
    int b = getValue(2);
    int c = getValue(3);

    return new Triple(a, b, c);
}
```

Because it is an override, the method has the return type of `Object`, which is the return type of the `clone()` method defined by class `Object`.

Creating a `Triple` clone is straightforward. First variables a, b, and c are initialized with the attribute values of the `Triple` object that invoked method `clone()`. The return value is produced by creating a new `Triple` object with attribute values a, b, and c. The following code segment makes use of method `clone()` to initialize variable t2.

```
Triple t1 = new Triple(9, 28, 29);
Triple t2 = (Triple) t1.clone();
System.out.println("t1 = " + t1);
System.out.println("t2 = " + t2);
```

Although `Triple` method `clone()` returns a `Triple` object, its return type is `Object`. Therefore, the return value must be cast to `Triple` to use that value appropriately.

The segment output shows that the objects referenced by t1 and t2 have the same attributes.

```
Triple[9 , 28 , 29]
Triple[9 , 28 , 29]
```

Copy construction

While Java programmers tend to use a `clone()` method to produce a duplicate of an object, programmers in other object-oriented languages such as C++ tend to use a *copy constructor*. A copy constructor expends a single parameter of its class type and creates a duplicate of that object. Although the two mechanisms are different in syntax, they are equivalent.

The `Triple` class definition overrides the `Object` class `equals()` method because the inherited `equals()` does not meet our purposes. Consider the following code segment that defines `Triple` variables t1 and t2 that reference similarly constructed objects.

```
Triple t1 = new Triple(9, 28, 29);
Triple t2 = new Triple(9, 28, 29);
```

The representation of t1 and t2 would be

The inherited Object class equals() method reports if the two object references are the same rather than reporting whether the referenced objects have equivalent attributes. With Object class equals() method in effect, the following code segment displays **false**—variables t1 and t2 contain different references.

```
System.out.println(t1.equals(t2));
```

Object method equals() is equivalent to the == operator. Both test whether the objects in question are in fact the same object.

The Triple implementation of equals() instead determines whether its parameter is a Triple object with attributes that are *equivalent* to the invoking Triple object. The Triple implementation follows the standard form of an equals() method.

```
// equals(): equal facilitator
public boolean equals(Object v) {
    if (v instanceof Triple) {
        int a1 = getValue(1);
        int b1 = getValue(2);
        int c1 = getValue(3);

        Triple t = (Triple) v;
        int a2 = t.getValue(1);
        int b2 = t.getValue(2);
        int c2 = t.getValue(3);

        return (a1 == a2) && (b1 == b2) && (c1 == c2);
    }
    else {
        return false;
    }
```

The implementation begins by testing whether its parameter v references a Triple object. Operator **instanceof** returns **true** when the type of object referenced by the left operand is either that of the right operand or derived from the right operand; otherwise, the operator returns **false**. (The **null** reference is never considered an instance of a class.)

If v is not referencing a Triple object, then the test expression evaluates to **false** causing the **else** part to be executed. The **else** part returns **false** as the object cannot be equal to the Triple object invoking the equals() method.

If the test expression evaluates to **true**, then v is referencing a non-**null** Triple object. As such, the method can determine whether the corresponding attributes of the two Triple objects match.

Variables a1, b1, and c1 and a2, b2, and c2 represent respectively the attributes of the object invoking the equals() method and the Triple object referenced by parameter v.

```
int a1 = getValue(1);
int b1 = getValue(2);
int c1 = getValue(3);

Triple t = (Triple) v;
int a2 = t.getValue(1);
int b2 = t.getValue(2);
int c2 = t.getValue(3);
```

By testing whether a1 equals a2, b1 equals b2, and c1 equals c2, the method can signal whether the two objects represent objects with identical attribute values.

```
return (a1 == a2) && (b1 == b2) && (c1 == c2);
```

You may have wondered why the code defines a variable t that is a cast of v. Although it must be the case at this point in the method that parameter v references a Triple object, Java still requires an explicit cast to treat v as something other than an Object. Therefore, the statement

```
int a2 = v.getValue(1);
```
◄——— *The invocation does not compile because the apparent type of the object referenced by v is Object, which does not have a method getValue()*

would not compile—an Object does not have a method getValue(). The cast allows the Triple attributes of the object referenced by v to be obtained.

Consider the following code segment.

```
Triple e = new Triple(4, 6, 10);
Triple f = new Triple(4, 6, 11);,
Triple g = new Triple(4, 6, 10);
Triple h = new Triple(4, 5, 11);

boolean flag1 = e.equals(f);
boolean flag2 = e.equals(g);
boolean flag3 = g.equals(h);
```

Before reading on, determine the values to which variables flag1, flag2, and flag3 are initialized.

Keep things private

When designing your own classes, keep in mind that instance variables are declared normally to be **private**. This convention requires that any access or modification to the instance variables by other classes be through the accessors and mutator methods. This information hiding helps ensure the integrity of the variables and also normally makes it possible to update or correct the class without requiring changes to other classes that use your class.

Method equals()

In implementing an `equals()` method, the Java standard suggests that the following properties hold typically:

- *Reflexivity*: `x.equals(x)` should be always true.
- *Symmetry*: If `x.equals(y)` is true, then `y.equals(x)` should be true.
- *Transitivity*: If `x.equals(y)` and `y.equals(z)` are true then `x.equals(z)` should be true.
- *Consistency*: While the objects to which x and y refer are unchanged, repeated evaluations of `x.equals(y)` should return the same value.
- *Physicality*: `x.equals(null)` should return **false**.

Based on their initialization, variables e, f, g, and h have representations

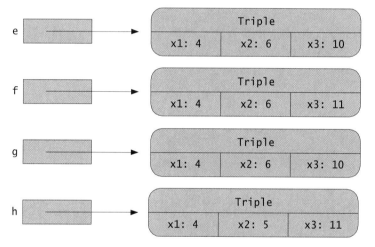

The objects referred to by e and f are different because their x3 attributes are different ($10 \neq 11$). The objects referred to by e and g are equivalent because the corresponding attribute values are the same. The objects referred to by g and h are different because their x2 attributes different ($6 \neq 5$). Thus, variables `flag1`, `flag2`, and `flag3` have depiction

This discussion concludes our analysis of overriding `toString()`, `clone()`, and `equals()`. We now turn our attention scope and name reuse.

7.5   SCOPE AND REUSE

Consider the following class definition. Why doesn't the program compile?

```
// Illegal variable referencing
class Scope {
    public static void main(String[] args) {
        int i = 10;               // local definition
        f(i);                     // invoking f() with i as parameter
        System.out.println(a);    // illegal reference
        System.out.println(b);    // illegal reference
    }

    public static void f(int a) {
        int b = 1;                // local definition
        System.out.println(a);    // print 10
        a = b;                    // update a
        System.out.println(a);    // print 1
    }
}
```

The program does not compile, because the references to variables a and b in method `main()` are illegal as seen in the activation record for `main()`.

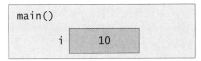

Variables a and b do not exist in the *scope* of method `main()`. According to the Java language specification, a method's parameters and variables can be used only within the method itself. The parameters and variables are said to be *local* to the method. Depending on where the definition occurs and what other definitions occur within the method, other scope rules can further limit a local variable to particular sections of code within the method.

7.5.1   LOCAL SCOPE RULES

A *block* is a list of statements nested within braces. By this definition, a method body is a block. It is legal in Java to put a statement block anywhere a statement would be legal, and there is no restriction on what type of statements a block can include. This flexibility enables us to have a block within a block within a block and so on. A block contained within another block is called a *nested* block.

The statement list that comprises a block is delimited naturally, or *terminated* in Java terminology, from the statement that follows it by the right brace. Thus, no semicolon is needed after the right brace. The property is shown in the following example:

```
{
    int a = 1; // semicolon is necessary
```

```
}              // semicolon is not necessary
int b = 2;     // semicolon is necessary
```

Java's scope rules state that a local variable can be used only in the block and in the nested blocks of the block in which it has been defined. In particular, a local variable can be used only in a statement or nested block that occurs after its definition. Java considers a formal parameter to be defined at the beginning of its associated method body. That is why a formal parameter can be used throughout its method.

There is a scope rule that limits the statements in which a variable can be used. The limitation has to do with the reuse of a variable's name. Although it often seems disconcerting to beginning programmers to reuse names, imagine how difficult it would be to write programs if name reuse was not permitted. Programmers would then need to be aware of the name of every variable used in every method in the software project, regardless of the method's author. Not only would this task tend to be unmanageable; it would encourage poor names for the sake of uniqueness.

Informally, Java allows an identifier name to be reused as long as the blocks containing the duplicate declarations are not nested one within the other. This policy means that the following class definition is legal.

```
class Scope2 {
    public static void main(String[] args) {
        int a = 10;            // local definition
        f(a);                  // invoking f() with a as parameter
        System.out.println(a); // print 10
    }

    public static void f(int a) {
        System.out.println(a); // print 10
        a = 1;                 // update a
        System.out.println(a); // print 1
    }
}
```

Method main()'s local variable a is different from the formal parameter a of method f(). The local variable a of main() exists only within main()'s statement block, and the formal parameter a of f() exists only within f()'s statement block.

The name reuse is reflected in the activation records for the two methods. They both contain entries for an a, but the a in one method is independent of the a in the other method. The activation records would have the following depiction when the **return** statement of method f() is about to be executed.

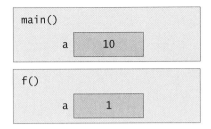

The output of the program is

```
10
1
10
```

Name reuse within the same method is permitted as long as the reuse occurs in distinct blocks. For example, while it is hard to understand, method g() is legal Java.

```
public void g() {
   {
      int j = 1;                // define j
      System.out.println(j);    // print 1
   }
   {
      int j = 10;               // define a different j
      System.out.println(j);    // print 10
   }
   {
      char j = '@';             // define a different j
      System.out.println(j);    // print '@'
   }
}
```

The three variable j's are defined in three different blocks none of which are nested with respect to the others.

Because the three variable j's exist only within their respective blocks, we cannot move the println() statements to display their values as in method h().

```
public void h() {
   {
      int j = 1;                // define j
   }
   System.out.println(j);       // illegal: no j in scope
   {
      int j = 10;               // define a different j
   }
   System.out.println(j);       // illegal: no j in scope
   {
      char j = '@';             // define a different j
   }
   System.out.println(j);       // illegal: no j in scope
}
```

Shadowing

Name reuse is permitted within nested blocks if one of the blocks is a class definition block. The following class ShadowDemo demonstrates this practice.

```
public class ShadowDemo {
    static int n = 0;
    public static void main(String[] args) {
        int n = 0;      // local n shadows the class variable n
        n = 10;         // local n is updated
        System.out.println(n);
        System.out.println(ShadowDemo.n);
    }
}
```

ShadowDemo has a class variable n and its method main() has a local variable n. Within method main(), the name n by itself refers to the local variable. We say that the local variable n *shadows* (obscures) the class variable n. Access to the class variable requires its class specification (i.e., ShadowDemo.n). Therefore, the assignment in method main() updates the local variable and not the class variable. The program output is therefore

```
0
10
```

Because of its potential for reader and programmer confusion, the shadowing of variables is not recommended generally.

In the next example, method k() does not compile because one of the definitions of j is nested within a block that has already defined j.[†]

```
public void k() {
    int j = 1;
    {
        int j = 10;      // illegal: j already defined locally
        System.out.println(j);
    }
    System.out.println(j);
}
```

Now considering the following **for** loop using a local variable j. What is its output?

```
for (int i = 0; i < 3; ++i) {
    int j = 0;
    ++j;
    System.out.println(j);
}
```

The segment output is

```
1
1
1
```

[†]   Java naming requirements are more restrictive than other languages (e.g., C++).

The scope of variable j is the body of the **for** loop. Variable j is not in scope when the **for** post expression ++i and test expression i < 3 are evaluated. Therefore, variable j is redefined and reinitialized with each iteration of the loop.

Just because name reuse is permitted does not mean that it should be used. Variable names should reflect their intended purpose and name reuse within a method should be limited normally to loop index variables.

7.6   OVERLOADING

In Chapter 2, we discussed how Java has *overloaded* operators. That is, what an operator does depends on the type of its operands. For example, the division operator (/) performs integer or floating-point division depending on whether its operands are respectively integer or floating-point. Similarly, the plus operator (+) is overloaded. If its operands are numeric then addition is performed; and if its operands are strings then concatenation is performed.

Java also supports *method overloading*. It allows us to create methods that have the same name but behave differently. Method overloading is useful when we need to write methods that perform similar tasks but need to operate on either different types or on different numbers of parameters. Java allows a method name to be overloaded as long as the signature of the new definition is different from the other methods for the class to which it belongs (i.e., the two signatures must differ in the names, types, number, or order of the parameters).

For example, package java.lang.Math overloads the method name min() four times—there are methods operating on **int**, **long**, **float**, and **double** parameters. Their signatures are respectively min(**int, int**), min(**long, long**), min(**float, float**), and min(**double, double**).

The min(**int, int**) and min(**double, double**) methods are demonstrated in the following code segment.

```
BufferedReader stdin = new BufferedReader(
        new InputStreamReader(System.in);

System.out.println("Enter two integers (one per line):");
int i1 = Integer.parseInt(stdin.readLine());
int i2 = Integer.parseInt(stdin.readLine());
int imin = Math.min(i1, i2);
System.out.println("Min of " + i1 + " and " + i2 + " is "
        + imin);

System.out.println("Enter two decimal values"
        + "(one per line):");
double d1 = Double.parseDouble(stdin.readLine());
double d2 = Double.parseDouble(stdin.readLine());
double dmin = Math.min(d1, d2);
System.out.println("Min of " + d1 + " and " + d2 + " is "
        + dmin);
```

Continuing with the `min()` example, the class `Tools` of Listing 7.7 defines in part two methods named `min()`. These two methods are class methods that operate respectively with three and four **int** parameters.

The use of these `min()` methods is demonstrated in `MinDemo.java` of Listing 7.8. When the compiler encounters a call to a method `Tools.min()` in method `main()`, there is no ambiguity on which method to invoke—the compiler examines the parameter list of the method call, and it invokes the method whose signature best matches the actual parameter list. The process of determining which method to invoke is known as *overloading resolution*. For class `Tools`, there is only one method `min()` with a three-parameter signature and only one method `min()` with a four-parameter signature. Thus, the `Tools` method with signature

```
min(int, int, int)
```

is invoked in statement

```
int imin = Tools.min(i1, i2, i3);
```

and the `Tools` method with signature

```
min(int, int, int, int)
```

is invoked in the statement

```
int jmin = Tools.min(j1, j2, j3, j4);
```

It is interesting to observe that the `Tools` three-parameter method `min()` makes two uses of `Math.min()` to achieve its result.

```
return Math.min(a, Math.min(b, c));
```

The method returns whatever is minimum—a or the minimum of b or c. This method also demonstrates that a return value can be an arbitrary expression and not just a variable.

The four-parameter method `min()` uses both the `Math.min()` and the `Tools` three-parameter `min()` to achieve its result.

```
return Math.min(a, min(b, c, d));
```

The four parameter `min()` method returns whatever is minimum—a or the minimum of b, c, or d. There is no need to write the **return** statement as

```
return Math.min(a, Tools.min(b, c, d));
```

Because the default scope is the class scope, the Tools scope specifier is unnecessary

because by default, the `Tools` class uses `Tools` methods.

Listing 7.7   Tools.java

```
1.  // Defines some helpful methods
2.
3.  public class Tools {
4.      // min(): returns the min of its three parameters
5.      public static int min(int a, int b, int c) {
6.          return Math.min(a, Math.min(b, c));
7.      }
8.
9.      // min(): returns the min of its four parameters
10.     public static int min(int a, int b, int c, int d) {
11.         return Math.min(a, min(b, c, d));
12.     }
13.
14.     // power(): returns x ^ n
15.     public static int power(int x, int n) {
16.         int result = 1;
17.         for (int i = 1; i <= n; ++i) {
18.             result *= x;
19.         }
20.         return result;
21.     }
22.
23.     // power(): returns x ^ n
24.     public static double power(double x, int n) {
25.         double result = 1;
26.         for (int i = 1; i <= n; ++i) {
27.             result *= x;
28.         }
29.         return result;
30.     }
31.
32.     // isInteger(): returns whether s is a number
33.     public static boolean isInteger(String s) {
34.         // is there a nonempty string to consider
35.         if ((s == null) || (s.length() == 0)) {
36.             return false;
37.         }
38.
39.         // ignore sign if there is one
40.         if ((s.charAt(0) == '+') || (s.charAt(0) == '-')) {
41.             s = s.substring(1);
42.             // make sure what's left is nonempty
43.             if (s.length() == 0) {
44.                 return false;
45.             }
46.         }
47.
48.         // make sure the rest is digits
49.         for (int i = 0; i < s.length(); ++i) {
50.             // is current character a digit
51.             if (! Character.isDigit(s.charAt(i))) {
52.                 return false;
53.             }
54.         }
```

Listing 7.7   Tools.java (Continued)

```
55.
56.          // number checked out
57.          return true;
58.      }
59. }
```

Listing 7.8   MinDemo.java

```
1.  // Demonstrates overloading method usage
2.
3.  import java.io.*;
4.
5.  public class MinDemo {
6.
7.      // main(): application entry point
8.      public static void main(String[] args) throws IOException {
9.          BufferedReader stdin = new BufferedReader(
10.             new InputStreamReader(System.in));
11.
12.         System.out.println("Enter three integers (one per line):");
13.         int i1 = Integer.parseInt(stdin.readLine());
14.         int i2 = Integer.parseInt(stdin.readLine());
15.         int i3 = Integer.parseInt(stdin.readLine());
16.         int imin = Tools.min(i1, i2, i3);
17.         System.out.println("Min of " + i1 + ", "+ i2 + ", and " + i3
18.             + " is " + imin);
19.
20.         System.out.println("Enter four integers (one per line):");
21.         int j1 = Integer.parseInt(stdin.readLine());
22.         int j2 = Integer.parseInt(stdin.readLine());
23.         int j3 = Integer.parseInt(stdin.readLine());
24.         int j4 = Integer.parseInt(stdin.readLine());
25.         int jmin = Tools.min(j1, j2, j3, j4);
26.         System.out.println("Min of " + j1 + ", "+ j2 + ", " + j3
27.             + ", and " + j4 + " is " + jmin);
28.     }
29. }
```

As another example of method overloading, class Tools defines two methods named power() that calculate x^n. One method has an integer base parameter x and the other method has a floating-point base parameter x. In addition, both power() methods require an integer exponent parameter n. (Both methods assume implicitly n is positive.)

```
public static int power(int x, int n) {
    int result = 1;
    for (int i = 1; i <= n; ++i) {
        result *= x;
    }
    return result;
}

public static double power(double x, int n) {
    double result = 1;
    for (int i = 1; i <= n; ++i) {
```

```
            result *= x;
            }
        return result;
    }
```

Even though both power() methods take two parameters, they have different signatures: power(**int**, **int**) and power(**double**, **int**).

Listing 7.9   PowerDemo.java

```
1.  // Demonstrates method overloading usage
2.
3.  import java.io.*;
4.
5.  public class PowerDemo {
6.
7.      // main(): application entry point
8.      public static void main(String[] args) throws IOException {
9.          BufferedReader stdin = new BufferedReader(
10.             new InputStreamReader(System.in));
11.
12.         System.out.print("Enter an integer base: ");
13.         int i1 = Integer.parseInt(stdin.readLine());
14.         System.out.print("Enter a positive integer power: ");
15.         int i2 = Integer.parseInt(stdin.readLine());
16.         int ipow = Tools.power(i1, i2);
17.         System.out.println(i1 + " to the power "+ i2 + " is "
18.             + ipow);
19.
20.         System.out.print("Enter a floating-point base: ");
21.         double d = Double.parseDouble(stdin.readLine());
22.         System.out.print("Enter a positive integer power: ");
23.         int n = Integer.parseInt(stdin.readLine());
24.         double dpow = Tools.power(d, n);
25.         System.out.println(d + " to the power "+ n + " is " + dpow);
26.     }
27. }
```

Program PowerDemo.java of Listing 7.9 uses both Tools methods power(). Its method main() first invokes the Tools method power() requiring two **int** parameters.

```
System.out.print("Enter an integer base: ");
int i1 = Integer.parseInt(stdin.readLine());
System.out.print("Enter a positive integer power: ");
int i2 = Integer.parseInt(stdin.readLine());
int ipow = Tools.power(i1, i2);
System.out.println(i1 + " to the power "+ i2 + " is "
    + ipow);
```

Method main() then invokes the Tools method power() requiring a **double** parameter and an **int** parameter.

```
System.out.print("Enter a floating-point base: ");
double d = Double.parseDouble(stdin.readLine());
System.out.print("Enter a positive integer power: ");
int n = Integer.parseInt(stdin.readLine());
```

```
       double dpow = Tools.power(d, n);
       System.out.println(d + " to the power "+ n + " is " + dpow);
```

As it was for MinDemo.java with the min() methods, there is no problem for the compiler in determining which method power() is to be invoked in statement

```
       int ipow = Tools.power(i1, i2);
```

and in statement

```
       double dpow = Tools.power(d, n);
```

When the compiler encounters the invocation Tools.power(i1, i2) in method main(), clearly the best match is the Tools method power() with two **int** parameters. Thus, the Tools method with signature

```
       power(int, int)
```

is used to calculate Tools.power(i1, i2).

Similarly, when the compiler encounters the invocation Tools.power(d, n) in method main(), there is again no ambiguity on which method to invoke—the best match is the Tools method power() with one **double** parameter and one **int** parameter; that is, the Tools method with signature

```
       power(double, int)
```

Now consider the program OverloadingDemo.java of Listing 7.10. The program defines two methods f(). One f() method requires two **int** parameters and the other requires two **double** parameters. The f() method with two **int** parameters displays the sum of its parameters; the f() method with two **double** parameters displays the difference of its second parameter from its first parameter.

Listing 7.10   OverloadingDemo.java

```
 1.  // Demonstrates method overloading
 2.
 3.  public class OverloadingDemo {
 4.
 5.      // main(): application entry point
 6.      public static void main(String[] args) {
 7.          int i = 19;
 8.          double x = 54.0;
 9.
10.          f(i, x);      // which f() is invoked?
11.      }
12.
13.      // f(): display a + b
14.      public static void f(int a, int b) {
15.          System.out.println(a + b);
16.      }
17.
18.      // f(): display a - b
19.      public static void f(double a, double b) {
20.          System.out.println(a - b);
21.      }
22.  }
```

So which of the f() methods gets invoked at line 10 of method main()?

```
f(i, x);
```

Unlike our previous overloading examples, there is no perfect match in terms of the invocation and the method signatures. However, there is a best match. The compiler would cause the method f() with signature

```
f(double, double)
```

to be invoked. It does so, because there is an automatic conversion that maps the **int** value i to the **double** version of i. This conversion produces parameters suitable for method f(**double** a, **double** b). This match is the best match because there are no automatic conversions that could produce parameters suitable for method f(**int** a, **int** b). Thus, the output of the program is

```
-35.0
```

A good programming practice is to not rely on automatic conversion. Instead make explicit conversions. That way readers of the code have an easier time determining which method is being invoked. For example, line 10 of method main() from Overloading-Demo.java can be written as

```
f((double) i, x);
```

Overloading

When method overloading, Java requires that the parameter lists for the methods be different. Therefore, the following class BadDemo does not compile.

```java
public class BadDemo {
    public double f(int a, int b) {
        return 2.5 * (a + b);
    }

    public int f(int a, int b) {  // illegal overloading
        return (a + b);
    }

    public static void main(String[] args) {
        double x = f(2, 4);
        int i = f(2, 4);
    }
}
```

Java does not consider the different return types of the two methods f() as a distinguishing factor for allowing the overloading.

7.7 ILLUSTRATIONS

We next present several small classes for illustrative purposes. Each of the classes demonstrates a nuance with regard to class behavior in Java.

First consider class A. Class A has four instance variables named `data1`, `data2`, `data3`, and `data4`. These four variables are of type **int**, **double**, **boolean**, and **String** respectively and the latter three variables have no explicit initialization. There is also a default constructor that performs no explicit work and accessors for each of the instance variables.

```java
public class A {
    private int data1 = 1;
    private double data2;
    private boolean data3;
    private String data4;

    public A() {
        // no body used
    }

    public int getData1() {
        return data1;
    }

    public double getData2() {
        return data2;
    }

    public boolean getData3() {
        return data3;
    }

    public String getData4() {
        return data4;
    }
}
```

Before reading our analysis try to determine the output of the following program `ADemo.java`. Understanding what output is produced should reinforce your understanding of instance variable initialization.

```java
public class ADemo {
    public static void main(String[] args) {
        A a = new A();
        System.out.println(a.getData1());
        System.out.println(a.getData2());
        System.out.println(a.getData3());
        System.out.println(a.getData4());
    }
}
```

As noted previously, immediately before a constructor begins executing its statement body, its instance variables are initialized. If the instance variable definition includes an explicit initialization value as does the definition of data1, then that value is used. If a variable definition does not specify an explicit initialization value, then it is initialized to 0 if it is a primitive numeric variable, to **false** if it is a **boolean** variable, or to **null** if it is a reference type variable.

```
private int data1 = 1;
private double data2;
private boolean data3;
private String data4;
```

Thus, in regard to the new object to which variable a refers, **int** instance variable data1 is initialized explicitly to 1; **double** instance variable data2 is default initialized to 0.0, **boolean** instance variable data3 is default initialized to **false**, and String instance variable data4 is default initialized to **null**. The result is that program ADemo.java outputs

```
1
0.0
false
null
```

Now consider the following class B with a class variable counter1 and an instance variable counter2.

```
public class B {
    private static int counter1 = 0;
    private int counter2;

    public B(int n) {
        counter2 = n;
    }

    public void incrementCounter1() {
        ++counter1;
    }

    public void incrementCounter2() {
        ++counter2;
    }

    public int getCounter1() {
        return counter1;
    }

    public int getCounter2() {
        return counter2;
    }
}
```

Before reading our analysis try to determine the output of program BDemo.java that uses class B. If you understand what output it produces, you should understand the important difference between class and instance variables.

```
public class BDemo {
    public static void main(String[] args) {
        B b1 = new B(0);
```

```
        B b2 = new B(0);

        b1.incrementCounter1();
        b1.incrementCounter2();
        b1.incrementCounter2();
        b1.incrementCounter2();

        b2.incrementCounter1();
        b2.incrementCounter2();

        System.out.println(b1.getCounter1());
        System.out.println(b1.getCounter2());
        System.out.println(b2.getCounter1());
        System.out.println(b2.getCounter2());
    }
}
```

Program `BDemo.java` begins by defining two B reference variables `b1` and `b2`. The variables reference distinct newly created B objects. These objects each have an instance variable `counter2` with value 0. These same objects share access to a class variable `counter1` with value 0. A series of `incrementCounter1()` and `increment-Counter2()` invocations then is made.

The effect of invocations

```
b1.incrementCounter1();
b1.incrementCounter2();
b1.incrementCounter2();
b1.incrementCounter2();
```

is to increment class variable `counter1` from 0 to 1 and to increment the instance variable `counter2` of the object to which `b1` refers from 0 to 3.

The effect of invocations

```
b2.incrementCounter1();
b2.incrementCounter2();
```

is to further increment class variable `counter1` from 1 to 2 and to increment instance variable `counter2` of the object to which `b2` refers from 0 to 1.

Therefore, the output of the program is

```
2
3
2
1
```

The output confirms our analysis. Because `counter1` is a class variable, regardless whether it is accessed via `b1` or `b2` it is the same value being manipulated. As this class variable was incremented two times over the course of the program, its value went from 0 to 2. Because `counter2` is an instance variable, each B object has its own `counter2` data field to hold its value. As `b1` and `b2` reference different objects, their increment operations affected different instances of `counter2`. Because three increments were applied to the object referenced by `b1` and one increment was applied to object referenced by `b2`, their `counter2` values are respectively 3 and 1 at the end of the program.

Next suppose class C has definition

```
public class C {
    private int count = 0;

    public C(int n) {
        count = n;
    }

    public void f(int n) {
        count = n;
    }

    public void g(int n) {
        int count = n;
        count += n;
    }
}
```

Our interest in this class concerns its manipulation of the **private** instance variable count. Before reading our analysis try to determine your own answers to the following questions.

- Which methods in C are in principle allowed to access instance variable count?

- Which of the methods in C legally set instance variable count.

- Which of the methods in C illegally attempt to set the instance variable count?

- Which of the methods in C do not make any attempt to modify the instance variable count?

The answer to the first question is that all of the methods are in principle allowed to modify instance variable count. They are allowed to do so because all of the methods are instance methods, and regardless of the access attribute of an instance method (e.g., **public** or **private**), an instance method is allowed to access any instance variable of its class.

To determine the answers to the other questions, we first make several observations. Both constructor C() and method f() consist of the single statement

```
count = n;
```

The count being used here is the instance variable count of the invoking object. This association is the case because of the following facts: count was not declared previously within either the C() constructor or method f(), and every C object has an instance variable count.

The definition of method g() defines a local variable count. Furthermore, the assignment that follows increments that local variable.

```
int count = n;
count += n;
```

It increments the local variable rather than the instance variable because the local definition takes precedence over definitions from other scopes (i.e., it shadows them). Thus, method g() does not reference instance variable count.

Based on our observations, we know that methods C() and f() manipulate instance variable count, method g() does not manipulate instance variable count; and none of the methods have any illegal statements.

We next consider two classes D and E. It will be the case that both of these classes define a String instance variable named data and a method get(). Furthermore, the definitions of get() methods are identical—they return the value of their instance variable data. However, the two classes do define different overridings of a clone() method. The definition of class D is

```
public class D {
    private String data;

    public D(String s) {
        data = s;
    }

    public String get() {
        return data;
    }

    public Object clone() {
        String val = get();
        return new D(val);
    }
}
```

and the definition of class E is

```
public class E {
    private String data;

    public E(String s) {
        data = s;
    }

    public String get() {
        return data;
    }

    public Object clone() {
        String str = get();
        String val = new String(str);
        return new E(val);
    }
}
```

Before reading the analysis that follows, try to determine the output of the following program DEDemo.java that uses classes D and E. Understanding what output it produces should reinforce your understanding of cloning.

```
public class DEDemo {
    public static void main(String[] args) {
        String word = "strengths";
        D d1 = new D(word);
        E e1 = new E(word);
```

```
        D d2 = (D) d1.clone();
        E e2 = (E) e1.clone();

        boolean flag1 = d1.get() == d1.get();
        boolean flag2 = d1.get() == d2.get();
        boolean flag3 = e1.get() == e1.get();
        boolean flag4 = e1.get() == e2.get();

        System.out.println(flag1);
        System.out.println(flag2);
        System.out.println(flag3);
        System.out.println(flag4);
    }
}
```

The program begins by defining two D reference variables d1 and d2, and two E reference variables e1 and e2. The object to which d2 refers is a clone of d1 and the object to which e2 refers is a clone of e1. All four objects have a String instance variable string that refers to a representation of "strengths". Three of these instance variables refer to the same String object and one does not.

In creating the object to which d1 refers, its instance variable data is initialized to reference the same object as word.

```
        data = s;
```

This assignment value occurs because the actual value of formal constructor parameter s is the value of word. The depiction of memory at this point is

This depiction is correct because d1 references a new D object. This new object has an instance variable data of type String, which references the same String as word.

For similar reasons, the object to which e1 refers has an instance variable data that is initialized to reference the same instance variable as word.

```
        data = s;
```

Localization

The use of accessors and mutators rather than direct access of instance variables insulates an implementation. This localization generally makes it simpler to incorporate changes in the data representation. It also ensures consistent checking for the validity of new instance variable values.

Thus, after this construction, variables `word`, `d1.data`, and `e1.data` all reference the same object. The depiction of memory at this point is

In creating the clone of the object to which `d1` refers, a new D object is created. This new D object has an instance variable `data` that references the same object as `clone()` method local variable `val` references.

```
String val = get();
return new D(val);
```

But, `val` references the same `String` object as that which `d1.data` references. It does so because the value of the current object is the value of `d1`, which means the `get()` operation returns `d1.data`. Therefore, variables `word`, `d1.data`, `d2.data`, and `e1.data` all reference the same object. The depiction of memory at this point is

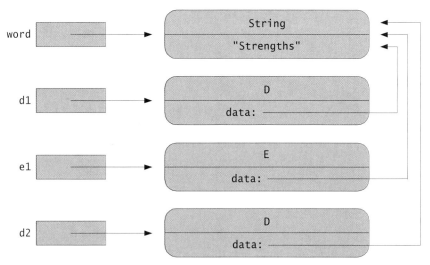

In creating the clone of the object to which `e1` refers, a new E object is created. This new E object has an instance variable `data` that references the same `String` object as `val` references.

```
String str = get();
String val = new String(str);
return new E(val);
```

However, `val` does not reference the same `String` object that `e1.data` does. While `str` references the same object that `e1.data` does; variable `val` references a new object. Although this new object has the same representation as the object to which `e1.data` references, it is a different object. Therefore `e2.data` is not referencing the same `String` as `e1.data`.

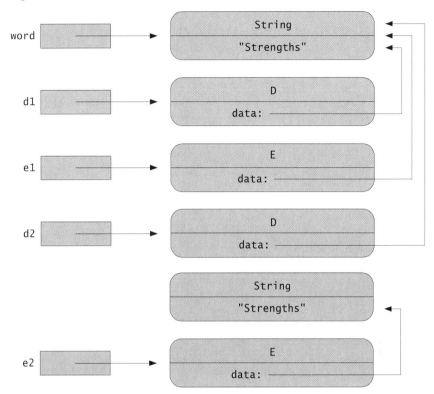

Thus, the output of the program is

```
true
true
true
false
```

This discussion completes our introduction to classes and methods.

7.8 REVIEW

- There are two types of methods in Java—instance methods and class methods. An instance method operates on an object and a class method is a service provided by a class that is not associated with a particular object.

- When a method is invoked, flow of control is transferred temporarily to that method. The actual parameters in the invocation are used to initialize the formal parameters in the method's definition.

- For each method invocation, Java sets aside memory—known as the activation record—for that particular invocation. The activation record stores, among other things, the values of the formal parameters.

- Java uses value parameter passing in an invocation. Once the actual parameters have been used to initialize the formal parameters, the actual parameters and formal parameters are independent of each other. If a method updates the value of a formal parameter, the change does not affect the actual parameter. The change is limited to the activation record containing the value of the formal parameter.

- Java divides the memory allocated to a program into two portions—the stack and the heap. Activation records are maintained in the stack and the space for objects comes from the heap.

- A method's parameters and variables can be used only within the method itself. The parameters and variables are said to be local to the method.

- To invoke a method, a programmer supplies actual parameters of the correct types. If the actual parameters do not match the types of the formal parameters, the compiler attempts to perform conversions to put the actual parameters in the correct form.

- Instance variables are declared normally to be **private**. This convention requires that any access or modification to the instance variables by other classes be through the accessors and mutator methods. This information hiding helps ensure the integrity of the variables and also normally makes it possible to update or correct the class without requiring changes to other classes that use your class.

- A class normally uses its accessors and mutators to manipulate its instance variables. This localization makes it simpler to incorporate changes in the data representation. It also ensures consistent checking for the validity of new instance variable values.

- Class NumberFormat also provides methods for formatting the display of a number.

- A statement block is a list of statements within braces.

- A nested block is a statement block occurring within another statement block.

- A local variable is a variable defined within a statement block.

- Names can be reused as long as the declarations associated with the names occur in different blocks (i.e., neither of the blocks is nested within the other).

- Method overloading occurs when two or more methods defined in a class have the same name. Java allows a method name to be overloaded as long as the signature of the new definition is different from the other methods for the class to which it belongs (i.e., there must be a difference in the types, number, or order of the parameters).

- The compiler resolves overloaded method calls by calling the method whose signature best matches that of the invocation.

- Keyword **this** is a reference to the object being acted upon. In a constructor, **this** references the object under construction; in an instance method, **this** references the object being manipulated.

- A constructor of a class can invoke another constructor of its class to assist in the creation of the new object. Java requires that such assistance be at the beginning of the statement body. To invoke another constructor for assistance, keyword **this** is used.

- If a class does not define any constructors, then Java will create a default constructor for the class. The provided default constructor will invoke the default constructor of the direct superclass for the new class.

- A facilitator method performs a task that depends in part on the attributes of an object.

- Methods with the modifier **static** are known as class methods; methods without the modifier **static** are instance methods.

- A class variable or class constant is a common value to which all objects of the class share access. Class variables and class constants represent collective information that is not specific to individual objects of the class. The modifier **static** indicates that the value being represented is a class variable or constant.

- An instance method can access both class variables and the instance variables of the object on which the method operates.

- It is generally the responsibility of a mutator to validate manipulation requests. If the manipulation does not make sense, it is standard practice to generate an exception.

- Operator **instanceof** returns **true** when the type of its left operand is either the right operand or derived from the right operand; otherwise, the operator returns **false**.

- All classes inherit methods toString(), equals(), and clone(). It is standard for a class to override these three methods.

- In overriding the clone() method, the return type is Object, which is the return type of the clone() method defined for the class Object.

- It is generally expected when implementing an equals() method that the following properties will hold:

  - Reflexivity: For any object x, x.equals(x) should be true.
  - Symmetry: For any objects x and y, if x.equals(y) then y.equals(s).
  - Transitivity: For any objects x, y, and z, if x.equals(y) and y.equals(z), then x.equals(z).
  - Consistency: For any unchanging objects x and y, repeated evaluations of x.equals(y) should return the same value.
  - Physicality: For any object x, x.equals(**null**) should return **false**.

SELF-TEST

S7.1 Rewrite Listing 7.7's method `min()` with signature

```
min(int, int, int, int)
```

so that the method body uses only `Math.min()`.

S7.2 What is the output of the following program? Explain.

```java
public class CounterTest {
    public static void f(int counter) {
        ++counter;
    }

    public static void g(int counter) {
        f(counter);
        f(counter);
    }

    public static void h(int counter) {
        f(counter);
        g(counter);
        f(counter);
    }

    public static void main(String[] args) {
        int counter = 0;
        f(counter);
        System.out.println(counter);
        g(counter);
        System.out.println(counter);
        h(counter);
        System.out.println(counter);
    }
}
```

S7.3 The formula for a line is given normally as $y = mx + b$. Write a method `line()` that expects three **double** parameters, a slope m, a y-intercept b, and an x-coordinate x. The method computes the y-coordinate associated with the line specified by m and b at x-coordinate x.

S7.4 Can you write a **void** method `swap()` that swaps the values of its two actual parameters? For example, the desired output of the following code segment

```java
int a = 1;
int b = 2;
swap(a, b);
System.out.println(a + " "+ b);
```

is

2 1

S7.5 Design and implement a console-based program `TriangleArea.java` that prompts and extracts for the sides *a*, *b*, and *c* of a triangle. If the sides do not represent a triangle, then an appropriate message is displayed. Otherwise, the program displays the area of the associated triangle. The program should define and use a method `area()`. Method `area()` takes three parameters representing the sides of a possible triangle. The sides represent a valid triangle if they are positive and the sum of the lengths for any two sides is greater than the length of the remaining side. The area of a triangle can be computed from its sides using the formula

$$\sqrt{s \cdot (s-a) \cdot (s-b) \cdot (s-c)}$$

where s is half of the sum of the sides (i.e., it is half the perimeter).

S7.6 Develop a class `Cast.java` that offers conversions from the fundamental types to its string representation and vice versa. For example, `Cast.toInt(s)` returns the **int** value represented through `String` variable s.

S7.7 Consider the following class declaration.

```java
public class C {
    private int data1 = 0;
    private int data2 = 0;
    public int data3 = 0;
    public C() {
        // no body used
    }
    public void setData1(int n) {
        data1 = n;
    }
    public void getData2() {
        return data2;
    }
    public void getData3() {
        return data3;
    }
    private void setData3(int n) {
        data3 = n;
    }
}
```

Explain all errors in classes `C` and `CDemo.java`.

```java
public class CDemo {
    public static void main(String[] args) {
        C c1 = new C();
        C c2 = new C(1, 2, 3);
        c1.setData1(4);
        c1.setData3(5);
        int n1 = c1.getData2();
        int n2 = c1.getData3();
        int n3 = c1.data1;
        int n4 = c1.data2;
        int n5 = c1.data3;
    }
}
```

7.10   EXERCISES

7.1   What is the purpose of name reuse?

7.2   Describe what happens during a method invocation.

7.3   What is an activation record?

7.4   What is a local variable?

7.5   What is a signature?

7.6   Can the name of a formal parameter be the same name as an actual parameter? Explain.

7.7   Discuss the transfers of flow of control during method invocation and completion.

7.8   Speculate on possible parameter-passing styles other than pass by value. Discuss how they could be effective.

7.9   Why is the information-hiding principle so important to the object-oriented programming paradigm?

7.10   What methods does a client program have access to? Why?

7.11   Does every class have a constructor? Why?

7.12   Should a **void** method necessarily contain a **return** statement? Explain.

7.13   Can a non-**void** method have a **return** statement? Explain.

7.14   What is it called when two methods have the same name? Under what situations can two methods have the same name?

7.15   Write a method `barrelsToTeaspoons()` with a **double** parameter **b** representing a number of barrels of petroleum. The method returns the equivalent number of teaspoons of oil. For your information,

- 1 barrel petroleum = 158.98729 liters
- 1 teaspoon = 0.004928922 liters

7.16   Write a method `pointsToMeters()` with a **double** parameter **p** representing a number of points. The method returns the distance in meters. For your information,

- 1 typographical point = 0.3514598 millimeters

7.17   Write a **int** method `cube()` that returns the cube of its single **int** formal parameter n.

7.18   Write a **double** method `triangle()` that computes the area of a triangle using its two **double** formal parameters h and w, where h is the height and w is the length of the base of the triangle.

7.19   Write a **double** method `rectangle()` that computes and returns the area of a rectangle using its two **double** formal parameters h and w, where h is the height and w is the width of the rectangle.

7.20   Write a **void** method `doubleSpace()` that inserts two newline characters (`'\n'`) to standard output.

7.21 Write a **void** method endLine() with a single **int** formal parameter n that indicates the number of newline characters to be displayed to standard output by the method.

7.22 Write a **boolean** method intersect() with four **double** parameters m1, b1, m2, and b2. The parameters come conceptually in two pairs. The first pair contains the coefficients describing one line; the second pair contains coefficients describing a second line. The method returns **true** if the two lines intersect; otherwise, the method returns **false**.

7.23 Write a **boolean** method parallel() with four **double** parameters m1, b1, m2, and b2. The parameters come conceptually in two pairs. The first pair contains the coefficients describing one line; the second pair contains coefficients describing a second line. The method returns **true** if the two lines are parallel; otherwise, the method returns **false**. Why does the method take four parameters?

7.24 Write a **boolean** method isPrime() that has a single parameter i of type integer. The method returns **true** if i is a prime number; otherwise, the method returns **false**.

7.25 Write a **boolean** method isEndOfSentence() that has a single value **char** parameter c. The method returns **true** if c is either a period, a question mark, or an exclamation point; otherwise, the method returns **false**.

7.26 Write an **int** method sum() that expects a single integer number as its parameter. The method should return the sum of the integers from 1 to that number.

7.27 Write a **void** method printChar() that expects two parameters: a character object c and an integer amount n. The method should make n copies of the character c to the standard output stream.

7.28 Write a **double** method evaluateQuadraticPolynomial() that expects four **double** parameters a, b, c, and x. The method should return the value

$$ax^2 + bx + c$$

7.29 Write a **double** method cubicArea() that computes the area under the curve for the cubic polynomial $a_3x^3 + a_2x^2 + a_1x + a_0$ along the x-interval (s, t).

7.30 Write a double method quarticArea() that computes the area under the curve for the quartic polynomial $a_4x^4 + a_3x^3 + a_2x^2 + a_1x + a_0$ along the x-interval (s, t).

7.31 An angle is measured normally in either degrees or in radians where 360 degrees equal 2π radians. Write **double** methods degreesToRadians() and radiansToDegrees() that each expect a single **double** parameter. Method degreesToRadians() treats its parameter as a value in degrees and returns the equivalent number of radians. Method radiansToDegrees() treats its parameter as a value in radians and returns the equivalent number of degrees.

7.32 Write a method stripVowels() that extracts and processes the current input line. The method returns, as a string, the consonant portion of the input.

7.33 Write a method distanceToLightYears() that takes a distance in kilometers and returns the amount in light-years to travel that distance. The speed of light is approximately $2.997925 * 10^8$ meters per second. What types should the parameter and return value be? Why?

7.34 Write a String method pigLatin() with a single parameter w of type String. The method returns the translation of the word represented by w into Pig Latin. Pig Latin translates words in the following way: words that start with consonants have the consonants stripped and added as a suffix along with the string "ay"; words that start with a vowel are appended with the string "ay".

7.35 Suppose you must create a library to facilitate computer-assisted telephone calls. What methods should be in the library to support client applications?

7.36 Suppose you must create a library to facilitate computer-assisted checkbook management. What methods should be in the library to support client applications?

7.37 Specify two application areas other than telephony and checkbook management where computing assistance is appropriate. What methods should be in these libraries to support client applications?

7.38 Write methods for the following tasks. Discuss your choice of which values are parameters, which values are local constants, and what their types should be.

a) speed(): Compute the speed of an object after t seconds of acceleration given that the object was traveling initially at v_0 meters per second and then accelerated at a meters per second per second, where $speed = v_0 + at$.

b) distance(): Compute the distance traveled in t seconds by an object that started at rest and then accelerated at a meters per second per second, where $distance = at^2/2$.

7.39 Write a program CompoundInterest.java that gets from its users a deposit amount, an interest rate, and a term of deposit. The program then computes and displays how the principal will change. The program should define and use a method compoundAnnual() with three parameters: a starting amount, an interest rate represented as a percentage, and the number of years. After acquiring these values, the program then computes and displays how the principal will change. The formula for computing interest compounded on an annual basis is as follows:

$$StartingAmount \cdot (1 + InterestRate/100)^{Years}$$

7.40 Write a program SwissCheese.java that gets from its user eight values that specify the characteristics of a rectangular hunk of cheese: width w, length l, height h, m internal spherical air bubbles of radius b, and n surface cylindrical holes of radius r and height d. The program then computes and displays the volume of the associated hunk of Swiss cheese. In developing the program, you should define and use methods

- cylinderVolume(): computes using its radius and height parameters, the volume of the associated cylinder. The volume of a cylinder with radius r and height h is $\pi r^2 h$.

- barVolume(): computes using its width, height, and length parameters, the volume of the associated bar. The volume of a bar is the product of its width, height, and length.

- sphereVolume(): computes using its radius parameter, the volume of the associated sphere. The volume of sphere with radius r is $4\pi r^3/3$.

7.41 Develop a program Euler.java that uses the method factorial() to compute an approximation of e (Euler's number). Base your approximation on the following formula for e:

$$1 + \frac{1}{1!} + \frac{1}{2!} + \frac{1}{3!} + \ldots.$$

For Exercises 7.42 – 7.44 consider the following class Overload.java.

```java
public class Overload {
    public static void f(int a, double b) {
        System.out.println("f(int, double): a = " + a);
        System.out.println("f(int, double): b = " + b);
    }

    public static void f(int a, int b) {
        System.out.println("f(int, int): a = " + a);
        System.out.println("f(int, int): b = " + b);
    }

    public static void f(double a, double b) {
        System.out.println("f(double, double): a = " + a);
        System.out.println("f(double, double): b = " + b);
    }
}
```

7.42 What is output (if any) by the following program? Explain.

```java
public class OverloadDemo1 {
    public static void main(String[] args) {
        int i = 1;
        int j = 2;
        double x = 3.5;
        double y = 10.2;
        Overload.f(i, j);
        Overload.f(i, y);
        Overload.f(y, x);
    }
}
```

7.43 What is output (if any) by the following program? Explain.

```java
public class OverloadDemo2 {
    public static void main(String[] args) {
        Overload.f(1, 2.3);
        Overload.f(2, 4);
        Overload.f(2.6, 10.5);
    }
}
```

7.44   What is output (if any) by the following program? Explain.

```
public class OverloadDemo3 {
    public static void main(String[] args) {
        Overload.f(1, 2.3);
        Overload.f(2.3, 4);
        Overload.f(2.6, 10.5);
    }
}
```

7.45   Rewrite our method min() with signature

   min(int, int, int)

from Listing 7.7 using **if** statements.

7.46   Rewrite our method min() with signature

   min(int a, int b, int c, int d)

from Listing 7.7 using **if** statements.

7.47   Reimplement power() so that if the values of its parameters require it, the method appropriately returns values Double.NaN, Double.NEGATIVE_INFINITY, and Double.POSITIVE_INFINITY.

7.48   Explain why two classes referenced by the same program can have methods with identical names.

7.49   Explain why two classes referenced by the same program can have constructors with identical names.

For Exercises 7.50 – 7.53 the following definition is in effect.

```
class A {
    private int count = 0;
    public A(int n) {
        count = n;
    }
    public static void d() {
        count = 5;
    }
    public void e(int n) {
        { count = n; }
    }
    public void f(int n) {
        { int count = n; }
        ++count;
    }
    public static void g(int n) {
        count = n;
    }
    public static void h(int n) {
        count = n;
    }
}
```

7.50   Which of the methods in A that are in principle allowed to modify the instance variable count? Why?

7.51 Which of the methods in A, if any, legally modify the instance variable `count`? Why?

7.52 Which of the methods in A, if any, illegally attempt to modify the instance variable `count`? Why?

7.53 Which of the methods in A, if any, do not make any attempt to modify the instance variable `count`. Why?

7.54 Suppose class B1 has definition

```java
public class B1 {
    private String string = "";
    public B1(String s) {
        string = s;
    }
    public String getS() {
        return string;
    }
    public void clone() {
        return new B1(getS());
    }
}
```

and class B2 has definition

```java
public class B2 {
    private String string = "";
    public B2(String s) {
        string = s;
    }
    public String getS() {
        return string.clone();
    }
    public Object clone() {
        return new B2(getS());
    }
}
```

What is the output of the following program? Why?

```java
public class BDemo
    public static void main(String[] args) {
        String s = "tsktsking";
        B1 u1 = new B1(s);
        B1 u2 = u1.clone();
        B2 u3 = new B2(s);
        B2 u4 = u3.clone();
        boolean flag1 = (u1.getS() == u3.getS());
        boolean flag2 = (u2.getS() == u4.getS());

        System.out.println(flag1);
        System.out.println(flag2);
    }
}
```

7.55 Suppose class C has definition

```java
public class C {
```

```
                    private int data1;
                    private int data2;
                    private Point data3;
                    private Point data4 = new Point();
                    public C() {
                       data2 = 1;
                    }
                    public int getData1() {
                       return data1;
                    }
                    public int getData2() {
                       return data2;
                    }
                    public Point getData3() {
                       return data3;
                    }
                    public Point getData4() {
                       return data4.toString();
                    }
                 }
```

What is the output of the following program? Why?

```
           public class CDemo {
              public static void main(String[] args) {
                 C c = new C();
                 System.out.println(c.getData1());
                 System.out.println(c.getData2());
                 System.out.println(c.getData3());
                 System.out.println(c.getData4());
              }
           }
```

7.56 Suppose class D has definition

```
           public class D {
              private static int counter1 = 0;
              private int counter2 = 0;
              public D() {
                 // no body needed
              }
              public void increment() {
                 ++counter1;
                 ++counter2;
              }
              public int getCounter1() {
                 return counter1;
              }
              public int getCounter2() {
                 return counter2;
              }
           }
```

What is the output of the following program? Why?

```java
public static class DDemo {
    public void main(String[] args) {
        D d1 = new D();
        D d2 = new D();
        d1.increment();
        d1.increment();
        d2.increment();
        d2.increment();
        System.out.println(d1.getCounter1());
        System.out.println(d1.getCounter2());
        System.out.println(d2.getCounter1());
        System.out.println(d2.getCounter2());
    }
}
```

For Exercises 7.57 and 7.58 the following definition is in effect

```java
public class E {
    private int data = 0;
    public E() {
        // no body used
    }
    public void f() {
        data = 1;
        // f comment
    }
    public void g() {
        data = 2;
        // g comment
    }
}
```

7.57 If the comment in method f() is replaced with the following statement will class E successfully compile? Why?

```java
g();
```

7.58 If the comment in method g() is replaced with the following statement will class E successfully compile? Why?

```java
f();
```

7.59 Design and implement a data abstraction for representing the days of the week. Justify why your design and implementation are reasonable.

7.60 Reimplement the power() methods of Listing 7.7 to work for an arbitrary integer power *n*.

7.11   PROGRAMMING PROJECT — AUTOMOBILE FINANCING

Suppose you want borrow an amount d to purchase an automobile and your lending institution offers you a loan with n monthly payments at annual interest rate of $i\%$. The formula to determine your monthly payment p is

> The objective of this case study is to practice the design and development of methods

$$p = \frac{d \cdot i \cdot a^n}{a^n - 1}, \text{ where } a = 1 + i/12$$

If your automobile loan is a *simple interest* loan, then your interest charge each month is based on your current balance. Your balance $b(m)$ after the month m is

$$b(m) = d \cdot a^m - p \cdot a^{m-1}/i$$

If you decided, to make a balloon payment of $b(m)$ at month m (a final payment that finishes off the loan), then your total interest charges $c(m)$ would have been

$$c(m) = d - p \cdot (m - 1) + b(m)$$

Table 7.1 provides an *amortization table* for a $10,000 simple interest loan at 7% for 36 months. Each row in the table indicates for the given month: opening balance, monthly payment, amount of payment applied to principal, amount of payment applied to interest, and closing balance. Thus, if you decided to retire the loan at the 12th month you would have paid previously the amount $11 \times \$308.77 = \$3,396.47$ and would have to make a balloon payment of $7,163.41. Your total outlay would be $10,559.88.

Most automobile loans are not simple interest loans. They are instead *precomputed loans*. For such loans, the total interest to be paid is more front loaded. The loading is based on the *Rule of 78s*. (Because of the excessive prepayment penalties associated with the Rule of 78s, the United States has banned its use for loans with terms longer than 61 months.)

The term Rule of 78s arose in how the interest is charged for a precomputed loan with a twelve-month term. If such a loan goes its full term, then the total interest to be paid is $c(12)$, which is the same amount for a simple loan. However, with precomputed loans, the lender requires that $12/78$ of $c(12)$ be paid in interest the first month, $11/78$ of $c(12)$ be paid the second month, $10/78$ of $c(12)$ be paid in the third month, and so on. Leaving the last month to pay $1/78$ of $c(12)$ to be paid in interest the last month. (78 is the sum of $1 + 2 + \dots + 12$.) For example, in the first three payments of a twelve-month loan, the borrower is obligated to pay 42.3% of the finance charges ($0.423 \cong (12 + 11 + 10)/78$).

The Rule of 78s can be generalized for a loan with a term of t months. For such loans, $t/(t(t+1)/2)$ of $c(t)$ is paid the first month, $(t-1)/(t(t+1)/2)$ of $c(t)$ is paid the second month, $(t-2)/(t(t+1)/2)$ of $c(t)$ is paid the third month, and so on. As a result of how interest is charged, a precomputed loan's monthly balance formula $f(m)$ is different

Table 7.1   Amortization for simple interest 7% loan.

Month	Opening Balance	Payment	Principal	Interest	Closing Balance
1	$10,000.00	$308.77	$250.44	$58.33	$9,749.56
2	$9,749.56	$308.77	$251.90	$56.87	$9,497.66
3	$9,497.66	$308.77	$253.37	$55.40	$9,244.29
4	$9,244.29	$308.77	$254.84	$53.93	$8,989.45
5	$8,989.45	$308.77	$256.33	$52.44	$8,733.12
6	$8,733.12	$308.77	$257.83	$50.94	$8,475.29
7	$8,475.29	$308.77	$259.33	$49.44	$8,215.96
8	$8,215.96	$308.77	$260.84	$47.93	$7,955.12
9	$7,955.12	$308.77	$262.37	$46.40	$7,692.75
10	$7,692.75	$308.77	$263.90	$44.87	$7,428.85
11	$7,428.85	$308.77	$265.44	$43.33	$7,163.41
12	$7,163.41	$308.77	$266.98	$41.79	$6,896.43
13	$6,896.43	$308.77	$268.54	$40.23	$6,627.89
14	$6,627.89	$308.77	$270.11	$38.66	$6,357.78
15	$6,357.78	$308.77	$271.68	$37.09	$6,086.10
16	$6,086.10	$308.77	$273.27	$35.50	$5,812.83
17	$5,812.83	$308.77	$274.86	$33.91	$5,537.97
18	$5,537.97	$308.77	$276.47	$32.30	$5,261.50
19	$5,261.50	$308.77	$278.08	$30.69	$4,983.42
20	$4,983.42	$308.77	$279.70	$29.07	$4,703.72
21	$4,703.72	$308.77	$281.33	$27.44	$4,422.39
22	$4,422.39	$308.77	$282.97	$25.80	$4,139.42
23	$4,139.42	$308.77	$284.62	$24.15	$3,854.80
24	$3,854.80	$308.77	$286.28	$22.49	$3,568.52
25	$3,568.52	$308.77	$287.95	$20.82	$3,280.57
26	$3,280.57	$308.77	$289.63	$19.14	$2,990.94
27	$2,990.94	$308.77	$291.32	$17.45	$2,699.62
28	$2,699.62	$308.77	$293.02	$15.75	$2,406.60
29	$2,406.60	$308.77	$294.73	$14.04	$2,111.87
30	$2,111.87	$308.77	$296.45	$12.32	$1,815.42
31	$1,815.42	$308.77	$298.18	$10.59	$1,517.24
32	$1,517.24	$308.77	$299.92	$8.85	$1,217.32
33	$1,217.32	$308.77	$301.67	$7.10	$915.65
34	$915.65	$308.77	$303.43	$5.34	$612.22
35	$612.22	$308.77	$305.20	$3.57	$307.02
36	$307.02	$308.81	$307.02	$1.79	$0.00
Totals		$11,115.76	$10,000.00	$1,115.76	

Table 7.2 Amortization for precomputed interest 7% loan.

Month	Opening Balance	Payment	Principal	Interest	Closing Balance
1	$10,000.00	$308.77	$248.46	$60.31	$9,751.54
2	$9,751.54	$308.77	$250.14	$58.63	$9,501.40
3	$9,501.40	$308.77	$251.81	$56.96	$9,249.59
4	$9,249.59	$308.77	$253.49	$55.28	$8,996.11
5	$8,996.11	$308.77	$255.16	$53.61	$8,740.94
6	$8,740.94	$308.77	$256.84	$51.93	$8,484.11
7	$8,484.11	$308.77	$258.51	$50.26	$8,225.59
8	$8,225.59	$308.77	$260.19	$48.58	$7,965.41
9	$7,965.41	$308.77	$261.86	$46.91	$7,703.54
10	$7,703.54	$308.77	$263.54	$45.23	$7,440.01
11	$7,440.01	$308.77	$265.21	$43.56	$7,174.79
12	$7,174.79	$308.77	$266.89	$41.88	$6,907.90
13	$6,907.90	$308.77	$268.56	$40.21	$6,639.34
14	$6,639.34	$308.77	$270.24	$38.53	$6,369.10
15	$6,369.10	$308.77	$271.91	$36.86	$6,097.19
16	$6,097.19	$308.77	$273.59	$35.18	$5,823.60
17	$5,823.60	$308.77	$275.26	$33.51	$5,548.33
18	$5,548.33	$308.77	$276.94	$31.83	$5,271.39
19	$5,271.39	$308.77	$278.62	$30.15	$4,992.78
20	$4,992.78	$308.77	$280.29	$28.48	$4,712.49
21	$4,712.49	$308.77	$281.97	$26.80	$4,430.52
22	$4,430.52	$308.77	$283.64	$25.13	$4,146.88
23	$4,146.88	$308.77	$285.32	$23.45	$3,861.56
24	$3,861.56	$308.77	$286.99	$21.78	$3,574.57
25	$3,574.57	$308.77	$288.67	$20.10	$3,285.90
26	$3,285.90	$308.77	$290.34	$18.43	$2,995.56
27	$2,995.56	$308.77	$292.02	$16.75	$2,703.54
28	$2,703.54	$308.77	$293.69	$15.08	$2,409.85
29	$2,409.85	$308.77	$295.37	$13.40	$2,114.48
30	$2,114.48	$308.77	$297.04	$11.73	$1,817.44
31	$1,817.44	$308.77	$298.72	$10.05	$1,518.72
32	$1,518.72	$308.77	$300.39	$8.38	$1,218.33
33	$1,218.33	$308.77	$302.07	$6.70	$916.26
34	$916.26	$308.77	$303.74	$5.03	$612.51
35	$612.51	$308.77	$305.42	$3.35	$307.09
36	$307.09	$308.77	$307.09	$1.68	$0.00
Totals		$11,115.72	$10,000.00	$1,115.72	

from the formula for the monthly balance $b(m)$ of a simple loan. For a precomputed loan, the balance $f(m)$ is

$$f(m) = d - p \cdot m + c(t) \cdot \frac{m(2t - m + 1)}{t(t + 1)}.$$

Table 7.2 provides an amortization table for a $10,000 precomputed interest loan at 7% for 36 months. If you compare the difference in entries in Table 7.1, you will see that there is an interest penalty associated with the early pay back of a precomputed interest loan as compared to what happens with a simple interest loan. For example, the balloon payment for the loan at the twelfth month is $7,174.79. For a comparable simple interest loan the balloon payment was only $7,163.41.

PROBLEM STATEMENT

For this case study, implement an automobile loan calculator. The calculator should expect the user to provide: a loan amount, interest rate, term, and indication of whether the finance charges are simple interest or precomputed interest. The program should display an amortization table for the loan.

IMPLEMENTATION

Your program should be named `CarLoan.java`. Your program should consist of an application entry point method `main()`. Method `main()` manages the program interaction. In doing its work it invokes several other methods. At a minimum you need to make the following methods available.

`double b(double m, double d, double i, double t)`

Computes the balance $b(m)$ at m months for a simple interest loan of amount d at annual interest i with a term of t months

`double f(double m, double d, double i, double t)`

Computes the balance $f(m)$ at m months for a precomputed interest loan of amount d at annual interest i with a term of t months

`double p(double d, double i, double t)`

Computes the monthly payment for a loan of amount d at annual interest i with a term of t months

`double c(double m, double d, double i, double t)`

Computes the total interest paid $b(m)$ at m months for a simple interest loan of amount d at annual interest i with a term of t months.

TESTING

The World Wide Web has many sites that provide loan calculators that compute amortization tables. Search the Web for such calculators, compare your calculator's results to one of the calculators that you find. Document the various test cases that you considered and the calculator that was used in the comparison.

DOCUMENTATION

You should document both your design and implementation. In documenting your design, justify the access specification of all members. You should also justify your approach and explain the behaviors and nuances of your methods. This documentation requirement has been added to the case study because of the complexity of your design task. Previous case studies were specified to such a degree that class members were specified fully.

7.12   SELF-TEST ANSWERS

S7.1   Method `min()` can be reimplemented in the following manner

```
min(int a, int b, int c, int d) {
    return Math.min(Math.min(a, b), Math.min(c, d));
}
```

S7.2   The output of the program is

```
0
0
0
```

This output is produced because Java uses value parameters. The value of the actual **int** parameter is unaffected by changes to the formal **int** parameter.

S7.3   Method `line()` can be implemented in the following manner

```
public double line(double m, double b, double x) {
    return m*x + b;
}
```

S7.4   No. Because Java uses call-by-value parameter passing, the actual parameters cannot be affected by a method invocation.

S7.5   `TriangleArea.java` can be implemented in the following manner.

```
import java.io.*;

public class TriangleArea {
    public static void main(String[] args)
            throws IOException {
        BufferedReader stdin = new BufferedReader(
            new InputStreamReader(System.in));

        System.out.println("Enter triangle sides: "
            + "(one per line): ");
        double a = Double.parseDouble(stdin.readLine());
        double b = Double.parseDouble(stdin.readLine());
        double c = Double.parseDouble(stdin.readLine());

        double val = area(a, b, c);

        if (! Double.isNaN(val)) {
            System.out.println("A triangle with sides "
                + a + ", " + b + ", and " + c
                + " has area " + val);
        }
        else {
            System.out.println(a + ", " + b + ", and " + c
                + " do not represent sides of a triangle");
        }
    }

    public static double area(double a, double b, double
c) {
        boolean ok = (a > 0) && (b > 0) && (c > 0)
```

```
                                && (a + b > c) && (a + c > b) && (b + c > a);

                    if (ok) {
                        double s = (a + b + c) / 2;
                        return Math.sqrt(s*(s - a)*(s - b)*(s - c));
                    }
                    else {
                        return Double.NaN;
                    }
                }
            }
```

S7.6 Class Cast can be implemented in the following manner.

```
        public class Cast {

            static public char toChar(String s) {
                return s.charAt(0);
            }

            static public boolean toBoolean(String s) {
                return Boolean.valueOf(s).booleanValue();
            }

            static public short toShort(String s) {
                return Short.valueOf(s).shortValue();
            }

            static public int toInt(String s)
                            throws NumberFormatException {
                return Integer.valueOf(s).intValue();
            }

            static public long toLong(String s) {
                return Long.valueOf(s).longValue();
            }

            static public float toFloat(String s) {
                return Float.valueOf(s).floatValue();
            }

            static public double toDouble(String s) {
                return Double.valueOf(s).doubleValue();
            }

            static public String toString(short val) {
                return String.valueOf(val);
            }

            static public String toString(int val) {
                return String.valueOf(val);
            }

            static public String toString(long val) {
                return String.valueOf(val);
            }
```

```
static public String toString(float val) {
   return String.valueOf(val);
}

static public String toString(double val) {
   return String.valueOf(val);
}

static public String toString(char val) {
   return String.valueOf(val);
}

static public String toString(boolean val) {
   return String.valueOf(val);
}
}
```

S7.7   With regard to `CDemo.java`:

- The definition of `c1` is legal because C has a **public** default constructor.

- The definition of `c2` is illegal because C does not have a constructor taking three parameters.

- The invocation `c1.setData1(4)` is legal because C mutator method `setData1()` is **public** and takes one integer parameter. It makes no difference that the mutator is setting a **private** instance variable.

- The invocation `c1.setData3(4)` is illegal because C mutator method `setData3()` is **private**. It makes no difference that the mutator is setting a **public** instance variable.

- The definition of `n1` is legal because C accessor method `getData2()` is **public**.

- The definition of `n2` is legal because C accessor method `getData3()` is **public**.

- The definition of `n3` is illegal because C instance variable `data1` is **private**.

- The definition of `n4` is illegal because C instance variable `data2` is **private**.

- The definition of `n5` is legal because C instance variable `data3` is **public**.

8 ARRAYS AND COLLECTIONS

A programmer often needs the ability to represent a group of values as a list. For such tasks, Java provides several list representation alternatives. Our examination of lists begins with the array, which is the basic Java list mechanism. Java arrays have features that make them more robust than arrays in other common programming languages: the size of array can be specified at run time; automatic bounds checking to ensure that any reference to an array element is valid; and a data field `length` that specifies the number of elements in the list. Furthermore, because an array is an object, an array also has the features common to all other objects (e.g., the ability to clone). Our examination of lists also considers the `java.util` collection classes. The collection classes are important to programmers because they provide advanced data structures and algorithms that are useful in many problem-solving situations.

OBJECTIVES

- Define and initialize one-dimensional and multidimensional arrays.
- Reference and manipulate entire arrays and individual array elements.
- Use arrays and array elements as parameters to methods.
- Present algorithms for sorting and searching arrays.
- Consider the various collection classes.
- Explore the use of ArrayList.
- Explore the use of the collections algorithms.

8.1   BASIC LIST REQUIREMENTS

Suppose we want to find the minimum value of five integers represented by **int** variables `value1`, `value2`, through `value5`. The following code segment computes that value for us.

```
int minimumSoFar = value1;
if (value2 < minimumSoFar) {
   minimumSoFar = value2;
}
if (value3 < minimumSoFar) {
   minimumSoFar = value3;
}
if (value4 < minimumSoFar) {
   minimumSoFar = value4;
}
if (value5 < minimumSoFar) {
   minimumSoFar = value5;
}
```

Notice that a separate **if** statement is used for each value in the list—although the variable names are similar, each variable is independent of the other variables.

Now suppose that we need the minimum value of 1,000 integers represented by variables `value1` through `value1000`. Because of the variable independence, we cannot introduce simply iteration into the solution as was done for the number averaging problem of Chapter 6. And if we proceed as above, with a separate **if** statement for each individual value, the resulting very large code segment would be both clumsy and error prone. Instead what we require is a Java mechanism that enables us to create an object that can represent a list of values. Furthermore, we require the ability to manipulate collectively and individually the elements of a list in an intuitive manner.

Our examination of list types begins with the array, which is the basic Java mechanism for representing a list of values. Because Java considers an array to be an object, an array has the features common to all other objects. In particular, the value of an array variable is a reference to an array rather than being an array itself.

8.2   ONE-DIMENSIONAL ARRAYS

The individual values that make up an array are known as *elements*. Array elements can be referenced collectively or individually. They can be of any fundamental type, a previously defined class type, including an array type. One important language restriction on arrays is that all elements of an array have the same type, which is known as the *element type*.

8.2.1   DEFINITIONS

Arrays can be defined with or without initialization. If there is no initialization, then the definition has the form

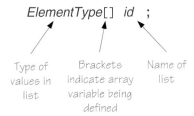

where *ElementType* is the type of the individual elements in the array and *id* is an identifier naming the array.

Our next code segment defines three local array variables a, b, and c without specifying initial values for these variables.

```
int[] a;
char[] b;
double[] c;
```

Like other local variable definitions that do not specify initial values, the values of these variables are undefined. Our representation of these variables is

An array variable definition can specify the array to which the variable is to reference. The most common such form is

The following code segment defines in part, three array variables number, value, and s. The variable definitions specify the arrays to which they reference.

```
BufferedReader stdin = new BufferedReader(
    new InputStreamReader(System.in));
int[] number = new int[3];
n = Integer.parseInt(stdin.readLine());
```

```
double[] value = new double[n];
String[] s = new String[n];
```

Variable number references a new array of three elements with element type **int**, variable value references a new array of n elements with element type **double**, and variable s references a new array of n elements with element type String, where the value for n has been extracted from the standard input stream. Each of the arrays is a collection of individual *array elements*. Each of the array elements can be used like a variable of the underlying element type.

If the value extracted for n is 5, then number, value, and s have representation

Variable number refers to a list of three elements and variables value and s both refer to lists of five elements. Because no initial values are specified for the elements themselves, the elements of the three arrays are default initialized. By default, numeric elements are initialized to 0; **boolean** elements are initialized to **false**; and object elements are initialized to **null**.

Suppose d and e are both **int** array variables. where d references an array with three elements whose values are initialized to 10, 20, and 30 and e references an array of two elements whose values are initialized to 40 and 50. Also suppose that f is a two-element **double** array whose elements are initialized to 1.1 and 2.2.[†] Our depiction of these arrays is

Because d and e are both of the same type, we can assign one to the other. For example, if

```
d = e;
```

is executed. Then the new value of d is the value of e; i.e., d and e now reference the same array of elements. Our depiction of the arrays is now

---

†   Explicit array initialization is considered in Section 8.2.3.

(The three-element array that d used to reference is returned automatically to the system by the Java garbage collector.)

The assignment

```
f = e;      // illegal
```

is illegal. Arrays e and f have different element types—e is an array of **int** values and f is an array of **double** values. Because the arrays have different types, one cannot be assigned to the other.

Unless it would cause confusion with regard to the particular example, in subsequent array depictions, we use a more succinct representation that does not show explicitly the reference. For example, if g is a three-element **char** array whose elements are 'a', 'b', and 'c', then our standard depiction of g is

g | 'a' | 'b' | 'c' |

Bracket placement

Java permits the brackets indicating an array variable definition to be placed alternatively after the variable name. Thus, array definition

```
double[] x;
```

can also be specified in the following manner

```
double x[];
```

It is our practice to use only the first form. This convention is the one followed by most Java programmers.

Remember array variables are reference variables

Beginning Java programmers sometimes forget that an array type variable holds a reference to an object. They mistakenly assume that the definition of the array type variable automatically provides the list of elements that are to be manipulated.

8.2.2   ELEMENT ACCESS

The act of referring to an individual array element is called *subscripting* or *indexing*. Just as brackets are used in a definition to indicate that an array is being created, so too are brackets used to subscript a particular element of an array. Each element of an array has its own subscript value. The first element of an array has subscript value 0, the second element of an array has subscript value 1, and so on. For array v defined below,

```
int[] v = new int[10]; // elements default initialized to 0s
```

the last element has a subscript value 9. The following figure shows a representation of v.

v | 0 | 0 | 0 | 0 | 0 | 0 | 0 | 0 | 0 | 0 |

    v[0] v[1] v[2] v[3] v[4] v[5] v[6] v[7] v[8] v[9]

The elements of array v can be referenced via the expressions v[0], v[1], v[2], …, v[9].

A subscript can be a nonnegative integer expression. For example, v[(low + high)/2], refers to the element of v with subscript value (low + high)/2. If low has value 0 and high has value 9, then v[(low + high)/2] refers to v[4].

In the following code segment, all references to array elements are legal.

```
int i = 7;
int j = 2;
int k = 4;
v[0] = 1;                    // element 0 of v given value 1
v[i] = 5;                    // element i of v given value 5
v[j] = v[i] + 3;             // element j of v given value
                             // of element i of v plus 3
v[j+1] = v[i] + v[0];        // element j+1 of v given value
                             // of element i of v plus
                             // value of element 0 of v
v[v[j]] = 12;                // element v[j] of v given
                             // value 12
System.out.println(v[2]);    // element 2 of v is displayed
v[k] = Integer.parseInt(stdin.readLine());
                             // element k of v given next
                             // extracted value
```

If the value extracted from the standard input was the value 3, then the effect of executing the preceding code segment is

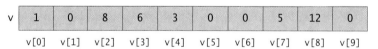

v	1	0	8	6	3	0	0	5	12	0
	v[0]	v[1]	v[2]	v[3]	v[4]	v[5]	v[6]	v[7]	v[8]	v[9]

Unlike many other programming languages, Java automatically checks that proper array subscripts are used. If a subscript is determined to be invalid, an exception of type IndexOutOfBoundsException is generated. For example, the following code segment contains two misuses of array b.

```
int[] b = new int[100];    // b has 100 elements: b[0], … b[99]
b[-1] = 0;                 // illegal: subscript too small
b[100] = 0;                // illegal: subscript too large
```

Unless a program provides exception handling code, an IndexOutOfBoundsException exception causes the program to terminate.

Exception handling is considered in Chapter 10

If the element type of an array is an object type, then the elements hold either the value **null** or references to element type values rather than holding element type values themselves. This situation is illustrated in the following example that defines and then initializes a two-element String array s.

```
String[] s = new String[2];
s[0] = "Brooklyn";
s[1] = "Memphis";
```

Element s[0] is a reference to a String representing "Brooklyn" and element s[1] is a reference to a String representing "Memphis". Array s has depiction

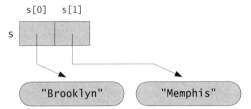

In our next example, we make use awt class Point.

```
Point[] p = new Point[3];
p[0] = new Point(0, 0);
p[1] = new Point(1, 1);
p[2] = new Point(2, 2);
```

Array p has depiction

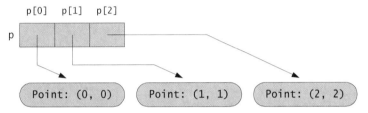

Because p[0], p[1], and p[2] are Point reference variables, they have access to Point member methods. For example, code segment

```
p[0].setX(1);
p[1].setY(p[2].getY());
```

causes the following update of p.

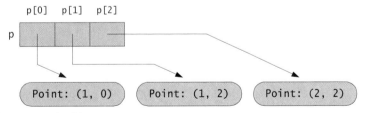

The update occurs in this manner:

- Expression p[0].setX(1) causes the object that p[0] references to set its x-coordinate data field to 1.
- Expression p[1].setY(p[2].getY()) causes the object that p[1] references to set its y-coordinate to the value of the y-coordinate of the object referenced by p[2].

The elements of p hold references. Therefore, an assignment to one of its elements modifies what that element references rather than modifying the object that had been referenced. For example, consider the following code segment that further updates array p.

```java
Point vertex = new Point(4,4);
p[1] = p[0];
p[2] = vertex;
```

The assignment of p[0] to p[1] causes p[1] to refer to the same object as p[0]; the assignment of vertex to p[2] causes p[2] to refer to the same object as vertex. Thus, memory has depiction

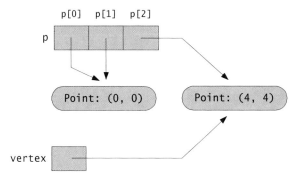

(Because Point objects (1, 1) and (2, 2) no longer have any variables referencing them, their memory is reclaimed automatically by the Java garbage collector.)

8.2.3 EXPLICIT INITIALIZATION

Java also provides a declaration form to specify explicitly the initial values of the elements of an array.

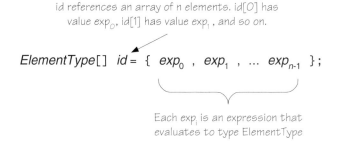

By using this feature, the following code segment specifies the initial values for the arrays referenced by variables fibonacci, puppy, and unit.

```java
int[] fibonacci = { 1, 1, 2, 3, 5, 8, 13, 21, 34, 55 };
String[] puppy = { "nilla", "buffer", "darby", "galen" };
int[] unit = { 1 };
```

The declaration of `fibonacci` causes it to reference an **int** array of 10 elements, the declaration of `puppy` causes it to reference a `String` array of four elements, and the declaration of `unit` causes it to reference an **int** array of one element. Functionally, the three declarations are equivalent to the following.

```
int[] fibonacci = new int[10];
fibonacci[0] = 1;
fibonacci[1] = 1;
fibonacci[2] = 2;
fibonacci[3] = 3;
fibonacci[4] = 5;
fibonacci[5] = 8;
fibonacci[6] = 13;
fibonacci[7] = 21;
fibonacci[8] = 34;
fibonacci[9] = 55;

String[] puppy = new String[4];
puppy[0] = "nilla";
puppy[1] = "buffer";
puppy[2] = "darby";
puppy[3] = "galen";

int[] unit = new int[1];
unit[0] = 1;
```

A single element list, like `unit`, is an array and is treated consistently by Java in that manner.

8.2.4 CONSTANT ARRAYS

As in other declarations, the modifier **final** can be applied in an array declaration. The modifier has the usual effect—after its initialization, the array variable is treated as a constant. In this case, the array variable cannot change which array it references. For example, the following declaration defines and initializes a constant two-element array B.

```
final int[] B = { 10, 100 };
```

Our depiction for B is

where the lock indicates that the value of the reference cannot be changed. With the constant declaration in effect, the following statement is invalid.

```
B = new int[2];          // illegal: a final object cannot be
                         // the target of an assignment
```

However, the values of the elements of the array can be changed.

```
B[1] = 20;               // legal: B[1] is not final
```

8.2.5   MEMBERS

Because an array is a Java object, an array has associated with it all of the member methods of an `Object` (e.g., `clone()` and `equals()`). However, the array `clone()` method is overridden specifically for arrays. In addition to member methods, an array also has a **public final** data field `length` specifying the number of elements in the array.

The Java language designers were particularly helpful to programmers by including array data field `length`—it is a convenience not found with arrays in many other programming languages. In the next code segment, we make use of the feature in the test expression of a **for** loop. The loop displays the elements of the array `puppy` to standard output.

```
for (int i = 0; i < puppy.length; ++i) {
   System.out.println(puppy[i]);
}
```

In the loop, `i` iteratively takes on the values 0, 1, 2, 3, and 4. Because the values 0, 1, 2, and 3 are all less than `puppy.length`, the statement

```
System.out.println(puppy[i]);
```

is executed four times. Each time a successive element of `puppy` is displayed. When `i` is 4, the expression `i < puppy.length` is **false**, which causes the loop to be exited.

Array method `clone()` returns a duplicate of the array. The new array object has the same number of elements as the invoking array. The values of these elements are duplicates of the invoking array. A clone produced in this manner is known as a *shallow copy*. The corresponding elements in the two arrays reference the same objects. The shallowness can be seen by viewing the representations of the array variables `u` and `v` defined in the following code segment.

```
Point[] u = { new Point(0, 0), new Point(1, 1),
                 new Point(2, 2) };
Point[] v = u.clone();
```

The code segment makes array `v` a clone of array `u`. Arrays `u` and `v` have representation

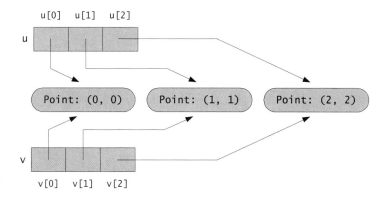

The shallowness of array cloning is further highlighted by the effect of the following statement on the arrays u and v.

```
u[2].setX(3);
```

Because elements u[2] and v[2] reference the same Point, the change to u[2] is visible through v[2].

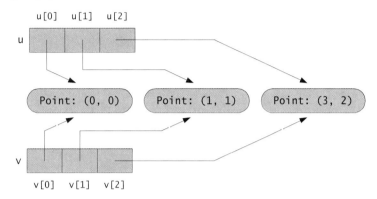

Although array v was created to be a clone to array u, there is no requirement that the elements of v reference the same Point objects as u.

For example, if statement

```
v[2] = new Point(4, 30);
```

is executed, then changes to u[2] do not affect v[2] and vice versa. This independence is in effect because u[2] and v[2] reference different objects.

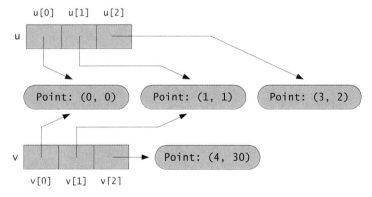

If a distinct element-by-element clone w of array u is needed, it can be created in the following manner.

```
Point[] w = new Point[u.length];
for (int i = 0; i < u.length; ++i) {
    w[i] = u[i].clone();
}
```

In this code segment, the definition of w causes a new array of the proper length to be created. Distinct copies of the elements of u are created by individually cloning its elements.

For this example, we say that array w is a *deep copy* of u—arrays u and w do not share any memory.

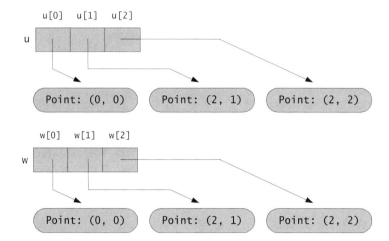

The next example demonstrates that using method clone() on an array with a primitive element type automatically produces a deep copy.

```
int[] x = { 0, 1, 2 };
int[] y = x.clone();
```

The two arrays have depiction

Because the elements of the two arrays hold **int** values and not **int** references, a change to array x does not affect array y and vice versa. A change to an element affects only its value. For example, if x[1] is modified

```
x[1] = 3;
```

then y[1] is unaffected (i.e., there are no side effects to the assignment of x[1]).

8.3	**SIMPLE ARRAY PROCESSING**

We now consider a series of code segments that accomplish three common tasks when using arrays. The segments support

- Extraction of input values to set up an array;
- Search an array of values to determine if a particular value is present;
- Find the minimum value in an array.

Each of these tasks is important and has many applications. For example, an online retailer needs to be able to read a list of merchandise in response to a user query. From that list, the merchandise matching the query request needs to be displayed with special attention given to the merchandise of least cost.

8.3.1	**EXTRACTION**

The first code segment extracts up to MAX_LIST_SIZE values from the standard input stream. Upon completion of the segment, the extracted values are represented by the elements of array data, where data.length equals the number of extracted values. In setting up array data, an array buffer temporarily stores the extracted values.

```
final int MAX_LIST_SIZE = 1000;

int[] buffer = new int[MAX_LIST_SIZE];

int listSize = 0;

for (int i = 0; i < MAX_LIST_SIZE; ++i) {
   String input = stdin.readLine();
   if (input != null) {
      int number = Integer.parseInt(input);
      buffer[i] = number;
      ++listSize;
   }
   else {
      break;
   }
}

int[] data = new int[listSize];
for (int i = 0; i < listSize; ++i) {
   data[i] = buffer[i];
}
```

Because the user does not provide necessarily that many values, a variable listSize keeps track of the number of elements in buffer that have been assigned extracted values. Variable listSize is initialized to zero to reflect that no values have been extracted as of yet.

A **for** loop processes the extractions. The loop iterates at most MAX_LIST_SIZE times. Each iteration a string extraction is attempted. The result of an extraction is assigned to a String variable input.

```
String input = stdin.readLine();
```

A test then determines whether input is non-**null**.

```
if (input != null) {
    int number = Integer.parseInt(input);
    buffer[i] = number;
    ++listSize;
}
else {
    break;
}
```

If input is non-**null**, then the user has supplied another value. If instead input is **null**, then the user has indicated no more values are being supplied.

If the user has supplied a value, then the value is converted to an **int** representation and assigned to variable number. Variable number is assigned to the next available element in array buffer, which is element buffer[i].

```
int number = Integer.parseInt(input);
buffer[i] = number;
++listSize;
```

To complete the processing of the input, variable listSize is incremented to reflect that another value has been added to array buffer.

If the user did not supply a value, then buffer already holds all of the values that the user is supplying. Therefore, the loop should terminate. The termination is accomplished with a **break** statement. As in a **switch** statement, the **break** in a looping construct indicates that the construct is finished. Execution continues immediately at the statement following the loop.

Suppose the input stream contains three values: 4, 9, and 5. The first time through the loop, i is 0, so buffer[0] is assigned the input value 4. The memory associated with buffer, input, number, and listSize looks like the following

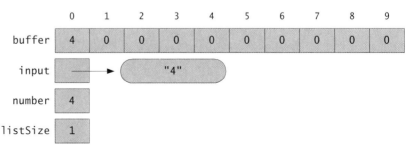

where the elements buffer[1] through buffer[9] contains 0s from the default initialization of the elements of buffer.

In the next iteration, i is incremented to 1, and buffer[1] is assigned the input value 9. The variable depiction is now

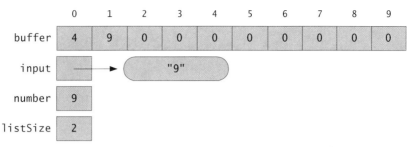

In the next iteration, i is incremented to 2, and buffer[2] and is assigned 5.

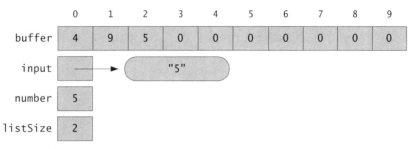

In the next iteration, the user does not supply a value and instead indicates end-of-file. As a consequence, input becomes **null** and the **else** part of the **if** statement terminates the loop. The variables now have depiction

The code segment then copies the input values to array data. Array data is created to hold listSize elements. The elements are copied in turn from array buffer.

```
int[] data = new int[listSize];
for (int i = 0; i < listSize; ++i) {
   data[i] = buffer[i];
}
```

After the segment has completed arrays `buffer` and `data` have the following depiction.

In particular, `data` is a correctly sized array holding the extracted input values.

You might have been tempted to say that we have accomplished our task of extracting the input values once the first **for** loop completed. However, array `buffer` has `buffer.length` elements and the number of extracted elements is `listSize`. These two values are not necessarily the same. It normally is incumbent upon a programmer to have the size of an array reflect the number of elements that have been assigned to it. It is easy to imagine that the input values will undergo significant and varied processing. In such cases, a list whose length does not reflect the number of elements to be processed can be misused. Thus, we copy the assigned elements of `buffer` to `data`.

8.3.2   SEARCHING FOR A KEY VALUE

In our next example, array `data` is searched for a particular value. The variable holding the value to be searched is called the *key*. As indicated at the start of this section, searching is an important list processing activity. For many applications the presence of a value indicates availability; for other applications the presence of a value indicates the list has a particular property associated with it.

```
System.out.println("Enter the search value (number): ");
int key = Integer.parseInt(stdin.readLine());

int i;
for (i = 0; i < data.length; ++i) {
    if (key == data[i]) {
        break;
    }
}

if (i != data.length) {
    System.out.println(key + " is the " + i + "-th element");
}
else {
    System.out.println(key + " is not in the list");
}
```

The code uses index variable `i` to represent the current subscript value. The value of `i` must be available after the loop, so variable `i` cannot be declared as part of the **for** loop. The loop examines in turn array elements `data[0]` through `data[data.length - 1]`.

Each iteration, another element of the array is tested for equivalence to the key value. If `data[i]` does not match the key value, then the loop proceeds with the next iteration. If `data[i]` does match the key value, then the **break** statement is executed.

By examining the value of `i` after the **for** loop has completed, the code determines whether one of the array elements of `data` has the same value as `key`.

If `i` does not have the value of `data.length`, then it must be the case that the **for** loop terminated because (`key == data[i]`) was **true** for some `i` with a value between 0 and `data.length - 1`. In this case, `data[i]` is the key value, and the appropriate message is inserted to the standard output stream.

If `i` has the value `data.length`, then the loop was terminated because there were no more elements to consider. (Remember that `data[0]` through `data[data.length - 1]` are the elements to consider.) In this case, the key value is not present, and an appropriate message is inserted to the output stream.

We now trace through the code segment using the following representation for `data`, `key`, and `i`.

In terms of execution, we are about to begin the **for** loop.

The initialization step of the **for** loop is first executed, and index `i` is assigned value 0.

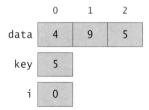

The **for** test expression then is evaluated. Because `i < data.length` (i.e., $0 < 3$), the **for** loop body is executed. Because `data[i]` does not equal `key` (i.e., $4 \,!\!= 5$), the loop does not terminate automatically. Index i then is incremented to 1 to prepare for the next evaluation.

The test expression is reevaluated. Because i < data.length (i.e., 1 < 3), the **for** loop body is executed again. Because data[i] does not equal key (i.e., 9 != 5), the loop does not terminate automatically. Index i then is incremented to 2 to prepare for the next evaluation.

The test expression is reevaluated. Because i < data.length (i.e., 2 < 3), the **for** loop body is executed again. Because data[i] equal key (i.e., 5 = 5), the **break** statement is executed and the loop is terminated.

The **if** statement following the **for** loop then is evaluated, and its test expression is found to be **true** (2 != 3). As a result, the following output occurs.

```
5 is the 2-th element
```

8.3.3   SEARCHING FOR THE MINIMUM VALUE

The key value search code segment is typical of array processing. There is initialization to prepare for the processing of the array, a loop to process each array element in turn, and a check to see how the list processing completed. For example, the next code segment finds the minimum value of a list sample where the list size of sample is at least 1.

```
int minimumSoFar = sample[0];
for (int i = 1; i < sample.length; ++i) {
   if (sample[i] < minimumSoFar) {
      minimumSoFar = sample[i];
   }
}
```

To find the minimum value in an array requires examining each element in turn. If the code segment keeps track of the minimum array element value seen so far, the lesser of that value and the current element is the minimum value seen so far. If this processing is done for each array element, then after the last array element has been considered, the minimum value seen so far is in fact the minimum. Observe that our code segment for finding the minimum of an arbitrarily sized list is even smaller than the code segment presented at the start of this chapter for finding the minimum of five values!

We now turn our attention to using arrays and array elements as method parameters and as return values. By providing methods for list manipulations, the previous code segments can be put to general use.

<table>
<tr><td>**8.4**</td><td>## ARRAYS AND METHODS</td></tr>
</table>

The syntax for expressing an array parameter definition is no different from that of a normal variable definition. An array parameter has form

ElementType[] *ParameterName*

A formal array parameter must include its name as part of its declaration

A formal array parameter must include its array type as part of its declaration

Evidence of this fact has been in all of our programs. For example, listing

```
// Authors: J. P. Cohoon and J. W. Davidson
// Purpose: display a quotation in a console window

public class DisplayForecast {

    // main(): application entry point
    public static void main(String[] args) {
        System.out.print("I think there is a world market for");
        System.out.println(" maybe five computers.");
        System.out.println("   Thomas Watson, IBM, 1943.");
    }
}
```

An array formal parameter specifies its element type, brackets, and parameter name

reproduces `DisplayForecast.java` of Chapter 1—the first program that we considered. As required by Java, its method `main()` has a single array parameter `args` with an element type of `String`.

Our consideration of methods using arrays as parameters or producing arrays as return values begins with methods `sequentialSearch()` and `binarySearch()`. These two methods for searching lists are part of `ArrayTools.java` that we develop in this chapter. Class `ArrayTools` is an API for accomplishing some common list tasks. For example, the API also contains methods to sort and displays lists. All of the methods in this API are **static**; that is, each method is a class method.

Clarity

Even the most experienced programmers are tempted to optimize their programs so they run faster. While efficiency is important, clarity and correctness are more important. Who wants to use a program that runs fast but produces incorrect results or is so difficult to understand that its correctness cannot be verified? Thus, we should not sacrifice clarity and correctness for efficiency. Furthermore, it is hard for a programmer to "tweak" a program so that it runs measurably faster. One rule of thumb in programming is that 90 percent of a program's running time is spent in 10 percent of the code. Consequently, without some idea of where a program spends most of its time, most changes to a program to speed it up will have little effect on the overall running time. If efficiency becomes an issue, a more effective approach is to wait until the program is complete and then use a special tool called a *profiler* to identify the program's hot spots. *Hot spots* are where the programs spends most of its time running. These areas of the program can be tuned to reduce the running time of the program.

8.4.1   SEQUENTIAL AND BINARY SEARCH

Method `sequentialSearch()` of Listing 8.1 has two formal parameters—the first parameter is an `int[]` array `data` and the second parameter is the search value `key`.

Listing 8.1   sequentialSearch() from ArrayTools.java

```
1.  // sequentialSearch(): examine unsorted list for a key
2.  public static int sequentialSearch(int[] data, int key) {
3.     for (int i = 0; i < data.length; ++i) {
4.        if (data[i] == key) {
5.           return i;
6.           }
7.     }
8.
9.     return -1;
10. }
```

Method `sequentialSearch()` is similar in form to the code segment that searched an array for a key value in Section 8.3.2. However, `sequentialSearch()` does not display a message indicating whether it found the value. If `sequentialSearch()` finds the key value in the array, it returns the subscript of the first matching element. If the key value is not among the array element values, `sequentialSearch()` returns the number of elements in the array. Because the array elements occupy subscript positions 0 through `data.length-1` in the array, the value –1 indicates that the key value is not in the array.

Suppose the array `score` has the following definition.

```
int[] score = { 6, 9, 82, 11, 29, 85, 11, 28, 91 };
```

It depiction is

	0	1	2	3	4	5	6	7	8
score	6	9	82	11	29	85	11	28	91

In the following code segment, the array `score` is searched for two values.

```
int i1 = ArrayTools.sequentialSearch(score, 11);  // 2
int i2 = ArrayTools.sequentialSearch(score, 30);  // -1
```

The first invocation initializes `i1` to 3 because the first match of the value 11 in the array `score` is with `score[3]`. The second invocation initializes `i2` to –1, because none of array elements `score[0]` through `score[8]` have value 30.

Although subscripts are not used when an array is used as an actual parameter, subscripts are used when an individual array element is passed as an actual parameter. The use of brackets is necessary because it is the subscript that enables a particular element to be specified. For example, consider the following code segment that use class method `max()` from the `java.lang.Math` API to display the larger of array elements `score[0]` and `score[2]`.

```
System.out.println(Math.max(score[0], score[2]));
```

Method `max()` expects two **int** parameters. Because the element type of array `score` is **int**, passing two `score` array elements to `max()` is appropriate.

Listing 8.2   **binarySearch() from ArrayTools.java**

```
1.  // binarySearch(): examine sorted list for a key
2.  public static int binarySearch(char[] data, char key) {
3.      int left = 0;
4.      int right = data.length - 1;
5.      while (left <= right) {
6.          int mid = (left + right)/2;
7.          if (data[mid] == key) {
8.              return mid;
9.          }
10.         else if (data[mid] < key) {
11.             left = mid + 1;
12.         }
13.         else {
14.             right = mid - 1;
15.         }
16.     }
17.
18.     return -1;
19. }
```

When the values of a list are in sorted order, there are better searches than method `sequentialSearch()` for determining if a particular value is in the list. For example, when you look up a name in the phone book, you do not start in the beginning and scan through until you find the name—you use the fact that the names are listed in sorted order and use some intelligence to jump quickly to the right page and then start scanning.

Method `binarySearch()` of Listing 8.2 conducts a series of tests that enable it to reduce repeatedly the portion of its array parameter `data` that possibly can contain the value of parameter `key`. The method follows the same convention as `sequentialSearch()`. If the key value is present, then `binarySearch()` returns the index of a matching element; if the key value is not present, then `binarySearch()` returns –1.

> The standard Java class Collections method binarySearch() behaves differently than our method—if the key is not in the list, that method returns the index where the key value should be located

The portion of the list that can contain the key value is represented by the indexes `left` and `right`. Prior to the first **if** test, any list element can contain the `key` value. For this reason, `left` is initialized to 0, and `right` is initialized to `data.length-1`. Suppose the list and key value have representation

key `'R'`

	0	1	2	3	4	5	6	7	8	9
data	`'E'`	`'I'`	`'O'`	`'P'`	`'Q'`	`'R'`	`'T'`	`'U'`	`'W'`	`'Y'`
	left									right

A **while** loop performs repeated tests to update indexes `left` and `right`. The loop iterates until either the `key` value has been found or it has been determined that no portion of the list contains the `key` value.

The **while** loop body starts by assigning the average of the current values of `left` and `right` to variable `mid`. If element `data[mid]` equals `key`, then `mid` is returned.

key `'R'`

	0	1	2	3	4	5	6	7	8	9
data	`'E'`	`'I'`	`'O'`	`'P'`	`'Q'`	`'R'`	`'T'`	`'U'`	`'W'`	`'Y'`
	left					mid				right

If element `data[mid]` is less than `key`, then because the list is sorted, all elements to the left of `data[mid]` are also less than `key`. If value of `key` is to be in the list, it must occur to the right of `data[mid]`. Therefore, index `left` is reset to be to the immediate right of `mid`; that is, `left` becomes `mid + 1`. For our example, the value of `key`, which is `'R'`, is greater than the value of `data[mid]`, which is `'Q'`. After the updating of `mid` at the start of the next iteration, the variables have depiction

key `'R'`

	0	1	2	3	4	5	6	7	8	9
data	`'E'`	`'I'`	`'O'`	`'P'`	`'Q'`	`'R'`	`'T'`	`'U'`	`'W'`	`'Y'`
							left		mid	right

The grayed portion indicates that those elements are no longer in consideration in finding the value of `key`.

If element data[mid] is neither equal to nor less than key, it must be greater than the key. As the list is sorted, all elements to the right of data[mid] are also greater than key. If the value of key is to be in the list, it must occur to the left of data[mid]. Therefore, in this case index right is reset to be to the immediate left of mid; that is, right becomes mid – 1. For the previously depicted situation, the value of key, which is 'R', is less than the value of data[mid], which is 'U'. After the updating of mid at the start of the next iteration, the variables have depiction

With this situation, the values of key and data[mid] test equal, so the method returns the value of mid.

It can be shown in the worst case that binarySearch() performs approximately $2 \cdot \log_2 n$ comparisons to process a list of n elements. Consequently, for a sorted list of 1,000 elements, 20 comparisons are sufficient for binarySearch() to determine whether the key value is present. It also means that for a sorted list of 1 million elements, binarySearch() can determine whether a particular value is present using no more than 40 comparisons! This ability is even more impressive when compared to sequentialSearch(), which can need up to 1 million comparisons! For interactive applications, the fast response time of binarySearch() is what users expect.

We next turn our attention to some of the implications of having an array reference be a parameter of a method.

8.4.2   ZEROING

Consider program ArrayDemo.java of Listing 8.3. In particular, pay attention to methods zeroInt() and zeroArray(). What is the output of the program? Do not examine the output until you have tried to determine it yourself.

The output of the program is

```
int i: 1
array z: 1 2 3
int i: 1
array z: 0 0 0
```

Why has z changed but not i? From previous chapters, you know that in the invocation of zeroInt(i) a copy of the **int** value of actual parameter i is passed to zeroInt() to initialize its formal parameter val. It is that copy that method zeroInt() modifies, leaving method main() variable i untouched. The following figure depicts the activation

---

Listing 8.3   ArrayDemo.java

```java
1.  // Demonstrates array parameter nuances
2.  public class ArrayDemo {
3.     public static void main(String[] args) {
4.        int i = 1;
5.        int[] z = { 1, 2, 3 };
6.
7.        System.out.println("int i: " + i);
8.        System.out.println("array z: " + z[0] + " " + z[1] + " "
9.               + z[2]);
10.
11.       zeroInt(i);
12.       zeroArray(z);
13.
14.       System.out.println("int i: " + i);
15.       System.out.println("array z: " + z[0] + " " + z[1] + " "
16.              + z[2]);
17.    }
18.
19.    public static void zeroInt(int val) {
20.       val = 0;
21.    }
22.
23.    public static void zeroArray(int[] list) {
24.       for (int j = 0; j < list.length; ++j) {
25.          list[j] = 0;
26.       }
27.    }
28. }
```

records for methods `main()` and `zeroInt()` immediately before `zeroInt()` completes.

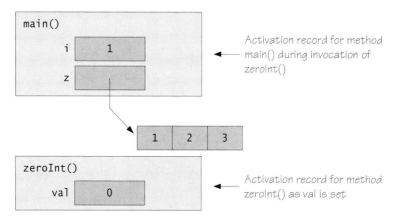

However, in invocation `zeroArray(z)`, a copy of the reference value of variable `z` is used to initialize parameter `list` of `zeroArray()`. In particular, the value is a reference to an array of three **int** elements. Thus, when method `zeroArray()` is executing, `list`

is referencing the same list as z. As a result, the activation records for main() and zeroArray() have the following depiction.

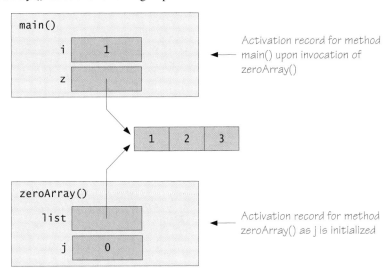

Therefore, whenever the **for** statement body is executed,

```
list[j] = 0;
```

method zeroArray() is changing the jth element of array z. The changes brought about by the **for** loop cause the activation records for methods main() and zeroAr-ray() to have the following depiction as method zeroArray() completes.

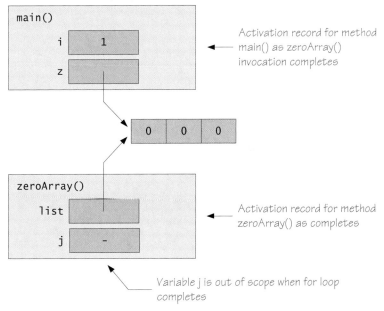

We make use of this ability of method to change the elements of the actual array parameter in Section 8.5.1 when we present a method to sort the values in an array.

We now consider three other methods from API `ArrayTools`. These methods are `putList()`, `getList()`, and `reverse()`. The first two of these methods are probably the most needed ones when doing list processing. Method `putList()` displays the elements of its array parameter to standard output; method `getList()` extracts a list of values from standard input and returns the list in array form; and method `reverse()` takes the elements of its array parameter and reverses the order of the values. The three methods are defined in Listing 8.4.

8.4.3   DISPLAY

Method `putList()` of `ArrayTools` is a useful method to have around. It is convenient when debugging a program to display the contents of an array.

This **void** method has a single parameter `data` of type `int[]`. The method uses a **for** statement to display iteratively the elements of the array one per line to standard output. As an example of its use, suppose array `score` has the following depiction.

	0	1	2	3	4	5	6	7	8
score	6	9	82	11	29	85	11	28	91

Then invocation

```
ArrayTools.putList(score);
```

displays the elements of the array `score`, one per line to standard output.

```
6
9
82
11
29
85
11
28
91
```

8.4.4   EXTRACTION AND REVERSAL

Method `getList()` of Listing 8.4 is the input extraction segment of Section 8.3 embedded with a method body. The method warrants no further discussion. The exercises consider alternative implementations.

Method `reverse()` of Listing 8.4 takes the elements of its array parameter and reverses the order of the values. The method has a **for** loop whose index variable i iterates over the first half of the array referenced by parameter `list`. The i th element from the front of the list is swapped with the i th element from the end of the list. The i th ele-

Listing 8.4   putList(), getList(), and revere() from ArrayTools.java

```
1.  // class constant
2.  private static final int MAX_LIST_SIZE = 1000;
3.
4.  // valueOf(): produces a string representation
5.  public static void putList(int[] data) {
6.      for (int i = 0; i < data.length; ++i) {
7.          System.out.println(data[i]);
8.      }
9.  }
10. // getList(): extract up to MAX_LIST_SIZE values and returns them
11. public static int[] getList() throws IOException {
12.     BufferedReader stdin = new BufferedReader(
13.             new InputStreamReader(System.in));
14.
15.     int[] buffer = new int[MAX_LIST_SIZE];
16.
17.     int listSize = 0;
18.
19.     for (int i = 0; i < MAX_LIST_SIZE; ++i) {
20.         String currentInput = stdin.readLine();
21.         if (currentInput != null) {
22.             int number = Integer.parseInt(currentInput);
23.             buffer[i] = number;
24.             ++listSize;
25.         }
26.         else {
27.             break;
28.         }
29.     }
30.
31.     int[] data = new int[listSize];
32.     for (int i = 0; i < listSize; ++i) {
33.         data[i] = buffer[i];
34.     }
35.
36.     return data;
37. }
38.
39. // reverse(): reverses the order of the element values
40. public static void reverse(int[] list) {
41.     int n = list.length;
42.
43.     for (int i = 0; i < n/2; ++i) {
44.         // swap element from front of list with corresponding element
45.         // from the end of the list
46.         int rmbr = list[i];
47.         list[i] = list[n-1-i];
48.         list[n-1-i] = rmbr;
49.     }
50. }
```

ment from the end of the list has index n-i-1, where n is the number of elements in the list.

Listing 8.5 Demo.java

```
1.  // Extracts and displays a list in forward and reverse order
2.  import java.io.*;
3.
4.  public class Demo {
5.      // main(): application entry point
6.      public static void main(String[] args) throws IOException {
7.          System.out.println("");
8.          System.out.println("Enter list of integers, one per line:");
9.          int[] number = ArrayTools.getList();
10.
11.         System.out.println("");
12.         System.out.println("Your list");
13.         ArrayTools.putList(number);
14.
15.         ArrayTools.reverse(number);
16.         System.out.println("");
17.         System.out.println("Your list in reverse");
18.         ArrayTools.putList(number);
19.         System.out.println();
20.     }
21. }
```

Methods getList(), putList(), and reverse() are used in program
Demo.java of Listing 8.5. An example of the program's input and output behavior is
depicted in Figure 8.1.

Figure 8.1 Demo snapshot.

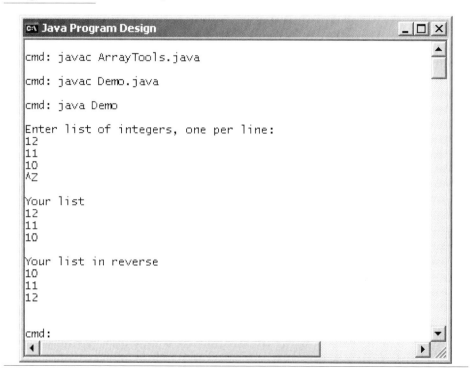

8.4.5   INCREASING REPRESENTATION CAPACITY

In some problem-solving situations, the case arises where new values need to be added to a list but the list is full. For example, suppose merchandise is a String array with definition

```
String[] merchandise = { "Music", "Books", "Magazines",
    "DVDs" };
```

There is no room to add additional items to list merchandise. Each element of the array already references a value. This problem can be alleviated with method doubleCapacity() of Listing 8.6. The method takes an array currList as its parameter and returns a new array with twice the capacity as currList, where the first half of the new array is initialized to the values of currList.

Listing 8.6   doubleCapacity() from ArrayTools.java

```
1.  // doubleCapacity(): create a duplicate list with extra capacity
2.  public static String[] doubleCapacity(String[] currList) {
3.     int n = currList.length;
4.     String[] biggerList = new String[2*n]; // get a bigger list
5.
6.     for (int i = 0; i < n; ++i) {
7.        biggerList[i] = currList[i];          // copy existing values
8.     }
9.
10.    return biggerList;
11. }
```

With method doubleCapacity(), the following actions are possible

```
merchandise = doubleCapacity(merchandise);
merchandise[4] = "Clothes";
merchandise[5] = "Shoes";
```

The depiction of merchandise before the code segment is

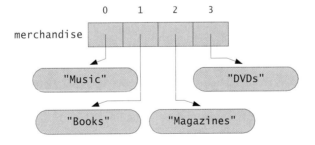

The depiction of merchandise after the code segment is

Method `doubleCapacity()` begins by determining the size of array represented by its formal parameter.

```
int n = currList.length;
```

A new bigger array then is created with twice the capacity.

```
String[] biggerList = new Object[2*n]; // get a bigger list
```

The elements then are copied from the old list to the new bigger array.

```
for (int i = 0; i < n; ++i) {
    biggerList[i] = currList[i];        // copy existing values
}
```

To complete its task, the method needs only to return the new list.

```
return biggerList;
```

8.5   SORTING

Chapter 5 introduced the notion of sorting in `SortTwo.java` and `SortThree.java`, which respectively displayed two and three input values in nondecreasing order. We used the term nondecreasing rather than increasing to allow for duplicate values. Here we consider the general sorting problem of arranging the values in a list of arbitrary size into nondecreasing order.

A sort is often an iterative process such that each iteration rearranges some of the values in the list v to be sorted. For example, on iteration i the method known as `selectionSort()` finds the element containing the ith smallest value of its list v and exchanges that element with v[i]. As another example, on iteration i the method known as `insertionSort()` correctly places the value of v[i] with respect to the values stored in elements v[0] through v[i-1].

In the next section, we present an implementation of `selectionSort()`. Method `insertionSort()` is considered in the exercises. In that discussion that follows, we assume that the list to be sorted is an array of **char** values. The sort can be modified easily to handle other types of values.

8.5.1   METHOD SELECTIONSORT()

As discussed in the previous section, on iteration i, selectionSort() finds the element containing the ith smallest value of array v and exchanges that element with element v[i]; that is, on the first iteration, the smallest element is placed correctly; on the second iteration, the second smallest element is placed correctly; and so on.

In looking for the smallest element, selectionSort() must consider all of the elements. The element containing the smallest considered value then is exchanged with v[0]. For example, suppose the list to be sorted is

then v[2], which contains an 'E', is exchanged with v[0], which contains a 'Q'. The result is

The yellow shading indicates that the element has been determined to be set correctly in the sorting of v.

In looking for the second smallest element, selectionSort() need not consider the element containing the smallest value. Because the element containing the smallest value is v[0], to find the second smallest element, selectionSort() needs only to find the smallest value among elements v[1] through v[n-1]. The element containing the smallest considered value then is exchanged with v[1]. In our example, v[7], which contains an 'I', is exchanged with v[1], which contains a 'W'. The result is

The yellow shading continues to indicate the elements that have been determined to be set correctly.

In looking for the third smallest element, selectionSort() need not consider the elements containing the smallest and second smallest values. Because the element containing the smallest value is v[0] and the element containing the second smallest value is v[1], to find the third smallest element, selectionSort() needs only to find the smallest value among elements among elements v[2] through v[n-1]. The element containing the smallest considered value then is exchanged with v[2]. In our example, v[8], which contains an '0', is exchanged with v[2], which contains a 'Q'. The result is

In general, looking for the ith smallest element, selectionSort() needs only to find the smallest value among elements among elements v[i] through v[n-1]. The element containing the smallest considered value then is exchanged with v[i]. The following code segment correctly finds the element containing the smallest value among elements v[i] through v[n-1].

```
// guess the location of the ith smallest element
int guess = i;
for (int j = i+1; j < v.length; ++j) {
   if (v[j] < v[guess]) // is guess ok?
      // update guess with index of smaller element
      guess = j;
}

// guess is now correct, so swap elements v[guess] and v[0]
```

The code is similar to our other array processing code. In particular, the code is most similar to the code that searches an array. The code segment begins defining **int** index variable guess. Variable guess represents where we believe the ith smallest element can be found. The definition initializes guess to i. The code segment then determines whether the value of guess is correct. The **for** loop body repeatedly tests whether v[j] < v[guess], with j iteratively taking on the values i + 1 through v.length - 1.

If it is determined that v[j] < v[guess], then our value for guess is wrong and it is updated with the value of j. At this point, guess is the index of the smallest value among elements v[i] through v[j]. Thus, completing the **for** loop assures that guess is the index of the ith smallest element.

To place the ith smallest element correctly, the values of v[i] and v[guess] are interchanged.

```
char rmbr = v[i];
v[i] = v[guess];
v[guess] = rmbr;
```

The outer **for** loop ends when i equals v.length-1; that is, no additional work is needed to place the largest element correctly once the other elements have been placed correctly. For our example, after placing the second largest element the array has depiction

	0	1	2	3	4	5	6	7	8	9
v	'E'	'I'	'0'	'P'	'Q'	'R'	'T'	'U'	'W'	'Y'

Because the search for the largest value in the array needs only to consider the final element, no additional work is needed—the largest value is already placed correctly.

	0	1	2	3	4	5	6	7	8	9
v	'E'	'I'	'O'	'P'	'Q'	'R'	'T'	'U'	'W'	'Y'

Based on this analysis, we present method selectionSort() from Array-Tools.java in Listing 8.7.

8.5.2 QUALITY OF SELECTIONSORT()

In analyzing a sorting algorithm, software developers are concerned normally with the total number of element comparisons and the total number of element copies/assignments performed by the sort. When i is 0 for selectionSort(), there are $n - 1$ element comparisons and 3 element copies/assignments, where n is the number of elements in array v. When i is 1, there are $n - 2$ element comparisons and 3 element copies/assignments. When i is 2, there are $n - 3$ element comparisons and 3 element copies/assignments. In general, on iteration i, there are $n - (i + 1)$ element comparisons and 3 element copies/assignments.

Listing 8.7 Method selectionSort() of ArrayTools.java

```
1.  // selectionSort(): sorts the elements of a
2.  public static void selectionSort(char[] v) {
3.      for (int i = 0; i < v.length-1; ++i) {
4.      // guess the location of the ith smallest element
5.          int guess = i;
6.          for (int j = i+1; j < v.length; ++j) {
7.              if (v[j] < v[guess]) { // is guess ok?
8.              // update guess to index of smaller element
9.                  guess = j;
10.             }
11.         }
12.
13.     // guess is now correct, so swap elements
14.         char rmbr = v[i];
15.         v[i] = v[guess];
16.         v[guess] = rmbr;
17.     }
18. }
```

The total number of element comparisons is therefore $n-1 + n-2 + \ldots + 2 + 1$, which is proportional to n^2. The total number of element copies/assignments is at most $3 + 3 + \ldots + 3$, which is proportional to n. Because the number of element comparisons is proportional to the square of the number of elements, we say that method selectionSort() has *quadratic* performance with respect to element comparisons. Because the number of element copies/assignments is proportional to the number of elements, we say that the algorithm has *linear* performance with respect to element copies/assignments. Because $n^2 > n$, we say that overall algorithm performs a quadratic number of element operations.

8.6	## COMMAND-LINE PARAMETERS

Many operating systems (e.g., Linux and Windows) provide command-line interpreters. These interpreters enable a user to type a command and then have the operating system execute it. For example, the following instruction uses the Linux/Windows command cd to change the current folder to folder code.

```
cmd: cd code
```

In the instruction, the string "code" is a *command-line parameter* to the command cd.

As another example, the following instruction runs the Java program Echo with the strings Genie, Donna, and Ave as its command-line parameters.

```
java Echo Genie Donna Ave
```

This program displays its parameters to standard output.

```
Genie Donna Ave
```

Thus, its operation is the same as the Linux/Windows commands echo.

Java provides a method for creating programs that use command-line parameters. The command-line parameters are communicated to a program via its method main(). To make this communication straightforward, Java requires that a program view the command-line parameters as an array of strings. The first element in the array is the first command-line parameter, the second element in the array is the second command-line parameter, and so on. For the Echo example, the array consists of references to the strings "Genie", "Donna", and "Ave".

Access to the array of strings representing the command-line parameters is through method main()'s array parameter.

```
public static void main(String[] args)
```

When a program is run, elements args[0] through args[args.length – 1] are initialized automatically to reference the strings representing the command-line parameters to the program. This initialization is depicted for the Echo example in Figure 8.2.

Listing 8.8 supplies the code for Echo.java. The command-line parameters passed to the program are displayed iteratively using a **for** loop that iterates once for each command-line parameter. Each parameter is displayed individually using method print(). Once the loop is finished, method println() causes a newline character to be displayed.

We now turn our attention to multidimensional arrays.

Figure 8.2   **Command-line parameter associations.**

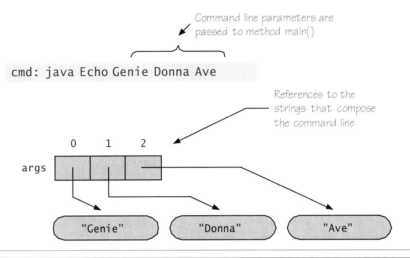

Listing 8.8   Echo.java

```
1.  // Mimics operating system command echo.
2.
3.  public class Echo {
4.      // main(): application entry point
5.      public static void main(String[] args) {
6.          // display parameters one after the other
7.          for (int i = 0; i < args.length; ++i) {
8.              System.out.print(args[i] + " ");
9.          }
10.
11.         System.out.println();
12.     }
13. }
```

Another program parameter example

Chapter 10 presents a version of the Windows command `type` (in Linux its known as `cat`). We delay its coverage until then because of its use of exception handling.

8.7   MULTIDIMENSIONAL ARRAYS

In addition to defining one-dimensional arrays, it is also possible to define multidimensional arrays. There are a great many problems whose solutions can be determined through the manipulation of multidimensional arrays. The application domains include matrices, graphical animation, economic forecast models, map representation, time studies of population change, and microprocessor design to name just a few.

The following definition initializes m to reference a two-dimensional array.

```
int[][] m = new int[3][4];
```

Two-dimensional array m should be viewed as consisting of three *component* arrays m[0], m[1], and m[2] with each of these components consisting of a four-element array. The *component type* of m is **int**[] and the element type of each of m[0], m[1], and m[2] is **int**. To be explicit, our definition of m is shorthand for

```
int[][] m = new int[3][];
m[0] = new int[4];
m[1] = new int[4];
m[2] = new int[4];
```

The components of a two-dimensional array are known as *rows*. To refer to an individual element of a row, an additional subscript is used. For example, m[i][j] is the jth element of the ith row in m. Array m has representation

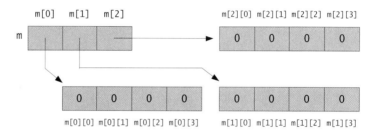

The representation indicates explicitly that m[0], m[1], and m[2] are all references to four-element arrays whose elements are default initialized to zero.

Suppose we wanted to set the elements of a two-dimensional array m using standard input. To do so, we would use nested **for** loops. The outer **for** loop would iterate once per subarray. For each such iteration, the inner **for** loop would iterate once for each element of the current subarray. Such nesting is demonstrated in the following code segment.

```
for (int r = 0; r < m.length; ++r) {
    for (int c = 0; c < m[r].length; ++c) {
        System.out.print("Enter a value: ");
        m[r][c] = Integer.parseInt(stdin.readLine());
    }
}
```

Notice that the outer **for** loop test expression is r < m.length, where r is the current row index. The expression term m.length has meaning because m consists of three one-dimensional subarrays. Similarly, the term m[r].length from the inner **for** loop test expression c < m[r].length has meaning because component m[r] is an **int**[] array.

Java does not require that the subarrays of a two-dimensional array have the same length. For example, the following code segment defines a two-dimensional array s of type `String[][]`. Array `s` consists of four rows. The first two rows both have two elements; the last two rows have four and three elements respectively.

```
String[][] s = new String[4][];
s[0] = new String[2];
s[1] = new String[2];
s[2] = new String[4];
s[3] = new String[3];
```

Array `s` has representation

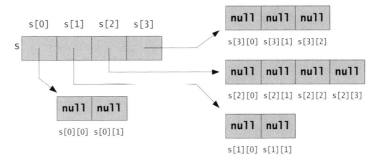

Arrays with more than two dimensions are also possible. However, in practice, arrays with three dimensions are used infrequently, and arrays with more than three dimensions are used rarely.

The definition of a multidimensional array can include initialization by specifying a block of values with each component of the array having its own initialization specification. For example, the following definitions initializes both `b` and `c` to be `int[][]` arrays.

```
int b[][] = {{1, 2, 3}, {4, 5, 6}, {7, 8, 9}};
int c[][] = {{1, 2}, {3, 4}, {5, 6}, {7, 8, 9}};
```

Array `b` consists of three components each of which is a three-element array.

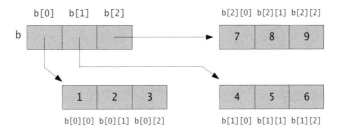

Array c consists of four components, the first three of which are two-element arrays and the fourth is a three-element array.

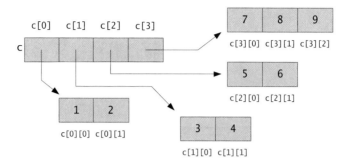

Methods with parameters that are multidimensional arrays are permitted. For example, the following method `zero()` sets to 0 all of the elements of the subarrays of its two-dimensional `int[][]` parameter array a.

```java
public void zero(int[][] a) {
   for (int r = 0; r < a.length; ++r)
      for (int c = 0; c < a[r].length; ++c)
         a[r][c] = 0;
}
```

It is also possible to use a subarray of a multidimensional array as a parameter. For example, we can invoke `ArrayTools` method `sequentialSearch()` on each of the components of the two-dimensional array m that was defined at the beginning of this section.

```java
System.out.println(ArrayTools.sequentialSearch(m[0], key));
System.out.println(ArrayTools.sequentialSearch(m[1], key));
System.out.println(ArrayTools.sequentialSearch(m[2], key));
```

We can make these invocations using the rows of m because each row of a two-dimensional array is a one-dimensional array.

The following example demonstrates a three-dimensional array alpha. Each element in alpha is assigned a value equal to the sum of its subscripts.

```java
int[][][] alpha = new int[10][5][3];
for (int i = 0; i < alpha.length; ++i) {
   for (int j = 0; j < alpha[i].length; ++j) {
      for (int k = 0; k < alpha[i][j].length; ++k) {
         alpha[i][j][k] = i + j + k;
      }
   }
}
```

8.7.1   MATRICES

A two-dimensional array is sometimes known as a *matrix* because it resembles that mathematical concept. A matrix a with m rows and n columns is represented mathematically in the following manner:

In the programming project of Section 8.15, a class Matrix is developed for matrix representation and manipulation

$$\begin{bmatrix} a_{1,1} & a_{1,2} & \cdots & a_{1,n} \\ a_{2,1} & a_{2,2} & \cdots & a_{2,n} \\ \cdots & & & \cdots \\ a_{m,1} & a_{m,2} & \cdots & a_{m,n} \end{bmatrix}$$

Addition is defined for matrices whose dimensions match. If a and b are both matrices with m rows and n columns, then their sum c has the following form:

$$\begin{bmatrix} a_{1,1}+b_{1,1} & a_{1,2}+b_{1,2} & \cdots & a_{1,n}+b_{1,n} \\ a_{2,1}+b_{2,1} & a_{2,2}+b_{2,2} & \cdots & a_{2,n}+b_{2,n} \\ \cdots & & & \cdots \\ a_{m,1}+b_{m,1} & a_{m,2}+b_{m,2} & \cdots & a_{m,n}+b_{m,n} \end{bmatrix}$$

Matrix addition is implemented in the following method add() whose body is a doubly nested **for** loop.

```
public static double[][] add(double[][] a, double[][] b) {
    // determine number of rows in solution
    int m = a.length;
    // determine number of columns in solution
    int n = a[0].length;

    // create the array to hold the sum
    double[][] c = new double[m][n];

    // compute the matrix sum row by row
    for (int i = 0; i < m; ++i) {
        // produce the current row
        for (int j = 0; j < n; ++j) {
            c[i][j] = a[i][j] + b[i][j];
        }
    }

    return c;
}
```

The outer **for** loop of add() supplies the index variable i to process the current row. The inner **for** loop supplies the index variable j to process the current column in the current row. Together the two indices enable the sum of a pair of elements from arrays a and b to be calculated and assigned to the corresponding array element of c. (A robust method add() would test that arrays a and b are sized consistently; that is, both arrays have m rows with n columns per row.)

If a is a matrix with m rows and n columns and b is a matrix with n rows and p columns, then the product of matrices a and b is a matrix c with n rows and p columns, where element $c_{i,j}$ has definition

$$c_{i,j} = a_{i,1}b_{1,j} + a_{i,2}b_{2,j} + \ldots + a_{i,n}b_{n,j}$$

Conceptually, element $c_{i,j}$ is the sum of terms produced by multiplying the matrix a elements in row i times the corresponding matrix b elements in column j.

Matrix multiplication is implemented in the following method `multiply()` whose body is a triply nested **for** loop.

```
public static double[][] multiply(double[][] a, double[][] b) {
    // determine the size of the matrices
    int m = a.length;
    int n = a[0].length;
    int p = b[0].length;

    // create array to hold the product
    double[][] c = new double[m][p]; // elements are initially 0

    // create the product row by row
    for (int i = 0; i < m; ++i) {
        // produce the current row
        for (int j = 0; j < p; ++j) {
            for (int k = 0; k < n; ++k) {
                c[i][j] += a[i][k] * b[k][j];
            }
        }
    }

    return c;
}
```

(A robust method `multiple()` would test that arrays a and b are sized consistently; that is, array a has m rows and n columns per row and array b has n rows with p columns per row.) The exercises consider other matrix operations.

We now turn our attention to the collections framework. The framework is a collection of classes and interfaces that support list representation and manipulation. Informally, an *interface* is a template describing features of a class. Interfaces are discussed in Section 9.6.

8.8   COLLECTIONS FRAMEWORK

Although arrays in Java are more robust than arrays in other languages they suffer from the traditional shortcoming—they cannot be resized; that is, there are no Java array operations that support the insertion of a new elements or the deletion of existing elements.

For software projects being developed in other languages, the restrictions on arrays often forced developers to use nonportable alternative list representations. The cost of using nonportable representations can be quite high because developers must create and support multiple versions of their software.

Through its *collections framework*, Java has a rich set of list representations. With this framework, Java software developers typically can avoid the expense of developing new list representations. In addition, because the framework provides an extensive collection of algorithms for examining and manipulating its list representations, software developers can rely on the correctness of these data structures and concentrate their resources on the problem-specific aspects of their project.

There are two types of list representations in the collections framework—those that implement the interface `java.util.Collection` and those that implement the interface `java.util.Map`.

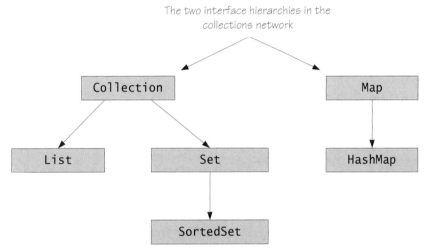

Classes that implement one of the derived `Collection` interfaces `List`, `Set`, and `SortedSet` represent lists as we normally imagine them. Such classes support a view of a list as a group of elements. Classes that implement the `Map` interface or its derived interface `HashMap` take a more associative view; that is, these classes provide the means to associate "keys" with values. The `Map`-based classes also provides the means to determine the value associated with a key and vice versa.

8.9   ARRAYLIST

Our focus here will be on the class `ArrayList`. Class `ArrayList` provides a resizeable list representation that implements the `List` interface. The name `ArrayList` is intended to be suggestive doubly. An `ArrayList` uses an array to represent the elements of its list. In addition, an `ArrayList` has been designed so that its element accessor and mutator methods are guaranteed to be very efficient. In computer science parlance, we say that the element accessor and mutator methods run in *constant time*.

Nothing magical

Associated with each `ArrayList` is a *capacity*, which is the maximum number of elements that the list can store currently without growing. The capacity is the size of the array the `ArrayList` is using currently to store the elements of the list. If the capacity of that array becomes insufficient, then a new array is created with greater capacity for the `ArrayList` and the values from the old list are copied to it. The operation is much like method `doubleCapacity()` of Listing 8.6.

In addition to its accessor and mutator methods, `ArrayList` provides the ability to add (*append*) an element to the end of the list. The append operation is guaranteed to be fast on average (i.e., an append opera-

A complete description of `ArrayList` capabilities is provided in Appendix D

tion operates in constant time on average). The class also provides a number of other methods for inserting and deleting elements to the list. These other methods can require time proportional to the number of elements in the list to perform their tasks. In computer science parlance, we say that these methods run in *linear time*. A partial list of the capabilities of `ArrayList` is provided in Table 8.1.

The following code segment defines and initializes two `ArrayList` variables c and d. We shall use these variables in several subsequent code segments.

```
ArrayList c = new ArrayList();
ArrayList d = new ArrayList(20);
```

Variable c references a new `ArrayList`. This list has no elements. In terms of its internal configuration, the new `ArrayList` has been set up so that it has the ability to represent up to 10 elements before it will need to update its internal capacity. Variable d references another new `ArrayList`, which also has no elements. In terms of its internal configuration, this new `ArrayList` has been set up so that it has the ability to represent up to 20 elements before it will need to update its internal capacity.

Suppose we wanted to add two elements to the list referenced by c, where these elements represent the strings `"Brooklyn"` and `"Wichita Falls"`. The following code will accomplish this.

```
c.add("Brooklyn");
c.add("Wichita Falls");
```

Based on the method invocations, `ArrayList` variable c has representation

---

Table 8.1 **Selected ArrayList constructors and methods.**

public void add(int i, Object v)
> Inserts value v into the list such that v has index i. Any preexisting elements with indices i or greater are shifted backward by one element position.

public boolean add(Object v)
> Appends the list with a new element with value v and returns **true**.

public void clear()
> Removes all elements from the list.

public Object clone()
> Returns a shallow copy of this list.

public Object get(int i)
> If i is a valid index, it returns the ith element; otherwise an exception is generated.

public boolean isEmpty()
> Returns **true** if there are no elements; otherwise, it returns **false**.

public Object remove(int i)
> If i is a valid index, it removes the ith element from the list by shifting forward elements i + 1 and on. In addition, the removed value is returned. Otherwise, an exception is generated.

public Object set(int i, Object v)
> If i is a valid index, then ith element is set to v and the previous value of the element is returned. Otherwise, an exception is thrown.

public int size()
> Returns the numbers of elements in the list.

The representation indicates that variable c references an ArrayList object. This object currently represents a list with two elements. The first element references the string "Brooklyn" and the second element references the string "Wichita Falls".

Suppose we wanted ArrayList variable d to a reference a list whose elements represented the integers 0, 1, and 2. The following code segment accomplishes this task.

```
for (int i = 0; i < 3; ++i) {
   d.add(new Integer (i));
}
```

Because an **int** value is not an object, we cannot directly add the values 0, 1, and 2 to the list. Instead, we must add objects representing those values. The natural way to do so is to use class Integer.

Based on the code segment, ArrayList variable d has representation

The representation indicates that variable d references an ArrayList object. This object currently represents a list with three elements. The first element references an Integer representing the value 0, the second element references an Integer representing the value 1, and the third element references an Integer representing the value 2.

To access the elements of an ArrayList we can use method get(). This method behaves in practice like the array subscript operator []. For example, the following class method displayList() from ArrayListTools.java of Listing 8.9 displays the values of its ArrayList parameter.

```java
public static void displayList(ArrayList a) {
    for (int i = 0; i < a.size(); ++i) {
        System.out.println(a.get(i));
    }
}
```

Observe that we used ArrayList member method size() in the **for** loop test expression. Method size() returns the number of elements represented by the list. An examination of the use of index variable i indicates that the elements of an ArrayList are numbered in the same manner as the elements of an array. The first element has index 0, the second element has index 1, and so on.

Invocation

```java
ArrayListTools.displayList(c);
```

uses displayList() to display the elements of c. The output produced by the invocation is

```
Brooklyn
Wichita Falls
```

ArrayList method set() is used to change the value of an element. For example, the following code segment changes the value of the second element in c and then displays the list.

```java
c.set(1, "Glen Rock");
ArrayListTools.displayList(c);
```

The output produced by the segment is

```
Brooklyn
Glen Rock
```

Listing 8.9   **ArrayListTools.java**

```
1.  // Provide some ArrayList services
2.
3.  import java.util.*;
4.  import java.io.*;
5.
6.  public class ArrayListTools {
7.      // displayList(): print an ArrayList
8.      public static void displayList(ArrayList a) {
9.          for (int i = 0; i < a.size(); ++i) {
10.             System.out.println(a.get(i));
11.         }
12.     }
13.
14.     // getList(): get ArrayList values from standard input
15.     public static ArrayList getList() throws IOException {
16.         BufferedReader stdin = new BufferedReader(
17.                 new InputStreamReader(System.in));
18.
19.         ArrayList a = new ArrayList();
20.
21.         String s = stdin.readLine();
22.         while (s != null) {
23.             a.add(s);
24.             s = stdin.readLine();
25.         }
26.
27.         return a;
28.     }
29.
30.     // convertToInteger(): converts strings to Integers
31.     public static void convertToInteger(ArrayList a) {
32.         for (int i = 0; i < a.size(); ++i) {
33.             String s = (String) a.get(i);
34.             Integer v = Integer.valueOf(s);
35.             a.set(i, v);
36.         }
37.     }
38. }
39.
```

Class `ArrayListTools` also provides two class methods `getList()` and convertToInteger(). Method `getList()` reads the input lines that make up standard input and returns a new `ArrayList` whose elements represent those lines. Method `convertToInteger()` takes its `ArrayList` parameter a and modifies its elements so that their representation is `Integer`.

`ArrayListTools` method `getList()` is similar in purpose to `ArrayTools` method `getList()` of Listing 8.4.

```
public static ArrayList getList() throws IOException {
    BufferedReader stdin = new BufferedReader(
        new InputStreamReader(System.in);

    ArrayList a = new ArrayList();
```

```
String s = stdin.readLine();
while (s != null) {
    a.add(s);
    s = stdin.readLine();
}

return a;
}
```

However, its implementation is far simpler. The simplicity is possible because of the capabilities of the ArrayList methods. In particular, the append behavior of method add() enables each additional input value to be incorporated easily into the list.

If standard input contains the following values

```
28
1
18
```

then statement

```
d = ArrayListTools.getList();
```

extracts those values into an ArrayList representation and assigns a reference to the list to ArrayList variable d. The representation of variable d is

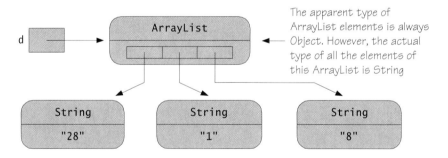

In accessing and manipulating the values in the list represented by d, casting and conversions are necessary to change the representation of the elements from String to Integer. This process can be accomplished using ArrayListTools class method convertToInteger().

```
public static void convertToInteger(ArrayList a) {
    for (int i = 0; i < a.size(); ++i) {
        String s = (String) a.get(i);
        Integer v = Integer.valueOf(s);
        a.set(i, v);
    }
}
```

Method convertToInteger() uses a **for** loop to convert iteratively the elements of its parameter a to Integer form. For ease of understanding, the loop uses three statements to perform a conversion. The first statement gets the value of the current element using `ArrayList` method `get()`. Because the return type of `get()` is `Object`, a cast is necessary to convert the value from its *apparent type* to its *actual type*, which is `String`.

    String s = (String) a.get(i);

An `Integer` representation of the `String` is produced using `Integer` class method `valueOf()`.

    Integer v = Integer.valueOf(s);

The `Integer` representation is used to update the value of the `ArrayList` element.

    a.set(i, v);

With the conversion, variable d has representation

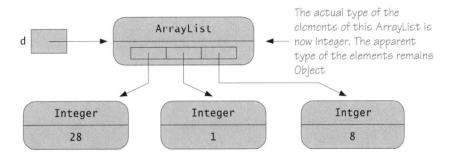

8.10   COLLECTIONS ALGORITHMS

As indicated at the beginning of our collections frame-work discussion, the framework includes a collection of algorithms for performing standard list operations. The algorithms are implemented as class methods of the class `java.util.Collections`. A summary of the most commonly useful methods is included in Table 8.2.

A complete list of
`Collections` capabilities is
provided in Appendix D

Several of the methods make use of the interfaces `java.util.Comparable` or `java.util.Comparator` when examining list elements (e.g., `min()`, `max()`, and `sort()`). Interface `Comparable` calls for a method `compareTo()` with the following characteristics.

    public int compareTo(Object v)

> Returns a negative value if this object is less than v; returns zero if the two objects are equal; and returns a positive value if this object is greater than v.

Interface `Comparator` calls for methods `equals()` and `compare()`. A class's implementation of these methods is expected to have the following two characteristics.

    public int compare(Object v1, Object v2)

> Returns a negative value if v1 is less than v2; returns zero if the two values are equal; and returns a positive value if v1 is greater than v2.

    public boolean equals(Object v)

> Returns whether v is equal to this `Comparator`.

Table 8.2   **Some Collections algorithms.**

```
static Object max(Collection a)
```
   Returns the maximum-valued element of collection a. The determination of the
   value is based on the natural ordering of the elements (i.e., the ordering based on
   their Comparable interface method compareTo()).
```
static Object max(Collection a, Comparator c)
```
   Returns the maximum-valued element of collection a based on the ordering
   using comparator c.
```
static Object min(Collection a)
```
   Returns the minimum-valued element of collection a. The determination of the
   value is based on the natural ordering of the elements (i.e., the ordering based on
   their Comparable interface method compareTo()).
```
static Object min(Collection a, Comparator c)
```
   Returns the minimum-valued element of collection a based on the ordering using
   comparator c.
```
static void reverse(List a)
```
   Reverses the order of the elements in list a.
```
static void shuffle(List a)
```
   Randomly permutes list a.
```
static void sort(List a)
```
   Sorts list a into its natural ordering of the elements (i.e., the ordering based on
   their Comparable interface method compareTo()).
```
static void sort(List a)
```
   Sorts list a into its natural ordering of the elements (i.e., the ordering based on
   their Comparable interface method compareTo()).
```
static void sort(List a, Comparator c)
```
   Sorts list a into nondescending order with respect to comparator c.

Many of the standard classes implement the Comparable interface including String,
Integer, and Double. The comparison methods for these classes work as you expect.
For example, the compareTo() methods of the numeric classes (e.g., Integer and
Double) order values numerically and the compareTo() method of String orders val-
ues lexicographically.

Program CollectionsTest.java of Listing 8.10 demonstrates some of the Collections algorithms. The program begins by defining an ArrayList variable a that
reference an ArrayList whose elements are Integer objects represent the integer values 0 ... 9.

```
// initialize a to represent the integers 0 … 9
ArrayList a = new ArrayList();
for (int i = 0; i < 10; ++i) {
   a.add(new Integer(i));
}
```

The program then displays the ArrayList using a println() invocation.

```
// display a to demonstrate its current configuration
System.out.println("Original: " + a);
```

Listing 8.10 CollectionsTest.java

```
1.  // Demonstrate Collections usefulness
2.
3.  import java.util.*;
4.
5.  public class CollectionsTest {
6.      // main(): application entry point
7.      public static void main(String[] args) {
8.          // initialize a to represent the integers 0 … 9
9.          ArrayList a = new ArrayList();
10.         for (int i = 0; i < 10; ++i) {
11.             a.add(new Integer(i));
12.         }
13.
14.         // display a to demonstrate its current configuration
15.         System.out.println("Original: " ı a);
16.
17.         // put a into reverse order
18.         Collections.reverse(a);
19.
20.         // display a to demonstrate its current configuration
21.         System.out.println("Reversed: " + a);
22.
23.         // put a into random order
24.         Collections.shuffle(a);
25.
26.         // display a to demonstrate its current configuration
27.         System.out.println("Shuffled: " + a);
28.
29.         // sort a
30.         Collections.sort(a);
31.
32.         // display a to demonstrate its current configuration
33.         System.out.println("Sorted:    " + a);
34.     }
35. }
```

The values of the elements then are put into reverse order using Collections method reverse().

```
// put a into reverse order
Collections.reverse(a);
```

The program then redisplays the ArrayList using another println() invocation.

```
// display a to demonstrate its current configuration
System.out.println("Reverse: " + a);
```

The values of the elements are rearranged randomly using Collections method shuffle().

```
// put a into random order
Collections.shuffle(a);
```

The program then redisplays the ArrayList using another println() invocation.

```
// display a to demonstrate its current configuration
```

```
System.out.println("Shuffled: " + a);
```

In a sample run of the program, the program output up to this point was

```
Original: [0, 1, 2, 3, 4, 5, 6, 7, 8, 9]
Reversed: [9, 8, 7, 6, 5, 4, 3, 2, 1, 0]
Shuffled: [3, 0, 1, 9, 5, 2, 8, 6, 7, 4]
```

The output indicates that the elements of the `ArrayList` were configured, reversed, and scrambled correctly.

Program `CollectionsTest.java` then sorts the values by using `Collections` method `sort()`.

```
// sort a
Collections.sort(a);
```

Finally, the program redisplays the `ArrayList` a last time.

```
// display a to demonstrate its current configuration
System.out.println("Sorted: " + a);
```

For the same run depicted only partially before, the complete output of the program was

```
Original: [0, 1, 2, 3, 4, 5, 6, 7, 8, 9]
Reversed: [9, 8, 7, 6, 5, 4, 3, 2, 1, 0]
Shuffled: [3, 0, 1, 9, 5, 2, 8, 6, 7, 4]
Sorted:   [0, 1, 2, 3, 4, 5, 6, 7, 8, 9]
```

The output shows that the elements of the `ArrayList` end up being sorted.

This discussion completes our introduction to the collections framework. We now turn our attention to data visualization. That example will complete our introduction to array and list mechanisms.

8.11 CASE STUDY — PIE CHARTS

Visualization of data is an important area of computing and statistical research. Two standard visualization techniques are histograms and pie charts. We consider a pie chart representation here and leave a histogram representation to the exercises. An array will be used to store the data. Therefore, methods will be needed for extracting inputs and converting those inputs to a pie chart representation.

> The objective of this case study is practice with arrays, and class design and implementation in the context of data visualization

A pie chart shows graphically the relative sizes of a set of numeric values. Each value is represented as a slice of pie with the size of a slice proportional to the ratio of the associated value to the sum of the values. Accompanying the pie is a legend describing the data set.

As an example of a data set, consider Table 8.3, which reports preferred musical tastes as reported by the Recording Industry Association of America. A pie chart for this data is given in Figure 8.3. The pie chart was produced by program `MusicChart.java` of Listing 8.11. The program makes use of a class `PieChart` that we design and develop.

Table 8.3 **USA musical preferences.**

Genre	%	Genre	%
Classical	3.2	Religious	6.7
Country	10.5	Rock	24.4
Jazz	3.4	Urban and R&B	10.6
Pop	12.1	Other	17.7
Rap and Hip-Hop	11.4		

The pie chart does a better job of showing the various similarities and disparities. When analyzing data, a visual representation typically enables relationships to be recognized more easily.

ANALYSIS AND DESIGN

If you consider how users may want to generate pie charts, you will see the utility of at least two types of constructors—a constructor where just the data and legend information are supplied and a constructor that also requires coloring information.

```
public PieChart(double[] d, String[] s)
```
> Generates a default-color pie chart representation for data list d, where s[i] is the legend text associated with value d[i].

```
public PieChart(double[] d, String[] s, Color[] c)
```
> Generates a pie chart representation for data list d, where s[i] is the legend text associated with value d[i] and c[i] is the color associated with d[i].

Figure 8.3 **Pie chart produced by MusicChart.java.**

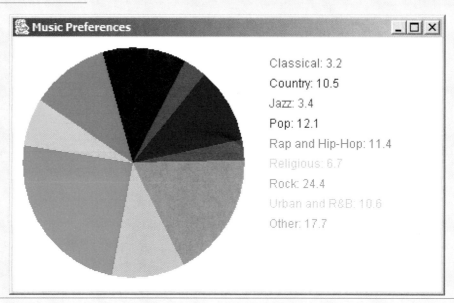

Listing 8.11 MusicChart.java

```
1.  // Produces a pie chart of music preferences
2.
3.  import java.awt.*;
4.  import javax.swing.*;
5.  import java.io.*;
6.
7.  public class MusicChart {
8.      // main()" application entry point
9.      public static void main(String[] args) throws IOException {
10.         JFrame w = new JFrame("Music Preferences");
11.         w.setSize(450, 280);
12.         w.setVisible(true);
13.         w.setDefaultCloseOperation(JFrame.EXIT_ON_CLOSE);
14.         Container c = w.getContentPane();
15.         c.setBackground(Color.WHITE);
16.         Graphics g = c.getGraphics();
17.
18.         double[] choice = { 3.2, 10.5, 3.4, 12.1, 11.4, 6.7, 24.4,
19.                             10.6, 17.7 };
20.         String[] genre = { "Classical", "Country", "Jazz", "Pop",
21.                 "Rap and Hip-Hop", "Religious", "Rock",
22.                             "Urban and R&B", "Other" };
23.
24.         System.out.println("Hit enter when ready");
25.         System.in.read();
26.
27.         PieChart chart = new PieChart(choice, genre);
28.         chart.paint(g);
29.     }
30. }
```

In the implementation that we develop here, only array representations are considered for the data, legend, and color lists. The exercises consider constructors where the data, legend, and color lists are represented using `ArrayList` objects.

A variety of accessors, mutators, and facilitators should be present if the `PieChart` representation is to have general utility. For example, the class should provide the means for getting and setting the various pie chart characteristics including such characteristics as pie position, radius, and legend position. The class should also provide the means for rendering the entire pie chart and the individual rendering of the pie and the legend.

We leave the implementation of accessors and mutators to the exercises. Our discussion concentrates on implementing the constructors and the following rendering facilitators.

`public void paint(Graphics g)`

Renders a graphical representation of the pie chart to graphic context `g`.

`public void paintPie(Graphics g, int x, int y, int r)`

Renders a graphical representation of the pie to graphical context `g`, where the radius of the pie is `r` and the upper-left-hand corner of the bounding box of the pie is (`x`, `y`).

`public void paintLegend(Graphics g, int x, int y, int delta)`

Renders a graphical representation of the pie legend to graphical context `g`, where the first line of the legend begins at location (`x`, `y`) and successive lines are each offset by an additional `delta` pixels downward.

In support of these rendering behaviors, the following `PieChart` attributes are appropriate.

`private double[] data`

Reference to the list of numeric values being represented in the pie chart.

`private String[] name`

Reference to the list of names to be used in the pie chart, where `name[i]` is the basis for the legend entry for value `data[i]`.

`private Color[] color`

Reference to the list of colors to be used in the pie chart, where the color associated with value `data[i]` is `color[i]`.

`private int radius`

The radius of the pie in the pie chart.

`private Point pieLocation`

Reference to the location where the pie is to be placed in the pie chart.

`private Point legendLocation`

Reference to the location where the legend is to be placed in the pie chart.

`private int lineSpacing`

Number of pixels separating successive legend lines in the pie chart.

IMPLEMENTATION

Because one of the `PieChart` constructors automatically assigns the colors in the pie chart, it is appropriate for the class `PieChart` to maintain a list of available colors. The list can be represented using a class constant `DEFAULT_PIE_COLOR`.

```
private static final Color[] DEFAULT_PIE_COLOR = {
    Color.RED, Color.BLUE, Color.MAGENTA, Color.BLACK,
    Color.GREEN, Color.YELLOW, Color.CYAN, Color.PINK,
```

```
       Color.GRAY, Color.ORANGE, Color.DARK_GRAY, Color.WHITE };
```

To make the construction of a pie chart simple for a `PieChart` user, it is also appropriate to have constants that specify default layout characteristics of the pie chart.

```
private static final int DEFAULT_RADIUS = 115;
private static final int DEFAULT_LINE_SPACING = 20;
private static final int DEFAULT_PIE_LOCATION
                           = new Point (10, 10);
private static final int DEFAULT_LEGEND_LOCATION
                           = new Point (495, 35);
```

(The exercises investigate alternatives to using these values through the use of mutator methods.) These class constants serve the following purposes:

- `DEFAULT_RADIUS`: the default pie radius;

- `DEFAULT_LINE_SPACING`: the default spacing in pixels between successive lines of the legend;

- `DEFAULT_PIE_LOCATION`: the default location of the upper-left-hand corner of the bounding box of the pie;

- `DEFAULT_LEGEND_LOCATION`: the default location of the upper-left-hand corner of the bounding box of the legend.

With `DEFAULT_PIE_COLOR`, the initialization required of the first `PieChart` constructor can be accomplished through an invocation of the other `PieChart` constructor.

```
// PieChart(): constructor for case when colors are not supplied
public PieChart(double[] d, String[] s) {
   this(d, s, DEFAULT_PIE_COLOR);
}
```

Defining one constructor in terms of another is a standard software engineering practice.

The other `PieChart` constructor uses its parameters to set respectively the data values, legend text, and colors to be used in the pie chart. The class constants are used to set the other attributes of the pie chart.

```
// PieChart(): constructor using given data, names, colors
public PieChart(double[] d, String[] s, Color[] c) {
   if ((d.length == 0) || (d.length > s.length)
             || (d.length > c.length)) {
       System.err.println("PieChart: invalid data");
       System.exit(1);
   }

   data = d;
   name = s;
   color = c;

   radius = DEFAULT_RADIUS;
   pieLocation = DEFAULT_PIE_LOCATION;
   legendLocation = DEFAULT_LEGEND_LOCATION;
   lineSpacing = DEFAULT_LINE_SPACING;
}
```

As an examination of the constructor body indicates, the implementation is straight-forward. A test first determines whether the parameters are sensible. If there are no data values or an insufficient number of legend entries or colors, then the constructor issues an error message and terminates the program. Otherwise, the constructor sets the various attributes of the pie chart.

We now turn our attention to implementing the three rendering facilitators specified in the problem design section. As a reminder, renderer `paint()` displays the complete pie chart; renderer `paintPie()` displays the pie itself; and renderer `paintLegend()` displays the legend associated with the pie chart.

Renderer method `paint()` needs to display the pie chart in the graphical context specified by its parameter g. It can so by invoking rendering methods `paintPie()` and and `paintLegend()` with appropriate parameters.

```
// paint(): render chart and legend
public void paint(Graphics g) {
    // set pie chart characteristics
    int r = getRadius();
    Point pie = getPieLocation();
    Point legend = getLegendLocation();
    int spacing = getLineSpacing();

    // paint the chart
    paintPie(g, pie.x, pie.y, r);
    paintLegend(g, legend.x, legend.y, spacing);
}
```

Our implementation of method `paint()` begins by using `PieChart` accessors `getRadius()` and `getPieLocation()` to determine the size of the pie and its location.[†]

```
int r = getRadius();
Point pie = getPieLocation();
```

It then uses accessors `getPieLocation()` and `getLegendSpacing()` to determine the location of the legend and the number of pixels separating successive legend lines.

```
Point legend = getLegendLocation();
int spacing = getLineSpacing();
```

With these values, the pie renderer `paintPie()` and the legend renderer `paintLeg-end()` then can be invoked to display the pie chart.

```
paintPie(g, pie.x, pie.y, r);
paintLegend(g, legend.x, legend.y, spacing);
```

The implementation of method `paintPie()` iteratively displays the slices one at a time.

```
// paintPie(): render the pie
public void paintPie(Graphics g, int x, int y, int r) {
```

---

†   The accessors are considered in the self-test section with their implementation included in List-ing 8.12, which starts on page 451. Listing 8.12 provides a complete definition of `Pie-Chart.java`.

```
final int CIRCLE_DEGREES = 360;

// determine number of values
int n = getSampleSize();

// compute sum of the values
double dataSum = 0;
for (int i = 0; i < n; ++i) {
   dataSum += getData(i);
}

// draw slices one by one starting from origin
int startAngle = 0;

for (int i = 0; i < n; ++i) {
   // how much of the pie does the next slice take
   double percent = getData(i) / dataSum;
   int arcAngle = (int) Math.round(percent * CIRCLE_DEGREES);

   // set the slice color
   Color c = getColor(i);
   g.setColor(c);

   // render the slice
   g.fillArc(x, y, 2*r, 2*r, startAngle, arcAngle);

   // record where next slice starts
   startAngle += arcAngle;
   }
}
```

In doing its slice display, the `paintPie()` implementation makes use of one local constant. The constant specifies the number of degrees in a circle.

```
final int CIRCLE_DEGREES = 360;
```

Because the size of a slice is proportional to the ratio of its associated value to the sum of the values, `paintPie()` first uses `PieChart` accessors to determine the number of data values n and the sum `dataSum` of the data values.

```
// determine number of values
int n = getSampleSize();

// compute sum of the values
double dataSum = 0;
for (int i = 0; i < n; ++i) {
   dataSum += getData(i);
}
```

The implementation uses a variable `startAngle` to represent the starting angle orientation of the next slice to be displayed, where the first slice has a starting orientation of 0 degrees.

```
// draw slices one by one starting from origin
int startAngle = 0;
```

Figure 8.4 Method fillArc() rendering.

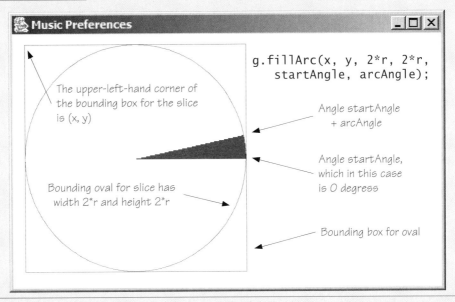

Method `paintPie()` uses a **for** loop to display the slices, with the `i`th iteration displaying the slice associated with the `i`th data value. Each iteration begins by determining the width `arcAngle` of the current slice in degrees.

```
// how much of the pie does the next slice take
double percent = getData(i) / dataSum;
int arcAngle = (int) Math.round(percent * CIRCLE_DEGREES);
```

The width of the angle equals the product of the number of degrees in a circle and the relative size of the current data value to the sum of the data values.

The **for** loop body then sets the color of the slice in the desired graphical context.

```
// set the slice color
Color c = getColor(i);
g.setColor(c);
```

The slice then is rendered using `Graphics` member method `fillArc()`.

```
// render the slice
g.fillArc(x, y, 2*r, 2*r, startAngle, arcAngle);
```

`Graphics` method `fillArc()` expects six parameters. The first two parameters specify the x- and y- coordinates of the upper-left-hand corner of the bounding box associated with the oval that contains the slice. The next two parameters specify width and height of that oval. The next parameter specifies the starting angle of the slice and the last parameter specifies the width of the angle. The method renders the slice counterclockwise from the start angle. The roles of the parameters is demonstrated in Figure 8.4.

In the `paintPie()` invocation of `fillArc()`, the coordinates of the upper-left-hand corner of the bounding box come from parameters x and y of `paintPie()`. Because the pie is to be a circle, the width and height values are both `2*r`, where r is also one of the parameters of `paintPie()`. The starting angle and the width angle are respectively `startAngle` and `arcAngle`.

To prepare for the display of the next slice, the **for** loop body ends with an updating of `startAngle`. Its new value is to be where the last slice ended.

```
// record where next slice starts
startAngle += arcAngle;
```

Like method `paintPie()`, the implementation of method `paintLegend()` uses a **for** loop to display iteratively its elements.

```
// paintLegend(): render the legend for the pie
public void paintLegend(Graphics g, int x, int y, int delta) {
    // determine number of values
    int n = getSampleSize();

    for (int i = 0; i < n; ++i) {
        // set up the current legend line
        Color c = getColor(i);
        String s = getName(i) + ": " + getData(i);

        // render the line
        g.setColor(c);
        g.drawString(s, x, y);

        // set up the y-coordinate location of the next line
        y += delta;
    }
}
```

Its parameters x and y specify the starting location for the first line of the legend and its parameter `delta` specifies how far apart are successive legend lines.

For each of the n values in the data set, the associated color and entry for the legend is determined.

```
// set up the current legend line
Color c = getColor(i);
String s = getName(i) + ": " + getData(i);
```

The legend line is rendered using `Graphics` method `drawString()`.

```
// render the line
g.setColor(c);
g.drawString(s, x, y);
```

Method `drawString()` takes three parameters. The first parameter supplies the string to be rendered and the next two parameters specify where the rendering is to begin.

This discussion completes both our analysis of class `PieChart` and our introduction to Java array and list mechanisms. A complete definition of `PieChart` is given in Listing 8.12 of the self-test answer section.

| 8.12 | **REVIEW** |

- An array is the basic Java list mechanism. Because Java considers an array to be an object, it has the features common to other objects.

- The value of an array variable is a reference to an array rather than being an array itself.

- The individual objects that make up an array are known as elements. Array elements can be accessed collectively or individually. They can be of any fundamental type, a previously defined class type, or even an array type.

- An important language restriction on arrays is that all elements of an array must have the same type, which is known as the element type.

- An array element can be used like a variable of the underlying element type.

- An array whose elements are arrays is a multidimensional array.

- An array variable definition does not provide automatically a list of elements to be manipulated.

- Like other objects, arrays can be defined either with or without initialization. If there is no initialization, then the definition has the form

$$ElementType[]\ id\ ;$$

where *ElementType* is the type of the individual elements in the array and *id* is an identifier that is the name of the array.

- An array variable definition can specify the initial array that the variable is to reference. The most common such form is

$$ElementType[]\ id\ =\ \textbf{new}\ ElementType[exp]\ ;$$

- Java also provides a declaration form to specify initial values for a new array.

$$ElementType[]\ id\ =\ \{\ exp_0\ ,\ exp_1\ ,\ \ldots\ exp_{n-1}\ \}\ ;$$

- The act of referring to an individual array element is called *subscripting* or *indexing*. A subscript can be a nonnegative integer expression. Just as brackets are used in a definition to indicate that an array is being created, so too are brackets used to subscript a particular element of an array. Each element of an array has its own subscript value. The first element of an array has subscript value 0, the second element of an array has subscript value 1, and so on.

- Unlike many other programming languages, Java automatically checks that proper array subscripts are used. If a subscript is determined to be invalid, an exception of type `IndexOutOfBoundsException` is generated.

- If the element type of an array is an object type, then the elements of the array hold references to values of the element types.

- An array has a **public final** data field `length` that specifies the number of elements in the array.

- Because an array is an object, an array has associated with it all of the methods of class `Object`. The `clone()` method of an array is one tailored specifically for arrays to produce a shallow copy of the array.

- There are no methods to resize an array—an array's size is fixed at its creation.

- When used as a parameter, a reference to the array is passed. If code modifies the elements of that formal parameter, the changes are visible to the elements of the actual parameter.

- Java provides a method for creating programs that use command-line parameters. The command-line parameters are communicated to a program via its method `main()`. To make this communication straightforward, Java requires that a program view the command line parameters as an array of strings.

- A sort is often an iterative process such that each iteration rearranges some of the values in the list `a` to be sorted. For example, on iteration `i`, the method known as `selectionSort()` finds the element containing the `i`th smallest value of the list and exchanges that element with the `i`th element.

- The total number of element comparisons made by `selectionSort()` is proportional to n^2, where n is the number of elements in array `a`. Because the number of element comparisons is proportional to the square of the number of elements, we say that method `selectionSort()` has quadratic performance with respect to element comparisons. Because the number of element copies/assignments is proportional to the number of elements, we say that the algorithm has linear performance with respect to element copies/assignments. Overall, the algorithm has quadratic performance.

- The components (subarrays) of a two-dimensional array are known as rows. To refer to an individual element of a row, an additional subscript is used. For example, `m[i][j]` is the `j`th element of the `i`th row in `m`.

- A two-dimensional array is sometimes known as a matrix because it resembles that mathematical concept.

- Java does not require that the components of a two-dimensional array have the same length.

- The definition of a multidimensional array can include initialization. For a two-dimensional array whose base type is a fundamental type, the array initialization is given as collections of initial row values.

- Arrays in Java suffer from the traditional shortcoming—they cannot be resized—there are no Java array operations that support the insertion of a new elements or the deletion of existing elements.

- Java also provides a rich set of alternative list representations, know as the collections framework. There are two types of list representations in the collections framework—those that implement the interface `java.util.Collection` and those that implement the interface `java.util.Map`.

- Classes that implement one of the derived `Collection` interfaces `List`, `Set`, and `SortedSet` represent lists as we normally imagined them. Such classes support a view of a list as a group of elements. Classes that implement the Map interface or its derived interface HashMap take a more associative view; that is, these classes provide the means to associate "keys" with values. The Map-based classes also provides the means to determine the value associated with a key and vice versa.

- Class ArrayList provides a resizeable list representation that implements the List interface. The name ArrayList is intended to be suggestive doubly. An ArrayList uses an array to represent the elements of its list. In addition, an ArrayList has been designed so that its element accessor and mutator methods are guaranteed to run in constant time.

- ArrayList provides the ability to append an element to the end of the list. The append operation takes a constant amount of time on average. The class also provides a number of other methods for inserting and deleting elements to the list. These other methods are guaranteed to run in at most linear time.

- The collections framework through its class Collections provide a collection of algorithms for performing standard list operations. For example, the class provide methods that search, copy, reverse, and shuffle a list. There are also methods to determine the minimum and maximum and methods to swap individual elements.

8.13   SELF-TEST

S8.1   Assume that a and b are **int** arrays that have been initialized and that i, j, and k are **int** variables that have been initialized.

- Write the statement that adds 6 to element k of a.
- Write the statement that copies element i of b to element k+1.
- Write the statement that sums elements i and k of a and places the result in element j+5 of b.

S8.2   Write the appropriate definitions.

- Define an array named stackElements that can hold 50 values of type **double**.
- Define an array named testData that can hold 500 values of type String.

S8.3   Write an array definition for an array coefficient that is initialized with the following values: 1.4, 4.30, 5.12, 6.9, 6.21, 7.31, 11.4, 11.28, and 11.29.

S8.4   Implement a method max() that takes an array of integers as its parameter. The method returns the largest value in the list.

S8.5   Implement a method called isSorted() that takes an integer array as a parameter. The method returns **true** if the list is in nondecreasing order; otherwise it returns **false**.

S8.6   Because of its simplicity, a popular sorting algorithm is *BubbleSort*. Bubblesort is so named because the smallest item "bubbles" to the top of the array when the algorithm is applied. The basic idea is to compare successively adjacent elements and swap them if the they are out of order. If we are sorting the list into ascending order (smallest elements appear first in the array), the smaller elements slowly "bubble" to the top, while the largest elements sink to the bottom. After the first pass through the elements, the maximal value is guaranteed to be in its correct position. After the second pass, the next most maximal element is guaranteed to be in its correct position, and so on. Implement a Java version of `bubbleSort()`.

S8.7 Implement a program `ExpressionEvaluate.java` that evaluates its three command-line parameters as a binary arithmetic expression. An example sample run could be

```
java ExpressionEvaluate 12.3 * 4.56
```

S8.8 Implement a `void` method `printMatrix()` the prints the values of its integer matrix parameter row by row.

S8.9 What happens if the following code using class `PieChart` is executed?

```
double[] d = null;
String[] s = null;
PieChart piechart = new PieChart(d, s);
JFrame w = new JFrame("Test");
Graphics g = w.getContentPane().getGraphics();
piechart.paint(g);
```

How should class `PieChart` be modified to correct this problem?

S8.10 Implement the following accessors for class `PieChart`.

```
public double getData(int i)
```
Returns the `i`th value from the data set being represented.

```
public String getName(int i)
```
Returns the associated legend name for the `i`th value from the data set being represented.

```
public Color getColor(int i)
```
Returns the associated color for the `i`th value from the data set being represented.

```
public int getRadius()
```
Returns the radius of the pie chart.

```
public Point getPieLocation()
```
Returns the location of the upper-left hand corner of the bounding box for the pie.

```
public Point getLegendLocation()
```
Returns the location of where the display of the legend is to start.

```
public int getLineSpacing()
```
Returns the interline spacing in pixels between successive legend lines.

8.14   EXERCISES

8.1   Which operator is used to refer to a particular element of an array?

8.2   Can an array represent more than one type of value? Explain.

8.3   Can an array be a parameter? Explain.

8.4   Does a local array with a base type that is a fundamental type have its elements automatically initialized? Explain.

8.5   Write a code segment that does the following:

   a) Defines a constant `MAX_SIZE` equal to 20.

   b) Defines an array `list` with `MAX_SIZE` elements.

   c) Sets the first element of `list` to the value 19.

   d) Sets the last element of `list` to the value 54.

   e) Sets the other elements of `list` to 0.

   f) Displays `list`.

8.6   Write a code segment that does the following:

   a) Defines an array `score` with 40 elements. The element type of the array is **double**.

   b) Sets the value of each element in `score` so that it matches its subscript value.

   c) Displays the values of the last five element of `scores`.

   d) Is the value 3.1415 a legal element value for `score`? Explain.

   e) Is the value 3.1415 a legal subscript value for `score`? Explain.

8.7   Explain why `a[3]` does not access the third element of the array `a`.

8.8   What is the output of the following program fragment?

```
int[] a = new int[5];
a[0] = 0;
for (int i = 1; i <= 4; ++i) {
   a[i] = a[i-1] + i;
}
System.out.println(a[3]);
```

8.9   Write a code segment that does the following:

   a) Defines constants `MAX_ROWS` equal to 25 and `MAX_COLUMNS` equal to 10.

   b) Defines an two-dimensional **boolean** array `Data` with 25 rows, where each row consists of 10 elements.

   c) Initializes array `data` so that the elements whose row subscript values are odd have the value **true** and initializes the other elements to **false**.

For Exercises 8.10–8.21, suppose the following definitions are in effect.

   ■ a is an **int** array with 10 elements;

   ■ b and c are **int** arrays with 20 elements;

   ■ d is a **double** array with 20 elements.

8.10 Is the following legal? Explain.

```
a[1] = a[9];
```

8.11 Is the following legal? Explain.

```
a[1] = a[10];
```

8.12 Is the following legal? Explain.

```
a[1] = b[1];
```

8.13 Is the following legal? Explain.

```
a[1] = d[1];
```

8.14 Is the following legal? Explain.

```
d[1] = a[1];
```

8.15 Is the following legal? Explain.

```
b = c;
```

8.16 Is the following legal? Explain.

```
a = b;
```

8.17 Is the following legal? Explain.

```
b = a;
```

8.18 Is the following legal? Explain.

```
d = b;
```

8.19 Is the following legal? Explain.

```
b = d;
```

8.20 Is the following legal? Explain.

```
int m = a.length;
```

8.21 Is the following legal? Explain.

```
int n = a.size();
```

The following definition of method f() is in effect for Exercises 8.22–8.25.

```
public int f() {
    BufferedReader stdin = new BufferedReader
        new InputStreamReader(System.in));
    int[] a = new int[10];
    for (int i = 0; i < a.length; ++i) {
        a[i] = Integer.parseInt(stdin.readLine());
    }
    int guess = -1;
    for (int i = 0; i < a.length; ++i) {
        if (guess < a[i]) {
            guess = a[i];
        }
    }
    return guess;
}
```

8.22 If the values in a are all positive, does method f() correctly determine the maximum value in a? Explain.

8.23 If the values in a are all negative, does method f() correctly determine the maximum value in a? Explain.

8.24 If the definition of guess is replaced with the following statement, does method
      f() determine correctly the maximum value in a? Explain.

      `int guess = a[0];`

8.25 If the definition of guess is replaced with the following statement, does method
      f() determine correctly the maximum value in a? Explain.

      `int guess = a[9];`

8.26 Design and implement a **double** method min() with formal parameter **double**
      array a. The method returns the minimum element value in a.

8.27 Design and implement a String[] method deepCopy() with a formal parameter
      String array s. The method returns a deep copy of s.

8.28 Design and implement a **void** method initialize() with two formal parame-
      ters: an **int** array a and an **int** value v. The method sets each of the n elements of
      a to val.

8.29 Design and implement an **int** method numberLessThan() with two formal
      parameters: an **int** array a and an **int** value v. The method returns the number of
      elements in a that are less than v.

8.30 Design and implement the following statistical methods. Each of the methods
      returns a **double** value and has an **int** array a.

      a) Method mean(): returns the average of the n values in the list.

      b) Method median(): returns the middle value of the values in the list if the size
         of the list is odd; otherwise, it returns the average of the two middle values of
         the list. In performing its computation, the method does not alter the elements
         of a (i.e., it makes a copy of a and manipulates the copy).

      c) Method mode(): returns a value in the list that occurs most frequently. If there
         is more than one such value, any of the possible modes can be returned.

8.31 Implement a variant of searching method sequentialSearch(). The variant
      method has four formal parameters: **int** array a and **int** parameters key, m, and n.
      The variant searches elements a[m] through a[n] for the key value. If the value is
      present, then the method returns the minimal index k in m … n such that a[k]
      equals key. If the value is not present, then the method returns n+1.

8.32 Design and implement a **void** method listAll() that has two formal parame-
      ters: an **int** array a and an **int** value key. Method listAll() displays the
      indexes of all elements in a that are equal to key. Method listAll() accom-
      plishes its task through a series of iterative calls to the modified method sequen-
      tialSearch() of Exercise 8.31.

8.33 Implement the iterative sorting method insertionSort(). The method has one
      formal parameter: **int** array a. On its ith iteration, this method correctly places the
      value of a[i] with respect to elements a[0] through a[i-1].

8.34 Implement a variant of sorting method insertionSort(). The variant method
      has three formal parameters: **int** array a and **int** parameters m and n. The variant
      sorts only elements a[m] through a[n].

8.35 Implement a method `zeroMatrix()` that takes two **int** parameters m and n. The method returns a two-dimensional array with m rows and n columns with element type **double**. All elements are initialized to 0.

8.36 Implement a method `identityMatrix()` that takes one **int** parameter m. The method returns a two-dimensional array with m rows and columns with element type **double**. All elements are initialized to 0 except for those elements on the *main diagonal* (i.e., elements whose row index equals its column index). Elements on the main diagonal are initialized to 1.

8.37 Implement a **boolean** method `isUpperTriangular()` that takes one **double**[][] parameter m. The method returns **true** if all elements below the main diagonal are 0 and returns **false**, otherwise. (See Exercise 8.36 for a definition of main diagonal.)

8.38 Redesign and reimplement `getList()` so that it takes account that there is no need to copy the elements of buffer to data when listSize equals MAX_LIST_SIZE. For this case, it is sufficient to return the value of buffer to accomplish the method's task.

8.39 Redesign and reimplement `getList()` so that it takes one **int** parameter n. The parameter specifies the maximum number of values to extract.

8.40 Redesign and reimplement `ArrayTools` method `getList()` so that it can extract all remaining values from standard input. Hint: you may find method like `doubleCapacity()` helpful.

8.41 Implement the following constructors for class `PieChart`. Your implementation of the constructors should neither introduce any additional instance variables nor require modification to any of the `PieChart` methods.

   a) **public** `PieChart(ArrayList d, ArrayList s)`: Generates a default-color pie chart representation for data list d, where s[i] represents the legend text associated with the value d[i].

   b) **public** `PieChart(ArrayList d, ArrayList s, ArrayList c)`: Generates a pie chart representation for data list d, where s[i] represents the legend text associated with value d[i] and c[i] represents the color associated with d[i].

8.42 Implement the following methods for class `PieChart`.

   a) **public double** `setData(int i, double v)`: sets the ith value of the data set being represented to v.

   b) **public double** `setName(int i, String s)`: sets the associated legend name for the ith value of the data set being represented to s.

   c) **public double** `setColor(int i, Color c)`: sets the associated color for the ith value of the data set being represented to c.

   d) **public void** `setRadius(int r)`: sets the radius of the associated pie chart to r.

   e) **public void** `setPieLocation(Point p)`: sets the location of the bounding box for the pie slices of the associated pie chart to p.

    f) **public void** setLegendLocation(Point p): sets the location of the legend of the associated pie chart to p.

    g) **public void** setLineSpacing(**int** n): sets the interline spacing between successive legend lines to n pixels.

8.43 Implement the following methods for class PieChart. As part of your implementation ensure that the rendering methods attempt only to paint a sensible pie chart representation.

    a) **public double** setData(**double**[] d): sets the data set being represented to d.

    b) **public double** setName(String[] s): sets the legend names for the data set being represented to s.

    c) **public double** setColor(Color[] c): sets the colors for data set being represented to c.

8.44 In class PieChart, the pie slice rendered for each data value may be only an approximation. Inaccuracy can be introduced both because an integer angle width is being derived from a floating-point data value and because the angle widths and data values come from different numeric ranges. In the case of the music chart data of Table 8.3, the last rendered pie slice paints over the first rendered pie slice by one degree. This condition is demonstrated in the following diagram.

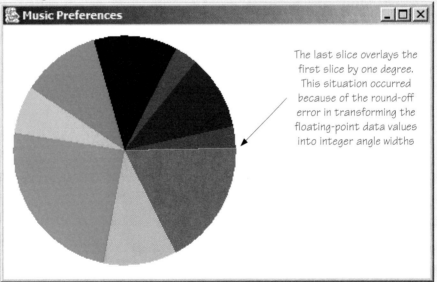

For other data sets, the last slice may not complete the circle. Reimplement method paintPie() of PieChart so that a complete pie with no overlap is rendered. One possibility is to render the last slice outside of the loop and have that slice complete the pie. Another possibility is to render the largest slice last. To do so, use one **for** loop to render pie slices counterclockwise toward the largest slice and use another loop to render pie slices clockwise toward the largest slice. The largest slice is rendered in the unfilled section of the circle. Why might one of these possible implementations be preferred over the other?

8.45   Reimplement constructor `PieChart(double[], String[], Color[])` so that the constructor checks whether formal parameters d, s, and c are all non-**null** array references before its checks whether the lengths of the associated arrays are sensible.

8.46   Design and implement a class `Histogram` with functionality similar to `PieChart`. A histogram displays its values as height-varying rectangles with unit width. The height of a rectangle is proportional to its value.

8.15   PROGRAMMING PROJECT — MATRICES

Our representation of matrices in Section 8.7.1 did not take an object-oriented design approach. This programming project takes an object-oriented view of a matrix.

The objective of this case study is practice with arrays and class design in implementing a matrix representation

As indicated there, a matrix is a collection of numeric values arrange in rows. In a given matrix, each row has the same number of columns.

ANALYSIS AND DESIGN

To represent a matrix, you need to represent its rows and columns with the natural underlying representation being a two-dimensional array. For this project, the elements of a matrix are represented using is two-dimensional **double** array `element`.

`private double[] element`

Represents the element values of the matrix, where `elementi][j]` represents the value in the `j`th column of the `i`th row.

Previous experience with matrices numbers and other Java APIs tells us that the `Matrix` abstraction should provide methods to initialize and manipulate a rational number object in at least the following ways:

`public Matrix()`

Construct a new matrix of size 10×10 (i.e., 10 rows with 10 columns per row). Each element in the matrix has value 0.

`public Matrix(int m, int n)`
`public Matrix(int m, int n, double v)`

Construct a new matrix of size $m \times n$, where m and n represent the number of rows and columns respectively. Each element in the matrix has value v.

`public Matrix(double[][] a)`

Construct a new matrix of size $m \times n$ whose elements are initialized using two-dimensional array parameter a, where m is the number of rows in array a and n is the number of columns per row.

`public Matrix add(Matrix a)`

Returns the matrix addition of this matrix and matrix a.

`public Matrix multiply(Matrix a)`

Returns the matrix product of this matrix and matrix a.

`public int getNumberRows()`

Returns the number of rows of this matrix.

```
public int getNumberColumns()
```
Returns the number of columns of this matrix.
```
public double get(int i, int j)
```
Represents the value of element in the jth column of the ith row of this matrix.
```
public Object clone()
```
Returns a new matrix that is a duplicate of this matrix.
```
public String toString()
```
Returns a text representation of this matrix.
```
public boolean equals(Object v)
```
Returns whether object v is a matrix of the same dimensions as this matrix and whose element values correspond to the element values of this matrix.
```
public void fill(double v)
```
Sets all elements of this matrix to v.
```
public static Matrix identityMatrix(int m)
```
Returns a new square Matrix with m rows and columns. All elements are initialized to 0 except for those elements on the *main diagonal* (i.e., elements whose row index equals its column index). Elements on the main diagonal are initialized to 1.
```
public static Matrix getMatrix(int m, int n)
```
Returns a new Matrix with m rows and n columns. The element values for the matrix are extracted from the standard input stream. The input values fill in the new matrix in a row by row manner.

TESTING AND DOCUMENTATION

In addition, develop a test program MatrixDemo.java that illustrates and tests all of the constructors and methods of your class Matrix. The test program should also highlight the robustness of your constructors and methods.

In documenting your implementation, be sure to explain the behaviors and nuances of your methods. Also explain how you ensured that your methods are robust.

8.16   SELF-TEST ANSWERS

S8.1   The statements are
```
a[k] += 6;
b[k+1] = b[i];
b[j+5] = a[i] + a[k];
```

S8.2   The definitions of stackElements and testData are
```
double stackElements = new double[50];
String testData = new String[500];
```

S8.3   Array coefficient can be defined as follows.
```
double coefficient = {1.4, 4.30, 5.12, 6.9, 6.21, 7.31,
                      11.4, 11.28, 11.29};
```

S8.4 Method max() can be implemented as follows.

```java
public static int max(int[] a) {
    int guess = a[0];
    for (int i = 1; i < a.length; ++i) {
        if (guess < a[i]) {
            guess = a[i];
        };
    }
    return guess;
}
```

S8.5 Method isSorted() can be implemented as follows.

```java
public static boolean isSorted(int[] a) {
    for (int i = 0; i < a.length - 1; ++i) {
        if (a[i] > a[i+1]) {
            return false;
        }
    }

    return true;
}
```

S8.6 Method bubbleSort() can be implemented as follows.

```java
public static void bubbleSort(int[] a) {
    boolean bubbling;
    do {
        bubbling = false;
        for (int i = 0; i < a.length - 1; ++i) {
            if (a[i+1] < a[i]) {
                int rmbr = a[i];
                a[i] = a[i+1];
                a[i+1] = rmbr;
                bubbling = true;
            }
        }
    } while (bubbling);
}
```

S8.7 Program ExpressionEvaluate.java can be implemented as follows.

```java
public class ExpressionEvaluate {
    public static void main(String args[]) {
        if (args.length == 3) {
            double op1 = Double.parseDouble(args[0]);
            double op2 = Double.parseDouble(args[2]);
            if (args[1].length() != 1) {
                System.err.println("Unrecognized operator: "
                    + args[1]);
                return;
            }
            char operator = args[1].charAt(0);
            double result;
            switch ( operator ) {
                case '+':
                    result = op1 + op2;
                    break;
```

```
            case '-':
                result = op1 - op2;
                break;
            case '*':
                result = op1 * op2;
                break;
            case '/':
                result = op1 / op2;
                break;
            default:
                System.err.println("Illegal operation");
                return;
            }
            System.out.println(args[0] + " " + args[1]
                + " " + args[2] + " = " + result);
        }
        else {
            System.err.println("Malformed expression");
        }
    }
}
```

S8.8 Method `printMatrix)` can be implemented as follows.

```
public static void printMatrix(int[][] a) {
    for (int i = 0; i < a.length; ++i) {
        for (int j = 0; j < a[i].length; ++j) {
            System.out.print(a[i][j] + " ");
        }
        System.out.println();
    }
}
```

S8.9 The code segment generates an exception (error) in constructor `PieChart(dou-ble[], String[], Color[])` while attempting to access the length of a nonexistent array. The situation can be corrected by first ensuring that the formal parameters d, s, and c are all non-**null** array references and then checking whether the lengths of the associated arrays are sensible.

S8.10 The implementation of the requested accessors is included in the definition of `PieChart.java` of Listing 8.12.

Listing 8.12 PieChart.java

```
1.  // Supports the representation of a statistical pie chart
2.
3.  import java.awt.*;
4.
5.  public class PieChart {
6.      // default characteristics
7.      private static final Color[] DEFAULT_PIE_COLOR = {
8.          Color.RED, Color.BLUE, Color.MAGENTA, Color.BLACK,
9.          Color.GREEN, Color.ORANGE, Color.CYAN, Color.PINK,
10.         Color.GRAY, Color.YELLOW, Color.DARK_GRAY, Color.WHITE };
11.
12.     private static final int DEFAULT_RADIUS = 115;
13.     private static final int DEFAULT_LINE_SPACING = 20;
```

Listing 8.12   PieChart.java (Continued)

```java
14.     private static final Point DEFAULT_PIE_LOCATION
15.                               = new Point (10, 10);
16.     private static final Point DEFAULT_LEGEND_LOCATION
17.                               = new Point (265, 35);
18.
19.     // individual pie chart characteristics
20.     private double[] data;          // data to be represented
21.     private String[] name;          // legend names for data
22.     private Color[] color;          // colors representing data
23.     private int radius;             // radius of the pie
24.     private Point pieLocation;      // pie location
25.     private Point legendLocation;   // legend location
26.     private int lineSpacing;        // spacing between legend lines
27.
28.     // PieChart(): default constructor
29.     public PieChart(double[] d, String[] s) {
30.        this(d, s, DEFAULT_PIE_COLOR);
31.     }
32.
33.     // PieChart(): constructor using given data, names, colors
34.     public PieChart(double[] d, String[] s, Color[] c) {
35.        if ((d.length == 0) || (d.length > s.length)
36.                || (d.length > c.length)) {
37.            System.err.println("PieChart: invalid data");
38.            System.exit(1);
39.        }
40.
41.        data = d;
42.        name = s;
43.        color = c;
44.
45.        radius = DEFAULT_RADIUS;
46.        pieLocation = DEFAULT_PIE_LOCATION;
47.        legendLocation = DEFAULT_LEGEND_LOCATION;
48.        lineSpacing = DEFAULT_LINE_SPACING;
49.     }
50.
51.     // getSampleSize(): return the number of data values
52.     public int getSampleSize() {
53.        return data.length;
54.     }
55.
56.     // getColor(): return the ith color
57.     public Color getColor(int i) {
58.        return color[i];
59.     }
60.
61.     // getData(): return the ith data value
62.     public double getData(int i) {
63.        return data[i];
64.     }
65.
66.     // getName(): return the ith legend name
67.     public String getName(int i) {
```

Listing 8.12 **PieChart.java (Continued)**

```
68.            return name[i];
69.        }
70.
71.        // getRadius(): return the pie radius
72.        public int getRadius() {
73.            return radius;
74.        }
75.
76.        // getPieLocation(): return the location of the pie
77.        public Point getPieLocation() {
78.            return pieLocation;
79.        }
80.
81.        // getLegendLocation(): return the location of the legend
82.        public Point getLegendLocation() {
83.            return legendLocation;
84.        }
85.
86.        // getLineSpacing(): return space between legend lines
87.        public int getLineSpacing() {
88.            return lineSpacing;
89.        }
90.
91.        // paint(): render chart and legend
92.        public void paint(Graphics g) {
93.            // get pie chart characteristics
94.            int r = getRadius();
95.            Point pie = getPieLocation();
96.            Point legend = getLegendLocation();
97.            int spacing = getLineSpacing();
98.
99.            // paint the chart
100.           paintPie(g, pie.x, pie.y, r);
101.           paintLegend(g, legend.x, legend.y, spacing);
102.       }
103.
104.       // paintPie(): render the pie
105.       public void paintPie(Graphics g, int x, int y, int r) {
106.           final int CIRCLE_DEGREES = 360;
107.
108.           // determine number of values
109.           int n = getSampleSize();
110.
111.           // compute sum of the values
112.           double dataSum = 0;
113.           for (int i = 0; i < n; ++i) {
114.               dataSum += getData(i);
115.           }
116.
117.           // draw slices one by one starting from origin
118.           int startAngle = 0;
119.
120.           for (int i = 0; i < n; ++i) {
121.               // how much of the pie does the next slice take
```

Listing 8.12   **PieChart.java (Continued)**

```java
122.            double percent = getData(i) / dataSum;
123.            int arcAngle = (int) Math.round(percent * CIRCLE_DEGREES);
124.
125.            // set the slice color
126.            Color c = getColor(i);
127.            g.setColor(c);
128.
129.            // render the slice
130.            g.fillArc(x, y, 2*r, 2*r, startAngle, arcAngle);
131.
132.            // record where next slice starts
133.            startAngle += arcAngle;
134.        }
135.    }
136.
137.    // paintLegend(): render the legend for the pie
138.    public void paintLegend(Graphics g, int x, int y, int delta) {
139.        // determine number of values
140.        int n = getSampleSize();
141.
142.        for (int i = 0; i < n; ++i) {
143.            // set up the current legend line
144.            Color c = getColor(i);
145.            String s = getName(i) + ": " + getData(i);
146.
147.            // render the line
148.            g.setColor(c);
149.            g.drawString(s, x, y);
150.
151.
152.            // set up the y-coordinate location of the next line
153.            y += delta;
154.        }
155.    }
156. }
```

9

INHERITANCE AND POLYMORPHISM

Inheritance and polymorphism are two powerful mechanisms of object-oriented languages. *Inheritance* is the ability to define a new class using an existing class as a basis. The new class, called the *subclass*, inherits the attributes and behaviors of the class on which it is based, the *superclass*. The subclass also *extends* the superclass representation by introducing new attributes and behaviors that are specific to the subclass. Polymorphism is a programming language behavior where the same code expression can invoke different methods depending on the type of objects using the code. In this chapter, we begin our introduction of these two mechanisms by extending the standard class `Point`.

OBJECTIVES

- Explore the role of inheritance in object-oriented design.
- Demonstrate the power of polymorphism and the late binding of methods.
- Develop a series of classes demonstrating the power of the inheritance and polymorphism mechanisms.
- Explore the nuances of superclasses and subclasses in Java.
- Consider the roles of protected access and default access in information hiding.
- Introduce abstract classes and interfaces.
- Provide an appreciation for the use of modifier final with classes and methods.

9.1   OBJECT-ORIENTED DESIGN

We are all familiar with the concept of biological inheritance. Living things inherit characteristics from their ancestors. For example, you may have one parent's eye color and the other parent's smile. These characteristics may have been unique to your parents, or ones your parents inherited from their parents.

The concept of inheritance is important in the design of software systems. It provides a way of organizing the components of the system in a hierarchical manner. The hierarchy helps us understand the system. In addition, it provides a framework for reusing code.

Inheritance is used typically to organize abstractions in a top-down fashion from most general to least general. For example, Figure 9.1 contains a partial outline of a hierarchical organization for different types of musical instruments. The hierarchy is organized according to how the instruments make their sound. Understanding the hierarchy enables us to recognize and distinguish shared and differing musical instrument characteristics.

As the figure indicates, musical instruments fall in one of five categories: idiophones, membranophones, aerophones, chordophones, or electrophones.

- Idiophones: Solid instruments that are intrinsically sonorous, e.g., bell and cymbal;

- Membranophones: Instruments with taut membranes, e.g., drum and kazoo;

- Aerophones: Instruments that enclose and free masses of air, e.g., clarinet and whistle;

- Chordophones: Instruments with stretched strings, e.g., lyre and violin;

- Electrophones: Instruments with oscillating electric circuits, e.g. synthesizer and electric piano.

Figure 9.1   A partial outline of a musical instrument hierarchy.

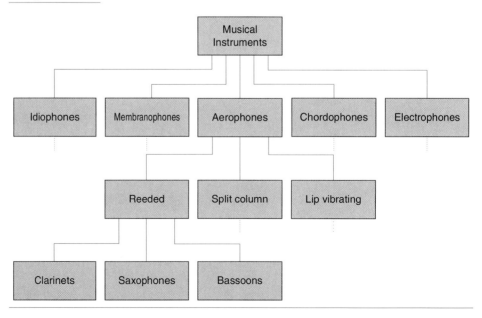

We can refine our notions of each of the categories. For example, aerophones are classified into three subcategories: reeded, split column, and lip vibrating. Clarinets and saxophones are examples of reeded aerophones; whistles and flutes are examples of split-column aerophones; and tubas and trumpets are lip-vibrating aerophones. As another example, chordophones are classified into one of three subcategories: flat-bodied, necked, and plucked. Zithers and dulcimers are examples of flat-bodied chordophones; violins and guitars are examples of necked chordophones; and lyres and harps are examples of plucked chordophones.

In object-oriented programming languages, a class created by extending another class is known as a *subclass*. The class used as a basis for a subclass is its *superclass*. A superclass is also referred to as the *base* class and the subclass is also referred to as the *derived* class. In general, a subclass can provide both additional data fields and methods. Figure 9.2 shows the subclass and superclass relationships between clarinets, reeded instruments, membranophones, and musical instruments.

Figure 9.2   Some relationships in the musical hierarchy.

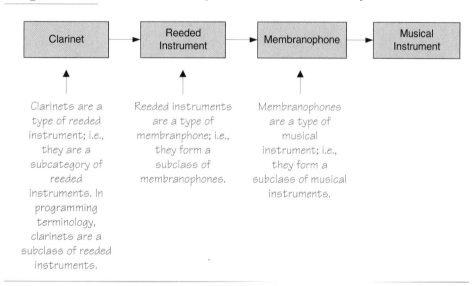

One complication with regard to inheritance for beginning programmers is the fact that a subclass object has multiple types. The subclass object *is* a specialized superclass type object. Therefore, the subclass object is of both the subclass and superclass types. With inheritance, we say there is an *is-a relationship* between the subclass type and its superclass type. A clarinet is a reeded instrument and it is a membranophone.

Now that you understand the concept of inheritance, we turn our attention to using inheritance as a programming mechanism. In our first examples, we extend the awt class to support several different application needs. In particular, we use inheritance to extend Java's Point class to create a three-dimensional point class and a colored point class.

9.1.1   THREEDIMENSIONALPOINT

The awt class Point provides a representation of a two-dimensional point that we have used several times throughout the text. With inheritance, it is easy to build upon this two-dimensional point representation to create a three-dimensional point class representation, ThreeDimensionalPoint. The new class ThreeDimensionalPoint *extends* class Point by adding a new property that the Point class does not have—a z-coordinate value.

The property can be maintained using a **public** data field z. To support encapsulation and information hiding, the class ThreeDimensionalPoint provides an accessor method getZ() and a mutator method setZ() for the new z-coordinate property.

As we are extending class ThreeDimensionalPoint from Point, ThreeDimensionalPoint inherits the Point x-coordinate and y-coordinate attributes and Point accessor and mutator methods getX(), getY(), setX(), and setY(). We will use the accessors and mutators methods in our implementation of ThreeDimensionalPoint. The use of these methods is not strictly necessary because the Point class makes its attributes **public** (and this is why we made z a **public** data field). Our implementation uses them because the use of the accessors and mutators is good practice—superclass attributes are almost always **private** (Point is a rare exception to the rule). In the typical case, a subclass cannot access directly the attributes, and instead must use the available superclass accessors and mutators to manipulate the superclass attributes.

Unless we indicate otherwise, the ThreeDimensionalPoint class also inherits the Point facilitators, e.g., translate(), toString(), equals(), and clone(). However, these Point facilitators are unsuitable for a three-dimensional context—they are not cognizant of the z-coordinate value. Therefore, the ThreeDimensionalPoint class must provide its own versions of these methods.

For the ThreeDimensionalPoint method translate(), there will be three parameters. The parameters represent the increment in x-coordinate value, increment in y-coordinate value, and increment in z-coordinate value by which the point will be shifted. Because the method signatures of the ThreeDimensionalPoint and Point versions of translate() are different, the method name translate() is overloaded in the ThreeDimensionalPoint class. Thus, with a ThreeDimensionalPoint object both methods are available. Java determines which method is in use by the number of parameters in the given invocation.

```
ThreeDimensionalPoint a = new ThreeDimensionalPoint(6, 21, 54);
a.translate(1, 1);      // invocation of superclass translate()
a.translate(2, 2, 2);   // invocation of subclass translate()
```

It's all inheritance

Remember that all classes are either explicitly or implicitly an extension of the class `Object`. The relationship between `ThreeDimensionalPoint`, `Point`, and `Object` are illustrated by the following diagram.

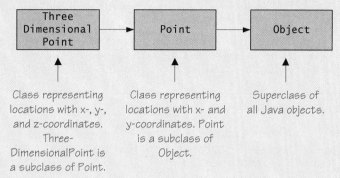

Class `Object` provides basic versions of several methods. In particular, it has methods `toString()`, `equals()`, and `clone()`. It also has methods `finalize()`, `get-Class()`, `hashCode()`, `notify()`, `notifyAll()`, and `wait()`. These are all inherited by the subclasses of `Object`.

The `ThreeDimensionalPoint` versions of `toString()`, `equals()`, and `clone()` should *not* have different signatures from the `Point` versions. By having the same signatures as their superclass counterparts, the subclass methods override the superclass definitions for `ThreeDimensionalPoint` objects. The overriding enables the subclass-specific nature of the `ThreeDimensionalPoint` objects to be considered.

```
ThreeDimensionalPoint c = new ThreeDimensionalPoint(1, 4, 9);

ThreeDimensionalPoint d = (ThreeDimensionalPoint) c.clone();

String s = c.toString();

boolean b = c.equals(d);
```

Cast is necessary as apparent type of return value of subclass method clone() is Object

Invocation of subclass toString() method

Invocation of subclass equals() method

Now that the subclass requirements are clear, we give the definition of `ThreeDimensionalPoint.java` in Listing 9.1.

`ThreeDimensionalPoint.java` begins with a **package** statement. A **package** statement indicates that the definitions that follow are part of a bigger collection known as a *package*. In particular, `ThreeDimensionalPoint` is part of the package `geometry`.

```
package geometry ;
```

Package name

Keyword package indicates that definitions that follow are part of a package. An element of a package has special access rights with regard to the other elements of the package

Listing 9.1   ThreeDimensionalPoint.java

```
1.  // Represents a three-dimensional point
2.
3.  package geometry;
4.
5.  import java.awt.*;
6.
7.  public class ThreeDimensionalPoint extends Point {
8.     // private class constant
9.     private final static int DEFAULT_Z = 0;
10.
11.    // private instance variable
12.    public int z = DEFAULT_Z;
13.
14.    // ThreeDimensionalPoint(): default constructor
15.    public ThreeDimensionalPoint() {
16.       super();
17.    }
18.
19.    // ThreeDimensionalPoint(): specific constructor
20.    public ThreeDimensionalPoint(int a, int b, int c) {
21.       super(a, b);
22.       setZ(c);
23.    }
24.
25.    // getZ(): z-coordinate accessor
26.    public double getZ() {
27.       return z;
28.    }
29.
30.    // setZ(): y-coordinate mutator
31.    public void setZ(int value) {
32.       z = value;
33.    }
34.
35.    // translate(): shifting facilitator
36.    public void translate(int dx, int dy, int dz) {
37.       translate(dx, dy);
38.
39.       int zValue = (int) getZ();
40.
41.       setZ(zValue + dz);
42.    }
43.
44.    // toString(): conversion facilitator
45.    public String toString() {
46.       int a = (int) getX();
47.       int b = (int) getY();
48.       int c = (int) getZ();
49.       return getClass() + "[" + a + ", " + b + ", " + c + "]";
50.    }
51.
52.    // equals(): equality facilitator
53.    public boolean equals(Object v) {
54.       if (v instanceof ThreeDimensionalPoint) {
```

Listing 9.1 ThreeDimensionalPoint.java (Continued)

```
55.          ThreeDimensionalPoint p = (ThreeDimensionalPoint) v;
56.          int z1 = (int) getZ();
57.          int z2 = (int) p.getZ();
58.
59.          return super.equals(p) && (z1 == z2);
60.      }
61.      else {
62.          return false;
63.      }
64.  }
65.
66.  // clone(): clone facilitator
67.  public Object clone() {
68.      int a = (int) getX();
69.      int b = (int) getY();
70.      int c = (int) getZ();
71.
72.      return new ThreeDimensionalPoint(a, b, c);
73.  }
74. }
```

We have used packages (e.g., swing, awt, math, io) in many of our programs. However, class ThreeDimensionalPoint is the first class that we have defined to be part of a package.

Programmers put classes and interfaces into a package for two basic reasons—*organization* and *special access to members*. By organizing classes and interfaces with a related purpose into a package, you make it easier for users to find them—classes and interfaces with the same package name are stored in the same folder. In addition, Java puts the classes of one package in a different *namespace* (scope) than it puts the classes of another package. As a result, the names in a package do not conflict with names in other packages.

When defining members of a class or interface, Java does not require an explicit access specification. The implicit specification is known as *default access*. Members of a class with default access can be accessed only by members of the package.

If a Java file does not begin with a **package** statement, then all definitions in that file are considered to be part of a **package** unique to that file.

The next statement in Listing 9.1 of ThreeDimensionalPoint begins the class definition of ThreeDimensionalPoint.

public class ThreeDimensionalPoint **extends** Point {

Keyword extends indicates that class
ThreeDimensionalPoint is a subclass of
its superclass Point

Keyword **extends** is Java's mechanism for deriving a new class from an existing class. Programmers often read this statement as "ThreeDimensionalPoint is a kind of Point." Except for the use of the **extends**, defining a subclass is not very different from defining a superclass. When differences do arise, they are found normally in the constructor definitions.

The ThreeDimensionalPoint class first defines a **private** class constant DEFAULT_Z and a **public** instance variable z. Adding a member to a subclass does not require special syntax. Therefore, the DEFAULT_Z and z definitions have the expected form.

```
// private class constant
private final static int DEFAULT_Z = 0;

// private instance variable
public int z = DEFAULT_Z;
```

The definitions of the ThreeDimensionalPoint constructors differ from the definitions of previous constructors in their use of keyword **super**.

```
// ThreeDimensionalPoint(): default constructor
public ThreeDimensionalPoint() {
        super();          Invocation of default
        setZ(DEFAULT_Z);  superclass constructor
}

// ThreeDimensionalPoint(): specific constructor
public ThreeDimensionalPoint(int a, int b, int c) {
        super(a, b);
        setZ(c);          Invocation of specific
}                         superclass constructor
```

Because a ThreeDimensionalPoint object is an extended version of a Point object, the construction of a ThreeDimensionalPoint object begins with the construction of its superclass attributes (i.e., x- and y-coordinate values). To initialize these attributes, a superclass constructor must be invoked. The superclass invocation can be explicit or implicit.

As we discussed, a subclass is a specialization of the superclass. Consequently, a constructor for the superclass must be invoked to create a superclass object before the constructor for the subclass can do its specialization. If you think about what inheritance means for a moment, this sequence makes sense. The superclass object must exist before it can be turned into a specialized subclass object.

To invoke explicitly a superclass constructor for the object under construction, we use the keyword **super**. Keyword **super** is the Java mechanism for viewing the current object as an instance of the superclass. Therefore, statement

```
super();
```

from the ThreeDimensionalPoint default constructor definition is an invocation of the superclass's default constructor on the object under construction. Because the superclass of ThreeDimensionalPoint is Point, it is the Point default constructor that is invoked for the object under construction. The Point default constructor takes care of the initialization of the x- and y-coordinate values. This action is the only explicit work required for the initialization process, because the z-coordinate instance variable definition specifies the initial value for instance variable z.

The other `ThreeDimensionalPoint` constructor initializes the object under construction to the given x-, y-, and z-coordinate values. This constructor also explicitly invokes a superclass constructor.

```
super(a, b);
```

The invocation uses the `Point` constructor to set properly the x- and y-coordinate values. To complete the initialization, the z-coordinate is set to the desired value using mutator `setZ()`.

```
setZ(c);
```

If a subclass constructor does not invoke explicitly a superclass constructor, then Java automatically invokes the superclass's default constructor to initialize the superclass attributes. Therefore, we could have written our `ThreeDimensionalPoint` default constructor definition without explicitly invoking **super()**.

```
public ThreeDimensionalPoint() {
    // implicit super() invocation before mutator invocation
}
```

Because its simpler to omit the explicit invocation than to key it in, most constructor code makes use of the implicit invocation of **super()**.

An interesting thing to observe about these constructors is that they are very short. It is possible to be succinct because we are able to reuse the code that we developed for the superclass. Although with this simple subclass the savings are not that great, it is important to realize that with more complex classes, the savings can be substantial.

The Listing 9.1 definitions of accessor `getZ()`, mutator `setZ()` and facilitator `clone()` are all straightforward and warrant no special analysis. However, the definitions of `toString()`, `equals()`, and `translate()` are interesting. Therefore, we consider them next.

Method `toString()` of class `ThreeDimensionalPoint` makes use of its `Object` inherited method `getClass()` in displaying its debugging representation.

```
// toString(): conversion facilitator
public String toString() {
    int a = (int) getX();           Casts are necessary as Point
    int b = (int) getY();           accessors return the int-valued
    int c = (int) getZ();           data fields as double values
    return getClass() + "[" + a + ", " + b + ", " + c + "]";
}
```

Method `getClass()` returns a `String` description of the object's type. For example, the following code segment

```
ColoredPoint c = new ColoredPoint();
System.out.println(c);
```

displays

```
class geometry.ThreeDimensionalPoint(0, 0, 0)
```

String produced by invocation
getClass()

ThreeDimensionalPoint method equals() uses superclass method equals() in determining whether parameter v is the same as the **this** object.

```
// equals(): equality facilitator
public boolean equals(Object v) {
    if (v instanceof ThreeDimensionalPoint) {
        ThreeDimensionalPoint p = (ThreeDimensionalPoint) v;
        int z1 = (int) getZ();
        int z2 = (int) p.getZ();

        return super.equals(p) && (z1 == z2);
    }
    else {                          Invocation of superclass
        return false;               method equals()
    }
}
```

For the ThreeDimensionalPoint method equals() to use its superclass Point method equals(), a special syntax is needed. Special syntax is required because by default the subclass version overrides normal access to the superclass version. Using the keyword **super** indicates explicitly that the superclass member is to be referenced.

ThreeDimensionalPoint method translate() uses the superclass method translate() to assist in the shifting of position. However, keyword **super** is not required to invoke the superclass translate(). Because the superclass version uses two parameters and the subclass version uses three parameters, Java can tell by context that it is the superclass method translate() being invoked within the definition.

```
// translate(): shifting facilitator
public void translate(int dx, int dy, int dz) {
    translate(dx, dy);
    int zValue = (int) getZ();
    setZ(zValue + dz);
}
```

Because there are two parameters present, it
is the superclass method translate() being
invoked

The following code segment demonstrates some uses of class ThreeDimensionalPoint.

```
ThreeDimensionalPoint c = new ThreeDimensionalPoint();
c.translate(2, 2, 2);
ThreeDimensionalPoint d = new ThreeDimensionalPoint(1, 2, 3);
ThreeDimensionalPoint e = (ThreeDimensionalPoint) d.clone();

System.out.println(c);
System.out.println(d);
```

```
System.out.println(e);

System.out.println(d.equals(c));
System.out.println(d.equals(e));
```

The segment produces output

```
class geometry.ThreeDimensionalPoint[2, 2, 2]
class geometry.ThreeDimensionalPoint[1, 2, 3]
class geometry.ThreeDimensionalPoint[1, 2, 3]
false
true
```

9.1.2   COLOREDPOINT

Suppose an application calls for the use of colored points. For example, we can use colored points to represents the pixels of some images. It makes sense to consider using inheritance to create a class to represent colored points. Listing 9.2 of `Colored-Point.java` defines a class `ColoredPoint` that extends `Point` in the natural manner to provide a representation of a colored point. The class adds data field `color` to represent the color attribute and an appropriate accessor and mutator for that property. The class also provides overrides of `equals()`, `clone()`, and `toString()`.

The following code segment demonstrates some uses of class `ColoredPoint`.

```
ColoredPoint c = new ColoredPoint();
ColoredPoint d = new ColoredPoint(1, 2, Color.BLACK);
ColoredPoint e = (ColoredPoint) d.clone();
System.out.println(c);
System.out.println(d);
System.out.println(e);
System.out.println(d.equals(c));
System.out.println(d.equals(e));
```

The segment produces output

```
class geometry.ColoredPoint[0, 0, java.awt.Color[r=0,g=0,b=255]]
class geometry.ColoredPoint[1, 2, java.awt.Color[r=0,g=0,b=0]]
class geometry.ColoredPoint[1, 2, java.awt.Color[r=0,g=0,b=0]]
false
true
```

Suppose we are now interested in colored, three-dimensional points. The question you should be asking yourself is whether there is a way to create a class `Colored3DPoint` that extends from *both* `ThreeDimensionalPoint` and `Colored-Point`? The answer is no. Java supports *single inheritance* but does not support *multiple inheritance*. Because of its complexity, Java language designers decided explicitly not to support multiple inheritance. For example, suppose we were to create `Colored3DPoint` by extending it from both `ThreeDimensionalPoint` and `ColoredPoint`. Should our new class have two sets of x- and y-coordinate values because `ThreeDimension-`

Listing 9.2 ColoredPoint.java

```java
1.  // Represents a colored two-dimensional point
2.
3.  package geometry;
4.
5.  import java.awt.*;
6.
7.  public class ColoredPoint extends Point {
8.      // instance variable
9.      Color color;
10.
11.     // ColoredPoint(): default constructor
12.     public ColoredPoint() {
13.         super();
14.         setColor(Color.blue);
15.     }
16.
17.     // ColoredPoint(): specific constructor
18.     public ColoredPoint(int x, int y, Color c) {
19.         super(x, y);
20.         setColor(c);
21.     }
22.
23.     // getColor(): color property accessor
24.     public Color getColor() {
25.         return color;
26.     }
27.
28.     // setColor(): color property mutator
29.     public void setColor(Color c) {
30.         color = c;
31.     }
32.
33.     // clone(): clone facilitator
34.     public Object clone() {
35.         int a = (int) getX();
36.         int b = (int) getY();
37.         Color c = getColor();
38.         return new ColoredPoint(a, b, c);
39.     }
40.
41.     // toString(): string representation facilitator
42.     public String toString() {
43.         int a = (int) getX();
44.         int b = (int) getY();
45.         Color c = getColor();
46.         return getClass() + "[" + a + ", " + b + ", " + c + "]";
47.     }
48.
49.     // equals(): equal facilitator
50.     public boolean equals(Object v) {
51.         if (v instanceof ColoredPoint) {
52.             Color c1 = getColor();
53.             Color c2 = ((ColoredPoint) v).getColor();
54.             return super.equals(v) && c1.equals(c2);
```

Listing 9.2 **ColoredPoint.java (Continued)**

```
55.        }
56.        else {
57.            return false;
58.        }
59.    }
60. }
```

---

alPoint and ColoredPoint both have x- and y-coordinate values or should it have one set of x- and y-coordinate values because ThreeDimensionalPoint and Colored-Point are both extended from Point? Rather than making programmers deal with such issues, Java does not permit multiple inheritance.

So if we want a colored-three dimensional point representation Colored3DPoint, we would either extend ThreeDimensionalPoint to provide a color attribute or extend ColoredPoint to provide a z-coordinate attribute. The former alternative is demonstrated in Listing 9.3.

Why not add rather than extend?

You may have already asked yourself, why bother with inheritance. Why not just modify the existing class to cover the new features? For example, we could give the Point class a z-coordinate value. However, the approach of adding features is generally not the preferred one, and sometimes it is not even an option.

Simply adding features can make a class too complex to understand or build. Imagine if such an approach were taken with musical instruments—whenever a new sound is desired, an existing instrument is modified to also make that sound. Such a combined musical instrument would be too unwieldy to use effectively.

Another factor discouraging addition is user confidence and cost. Complex classes are difficult to build, maintain, and test. Programmers are understandably skeptical regarding the use of a massive API. Furthermore, if the source code to an existing class is not available, then adding new features to that class is not an option. Consider the fact that most libraries are distributed as compressed archives or as .class files with the .java versions unavailable—developers often keep the .java versions to themselves to protect their intellectual investment.

Listing 9.3 Colored3DPoint.java

```
1.  // Represents a colored, three-dimensional point
2.
3.  package geometry;
4.
5.  import java.awt.*;
6.
7.  public class Colored3DPoint extends ThreeDimensionalPoint {
8.      // instance variable
9.      Color color;
10.
11.     // Colored3DPoint(): default constructor
12.     public Colored3DPoint() {
13.        setColor(Color.blue);
14.     }
15.
16.     // Colored3DPoint(): specific constructor
17.     public Colored3DPoint(int a, int b, int c, Color d) {
18.        super(a, b, c);
19.        setColor(d);
20.     }
21.
22.     // getColor(): color property accessor
23.     public Color getColor() {
24.        return color;
25.     }
26.
27.     // setColor(): color property mutator
28.     public void setColor(Color c) {
29.        color = c;
30.     }
31.
32.     // clone(): clone facilitator
33.     public Object clone() {
34.        int a = (int) getX();
35.        int b = (int) getY();
36.        int c = (int) getZ();
37.        Color d = getColor();
38.        return new Colored3DPoint(a, b, c, d);
39.     }
40.
41.     // toString(): string representation facilitator
42.     public String toString() {
43.        int a = (int) getX();
44.        int b = (int) getY();
45.        int c = (int) getZ();
46.        Color d = getColor();
47.        return getClass() + "[" + a + ", " + b + ", " + c + ", "
48.           + d + "]";
49.     }
50.
51.     // equals(): equal facilitator
52.     public boolean equals(Object v) {
53.        if (v instanceof Colored3DPoint) {
54.           Color c1 = getColor();
```

Listing 9.3   **Colored3DPoint.java (Continued)**

```
55.             Color c2 = ((Colored3DPoint) v).getColor();
56.             return super.equals(v) && c1.equals(c2);
57.         }
58.         else {
59.             return false;
60.         }
61.     }
62. }
```

<table>
<tr><td>**9.2**</td><td>**POLYMORPHISM**</td></tr>
</table>

We use all four point classes—Point, ThreeDimensionalPoint, ColoredPoint, and Colored3DPoint—in the program PolymorphismDemo.java of Listing 9.4. The **for** loop of method main() in conjunction with the program output demonstrates one of the important features of object-oriented programming—*a code expression can invoke different methods depending on the types of objects using the code*. This language feature is known as *polymorphism*

Some people view method overloading as *syntactic* or *primitive* polymorphism. With method overloading, Java can determine which method to invoke at compile time. The decision is based on the invocation signature. However, true polymorphism—or as it is sometimes known, *pure* polymorphism—generally requires the decision to be delayed until run time.

The polymorphic code in the **for** loop is invocation expression p[i].toString().

```
String s = p[i].toString();
```

In Java, *it is not the variable type that determines the invocation, but the type of object at the location to which the variable refers.* The code is polymorphic because array p is a *heterogeneous* list; that is, its element reference values of different types.

That array p is a heterogeneous list is a result of how its elements are set. For example, Point variable p[0] is set using statement

```
p[0] = new Colored3DPoint(4, 4, 4, Color.BLACK);
```

The assignment makes sense because Colored3DPoint has an *is-a* relationship with Point. Colored3DPoint extends from ThreeDimensionalPoint, which extends from Point. Thus, Point variable p[0] refers to a Colored3DPoint object.

Similarly, the assignment

```
p[1] = new ThreeDimensionalPoint(2, 2, 2);
```

causes variable p[1] to refer to a ThreeDimensionalPoint object. The other two assignments cause p[2] and p[3] to refer respectively to ColoredPoint and Point

---

Listing 9.4   PolymorphismDemo.java

```
1.  // Demonstrates polymorphism using various point classes
2.
3.  import java.awt.*;
4.  import geometry.*;
5.
6.  public class PolymorphismDemo {
7.     // main(): application entry point
8.     public static void main(String[] args) {
9.        Point[] p = new Point[4];
10.
11.       p[0] = new Colored3DPoint(4, 4, 4, Color.BLACK);
12.       p[1] = new ThreeDimensionalPoint(2, 2, 2);
13.       p[2] = new ColoredPoint(3, 3, Color.RED);
14.       p[3] = new Point(4, 4);
15.
16.       for (int i = 0; i < p.length; ++i) {
17.          String s = p[i].toString();
18.          System.out.println("p[" + i + "]: " + s);
19.       }
20.
21.       return;
22.    }
23. }
```

---

objects.

```
       p[2] = new ThreeDimensionalPoint(3, 3, Color.RED);
       p[3] = new Point(4, 4);
```

Because array p is heterogeneous, the `toString()` method that is invoked in expression `p[i].toString()` depends on the type of `Point` object to which `p[i]` refers. For i equal to 0, the expression `p[i].toString()` invokes the `Colored3DPoint` method `toString()`; for i equal to 1, expression `p[i].toString()` invokes the `ThreeDimensionalPoint` method `toString()`; for i equal to 2, the expression `p[i].toString()` invokes the `ColoredPoint` method `toString()`; and for i equal to 3, the expression `p[i].toString()` invokes the `Point` method `toString()`.

Therefore, the program outputs

```
class geometry.Colored3DPoint[4, 4, 4, java.awt.Color[r=0,g=0,b=0]]
class geometry.ThreeDimensionalPoint(2, 2, 2)
class geometry.ColoredPoint[3, 3, java.awt.Color[r=255,g=0,b=0]]
java.awt.Point[x=4,y=4]
```

Flexibility for future enhancements

With polymorphism, the decision on which method to invoke in an expression may have to be determined at run time. This capability makes it possible to compile a method that performs a method invocation in its body even though the subclass eventually supplying the method has not yet been implemented or even defined!

Design with inheritance in mind

When designing a collection of new but related classes, pay attention to what are the common behaviors and characteristics. This process is known as *factorization*. Then try to create a coherent base class that provides this commonality. From this base class, sub-classes can be defined to provide the special behaviors and characteristics. Your current work effort should be reduced as common behaviors are implemented just once. Future work efforts should also be minimized as new features can be added by extending the existing classes.

9.3   INHERITANCE NUANCES

Before developing a data abstraction, we first present several small classes for illustrative purposes. Each of the classes demonstrate some important nuance with regard to inherit-ance behavior in Java. Our examination begins with construction.

Consider the following class B composed of two constructors. Both constructors pro-duce output when invoked.

```java
public class B {
   // B(): default constructor
   public B() {
      System.out.println("Using B's default constructor");
   }

   // B(): specific constructor
   public B(int i) {
      System.out.println("Using B's int constructor");
   }
}
```

Before reading the analysis that follows, try to determine the output of the following program C.java whose class C extends B. If you understand what output it produces, you should better understand how object construction is always a two-step process. The first step constructs the superclass view of the object. The second step constructs the subclass view of the object.

```java
public class C extends B {
   // C(): default constructor
   public C() {
      System.out.println("Using C's default constructor");
      System.out.println();
   }

   // C(int a): specific constructor
   public C(int a) {
      System.out.println("Using C's int constructor");
      System.out.println();
   }
```

```
    // C(int a, int b): specific constructor
    public C(int a, int b) {
       super(a + b);
       System.out.println("Using C's int-int constructor");
       System.out.println();
    }

    // main(): application entry point
    public static void main(String[] args) {
       C c1 = new C();
       C c2 = new C(2);
       C c3 = new C(2,4);
       return;
    }
 }
```

Method `main()` of program `C.java` begins by defining three C variables `c1`, `c2`, and `c2`. Each of the objects is constructed using a different C constructor. Because construction is a two-step process, the construction of each C object begins with the construction of its superclass attributes. Neither of the constructors for the objects referenced by `c1` and `c2` explicitly invoke a superclass constructor. Therefore, Java automatically invokes C's superclass default constructor for these objects.

Because the constructor of the object referenced by `c2` explicitly invokes a superclass constructor, Java does not automatically invoke C's superclass default constructor for that object. Therefore, the program produces the following output.

```
Using B's default constructor
Using C's default constructor

Using B's default constructor
Using C's int constructor

Using B's int constructor
Using C's int-int constructor
```

9.3.1   CONTROLLING ACCESS

Up to this point our member variables and methods have always had either **public** or **private** access rights. A **public** member has no restrictions on its access. A **private** member can be used only by the class that defines that member. With respect to **public** and **private** access rights, a subclass is treated no differently than any other Java class—a subclass can access the superclass's **public** members and cannot access the superclass's **private** members. Java also supports two other access rights. They are **protected** access and default access.

Besides being accessible in its own class, a **protected** variable or method can be used by subclasses of its class.

For example, consider class P from package demo with a **private** instance variable data, a **public** default constructor, a **public** accessor getData(), a **protected** mutator setData(), and a facilitator print() with default access.

```
package demo;

public class P {
    // instance variable
    private int data;

    // P(): default constructor
    public P() {
        setData(0);
    }

    // getData(): accessor
    public int getData() {
        return data;
    }

    // setData(): mutator
    protected void setData(int v) {
        data = v;
    }

    // print(): facilitator
    void print() {
        System.out.println();
    }
}
```

Class Q, which extends P, can invoke P's default constructor, accessor getData(), and mutator setData(). However, class Q cannot access directly P's instance variable data.

```
import demo.P;

public class Q extends P {
    // Q(): default constructor
    public Q() {
        super();          ◄──────  Q can access superclass's public default constructor
    }

    // Q(): specific constructor
    public Q(int v) {
        setData(v);       ◄──────  Q can access superclass's protected mutator
    }

    // toString(): string facilitator
    public String toString() {
        int v = getData();   ◄──────  Q can access superclass's public accessor
        return String.valueOf(v);
    }

    // invalid1(): illegal method
    public void invalid1() {
```

```
        data = 12;          ◄─────────  Q cannot access directly superclass's private data
    }                                    field

    // invalid2(): illegal method
    public void invalid2() {
        print();            ◄─────────  Q cannot access directly superclass's default access
    }                                    method print()
}
```

With regard to default access, only two classes in the same package can access each other's default-access members. Therefore, class Q, which is not part of package demo, cannot access P facilitator print().

Now consider class R of package demo, R's methods can invoke P's **public** default constructor and accessor getData(); **protected** mutator setData(); and default-access facilitator print(). However, class R cannot access directly P's **private** instance variable data.

```
package demo;

public class R {
    // instance variable
    private P p;

    // R(): default constructor
    public R() {
        p = new P();        ◄─────────  R can access P's public default constructor
    }

    // set(): mutator
    public void set(int v) {
        p.setData(v);       ◄─────────  R can access P's protected mutator
    }

    // get(): accessor
    public int get() {
        return p.getData(); ◄─────────  R can access P's public accessor
    }

    // use(): facilitator
    public void use() {
        p.print();          ◄─────────  R can access P's default access method
    }

    // invalid(): illegal method
    public void invalid() {
        p.data = 12;        ◄─────────  R cannot access directly P's private data field
    }
}
```

Next consider class S that is neither part of package demo nor is it extended directly or indirectly from class P. Therefore, class S can invoke only P's **public** default constructor and accessor getData().

```
import demo.P;

public class S {
```

```
// instance variable
private P p;

// S(): default constructor
public S() {
    p = new P();        ◄───────    S can access P's public default constructor
}

// get(): inspector
public int get() {
    return p.getData();   ◄───────   S can access P's public accessor
}

// illegal1(): illegal method
public void illegal1(int v) {
    p.setData(v);       ◄───────    S cannot access P's protected mutator
}

// illegal2(): illegal method
public void illegal2() {
    p.data = 12;        ◄───────    S cannot access directly P's private data field
}

// illegal3(): illegal method
public void illegal3() {
    p.print();          ◄───────    S cannot access directly P's default access print()
}
}
```

Access rights of classes are summarized in Table 9.1.

Table 9.1   **Class access rights.**

Member Restriction	`this`	Subclass	Package	General
`public`	√	√	√	√
`protected`	√	√	√	—
`default`	√	—	√	—
`private`	√	—	—	—

9.3.2   DATA FIELDS

Consider the following class D with a single **protected int** instance variable d. Because the variable is **protected**, classes extending D have direct access to it. The D default constructor explicitly sets d to 0. The other D constructor sets d to the value of its parameter v. We will use class D as the base class for classes E and F.

```
public class D {
    // D instance variable
    protected int d;

    // D(): default constructor
    public D() {
        d = 0;
    }

    // D(): specific constructor
    public D(int v) {
        d = v;
    }

    // printD(): facilitator
    public void printD() {
        System.out.println("D's d: " + d);
        System.out.println();
    }
}
```

Although class E extends D, it does not introduce any new instance variables. However, class E does define a single constructor and a method `printE()`.

```
public class E extends D {
    // E(): specific constructor
    public E(int v) {
        d = v;
        super.d = v*100;
    }

    // printE(): facilitator
    public void printE() {
        System.out.println("D's d: " + super.d);
        System.out.println("E's d: " + this.d);
        System.out.println();
    }
}
```

For class E, both d and super.d access superclass instance variable d

In contrast, class F both extends D and introduces a new instance variable. Because the new variable has the same name d as the superclass instance variable, the superclass variable is *hidden* in class F. Class F also defines a constructor, facilitator, and class method `main()` that enables the class to serve as an application program.

Before reading our analysis, determine the output of program `F.java`.

```
public class F extends D {
    // F instance variable
    int d;

    // F(): specific constructor
    public F(int v) {
        d = v;
        super.d = v*100;
```

```
    }

    // printF(): facilitator
    public void printF() {
        System.out.println("D's d: " + super.d);
        System.out.println("F's d: " + this.d);
        System.out.println();
    }

    // main(): application entry point
    public static void main(String[] args) {
        E e = new E(1);
        F f = new F(2);
        e.printE();
        f.printF();
        return;
    }
}
```

Because E does not define any instance variables itself, the instance variable it manipulates is its superclass's instance variable. Thus, the two assignments in constructor

```
public E(int v) {
    d = v;                      ⎫   Two separate modifications of
    super.d = v*100;            ⎭   superclass's instance variable d
}
```

are both manipulating the same variable. When the constructor completes, the value of that variable is based on the second assignment. The fact that d and **super**.d are referencing the same variable means that E's facilitator

```
public void printE() {
    System.out.println("D's d: " + super.d);
    System.out.println("E's d: " + this.d);
    System.out.println();
}
```

prints the same value twice. In the case of the E object referenced by e from F's method main(), the value 100 is displayed twice.

```
E e = new E(1);
```

Because F defines an instance variable d, that definition results in the superclass instance variable being hidden. Inside an F method, the expression d refers to the F instance variable and not the superclass instance variable. Thus, the two assignments in constructor

```
                         Modification of this's d

public F(int v) {
    d = v;                ◄─────────────┐
    super.d = v*100;      ◄──────────┐  │
}

                         Modification of superclass's d
```

manipulate different instance variables. When the constructor completes, the value of the object's F variable d is equal to v and the value of the object's superclass variable d is equal to 100*v. So unless v equals 0, when method printF()

```java
public void printF() {
    System.out.println("D's d: " + super.d);
    System.out.println("E's d: " + this.d);
    System.out.println();
}
```

— Accessing superclass's d

— Accessing this's d

is invoked, two different values are displayed. In the case of the F object referenced by f from F's method

```java
F f = new F(2);
```

main(), the values 200 and 2 are displayed. So the output produced by the program is

```
D's d: 100
E's d: 100

D's d: 200
F's d: 2
```

9.3.3   TYPING

Consider the following class X. Class X provides a default constructor, a **boolean** class method isX() that reports whether its parameter v is of type X, and a **boolean** class method isObject() that reports whether its parameter v is of type Object.

```java
public class X {
    // default constructor
    public X() {
        // no body needed
    }

    // isX(): class method
    public static boolean isX(Object v) {
        return (v instanceof X);
    }

    // isObject(): class method
    public static boolean isObject(X v) {
        return (v instanceof Object);
    }
}
```

Now consider program Y.java. Class Y extends class X. Besides defining method main(), class Y provides a default constructor and a **boolean** class method isY() that reports whether its parameter v is of type Y.

Before reading the analysis that follows, determine the output of program Y.java. Understanding what output is produced should contribute to your understanding of inheritance with respect to object types.

```java
public class Y extends X {
    // Y(): default constructor
    public Y() {
        // no body needed
    }

    // isY(): class method
    public static boolean isY(Object v) {
        return (v instanceof Y);
    }

    public static void main(String[] args) {
        X x = new X();
        Y y = new Y();
        X z = y;

        System.out.println("x is an Object: " + X.isObject(x));
        System.out.println("x is an X: " + X.isX(x));
        System.out.println("x is a Y: " + Y.isY(x));
        System.out.println();

        System.out.println("y is an Object: " + X.isObject(y));
        System.out.println("y is an X: " + X.isX(y));
        System.out.println("y is a Y: " + Y.isY(y));
        System.out.println();

        System.out.println("z is an Object: " + X.isObject(z));
        System.out.println("z is an X: " + X.isX(z));
        System.out.println("z is a Y: " + Y.isY(z));
        return;
    }
}
```

The definition of variable x assigns it to a new object of type X. Because all classes in Java are extensions of class Object, both X.isObject(x) and X.isX(x) report true. Class X is not extended directly or indirectly from class Y, so Y.isY(x) reports false.

Because variable y is defined to be of class type Y, where Y is a subclass of X, each of X.isX(y), Y.isY(y), and X.isObject(y) reports true.

Although the apparent type of z is X, the object referenced by z is the same object that y references. Therefore, variable z references a Y object and the tests regarding z report the same results as the tests regarding y. Therefore, the program outputs

```
x is an Object: true
x is an X: true
x is a Y: false

y is an Object: true
y is an X: true
y is a Y: true

z is an Object: true
```

```
z is an X: true
z is a Y: true
```

9.3.4   LATE BINDING

Consider the following class L.

```java
public class L {
    // L(): default constructor
    public L() {
    }

    // f(): facilitator
    public void f() {
        System.out.println("Using L's f()");
        g();
    }

    // g(): facilitator
    public void g() {
        System.out.println("using L's g()");
    }
}
```

Also consider class M that extends L. Together, classes L and M further demonstrate the power of polymorphism in Java.

```java
public class M extends L {
    // M(): default constructor
    public M() {
        // no body needed
    }

    // g(): facilitator
    public void g() {
        System.out.println("Using M's g()");
    }

    // main(): application entry point
    public static void main(String[] args) {
        L l = new L();
        M m = new M();
        l.f();
        m.f();
        return;
    }
}
```

The statements of interest in method main() are

```java
l.f();
m.f();
```

Because class M does not override superclass method f(), both f() invocations are invocations of L's method f(). However, the invocations produce different results!

The invocation l.f() causes statements

```
System.out.println("Using L's f()");
g();
```

from the L definition of f() to be executed with respect to the object referenced by variable l. Because l references an L object, it is L method g() that is invoked. Thus, the first two output lines produced by the program are

```
Using L's f()
using L's g()
```

The invocation m.f() again causes statements

```
System.out.println("Using L's f()");
g();
```

from the L definition of f() to be executed. They are executed with respect to the object referenced by variable m. Because m references an M object, it is M method g() that is invoked. Thus, the program output is

```
Using L's f()
using L's g()
Using L's f()
Using M's g()
```

9.3.5   FINALITY

Just as Java permits a constant data field to be defined through the use of the keyword **final**, so it permits **final** methods and classes. A **final** class is a class that cannot be extended. A **final** method is a method that cannot be overridden.

The developer of a class might make it **final** for economic or security reasons. If clients have access only to the .class version of a **final** class, then they must look to the developer for additional features. As another example, a class or method may be crucial to a system. By declaring the class or method in question to be **final**, it is harder to tamper with the system by introducing classes that override the existing code.

For example, the following class U is a **final** class. Therefore, class U cannot be extended.

```
final public class U {
    // U(): default constructor
    public U() {
    }

    // f(): facilitator
    public void f() {
        System.out.println("f() can't be overridden: U is final");
    }
}
```

As another example, method f() of class V is a **final** method. Therefore, f() cannot be overridden if V is extended.

```
public class V {
   // V(): default constructor
   public V() {
   }

   // f(): facilitator
   final public void f() {
      System.out.println("f() can't be overridden: it is final");
   }
}
```

We now turn our attention to a data abstraction ImprovedReader that extends Java input/output functionality through inheritance. In particular, ImprovedReader extends class BufferedReader. For subsequent convenience and ease of use, ImprovedReader is packaged in an API named ez.

9.4	CASE STUDY — EXTENDING BUFFEREDREADER

When developing interactive console applications, we have used the class `BufferedReader` to extract input. However, this class provides minimal support for extracting values. Its two principal extraction methods are methods `read()` and `readLine()`.

> The objective of this case study is practice using inheritance in the context of stream specialization

```
int read()
```

If there is a character available for extraction (i.e., end of file has not been reached), then the value of that character is returned; otherwise, the method returns –1.

```
String readLine()
```

If there is a line of characters available for extraction, then the next line of characters is returned as a `String` (the line feed at the end of that line is extracted but is not part of the return value); otherwise, **null** is returned.

ANALYSIS AND DESIGN

Many Java programmers dislike the `BufferedReader` class because it does not provide methods to extract integer, floating-point, and boolean values. The class's limited functionality forces the programmer to supply code to convert a `String` extraction to a value of the desired type. The limitations are demonstrated in the following code segment that initializes **int**, **double**, and **boolean** variables with values from standard input.

```
BufferedReader stdin = new BufferedReader(
     new InputStreamReader(System.in));
String s = stdin.readLine();
int i = Integer.parseInt(s);
String t = stdin.readLine();
double d = Double.parseDouble(t);
String u = stdin.readLine();
boolean b = Boolean.getBoolean(u);
```

Our initial attempt at extending `BufferedReader` is class `ImprovedReader` of Listing 9.5. Class `ImprovedReader` provides two constructors. One class is a convenience constructor that takes an `Input-Stream` as a parameter (`System.in` is of type `InputStream`). The other constructor mirrors the standard `BufferedReader` constructor and takes a `Reader` as its parameter, where `Reader` is the Java superclass for all character reading streams.

> In Chapter 10 we develop a stream reader class EzReader with greater functionality

IMPLEMENTATION

The definition of the `ImprovedReader` convenience constructor is straightforward—it invokes the other `ImprovedReader` constructor using an `InputStreamReader` parameter based on its parameter `in`.

```
public ImprovedReader(InputStream in) {
     this(new InputStreamReader(in));
}
```

> Invoking the other ImprovedReader constructor to do the actual configuration

Listing 9.5 ImprovedReader.java

```
1.  // ImprovedReader: initial attempt at extending BufferedReader
2.
3.  package ez;
4.
5.  import java.io.*;
6.
7.  public class ImprovedReader extends BufferedReader {
8.
9.      public ImprovedReader(InputStream in) {
10.         this(new InputStreamReader(in));
11.     }
12.
13.     public ImprovedReader(Reader in) {
14.         super(in);
15.     }
16.
17.     public short getShort() throws IOException {
18.         String s = readLine();
19.         return Short.parseShort(s);
20.     }
21.
22.     public int getInt() throws IOException {
23.         String s = readLine();
24.         return Integer.parseInt(s);
25.     }
26.
27.     public long getLong() throws IOException {
28.         String s = readLine();
29.         return Long.parseLong(s);
30.     }
31.
32.     public float getFloat() throws IOException {
33.         String s = readLine();
34.         return Float.parseFloat(s);
35.     }
36.
37.     public double getDouble() throws IOException {
38.         String s = readLine();
39.         return Double.parseDouble(s);
40.     }
41.
42.     public boolean getBoolean() throws IOException {
43.         String s = readLine();
44.         return Boolean.getBoolean(s);
45.     }
46. }
```

The other ImprovedReader constructor is also straightforward—it just invokes the corresponding superclass constructor of BufferedReader. No other work is needed from the constructor as the class's extended functionality comes strictly from its member methods.

```
public ImprovedReader(Reader in) {
    super(in);
```

```
}
```

There are six subclass methods provided by ImprovedReader. These methods are getShort(), getInt(), getLong(), getFloat(), getDouble(), and getBoolean() and they return respectively a **short**, **int**, **long**, **float**, **double**, and **boolean**.

Each of the six methods can throw an IOException because BufferedReader method readLine() throws an IOException if an I/O error occurs. Each of the methods consists of two lines—the definition of a String variable s and a **return** statement.

All six methods define String variable s in the same way. Variable s is initialized with the next line from the input stream using superclass method readLine().

```
String s = readLine();
```

The **return** statement depends on the particular method. For example, for method getShort(), the **return** statement is

```
return Short.parseShort(s);
```

Method parseShort() is a Short class method. If s has the form of a decimal integer, then parseShort() returns the **short** value of that integer. Otherwise, an exception of type java.lang.NumberFormatException is thrown.

There are comparable parse methods for the other numeric types—parseInt(), parseLong(), parseFloat(), and parseDouble(). However, the method to convert a String to a **boolean**, is named getBoolean() (e.g., Boolean.getBoolean("true") returns **true**).

With class ImprovedReader, we can rewrite our earlier code segment from the beginning of this section for extracting values for variables i, d, and b as follows.

```
ImprovedReader reader = new ImprovedReader(System.in);
int i = reader.getInt();
double d = reader.getDouble();
boolean b = reader.getBoolean();
```

The new code segment is definitely more readable than the earlier code segment.

Another demonstration of ImprovedReader is given in Listing 9.6. The program computes the sum of 10 values extracted from standard input.

Although class ImprovedReader extends BufferedReader functionality, it has some significant limitations. For example, a user can provide only one input value per line. Chapter 10 considers both how to remove these limitations and how to provide straightforward file processing.

Listing 9.6   *SumTen.java*

```java
1.  // Computes the sum of ten input values
2.
3.  import java.io.*;
4.  import ez.ImprovedReader;
5.
6.  public class SumTen {
7.
8.      // main(): application entry point
9.      public static void main(String[] args) throws IOException {
10.
11.         // set up input stream
12.         ImprovedReader reader = new ImprovedReader(System.in);
13.
14.         // initially no values have been processed
15.         System.out.println("Enter 10 values one per line");
16.         double valueSum = 0;
17.
18.         // process values one by one
19.         for (int i = 0; i < 10; ++i) {
20.             valueSum += reader.getDouble();
21.         }
22.
23.         // display sum
24.         System.out.println("Sum of inputs: " + valueSum);
25.     }
26. }
```

9.5   ABSTRACT BASE CLASSES

When doing program development, a need sometimes arises for defining a superclass where for some of its methods there are no sensible definitions; that is, it is necessary to make some methods part of the superclass so that other code can exploit Java's polymorphic capabilities. Such classes are known as *abstract* classes. For example, in developing a geometric shape hierarchy, a suitable superclass `GeometricObject` for the hierarchy might have two data fields:

`Point position`

> Upper northwest corner of the shape's bounding box.

`Color color`

> Color of the shape.

The following methods are reasonable for the superclass `GeometricObject`. (Other methods could also be reasonable.)

`Point getPosition()`

> Returns the upper northwest corner of the shape's bounding box.

`void setPosition(Point p)`

> Sets the upper northwest corner of the shape's bounding box to p.

`Color getColor()`

> Returns the color of the shape.

`void setColor(Color c)`

> Sets the color of the shape to c.

`void paint(Graphics g)`

> Renders the shape in graphics context g.

However, we can define sensible implementations only for methods `getPosition()`, `setPosition()`, `getColor()`, and `setColor()`.

```
// getPosition(): return object position
Point getPosition() {
   return position;
}

// setPosition(): update object position
void setPosition(Position p)
   position = p;
}

// getColor(): return object color
Color getColor() {
   return color;
}

// setColor(): update object color
void setColor(Color c) {
   color = c;
}
```

Method `paint()` has no sensible implementation because it is shape-specific—the rendering of a rectangle is different from the rendering of a line, which is different from

---

Listing 9.7 **GeometricObject.java**

```
1.  // GeometricObject: abstract superclass for geometric shapes
2.
3.  import java.awt.*;
4.
5.  abstract public class GeometricObject {
6.      // instance variables
7.      Point position;
8.      Color color;
9.
10.     // getPosition(): return object position
11.     public Point getPosition() {
12.         return position;
13.     }
14.
15.     // setPosition(): update object position
16.     public void setPosition(Point p) {
17.         position = p;
18.     }
19.
20.     // getColor(): return object color
21.     public Color getColor() {
22.         return color;
23.     }
24.
25.     // setColor(): update object color
26.     public void setColor(Color c) {
27.         color = c;
28.     }
29.
30.     // paint(): render the shape to graphics context g
31.     abstract public void paint(Graphics g);
32. }
```

---

the rendering of a circle. Because there is no sensible implementation for `paint()`, it makes sense to use the Java modifier **abstract** to make `GeometricObject` an **abstract** class and to make its method `paint()` and an **abstract** method. A complete definition of the abstract class `GeometricObject` is given in Listing 9.7. Definitions of its subclasses `Box` and `Circle` are given in Listing 9.8 and Listing 9.9.

The keyword **abstract** at the start of a class definition indicates that the class can be instantiated; i.e., we cannot create directly a new `GeometricObject`.

The keyword **abstract** at the front of a method declaration indicates that the definition of the method will not be supplied. Non-**abstract** subclasses of the **abstract** superclass *must* provide their own definitions of the **abstract** method, which would not have been the case if the superclass had instead defined the method with an empty statement list for its method body.

Because classes `Box` and `Circle` both define a method `paint()`, the classes are non-**abstract** and can be instantiated.

```
Circle c = new Circle(1, new Point(0, 0), Color.blue);
Box r = new Box(1, 2, new Point(3, 4), Color.red);
```

Listing 9.8   Box.java

```
1.  // Box: rectangle shape representation
2.
3.  import java.awt.*;
4.
5.  public class Box extends GeometricObject {
6.      // instance variables
7.      int length;
8.      int height;
9.
10.     // Box(): default constructor
11.     public Box() {
12.         this(0, 0, new Point(), Color.black);
13.     }
14.
15.     // Box(): specific constructor
16.     public Box(int l, int h, Point p, Color c) {
17.         setLength(l);
18.         setHeight(h);
19.         setPosition(p);
20.         setColor(c);
21.     }
22.
23.     // getLength(): get the rectangle length
24.     public int getLength() {
25.         return length;
26.     }
27.
28.     // getHeight(): get the rectangle height
29.     public int getHeight() {
30.         return height;
31.     }
32.
33.     // setLength(): set the rectangle length to l
34.     public void setLength(int l) {
35.         length = l;
36.     }
37.
38.     // setHeight(): get the rectangle height to h
39.     public void setHeight(int h) {
40.         height = h;
41.     }
42.
43.     // paint(): render the rectangle to graphics context g
44.     public void paint(Graphics g) {
45.         Point p = getPosition();
46.         Color c = getColor();
47.         int    l = getLength();
48.         int    h = getHeight();
49.
50.         g.setColor(c);
51.         g.fillRect((int) p.getX(), (int) p.getY(), l, h);
52.     }
53. }
```

Listing 9.9   Circle.java

```
1.  // Circle: circle shape representation
2.
3.  import java.awt.*;
4.
5.  public class Circle extends GeometricObject {
6.      // instance variable
7.      int radius;
8.
9.      // Circle(): default constructor
10.     public Circle() {
11.         this(0, new Point(), Color.black);
12.     }
13.
14.     // Circle(): specific constructor
15.     public Circle(int r, Point p, Color c) {
16.         setRadius(r);
17.         setPosition(p);
18.         setColor(c);
19.     }
20.
21.     // getRadius(): get the circle radius
22.     public int getRadius() {
23.         return radius;
24.     }
25.
26.     // setRadius(): set the circle radius to r
27.     public void setRadius(int r) {
28.         radius = r;
29.     }
30.
31.     // paint(): render the circle to graphics context g
32.     public void paint(Graphics g) {
33.         Point p = getPosition();
34.         Color c = getColor();
35.         int   r = getRadius();
36.
37.         g.setColor(c);
38.
39.         g.fillOval((int) p.getX(), (int) p.getY(), r, r);
40.     }
41. }
```

Abstract classes are valid types. Therefore, we can initialize a variable of an **abstract** type to reference an existing subclass object of that type.

```
GeometricObject g = c;     // A Circle is a GeometricObject
```

We can also use an abstract base type to define a polymorphic method.

```
public void renderShapeInBlue(Graphics g, GeometricObject s) {
    g.setColor(Color.blue);
    s.paint(g);     // drawing is based on s's subclass type
}
```

Here the method will set the color for current graphical context g to blue and then draw the object referenced by s in that context. Because Java invokes the `paint()` method for the type of object to which parameter s references, the type of drawing depends on the `GeometricObject` subclass type of s.

| 9.6 | ## INTERFACES |

Besides allowing programmers to define **abstract** classes, Java also allows programmers to define *interfaces*. An **interface** is not a class but is instead a partial template of what must be in a class that *implements* the interface. An **interface** is a Java type and can be used as such.

```
public interface name {
     // constants   ◄

     // method declarations

}
                     ◄
```

All variables are either explicitly or implicitly public class constants (i.e., public static final)

All listed methods are either explicitly or implicitly public

An interface definition differs from an **abstract** class definition in three important ways.

- An **interface** cannot specify any method implementations;
- All of the methods of an **interface** are **public**;
- All 'of the variables defined in an **interface** are **public**, **final**, and **static**.

So why use an **interface** when an **abstract** class offers greater flexibility? The answer is twofold. First, Java allows a class to implement more than one **interface**, whereas a class can extend only one superclass. Second, because an **interface** is not a class, it is not part of a class hierarchy. Two unrelated classes can implement the same interface with objects of those unrelated classes having the same type—the **interface** their class types implement.

Listing 9.10 Colorable.java

```
1.  package geometry;
2.
3.  import java.awt.*;
4.
5.  public interface Colorable {
6.      // getColor(): return the color of the object
7.      public Color getColor();
8.      // setColor(): set the color of the object
9.      public void setColor(Color c);
10. }
```

As an example, consider **interface** `Colorable` of Listing 9.10. Implementing the interface requires two methods—`getColor()` and `setColor()`. The methods' intended purposes are to serve respectively as a color accessor and mutator. Classes `Colorable-Point` and `Colorable3DPoint` of Listing 9.11 and Listing 9.12 are respectively reworkings of classes `ColoredPoint` and `Colored3DPoint` of Listing 9.2 and Listing 9.3. Except for the cosmetic differences of `ColorablePoint` versus `ColoredPoint` and `Colorable3DPoint` versus `Colored3DPoint`, the only other difference is that `ColorablePoint` and `Colorable3DPoint` indicate that they implement `Colorable`.

Because both `ColorablePoint` and `Colorable3DPoint` indicate they implement interface `Colorable`, a polymorphic code segment such as the following is possible

```
ColorablePoint u = new ColorablePoint();
Colorable3DPoint v = new Colorable3DPoint();
Colorable w = u;
w.setColor(Color.BLACK);          ColorablePoint method
                                  setColor() is invoked
w = v;
w.setColor(Color.RED);            Colorable3DPoint method
                                  setColor() is invoked
```

In this segment, variable w is used in the invocation of two different `setColor()` methods. This polymorphic circumstance is possible because points u and v share the common interface type `Colorable`.

Similarly, a polymorphic method can be defined to take advantage of interface-implemented commonality. Consider the following class `Blue` with polymorphic class method `setBlue()`.

```
public class Blue {
    public static void setBlue(Colorable p) {
        p.setColor(Color.BLUE);
    }
}
```

Class method `setBlue()` can have either a `ColorablePoint` or a `Colorable3DPoint` as its actual parameter, both of which are demonstrated in the following code segment.

```
ColorablePoint a = new ColorablePoint();
Colorable3DPoint b = new Colorable3DPoint();
Blue.setBlue(a);
Blue.setBlue(b);
```

Thus, the `setColor()` method invoked with `setBlue()` depends on the actual type of the `Colorable` parameter.

Even though both `ColoredPoint` and `Colored3DPoint` implement `getColor()` and `setColor()` methods, comparable code segments with `ColoredPoint` and `Colored3DPoint` being used is not possible. `ColoredPoint` and `Colored3DPoint`

Listing 9.11 ColorablePoint.java

```
1.  package geometry;
2.
3.  import java.awt.*;
4.
5.  public class ColorablePoint extends Point implements Colorable {
6.      // instance variable
7.      Color color;
8.
9.      // ColorablePoint(): default constructor
10.     public ColorablePoint() {
11.         super();
12.         setColor(Color.blue);
13.     }
14.
15.     // ColorablePoint(): specific constructor
16.     public ColorablePoint(int x, int y, Color c) {
17.         super(x, y);
18.         setColor(c);
19.     }
20.
21.     // getColor(): color property accessor
22.     public Color getColor() {
23.         return color;
24.     }
25.
26.     // setColor(): color property mutator
27.     public void setColor(Color c) {
28.         color = c;
29.     }
30.
31.     // clone(): clone facilitator
32.     public Object clone() {
33.         return new ColorablePoint(x, y, getColor());
34.     }
35.
36.     // toString(): string representation facilitator
37.     public String toString() {
38.         Color c = getColor();
39.         return "[" + super.toString() + ", " + c.toString() + "]";
40.     }
41.
42.     // equals(): equal facilitator
43.     public boolean equals(Object v) {
44.         if (v instanceof ColorablePoint) {
45.             Color c1 = getColor();
46.             Color c2 = ((ColoredPoint) v).getColor();
47.             return super.equals(v) && c1.equals(c2);
48.         }
49.         else {
50.             return false;
51.         }
52.     }
53. }
```

Listing 9.12 **Colorable3DPoint.java**

```java
1.  package geometry;
2.
3.  import java.awt.*;
4.
5.  public class Colorable3DPoint extends ThreeDimensionalPoint
6.                                     implements Colorable {
7.      // instance variable
8.      Color color;
9.
10.     // Colorable3DPoint(): default constructor
11.     public Colorable3DPoint() {
12.         setColor(Color.blue);
13.     }
14.
15.     // Colorable3DPoint(): specific constructor
16.     public Colorable3DPoint(int x, int y, int z, Color c) {
17.         super(x, y, z);
18.         setColor(c);
19.     }
20.
21.     // getColor(): color property accessor
22.     public Color getColor() {
23.         return color;
24.     }
25.
26.     // setColor(): color property mutator
27.     public void setColor(Color c) {
28.         color = c;
29.     }
30.
31.     // clone(): clone facilitator
32.     public Object clone() {
33.         return new Colorable3DPoint(x, y, z, getColor());
34.     }
35.
36.     // toString(): string representation facilitator
37.     public String toString() {
38.         Color c = getColor();
39.         return "[" + super.toString() + ", " + c.toString() + "]";
40.     }
41.
42.     // equals(): equal facilitator
43.     public boolean equals(Object v) {
44.         if (v instanceof Colorable3DPoint) {
45.             Color c1 = getColor();
46.             Color c2 = ((Colorable3DPoint) v).getColor();
47.             return super.equals(v) && c1.equals(c2);
48.         }
49.         else {
50.             return false;
51.         }
52.     }
53. }
```

are not of type `Colorable`, whereas `ColorablePoint` and `Colorable3DPoint` are.

```
ColoredPoint c = new ColoredPoint();
Colored3DPoint d = new Colored3DPoint();
Colorable e = c;          ———————— Illegal: c does not reference a Colorable object
e.setColor(Color.black);
e = d;                    ———————— Illegal: d does not reference a Colorable object
e.setColor(Color.red);
Blue.setBlue(c);          ———————— Illegal: c does not reference a Colorable object
Blue.setBlue(d);          ———————— Illegal: d does not reference a Colorable object
```

9.7   PREPARING THE AQUARIUM

One of the examples that we will consider in Chapter 12 is an aquarium simulation. For the simulation to be interesting, it will need to be able to draw fish and plants. To help in that task, we create now an interface `Drawable`. Implementing interface `Drawable` of Listing 9.13 requires three methods: `getX()`, `getY()`, and `paint()`. The purposes of methods `getX()` and `getY()` are to return respectively the x- and y-coordinates of the position of the object. The purpose of the method `paint()` is to render its object in the graphics context specified by its parameter.

Listing 9.13   Drawable.java

```
1.  import java.awt.*;
2.
1.  public interface Drawable {
2.      // getX(): returns the x-coordinate of the object
3.      public int getX();
4.
5.      // getY(): returns the y-coordinate of the object
6.      public int getY();
7.
8.      // paint(): draw the object in context g at coordinate
9.      // (getX(), getY())
10.     public void paint(Graphics g);
11. }
```

We will use interface `Drawable` in our definition of the class `Fish`. For our purposes, a fish is a drawable shape of specified color located at a particular position. To specify the color and shape, we use `awt` classes `Color` and `Polygon`. To specify the x- and y-coordinates, we use **int** values.

Before describing class `Fish`, we briefly review class `Polygon`. Class `Polygon` represents a shape using an ordered list of points. For example, with three points a triangle can be represented (e.g., `ColoredTriangle` of Chapter 5), with four points a quadrilateral can be represented, and so on. To support the creation of shapes, class `Polygon` has a constructor that takes three parameters—an array of x-coordinates, and an array of y-coordinates, and the number of points.

```
public Polygon(int[] x, int[] y, int n)
```
Constructs a polygon whose ith endpoint has location (x[i], y[i]). The number of points in the new polygon is n.

The following code segment uses Polygon to define both an equilateral triangle and a house-shaped pentagon.

```
int[] triangleX = { 10, 20, 30 };
int[] triangleY = { 20, 10, 20 };
Polygon triangle = new Polygon(triangleX, triangleY, 3);
int[] pentalateralX = { 100, 100, 150, 200, 200 };
int[] pentalateralY = { 200, 100,  75, 100, 200 };
Polygon house = new Polygon(pentalateralX, pentalateralY, 5);
```

Among its members, a Polygon has three **public** instance variables—xpoints, ypoints, and npoints. These instance variables represent respectively the array of x-coordinates, the array of y-coordinates, and the number of points in the polygon.

As indicated, one of the data fields of a Fish is a Polygon. In particular, instance variable fishShape references a Polygon. The other Fish instance variables are fishColor, currentX and currentY.

```
private Color fishColor
```
Represents the color of the fish.
```
private Polygon fishShape
```
Represents the shape of the fish.
```
private int currentX;
```
Represents the current x-coordinate of the fish's position.
```
private int currentY;
```
Represents the current y-coordinate of the fish's position.

To support the construction of fish, the class provides two constructors.
```
public Fish()
```
Creates a default fish using class method makeRandomColoredFish().
```
public Fish(Color c, Polygon p, int x, int y)
```
Creates a fish with color c and shape p at coordinate (x, y).

To support information hiding, the class provides accessors and mutators for fish attributes.
```
public Color getColor()
```
Returns the color of the fish.
```
public void setColor(Color c)
```
Sets the color of the fish to c.
```
public Polygon getShape()
```
Returns the shape of the fish.
```
public void setShape(Polygon p)
```
Sets the shape of the fish to be a clone of p.
```
public int getX()
```
Returns the x-coordinate of the fish's position.
```
public void setX(int x)
```
Sets the x-coordinate of the fish's position to x.
```
public int getY()
```
Returns the y-coordinate of the fish's position.

```
public void setY(int y)
```
      Sets the y-coordinate of the fish's position to y.
```
public void setPosition(int x, int y)
```
      Sets the fish's position to (x, y).

Because the class implements the interface `Drawable`, it also defines method `paint()`. (Methods `getX()` and `getY()` have already been accounted for.)
```
public void paint(Graphics g)
```
      Draws a representation of the fish to context g at position (`getX()`, `getY()`).

In addition to its instance variables and member methods, there is the single class method `makeRandomColoredFish()`.
```
public static Fish makeRandomColoredFish()
```
      Creates a "fishy" shape of random color that is positioned at coordinate (0, 0).

The definition of class `Fish` is given in Listing 9.14. Based on the preceding specifications, the implementation of most methods are straightforward. Discussion is warranted only for methods `paint()` and `makeRandomColoredFish()`.

In drawing its fish, member method `paint()` must recognize that the `Polygon` referenced by `fishShape` represents only a template for describing the outline of the fish. In particular, the points that make up that `Polygon` represent the *relative* positions of the line segment endpoints to each other. To draw the fish at its current position, those relative positions must be offset by its current position. For example, if the tip of the fish's nose has relative coordinate (130, 30) and the fish's current position is given by coordinate (50, 75), then the tip of nose is rendered at (130+50, 30+75) = (180, 105).

The figure shifting is accomplished by method `paint()`. It first copies the arrays of x-coordinates and y-coordinates that represent the shape of the fish. The copies are made by cloning the **public** data fields `xpoints` and `ypoints` for the `Polygon` describing the fish shape. Clones are made because the shifting should be evident only in `paint()`.

```
Polygon p = getShape();
int[] x = (int[]) p.xpoints.clone();
int[] y = (int[]) p.ypoints.clone();
int n = p.npoints;
```

A **for** loop then shifts the copies of the x-coordinates and y-coordinates by `getX()` and `getY()` respectively.

```
for (int i = 0; i < n; ++i) {
   x[i] += getX();
   y[i] += getY();
}
```

A new polygon then is constructed using the shifted points.

```
p = new Polygon(x, y, n);
```

To do the actual drawing, the color of the fish is determined; the graphical context has its active color set to that color, and a filled polygon is rendered.

```
Color c = getColor();
g.setColor(c);
g.fillPolygon(p);
```

Listing 9.14 Fish.java

```
1.  // Representation of a fish
2.
3.  import java.awt.*;
4.  import java.util.*;
5.
6.  public class Fish implements Drawable {
7.      // instance variables
8.      Color fishColor;
9.      Polygon fishShape;
10.     int currentX;
11.     int currentY;
12.
13.     // Fish(): default constructor
14.     public Fish() {
15.         Fish fish = makeRandomColoredFish();
16.         setColor(fish.getColor());
17.         setShape(fish.getShape());
18.         setPosition(fish.getX(), fish.getY());
19.     }
20.
21.     // Fish(): constructor for specified color, shape, and position
22.     public Fish(Color c, Polygon p, int x, int y) {
23.         setColor(c);
24.         setShape(p);
25.         setPosition(x, y);
26.     }
27.
28.     // getColor(): returns the color of the fish
29.     public Color getColor() {
30.         return fishColor;
31.     }
32.
33.     // setColor(): sets the color of the fish to c
34.     public void setColor(Color c) {
35.         fishColor = c;
36.     }
37.
38.     // getShape(): returns the shape of the fish
39.     public Polygon getShape() {
40.         return fishShape;
41.     }
42.
43.     // setShape(): sets the shape of the fish to a clone of p
44.     public void setShape(Polygon p) {
45.         fishShape = new Polygon(p.xpoints, p.ypoints, p.npoints);
46.     }
47.
48.     // getX(): returns the fish's x-coordinate position
49.     public int getX() {
50.         return currentX;
51.     }
52.
53.     // setX(): sets the fish's x-coordinate position
54.     public void setX(int x) {
```

Listing 9.14 Fish.java (Continued)

```
55.          currentX = x;
56.      }
57.
58.      // getY(): returns the fish's y-coordinate position
59.      public int getY() {
60.          return currentY;
61.      }
62.
63.      // setY(): sets the fish's y-coordinate position
64.      public void setY(int y) {
65.          currentY = y;
66.      }
67.
68.      // setPosition(): sets the fish's x- and y-coordinate position
69.      public void setPosition(int x, int y) {
70.          setX(x);
71.          setY(y);
72.      }
73.
74.      // paint(): draws the fish in graphical context g
75.      public void paint(Graphics g) {
76.          Polygon p = getShape();
77.          int[] x = (int[]) p.xpoints.clone();
78.          int[] y = (int[]) p.ypoints.clone();
79.          int n = p.npoints;
80.
81.          for (int i = 0; i < n; ++i) {
82.              x[i] += getX();
83.              y[i] += getY();
84.          }
85.
86.          p = new Polygon(x, y, n);
87.
88.          Color c = getColor();
89.          g.setColor(c);
90.          g.fillPolygon(p);
91.      }
92.
93.      // makeRandomColoredFish(): create fish with random color
94.      public static Fish makeRandomColoredFish() {
95.          int[] x = {   0,  30,  40,  50,  60,  70,  90, 100, 115,
96.                      130, 115, 100,  90,  70,  60,  50,  40,  30,
97.                        0,  15 };
98.          int[] y = {   5,  15,  10,   7,   0,   7,  12,  15,  22,
99.                       25,  28,  35,  40,  43,  50,  43,  40,  35,
100.                       45,  25 };
101.
102.          Random die = new Random();
103.          int red = die.nextInt(255);
104.          int yellow = die.nextInt(255);
105.          int green = die.nextInt(255);
106.
107.          Color c = new Color(red, yellow, green);
108.
```

Listing 9.14 **Fish.java (Continued)**

```
109.        Polygon p = new Polygon(x, y, x.length);
110.
111.        return new Fish(c, p, 0, 0);
112.    }
113. }
```

Class method `makeRandomColoredFish()` operates in the following manner. It first defines array variables `x` and `y` that are initialized respectively with the x- and y-coordinates of the points that make up the polygon describing the shape of the fish.

```
int[] x = {   0,  30,  40,  50,  60,  70,  90, 100, 115,
            130, 115, 100,  90,  70,  60,  50,  40,  30,
              0,  15 };
int[] y = {   5,  15,  10,   7,   0,   7,  12,  15,  22,
             25,  28,  35,  40,  43,  50,  43,  40,  35,
             45,  25 };
```

The method then constructs an object of type `Random` that is referenced by variable `die`.

```
Random die = new Random();
```

Standard Java class `Random` provides the means to generate pseudorandom numbers. The class `Random` is part of the Java package `java.util`.

The `Random` object referenced by `die` is used to generate **int** values in the interval 0 … 255.

```
int red = die.nextInt(256);
int yellow = die.nextInt(256);
int green = die.nextInt(256);
```

This interval corresponds to the legal values for the three settings in a `Color` representation. The `Random` method used to generate the values is one of several `nextInt()` class methods. The particular `nextInt()` method takes a value n and returns a pseudorandom value from the interval $0 … n-1$.

See Appendix D for a complete description of class Random

By generating three pseudorandom values, a pseudorandom color can be constructed.

```
Color c = new Color(red, yellow, green);
```

Using `c` and a polygon constructed from `x`, `y`, and `x.length`, a fish with pseudorandom color can be generated, where the fish is positioned at the origin.

```
Polygon p = new Polygon(x, y, x.length);
return new Fish(c, p, 0, 0);
```

To illustrate the drawing process of a fish, program `FishDemo.java` of Listing 9.15 first creates a window and a *canvas* in that window, where a canvas is rectangular drawing area to which drawing commands can be issued. The program then creates a fish and draws the fish on the canvas at two different positions. A sample window produced by the program is depicted in Figure 9.3.

The canvas is produced using awt class `Canvas`. A `Canvas` object can be sized using

Listing 9.15 FishDemo.java

```
1.  // Demonstrates fish and canvas features
2.
3.  import java.awt.*;
4.  import javax.swing.*;
5.  import java.io.*;
6.
7.  public class FishDemo {
8.      // main(): application entry point
9.      public static void main(String[] args) throws IOException {
10.         JFrame window = new JFrame("Fish still life");
11.         window.setDefaultCloseOperation(JFrame.EXIT_ON_CLOSE);
12.         window.setSize(200, 200);
13.         window.setVisible(true);
14.
15.
16.         Canvas canvas = new Canvas();
17.         canvas.setSize(200, 200);
18.         canvas.setBackground(Color.BLUE);
19.
20.         Container c = window.getContentPane();
21.
22.         FlowLayout manager = new FlowLayout();
23.         c.setLayout(manager);
24.
25.         c.add(canvas);
26.
27.         System.out.print("Enter any character when ready.");
28.         System.in.read();
29.
30.         Graphics g = canvas.getGraphics();
31.
32.         Fish fish = new Fish();
33.         fish.setPosition(12, 25);
34.         fish.paint(g);
35.         fish.setPosition(45, 95);
36.         fish.paint(g);
37.     }
38. }
```

member method setSize() and its background can be colored using member method
setBackground().

```
Canvas canvas = new Canvas();
canvas.setSize(200, 200);
canvas.setBackground(Color.blue);
```

To make the canvas a part of the window we must *add* the canvas to the window. In
particular, we must add the canvas to the content part of the window.

```
Container c = window.getContentPane();

FlowLayout manager = new FlowLayout();
c.setLayout(manager);

c.add(canvas);
```

Figure 9.3   FishDemo window.

Random values

Random number sequences have an important role in many computer applications. For example, they are used in games to ensure that players do not experience the same situations each time they play the game. Random number sequences are also used in the design of complex systems such as a new highway. Before a highway is constructed, it is typically modeled and simulated on a computer. By using random number sequences that reflect the expected frequency and behavior of automobiles on the proposed highway, designers can estimate the impact of adding a lane or an interchange.

A particularly useful random number sequence is the *uniform random number sequence*. A uniform random number sequence has a specified set of numbers from which the sequence takes or *draws* its random numbers. In each position of the random number sequence, any number from the set is equally likely to occur.

Suppose you wanted to create a uniformly distributed random number sequence drawn from the set {1, 2, 3, 4, 5, 6}. One way to do so is to get a normal six-sided die that has each of its sides labeled with a different element from that set. When the die is thrown, one of its sides will be facing up after the throw. For any given throw, each side is equally likely to be facing up. The sequence of values appearing on the face-up side will be a uniform random number sequence from the set {1, 2, 3, 4, 5, 6}.

Because a random number sequence is supposed to be random, there cannot be any computer algorithm that iteratively computes truly random numbers. The instructions that constitute an algorithm are deterministic rules—knowing them tells you the next number. However, there are methods that produce sequences of numbers that appear to be random. These sequences are more properly called *pseudorandom number sequences*, although most people are imprecise and drop the prefix *pseudo*.

Although our program only adds one element to the Container representing the content pane, there are generally multiple elements added to a Container. To arrange its elements, a Container uses a layout manager. Program FishDemo.java uses awt class FlowLayout for element positioning. A FlowLayout manager arranges the elements in a top-to-bottom, left-to-right manner in the order they are added to the window.

Figure 9.4 depicts that same window of Figure 9.3 as part of a desktop. The window is obscured partially by the console window that initiated the program. Figure 9.5 shows that same desktop after the console window has been moved. Observe that the fish rendering is no longer complete. The reason the now exposed portions of the fish are missing is that the program had not been configured to *repaint* the canvas with the two fish renderings whenever an exposure event occurs. As written, the program displays the two fish only once.

Figure 9.4   **FishDemo window obscured partially by console window.**

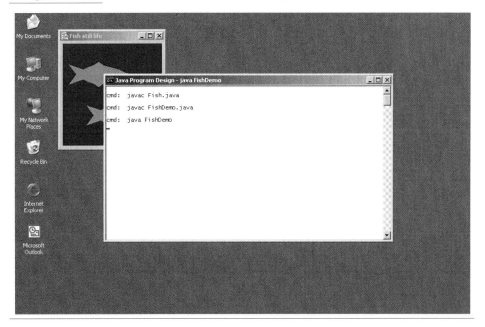

Although every Canvas object has a method paint() that is invoked automatically whenever an exposure event occurs in relation to the object, the paint() method defined by Canvas performs no actions. It is a placeholder that is to be overridden by a specialized Canvas for the task at hand.

As an example of a specialized canvas, Listing 9.16 gives FishCanvas.java. Class FishCanvas extends Canvas so that is produces a picture of a fish centered within the canvas. For that purpose, the class defines an instance variable fish of type Fish. The FishCanvas default constructor both configures the canvas (i.e., size and background) and positions the fish for the canvas. FishCanvas member method paint() simply draws the fish in the current graphical context.

Figure 9.5 **FishDemo window after console window has shifted.**

To demonstrate its specialization, FishCanvas provides a class method main() that defines an instance of FishCanvas and adds that canvas to a JFrame. Figure 9.6 shows the program window as part of a desktop. In the figure, the program is obscured partially by the console window. Figure 9.7 shows the program window after the console window has been shifted rightward on the desktop. Observe that FishCanvas method paint() correctly handled the rendering of the canvas after the exposure event occurred.

This analysis completes our introduction to inheritance and polymorphism.

Listing 9.16 FishCanvas.java

```
1.  // Demonstrates specialized canvas redrawing
2.
3.  import java.awt.*;
4.  import javax.swing.*;
5.
6.  public class FishCanvas extends Canvas {
7.
8.      // instance variables
9.      Fish fish = new Fish();
10.
11.     // FishCanvas(): default constructor
12.     public FishCanvas() {
13.         // configure canvas attributes
14.         setSize(200, 200);
15.         setBackground(Color.blue);
16.
17.         // position fish
18.         int fishWidth =
19.             (int) fish.getShape().getBounds().getWidth();
20.         int fishHeight =
21.             (int) fish.getShape().getBounds().getHeight();
22.         int w = getWidth();
23.         int h = getHeight();
24.         fish.setPosition((w - fishWidth)/2, (h - fishHeight)/2);
25.     }
26.
27.     // paint(): draw the fish
28.     public void paint(Graphics g) {
29.         fish.paint(g);
30.     }
31.
32.     // main(): application entry point
33.     public static void main(String[] args) {
34.         FishCanvas fishCanvas = new FishCanvas();
35.
36.         JFrame window = new JFrame("Canvas demo");
37.         window.setSize(200, 200);
38.         window.setDefaultCloseOperation(JFrame.EXIT_ON_CLOSE);
39.
40.         Container c = window.getContentPane();
41.
42.         FlowLayout manager = new FlowLayout();
43.         c.setLayout(manager);
44.
45.         c.add(fishCanvas);
46.
47.         window.setVisible(true);
48.     }
49. }
```

Figure 9.6   **FishCanvas window obscured partially by console window.**

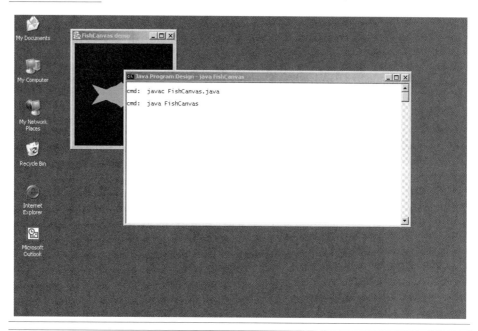

Figure 9.7   **FishCanvas window after console window has shifted.**

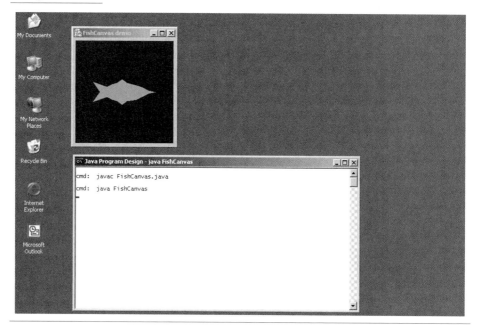

9.8　REVIEW

- Inheritance is a powerful mechanism in the object-oriented design methodology. Inheritance is the ability to define a new class using an existing class as a basis. The new class, called the subclass, inherits the attributes and behaviors of the class on which it is based, the superclass. The subclass also extends the superclass representation by introducing new attributes and behaviors that are specific to the subclass.
- Keyword **extends** is Java's mechanism for deriving a new class from an existing class.
- Inheritance is often used to organize abstractions in a top-down fashion from most general to least general.
- A superclass is also referred to as the base class and the subclass is also referred to as the derived class.
- A subclass can provide additional data fields and methods
- A subclass object has multiple types. The subclass object is a specialized superclass type object. Therefore, the subclass object is of both the subclass and superclass types.
- With inheritance, there is an is-a relationship between the subclass type and its superclass.
- All classes are either explicitly or implicitly extensions of the class `Object`.
- A subclass method overrides a superclass method if the two methods have the same signature.
- A subclass constructor essentially adds to a superclass object the features needed to make that object into a subclass object; that is, a subclass is a specialization of the superclass. A superclass constructor must be called to create a superclass object before the subclass constructor can do its job.
- To invoke explicitly a superclass constructor for the object under construction, we use the keyword **super**. Keyword **super** is the Java mechanism for viewing the current object as an instance of the superclass.
- If a subclass constructor does not invoke explicitly a superclass constructor, then Java automatically invokes the superclass's default constructor to initialize the superclass attributes.
- If a subclass overrides a method, the subclass can access the overridden method through the use of the keyword **super**.
- Java supports single inheritance but does not support multiple inheritance; that is, a subclass can be extended directly from only one class.
- A code expression is polymorphic if it can invoke different methods depending on the types of objects using the code.
- In Java, it is not the variable type that determines which method is invoked, but the type of object at the location to which the variable refers.
- Java's support for polymorphism makes it possible to compile a method that performs a method invocation in its body even though the subclass that eventually will supply

the method has not yet been implemented or even defined. This capability is important for software vendors who design libraries where the source code is to be kept proprietary. A library client can extend classes and have them make use of the vendor methods without the client needing access to vendor implementation files.

■ Object construction is always a two-step process. The first step constructs the superclass view of the object. The second step constructs the subclass view of the object.

■ With respect to **public** and **private** access rights, a subclass is treated no differently than any other Java class—a subclass can access the superclass's **public** members and cannot access the superclass's **private** members.

■ Besides being accessed by its own class, a **protected** variable or method can be used by subclasses of its class.

■ A **package** statement indicates that the definitions that follow are part of a bigger collection known as a package. Programmers put classes and interfaces into a package for two basic reasons—organization and special access to members. By organizing classes and interfaces with a related purpose into a package, you make it easier for users to find them—classes and interfaces with the same package name are stored in the same folder.

■ Java puts the classes of one package in a different namespace (scope) than it puts the classes of another package. As a result, the names in a package do not conflict with names in other packages.

■ When defining members of a class or interface, Java does not require an explicit access specification. The implicit specification is known as default access or package access. Members of a class with default access can be accessed only by members of the package.

■ If a Java file does not begin with a **package** statement, then Java automatically considers all definitions in that file to be part of a **package** unique to that file.

■ Two classes that are part of the same package can access each other's **public**, **protected**, and default access members.

■ Just as Java permits a constant data field to be defined through the use of the keyword **final**, so it permits **final** methods and classes. A **final** class is a class that cannot be extended. A **final** method is a method that cannot be overridden.

■ Developers of classes sometimes make them **final** for economic or security reasons.

■ The keyword **abstract** at the start of a class definition indicates that the class is not to be instantiated. The class exists to be a superclass of other classes. By having a common base for the specialized classes, the inheritance and polymorphism mechanisms can be exploited.

■ The keyword **abstract** at the front of a method declaration indicates that the definition of the method will not be supplied. Non-**abstract** subclasses of the **abstract** superclass must provide their own definitions.

■ Because **abstract** classes are valid types, we can initialize a variable of an **abstract** type variable to reference an existing subclass object of that type.

■ Besides allowing programmers to define **abstract** classes, Java also allows programmers to define and implement interfaces. An **interface** is not a class but is instead a partial template of what must be in a class.

```
public interface name {
        // constants          ◄──────────
        // method declarations
}                               ◄──────────
```

All variables are either explicitly or implicitly public class constants (i.e., public static final)

All listed methods are either explicitly or implicitly public

■ An **interface** differs from an **abstract** class in three important ways.

  – An **abstract** class can have complete method definitions, while an **interface** cannot specify any method implementations;

  – The methods and variables of an **abstract** class can have different access specifications, while the methods and variables of an interface are all **public**;

  – There are no restrictions on the kinds of variables an **abstract** class defines, while any variables defined in **interface** are **final** and **static**.

■ A class can extend only one class, but it can implement multiple interfaces.

■ Most applications that use class **Canvas** extend its definition to include an application-specific **paint()** method.

9.9 SELF-TEST

S9.1 What is the relationship that implies inheritance? A class that is created from another class via inheritances is called a _____. The class at the top of the inheritance hierarchy is known as the _____.

S9.2 Fill in the following table to show how the different inheritance access specifiers affect the ability of the derived class's member functions to access a base class's members.

Member Restriction	this	Subclass	Package	General
public				
protected				
default				
private				

S9.3   Consider classes D and F from Section 9.3.2. What is the output of the following code segment? Why?

```
F f = new F(2);
D d = f;
d.printD();
f.printF();
```

S9.4   Suppose classes U.java contains the following definitions. What does the program output?

```
class S {
    private int value;

    public S(int x) {
        value = x;
        System.out.println("Made an S: " + value);
    }

    public int getValue() {
        return value;
    }
}

class T {
    private S s;

    public T(int x) {
        s = new S(x);
    }

    protected S getValue() {
        return s;
    }
}

public class U extends T {
    private U(int y) {
        super(y);
    }

    private void print() {
        S s = getValue();
        System.out.println(s.getValue());
    }

    public static void main(String[] args) {
        U u = new U(1128);
        u.print();
    }
}
```

9.10   EXERCISES

9.1   Design a hierarchy of toys. Examples of possible specialized subclasses are stuffed toy, battery-powered toy, and mechanical toy. Illustrate your hierarchy by drawing a diagram like the one in Figure 9.1.

9.2   Design an inheritance hierarchy for lights. For example, there are electric lights, combustible lights (kerosene lanterns, propane lanterns, etc.), and electrolumines-cent lights. Illustrate your hierarchy by drawing a diagram like the one in Figure 9.1.

9.3   Design an inheritance hierarchy for shoes. The first level of your hierarchy should be men's and women's shoes. Illustrate your hierarchy by drawing a diagram like the one in Figure 9.1.

9.4   Design an inheritance hierarchy of clocks. After you have designed the hierarchy, design classes for each type of clock. Do not implement the member functions of the classes.

9.5   Consider the classes A and B. Identify the errors and explain them.

```
1. public class A {
2.     private int n;
3.     protected int m;
4.
5.     public A() {
6.         super(0, 0);
7.     }
8.
9.     private A(int a) {
10.         this(a, 0);
11.     }
12.
13.     protected A(int a, int b) {
14.         super(a, b);
15.     }
16. }
17.
18. public class B {
19.     public A() {
20.         super(0);
21.     }
22.
23.     public B(int a) {
24.         this(a, 0);
25.     }
26.
27.     private B(int a, int b) {
28.         A(a, b);
29.     }
30. }
```

9.6   Consider the following file C.java.

```
public class C {
```

```
      protected int m;
      private int n;

      public C() {
         this(0, 0);
      }

      C(int n) {
         this(n, 0);
      }

      protected C(int a, int b) {
         this(n, 0);
      }

      int look1() {
         return m;
      }
      int look2() {
         return n;
      }
   }
```

Suppose class D is extended from C. Which members of C can be accessed by D? How would your answer change (if at all), if class D was defined in the same file as C?

9.7   Suppose class X has the following definition.

```
   public class X {
      private int data;
      public X(int n) {
         data = n;
      }

      public int getData() {
         return data;
      }
   }
```

Also suppose Y has the following definition.

```
   public class Y {
      private int value;
      public Y(int n) {
         value = n;
      }

      public int getValue() {
         return value;
      }
   }
```

If it is necessary, correct the following class definition that attempts to define a class Z that has two data fields representing respectively X and Y objects.

```
   public class Z extends X, Y {
      public Z(int x, int y) {
```

```
        super.X(x);
        super.Y(y);
    }
}
```

9.8 Suppose class F has the following definition

```
public class F {
    private int value;
    public F(int x) {
        value = x;
        System.out.println("Made F: " + value);
    }
}
```

What is the output of the following program?

```
public class G extends F {
    private F value;

    public G(int x, int y) {
        super(x);
        value = new F(y);
    }

    public static void main(String[] args) {
        G g = new G(11, 28);
    }
}
```

9.9 Consider class E from Section 9.3.2. How many times is its instance variable set during the construction process? Explain.

9.10 Defend Java's decision not to give subclasses special access rights with regard to **private** members.

9.11 Defend Java's decision to give subclasses special access rights with regard to **protected** members.

9.12 Does awt class `Polygon` support encapsulation and information hiding?

9.13 Defend Java's decision to give the classes of a package special access rights with regard to default access members.

9.14 Consider class Y Section 9.3.3. Which of the following statements could be the fourth statement in method `main()`? Explain.

a) x = y;

b) x = (X) y ;

c) y = x;

d) y = (Y) x;

9.15 Suppose the following method `main()` was added to class `Colored3DPoint`. What would the program output be?

```
public static void main(String[] args) {
    Colored3DPoint c = new Colored3DPoint();
    Colored3DPoint d =
        new Colored3DPoint(1, 2, 3, Color.black);
```

```
            Colored3DPoint e = (Colored3DPoint) d.clone();
            System.out.println(c);
            System.out.println(d);
            System.out.println(e);
            System.out.println(d.equals(c));
            System.out.println(d.equals(e));
            return;
      }
```

9.16   Why is the decision on which method to invoke often made at run time rather than at compile time?

9.17   Extend class `Polygon` by defining a subclass `Triangle` that implements the `Drawable` interface for representing triangles embedded in coordinate space.

9.18   Speculate on why abstract methods are used rather than methods that simply do an immediate return. Consider what would happen if a derived class did not have an overriding definition.

9.19   Our concern here is developing a representation for vehicles.

   a)   Design an interface hierarchy for the types of vehicle ownership: commercial, individual, or governmental.

   b)   Define a movement interface hierarchy: wheeled and nonwheeled.

   c)   Define a class hierarchy for vehicles based on energy source—fossil fuel, solar, chemical, steam, electric, or nuclear—that also takes into account ownership and movement. Further develop the hierarchy for classes for snowmobiles, school buses, and station wagons. Justify which classes and methods are **abstract** or **final** (if any).

9.20   Use instances of classes `Polygon`, `Circle`, and `Box` along with `Triangle` from Exercise 9.17 to paint a canvas with the following image.

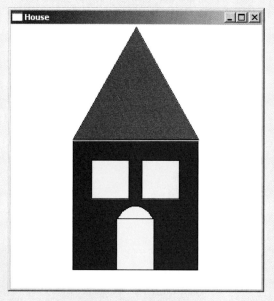

9.21 Use instances of classes `Polygon`, `Circle`, and `Box` along with `Triangle` from Exercise 9.17 to paint a canvas with the following image whenever an exposure event occurs.

PROGRAMMING PROJECT — CHANGE MAKER

In this case study, we explore the notion of inheritance by developing a collection of coin classes and then use those classes in producing a change-making program. The utility of a change-making algorithm is evident whenever we use a commercial food or beverage dispensor. After inserting coins and making our selection, we expect both the right product and the correct amount of change.

> The objective of this case study is to design and implement a hierarchy structure in the context of problem solving

A major part of this assignment is documenting your design decisions regarding the classes you create. This case study gives you more of a chance to be a designer than previous case studies did. With a good design for this assignment, the methods you specify will have straightforward implementations.

ANALYSIS AND DESIGN

Suppose the superclass for your collection of coin classes is `Coin`. What attributes (if any) should be associated with class `Coin`? In particular, should there be attributes `valueOf` and `name` or should only the classes derived from `Coin` have attributes `valueOf` and `name`? Should the attributes be instance variables, class variables, instance constants, or class constants?

What methods (if any) should be associated with class `Coin`? For example, should there be an accessor and a mutator giving and setting the coin's worth? For the methods that do exist, should they have **public**, **private**, **protected**, or default access? There are other questions to consider in regard to class `Coin`. For example, should the `Coin` class be abstract?

From class `Coin` you should derive the unit coin for your monetary system (e.g., the cent in the United States and the centavo in Mexico).

The other coin types from your monetary system should also be derived. It is up to you whether they are derived from `Coin` or from the unit coin class. However, your documentation should justify this design decision. Also document whether the classes are part of a package.

To facilitate the change-making program, you should also develop a class `Change`. Class `Change` has an instance variable associated with each of the coin types of your monetary system. The instance variable associated with a particular coin type indicates the number of its coins that are part of the change.

IMPLEMENTATION

As part of its definition, class `Change` should have a constructor that takes a single **int** parameter n. The constructor initializes the object so that its instance variables are configured to make change for the amount n. In configuring the instance variables, the minimum number of coins should be used for the specified amount. For example, if we are using the U.S. monetary system and n has the value 138, then the `Change` object should be initialized to indicate one dollar, no half-dollars, one quarter, one dime, no nickels, and three cents. Any other way of making change for 138 uses more coins.

In designing your classes, take care to consider what superclass and `Object` methods (if any) they should override (e.g., `clone()`, `equals()`, and `toString()`)?

Demonstrate a use of your classes by also developing a program `Change-Maker.java` that displays how to make change for a user-specified amount. Possible interfaces are depicted in Figure 9.8 and Figure 9.9.

TESTING

We recommend *unit testing* for this assignment. In unit testing, each class separately is tested for correctness. If the classes have been implemented correctly, and encapsulation and information hiding is practiced, then their use in combinations should also be correct. Thus, before testing `ChangeMaker.java`, it is important that you know class `Change` is correct. Because the correctness of class `Change` is dependent on the correctness of your implementation of the coin hierarchy, the coin hierarchy classes must also be tested.

Although exhaustively testing all these classes is not possible, there is a reasonable test that will give confidence of the correctness of many of the methods of your `Change`

Figure 9.8   **Changemaker screen shot.**

```
cmd:   javac coin/*.java

cmd:   javac ChangeMaker.java

cmd:   java ChangeMaker

Enter change amount: 1234

Amount 1234 can be refunded in the following manner
       12 dollars(s)
        0 half-dollars(s)
        1 quarter(s)
        0 dime(s)
        1 nickel(s)
        4 cent(s)


cmd:
```

Figure 9.9   **Changemaker screen shot.**

and coin classes. The test involves a **for** loop that iterates for all amounts *i* in the interval 0 ... 2*n*, where *n* is the value of your largest coin. For each amount *i*, construct a Change object with *i* as its parameter and then display that object. You can then manually verify the correctness of the output. Testing and debugging are considered in detail in Chapter 13.

POSSIBLE EXTENSIONS

In practice, a change maker is constrained to make change using the coins held in storage. As such, the optimal way to make change may not be possible using the available coins.

Modify class `Change` so that its initialization supports specifying the number of coins for each coin type that are available. The algorithm for making change should take into account coin availability.

DOCUMENTATION

Besides documenting all design decisions and methods, also document your testing process.

| 9.12 | SELF-TEST ANSWERS |

S9.1 The relationship is is-a. A class created from another class via inheritances is called a subclass. The class at the top of an inheritance hierarchy is known as the super-class.

S9.2 The table has the following specification.

Member Restriction	this	Subclass	Package	General
public	√	√	√	√
protected	√	√	√	—
default	√	—	√	—
private	√	—	—	—

S9.3 The segment displays

```
fd.d is 200
d.d is 2
```

S9.4 The program displays

```
The output is Made an S: 1128
1128
```

II GUI-BASED PROGRAMMING

This chapter continues our gentle introduction to graphical user interfaces (GUIs) by first exploring the object-oriented design and development of a psychometric-like tool. The chapter then begins the object-oriented design and development of a guessing game. The completion of the game is left as a programming project.

OBJECTIVES

- To consider two significant GUI-based tools using the principles of object-oriented programming.

G.II.1   CASE STUDY — PERSONALITY TYPING

We now turn our attention to the development of a GUI-based program `TypeIndica-tor.java` that attempts to estimate the user's psychological type. The examination is intended for fun and to gain experience with program design and implementation. The program is not a true psychometric tool. We caution that the development of a true tool requires significant interaction with psychologists and extensive testing in controlled environments to calibrate the validity of the tool. Screen snapshots of the tool are depicted in Figure II.1 and Figure II.2.

Figure G.II.1   **Screen snapshot of TypeIndicator.java's first query.**

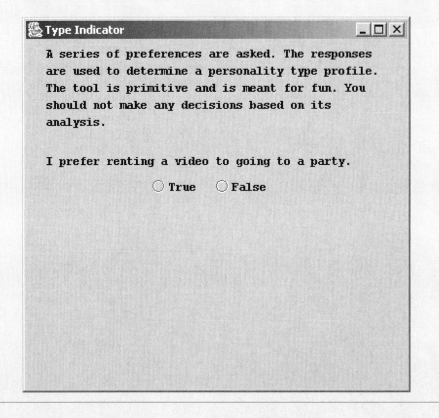

G.II.1.1   BACKGROUND

A major activity of psychological research is developing a psychological type model for explaining the structure of human personality. An early major effort was conducted by Carl Jung in the 1920s. Jung believed people primarily differed in whether they were *extroverted* or *introverted*; that is, whether they preferred to be outward or inward look-

Figure G.II.2 **Screen snapshot of TypeIndicator.java's analysis.**

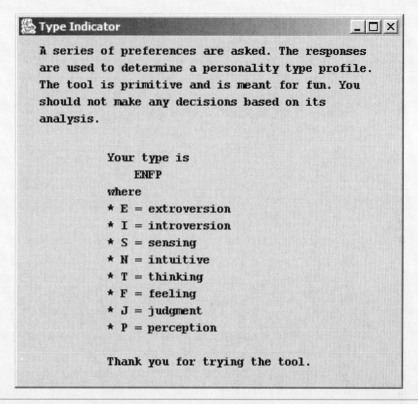

ing. Jung believed that two other important ways of categorizing people were according to their preferences regarding perception and judgment. In particular, he viewed that judgments tended to arise from processes that were based primarily on either *thinking* or *feeling*. He also viewed that people tended to have a preference for perception that was based primarily on either *physical sensing* or *intuition*.

Another major psychological typing effort began in the 1940s. This effort was conducted by Isabel Myers-Briggs and her mother Katherine Briggs. Their model classified people according to four preferences. Besides using Jung's three preferences, Myers-Briggs and Briggs also classified people with respect to their attitude toward life— whether *perception* or *judgment* was dominant. Based on the dominating characteristic for each of these four preferences, they would classify people into 1 of 16 personality types. Myers-Briggs and Briggs also developed a test now known the MBTI for determining a person's personality type. The test proved to be enormously popular and remains today an important psychometric tool. Research on improving the MBTI and other type indicator tests such as Keirsey Temperament Sorter is an important psychology research activity.

The 16 Myers Briggs and Briggs personality types are ISTJ, ISTP ISFJ, ISFP, INTJ, INTP INFJ, INFP, ESTJ, ESTP ESFJ, ESFP, ENTJ, ENTP, ENFJ, and ENFP, where I indicates introversion is dominant to extroversion, E indicates extroversion is dominant to introversion, S indicates sensing is dominant to intuition, N indicates intuition is dominant to sensing, T indicates that thinking is dominant to feeling, F indicates feeling is dominant to thinking, J indicates judgment is dominant to perception, and P indicates perception is dominant to judgment.

A major consequence of accepting the existence of these various types is being to able make inferences regarding individuals's interests and behaviors. Of course, caution must be taken in making such inferences—people are unique and their specific actions and reactions are a holistic sum of their entire makeup. However, a person's tendencies can sometimes be understood by knowing her or his personality type. The following summaries of the 16 Myers Briggs and Briggs personality types are based on the work *Gifts Differing: Tenth Anniversary Edition* by Isabel Myers-Briggs with Peter Briggs, Consulting Psychologists Press, 1980.

- ENFJ: Forceful, outstanding leader; can be aggressive at helping others. Five percent of the total population have this type.
- ENFP: Empathic; uncanny sense of the motivations of others; views life as an exciting drama; emotionally warm. Five percent of the total population have this type.
- ENTJ: Enjoys leading and problem solving; basic driving force is to lead; tends to seek positions of responsibility. Five percent of the total population have this type.
- ENTP: Innovative nonconformist; enthusiastic interest in everything; sensitive to possibilities. Five percent of the total population have this type.
- ESFJ: Most sociable type; nurturer of harmony; outstanding host or hostesses. Thirteen percent of the total population have this type.
- ESFP: Radiates warmth and optimism; witty, charming, clever; generous. Thirteen percent of the total population have this type.
- ESTJ: In touch with external environment; very responsible; pillar of strength. Thirteen percent of the total population have this type.
- ESTP: initiator; fiercely competitive; entrepreneur; uses shock effect to get attention; effective negotiator. Thirteen percent of the total population have this type.
- INFJ: Motivated and fulfilled by helping others; complex personality. One percent of the total population have this type.
- INFP: High capacity for caring. Calm and pleasant face to the world. Sense of honor comes from internal values. One percent of the total population have this type.
- INTJ: Very self-confident and pragmatic; decisions made easily; builder of systems and the applier of theoretical models. One percent of the total population have this type.
- INTP: Great precision in thought and language; readily discerns contradictions and inconsistencies; world exists to be understood. One percent of the total population have this type.
- ISFJ: Desires to be of service and to minister to individual needs; extremely loyal. Six percent of the total population have this type.
- ISFP: Interested in the fine arts; expression through action or art form; keen senses. Five percent of the total population have this type.

- ISTJ: Decisive in practical affairs; protector of institutions; dependable. Six percent of the total population have this type.

- ISTP: Impulsive, fearless, spontaneous; action is an end to itself; craves excitement; master of tools. Five percent of the total population have this type.

ANALYSIS AND DESIGN

The tool should have the following features.

> The objective of this case study is to practice the design and development of a significant class

- Is GUI-based.

- Presents introductory information on the tool and its limitations.

- Quizzes the user about preferences regarding extro-version versus introversion, sensing versus intuition, thinking versus feeling, and perception versus judgment.

- Analyzes and displays the results of the testing to estimate the associated personality type. The display indicates the associated personality type along with a summary of that type. Included in the description is a caveat warning of the tool's limitations.

These requirements indicate that the following elements should be part of the `TypeIndicator` GUI (i.e., they are `TypeIndicator` instance variables).

`private JFrame window`

Represents the window displaying the GUI.

`private JTextArea legendArea`

Represents the text message displaying tool usage and limitations.

`private JTextArea resultArea`

Represents the text message summary of the personality type test.

`private JTextArea statementPad`

Represents the text for the current preference being determined.

`private JRadioButton trueButton`

Represents the toggle indicating a true response to the current preference.

`private JRadioButton falseButton`

Represents the toggle indicating a false response to the current preference.

The buttons objects are of class type `JRadioButton`, which is a class that we have not used previously. `JRadioButton` is a `swing` button class whose behavior is like that of a toggle. The class name was chosen because the button supports the selection of mutually exclusive options—like the different buttons on an automobile radio cause different radio stations to be selected.

A `JRadioButton` is in one of two *states*—*selected* or *unselected*. By default, a `JRadioButton` is unselected when initialized.

To assist applications that require at most one `JRadioButton` object to be selected at a time, the `swing` API provides the class `ButtonGroup` for defining a logical grouping of buttons. When some button in a `ButtonGroup` is selected, the previously selected button from the group is made unselected.

As a reply to a trait query requires that a single response be selected, it is appropriate for class TypeIndicator to have a ButtonGroup element.

`private ButtonGroup buttonGroup`

Manages button selection behavior.

Once some button is selected from its group, a ButtonGroup requires that there be a selected button. Because we want neither the true button nor the false button to be selected when a new trait query is presented initially, TypeIndicator uses a third JRadioButton to be the selected button when a new query is made.

`private JRadioButton hiddenButton`

Represents the hidden alternative to true and false.

This JButton is never added to the GUI, so its presence is unknown to a program user. The user just sees and must pick from one of the other two radio buttons.

I prefer renting a video to going to a party.

◯ True   ◯ False

In addition, to the GUI elements, the results of the trait testing must be available to the TypeIndicator object so that it can create the appropriate display. Because the results are specific to the particular testing, they too are instance variables.

`private boolean introvert;`

Indicates whether testing shows introversion is dominant to extroversion.

`private boolean senser;`

Indicates whether testing shows sensing is dominant to intuition.

`private boolean thinker;`

Indicates whether testing shows thinking is dominant to feeling.

`private boolean judger;`

Indicates whether testing shows judging is dominant to perception.

We now turn our attention from TypeIndicator instance variables to TypeIndicator behaviors.

The TypeIndicator class is not intended to be of use to other classes. It is a standalone class whose purpose is to administer and determine the results of its personality type test. Thus, it is sufficient for the class's **public** interface to consists of two methods—a default constructor that carries out an occurrence of the testing process and a class method main() that defines an instance of the class.

`public main(String[] args)`

Creates an instance of the TypeIndicator class.

`public TypeIndicator()`

Conducts a personality type indicator test.

For simplicity, we suggest the following *top-level* algorithm for the default constructor.

- Configure and display GUI.
- Test whether extroversion or introversion is dominant.
- Test whether sensing or intuition is dominant.
- Test whether thinking or feeling is dominant.
- Test whether perception or judgment is dominant.

■ Display testing summary.

Programmers commonly expect that high-level activities correspond to the major methods of the class's implementation. We take such a view for `TypeIndicator`. The six steps are handled by different instance methods.

`private configureAndDisplayGUI()`

> Configures and displays the initial representation of the GUI.

`private boolean isIntroversionDominant()`

> Reports whether introversion is dominant over extroversion.

`private boolean isSensingDominant()`

> Reports whether sensing is dominant over intuition.

`private boolean isThinkingDominant()`

> Reports whether thinking is dominant over feeling.

`private boolean isJudgingDominant()`

> Reports whether judging is dominant over thinking.

`private void presentResults()`

> Displays the result of the test.

The methods are all **private** as their use in isolation does not make sense.

To determine whether the user has a particular characteristic (e.g., introversion), the program presents the user with a series of five statements. For each statement, the user selects one of two responses in reaction. By summarizing the responses we can get an indication of the dominant trait. A summary value of **true** means the trait in question is dominant and a summary value of **false** means the alternative trait is dominant (e.g., extroversion). By using a summary value as the return value for a trait test, the personality type instance variables can be initialized properly.

```
introvert = isIntroversionDominant();

senser = isSensingDominant();

thinker = isThinkingDominant();

judger = isJudgingDominant();
```

If you think about it, you should be see that the trait testers are doing the same type of work but asking different questions. This commonality suggests that the class have an instance method `doTraitTest()` that performs the trait testing. Through its parameters, it can be given the specific queries to be used in the current trait test. Furthermore, because a trait test involves making repeated queries, an instance method `getTrueOrFalseResponse()` is appropriate—the method poses an individual query and returns the response. Method `doTraitTest()` can accomplish its testing through five invocations of `getTrueOrFalseResponse()`.

`private boolean doTraitTest(String s1, String s2, String s3, String s4, String s5)`

> Conducts a trait test. The five statements involved in the five trait queries are represented by `s1`, `s2`, `s3`, `s4`, and `s5`. The method returns **true**, if the majority of the trait queries return **true**; otherwise, the method returns **false**.

```
private boolean getTrueOrFalse(String statement)
```

Displays a trait query and determines the user's response. The method returns a **boolean** value reflecting that response.

We now consider some of the important implementation details.

IMPLEMENTATION

TypeIndicator.java is given in Listing II.1. In terms of intellectual content, methods isIntroversionDominant(), isSensingDominant(), isThinkingDominant(), and isJudgingDominant() are all equivalent. Therefore, we discuss only isIntroversionDominant(). We also discuss configureAndDisplayGUI(), doTrait-Test(), and getTrueOrFalseResponse(). The other methods do not warrant specific discussion. The method examination begins with configureAndDisplayGUI().

Our particular interest in method configureAndDisplayGUI() (lines 57–94 of TypeIndicator.java) is its initial configuring of the GUI elements involved in assessing personality traits.

```
statementPad.setVisible(false);
statementPad.setEditable(false);
statementPad.setBackground(window.getBackground());

trueButton.setVisible(false);
falseButton.setVisible(false);
buttonGroup.add(trueButton);
buttonGroup.add(falseButton);
buttonGroup.add(hiddenButton);
```

JTextArea variable statementPad represents the JTextArea that is reset repeatedly with the current preference query.

> I prefer renting a video to going to a party.

This JTextArea is configured to be invisible initially. It is made visible only when there is a query to be made. (Because the code executes so fast, the user is unaware of the delay between the initial display of the GUI and the start of the first trait test.)

For the same reason, the JRadioButton objects are configured to be invisible initially. Because only one response is permitted, the two buttons are put in the Button-Group referenced by variable buttonGroup. The buttons are added one at a time using ButtonGroup instance method add(). Because a ButtonGroup is a logical grouping rather than a physical grouping, the group is not added to the GUI as an entity in itself.

We now consider methods isIntroversionDominant() and doTraitTest().

In order to conduct its test, method isIntroversionDominant() (lines 96–105 of Listing II.1) defines several String variables to represent statements that an introvert might find true.

```
String s1 = "I prefer renting a video to going to a party.";
String s2 = "I am happy when house guests leave.           ";
String s3 = "Meeting new people makes me tense.             ";
String s4 = "I enjoy being alone.                           ";
String s5 = "Crowds suck the life out of me.                ";
```

Listing G.II.1 TypeIndicator.java

```java
1.  // A simple psychometric-like type tool
2.
3.  import javax.swing.*;
4.  import java.awt.*;
5.  import java.awt.event.*;
6.
7.  public class TypeIndicator {
8.      // class constants
9.      private final int WINDOW_WIDTH = 400;
10.     private final int WINDOW_HEIGHT = 375;
11.     private final int AREA_WIDTH = 50;
12.
13.     private final String LEGEND =
14.         "A series of preferences are asked. The responses are "
15.         + "used to determine a personality type profile. The tool "
16.         + "is primitive and is meant for fun. You should not make "
17.         + "any decisions based on its analysis. ";
18.
19.     // instance GUI variables
20.     private JFrame window = new JFrame("Type Indicator");
21.     private JTextArea legendArea =
22.         new JTextArea(LEGEND, 6, AREA_WIDTH);
23.     private JTextArea resultArea = new JTextArea();
24.     private JTextArea statementPad =
25.         new JTextArea(LEGEND, 1, AREA_WIDTH);
26.     private JRadioButton trueButton = new JRadioButton("True ");
27.     private JRadioButton falseButton = new JRadioButton("False");
28.     private JRadioButton hiddenButton = new JRadioButton("");
29.     private ButtonGroup buttonGroup = new ButtonGroup();
30.
31.     // instance test variables
32.     private boolean introvert;
33.     private boolean senser;
34.     private boolean thinker;
35.     private boolean judger;
36.
37.     // main(): application entry point
38.     public static void main(String[] args) {
39.         TypeIndicator testInstrument = new TypeIndicator();
40.     }
41.
42.     // TypeIndicator(): default constructor
43.     public TypeIndicator() {
44.         configureAndDisplayGUI();
45.
46.         introvert = isIntroversionDominant();
47.
48.         senser = isSensingDominant();
49.
50.         thinker = isThinkingDominant();
51.
52.         judger = isJudgingDominant();
53.
54.         presentResults();
```

Listing G.II.I TypeIndicator.java (Continued)

```
55.     }
56.
57.     // configureAndDisplayGUI(): set up the GUI
58.     private void configureAndDisplayGUI() {
59.        // configure elements
60.        window.setSize(WINDOW_WIDTH, WINDOW_HEIGHT);
61.        window.setDefaultCloseOperation(JFrame.EXIT_ON_CLOSE);
62.
63.        legendArea.setEditable(false);
64.        legendArea.setLineWrap(true);
65.        legendArea.setWrapStyleWord(true);
66.        legendArea.setBackground(window.getBackground());
67.
68.        statementPad.setVisible(false);
69.        statementPad.setEditable(false);
70.        statementPad.setBackground(window.getBackground());
71.
72.        trueButton.setVisible(false);
73.        falseButton.setVisible(false);
74.        buttonGroup.add(trueButton);
75.        buttonGroup.add(falseButton);
76.        buttonGroup.add(hiddenButton);
77.
78.        resultArea.setEditable(false);
79.        resultArea.setBackground(window.getBackground());
80.
81.        // add elements to window's content pane
82.        Container c = window.getContentPane();
83.
84.        c.setLayout(new FlowLayout());
85.
86.        c.add(legendArea);
87.        c.add(statementPad);
88.        c.add(trueButton);
89.        c.add(falseButton);
90.        c.add(resultArea);
91.
92.        // ready to display GUI
93.        window.setVisible(true);
94.     }
95.
96.     // isIntroversionDominant(): is introversion is dominant to
97.     // extroversion
98.     private boolean isIntroversionDominant() {
99.        String s1 = "I prefer renting a video to going to a party.";
100.       String s2 = "I am happy when house guests leave.          ";
101.       String s3 = "Meeting new people makes me tense.           ";
102.       String s4 = "I enjoy being alone.                         ";
103.       String s5 = "Crowds suck the life out of me.              ";
104.       return doTraitTest(s1, s2, s3, s4, s5);
105.    }
106.
107.    // isSensingDominant(): is sensing is dominant to intuition
108.    private boolean isSensingDominant() {
```

Listing G.II.I TypeIndicator.java (Continued)

```
109.        String s1 = "Facts are more interesting than ideas.        ";
110.        String s2 = "I need the details more than the big picture.";
111.        String s3 = "I always measure, I never estimate.        ";
112.        String s4 = "Seeing is believing.        ";
113.        String s5 = "If you cannot touch it, it's not real.        ";
114.        return doTraitTest(s1, s2, s3, s4, s5);
115.    }
116.
117.    // isThinkingDominant(): test whether thinking is dominant to
118.    // feeling
119.    private boolean isThinkingDominant() {
120.        String s1 = "I prefer page 1 to the comics in a newspaper.";
121.        String s2 = "I think therefore I am.        ";
122.        String s3 = "I am not an emotional person.        ";
123.        String s4 = "Tears will not cause me to change my mind.  ";
124.        String s5 = "I rather be Data than Troi.        ";
125.        return doTraitTest(s1, s2, s3, s4, s5);
126.    }
127.
128.    // isJudgingDominant(): is judging is dominant to perceiving
129.    private boolean isJudgingDominant() {
130.        String s1 = "It is easy to make a decision.        ";
131.        String s2 = "My first impressions are right usually.    ";
132.        String s3 = "Wrong decisions are better than none.        ";
133.        String s4 = "I seldom have second thoughts.        ";
134.        String s5 = "Uncertainty makes me uncomfortable.        ";
135.        return doTraitTest(s1, s2, s3, s4, s5);
136.    }
137.
138.    // doTraitTest(): test for dominant response for a type category
139.    private boolean doTraitTest(String s1, String s2, String s3,
140.        String s4, String s5) {
141.        // create running totals for responses
142.        int choiceTrue = 0;
143.        int choiceFalse = 0;
144.
145.        // pose queries and get responses
146.        if (getTrueorFalseResponse(s1)) {  // do query 1
147.            ++choiceTrue;
148.        }
149.        else {
150.            ++choiceFalse;
151.        }
152.
153.        if (getTrueorFalseResponse(s2)) {  // do query 2
154.            ++choiceTrue;
155.        }
156.        else {
157.            ++choiceFalse;
158.        }
159.
160.        if (getTrueorFalseResponse(s3)) {  // do query 3
161.            ++choiceTrue;
162.        }
```

Listing G.II.I TypeIndicator.java (Continued)

```
163.          else {
164.              ++choiceFalse;
165.          }
166.
167.          if (getTrueorFalseResponse(s4)) {   // do query 4
168.              ++choiceTrue;
169.          }
170.          else {
171.              ++choiceFalse;
172.          }
173.
174.          if (getTrueorFalseResponse(s5)) {   // do query 5
175.              ++choiceTrue;
176.          }
177.          else {
178.              ++choiceFalse;
179.          }
180.
181.          // produce test result
182.          return choiceTrue > choiceFalse;
183.      }
184.
185.      // getTrueorFalseResponse(): pose a statement and get response
186.      private boolean getTrueorFalseResponse(String statement) {
187.
188.          statementPad.setText(statement);
189.          hiddenButton.setSelected(true);
190.          statementPad.setVisible(true);
191.          trueButton.setVisible(true);
192.          falseButton.setVisible(true);
193.
194.          for (; ;) {
195.              if (trueButton.isSelected() || falseButton.isSelected()) {
196.                  break;
197.              }
198.          }
199.
200.          statementPad.setVisible(false);
201.          trueButton.setVisible(false);
202.          falseButton.setVisible(false);
203.
204.          return trueButton.isSelected();
205.      }
206.
207.      // presentResults(): display testing results
208.      private void presentResults() {
209.          // setup text
210.          String result = "Your type is\n"
211.              + "      "
212.
213.              + ((introvert) ? "I" : "E")
214.              + ((senser)   ? "S" : "N")
215.              + ((thinker)  ? "T" : "F")
216.              + ((judger)   ? "J" : "P")
```

Listing G.II.1 **TypeIndicator.java (Continued)**

```
217.            + "\n"
218.
219.            + "where\n"
220.            + "* E = extroversion \n"
221.            + "* I = introversion \n"
222.            + "* S = sensing \n"
223.            + "* N = intuitive \n"
224.            + "* T = thinking \n"
225.            + "* F = feeling \n"
226.            + "* J = judgment \n"
227.            + "* P = perception \n"
228.            + "\n"
229.
230.            + "Thank you for trying the tool.";
231.
232.        // display text and quit button
233.        resultArea.setText(result);
234.
235.        window.show();
236.    }
237. }
```

The method then invokes doTraitTest() (lines 138–183 of Listing II.1) using the five statements as parameters. The return value of the invocation is the return value for testing whether introversion is dominant.

```
return doTraitTest(s1, s2, s3, s4, s5);
```

For each invocation, method doTraitTest() first defines two **int** variables choiceTrue and choiceFalse.

```
int choiceTrue = 0;
int choiceFalse = 0;
```

The variables are used to represent respectively the number of true responses and false responses to the statements in the current trait test.

The method then processes the first query of the current trait test.

```
// pose queries and get responses
if (getTrueorFalseResponse(s1)) {  // do query 1
   ++choiceTrue;
}
else {
   ++choiceFalse;
}
```

The invocation getTrueorFalseResponse(s1) causes in part statementPad's text label to be set to s1. The method returns **true** if the user indicated true to the new query and returns **false** if the user instead indicated false to the new query. Thus, based on the return value of the invocation, choiceTrue or choiceFalse can be updated appropriately.

The method then repeats this process four times to handle the other parts of this trait test using s2, s3, s4, and s5 as the statements to be displayed.

```
if (getTrueorFalseResponse(s2)) {   // do query 2
   ++choiceTrue;
}
else {
   ++choiceFalse;
}

if (getTrueorFalseResponse(s3)) {   // do query 3
   ++choiceTrue;
}
else {
   ++choiceFalse;
}

if (getTrueorFalseResponse(s4) {   // do query 4
   ++choiceTrue;
}
else {
   ++choiceFalse;
}

if (getTrueorFalseResponse(s5)) {   // do query 5
   ++choiceTrue;
}
else {
   ++choiceFalse;
}
```

The result of the current trait test then is reported by comparing choiceTrue and choiceFalse.

```
// produce test result
return choiceTrue > choiceFalse;
```

We now consider method getTrueOrFalseResponse() (lines 185–205 of Listing II.1). The method begins by configuring the GUI elements related to trait testing—the objects referenced by instance variables statementPad, trueButton, falseButton, and hiddenButton.

```
statementPad.setText(statement);
hiddenButton.setSelected(true);
statementPad.setVisible(true);
trueButton.setVisible(true);
falseButton.setVisible(true);
```

The JTextArea referenced by statementPad has its text set to the statement specified by parameter s, where s is current statement to which the user is to respond. The radio button referenced by hiddenButton then is set to the selected state. Because the three radio buttons are all part of the same button group, this selection has the effect of causing the true and false buttons to be unselected. To complete the configuration, the query statement, true button, and false button are made visible to the user.

A **for** loop then iterates until one of the buttons referenced by `trueButton` or `falseButton` has been selected.

```
for (; ;) {
    if (trueButton.isSelected() || falseButton.isSelected()) {
        break;
    }
}
```

Because an empty **for** test expression is equivalent to **true**, loop termination must come from the body of the **for** loop. The **if** statement in the loop body uses `JRadioButton` instance method `isSelected()` to test whether the radio button referenced by `true-Button` or the radio button referenced by `falseButton` has been selected. If one of those buttons has been selected, then the **break** statement executes and the loop terminates. Otherwise the loop continues to iterate. Because there is effectively no pause between the repeated evaluations of the **if** statement, this type of loop is known as a *busy-wait loop*.

Once the user has made a response, the GUI elements related to the query are made invisible.

```
statementPad.setVisible(false);
trueButton.setVisible(false);
falseButton.setVisible(false);
```

The return value for `getTrueorFalseResponse()` is based on expression `true-Button.isSelected()`.

```
return trueButton.isSelected();
```

The expression returns **true** if the true has been selected by the user and returns **false** otherwise (i.e., the false button has been selected indicating a false indication to the statement).

This discussion completes our analysis of the code.

TESTING AND ETHICS

To see whether our effort was more than an exercise in developing a Java program, you can test the program on willing participants. Because of the nature of the program, you must tell them of its limitations—it was developed by computer scientists rather than psychologists and that it has not been calibrated. If you do such testing, you must treat your participants confidentially.

When using human subjects for your own software projects, you should take similar care to give full disclosure. For information on how a professional computer scientist should behave visit `http://www.acm.org/constitution/code.html`.

REFERENCES

For further information on psychological typing, the following references should prove helpful.

- Association for Psychological Type, `http://www.aptcentral.org/`, 2002.
- Center for the Applications of Personality Type, `http://www.capt.org/`, 2001.

- Collected Works of C. G. Jung: Volume 6. Psychological Types, Carl Jung, Editors and translators: Gerhard Adler and R.F.C. Hull, Princeton University Press, 1976.

- Do What You Are: Second Edition, Paul Tieger and Barbara Barron-Tieger, Little Brown & Company, 2001.

- Please Understand Me II: Temperament, Character, and Intelligence, David Keirsey, Prometheus Books, 1998.

We now turn our attention to the design and partial development of a word guessing game.

| G.II.2 | **PROGRAMMING PROJECT — SMILEY GUESSING GAME** |

The Smiley guessing game follows the same rules as popular word guessing game Hangman. The player makes repeated attempts at trying to guess the letters in a mystery word. Each guess must be a single letter. If the guessed letter is part of the word, then all occur-

The objective of this case study is to practice the design and development of a significant class

rences of the letter are revealed. If the guessed letter is not part of the word, then a face feature is drawn.

If the word is guessed correctly before the face is drawn completely, then the game ends and the player wins. If instead, the word is not guessed correctly before the face is drawn completely, then the game ends and the player loses.

In the Smiley game, the face is drawn completely with the seventh errant guess. The first errant guess draws the contour of a face, the second errant guess draws the left eye, the third errant guess draws the left eyebrow, the fourth errant guess draws the right eye, the fifth errant guess draws the right eyebrow, the six error guess draws the nose, and the last errant guess draws the mouth to complete the face. Some snapshots of the game are given in Figure II.3.

To implement the game, you will need a GUI to represent the game display, update mechanisms, and an initialization process. We consider each of these needs in turn.

Our implementation uses a single class. However, given the complexity of the problem being solved, a design and implementation using two or more classes could be appropriate. For example in an alternative implementation, there can be one class for the GUI display and another class for controlling the flow of the game.

ANALYSIS AND DESIGN

We envision the game display as consisting of several graphical elements along with the window that holds them. The elements represent the mystery word, the current guess, an update signaller, the face, the past guesses, a quit signaler, and a status message.

The entries for the mystery word, current guess, and pass guesses can all be represented using class `JTextField` and the labels for those entries using class `JLabel`. The face can be drawn on a `Canvas` using the rendering methods of class `Graphics`. The game update signal can be generated using a `JButton`. Last, the game status message can be represented using class `JLabel`.

```
private JFrame window
```
Represents the container for Smiley game GUI.
```
private JTextField answerPad
```
Represents the current state of the mystery word solution.
```
private JTextField guessPad
```
Represents the entry area for entering a guess of a letter.
```
private JButton updateButton
```
Signaler for making a guess.
```
private Canvas facePad
```
Represents the drawing area for indicating bad guesses.

Figure G.II.3 Screen snapshots of the Smiley game.

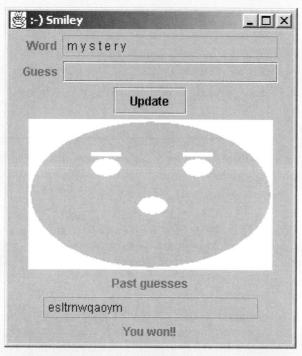

```
private JTextField pastPad
```
Represents the list of past guesses.
```
private JLabel resultPad
```
Represents a status message on the outcome of the game.
```
private JLabel answerLabel
```
Provides a label identifying the entry area for the current state of the mystery word solution.
```
private JLabel guessLabel
```
Provides a label identifying the entry area where a letter guess is made.
```
private JLabel pastLabel
```
Provides a label identifying the entry area for past guesses

To assist in the initialization of these instance variables, the following class constants should prove helpful. `String` constant `WORD_LIST` represents the name of the file containing the lists of possible words to be guessed. Constant `FIELD_WIDTH` represents the width of the `JTextField` entry areas. Constants `CANVAS_WIDTH` and `CANVAS_HEIGHT` represent the width and height respectively of the drawing area for the face. Constants `WINDOW_WIDTH` and `WINDOW_HEIGHT` represent the width and height respectively of the window containing the GUI. Constant `SKY_BLUE` represents the background color of the components of the GUI. `OFFSET` represents a pixel offset for drawing parts of the face. We discuss the role of `OFFSET` later.

```
private final static String WORD_LIST = "words.txt";
private final static int OFFSET = 2;
private final static int FIELD_WIDTH = 20;
private final static int CANVAS_WIDTH = 250;
private final static int CANVAS_HEIGHT = 150;
private final static int WINDOW_WIDTH = 300;
private final static int WINDOW_HEIGHT = 340;
private final static Color SKY_BLUE = new Color(198, 198, 255);
```

When the player clicks the `JButton`, the player is signaling a request to update the game using the new guess. If the new guess is a previously unseen letter, then either the mystery word or the face requires updating. In addition, the display of past guesses requires updating. If instead the new guess in not a previously unseen letter, then it is to be ignored. These activities can be supported through instance methods.

```
private boolean isValid(String s)
```
Determines whether s represents a new valid guess.
```
private void updateAnswer()
```
Displays occurrences of the new guess in the mystery word and the number of letters still to be guessed. If there are no occurrences of the guess in the mystery word, then the number of errant guesses has increased by one.
```
private void updateFace()
```
Updates drawing of the face based on the number of errant guesses.
```
private void updatePast()
```
Adds the current guess to the list of past guesses.

To support the drawing of the various features required by `updateFace()`, the following instance methods are appropriate.

```
private void drawContour()
```
Draws the basic shape of the face.
```
private void drawRightEye()
```
Draws the right eye.
```
private void drawLeftEye()
```
Draws the left eye.
```
private void drawRightEyebrow()
```
Draws the right eyebrow.
```
private void drawLeftEyebrow()
```
Draws the left eyebrow.
```
private void drawNose()
```
Draws the nose.
```
private void drawMouth()
```
Draws the mouth.

To support debugging and analysis, inherited method `toString()` should be overridden.
```
public toString()
```
Returns a `String` representation of the state of the game.

To make the game interesting, there must be some mechanism to choose a random mystery word.
```
private String getRandomWord()
```
Returns a random mystery word.

Therefore, the game must have access to a list of words. Our list is in the file `words.txt`. The first line of the file is the number of words that follows. The words occur one per line and there are approximately 200 listed words.

In addition, to the GUI instance variables listed previously, the methods we have proposed need access to the following *state information* about the game: the word to be guessed, what portion of the word has been guessed so far, the current guess, how many errant guesses have their been, how many letters are left to be guessed, and whether the game is over. This information on the state of the game can be maintained using instance variables
```
String word
```
Represents word to be guessed.
```
StringBuffer answer
```
Represents the portion of word guess so far.
```
char guess
```
Current letter guess.
```
int errors
```
Indicates how many bad guesses so far.
```
int lettersLeft
```
Indicates how many letters still needed.
```
boolean gameOver
```
Indicates has the game been won or lost.

A `StringBuffer` representation of the guessed portion of the word is maintained with variable `answer`. A `StringBuffer` is used because the display of the mystery word needs to be modified as the user makes correct guesses. Using a `String` would also be possible, however, keeping track of the updates is simpler with a `StringBuffer`.

Class `StringBuffer` provides a *mutable* representation of a character sequence; that is, there are methods that allow the representation to be modified (e.g., instance method `setCharAt()` allows the character at a specified index to be modified).

Three other methods of interest in regard to Smiley are accessors `charAt()` and `length()`, and facilitator `toString()`.

```
public void setCharAt(int i, char c)
```
> Sets the character in the sequence with index i to c.

```
public char charAt(int i)
```
> Returns the character at index i in the sequence.

```
public int length()
```
> Returns the number of characters in the sequence.

```
public String toString()
```
> Returns a `String` representation of the character sequence.

To play the game, we must be able to create instances of it. We suggest two constructors.

```
public Smiley()
```
> Invokes **this(null)**.

```
public Smiley(String w)
```
> Creates an instance of the Smiley game. If w is non-**null**, then it is the word to be guessed. If instead w is **null**, then a random word from WORD_LIST is used as the mystery word.

While it may seem strange to have a constructor where the mystery word is known, such a constructor is convenient for code debugging.

We now turn our attention to game implementation.

IMPLEMENTATION

The implementation of the class is in part your responsibility. We describe briefly versions of several `Smiley` methods. These methods are

```
public Smiley(String w)
private boolean isValid(String s)
private void updateAnswer()
private void drawContour()
private void drawLeftEye()
```

The general constructor `Smiley(String s)` begins by processing its parameter s.

```
// process parameter
if (w != null) {
    word = w;
}
else {
    word = getRandomWord();
}
```

If parameter s is non-**null**, then it represents the mystery word to be guessed. If instead s is **null**, then a random word is used as the mystery word.

The constructor then creates the initial state of the game.

```
// initialize state information

// record number of letters still unfound
lettersLeft = word.length();

// current guess placeholder
guess = ' ';

// no errant guesses as of yet
errors = 0;

// the game is not over
gameOver = false;

// create mystery word representation, e.g., _ _ _ _ _ _ _
String s = "";
for (int i = 0; i < word.length(); ++i) {
    s += " _";
}
answer = new StringBuffer(s);
```

With this state information, the GUI can be configured. The configuration begins with the window that holds the other GUI components. In particular, the window is sized, colored, and has its closing policy set.

```
// configure GUI
window.setSize(WINDOW_WIDTH, WINDOW_HEIGHT);
window.setDefaultCloseOperation(JFrame.EXIT_ON_CLOSE);
window.setBackground(SKY_BLUE);
```

The components of the GUI are then colored to match the window.

```
Container c = window.getContentPane();

c.setBackground(window.getBackground());
guessPad.setBackground(c.getBackground());
answerPad.setBackground(c.getBackground());
resultPad.setBackground(c.getBackground());
pastPad.setBackground(c.getBackground());
updateButton.setBackground(c.getBackground());
```

The GUI elements requiring configuration are then set.

```
answerPad.setText(answer.toString());

updateButton.addActionListener(this);

facePad.setSize(CANVAS_WIDTH, CANVAS_HEIGHT);
facePad.setBackground(Color.white);

answerPad.setEditable(false);
pastPad.setEditable(false);

c.setLayout(new FlowLayout());
```

To complete the GUI, the configured elements are added to its content pane and the GUI is made visible.

```
c.add(answerLabel);
c.add(answerPad);
c.add(guessLabel);
c.add(guessPad);
c.add(updateButton);
c.add(facePad);
c.add(pastLabel);
c.add(pastPad);
c.add(resultPad);

window.setVisible(true);
```

Facilitator method `isValid()` determines whether the current guess is valid. The method begins the validation by examining the string s in the text area of `guessPad`.

```
// guess must be a single unseen letter
if (guess.length() != 1) {
    // not a single character
    return false;
}
else if (! Character.isLetter(guess.charAt(0))) {
    // not a letter
    return false;
}
else { // its a letter -- is it previously unseen
    String past = pastPad.getText();
    char c = Character.toLowerCase(guess.charAt(0));
    String s = "" + c;
    // indexOf() only returns -1 if the s is not there
    return (past.indexOf(s) == -1);
}
```

If the length of the guess s is not equal to 1, then the guess does not correspond to a single character and **false** is returned. Also, if the guess is not a letter, **false** is returned. Otherwise, a lowercase version of the guess is compared to the previous guesses. The return value for this case is based on whether the guess can be found among the previous guesses.

The purpose of method `updateAnswer()` is to update the state instance variables and `answerPad` with respect to the current guess. The method begins by assuming the guess is not part of the mystery word by setting local variable `foundMatch` to **false**.

```
// assume the character is not there
boolean foundMatch = false;
```

A **for** loop then considers the mystery word letter-by-letter. If the current letter in the word matches the guess, then `foundMatch` is set to **true** and the corresponding position in instance variable `answer` is set to the guess, thus revealing the letter to the user. In addition, the number of letters left to be guessed is decremented by one.

```
// go through word character by character and look for
// matches with guess
for (int i = 0; i < word.length(); ++i) {
```

```
    if (word.charAt(i) == guess) { // got a match
       foundMatch = true;
       --lettersLeft;
       answer.setCharAt(2*i + 1, guess);
    }
}
```

After the loop is finished, a test determines whether the number of errant guesses needs to be increased.

```
// update errors and gameOver as needed
if (! foundMatch) {
   ++errors;
}
else if (lettersLeft == 0) {
   gameOver = true;
}
```

If foundMatch is **false**, then the guess was not part of the mystery word and instance variable errors is incremened by one. If instead a match was found, then it may be the case that all letters have been guessed. If this condition is **true**, then instance variable gameOver is set to **true**.

Once these cases have been processed, all that remains for updateAnswer() to do is to use the updated value of answer to set the text area of answerPad.

```
// update GUI
answerPad.setText(answer.toString());
```

We next consider how to draw the face contour and the left eye. The face contour is an oval drawn by method drawContour(). The oval is to be slightly smaller than the size of the drawing canvas represented by Canvas instance variable facePad.

```
// drawContour(): draw the outline of the face
private void drawContour() {
   int w = facePad.getWidth();
   int h = facePad.getHeight();
   int ow = w - 2*OFFSET;
   int oh = h - 2*OFFSET;
   Graphics g = facePad.getGraphics();
   g.setColor(window.getBackground());
   g.fillOval(OFFSET, OFFSET, ow, oh);
}
```

Using facePad methods getWidth() and getHeight(), we can determine the width w and height h of the drawing canvas. The upper-left-hand corner of the oval's bounding box, will be at coordinate (OFFET, OFFSET) of the Canvas. By making the oval width ow equal to w - 2*OFFSET and the oval height oh equal to h - 2*OFFSET, the oval will be centered in the drawing canvas. (The use of OFFSET is depicted in Figure II.4.)

To draw the oval, the graphics context g of the canvas is first determined using method getGraphics(). By then invoking Graphics methods setColor() and fillOval() appropriately, the drawing color can be set and the oval can be rendered on the canvas.

Figure G.II.4 **A use of OFFSET for drawing.**

Method `drawLeftEye()` is used to draw a left eye. The method draws an oval that is 1/8 of the width and height of the drawing canvas. The upper-left-hand corner of the oval's bounding box is positioned 1/4 of the way down and 1/4 of the way over from the upper-left-hand corner of the oval representing the face contour. The actual rendering follows the same scheme as `drawContour()`.

```
// drawLeftEye(): draw the draw left eye
private void drawLeftEye() {
   int w = facePad.getWidth();
   int h = facePad.getHeight();
   int ow = w/8;
   it oh = h/8;
   Graphics g = facePad.getGraphics();
   g.setColor(Color.white);
   g.fillOval(OFFSET + w/4, OFFSET + h/4, ow, oh);
}
```

Method `drawNose()` is used to draw a nose. The method draws an oval that is 1/8 of the width and height of the drawing canvas. The upper-left-hand corner of the oval's bounding box is positioned approximately 1/2 of the way down and 1/2 of the way over from the upper-left-hand corner of the oval representing the face contour. The rendering follows the same scheme as `drawContour()` and `drawLeftEye()`.

```
// drawNose(): draw the nose for our face
private void drawNose() {
```

```
        int w = facePad.getWidth();
        int h = facePad.getHeight();
        int ow = w/8;
        int oh = h/8;
        Graphics g = facePad.getGraphics();
        g.setColor(Color.white);
        g.fillOval(OFFSET + w/2 - ow/2, OFFSET + h/2, ow, oh);
    }
```

IMPLEMENTATION RESPONSIBILITIES

Complete the partial implementation provided in Listing II.2. In particular, the following methods require design and implementation.

```
public void actionPerformed(ActionEvent e)
private void updatePast()
private void resetGuess()
private void updateStatus()
private void updateFace()
private void drawLeftEyebrow()
private void drawRightEye()
public void drawRightEyebrow()
private void drawMouth()
private String getRandomWord()
```

Of these methods, we discuss only `getRandomWord()`. Method `getRandomWord()` must return a random mystery word from file `"words.txt"`. There are two simple ways to accomplish this task. One way is to assign the possible words to an `ArrayList` and then use `Collections` class method `shuffle()` to arrange the words into a random order. Method `getRandomWord()` can then return the first word in the list. A second way is to choose a random number i from the interval $1 \ldots n$, where n is the number of words in the file. The ith word in the file, can then be returned. To generate the value of i, a `java.util.Random` object can be used. A `Random` object has several methods named `nextInt()` that should prove useful in initializing i.

TESTING

You should document any changes to our design and document your implementation. Also, document your program's behavior with print-screen snapshots of games in progress.

You may consider modifying method `main()` to support selection of the word to be guessed. That way the program can be tested easily for correctness—the tester knows ahead of time whether a guess should be valid and in what positions it appears.

Listing G.II.2 Smiley.java

```
1.  // Plays a game similar to hangman
2.
3.  import java.io.*;
4.  import java.util.*;
5.  import java.awt.*;
6.  import java.awt.event.*;
7.  import javax.swing.*;
8.
9.  public class Smiley implements ActionListener {
10.
11.     // class constants
12.     private final static String WORD_LIST = "words.txt";
13.     private final static int OFFSET = 2;
14.     private final static int FIELD_WIDTH = 20;
15.     private final static int CANVAS_WIDTH = 250;
16.     private final static int CANVAS_HEIGHT = 150;
17.     private final static int WINDOW_WIDTH = 300;
18.     private final static int WINDOW_HEIGHT = 340;
19.     private final static Color SKY_BLUE = new Color(198, 198, 255);
20.
21.     // GUI instance variables
22.
23.     // window: frame for GUI
24.     private JFrame window = new JFrame(" :-) Smiley");
25.
26.     // answerLabel and answerPad: area for displaying mystery word
27.     private JLabel answerLabel = new JLabel(" Word");
28.     private JTextField answerPad = new JTextField(FIELD_WIDTH);
29.
30.     // guessLabel and guessPad: entry area to make a guess
31.     private JLabel guessLabel = new JLabel("Guess");
32.     private JTextField guessPad = new JTextField(FIELD_WIDTH);
33.
34.     // updateButton: signaler that a new guess has been made
35.     private JButton updateButton = new JButton("Update");
36.
37.     // facePad: drawing area for face
38.     private Canvas facePad = new Canvas();
39.
40.     // pastLabel and pastPad: area for displaying past guesses
41.     private JLabel pastLabel = new JLabel("Past guesses");
42.     private JTextField pastPad = new JTextField(" ", FIELD_WIDTH);
43.
44.     // resultPad: status area for game result
45.     private JLabel resultPad = new JLabel(" ");
46.
47.     // game instance variables
48.     private String word;           // word to be guessed
49.     private StringBuffer answer;    // portion of word guess so far
50.     private char guess;            // current letter guess
51.     private int errors;            // how many bad guesses so far
52.     private int lettersLeft;       // how many letters still needed
53.     private boolean gameOver;      // has the game been won or lost
54.
```

Listing G.II.2 Smiley.java (Continued)

```
55.    // Smile(): word-specified constructor
56.    public Smiley(String w) throws IOException {
57.        // process parameter
58.        if (w != null) {
59.            word = w;
60.        }
61.        else {
62.            word = getRandomWord();
63.        }
64.
65.        // initialize state information
66.
67.        // record number of letters still unfound
68.        lettersLeft = word.length();
69.
70.        // current guess placeholder
71.        guess = ' ';
72.
73.        // no errant guesses as of yet
74.        errors = 0;
75.
76.        // the game is not over
77.        gameOver = false;
78.
79.        // create mystery word representation, e.g., _ _ _ _ _ _ _
80.        String s = "";
81.        for (int i = 0; i < word.length(); ++i) {
82.            s += " _";
83.        }
84.        answer = new StringBuffer(s);
85.
86.        // configure GUI
87.        window.setSize(WINDOW_WIDTH, WINDOW_HEIGHT);
88.        window.setDefaultCloseOperation(JFrame.EXIT_ON_CLOSE);
89.        window.setBackground(SKY_BLUE);
90.
91.        Container c = window.getContentPane();
92.
93.        c.setBackground(window.getBackground());
94.        guessPad.setBackground(c.getBackground());
95.        answerPad.setBackground(c.getBackground());
96.        resultPad.setBackground(c.getBackground());
97.        pastPad.setBackground(c.getBackground());
98.        updateButton.setBackground(c.getBackground());
99.
100.       answerPad.setText(answer.toString());
101.
102.       updateButton.addActionListener(this);
103.
104.       facePad.setSize(CANVAS_WIDTH, CANVAS_HEIGHT);
105.       facePad.setBackground(Color.white);
106.
107.       answerPad.setEditable(false);
108.       pastPad.setEditable(false);
```

Listing G.II.2 Smiley.java (Continued)

```
109.
110.          c.setLayout(new FlowLayout());
111.
112.          c.add(answerLabel);
113.          c.add(answerPad);
114.          c.add(guessLabel);
115.          c.add(guessPad);
116.          c.add(updateButton);
117.          c.add(facePad);
118.          c.add(pastLabel);
119.          c.add(pastPad);
120.          c.add(resultPad);
121.
122.          window.setVisible(true);
123.      }
124.
125.      // isValid(): is current guess valid
126.      private boolean isValid(String guess) {
127.          // guess must be a single unseen letter
128.          if (guess.length() != 1) {
129.              // not a single character
130.              return false;
131.          }
132.          else if (! Character.isLetter(guess.charAt(0))) {
133.              // not a letter
134.              return false;
135.          }
136.          else { // its a letter -- is it previously unseen
137.              String past = pastPad.getText();
138.              char c = Character.toLowerCase(guess.charAt(0));
139.              String s = "" + c;
140.              // indexOf() only returns -1 if the s is not there
141.              return (past.indexOf(s) == -1);
142.          }
143.      }
144.
145.      // updateAnswer(): see where current guess fits in word
146.      private void updateAnswer() {
147.          // assume the character is not there
148.          boolean foundMatch = false;
149.
150.          // go through word character by character and look for
151.          // matches with guess
152.          for (int i = 0; i < word.length(); ++i) {
153.              if (word.charAt(i) == guess) { // got a match
154.                  foundMatch = true;
155.                  --lettersLeft;
156.                  answer.setCharAt(2*i + 1, guess);
157.              }
158.          }
159.
160.          // update errors and gameOver as needed
161.          if (! foundMatch) {
162.              ++errors;
```

Listing G.II.2 Smiley.java (Continued)

```
163.          }
164.          else if (lettersLeft == 0) {
165.             gameOver = true;
166.          }
167.
168.          // update GUI
169.          answerPad.setText(answer.toString());
170.       }
171.
172.       // drawContour(): draw the outline of the face
173.       private void drawContour() {
174.          int w = facePad.getWidth();
175.          int h = facePad.getHeight();
176.          int ow = w - 2*OFFSET;
177.          int oh = h - 2*OFFSET;
178.          Graphics g = facePad.getGraphics();
179.          g.setColor(window.getBackground());
180.          g.fillOval(OFFSET, OFFSET, ow, oh);
181.       }
182.
183.       // drawLeftEye(): draw the draw left eye
184.       private void drawLeftEye() {
185.          int w = facePad.getWidth();
186.          int h = facePad.getHeight();
187.          int ow = w/8;
188.          int oh = h/8;
189.          Graphics g = facePad.getGraphics();
190.          g.setColor(Color.white);
191.          g.fillOval(OFFSET + w/4, OFFSET + h/4, ow, oh);
192.       }
193.
194.       // drawNose(): draw the nose for our face
195.       private void drawNose() {
196.          int w = facePad.getWidth();
197.          int h = facePad.getHeight();
198.          int ow = w/8;
199.          int oh = h/8;
200.          Graphics g = facePad.getGraphics();
201.          g.setColor(Color.white);
202.          g.fillOval(OFFSET + w/2 - ow/2, OFFSET + h/2, ow, oh);
203.       }
204.
205.       // main(): application entry point
206.       public static void main (String[] args) throws IOException {
207.          Smiley game = new Smiley();
208.       }
209.
210.       // ***************** methods to be completed *****************
211.
212.       // default constructor
213.       public Smiley() throws IOException {
214.          // to be completed
215.       }
216.
```

Listing G.II.2 Smiley.java (Continued)

```
217.    // getRandomWord(): choose a random word from word file. file
218.    // begins with number of words n, followed by n words
219.    private String getRandomWord() throws IOException {
220.        // to be completed
221.    }
222.
223.    // actionPerformed(): process interaction
224.    public void actionPerformed(ActionEvent e) {
225.        // to be completed
226.    }
227.    // updatePast(): add current guess to list of guesses
228.    private void updatePast() {
229.        // to be completed
230.    }
231.
232.    // resetGuess(): blank out current guess
233.    private void resetGuess() {
234.        // to be completed
235.    }
236.
237.    // updateStatus(): if game is over, report results
238.    private void updateStatus() {
239.        // to be completed
240.    }
241.
242.    // updateFace(): update the face based on error count
243.    private void updateFace() {
244.        // to be completed
245.    }
246.
247.    // drawLeftEyebrow(): draw the draw left eyebrow
248.    private void drawLeftEyebrow() {
249.        // to be completed
250.    }
251.
252.    // drawRightEye(): draw the draw right eye
253.    private void drawRightEye() {
254.        // to be completed
255.    }
256.
257.    // drawRightEyebrow(): draw the draw right eyebrow
258.    public void drawRightEyebrow() {
259.        // to be completed
260.    }
261.
262.    // drawMouth(): draw the mouth for our face
263.    private void drawMouth() {
264.        // to be completed
265.    }
266. }
267.
```

---

10 EXCEPTIONS

When a program is running, abnormal events can arise that prevent the intended program execution. Such events are known as *exceptions*. For example, suppose a program that computes quotients is given a denominator with value zero. Rather than producing an undefined result, Java generates—or in programing parlance, *throws*—an exception that indicates the arithmetic operation cannot be performed. Unless a program has been designed to *catch* and *handle* this exception, the program automatically terminates when the exception is thrown.

OBJECTIVES

- Consider some of the abnormal events that can occur during program execution.
- Explore the use of try blocks for code that may generate exceptions.
- Explore the use of catch blocks as exception handlers.
- Encourage robust programs that always end gracefully.

10.1   EXCEPTION HANDLING

An *exception* is an abnormal event that occurs during program execution. Some examples of abnormal events are attempts to manipulate nonexistent files, improper array subscripting, and improper arithmetic operations such as a divide by zero.

If an exception occurs and an *exception-handler* code segment is in effect for that exception, then flow of control is transferred to the handler. If an exception occurs and there is no handler for it, the program terminates.

Consider program A.java of Listing 10.1 that prompts and extracts the name of a file. From that file, two integer values are extracted, and their quotient is computed and displayed.

Listing 10.1   A.java

```
1.  import java.io.*;
2.
3.  public class A {
4.      // main(): application entry point
5.      public static void main(String[] args) throws IOException {
6.          // get filename
7.          BufferedReader stdin = new BufferedReader(
8.              new InputStreamReader(System.in));
9.          System.out.print("Filename: ");
10.         String s = stdin.readLine();
11.
12.         // set up file stream for processing
13.         BufferedReader filein = new BufferedReader(new FileReader(s));
14.
15.         // extract values and compute quotient
16.         int numerator = Integer.parseInt(filein.readLine());
17.         int denominator = Integer.parseInt(filein.readLine());
18.
19.         int quotient = numerator / denominator;
20.         System.out.println();
21.         System.out.println(numerator + " / " + denominator + " = "
22.             + quotient);
23.
24.         return;
25.     }
26. }
```

There is a **throws** expression in the method main() signature for class A. In fact, all of our previous interactive console programs have **throws** expressions in their method main() signatures (e.g., BMICalculator.java of Listing 2.10). Java requires the **throws** expression of any method that does not handle the I/O (input/output) exceptions it may generate. Its inclusion is a warning to users of the method. Such knowledge is important because if an invoked method does not handle an exception, then the exception is given to the invoking method to handle. If the invoking method does not handle the exception, then the *unwinding* process continues with the method that did the invoking of the invoking method, and so on. If no method is found in the unwinding process to handle the exception, then the program terminates.

Suppose program `A.java` is run and that the user specifies the file of interest to be a file `numbers.txt` containing the values 12 and 4 on successive lines. The I/O behavior of the program would be the following

```
cmd: java A
Filename: numbers.txt

12 / 4 = 3
```

In this run, the program's execution proceeded as planned—the user supplied a valid filename and the quotient was computed and displayed.

Now consider a program run, where the user misspells the intended filename.

```
cmd: java A
Filename: mumbers.txt
Exception in thread "main" java.io.FileNotFoundException:
   mumbers.txt (The system cannot find the file specified)
      at java.io.FileInputStream.open(Native Method)
      at java.io.FileInputStream.<init>(FileInputStream.java:103)
      at java.io.FileInputStream.<init>(FileInputStream.java:66)
      at java.io.FileReader.<init>(FileReader.java:39)
      at A.main(A.java:13)
```

Because file `mumbers.txt` does not exist, it cannot be opened for input processing. Therefore, the `BufferedReader` construction at line 13 of `A.java` cannot complete successfully. Under such circumstances, Java throws an exception of type `java.io.FileNotFoundException`, where `FileNotFoundException` is a subclass of `IOException`.

When an exception is thrown and not handled, Java generates a message to the standard error stream indicating where the exception occurred. When examining an exception message, it is sometimes easier to start with the last line of the message and work toward the first message line. The last line indicates the start of the process that caused the throwing of the exception.

The last message line in our example indicates that the exception was generated at line 13 of `A.java`. That line defines a `BufferedReader` variable `filein`. In reading the other message lines we see that in creating the `FileReader` used by the `Buffered-Reader` constructor, a `FileInputStream` was needed. This `FileInputStream` used a method `open()` that interacted with the file system. Because of the misspelled name, the file could not be opened. An exception reporting this problem was generated that eventually *propagated* to method `main()`. Because method `main()` did not handle the exception, Java terminated the program.

For this example, the program did not end *gracefully*—a user does not want to read the jargon of an exception message. An alternative is to use Java's **try-catch** mechanism. With this mechanism, code that deals with situations in which exceptions can arise is put in a **try** block, where a **try** block is a statement block with the keyword **try** preceding it. If an exception arises in a **try** block, Java will transfer control to the appropriate *exception handler* to handle the problem.

The exception handlers are **catch** blocks and they immediately follow the **try** block. A **catch** block is a statement block that begins with the keyword **catch** followed by a single parameter that specifies the type of exception to be handled by the block. There is usually a **catch** handler for each type of exception that can occur within the **try** block. The **catch** blocks are executed only if an exception is generated.

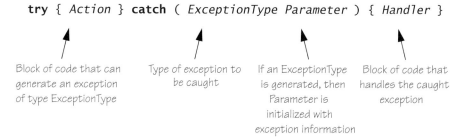

```
try { Action } catch ( ExceptionType Parameter ) { Handler }
```

Block of code that can generate an exception of type ExceptionType

Type of exception to be caught

If an ExceptionType is generated, then Parameter is initialized with exception information

Block of code that handles the caught exception

If an exception is thrown in a **try** block, then the first associated **catch** block whose parameter type matches the generated exception is used. If no **catch** block parameter matches the exception, then the invocation process is unwound automatically to find the appropriate exception handler. The unwinding process is depicted in Figure 10.1.

If a **catch** block is executed, then its parameter is initialized with information regarding the specifics of the exception. If the **catch** block does not end the program, then after the **catch** block completes, program execution continues with the statement following the **try**-**catch** construct.

As an example, the following code segment from program B.java of Listing 10.2 catches the exception generated by an invalid filename.

```java
// set up file stream for processing
BufferedReader filein = null;
try {
   filein = new BufferedReader(new FileReader(s));
}
catch (FileNotFoundException e) {
   System.err.println(s + ": cannot be opened for reading");
   System.exit(0);
}
```

The code segment defines the BufferedReader variable filein before the **try**-**catch** blocks so that it is available after the code segment. Like other block definitions, the scope of the definitions in a **try** or **catch** block is limited to that block.

The **try** block attempts to assign variable filein, a reference to a Buffered-Reader associated with the file indicated by variable s. If the BufferedReader construction runs as planned (i.e., the file can be opened), then program execution continues with the statement that follows the **try**-**catch** construct (line 23). The result is an I/O behavior similar to A.java.

```
cmd: java B
Filename: numbers.txt

12 / 4 = 3
```

Figure 10.1 **Exception-handling process.**

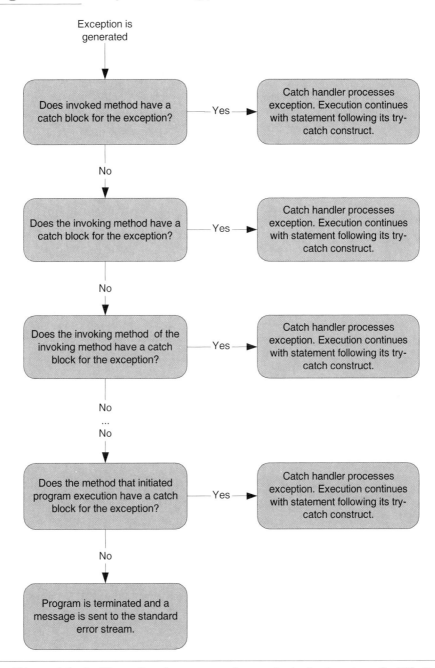

If instead the BufferedReader construction results in the throwing of a FileNot-FoundException, then the program handles the exception with its **catch** block.

Listing 10.2   B.java

```java
1.  import java.io.*;
2.
3.  public class B {
4.      // main(): application entry point
5.      public static void main(String[] args) throws IOException {
6.          // get filename
7.          BufferedReader stdin = new BufferedReader(
8.                  new InputStreamReader(System.in));
9.          System.out.print("Filename: ");
10.         String s = stdin.readLine();
11.
12.         // set up file stream for processing
13.         BufferedReader filein = null;
14.         try {
15.             filein = new BufferedReader(new FileReader(s));
16.         }
17.         catch (FileNotFoundException e) {
18.             System.err.println(s + ": cannot be opened for reading");
19.             System.exit(0);
20.         }
21.
22.         // extract values and compute quotient
23.         int numerator = Integer.parseInt(filein.readLine());
24.         int denominator = Integer.parseInt(filein.readLine());
25.
26.         int quotient = numerator / denominator;
27.         System.out.println();
28.         System.out.println(numerator + " / " + denominator + " = "
29.                 + quotient);
30.
31.         return;
32.     }
33. }
```

Because it does not make sense for the program to proceed without a valid filename, the **catch** block generates an error message and exits the program.

```
cmd: java B
Filename: mumbers.txt
mumbers.txt: cannot be opened for reading
```

A question you may have asked yourself is "Why does method main() of B.java have a **throws** expression if it is catching the FileNotFoundException?" It does so because it is still possible for the program to throw an IOException. In particular, any of the readLine() invocations in method main() can generate an IOException if there is a file-system failure.

To remove the necessity of having the **throws** expression as part of the method main() signature, the readLine() invocations need to be within **try** block(s). Program C.java of Listing 10.3 wraps the readLine() invocations within two **try** blocks. One **try** block performs the readline() invocation that attempts to extract the filename; the other **try** block performs the readline() invocations that attempt to extract the numerator and denominator.

Listing 10.3 **C.java**

```java
1.  import java.io.*;
2.
3.  public class C {
4.      // main(): application entry point
5.      public static void main(String[] args) {
6.          // get filename
7.          BufferedReader stdin = new BufferedReader(
8.              new InputStreamReader(System.in));
9.          System.out.print("Filename: ");
10.         String s = null;
11.         try {
12.             s = stdin.readLine();
13.         }
14.         catch (IOException e) {
15.             System.err.println("Cannot read input");
16.             System.exit(0);
17.         }
18.
19.         // set up file stream for processing
20.         BufferedReader filein = null;
21.         try {
22.             filein = new BufferedReader(new FileReader(s));
23.         }
24.         catch (FileNotFoundException e) {
25.             System.err.println(s + ": cannot be opened for reading");
26.             System.exit(0);
27.         }
28.
29.         // extract values and compute quotient
30.         try {
31.             int numerator = Integer.parseInt(filein.readLine());
32.             int denominator = Integer.parseInt(filein.readLine());
33.
34.             int quotient = numerator / denominator;
35.             System.out.println();
36.             System.out.println(numerator + " / " + denominator + " = "
37.                 + quotient);
38.         }
39.         catch (IOException e) {
40.             System.err.println(s + ": unable to read values");
41.             System.exit(0);
42.         }
43.
44.         return;
45.     }
46. }
```

With its IOException handling ability, it *appears* that program C.java is well-engineered to handle user miscues. However, suppose we run the program using the file values.txt, where values.txt consists of the lines

```
12
b
```

A program run using this file generates the following I/O behavior.

```
cmd: java C
Filename: values.txt
Exception in thread "main" java.lang.NumberFormatException: b
    at java.lang.Integer.parseInt(Integer.java:426)
    at java.lang.Integer.parseInt(Integer.java:476)
    at C.main(C.java:32)
```

The problem is one of input format—character 'b' is not the representation of an integer.

Suppose we run the program with the file one.txt that contains only the value 12. A program run using this file generates the following I/O behavior.

```
cmd: java C
Filename: one.txt
Exception in thread "main" java.lang.NumberFormatException: null
at java.lang.Integer.parseInt(Integer.java:394)
    at java.lang.Integer.parseInt(Integer.java:476)
    at C.main(C.java:32)
```

The problem is again one of input format—value **null** is not a reference to an integer representation.

Suppose we run the program using the file data.txt, where data.txt contains on separate lines, the values 12 and 0. A program run using this file generates the following I/O behavior.

```
cmd: java C
Filename: data.txt
Exception in thread "main" java.lang.ArithmeticException: / by
  zero
    at C.main(C.java:34)
```

The problem is now one of illegal arithmetic—division is not defined for a denominator with value 0.

The two *format* and one *arithmetic exceptions* arising in the preceding cases are examples of *runtime exceptions*. The superclass for all runtime exceptions is java.lang.RuntimeException. Because runtime exceptions can occur throughout a program and because the cost of implementing handlers for them typically exceeds the expected benefit, Java makes it optional for a method to catch them or to specify that it throws them.

Because runtime exceptions need not be caught, they are also known as *unchecked exceptions*. All other exceptions are known as *checked exceptions*. The checked exceptions that a method may generate must be either caught by one of its exception handlers or listed in the **throws** expression of the method.

Program D.java of Listing 10.4 continues with our quotient-calculating example and does handle the format and arithmetic exceptions that C.java did not handle. For this particular problem, the handling of these runtime exceptions is appropriate because well-crafted programs ensure the validity of their input. Program D.java's handling of the input validity exceptions is accomplished by adding two more **catch** blocks to the **try** block for computing the quotient.

Listing 10.4 D.java

```
1.  import java.io.*;
2.
3.  public class D {
4.      // main(): application entry point
5.      public static void main(String[] args) {
6.          // get filename
7.          BufferedReader stdin = new BufferedReader(
8.              new InputStreamReader(System.in));
9.          System.out.print("Filename: ");
10.         String s = null;
11.         try {
12.             s = stdin.readLine();
13.         }
14.         catch (IOException e) {
15.             System.err.println("Cannot read input");
16.             System.exit(0);
17.         }
18.
19.         // set up file stream for processing
20.         BufferedReader filein = null;
21.         try {
22.             filein = new BufferedReader(new FileReader(s));
23.         }
24.         catch (FileNotFoundException e) {
25.             System.err.println(s + ": cannot be opened for reading");
26.             System.exit(0);
27.         }
28.
29.         // extract values and compute quotient
30.         try {
31.             int numerator = Integer.parseInt(filein.readLine());
32.             int denominator = Integer.parseInt(filein.readLine());
33.
34.             int quotient = numerator / denominator;
35.             System.out.println();
36.             System.out.println(numerator + " / " + denominator + " = "
37.                 + quotient);
38.         }
39.         catch (IOException e) {
40.             System.err.println(s + ": unable to read values");
41.             System.exit(0);
42.         }
43.         catch (NumberFormatException e) {
44.             if (e.getMessage().equals("null")) {
45.                 System.err.println(s + ": doesn't contain two inputs");
46.             }
47.             else {
48.                 System.err.println(s + ": contains nonnumeric inputs");
49.             }
50.             System.exit(0);
51.         }
52.         catch (ArithmeticException e) {
53.             System.err.println(s + ": unexpected 0 input value");
54.             System.exit(0);
```

Listing 10.4   **D.java (Continued)**

```
55.        }
56.
57.        return;
58.     }
59. }
```

The first new **catch** block handler processes a NumberFormatException.

```
catch (NumberFormatException e) {
   if (e.getMessage().equals("null")) {
      System.err.println(s + ": doesn't contain two inputs");
   }
   else {
      System.err.println(s + ": contains nonnumeric inputs");
   }
   System.exit(0);
}
```

Because this exception can arise with either insufficient or malformed inputs, the handler tests the return value of Exception instance method getMessage(), where class java.lang.Exception is the superclass of all exception classes. This method returns a String message indicating why the exception was thrown. Because class method Integer.parseInt() throws an exception with message "null" only if its actual parameter has value **null**, the e.getMessage().equals("null") test is sufficient for determining why the exception was generated.

The second new **catch** block handler processes an ArithmeticException. For the **try** block, this exception is generated only if a divide-by-0 is attempted.

```
catch (ArithmeticException e) {
   System.err.println(s + ": unexpected 0 input value");
   System.exit(0);
}
```

The following I/O behavior shows three runs of program D.java using the previously described files one.txt, data.txt. and values.txt.

```
cmd: java D
Filename: one.txt
one.txt: doesn't contain two inputs

cmd: java D
Filename: data.txt
data.txt: unexpected 0 input value

cmd: java D
Filename: values.txt
values.txt: contains nonnumeric inputs
```

At this point, we can claim that we have a well-engineered solution to the quotient problem.

Why exception handle?

Although Java's exception-handling mechanism sometimes appears excessive to the beginning programmer, the mechanism truly is needed if programs are to follow the object-oriented programming paradigm. For example, suppose an error occurred within a method f() that was invoked by a method g() that was invoked by a method h(). Suppose further that to correct the error, method h() that initiated this invocation sequence must regain the flow of control. Without the exception-handling mechanism there would be no way to unwind the method invocations to enable corrective action to take place at the true problem source.

10.2 FINALLY AND THE COMMAND TYPE

Although not strictly necessary, Java provides a syntax for a handler block that is *always* run after the **try** block or **catch** handler have completed their tasks. The special handler is introduced through the keyword **finally**.

A **finally** handler is used by program Type.java of Listing 10.5. The program displays to standard output the contents of the files whose names are given to the program as command-line parameters. Thus, the program mimics the operation of the Windows command type and the Unix/Linux command cat.

The program begins with a **for** loop that iterates once for each of the command-line parameters to the program. The **for** loop body consists of nested **try-catch** blocks.

For each iteration i, the outer **try** block first attempts to define a BufferedReader variable filein that references the file stream with the name specified by args[i].

```
try {
   BufferedReader filein = BufferedReader(
      new FileReader(args[i]));
   // argv[i] is a readable filename
   ...
}
catch (FileNotFoundException e) {
   // argv[i] is not a valid filename
   System.err.println(args[i] + ": cannot be opened");
}
```

If the file stream cannot be opened, the **try** block throws a FileNotFoundException that is caught by the **catch** handler. The handler then displays an appropriate error message.

If the file stream can be opened, then the inner **try** block is attempted. This **try** block displays the contents of the file referenced by filein using a **while** loop that iter-

Listing 10.5   *Type.java*

```
1.  // Mimics operating system command type
2.
3.  import java.io.*;
4.
5.  public class Type {
6.
7.      // main(): application entry point
8.      public static void main(String[] args) {
9.          // each command-line parameter is treated as a filename
10.         // whose contents are displayed to standard output
11.         for (int i = 0; i < args.length; ++i) {
12.             // open input stream associated with i-th file parameter
13.             try {
14.                 BufferedReader filein = new BufferedReader(
15.                     new FileReader(args[i]));
16.                 // argv[i] is a readable filename
17.                 try {
18.                     String s = filein.readLine();
19.                     while (s != null) {
20.                         System.out.println(s);
21.                         s = filein.readLine();
22.                     }
23.                 }
24.                 catch (IOException e) {
25.                     System.err.println(args[i] + ": processing error");
26.                 }
27.                 finally {
28.                     try {
29.                         filein.close();
30.                     }
31.                     catch (IOException e) {
32.                         System.err.println(args[i] + ": system error");
33.                     }
34.                 }
35.             }
36.             catch (FileNotFoundException e) {
37.                 // argv[i] is not a valid filename
38.                 System.err.println(args[i] + ": cannot be opened");
39.             }
40.         }
41.     }
42. }
```

ates while `String` variable s is non-**null**.

```
        try {
            String s = filein.readLine();
            while (s != null) {
                System.out.println(s);
                s = filein.readLine();
            }
        }
        catch (IOException e) {
            System.err.println(args[i] + ": processing error");
        }
```

```
finally {
   try {
      filein.close();
   }
   catch (IOException e) {
      System.err.println(args[i] + ": system error");
   }
}
```

If an IOException is thrown by a readline() invocation, then there is a file-system error. The **catch** handler for the exception displays an appropriate message.

Regardless whether the file is displayed successfully or an exception is thrown, the file stream should be closed when either the **try** or **catch** block has completed. The **finally** block handles this activity. By using a **finally** block we do not need to repeat the close() invocation in both of the inner **try** and **catch** blocks. Because a close() invocation generates an IOException if there is a file-system problem. the close() invocation is embedded within its own **try-catch** construct.

```
finally {
   try {
      filein.close();
   }
   catch (IOException e) {
      System.err.println(args[i] + ": system error");
   }
}
```

We next turn our attention to the throwing of exceptions to indicate a malformed request.

10.3   CREATING AND THROWING EXCEPTIONS

The keyword **throw** has two uses in Java. Our use so far has been to head a **try** block. The other use is signaling an exception. A statement of the form

throw *exception* ;

is an exception-throwing statement, where *exception* specifies the necessary exception information. Our next example, class BankAccount makes use of this signaling mechanism. Class BankAccount throws NegativeAmountException exceptions, where class NegativeAmountException is a class that we also will define.

Class BankAccount maintains a bank account balance. Its constructors and methods throw a NegativeAmountException if there is an attempt to make the balance negative, deposit a negative amount, or withdraw a negative amount.

Class BankAccount supports two constructors—creating a new bank account with an empty balance and creating a new bank account with a positive balance.

`public BankAccount()`

Creates a new bank account with an empty balance.

> **public** BankAccount(**int** n) **throws** NegativeAmountException

Attempts to create a new bank account with an initial balance of n. If n is negative, a NegativeAmountException is thrown.

The class uses instance variable balance to keep track of the current bank account
balance.

> **private** balance

Represents the balance of this bank account.

Class BankAccount provides three instance methods to support balance access and
manipulation.

> **public int** getBalance()

Returns the balance of this bank account.

> **public void int** addFunds(**int** n) **throws** NegativeAmountException

Attempts to deposit a positive amount n into this bank account. If n is positive,
the balance is increased by amount n. If n is negative, a NegativeAmountException is thrown.

> **public void** removeFunds(**int** n) **throws** NegativeAmountException

Attempts to withdraw a positive amount n from this bank account. If n is negative, a NegativeAmountException is thrown. If n is positive and less than or
equal to the current balance, then the balance is increased by amount n; otherwise, a NegativeAmountException is thrown.

Listing 10.6 **NegativeAmountException.java**

```
1. // Represents an abnormal bank account event
2.
3. public class NegativeAmountException extends Exception {
4.    // NegativeAmountException(): creates exception with message s
5.    public NegativeAmountException(String s) {
6.       super(s);
7.    }
8. }
```

Class NegativeAmountException of Listing 10.6 is a specialized exception class
for indicating abnormal bank account manipulation. The behaviors wanted of a NegativeAmountException are just the normal exception behaviors (e.g., using inherited
method getMessage() to query an exception regarding its message).

> **public** NegativeAmountException(String s)

Creates a new NegativeAmountException with message s.

The definition of the NegativeAmountException constructor is straightforward. It
invokes the constructor of its superclass Exception with s as the message for the new
exception.

Listing 10.7 gives the definition of class BankAccount. With the existence of class
NegativeAmountException, the BankAccount constructors and methods all have
simple implementations. For example, the specific BankAccount constructor needs only

Listing 10.7 BankAccount.java

```
1.  // Represents a bank account balance
2.
3.  public class BankAccount {
4.     // instance variable
5.     int balance;
6.
7.     // BankAccount(): default constructor for a new empty balance
8.     public BankAccount() {
9.        balance = 0;
10.    }
11.
12.    // BankAccount(): specific constructor for a new balance n
13.    public BankAccount(int n) throws NegativeAmountException {
14.       if (n >= 0) {
15.          balance = n;
16.       }
17.       else {
18.          throw new NegativeAmountException("Bad balance");
19.       }
20.    }
21.
22.    // getBalance(): return the current balance
23.    public int getBalance() {
24.          return balance;
25.    }
26.
27.    // addFunds(): deposit amount n
28.    public void addFunds(int n) throws NegativeAmountException {
29.       if (n >= 0) {
30.          balance += n;
31.       }
32.       else {
33.          throw new NegativeAmountException("Bad deposit");
34.       }
35.    }
36.
37.    // removeFunds(): withdraw amount n
38.    public void removeFunds(int n) throws NegativeAmountException {
39.       if (n < 0) {
40.          throw new NegativeAmountException("Bad withdrawal");
41.       }
42.       else if (balance < n) {
43.          throw new NegativeAmountException("Bad balance");
44.       }
45.       else {
46.          balance -= n;
47.       }
48.    }
49. }
```

to examine its parameter n to determine if a new bank account is to be created with balance n or whether an exception is being thrown.

```
// BankAccount(): specific constructor for a new balance n
public BankAccount(int n) throws NegativeAmountException {
   if (n >= 0) {
      balance = n;
   }
   else {
      throw new NegativeAmountException("Bad balance");
   }
}
```

If the constructor is given a negative value for n, then **throw** statement

```
throw new NegativeAmountException("Bad balance");
```

is executed. This **throw** statement generates a new NegativeAmountException. Associated with the exception is the message "Bad Balance".

Similarly, method addFunds() needs only to examine its parameter n to determine if a deposit should be entered or whether an exception should be thrown.

```
// addFunds(): deposit amount n
public void addFunds(int n) throws NegativeAmountException {
   if (n >= 0) {
      balance += n;
   }
   else {
      throw new NegativeAmountException("Bad deposit");
   }
}
```

If the deposit is negative, then statement

```
throw new NegativeAmountException("Bad deposit");
```

is executed. This **throw** statement generates a new NegativeAmountException with message "Bad deposit".

Method removeFunds() processes a withdrawal. There are two ways a withdrawal can be improper: the withdrawal amount is negative or the withdrawal amount makes the balance negative.

```
// removeFunds(): withdraw amount n
public void removeFunds(int n) throws NegativeAmountException {
   if (n < 0) {
      throw new NegativeAmountException("Bad withdrawal");
   }
   else if (balance < n) {
      throw new NegativeAmountException("Bad balance");
   }
   else {
      balance -= n;
   }
}
```

Listing 10.8 Deposits.java

```
1.  // Demonstrates use of BankAccount and NegativeAmountException
2.
3.  import java.io.*;
4.
5.  public class Deposits {
6.      // main(): application entry point
7.      public static void main(String[] args)
8.          throws IOException, NegativeAmountException {
9.          BufferedReader stdin = new BufferedReader(
10.             new InputStreamReader(System.in));
11.
12.         BankAccount savings = new BankAccount();
13.
14.         System.out.print("Enter first deposit: ");
15.         int deposit = Integer.parseInt(stdin.readLine());
16.         savings.addFunds(deposit);
17.
18.         System.out.print("Enter second deposit: ");
19.         deposit = Integer.parseInt(stdin.readLine());
20.         savings.addFunds(deposit);
21.
22.         System.out.println("Closing balance: "
23.             + savings.getBalance());
24.     }
25. }
```

A negative withdrawal amount is handled by throwing an exception with message "Bad withdrawal".

```
throw new NegativeAmountException("Bad withdrawal");
```

And a withdrawal that would leave the balance negative is handled by throwing an exception with message "Bad balance".

```
throw new NegativeAmountException("Bad balance");
```

A demonstration of classes BankAccount and NegativeAmountException is given in program Deposits.java of Listing 10.8. The program creates a new BankAccount and then processes several deposit requests. Runs of the program are shown in Figure 10.2. The second run shows what happens if a negative deposit is made. The self-exercises consider adding a **try-catch** block construct to Deposits.java to handle NegativeAmountException exceptions.

We next turn our attention to a class ValueReader that provides extended input stream processing capabilities. Class ValueReader makes use of exception handling in accomplishing its tasks.

Figure 10.2 Sample Deposits.java runs.

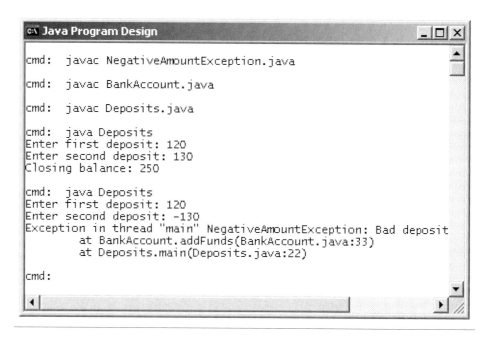

```
cmd:   javac NegativeAmountException.java

cmd:   javac BankAccount.java

cmd:   javac Deposits.java

cmd:   java Deposits
Enter first deposit: 120
Enter second deposit: 130
Closing balance: 250

cmd:   java Deposits
Enter first deposit: 120
Enter second deposit: -130
Exception in thread "main" NegativeAmountException: Bad deposit
        at BankAccount.addFunds(BankAccount.java:33)
        at Deposits.main(Deposits.java:22)

cmd:
```

10.4   CASE STUDY — VALUE-BY-VALUE EXTRACTION

When developing interactive console applications, we first used the class `BufferedReader` to extract input. Then in Chapter 9, we developed the class `ImprovedReader` of Listing 9.5 that extended `BufferedReader` functionality by providing methods `getInt()` and `getDouble()`. Both methods extract the next input line and return respectively the **int** or **double** value represented on that line.

> The objective of this case study is to practice exception handling, class design, and deriving specialized input stream representations

The extensions of class `ImprovedReader` definitely offer convenience. However, the class has the same significant limitation as `BufferedReader`—non-**char** input can be extracted only on a line-by-line basis.

We now design and implement a class `ValueReader` whose methods besides supporting character-by-character or line-by-line extraction also support the extracting of primitive value and string inputs on a value-by-value basis. A demonstration of class `ValueReader` is given with `ValueDemo.java` of Listing 10.9.

Listing 10.9   ValueDemo.java

```
1.  // ValueDemo: demonstrates use of ValueReader
2.
3.  import ez.ValueReader;
4.  import java.io.*;
5.
6.  public class ValueDemo {
7.      // main(): application entry point
8.      public static void main(String[] args) throws IOException {
9.          ValueReader filein = new ValueReader("names.txt");
10.         String word = filein.getString();
11.         while (! filein.EOF()) {
12.             System.out.println(word);
13.             word = filein.getString();
14.         }
15.     }
16. }
```

Program `ValueDemo.java` lists in a single column all of the words in the file, `names.txt`. For example, if `names.txt` contains

```
Hannah Jenna JJ
Emily Zachary
```

then the program output would be

```
Hannah
Jenna
JJ
Emily
Zachary
```

Another demonstration of class ValueReader is given with ValueSum.java of Listing 10.10 and the definition of class ValueReader is given in Listing 10.11. Program ValueSum.java sums all of the numbers provided in standard input. A sample run of the program is given in Figure 10.3.

Listing 10.10 ValueSum.java

```java
1.  // ValueSum: demonstrates use of ValueReader
2.
3.  import ez.ValueReader;
4.  import java.io.*;
5.
6.  public class ValueSum {
7.     // main(): application entry point
8.     public static void main(String[] args) throws IOException {
9.        ValueReader stdin = new ValueReader(System.in);
10.
11.       double inputSum = 0;
12.
13.       System.out.println("Enter numbers to be summed");
14.       String currentInput = stdin.getString();
15.       while (currentInput != null) {
16.          double number = Double.parseDouble(currentInput);
17.          inputSum += number;
18.          currentInput = stdin.getString();
19.       }
20.
21.       System.out.println("\n\n" + "Sum: " + inputSum);
22.    }
23. }
```

Figure 10.3 **Sample ValueSum.java run.**

Listing 10.11 ValueReader.java

```
1.   // ValueReader: extends BufferedReader for enhanced reading
2.
3.   package ez;
4.
5.   import java.io.*;
6.   import java.lang.*;
7.
8.   public class ValueReader extends BufferedReader {
9.       // instance variables
10.      private String inputLine = null;    // current input line
11.      private boolean haveEOF = false;    // do we have EOF
12.
13.      // ValueReader(): convenience constructor for an InputStream
14.      public ValueReader(InputStream in) {
15.          this(new InputStreamReader(in));
16.      }
17.
18.      // ValueReader(): convenience constructor for a filename
19.      public ValueReader(String s) throws FileNotFoundException {
20.          this(new FileReader(s));
21.      }
22.
23.      // ValueReader(): standard stream constructor
24.      public ValueReader(Reader in) {
25.          super(in);
26.      }
27.
28.      // getInt(): get next input value as an int
29.      public int getInt() throws IOException, NumberFormatException {
30.          String s = getString();
31.          return Integer.parseInt(s);
32.      }
33.
34.      // getDouble(): get next input value as a double
35.      public double getDouble()
36.                      throws IOException, NumberFormatException {
37.          String s = getString();
38.          return Double.valueOf(s).doubleValue();
39.      }
40.
41.      // getString(): get next whitespace-free string
42.      public String getString() throws IOException {
43.          // make sure the buffer has a string in it
44.          do {
45.              getInputAsNeeded();
46.              trimLeadingWhitespace();
47.          } while (!EOF() && (inputLine.length() == 0));
48.
49.          if (EOF()) { // no more input, so cannot return a string
50.              return null;
51.          }
52.
53.          // extract the first string from the nonempty buffer
54.          int n = inputLine.length();
```

Listing 10.11 ValueReader.java (Continued)

```
55.          for (int i = 1; i < n; ++i) {
56.              // if there is more than one string, then the first
57.              // string is followed by whitespace
58.              if (Character.isWhitespace(inputLine.charAt(i))) {
59.                  // found whitespace, so do the extraction
60.                  String s = inputLine.substring(0, i);
61.                  inputLine = inputLine.substring(i);
62.                  return s;
63.              }
64.          }
65.
66.          // no whitespace, so first and only string is the buffer
67.          String s = inputLine;
68.
69.          inputLine = "";
70.
71.          return s;
72.      }
73.
74.      // EOF(): is there a value to get
75.      public boolean EOF() {
76.          return haveEOF;
77.      }
78.
79.      // setEOF(): indicate that there are no more values to get
80.      protected void setEOF() {
81.          haveEOF = true;
82.      }
83.
84.      // trimLeadingWhitespace(): remove leading whitespace from
85.      // current input line
86.      protected void trimLeadingWhitespace() {
87.          // can only trim from a line that exists
88.          if (inputLine == null) {
89.              return;
90.          }
91.
92.          // can only trim a line with whitespace at the beginning
93.          while ((inputLine.length() > 0)
94.                  && Character.isWhitespace(inputLine.charAt(0))) {
95.              // trim the initial whitespace character
96.              inputLine = inputLine.substring(1);
97.          }
98.      }
99.
100.     // getInputAsNeeded(): update input line buffer if current
101.     // buffer has been used up
102.     protected void getInputAsNeeded() throws IOException {
103.         // test determine whether we need to get input
104.         if (EOF() || ((inputLine != null)
105.                     && inputLine.length() != 0)) {
106.             return;
107.         }
108.
```

Listing 10.11 **ValueReader.java (Continued)**

```
109.        // need to refill the buffer
110.        try {
111.           inputLine = super.readLine();
112.           if (inputLine == null) {
113.              // eof has been reached
114.              setEOF();
115.           }
116.        }
117.        catch (IOException e) {
118.           inputLine = null;
119.           setEOF();
120.           throw e;
121.        }
122.     }
123.
124.     // readLine(): override superclass method for returning
125.     // contents of input line buffer
126.     public String readLine() throws IOException {
127.        getInputAsNeeded();
128.        String result = inputLine;
129.        inputLine = null;
130.        return result;
131.     }
132.
133.     // read(): override superclass method for returning next
134.     // character from input line buffer
135.     public int read() throws IOException {
136.        getInputAsNeeded();
137.        if (EOF()) {
138.           // no character is available
139.           return -1;
140.        }
141.        else if (inputLine.length() == 0) {
142.           // buffer is used up, so return a linefeed
143.           inputLine = null;
144.           return '\n';
145.        }
146.        else {
147.           // got a character to extract from the buffer
148.           char result = inputLine.charAt(0);
149.           if (inputLine.length() == 1) {
150.              inputLine = "";
151.           }
152.           else {
153.              inputLine = inputLine.substring(1);
154.           }
155.           return result;
156.        }
157.     }
158. }
```

ANALYSIS AND DESIGN

Besides having methods that extract the next value from an input stream, programmers find it convenient to have a variety of constructors that support input processing. This preference means that `ValueReader` should support construction using an existing input stream or using a file whose name is specified by either a `String` or `File` representation. (The implementation of the `File`-based constructor is left to the exercises). `Value-Reader` should also provide a method `EOF()` that indicates whether end-of-file has been reached on the associated input stream.

`public ValueReader(InputStream in)`

Constructs a `ValueReader` from the stream referenced by `in`.

`public ValueReader(String s)`

Constructs a `ValueReader` from the file stream whose name is given by `s`.

`public ValueReader(Reader in)`

Constructs a `ValueReader` from the stream referenced by `in`, where `Reader` is the abstract base class in the Java hierarchy of streams with reading capability (e.g., `BufferedReader` and `FileReader`).

`public EOF()`

Indicates whether end-of-file has been reached on the input stream.

Our `ValueReader` implementation provides five methods for extracting values.

`public int getInt()`

Returns the next value from the input stream as an **int** value by returning `Integer.parseInt(getString())`.

`public double getDouble()`

Returns the next value from the input stream as a **double** value by returning `Double.parseInt(getString())`.

`public String getString()`

Returns the next maximal sequence of nonwhitespace characters from the input stream as `String`.

`public int read()`

If end-of-file has not been reached, the method returns the next previously unreturned character from the input stream as an **int** value. If end-of-file has been reached, the method returns –1. Thus, the method mimics the behavior of base class method `read()`.

`public String readLine()`

Returns the previously unreturned portion of the current input line.

The exercises consider the adding of methods (e.g., **short** and **long** extraction).

To support the constructors and methods, two instance variables are appropriate—`inputLine` and `haveEOF`.

`private String inputLine`

If non-**null**, the variable references the unreturned portion of the input line most recently extracted from the input stream. If **null**, the variable indicates the input line most recently extracted from the input stream has been returned completely. With this scheme, the initial value of the variable should be **null**.

`private boolean haveEOF`

Indicates whether end-of-file has been reached. As such, the variable is initialized to **false**.

We now turn our attention to the implementation of ValueReader.

IMPLEMENTATION

The ValueReader constructors all have straightforward implementations. The constructors ValueReader(InputStream in) and ValueReader(String s) both use constructor ValueReader(Reader in) to accomplish their construction.

```
public ValueReader(InputStream in) {
    this(new InputStreamReader(in));
}

// ValueReader(): convenience constructor for a filename
public ValueReader(String s) throws FileNotFoundException {
    this(new FileReader(s));
}
```

Because the instance variables have definitions

```
// instance variables
private String inputLine = null;    // current input line
private boolean haveEOF = false;    // do we have EOF
```

the only explicit action that constructor ValueReader(Reader in) must take is to
invoke the superclass constructor of BufferedReader.

```
// ValueReader(): standard stream constructor
public ValueReader(Reader in) {
    super(in);
}
```

The implementations of the stream accessors methods getInt() and getDouble()
are also straightforward—they both parse the value returned by a getString() invocation into a proper return type for their method.

```
// getInt(): get next input value as an int
public int getInt() throws IOException, NumberFormatException {
    String s = getString();
    return Integer.parseInt(s);
}

// getDouble(): get next input value as a double
public double getDouble()
                throws IOException, NumberFormatException {
    String s = getString();
    return Double.valueOf(s).doubleValue();
}
```

Because the implementation of getString() is not straightforward, we first present
and analyze the *pseudocode* (algorithm) that was the basis of our implementation of the
method.

```
do
    if inputLine is null then
        update inputLine with the next input line
    end
    Remove any leading whitespace in inputLine
while end-of-file has not occurred and inputLine is nonempty
```

```
if end-of-file has occurred then
    return null
end

for i = 1 to inputLine.getLength() do
    if the ith character in inputLine is whitespace then
        s = inputLine.substring(0, i)
        inputLine = inputLine.substring(i)
        return s
    end
end

s = inputLine
inputLine = null
```

return s

The algorithm begins with a loop that iterates either until end-of-file has been reached or until the `String` referenced by `inputLine` starts with a nonwhitespace character. The body of the loop acts in the following manner. If `inputLine` is currently **null**, then `inputLine` is assigned the next line of input (if any). Any leading whitespace then is deleted from the `String` referenced by `inputLine`. The whitespace deletion is necessary because `getString()` returns the next maximal sequence of nonwhitespace characters.

After the loop completes, a test determines how the loop terminated. If the loop terminated because of end-of-file, then no suitable string could be extracted and the method returns the **null** value. Otherwise, a search is made to determine whether the string referenced by `inputLine` contains embedded whitespace. If the string does contain embedded whitespace, then the portion of the string before the first whitespace character is the return value for the method. In addition, a reference to the remaining portion is assigned to `inputLine`

If the **for** loop completes, then it must be the case that the string referenced by `inputLine` has no embedded whitespace. Therefore, the entire contents of `inputLine` form the return value. This use means that `inputLine` must be emptied because all of its contents have been returned.

Our implementation of the `getString()` algorithm uses **protected** ValueReader facilitators `getInputAsNeeded()` and `trimLeadingWhitespace()`. The two methods have **protected** access rights because their purpose is to support the implementation of the **public** methods. In addition to these methods, class ValueReader also defines the **protected** mutator method `setEOF()`.

protected getInputAsNeeded()

If `inputLine` is non-**null** or if end-of-file has already occurred, then no action is taken. Otherwise, an attempt is made to update `inputLine` with the next line from the input stream. If there is no more input, then end-of-file status is set for the stream and `inputLine` is made **null**.

protected trimLeadingWhitespace()

> If inputLine is **null**, no action is taken. Otherwise, any leading whitespace in inputLine is removed. The method is **protected** as its purpose to support the implementation of the **public** methods.

protected setEOF()

> Sets haveEOF to **true**.

These methods together with Character method isWhitespace() allow the implementation of the getString() algorithm to be simple relatively.

```
// getString(): get next whitespace-free string
public String getString() throws IOException {
   // make sure the buffer has a string in it
   do {
      getInputAsNeeded();
      trimLeadingWhitespace();
   } while (!EOF() && (inputLine.length() == 0));

   if (EOF()) { // no more input, so cannot return a string
      return null;
   }

   // extract the first string from the nonempty buffer
   int n = inputLine.length();
   for (int i = 1; i < n; ++i) {
      // if there is more than one string, then the first
      // string is followed by whitespace
      if (Character.isWhitespace(inputLine.charAt(i))) {
         // found whitespace, so do the extraction
         String s = inputLine.substring(0, i);
         inputLine = inputLine.substring(i);
         return s;
      }
   }
}
```

The implementation of method getInputAsNeeded() requires some analysis. The method first tests whether end of file has occurred or inputLine is non-**null**. If either condition is true, then no action is required of the method.

```
// getInputAsNeeded(): update input line buffer if current
// buffer has been used up
protected void getInputAsNeeded() throws IOException {
   // test determine whether we need to get input
   if (EOF() || ((inputLine != null)
                        && inputLine.length() != 0)) {
      return;
   }

   // need to refill the buffer
   try {
      inputLine = super.readLine();
      if (inputLine == null) {
         // eof has been reached
         setEOF();
      }
```

```
      }
      catch (IOException e) {
         inputLine = null;
         setEOF();
         throw e;
      }
   }
```

If instead `inputLine` needs to be updated, then a **try** block attempts to assign `inputLine` with the next line from the input stream using `ValueReader` method `read-Line()`. If that assignment gives `inputLine` the value **null**, then end-of-file is set.

If the `readLine()` invocation in `getString()` throws an exception, then there is effectively no more input, so `inputLine` is made **null** and end-of-file is set. The exception is rethrown because the method has handled the exception the best it could and rethrows the exception so that the invoking methods can perform any other necessary processing.

We now turn our attention to the implementations of the `ValueReader` definitions that override `BufferedReader` methods `readLine()` and `read()`. The overloading by `ValueReader` is necessary because of `ValueReader`'s use of `inputLine` as an input buffer. For example, when `ValueReader` method `readLine()` is invoked, the return value should come from `inputLine`. Similarly, when `ValueReader` method `read()` is invoked, the return character should come from `inputLine`.

The definition of `ValueReader` method `readLine()` begins by invoking method `getInputAsNeeded()`.

```
// readLine(): override superclass method for returning
// contents of input line buffer
public String readLine() throws IOException {
   getInputAsNeeded();
   String s = inputLine;
   inputLine = null;
   return s;
}
```

This invocation properly ensures that `inputLine` references the unused portion of the current line from the input stream. Because an effect of `readLine()` invocation is to use up the current input line, a copy of that reference is used to initialize `String` variable `s`. Variable `inputLine` then is made **null** and the copied reference is returned.

The definition of `ValueReader` method `read()` also begins by invoking `get-InputAsNeeded()`. It does that to ensure that `inputLine` references the unused portion of the current line from the input stream.

```
// read(): override superclass method for returning next
// character from input line buffer
public int read() throws IOException {
   getInputAsNeeded();
   if (EOF()) {
      // no character is available
      return -1;
   }
   else if (inputLine.length() == 0) {
```

```
                    // buffer is used up, so return a linefeed
                    inputLine = null;
                    return '\n';
                }
                else {
                    // got a character to extract from the buffer
                    char result = inputLine.charAt(0);
                    if (inputLine.length() == 1) {
                        inputLine = "";
                    }
                    else {
                        inputLine = inputLine.substring(1);
                    }
                    return result;
                }
            }
```

To simulate BufferedReader method read() functionality, a test is made to determine whether end of file has occurred. If it has, then −1 is returned to match what BufferedReader method read() does in this case. If instead end of file has not been reached and inputLine has been emptied, then inputLine is set to **null** and a newline character is returned. The newline character is returned because that character originally had terminated the input line. Otherwise, it must be case that end of file has not been reached and inputLine has not been emptied. Therefore, the first character from inputLine is the return value. Also, depending whether inputLine has length 1, inputLine is either made empty or set to its unreturned portion.

The implementations of the other ValueReader methods do to not warrant any analysis.

This discussion completes both our analysis of class ValueReader and our introduction to exceptions. We revisit exception handling in Chapter 12. That chapter introduces thread programming. In Java, threads make extensive use of exceptions to control program flow.

10.5   REVIEW

- An exception is an abnormal event that occurs during program execution. If an exception occurs and an exception handler code segment is in effect for that exception, then flow of control is transferred to the handler. If an exception occurs and there is no handler for it, the program terminates.

- Java requires a **throws** expression for any method that does not handle the exceptions it may generate. If the invoking method does not handle the exception, then an exception-unwinding process continues with the method that did the invoking of the invoking method, and so on. If no method is found in the unwinding process to handle the exception, then the program terminates.

- When an exception is thrown and not handled, Java generates a message to the standard error stream indicating where the exception occurred.

- Programs should end gracefully. Users should not need to read the jargon of an exception message.

- Code that deals with situations in which exceptions can arise can be put in a **try** block. Following the **try** block should be a **catch** exception handler block for each type of exception that can occur within the **try** block.

```
try { Action } catch ( ExceptionType Parameter ) { Handler }
```

Block of code that can generate an exception of type ExceptionType

Type of exception to be caught

If an ExceptionType is generated then, Parameter is initialized with exception information

Block of code that handles the caught exception

- If an exception is thrown in a **try** block, then the first associated **catch** block whose parameter type matches the generated exception is used. If no **catch** block parameter matches the exception, then the invocation process is unwound automatically to find the appropriate exception handler.

- If a **catch** block is executed, then its parameter is initialized with information regarding the specifics of the exception. If the **catch** block does not end the program, then after the **catch** block completes, program execution continues with the statement following the **try**-**catch** construct.

- The superclass for all runtime exceptions is `java.lang.RuntimeException`. Because runtime exceptions can occur throughout a program and because the cost of implementing handlers for them typically exceeds the expected benefit, Java makes it optional for a method to catch them or to specify that it throws them.

- Format and arithmetic exceptions are examples of runtime exceptions.

- Runtime exceptions are also known as unchecked exceptions. All other exceptions are known as checked exceptions. The checked exceptions that a method may generate must be either caught by one of its exception handlers or listed in the **throws** expression of the method.

■ Java provides a syntax for a handler block that is always run after the **try** block or **catch** handler have completed their tasks. The special handler is introduced through the keyword **finally**.

10.6	**SELF-TEST**

S10.1 Identify where exceptions can be generated in program `AverageFive.java` of Listing 2.11.

S10.2 Reimplement `BMICalculator.java` of Listing 2.10 so that its method `main()` does not have a **throws** expression.

S10.3 Reimplement `ValueDemo.java` of Listing 10.9 so that its method `main()` does not have a **throws** expression.

S10.4 What is the purpose of a **throws** clause?

S10.5 What is an unchecked exception?

S10.6 Modify `Deposits.java` to catch `NegativeAmountException` exceptions.

10.7	**EXERCISES**

10.1 What is an exception? How do exceptions come about?

10.2 What is a **try** block?

10.3 What is a **catch** block?

10.4 What is a **finally** block?

10.5 What is a runtime exception?

10.6 What happens if a unchecked exception is not caught?

10.7 What happens if a checked exception is not caught?

10.8 Argue why using **if** statements to determine data validity is insufficient in robust programming.

10.9 Rewrite `C.java` so that there is only a single **try** block.

10.10 Add a constructor to `ValueReader` with the following specification.

```
public ValueReader(File f)
```
    Constructs a `ValueReader` from the file stream referenced by `f`.

10.11 Add the following methods to `ValueReader`.

```
public short getShort()
```
    Returns the next value from the input stream as a **short** value.

```
public long getLong()
```
    Returns the next value from the input stream as a **long** value.

```
public float getFloat()
```
    Returns the next value from the input stream as a **float** value.

10.12 Add the following methods to `ValueReader`.

> `public boolean getBoolean()`
>> Returns the next value from the input stream as a **boolean** value.
>
> `public char getChar()`
>> Returns the next value from the input stream as a **char** value.

10.13 Implement a program whose method `main()` does not have a **throws** expression that accomplished the following task. The program should prompt its user for a number of values *n*. The program should then extract *n* input lines from standard input. Finally, it should echo back to standard output copies of the *n* input lines.

10.8   PROGRAMMING PROJECT — A SECOND LOOK

Reimplement the classes `ColoredTriangle` of Listing 5.7 and `DataSet` of Listing 6.8 to make proper use of exceptions in their implementations. In the resulting classes, any remaining error message displays should be initiated by an exception handler.

> The objective of this case study is to practice exception handling and software modification

You should also develop test sets that demonstrate the exception handling abilities of your implementations. Document why your exception handling is sufficient for robust programming.

10.9   SELF-TEST ANSWERS

S10.1 Each of the five `stdin.readLine()` invocations can throw an `IOException` if there is a file system error. Each of the five `Integer.parseInt()` invocations can throw a `NumberFormatException` if in reaction to the associate prompt, the use does not provide an integer value or if the user signals end-of-file.

S10.2 The following definition has the desired property.

```
// Purpose: Compute BMI for user's weight and height

import java.io.*;

public class BMICalculator {
    // main(): application entry point
    public static void main(String[] args) {
        // defining constants
        final double KILOGRAMS_PER_POUND = 0.454;
        final double METERS_PER_FOOT = 0.3046;

        // displaying legend
        System.out.println("BMI Calculator\n");

        // set up input stream
```

```
        BufferedReader stdin = new BufferedReader(
            new InputStreamReader(System.in));

        // get person's characteristics
        double weight;
        double height;
        try {
            System.out.print("Enter weight (lbs): ");
            weight = Double.parseDouble(stdin.readLine());

            System.out.print("Enter height (feet): ");
            height = Double.parseDouble(stdin.readLine());
        }
        catch (IOException e) {
            System.err.println("Unable to read input");
            return;
        }

        // convert to metric equivalents
        double metricWeight = weight
                    * KILOGRAMS_PER_POUND;
        double metricHeight = height * METERS_PER_FOOT;

        // perform bmi calculation
        double bmi = metricWeight
                    / (metricHeight * metricHeight);

        // display result
        System.out.println("A person with");
        System.out.println(" weight " + weight
            + " (lbs)");
        System.out.println(" height " + height + " (ft)");
        System.out.println("has a BMI of " + bmi);
    }
}
```

S10.3 The following program has the desired property.

```
// ValueDemo: demonstrates use of ValueReader

import ez.ValueReader;
import java.io.*;

public class ValueDemo {
    // main(): application entry point
    public static void main(String[] args) {
        ValueReader filein = null;
        try {
            filein = new ValueReader("names.txt");
        }
        catch (FileNotFoundException e) {
            System.err.println("names.txt can't be "
                + "opened");
            System.exit(1);
        }

        try {
```

```
                    String word = filein.getString();
                    while (! filein.EOF()) {
                        System.out.println(word);
                        word = filein.getString();
                    }
                }
                catch (IOException e) {
                    System.err.println("names.txt can't be read");
                }
            }
        }
```

S10.4 A **throws** clause of a method specifies the uncaught exceptions that the method may generate—either directly or through invocation.

S10.5 Runtime exceptions are known as unchecked exceptions. The adjective unchecked refers to the fact that a method need not catch the exception or list its **throws** expression. Java does not require their handling because such exceptions can occur throughout a program and because the cost of implementing handlers for them typically exceeds the expected benefit.

S10.6 The following version of program `Deposits.java` catches abnormal bank account events.

```
// Demonstrates BankAccount & NegativeAmountException

import java.io.*;

public class Deposits {
    // main(): application entry point
    public static void main(String[] args)
            throws IOException {
        BufferedReader stdin = new BufferedReader(
            new InputStreamReader(System.in));

        BankAccount savings = new BankAccount();

        System.out.print("Enter first deposit: ");
        int deposit = Integer.parseInt(stdin.readLine());

        try {
            savings.addFunds(deposit);
        }
        catch (NegativeAmountException e) {
            System.err.println("Bad deposit: " + deposit);
        }

        System.out.print("Enter second deposit: ");
        deposit = Integer.parseInt(stdin.readLine());

        try {
            savings.addFunds(deposit);
        }
        catch (NegativeAmountException e) {
            System.err.println("Bad deposit: " + deposit);
        }
```

```
        System.out.println("Closing balance: "
          + savings.getBalance());
    }
}
```

11

RECURSIVE PROBLEM SOLVING

In this chapter we explore an elegant and powerful approach to problem solving—recursive problem solving. Recursive problem solving involves breaking a problem into identical, but smaller or simpler problem instances and solving those to obtain a solution to the original problem. Most programming languages, including Java, support the use of recursion to solve problems.

OBJECTIVES

- Explain the concept of a recursive definition.
- To learn to think recursively.
  - Develop an understanding and appreciation of recursive problem solving.
  - Explain the basic components of a recursive algorithm.
  - Learn to use recursion in Java to solve problems.
  - Develop an appreciation of the trade-offs between recursion and iteration.

11.1   RECURSIVE METHODS

A concise and elegant way to define a term or concept is to use a recursive definition. A recursive definition defines something in terms of itself. For example, a recursive definition of the term "descendants" is "A person's descendants is the person's children and all their descendants." Similarly, a concise and elegant method for solving a large class of problems is to use a recursive algorithm. A recursive algorithm is an algorithm that invokes or calls itself with smaller or simpler problem instances. The solution to the original problem is then obtained by applying simple operations to the solution of the smaller or simpler problem instances.

Java supports the use of recursion to solve problems. *Recursion* is the ability of a method to call itself. To illustrate what we mean by recursion and its use, let's reconsider the implementation of the factorial function. Our earlier definition of factorial

$$n! = \begin{cases} 1 & \text{if } n = 0 \\ n \times (n-1) \times \ldots \times 1 & \text{if } n \geq 1 \end{cases}$$

is not mathematically precise because we use an ellipsis (…). The ellipsis tells readers to use their intuition to recognize the pattern. A formal definition of factorial removes any ambiguity.

$$n! = \begin{cases} 1 & \text{if } n = 0 \\ n \times (n-1)! & \text{if } n > 0 \end{cases}$$

In the preceding formal definition, we see that factorial is defined in terms of itself. That is, if $n > 0$, then $n!$ is $n \times (n-1)!$. You should be able to verify that the two definitions are equivalent.

Using recursion, we can write a short and simple method that computes factorials. The method is

```java
public static int factorial(int n) {
    if (n == 0) {
        return 1;
    }
    else {
        return n * factorial(n-1);
    }
}
```

This method mirrors the mathematical definition of factorial. If the value of n is 0, the value 1 is returned. If the value of n is not equal to 0, the product of n and `factorial(n-1)` is returned.

To understand how recursion works, it is useful to visualize what is happening when a method calls itself. One way to do so is to picture the activation records that are created for each recursive call. Let's assume that we have the following method `main()` invoking `factorial()`

```java
public static void main(String[] args) throws IOException {
    BufferedReader stdin = new BufferedReader(
```

```
        new InputStreamReader(System.in));
    System.out.print("Enter a positive integer: ");
    int n = Integer.parseInt(stdin.readLine());
    System.out.println(n + "! = " + factorial(n));
}
```

In this initial invocation of `factorial()`, n is 3, so the **else** part

```
return n * factorial(n-1);
```

of the **if** statement is executed. The activation records are

Activation records

The **else** part invokes `factorial()` again, this time with an actual parameter with value 2. The activation records are

Activation records

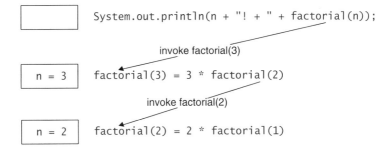

In this recursive invocation of `factorial()`, n is 2, so the **else** part

```
return n * dactorial(n-1);
```

of the **if** statement is executed with an actual parameter with value 1. As shown in Figure 11.1, the recursive invocation process continues until n equals 0. At this point, the **if** test expression evaluates to true, and

```
return 1;
```

is executed. The statement causes the recursion to start *unwinding* (i.e., no more recursive calls).

As the recursion unwinds, values are returned to the calling invocation of the method. In effect, the return value is substituted for the call. The process of the recursion unwinding is illustrated in Figure 11.2. Using the returned value, the factorial of the n (for this invocation) is computed and returned to the next level. This process continues until the call to `factorial()` from `main()` returns to `main()` with the value of 3! which is 6.

Figure 11.1 **Activation records for recursive invocations of factorial.**

Activation records

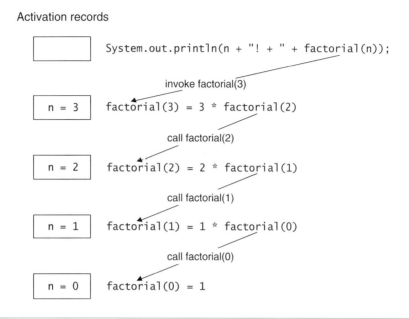

Figure 11.2 **Unwinding the recursive invocations of factorial.**

Activation records

When the first call to `factorial()` returns to `main()`, the insertion statement produces the following output:

```
3! = 6
```

One of the nice things about recursion is that it is a succinct way of expressing certain mathematical formulas, and the corresponding Java implementation is equally short. A recursive method generally has two parts:

- A termination part that stops the recursion. This is called the base case. The base case should have a simple or trivial solution.

- One or more recursive calls. This is called the recursive case. The recursive case calls the same method but with simpler or smaller arguments.

In the factorial code, the recursive call and the termination part were the two action parts of the **if-else** statement.

$$
\left.\begin{array}{l}
\texttt{if (n == 0)} \\
\qquad \texttt{return 1;}
\end{array}\right\} \textit{Base case}
$$

$$
\textit{Recursive case} \left\{\begin{array}{l}
\texttt{else} \\
\qquad \texttt{return n * factorial(n - 1);}
\end{array}\right.
$$

Let's now consider the development of a recursive implementation of method `power()` to compute x^n, where x and n are both integers.

We know that x^0 is 1 for all x. This fact will be the base case of our recursive method. We also know that $x^n = x \times x^{n-1}$ when $n > 0$, which will be the recursive part. Observe that because n is getting smaller, the recursion is sure to terminate. Writing the recursive version of the power method is simple.

```
public static int power(int x, int n) {
   if (n == 0) {
      return 1;
   }
   else {
      return x * power(x, n-1);
   }
}
```

11.1.1 FIBONACCI NUMBERS AND SQUARES

Our final example of simple recursion considers the Fibonacci sequence. We previously saw this number sequence in the self-test section of Chapter 6, when we developed iterative code to display the first n Fibonacci numbers. The sequence starts with the following numbers: 1, 1, 2, 3, 5, 8, 13, 21, 34, 55, 89, and 144. After the initial two 1s, each number in the sequence is the sum of the two previous numbers. For example, $1 + 1 = 2$, $1 + 2 = 3$, $2 + 3 = 5$, $3 + 5 = 8$, and so on.

Recursive algorithm design

A recursive algorithm always consists of at least two parts.
- A *base case* that deals with the simplest instance of the problem.
- A *recursive case* that deals with a simpler or smaller version of the problem.

There must always be one base case and one recursive case, but there can be more.

The Fibonacci numbers are interesting scientifically and socially because they model many things in nature. For example, they model the reproductive behavior of bees, the number of branches in a tree, and the number of petals on a flower (e.g., buttercups have 5 petals; some asters have 21 petals; and there are daisies with 34, 55, and 89 petals).

The first known investigation into the Fibonacci sequence was by the Italian mathematician Leonardo Pisano in 1202. Pisano was investigating how fast rabbits could breed under idealized circumstances. He assumed that a pair of male and female rabbits always breed and produce another pair of male and female rabbits. He also assumed that a rabbit becomes sexually mature after one month, and that the gestation period is also one month. With these assumptions, a pair of rabbits produces one new pair every month from its second month on. Pisano wanted to know the answer to the question how many rabbits would there be after one year?

We can work out a solution by hand. At the end of the first month, there is still only one pair. At the end of the second month, another pair is born so there are now two pairs. At the end of the third month, the original pair produces another pair, and the second pair has just matured, so there are only three pairs. At the end of the fourth month, the original pair has produced another pair and so has the second pair, so now there are five pairs. At the end of the fifth month, there will be eight pairs. In the sixth month, there will be 13 pairs. The sequence being generated is

  1, 1, 2, 3, 5, 8, 13, 21, 34, …

That is, the number of pairs for a month is the sum of the number of pairs in the two previous months. Therefore, at the end of one year, there will be 144 pairs of rabbits.

The mathematical definition of the *n*th Fibonacci number f_n is given by the recurrence

$$f_n = \begin{cases} f_n = 1 & \text{if } n = 1 \\ f_n = 1 & \text{if } n = 2 \\ f_n = f_{n-1} + f_{n-2} & \text{if } n > 2 \end{cases}$$

The definition is more complicated than our previous recursive methods, but we can still use the same strategy. The pattern for our previous recursive methods has been

```
if ( termination code satisfied ) {
    return value;
}
else {
    make simpler recursive call;
}
```

and this pattern also works for computing Fibonacci numbers. The code for the method is

```
public static int fibonacci(int n) {
```

```
        if (n <= 2) {
            return 1;
        }
        else {
            return fibonacci(n-1) + fibonacci(n-2);
        }
    }
```

The main difference between the current code and the code for the previous recursive methods is that the current code makes two recursive calls. We know that both of these recursive calls eventually unwind because every recursive call has a parameter that is less than the parameter of the invocation that spawned the call. Figure 11.3 depicts the recursive calls made by the method when computing f_5.

Figure 11.3 **Computation of f_5.**

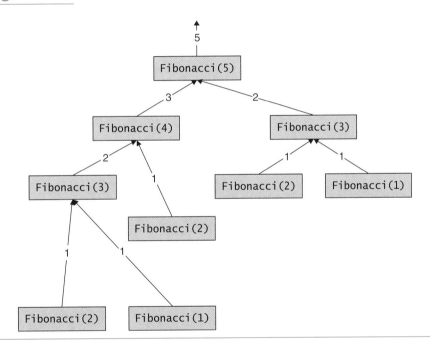

Fibonacci numbers arise in the rendering of some geometric art. Consider the picture in Figure 11.4(a). The squares have a Fibonacci relationship, which is made more explicit in the picture in Figure 11.4(b). The pictures are drawn by starting with two squares of size 1, one drawn to left of the other. Below these two squares, a square is drawn whose size is the sum of the two previously drawn squares (i.e., a square of size 2). Each succeeding square's size is the sum of the sizes of the two most previously drawn squares and its position is related in a counterclockwise manner to the square most previously drawn. Development of a program FibonacciSquares.java to produce a Fibonacci square picture is left to the exercises.

Figure 11.4   **Fibonacci art.**

(a) Geometric art.

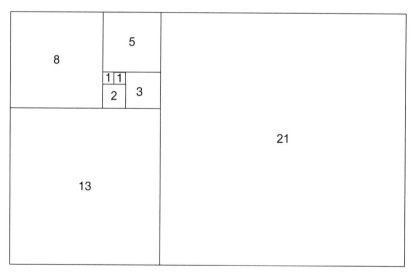

(b) The number in the squares indicate the length of a side.

Infinite recursion

A common programming error when using recursion is to not stop making recursive calls. The program will continue to recurse until it runs out of memory. Be sure that your recursive calls are made with simpler or smaller subproblems, and that your algorithm has a base case that terminates the recursion.

11.2   CASE STUDY — RECURSIVE BINARY SEARCH

We have all looked up a name in the telephone directory or a word in the dictionary. The fact that the directory or dictionary entries are in sorted order helps us find the number or word quickly. One fast strategy for finding an entry in a sorted list is called binary search. The basic idea is as follows. First, you compare the entry to the middle element of the list. If the entry matches the mid-

> The objective of this case study is to demonstrate the development a recursive algorithm to solve a common problem—searching for an entry in a list.

dle element, the desired entry has been located and the search is over. If the entry doesn't match, then if the entry is in the list it must be either to the left or right of the middle element. The correct sublist can be searched using the same strategy. This binary search strategy is illustrated by the diagram in Figure 11.5.

Figure 11.5   **Searching a sorted list.**

0	1	2	3	4	5	6
10	24	33	45	56	81	95

Compare entry to this element. If the entry matches, the search is successful. If the entry is less than 45, then the entry, if it is in the list, must be to the left in elements 0-2. If the entry is greater than 45, then the entry, if it is in the list, must be to the right in elements 4-6.

Consider searching for the number 24 in the list in Figure 11.5. The first comparison is with the middle element containing the value 45. Since 24 ≠ 45 and 24 < 45, we know that we should search the sublist to the left of element 3. We can apply the same search technique to the sublist consisting of elements 0 through 2. Again, we pick the middle element—element 1 in this case. The entry, 24, is equal to the value in `element[1]` so the search is successful.

The preceding search strategy can be implemented elegantly using recursion. The base case occurs when the entry is located or the sublist to search is empty. The previous paragraph discussed the case where the entry is located. Now we consider the case where the entry is not found. For example, if we searched the list in Figure 11.5 for 83, we would search the right sublist consisting of elements 4 through 6. Because 83 is greater than 81, we next search the sublist consisting of element 6, which also fails. There is no sublist to the left of element 6, so the search fails.

The recursive case is to search the appropriate sublist. Because a sublist is smaller than the size of the list, the condition that the recursive call has simpler or smaller element is satisfied.

To illustrate recursive binary search, we develop a class for searching a list of names and telephone numbers for a name. If the name is found, we print out the associated telephone number.

The following class defines an address book entry.

```
public class AddressEntry {
    private String personName;
    private String telephoneNumber;
    // default constructor
    public AddressEntry(String name, String number) {
        personName = name;
        telephoneNumber = number;
    }
    public String getName() {
        return personName;
    }
    public String getNumber() {
        return telephoneNumber;
    }
    public void setName(String Name) {
        personName = Name;
    }
    public void setTelephoneNumber(String number) {
        telephoneNumber = number;
    }
}
```

The class declaration follows our standard pattern for implementing a data abstraction. The class contains the standard inspector and mutator methods.

ANALYSIS AND DESIGN

We are now ready to begin the design of the recursive binary search class. Our class will not contain any instance variables. The job of this class is to provide a method for searching an array of `AddressEntry` objects when a name is provided. We will call the array an address book.

Our first step is to develop the interface to the method that initiates a search for a name in an address book. This step involves determining what arguments the method should accept and what type the method should return. Because the method is to locate the address entry for a person, it is appropriate that the search method return an `AddressEntry`. The method's parameters are the address book to search and the name of the person to look up. Thus, an appropriate interface to the search function is

```
public static AddressEntry recSearch(AddressEntry[]
    addressBook, String name)
```

We are now ready to design the interface to the recursive method that will perform the search and the algorithm to perform the search. The recursive method also returns an `AddressEntry`. The recursive method will also take as parameters the address book to search and the name to look up. In addition to those two parameters, the method will accept two integer parameters that indicate the sublist of the address book to search. Successive recursive calls to the method will search shorter and shorter sublists.

```
private static AddressEntry recSearch(AddressEntry[]
  addressBook, String name, int first, int last)
```

As we noted earlier, the base case of the algorithm consists of two subcases—the element is located and the list to search has length zero. In both cases, the recursion terminates. The recursive case also consists two subcases—the element, if it exists, is in the left half of the list or it is in the right half of the list. The algorithm then can be stated as follows:

Step 1.   If the list has no elements
             return null
Step 2.   Compute the midpoint of the list
Step 3.   If the name matches the name in the midpoint element
                 return the midpoint element
Step 4.   If the name is lexically less than the name in the midpoint element
                 recursively search the sublist to the left of the midpoint
Step 5.   Else the name is lexically greater than the name in the midpoint element
                 recursively and search the sublist to the right of the midpoint

Now that we have the interface and the high-level algorithm, the implementation will be easy.

IMPLEMENTATION

Listing 11.1 contains the implementation of methods `recSearch()`. The implementation of the public method `recSearch()` simply calls the private method with the length of the list.

```
public static AddressEntry recSearch(
  AddressEntry[] addressBook, String name) {
    return recSearch(addressBook, name, 0,
      addressBook.length-1);
}
```

The private method `recSearch()` does all the work. The first if statement decides whether the sublist to search is empty or not. If the list is empty, the method returns null. If the sublist is not empty, the midpoint of the sublist is computed and the name is compared to the name at the midpoint. If the names are the same, the method returns the address book entry. If the names are not the same, the code determines which side of the midpoint to search recursively. The use of the `String` method `compareToIgnore-Case()`. This methods compares two strings, but ignores whether letters are upper or lower case. Method `compareToIgnoreCase()` returns a negative integer if the string argument is lexically greater than this string, zero if the string argument is equal to this string, and a positive integer if the string argument is less than this string.

TESTING

Method `recSearch()` is simple and elegant, but it's operation is subtle. We should carefully test our implementation. To do so, we need to develop a set of cases to thoroughly test the code. After some consideration, we come up with the following situations that should be tested.

Listing 11.1 Recursive binary search method

```
1.  public static AddressEntry recSearch(AddressEntry[] addressBook,
2.    String name) {
3.      return recSearch(addressBook, name, 0, addressBook.length-1);
4.  }
5.  static AddressEntry recSearch(AddressEntry[] addressBook,
6.    String name, int first, int last) {
7.      // base case: if the array section is empty, not found
8.      if (first > last)
9.          return null;
10.     else {
11.         int mid = (first + last) / 2;
12.         // if we found the value, we're done
13.         if (name.equalsIgnoreCase(addressBook[mid].getName()))
14.             return addressBook[mid];
15.         else if (name.compareToIgnoreCase(
16.           addressBook[mid].getName()) < 0) {
17.             // if value is there at all, it's in the left half
18.             return recSearch(addressBook, name, first, mid-1);
19.         }
20.          else { // array[mid] < value
21.             // if value is there at all, it's in the right half
22.             return recSearch(addressBook, name, mid+1, last);
23.         }
24.     }
25. }
```

---

1. Locate a name that is in the first element of the address book.
2. Locate a name that is in the last element of the address book.
3. Attempt to locate a name that is not in the address book.
4. Locate a name that is in the middle of the address book.

Listing 11.2 gives the corresponding test harness. The first part of the code (lines 3–12) creates and initializes a list to search. The elements of the list are in sorted order because this is required by the binary search algorithm. The next parts of the code test various situations by searching for various names. The test harness searches for a name that is at the beginning of the list, then it searches for a name in the middle, and then a name at the end of the list. The final test makes sure the code works properly when searching for a name that is not in the address book.

The listed created in the test harness contains eight elements. To thoroughly test the code, a test should be created where a list containing an odd number of elements is created. Creating this additional test case is left to the exercises.

The binary search algorithm is very efficient. The efficiency of the search algorithm is represented by the binary tree in Figure 11.6. This tree is a full binary tree because no more nodes can be added without increasing the number of levels. If we think of each node in the tree as representing a comparison, we can use this tree to reason about the efficiency of binary search. At the top of the tree, a comparison divides the tree in half and similarly for subsequently levels until either the node is found or a leaf of the tree is reached. Hence the number of levels or height of the tree is the worst-case number of comparisons needed to find a entry in a sorted listed. We can see from Figure 11.6 that a binary tree with 31 nodes has a height of 5. Indeed, a binary tree that contains n nodes has

Listing 11.2 Recursive binary search test harness

```
1.  public static void main(String[] args) {
2.      // list must be in sorted order
3.      AddressEntry addressBook[] = {
4.          new AddressEntry("Audrey", "434-555-1215"),
5.          new AddressEntry("Emily" , "434-555-1216"),
6.          new AddressEntry("Jack"  , "434-555-1217"),
7.          new AddressEntry("Jim"   , "434-555-2566"),
8.          new AddressEntry("John"  , "434-555-2222"),
9.          new AddressEntry("Lisa"  , "434-555-3415"),
10.         new AddressEntry("Tom"   , "630-555-2121"),
11.         new AddressEntry("Zach"  , "434-555-1218")
12.     };
13.     AddressEntry p;
14.     // first element
15.     p = recSearch(addressBook, "Audrey");
16.     if (p != null) {
17.         System.out.println("Audrey's telephone number is " +
18.           p.getNumber());
19.     }
20.     else {
21.         System.out.println("No entry for Audrey");
22.     }
23.     // middle element
24.     p = recSearch(addressBook, "Jim");
25.     if (p != null) {
26.         System.out.println("Jim's telephone number is " +
27.           p.getNumber());
28.     }
29.      else {
30.         System.out.println("No entry for Jim");
31.     }
32.     // last element
33.     p = recSearch(addressBook, "Zach");
34.     if (p != null) {
35.         System.out.println("Zach's telephone number is " +
36.           p.getNumber());
37.     }
38.     else {
39.         System.out.println("No entry for Zach");
40.     }
41.     // non existent entry
42.     p = recSearch(addressBook, "Frank");
43.     if (p != null) {
44.         System.out.println("Frank's telephone number is " +
45.           p.getNumber());
46.     }
47.     else {
48.         System.out.println("No entry for Frank");
49.     }
50. }
```

a height of $\log_2 (n + 1)$. For example, this says that we can search a sorted list with up to 1 billion numbers with at most 30 comparisons.

Figure 11.6 **Efficiency of the binary search algorithm.**

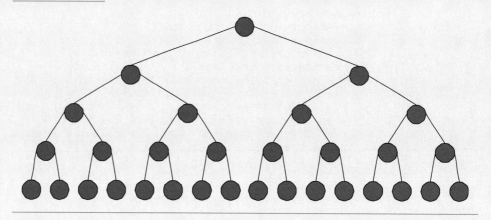

METHOD MERGESORT()

Although method `selectionSort()` described in Chapter 7 has reasonable performance characteristics, we can do better. In particular, time-critical client applications often use the `mergeSort()` or `quickSort()` methods. In this section, we discuss `mergeSort()` that is also part of `SortingAndSearching.java`. In the exercises, we consider how to develop `quickSort()`.

Method `mergeSort()` is a recursive sort that conceptually divides its list of n elements to be sorted into two sublists of size $n/2$. If a sublist contains more than one element, the sublist is sorted by a recursive call to `mergeSort()`. After the two sublists of size $n/2$ are sorted, they are merged together to produce a single sorted list of size n. This type of strategy is known as a *divide-and-conquer* strategy—the problem is divided into subproblems of lesser complexity and the solutions of the subproblems are used to produced the overall solution. The running time of method `mergeSort()` is proportional to $n \log n$. This performance is sometimes known as *linearithmic* performance.[†]

Suppose we are to again sort the following array:

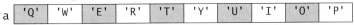

If we first sort the left and right sublists, the array would then look like

We are now left with the simpler task of merging the two sublists to produce the sorted array

a | 'E' | 'I' | 'O' | 'P' | 'Q' | 'R' | 'T' | 'U' | 'W' | 'Y'

For a client to invoke `mergeSort()` to sort array `a`, the invocation would be

`mergeSort(a);`

In our implementation of `mergeSort()`, this invocation will in turn cause the invocation

`mergeSort(a, 0, a.length - 1);`

to occur. As you can tell, our implementation overloads the name `mergeSort`. We do so, for client ease—a client should need not to worry about the mechanics of the sort. It is the responsibility of the API programmer to use the supplied information to accomplish the task at hand. In this case, the API translates the request to sort array `a` into the specific request of sorting from its first element through its last element; that is, elements `a[0]` through `a[9]`, where 9 equals `a.length - 1`.

[†]   Linearithmic is portmanteau of linear and logarithm coined by Robert Sedgwick.

Because this invocation will sort the array, there is nothing left for that method to do. Thus, its definition is straightforward.

```java
public static void mergeSort(char[] a) {
    mergeSort(a, 0, a.length - 1);
}
```

We now consider the other method `mergeSort()`, the method that does the actual sorting. This method has three parameters: the array a to be sorted and indices `left` and `right` that demark the portion of a to be sorted.

The method must first determine whether the sorting request involves any true work; i.e., are there are least two elements to consider. This determination can be made by testing whether `left < right`. If so, then are at least two elements two consider.

```java
if (left < right) {
    // there are multiple elements to sort.

        ...
}
```

If there are multiple elements to consider, we first recursively sort the left and right sublists. To do so, we calculate the middle index `mid` in the range `left … right`. Index mid has the value `(left + right) / 2`. Subrange `left … mid` are the indices of the left sublist and subrange `mid + 1 … right` are the indices of the right sublist.

```java
// first, recursively sort the left and right sublists
int mid = (left + right) / 2;
mergeSort(a, left, mid);
mergeSort(a, mid+1, right);
```

Although it is possible to merge the two sublists in place, it is far simpler to merge the sublists into another array `temp` and then copy array `temp` into a. Array `temp` needs to be only big enough to store the portion of a that we are sorting. Therefore, `temp` needs to be able to store only `right - left + 1` elements.

```java
// next, merge the sorted sublists into array temp
char[] temp = new char[right - left + 1];
```

Our code must keep track of which elements are left to consider in the left and right sublists. We will use index j to indicate the location of the smallest-valued element from the left sublist to be copied and index k to indicate the location of the smallest-valued element from the right sublist to be copied.

```java
int j = left;       // index of left sublist smallest element
int k = mid + 1;    // index of right sublist smallest element
```

A **for** loop can then be used to copy the elements from the two sublists into `temp`. The **for** loop will iterate `temp.length` times, where in each iteration the appropriate value from the sublists is copied into `temp`.

```java
for (int i = 0; i < temp.length; ++i) {
    // store the next smallest element
    // from the sublists into temp
```

```
        ...
    }
```

Case analysis is performed to determine where to get the next value to store into temp. If $j \leq mid$ and $k \leq right$, then both sublists have elements to be considered. If this is not the case, then only one of the sublists still has unconsidered elements.

```
    if ((j <= mid) && (k <= right)) {
        // need to grab the smaller of a[j] and a[k]
        ...
    }
    else if (j <= mid) { // can grab only from left half
        ...
    }
    else { // can grab only from right half
        ...
    }
```

For the case where both sublists have values to consider, a[j] is the least uncopied value of the left sublist and a[k] is the least uncopied value from the right sublist. The lesser of these two values needs to be copied into temp.

```
    if (a[j] <= a[k]) { // left has the smaller element
        temp[i] = a[j];
        ++j;
    }
    else { // right has the smaller element
        temp[i] = a[k];
        ++k;
    }
```

If a[j] is the lesser value then besides copying it to temp[i], we must also increment j. The increment reflects that another element from the left sublist has been copied. If instead a[k] is the lesser value, then besides copying it to temp[i], we must also increment k. The increment reflects that another element from the right sublist has been copied.

If this case does not apply (i.e., only one sublist has uncopied elements), then it must be determined which sublist has uncopied elements. If $j \leq mid$ then, it is the left sublist.

```
    else if (j <= mid) { // can only grab from left half
        temp[i] = a[j];
        ++j;
    }
```

Otherwise, it is the right sublist that has uncopied elements.

```
    else { // can only grab from right half
        temp[i] = a[k];
        ++k:
    }
```

Once all the elements have been copied into `temp`, all that remains to complete the sorting of `a[left]` through `a[right]` is to copy `temp` into that portion of a. The copying can be done in a straightforward manner using a **for** loop.

```
// lastly, copy temp into a
for (int i = 0; i < result.length ++i) {
   a[left + i] = temp[i];
}
```

Listing 11.3 contains the complete definitions of methods `mergeSort(`**char**`[] a)` and `mergeSort(`**char**`[] a, `**int** `left, `**int** `right)`. As we indicated previously, the methods are part of `SortingAndSearching.java`.

Figure 11.7 illustrates all the invocations of `mergeSort()` to arrange our list correctly. Each entry shows the values of parameters `left` and `right` at the start of an invocation. The invocation information is also presented in the following list. The invocations are listed in the order that they occur in the program. Like the figure, each entry provides the range of elements to be sorted by that invocation and the contents of the array immediately before and after the associated invocation.

```
0 ... 9:  QWERTYUIOP   EIOPQRTUWY
0 ... 4:  QWERTYUIOP   EQRTWYUIOP
0 ... 2:  QWERTYUIOP   EQWRTYUIOP
0 ... 1:  QWERTYUIOP   QWERTYUIOP
0 ... 0:  QWERTYUIOP   QWERTYUIOP
1 ... 1:  QWERTYUIOP   QWERTYUIOP
2 ... 2:  QWERTYUIOP   QWERTYUIOP
3 ... 4:  EQWRTYUIOP   EQWRTYUIOP
3 ... 3:  EQWRTYUIOP   EQWRTYUIOP
4 ... 4:  EQWRTYUIOP   EQWRTYUIOP
5 ... 9:  EQRTWYUIOP   EQRTWIOPUY
5 ... 7:  EQRTWYUIOP   EQRTWIUYOP
5 ... 6:  EQRTWYUIOP   EQRTWUYIOP
5 ... 5:  EQRTWYUIOP   EQRTWYUIOP
6 ... 6:  EQRTWYUIOP   EQRTWYUIOP
7 ... 7:  EQRTWUYIOP   EQRTWUYIOP
8 ... 9:  EQRTWIUYOP   EQRTWIUYOP
8 ... 8:  EQRTWIUYOP   EQRTWIUYOP
9 ... 9:  EQRTWIUYOP   EQRTWIUYOP
```

Listing 11.3 Mergesorting methods of SortandSearching.java

```
1.  // mergeSort(): sorts the elements of a
2.  public static void mergeSort(char[] a) {
3.      mergeSort(a, 0, a.length - 1);
4.  }
5.
6.  private static void mergeSort(char[] a, int left,
7.   int right) {
8.      if (left < right) {
9.          // there are multiple elements to sort.
10.
11.         // first, recursively sort the left and right sublists
12.         int mid = (left + right) / 2;
13.         mergeSort(a, left, mid);
14.         mergeSort(a, mid+1, right);
15.
16.         // next, merge the sorted sublists into array temp
17.         char[] temp = new char[right - left + 1];
18.
19.         int j = left;      // index of left sublist smallest element
20.         int k = mid + 1;   // index of right sublist smallest element
21.
22.         for (int i = 0; i < temp.length; ++i) {
23.             // store the next smallest element into temp
24.             if ((j <= mid) && (k <= right)) {
25.                 // need to grab the smaller of a[j] and a[k]
26.                 if (a[j] <= a[k]) { // left has the smaller element
27.                     temp[i] = a[j];
28.                     ++j;
29.                 }
30.                 else { // right has the smaller element
31.                     temp[i] = a[k];
32.                     ++k;
33.                 }
34.             }
35.             else if (j <= mid) { // can only grab from left half
36.                 temp[i] = a[j];
37.                 ++j;
38.             }
39.             else { // can only grab from right half
40.                 temp[i] = a[k];
41.                 ++k;
42.             }
43.         }
44.
45.         // lastly, copy temp into a
46.         for (int i = 0; i < temp.length; ++i) {
47.             a[left + i] = temp[i];
48.         }
49.     }
50. }
```

Figure 11.7 **Trace of mergeSort() when sorting string QWERTYUIOP.**

Invocation considers the elements
of EQRTWYUIOP with subscripts
from interval 5 ... 9 and produces
EQRTWIOPUY.

Initial invocation considers the elements
of QWERTYUIOP from interval 0 ... 9
and produces EIOPQRTUWY.

11.4   HOW FAST CAN WE SORT?

It is clear that mergeSort() is an improvement over selectionSort(). The question
remains, however, can we create an even better performing sorting method. It turns out
that all sorting algorithms that use comparisons to determine the ordering of the elements
must perform at least $n \log n$ element operations in the worst case. This fact about sorting
algorithms can be shown using what is known as an *information-theoretic* argument.

If a list is composed of n distinct values, then there are $n!$ possible orderings of the
values. When the first element comparison is made, one-half of the $n!$ orderings are still
candidates to be the sorted ordering. For example, if the ith element is smaller than the ith
element, then all orderings where the value of the ith element precedes the value of the
ith element are valid possibilities. After the second comparison, in the worst-case performance at least one-fourth of the $n!$ orderings are still candidates to be the sorted ordering.
After the third comparison, in the worst case at least one-eighth of the $n!$ orderings still

need to be considered. In a worst-case performance, we need at least $n \log n$ comparisons before only a single candidate ordering might remain to be considered. Therefore, any comparison-based sorting algorithm has a worst-case performance that is at least linearithmic in the number of comparisons.

11.5   RECURSION VERSUS ITERATION

How do we decide when to use iteration and when to use recursion? To get a handle on answering this question we need to understand the costs of recursion.

A recursive program accomplishes its task by making successive recursive calls with smaller subprograms. As we discussed in Chapter 4, a method call involves several steps. Three of these steps are to arrange for the values of the actual parameters to be passed to the invoked method, to create a new activation record, and to transfer control to the called method. When the called method returns, the return value (if any) is passed back to the calling method, the activation record must be removed, and control must be returned to the calling method. Combined these operations make method invocation relatively expensive compared to simple operations like evaluating an expression or looping to repeat a sequence of statements.

A second issue is the amount of memory used by a recursive program. Each time we make a recursive call a new activation record is created. If the program recurses deeply and the activation records for the method are large, substantial amounts of memory may be consumed. Depending on the amount of memory on the machine, this could be a potential problem.

To see concretely the potential inefficiency of a recursive solution, Table 11.1 gives some data about the execution characteristics of our Fibonacci code. The table gives the number of recursive calls made and the depth of the recursion (i.e., the number of activation records simultaneously on the stack). For an input value of 36, the program makes over 29 million recursive calls and the depth of the stack grows to 35.

Table 11.1   Fibonacci execution statistics.

n	Calls made	Call depth
5	9	4
6	15	5
12	287	11
18	5,167	17
24	92,735	23
30	1,664,079	29
36	29,860,703	35

For fibonacci, we can create a much more efficient iterative solution. The following method computes the *n*th Fibonacci number iteratively.

```java
public static int fibonacci(int n) {
    if (n <= 2) {
        return 1;
    }
    else {
        int f = 1;
        int f1 = 1;
        int f2 = 1;
        for (int i = 2; i <= n; ++i) {
            f = f1 + f2;
            f1 = f2;
            f2 = f;
        }
        return f;
    }
}
```

This solution is quite efficient and is also straightforward to understand.

So does this mean that one should avoid recursive solutions to problems? Not at all. Sometimes the easiest and least error-prone solution to a problem is a recursive one. Put another way, sometimes an iterative solution to a problem is much more difficult than a recursive solution. As an example, try solving the Towers of Hanoi problem in the exercises using iteration. An iterative solution is challenging, whereas the recursive solution is simple. Generally, our approach is to favor the solution that is easiest to understand. Later, if the chosen solution is inefficient to the extent it noticeably affects the overall performance of the application, we can investigate using a different solution approach. With today's modern compilers and the speed of machines, it is rare that a recursive solution is not fast enough.

11.6   CASE STUDY — STRING PERMUTATION

The Daily Jumble® is a popular two-part puzzle that appears everyday in many newspapers. Figure 11.8 reproduces a sample Daily Jumble puzzle. The first part of the puzzle gives a list of strings to be rearranged— each string in the list is to be unscrambled so that it forms a word. The second part of the puzzles poses a riddle regarding an accompanying cartoon. The answer to the riddle is formed by using selected letters from the words found in the first part.

> The objective of this case study is to demonstrate the development of both a recursive algorithm and an iterator

Figure 11.8   **Daily Jumble. Copyright, 2000, Tribune Media Services, Inc. All rights reserved. Reprinted with permission.**

ANALYSIS AND DESIGN

Our interest in the puzzle lies in how to automate unscrambling the letters to find the word. One approach is to generate all possible permutations of the letters in the scrambled word and then scan the list for legal words. For a string of length 5, the number of permutations can be computed as follows. There are five possibilities for the first letter.

This leaves four possibilities for the second letter, three possibilities for the third letter, two possibilities for the fourth letter, and one possibility for the last letter. Thus there are $5 \times 4 \times 3 \times 2 \times 1$ or 120 permutations of five letters. This computation should be familiar. It is just the computation of 5!. Indeed, in general, the number of permutations a string of length n is $n!$.

For example, if we generate the 120 permutations of the first scrambled word we get the following list of 120 words.

thiso	thios	thsio	thsoi	thois
thosi	tihso	tihos	tisho	tisoh
tiohs	tiosh	tshio	tshoi	tsiho
tsioh	tsohi	tsoih	tohis	tohsi
toihs	toish	toshi	tosih	htiso
htios	htsio	htsoi	htois	htosi
hitso	hitos	histo	hisot	hiots
hiost	hstio	hstoi	hsito	hsiot
hsoti	hsoit	hotis	hotsi	hoits
hoist	hosti	hosit	ithso	ithos
itsho	itsoh	itohs	itosh	ihtso
ihtos	ihsto	ihsot	ihots	ihost
istho	istoh	ishto	ishot	isoth
isoht	ioths	iotsh	iohts	iohst
iosth	iosht	sthio	sthoi	stiho
stioh	stohi	stoih	shtio	shtoi
shito	shiot	shoti	shoit	sitho
sitoh	sihto	sihot	sioth	sioht
sothi	sotih	sohti	sohit	soith
soiht	othis	othsi	otihs	otish
otshi	otsih	ohtis	ohtsi	ohits
ohist	ohsti	ohsit	oiths	oitsh
oihts	oihst	oisth	oisht	osthi
ostih	oshti	oshit	osith	osiht

Scanning the list of permutations we locate the word hoist.

Thus our plan for solving the Daily Jumble is to create a class called `PermuteString` that generates all permutations of a given string. We can then scan the generated list for legal English words. The exercises contain some problems that further automate our technique.

IMPLEMENTATION

Class `PermuteString` will be designed to be an iterator. An iterator is a type of class that produces successive values. For our problem, the successive values to generate are the permutations of the word. Typically, an iterator has the following methods.

- A constructor to create the generator.
- A method for returning the next value.
- A method that indicates if there are any more values to return.

Class `PermuteString` will have three methods.

`public PermuteString(String s)`

Default constructor that creates the permutation generator for `String s`.

`public String nextPermutation()`

Returns the next permutation of `String s`.

```
public boolean morePermutations()
```
Returns **false** if all permutations have been generated; otherwise **true** is returned.

Recall that to create a recursive solution we need two cases—the base case and the recursive case. For the permutation problem, the base case is the trivial case of a string that consists of a single letter. The permutation of a string of length one is the string. The recursive case is a little more complicated, but not much more. To generate the permutations of a string, we will select each letter of the string and concatenate it with all the permutations of the remaining letters (we will call this the substring). Notice that this definition satisfies the recursive case requirement that the recursive call have an argument that is simpler or smaller. The recursive call is being made with the substring that has one less character than the word.

To implement the permutation generator, we need to maintain state information to track the permutations generated thus far. We will need the following variables.

```
String word
```
The string being permuted.

```
int index
```
The position within the word of the character being selected to add to the permutations of the substring.

```
PermuteString substringGenerator()
```
A reference to the **PermuteString** generator for the substring of the word.

The constructor for **PermuteString** is:

```
// PermuteString: default constructor
public PermuteString(String s) {
    word = s;
    index = 0;
    if (s.length() > 1) {
        substringGenerator =
            new PermuteString(s.substring(1));
    }
}
```

The constructor initializes word to the string being permuted, and it sets index to 0. If the length of the string is greater than one, a **PermuteString** object is created for the substring of the word. Notice that this is a recursive call. Basically, when a **PermuteString** generator is created for a string, **PermuteString** generators are created for every substring of the word. For example, the invocation

```
PermuteString p = new PermuteString("ath");
```

creates the following objects.

The two generators for the substrings "th" and "h" will be invoked by method next-Permutation() to create permutations of these substrings as needed.

We now turn our attention to method morePermutations(). This method returns false if all permutations have been produced. The way we can tell whether all the permutations have been generated is by comparing index to the length of word. If we have selected every letter from instance variable word, then all permutations have been generated. Remember, our technique for generating the permutations is to select each letter of word and concatenate it with all the permutations of the substring. Consequently, the implementation of method morePermutations() is quite simple.

```
public boolean morePermutations() {
    return index < word.length();
}
```

When index is less than the length of word (i.e., there are still more characters in word to select), method morePermutations() returns **true**.

Now it is time to tackle method nextPermutation(), which is given in Listing 11.4. Like the constructor, method nextPermutation() will be recursive. The base case is when the instance variable word is length one (lines 17–21). For the base case, the instance variable word is the permutation. To indicate that there are no more permutations for this case, index is incremented so that it is equal to the size of the word.

For the recursive case, the code generates the permutation to return by taking the character at position index and concatenates it with the next permutation of the substring. This permutation is obtained by invoking the nextpermutation() method of the substring object (lines 22–23).

If there are no more permutations of the substring, then we need to advance index to the next character of word. If we are not at the end of the word, then we pick the character at that position, create the new substring (i.e., all the other characters in word), and create a PermuteString object for the new substring. Instance variable substring-Generator is a reference to the newly created PermuteString object. These steps are accomplished by lines 24–32. The final step is to return the permutation that was created by lines 23–24.

Listing 11.4 contains the complete implementation for class PermuteString. To help understand class PermuteString's operation, Figure 11.9 traces the production of the permutations of the string "tocs". A permutation can be found by tracing a path from the starting point on the left to a node on the right and reading off the letters in red. For example, the top path traces out the permutation "tocs", the next path (again starting from the left) traces out the permutation "tosc". Successive words can be found by reading the traces from the top to bottom. Thus, the last permutation generated would be "scot." The diagram illustrates how successive characters are chosen and a recursive call is made to create a generator for the resulting substring. For example, we see to produce the permutation "scot" that the last letter, "s" is selected from the original word "tocs" and a recursive call is made to generate the permutations of the remaining letters, "toc."

Listing 11.4 PermuteString.java

```java
1.  // generate the permutations of a string
2.  class PermuteString {
3.      private String word;
4.      private int index;
5.      private PermuteString substringGenerator;
6.
7.      // PermuteString: default constructor
8.      public PermuteString(String s) {
9.          word = s;
10.         index = 0;
11.         if (s.length() > 1)
12.             substringGenerator = new PermuteString(s.substring(1));
13.     }
14.
15.     // nextPermutation: return next permutation of word
16.     public String nextPermutation() {
17.         if (word.length() == 1) {
18.             ++index;
19.             return word;
20.         }
21.         else {
22.             String r = word.charAt(index)
23.              + substringGenerator.nextPermutation();
24.             if (!substringGenerator.morePermutations()) {
25.                 ++index;
26.                 if (index < word.length()) {
27.                     String tailString = word.substring(0, index)
28.                      + word.substring(index + 1);
29.                     substringGenerator = new PermuteString(tailString);
30.                 }
31.             }
32.             return r;
33.         }
34.     }
35.
36.     // morePermutations: return true of more permutations available
37.     public boolean morePermutations() {
38.         return index < word.length();
39.     }
40. }
```

Figure 11.9   **Generations of the permutations of string "tosc".**

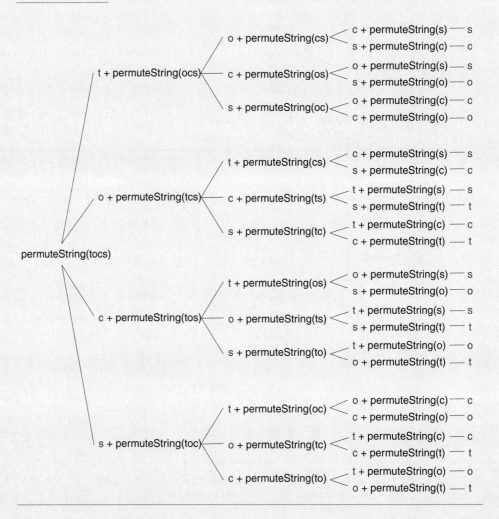

REVIEW

- Recursion is when a function calls itself. A recursive function must have two parts. It has a termination part that ends the recursion and a recursive call with simpler parameters.

- The termination part of a recursive algorithm is called the base case.

- The recursive part of a recursive algorithm is called the recursive case.

- Time-critical client applications with a sorting substep often use the mergeSort() method.

- Method mergeSort() is a recursive sort that conceptually divides its list of *n* elements to be sorted into two sublists of size *n*/2. If a sublist contains more than one element, the sublist is sorted by a recursive call to mergeSort(). After the two sublists of size *n*/2 are sorted, they are merged together to produce a single sorted list of size *n*. The running time of method mergeSort() is proportional to *n*log*n*. This performance is sometimes known as *linearithmic* performance.

- The mergeSort() strategy is known as a *divide-and-conquer* strategy—the problem is divided into subproblems of lesser complexity and the solutions of the subproblems are used to produced the overall solution.

- Any comparison-based sorting algorithm has a worst-case performance that is at least linearithmic in the number of comparisons. It can also be shown using an information-theoretic argument that any comparison-based searching algorithm is at least logarithmic in the number of comparisons.

- The binary search algorithm requires at most $\log_2 (N + 1)$ comparisons to search a sorted list with *N* elements.

- The height of a full binary tree of *N* nodes is $\log_2 (N + 1)$.

- The number of permutations of *n* distinct items is *n*!.

SELF-TEST

S11.1 What is the output of the following program?

```java
class SelfCheck1 {
    public static int f(int n) {
        if (n <= 1)
            return n;
        else
            return f(n-1) + f(n-2);
    }
    public static void main(String[] args) {
        System.out.println(f(4));
    }
}
```

S11.2 Write a recursive function `reverse()` that accepts two string arguments, s and r. Function `reverse()` uses recursion to reverse the characters in string s and place the reversed string in string r.

S11.3 Write a recursive function `printNumber()` that accepts an integer argument. Function `printNumber()` uses recursion to print out the value of its argument a character at a time.

S11.4 Give the names of the two types of cases every recursive algorithm must have.

S11.5 A full binary tree has 1023 nodes. What is the height of the tree?

11.9   EXERCISES

11.1 In the definition, "A person's descendants are the person's children and all their descendants", identify the base case and the recursive case.

11.2 Develop a recursive formula for the number of recursive calls made by `fibonacci()` in computing the nth Fibonacci number.

11.3 Rewrite method `fibonacci()` so that it performs the computation only if its parameter is nonnegative.

11.4 Redo the permutation generator using an iterative solution. Which solution is easier to understand?

11.5 Development a program `FibonacciSquares.java` to produce a Fibonacci square as depicted in the Figure 11.4. The number of squares to be displayed should be a user-supplied value. The colors of the squares should cycle through `Color.red`, `Color.yellow`, `Color.green`, and `Color.blue`, and the squares should be generated in a counterclockwise manner.

11.6 If we take the ratio of successive numbers in the Fibonacci sequence, we see that the ratio is approaching a particular value. For example, 5/3 is 1.66666...; 8/5 is 1.6; and 13/8 is 1.625. The value to which these ratios are converging is called the *golden ratio* or *golden mean*. Develop a program to compute an approximation of the golden mean. To get an accurate estimation of its value, compute the golden mean of successive pairs of Fibonacci numbers until the difference between the computed golden means is less than 0.0005.

11.7 Develop a program that prompts a user for a number n and then computes and displays for integer values i in the interval 1 through n the nearest integer to the expression

$$\frac{1}{\sqrt{5}} \cdot \left(\left(\frac{1 + \sqrt{5}}{2} \right)^i - \left(\frac{1 - \sqrt{5}}{2} \right)^i \right)$$

Compare the output of the program with the output of method `fibonacci()` for the same values. Discuss their similarity.

11.8 Rewrite function `factorial()` so that it returns a double value.

11.9 Develop a program that uses the function `factorial()` of Exercise 11.8 to compute an approximation of *e* (Euler's number). Base your approximation on the following formula for *e*:

$$1 + \frac{1}{1!} + \frac{1}{2!} + \frac{1}{3!} + ...$$

11.10 Write a recursive function to compute the greatest common divisor (gcd) of two integers. The gcd of two integers is the largest integer that divides them both. A working definition of gcd is

$$\gcd(m, n) = \begin{cases} n & \text{if } n \text{ divides } m \\ \gcd(n, \text{remainder of } m \text{ divided by } n) & \text{otherwise} \end{cases}$$

11.11 Implement a method `pivot()` with three formal parameters: **int** array a and **int** parameters m and n, where m is less than n. If a[n] is less than a[m], then the values of elements a[m] and a[n] are interchanged.

11.12 Develop an application that gives a solution to the Towers of Hanoi problem. There are three pegs with n disks on one of the pegs as in the following diagram.

Peg A   Peg B   Peg C

The problem to be solved is to come up with a set of moves that transfers the disks from Peg A to Peg C. A move must obey the following rules.

■ Only one disk can be moved at a time, and this disk must be top disk on a tower.

■ A larger disk cannot be placeD on the top of a smaller disk.

Your application should print out the moves necessary to move all the disks from Peg A to Peg C. The moves generated by the application should be of the form:

move a disk from Peg A to Peg B

11.13 Implement a method `partition()` with three formal parameters: **int** array a and **int** parameters m and n, where m is less than n. Method `partition()` first invokes method `pivot()` of Exercise 11.11. The list is then rearranged into three sublists or *partitions*. The middle sublist is composed of an element whose value is the *pivot value* a[m]; the values of the elements in the left sublist are no larger than the pivot value, and the values of the elements in the right sublist are no smaller than the pivot value. The method returns the location of the pivot value after the partitioning has completed.

11.14 Implement the `quickSort()` sorting method that uses in part, method `partition()` of Exercise 11.13. The method has three formal parameters: **int** array a and **int** parameters m and n. The method sorts elements a[m] through a[n] of a. If m ≥ n, the method simply returns. If m+1 equals n, then the method sorts the sublist directly. Otherwise, the method invokes `partition()`. Let k be the return value of the `partition()` invocation. To complete the sorting, method `quickSort()` makes two recursive calls to sort sublists a[m] through a[k-1] and a[k+1] through a[n].

11.15 Modify method `mergeSort()` so that it invokes the variant of `insertionSort()` of Exercise 8.33 if the number of elements to be sorted is 20 or less.

11.16 Modify method `quickSort()` of Exercise 11.15 so that it invokes the variant of `insertionSort()` of Exercise 8.33 if the number of elements to be sorted is 20 or less.

11.17 Create an additional test harness for the binary search method that searches a list with an odd number of elements.

11.18 A palindrome is a string that is identical to its reverse when differences in spacing, case of letters, and punctuation is ignored. Examples of palindromes are "level", "Was it a rat I saw", and "A man, a plan, a canal: Panama". Implement and test a Java method

   public static boolean isPalindrome(String phrase)

Method `isPalindrome()` returns true if its argument is a palindrome; otherwise it returns false. Include a test harness for your method.

11.19 Write a recursive method `sum(int m, int n)` that computes the sum of the integers m through n (i.e., $m + (m + 1) + (m + 2) + \ldots + (n - 2) + (n - 1) + n$). Write a test harness to exercise your code.

11.20 Modify the permutation generator so that it eliminates duplicate permutations. That is, the generator never returns the same string twice.

| 11.10 | **PROGRAMMING PROJECT — SIERPINSKI FRACTAL** |

Fractals are a geometric pattern where the curves or surfaces are independent of scale or self-similar. What that means from a visual standpoint is that if you took a fractal and magnified a section of it, the section would appear identical to the original.

> The objective of this programming project is to practice using recursion to create an interesting graphics image

Fractals have many uses in describing the mathematical properties of complex objects. However, most of us are more familiar with some of the beautiful images created using fractals. Figure 11.10 contains an image of a famous fractal named after the mathematician Benoit Mandelbrot.

Figure 11.10 **Mandelbrot fractal.**

In this programming case study, you will create a recursive program that renders another well known fractal—the Sierpinski fractal.

PROBLEM STATEMENT

A Sierpinski fractal or gasket is formed using the following algorithm.

Step 1.   *Draw a triangle.*

Step 2.   *Compute the midpoint of each of the triangle's sides.*

Step 3.   *Repeat for each smaller triangle that is formed by one vertex of the original triangle and the two closest midpoints. Stop when a predetermined number of steps is completed.*

The following diagram illustrates two levels of recursion.

Design and develop a program to render a Sierpinski fractal. Your program should program should prompt for and accept the depth of recursion from the console.

ANALYSIS AND DESIGN

Because we are developing a recursive solution, you should first determine the base and inductive cases. The base case occurs when the program has recursed to the depth input by the user. The recursive case draws the specified triangle, computes the midpoints of the triangle's three sides, and makes three recursive calls for each of the three new triangles. To make the image interesting and colorful looking, your program should alternate the colors used to render the triangles.

IMPLEMENTATION

Your program's name should be `SierpinskiFractal.java`.

What are objects and methods we need to create your Sierpinski fractal? Obviously, your program needs the capability to render a triangle. For this capability, it makes sense to use the `ColoredTriangle` class developed in Chapter 5. Class `ColoredTriangle` can be used to create and draw the necessary triangles. Recall that class `ColoredTriangle` has the following public methods:

`public ColoredTriangle()`

Constructs a default triangle representation. The default representation is a black triangle with points at coordinates (1, 1), (2, 2), and (3, 3).

`public ColoredTriangle(Point v1, Point v2, Point v3, Color c)`

Constructs a triangle using color `c` whose endpoints are equivalent to the points referenced by `p1`, `p2`, and `p3`.

`public Point getPoint(int i)`

Returns the `i`th point of the associated triangle.

`public void setPoint(int i, Point v)`

Sets the `i`th point of the associated triangle so that its value is equivalent to the point referenced by `v`.

`public Color getColor()`

Returns the color of the associated triangle.

`public void setColor(Color c)`

Sets the color of the associated triangle to `c`.

`public void paint(Graphics g)`

Renders the triangle to graphic context `g`.

The Sierpinski algorithm requires that we compute the midpoint of the sides of a triangle. Consequently, a method that computes the midpoint of line segment will be useful. Method `midPoint` has the following prototype:

```
public static Point midPoint(Point p1, Point p2)
```

Compute the midpoint of the line segment defined by endpoints `p1` and `p2`.

The two other methods necessary are method `main` and method `Sierpinski`. Method `main()` will prompt for and read the number of levels of triangles that should be drawn (i.e., the depth of recursion). It will then invoke the method `Sierpinski()`. Method `Sierpinski()` will do all the work. Its prototype is:

```
public static void Sierpinski(Graphics g, Point p1, Point p2,
    Point p3, Color c, int depth)
```

This method will draw a triangle of color `c` with points `p1`, `p2`, and `p3` in the graphics context `g`. The triangle should be color `c`. Parameter `depth` is the current depth of recursion. The method will recursively call itself to draw three new triangles.

The following diagram shows a Sierpinski fractal rendered using the colors blue and orange recursing to a depth of 6.

TESTING

Because you were able to reuse class `ColoredTriangle`, your program `Sierpinski-Fractal.java` is short and simple. Consequently, testing the program is straightforward. You should make sure your program does something reasonable if the recursion depth input is less than zero, zero, and one. You should also test to see what happens if different kinds of triangles are used. The previous diagram shows an equilateral triangle. Try an obtuse triangle. Does your program still work?

SELF-TEST ANSWERS

S11.1 3

S11.2

```java
class SelfCheckReverse {
   public static String reverse(String s) {
   if (s.length() <= 1)
      return s;
   else
      return reverse(s.substring(1, s.length()))
         + s.substring(0,1);
}

   public static void main(String[] args) {
      System.out.println(reverse("hello"));
   }
}
```

S11.3

```java
class SelfCheckPrintNumber {
   public static void printNumber(int n) {
      if (n < 10)
         System.out.print(n % 10);
      else {
         printNumber(n / 10);
         System.out.print(n % 10);
      }
   }
   public static void main(String[] args) {
      printNumber(231);
   }
}
```

S11.4 Every recursive algorithm must have at least one base case and at least one recursive case.

S11.5 10

12 THREADS

In state-of-the-art software, a program can be composed of multiple independent flows of control, where these flows of control are known commonly as *processes* or *threads*. For example, many document processing suites use multiple threads. The suites often use one thread to print a document while another thread enables a user to enter and format text. By separating these tasks into different flows of control, a user can continue to edit and format a document as it prints. In this chapter, we examine several Java mechanisms for creating, scheduling, managing, and running threads.

OBJECTIVES

- Develop programs with multiple, concurrent flows of control using threads.
  - Create threads that run at a time relative to the current time.
  - Create threads that run repeatedly.
  - Create threads that run at designated times.
- Schedule programs to pause for some specific time or event.
- Consider standard classes Timer, TimerTask, and Thread.
- Consider standard classes Date and Calendar.

12.1		**SCHEDULING**

Our programs thus far have consisted of single flows of control. For example with console-based programs, the flow of control started in the first statement of method `main()` and worked its way statement by statement to the last statement of method `main()`. Flow of control could be passed temporarily to other methods through invocations, but the control returned to `main()` after their completion. Programs with single flows of control are known as *sequential processes*.

```
Single-threaded Program {
    Statement 1;
    Statement 2;      ◄─────────
    ...
    Statement k;
}
```
Although the statements within a single flow of control may invoke other methods, the next statement is not executed until the current statement completes

The ability to run more than one process at the same time is an important characteristic of modern operating systems such us Linux, OS X, and Windows. For example, a user desktop may be running a browser, programming IDE, music player, and document preparation system. Figure 12.1 shows two snapshots of a Windows task manager: Figure 12.1(a) displays a list of applications running on some machine. Figure 12.1(b) displays some of the operating system and application processes required to run those applications.

Java supports the creation of programs with *concurrent* flows of control. These independent flows of control are called *threads*. Because threads run within a program and make use of its resources in their execution, these individual flows of control are also called *lightweight processes*. Figure 12.2 depicts a scenario where the main flow of control for a program spawns two threads to assist in the completion of its task. One of these threads spawns yet another thread to assist in its subtask.

Java has several classes that support the creation and scheduling of threads. Classes `java.util.Timer` and `java.util.TimerTask` are generally the easiest to use. They allow a thread to be created and run either at a time relative to the current time or at some specific time.

Class `Timer` has three methods named `schedule()` for creating threads after either some specified delay or at some specific time.

`public void schedule(TimerTask task, long m)`
> Runs `task.run()` after waiting m milliseconds.

`public void schedule(TimerTask task, long m, long n)`
> Runs `task.run()` after waiting m milliseconds. It then repeatedly reruns `task.run()` every **n** milliseconds.

`public void schedule(TimerTask task, Date y)`
> Runs `task.run()` at time t.

By extending **abstract** class `TimerTask` and specifying a definition for its **abstract** method `run()`, an application-specific thread can be created.

Figure 12.1 **Task manager snapshot.**

(a) Application listing

(b) Process listing.

Figure 12.2 **A multithreaded program.**

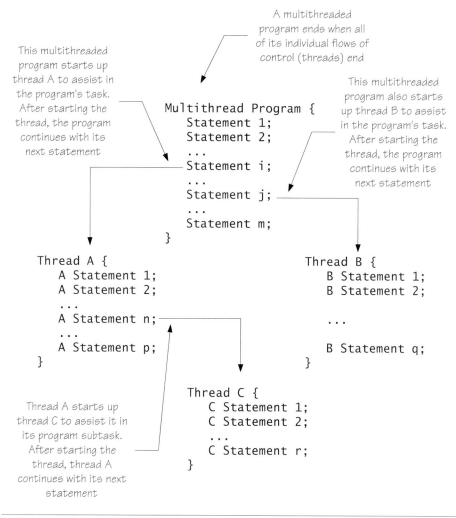

```
abstract void run()
```

Implements the action to be performed by this task.

12.1.1 RUNNING AFTER A DELAY

For our first thread example, we define a class `DisplayCharSequence` in Listing 12.1 that extends `TimerTask` to support the creation of a thread that displays 20 copies of some desired character (e.g., "H", "A", or "N").

Listing 12.1 DisplayCharSequence.java

```java
1.  // Displays characters in separate threads
2.
3.  import java.util.*;
4.
5.  public class DisplayCharSequence extends TimerTask {
6.      // instance variables
7.      private char displayChar;
8.      Timer timer;
9.
10.     // DisplayCharSequence(): construct a c displayer
11.     public DisplayCharSequence(char c) {
12.         displayChar = c;
13.         timer = new Timer();
14.         timer.schedule(this, 0);
15.     }
16.
17.     // run(): display the occurrences of the character of interest
18.     public void run() {
19.         for (int i = 0; i < 20; ++i) {
20.             System.out.print(displayChar);
21.         }
22.
23.         timer.cancel();
24.     }
25.
26.     // main(): application entry point
27.     public static void main(String[] args) {
28.         DisplayCharSequence s1 = new DisplayCharSequence('H');
29.         DisplayCharSequence s2 = new DisplayCharSequence('A');
30.         DisplayCharSequence s3 = new DisplayCharSequence('N');
31.     }
32. }
```

To assist with its behavior, a DisplayCharSequence object has two instance variables. They are **char** variable displayChar and Timer variable timer.

    private char displayChar

> The character to be displayed by the thread. Its value is specified during DisplayCharSequence construction.

    private Timer timer

> Represents the timer that schedules the thread.

The DisplayCharSequence class defines a single constructor.

    public DisplayCharSequence(char c)

> Schedules a thread whose task is to display 20 copies of the character c to standard output. The thread is scheduled to start after a delay of zero milliseconds; i.e., immediately.

Because class DisplayCharSequence extends TimerTask to support thread creation, DisplayCharSequence must define a method run().

    public void run()

> Displays 20 copies of displayChar.

To demonstrate its use as a thread creator, class DisplayCharSequence also defines a **static** method main() as a program entry point.

Figure 12.3 **DisplayCharSequence.java execution runs.**

```
cmd:   javac DisplayCharSequence.java

cmd:   java DisplayCharSequence
HHHHHHHHHHHHHHHHHHANAAAAAAAAAAAAAAANHHHHHNNNNNNNNNNAAAAAAANNNNNNNN

cmd:   java DisplayCharSequence
HHHHHHHHHHHHHHHHHHANANANANANANANANANNNNNNNNNNNNNNAAAAAAAAAAAAAAHHHH

cmd:   java DisplayCharSequence
HHHHHHHHHHHHHHHHHHANAAAAAAAAAAAAAAANHHHHHNNNNNNNNNNNNNNNNNNAAAAAA

cmd:
```

```java
public static void main(String[] args)
```
  Creates three DisplayCharSequence that display respectively the characters 'H', 'A', and 'N'.

By examining different runs of program DisplayCharSequence.java, it becomes obvious that there are different processes operating and producing output. Figure 12.3 depicts three runs of DisplayCharSequence.java. Each run produced a different output sequence.

The method definitions are worth analyzing. The DisplayCharSequence constructor configures the instance variables and schedule the thread.

```java
// DisplayCharSequence(): construct a c displayer
public DisplayCharSequence(char c) {
    displayChar = c;
    timer = new Timer();
    timer.schedule(this, 0);
}
```

The value of instance variable displayChar is given by parameter c; and the value of variable timer is obtained by constructing a new Timer. The new Timer then is used to the schedule a thread based on the new DisplayCharSequence object. Because the thread is to be based on the DisplayCharSequence object under construction, the first schedule() parameter is **this**. To schedule the new thread to run after a zero-millisecond delay from the current time, the second schedule() parameter has value 0.

A subclass implementation of TimerTask's **abstract** method run() has typically two parts. The first part defines the application-specific action the thread is to perform. The second part ends the thread. The thread is ended, because the application-specific

Timesharing

Most computer systems have a single central processing unit (CPU). On such systems, there can only be one process using the CPU at a time; i.e., there cannot be multiple processes running simultaneously. To simulate multiprocessing, uniprocessor computing systems normal practice *timesharing*. A timesharing computer system repeatedly gives each process a slice of time to use the CPU to make progress with respect to its action. Because the time slices are typically small and occur so frequently, the computing system has the appearance of simultaneous behavior.

action has completed. `DisplayCharSequence` method `run()` follows the standard form.

```java
// run(): display the occurences of the character of interest
public void run() {
    for (int i = 0; i < 20; ++i) {
        System.out.print(displayChar);      ⎫ Desired action to be
    }                                        ⎭ performed by thread

    timer.cancel();        ⎫ Desired action is
}                          ⎬ completed so thread
                           ⎭ is canceled
```

A **for** loop displays 20 copies of `displayChar`. Because the display completes the action wanted of the thread, the next statement uses `Timer` method `cancel()` to end the thread.

For class method `main()` to create the three character displaying threads, it needs only to define three instances of `DisplayCharSequence`.

```java
// main(): application entry point
public static void main(String[] args) {
    DisplayCharSequence s1 = new DisplayCharSequence('H');
    DisplayCharSequence s2 = new DisplayCharSequence('A');
    DisplayCharSequence s3 = new DisplayCharSequence('N');
}
```

12.1.2   RUNNING REPEATEDLY

Our next example demonstrates how to schedule a thread to run multiple times. We do so in `SimpleClock.java` of Listing 12.2. This program updates the display of a GUI-based clock every second.

Listing 12.2 SimpleClock.java

```
1.  // displays current time
2.
3.  import javax.swing.JFrame;
4.  import java.util.*;
5.  import java.text.*;
6.  import java.awt.*;
7.
8.  public class SimpleClock extends TimerTask {
9.      // class constants
10.     final static long MILLISECONDS_PER_SECOND = 1000;
11.
12.     // instance variables
13.     private JFrame window - new JFrame("Clock");
14.     private Timer timer = new Timer();
15.     private String clockFace = "";
16.
17.     // SimpleClock(): default clock constructor
18.     public SimpleClock() {
19.         // configure GUI
20.         window.setDefaultCloseOperation(JFrame.EXIT_ON_CLOSE);
21.         window.setSize(200, 60);
22.         Container c = window.getContentPane();
23.         c.setBackground(Color.white);
24.         window.setVisible(true);
25.
26.         // update GUI every second starting immediately
27.         timer.schedule(this, 0, 1*MILLISECONDS_PER_SECOND);
28.     }
29.
30.     // run(): updates clock display
31.     public void run() {
32.         Date time = new Date();
33.
34.         Graphics g = window.getContentPane().getGraphics();
35.
36.         g.setColor(Color.WHITE);
37.         g.drawString(clockFace, 10, 20);
38.
39.         clockFace = time.toString();
40.         g.setColor(Color.BLUE);
41.         g.drawString(clockFace, 10, 20);
42.     }
43.
44.     // main(): application entry point
45.     public static void main(String[] args) {
46.         SimpleClock clock = new SimpleClock();
47.     }
48. }
```

In producing its display, program SimpleClock.java makes uses of standard Java class Date. Class Date provides the following constructor and method of interest to us.

```
public Date()
```

Creates a date representation reflecting the current time to the millisecond.

```
public String toString()
```

Returns a textual representation of the date of the form

w c d h:m:s z y

where

- *w*: three-character representation of the day of the week;
- *c*: three-character representation of the calendar month of the year;
- *d*: two-digit representation of the day of the month;
- *h*: two-digit representation of the hour of the day;
- *m*: two-digit representation of the minute within the hour;
- *s*: two-digit representation of the second within the minute;
- *z*: three-character representation of the zone specification;
- y: four-character representation of the year.

Like `DisplayCharSequence.java`, program `SimpleClock.java` extends `TimerTask`. Class `SimpleClock` has three instance variables.

```
private JFrame window
```

Represents the window containing the GUI.

```
private String clockFace
```

Represents a string representation of the current date.

```
private Timer timer
```

Represents the timer that schedules this `SimpleClock` thread to run repeatedly every second.

The `SimpleClock` default constructor has two tasks: configure the GUI and schedule a thread whose task is to update the GUI every second.

```
// SimpleClock(): default clock constructor
public SimpleClock() {
    // configure GUI
    window.setSize(200, 60);
    Container c = window.getContentPane();
    c.setBackground(Color.white);
    window.setDefaultCloseOperation(JFrame.EXIT_ON_CLOSE);
    window.setVisible(true);

    // update GUI every second starting immediately
    timer.schedule(this, 0, 1*MILLISECONDS_PER_SECOND);
}
```

The GUI configuration of its window is straightforward—the window is sized properly, its background color is set, its closing policy is set, and it is made visible.

With the GUI arranged, `Timer` method `schedule()` then is used to schedule a thread that runs every second to update the GUI.

```
timer.schedule(this, 0, 1*MILLISECONDS_PER_SECOND);
```

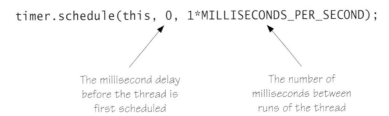

The millisecond delay before the thread is first scheduled

The number of milliseconds between runs of the thread

Standard class Timer and standard class Timer

Java provides two different standard classes named `Timer`. The class we have been using is part of the `util` API. There is also a `Timer` class that is part of `swing` API. In importing classes into `SimpleClock.java` we were careful not to import both `Timer` classes. The inclusion of both classes would make it ambiguous which `Timer` class was being used at line 14 of the program.

```
private Timer timer = new Timer();
```

Although we cannot import both `Timer` classes into a single Java source file, we can use both `Timer` classes in the same Java source file. The **import** statement exists to allow a syntactic shorthand when using Java resources; i.e., an **import** statement is not required to make use of Java resources. For example, by using fully qualified class names, the following code segment unambiguously uses both `Timer` classes.

```
java.util.Timer t1 = new java.util.Timer();
javax.swing.Timer t2 = new javax.swing.Timer();
```

The `schedule()` method invoked by `SimpleClock` is different from the method invoked by `DisplayCharSequence`. That `schedule()` method initiated a single thread run. The `schedule()` method invoked by `SimpleClock` causes a thread to be first run after a delay of 0 milliseconds (i.e., immediately) and then rerun every second.

The thread action associated with a `SimpleClock` is specified by its method `run()`.

```
// run(): updates clock display
public void run() {
   Date time = new Date();

   Graphics g = window.getContentPane().getGraphics();

   g.setColor(Color.WHITE);
   g.drawString(clockFace, 10, 20);

   clockFace = time.toString();
   g.setColor(Color.BLUE);
   g.drawString(clockFace, 10, 20);
}
```

Method `run()` first determines the current time by invoking a `Date` constructor.

```
Date time = new Date();
```

The GUI then is updated to reflect the current time. To do so, the method first redraws the previous time display using the background color. The redrawing effectively erases the only time display.

```
Graphics g = window.getContentPane().getGraphics();

g.setColor(Color.WHITE);
g.drawString(clockFace, 10, 20);
```

Instance variable `clockFace` then is updated to reflect the current time and the new time then is rendered using the foreground color.

```
clockFace = time.toString();
g.setColor(Color.BLUE);
g.drawString(clockFace, 10, 20);
```

There is no subsequent cancellation of the thread, because GUI updates are to occur every second.

For method `main()` of program `SimpleClock.java` to accomplish its task, it only needs to create a `SimpleClock` instance.

```
// main(): application entry point
public static void main(String[] args) {
    SimpleClock clock = new SimpleClock();
}
```

12.1.3   RUNNING AT A CHOSEN TIME

Our next thread example schedules two separate alerts for different times. The alerts are for two activities for the current day.

- Meeting of a prospective student at 9:30 AM.

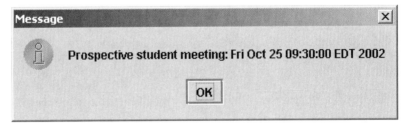

- Leave for dance recital at 6:15 PM.

The alerts are produced by program `DisplayAlert.java` of Listing 12.3. Class `DisplayAlert` provides a constructor that schedules the display of a message via a popup window. The parameters to the constructor are the message and the time the popup window is to appear.

```
public DisplayAlert(String s, Date t)
```

Displays a popup dialog window giving alert `s` at `time` t.

Listing 12.3 **DisplayAlert.java**

```java
1.  // Displays alert at specified time
2.
3.  import javax.swing.JOptionPane;
4.  import java.awt.*;
5.  import java.util.*;
6.
7.  public class DisplayAlert extends TimerTask {
8.      // instance variables
9.      private String message;
10.     private Timer timer;
11.
12.     // DisplayAlert(): display alert s at time t
13.     public DisplayAlert(String s, Date t) {
14.         message = s + ": " + t;
15.         timer = new Timer();
16.         timer.schedule(this, t);
17.     }
18.
19.     // run(): pop up alert
20.     public void run() {
21.         JOptionPane.showMessageDialog(null, message);
22.         timer.cancel();
23.     }
24.
25.     // main(): application entry point
26.     public static void main(String[] args) {
27.         Calendar c = Calendar.getInstance();
28.
29.         c.set(Calendar.HOUR_OF_DAY, 9);
30.         c.set(Calendar.MINUTE, 30);
31.         c.set(Calendar.SECOND, 0);
32.
33.         Date studentTime = c.getTime();
34.
35.         c.set(Calendar.HOUR_OF_DAY, 18);
36.         c.set(Calendar.MINUTE, 15);
37.         c.set(Calendar.SECOND, 0);
38.
39.         Date danceTime = c.getTime();
40.
41.         DisplayAlert alert1 = new DisplayAlert(
42.             "Prospective student meeting", studentTime);
43.
44.         DisplayAlert alert2 = new DisplayAlert(
45.             "Dance recital", danceTime);
46.     }
47. }
```

To support its activities, class `DisplayAlert` has two instance variables `message` and `timer`.

> `private String message`
>
> References the alert message to be displayed.

    `private` `Timer timer`

       References the timer that schedules the display of the alert.

The definition of the `DisplayAlert` constructor uses yet another of the `Timer` methods named `schedule()`.

```
// DisplayAlert(): display alert s at time t
public DisplayAlert(String s, Date t) {
   message = s + ": " + t;
   timer = new Timer();
   timer.schedule(this, t);
}
```

This `schedule()` method arranges a thread to be run at the time referenced by parameter t. If the indicated time has already passed, then the thread is run immediately.

The `DisplayAlert` thread defined by its method `run()` creates a popup dialog of type `JOptionPane`.

```
// run(): pop up alert
public void run() {
   JOptionPane.showMessageDialog(null, message);
   timer.cancel();
}
```

Swing class `JOptionPane` provides a rich collection of class methods for displaying dialogs of various standard forms. Class `DisplayAlert` creates the `JOptionPane` using `JOptionPane` class method `showMessageDialog()`. This method displays an *information-message* `JOptionPane`, where an information-message `JOptionPane` displays a stylized letter *i* icon along with the message of interest.

    `public static void showMessageDialog(Component c, Object s)`
      `throws HeadlessException`

      Displays an information popup dialog with message s in the frame of component c. If either c is **null** or has no associated frame, then a default frame is created for the dialog, A runtime `java.awt.HeadlessException` is thrown if the current environment does not support a keyboard, mouse, and display.

An alert demonstration is given by `DisplayAlert` class method `main()`.

```
// main(): application entry point
public static void main(String[] args) {
   Calendar c = Calendar.getInstance();

   c.set(Calendar.HOUR_OF_DAY, 9);
   c.set(Calendar.MINUTE, 30);
   c.set(Calendar.SECOND, 0);

   Date studentTime = c.getTime();

   c.set(Calendar.HOUR_OF_DAY, 18);
   c.set(Calendar.MINUTE, 15);
   c.set(Calendar.SECOND, 0);

   Date danceTime = c.getTime();

   DisplayAlert alert1 = new DisplayAlert(
       "Prospective student meeting", studentTime);
```

```
      DisplayAlert alert2 = new DisplayAlert(
         "Dance recital", danceTime);
}
```

Method `main()` creates alerts for two different times. The times are set by using standard class `java.util.Calendar`. Class `Calendar` is an **abstract** class that provides several class methods for manipulating calendar and date information. Its methods of interest to us are

```
static public Calendar getInstance()
```

Returns a new calendar representing the current time using the default time zone and locale.

```
public void set(int f, int v) throws
  ArrayIndexOutOfBoundsException
```

Sets the time field indicated by `f` to value `v`. The method throws an `ArrayIndexOutOfBoundsException` if `f` is not a valid time field indicator. The valid time field and associated values are given in Table 12.1.

To issue its alerts, method `main()` first creates a `Calendar` object representing the current time.

```
Calendar c = Calendar.getInstance();
```

To set up its two times alerts, method **main()** then modifies the time associated with `Calendar` variable `c`. The modifications are achieved using a `Calendar` member method `set()`.

The fields of interest for scheduling our alerts are `Calendar.HOUR`, `Calendar.MINUTE` and `Calendar.SECOND`. By first setting those fields respectively to 9, 30, and 0. The time for the prospective student appointment alert can be set.

```
c.set(Calendar.HOUR_OF_DAY, 9);
c.set(Calendar.MINUTE, 30);
c.set(Calendar.SECOND, 0);
```

The `Calendar` time then is converted to a `Date` representation suitable for scheduling a thread.

```
Date studentTime = c.getTime();
```

The calendar fields then are reset to arrange for the other alert.

```
c.set(Calendar.HOUR_OF_DAY, 18);
c.set(Calendar.MINUTE, 45);
c.set(Calendar.SECOND, 0);

Date danceTime = c.getTime();
```

Finally, two `DisplayAlert` objects are created.

```
DisplayAlert alert1 = new DisplayAlert(
   "Prospective student meeting", studentTime);

DisplayAlert alert2 = new DisplayAlert(
   "Dance recital", danceTime);
```

Table 12.1   Calendar fields and fields values.

Field	Purpose
AM_PM	Indicator whether the hour is before or after noon
DAY_OF_WEEK	Day of the week
MONTH	Month
DATE	Day of the month
HOUR	Hour of the morning or afternoon
MINUTE	Minute within the hour
SECOND	Second within the minute
MILLISECOND	Millisecond within the second
YEAR	Year
ZONE_OFFSET	Raw offset from GMT
WEEK_OF_MONTH	Week number within the month
WEEK_OF_YEAR	Week number within the year
DST_OFFSET	Daylight savings offset in milliseconds
ERA	Era (e.g., Gregorian.AD)
DAY_OF_WEEK_IN_MONTH	Day of the week within the month

Field Constant	Value
AM	Indicator of period midnight to just before noon
JANUARY	First month of the year
FEBRUARY	Second month of the year
APRIL	Fourth month of the year
MARCH	Third month of the year
MAY	Fifth month of the year
JULY	Seventh month of the year
JUNE	Sixth month of the year
AUGUST	Eighth month of the year
SEPTEMBER	Ninth month of the year
OCTOBER	Tenth month of the year
NOVEMBER	Eleventh month of the year
DECEMBER	Twelfth month of the year
UNDECIMBER	Thirteenth month of the lunar year
SUNDAY	Sunday
MONDAY	Monday
TUESDAY	Tuesday
WEDNESDAY	Wednesday
THURSDAY	Thursday
FRIDAY	Friday
SATURDAY	Saturday

Their creation schedules the threads that cause the alerts to appear on the desktop at the designated times.

12.2	**SLEEPING**

Thus far, our threads have performed some action. Threads are also used to pause a program for a time. For example, standard class `java.lang.Thread` has a class method `sleep()` for pausing a flow of control.

```
public static void sleep(long n) throws InterruptedException
```

> Pauses the current thread for n milliseconds. It then throws an `Interrupte-dException`.

For example, the following code segment twice gets and displays the current time. The two time acquisitions are separated by 10 seconds.

```
Date t1 = new Date();
System.out.println(t1);
try {
    Thread.sleep(10000);
}
catch (InterruptedException e) {
}
Date t2 = new Date();
System.out.println(t2);
```

A sample running of this code segment produced output

```
Fri Jan 31 19:29:45 EST 2003
Fri Jan 31 19:29:55 EST 2003
```

Observe that the two times were indeed acquired 10 seconds apart.

For programming convenience, Listing 12.4 defines a class `Sleep` as part of package `ez`. The class has two class methods `pauseSeconds()` and `pauseMilliseconds()`. The methods enable a programmer to pause the flow of control for a specified number of seconds or milliseconds respectively. Besides being a syntactic shorthand, the invocations of the methods do not require user code to catch an `InterruptedException`.

```
public static void pauseSeconds(long n)
```

> Pauses the flow of control for n seconds.

```
public static void pauseMilliseconds(long n)
```

> Pauses the flow of control for n milliseconds.

For example, by using `pauseSeconds()`, the previous code segment can be rewritten as

```
Date t1 = new Date();
System.out.println(t1);
ez.Sleep.pauseSeconds(10);
Date t2 = new Date();
System.out.println(t2);
```

Listing 12.4 **Sleep.java**

```java
 1.  // Supports waiting
 2.
 3.  package ez;
 4.
 5.  public class Sleep {
 6.     // class constant
 7.     private static final int MILLISECONDS_PER_SECOND = 1000;
 8.
 9.     // pauseMilliseconds(): pauses n milliseconds
10.     public static void pauseMilliseconds(long n) {
11.        if (n <= 0) {
12.           return;
13.        }
14.        else {
15.           try {
16.              Thread.sleep(n);
17.           }
18.           catch (java.lang.InterruptedException e) {
19.              return;
20.           }
21.        }
22.     }
23.
24.     // pauseSeconds(): pauses n seconds
25.     public static void pauseSeconds(long n) {
26.        pauseMilliseconds(n*MILLISECONDS_PER_SECOND);
27.     }
28.  }
```

The definitions of two Sleep methods are as expected. For example, method pauseMilliseconds() first examines its parameter n to determine whether it is nonnegative.

```java
// pauseMilliseconds(): pauses n milliseconds
public static void pauseMilliseconds(long n) {
   if (n <= 0) {
      return;
   }
   else {
      try {
         Thread.sleep(n);
      }
      catch (java.lang.InterruptedException e) {
         return;
      }
   }
}
```

If the value is negative, then the method immediately returns because no pause is required. Otherwise, a **try** block is entered and a Thread.sleep() invocation is made for n milliseconds. When the InterruptedException is thrown, the **catch** block performs a **return**.

We next turn our attention to the development of GUI-based programs with dynamic displays. In producing their animations, the programs make use of the Sleep class to introduce delays between display updates.

12.3   **ANIMATION**

Besides making use of the Sleep class, our animations will also make use of class Step of Listing 12.5. Class Step provides the constructors and methods to generate random, but directed, changes in position. In particular, the Step class provides member methods xShift() and yShift() that return pseudorandom values from particular x- and y-intervals. These values can be used as offsets by which an object is moved.

For example, the following definition creates a Step object where pseudorandom shifts in x-coordinate come from the integer interval 0 ... 1 and where pseudorandom shifts in the y-coordinate come from interval –1 ... 1.

```
Step step = new Step(0, 1, -1, 1);
```

With this Step object, we iteratively can invoke its xShift() and yShift() methods to generate a series of positions that when plotted correspond to a rightward pseudorandom walk.

```
int x = 0;
int y = 100;
System.out.println("Starting position: (" + x + ", " + y + ")");

for (int i = 0; i < 5; ++i) {
   // determine change in x and y
   x += step.xShift();
   y += step.yShift();

   System.out.println("New position: (" + x + ", " + y + ")");
}
```

One sample run produced output

```
Starting position: (0, 100)
New position: (1, 99)
New position: (1, 100)
New position: (2, 100)
New position: (3, 100)
New position: (4, 101)
```

and another sample run produced output

```
Starting position: (0, 100)
New position: (0, 99)
New position: (1, 98)
New position: (2, 99)
New position: (2, 99)
New position: (2, 98)
```

An examination of the Step listing indicates the following class elements.

Listing 12.5 Step.java

```java
1.  // generates changes in x and y from specified intervals
2.
3.  import java.util.*;
4.
5.  public class Step {
6.      // attributes and constant
7.      private static final Random DIE = new Random();
8.      private int minDeltaX;
9.      private int maxDeltaX;
10.     private int minDeltaY;
11.     private int maxDeltaY;
12.
13.     // Step(): step generator
14.     public Step(int lx, int ux, int ly, int uy) {
15.         minDeltaX = lx;
16.         maxDeltaX = ux;
17.         minDeltaY = ly;
18.         maxDeltaY = uy;
19.     }
20.
21.     // xShift(): returns a pseudorandom value from the x-interval
22.     public int xShift() {
23.         int a = getMinX();
24.         int b = getMaxX();
25.         return DIE.nextInt(b - a + 1) + a;
26.     }
27.
28.     // yShift(): returns a pseudorandom value from the y-interval
29.     public int yShift() {
30.         int a = getMinY();
31.         int b = getMaxY();
32.         return DIE.nextInt(b - a + 1) + a;
33.     }
34.
35.     // getMinX(): minimum change in x-coordinate
36.     public int getMinX() {
37.         return minDeltaX;
38.     }
39.
40.     // getMaxX(): maximum change in x-coordinate
41.     public int getMaxX() {
42.         return maxDeltaX;
43.     }
44.
45.     // getMinY(): minimum change in y-coordinate
46.     public int getMinY() {
47.         return minDeltaY;
48.     }
49.
50.     // getMaxY(): maximum change in y-coordinate
51.     public int getMaxY() {
52.         return maxDeltaY;
53.     }
54. }
```

```
public Step(int lx, int ux, int ly, int uy)
```

Produces a Step where the pseudorandom generated x-coordinate offsets come from the interval lx ... ux and where the pseudorandom generated y-coordinates offsets come from the interval ly ... uy.

```
public int xShift()
```

Returns a pseudorandom value from the interval getMinX() ... getMaxX().

```
public int yShift()
```

Returns a pseudorandom value from the interval getMinY() ... getMaxY().

```
public int getMinX()
```

Returns the minimum pseudorandom value that can be generated by xShift().

```
public int getMaxX()
```

Returns the maximum pseudorandom value that can be generated by xShift().

```
public int getMinY()
```

Returns the minimum pseudorandom value that can be generated by yShift().

```
public int getMaxY()
```

Returns the maximum pseudorandom value that can be generated by yShift().

In implementing these actions, class Step makes use of the following class constant and instance variables.

```
private static final Random DIE
```

Represents a pseudorandom number generator.

```
private minDeltaX
```

Represents the minimum pseudorandom x-coordinate offset to be generated.

```
private maxDeltaX
```

Represents the maximum pseudorandom x-coordinate offset to be generated.

```
private minDeltaY
```

Represents the minimum pseudorandom y-coordinate offset to be generated.

```
private maxDeltaY
```

Represents the maximum pseudorandom y-coordinate offset to be generated.

With these variables, the implementations of the Step constructor and member methods are straightforward and warrant no further discussion.

Listing 12.6 of program Wiggler.java and Listing 12.7 of program Slider.java demonstrate two uses of class Step. Both programs repeatedly render red circles after a brief delay. The points that position the circles are generated with Step methods xShift() and yShift().

The step size in Wiggler.java is the same as the step size in the earlier code segment. Its graphic display shows a circle sequence that does not vary very much in its vertical orientation. A running of the program gives the illusion of a growing line that is wiggling through the window. The **while** loop in Wiggler.java iterates until the

---

Listing 12.6 Wiggler.java

```
1.  // generate a series of slightly shifted circles
2.
3.  import javax.swing.*;
4.  import java.awt.*;
5.  import ez.Sleep;
6.
7.  public class Wiggler {
8.     // main(): application entry point
9.     public static void main(String[] args) {
10.        // define animation constants
11.        Color BACKGROUND_COLOR = Color.white;
12.        Color FOREGROUND_COLOR = Color.red;
13.        int PAUSE_TIME = 10;
14.        int CIRCLE_DIAMETER = 10;
15.
16.        // set up display
17.        JFrame window = new JFrame("Wiggling");
18.        window.setSize(200, 200);
19.        window.setDefaultCloseOperation(JFrame.EXIT_ON_CLOSE);
20.        window.setBackground(BACKGROUND_COLOR);
21.        window.setVisible(true);
22.        Container c = window.getContentPane();
23.        c.setBackground(BACKGROUND_COLOR);
24.
25.        // set up and draw first circle
26.        Graphics g = c.getGraphics();
27.        g.setColor(FOREGROUND_COLOR);
28.
29.        int x = 0;
30.        int y = c.getHeight()/2;
31.
32.        g.fillOval(x, y, CIRCLE_DIAMETER, CIRCLE_DIAMETER);
33.
34.        // set up generator for subsequent offsets
35.        Step step = new Step (0, 1, -1, 1);
36.
37.        // draw the shifted circles
38.        while (x < c.getWidth()) {
39.           x += step.xShift();
40.           y += step.yShift();
41.           g.fillOval(x, y, CIRCLE_DIAMETER, CIRCLE_DIAMETER);
42.           Sleep.pauseMilliseconds(PAUSE_TIME);
43.        }
44.     }
45.  }
```

---

upper-left-hand corner of the bounding box of the current circle lies beyond the right edge of the window.

```
// draw the shifted circles
while (x < c.getWidth()) {
   x += step.xShift();
   y += step.yShift();
   g.fillOval(x, y, 5, 5);
   Sleep.pauseMilliseconds(15);
```

```
      }
   }
```

To give the illusion of growth, the program pauses fifteen milliseconds after each circle rendering. Figure 12.4 gives a representative snapshot of each `Wiggler.java`.

Figure 12.4 **Snapshot of Wiggler.java.**

Program `Slider.java` is similar to `Wiggler.java`. The only consequential difference between the two programs occurs in the **while** loop body.

```
// draw the "sliding" circles
while (x < c.getWidth()) {
   g.setColor(BACKGROUND_COLOR);
   g.fillOval(x, y, CIRCLE_DIAMETER, CIRCLE_DIAMETER);
   g.setColor(FOREGROUND_COLOR);
   x += step.xShift();
   y += step.yShift();
   g.fillOval(x, y, CIRCLE_DIAMETER, CIRCLE_DIAMETER);
   Sleep.pauseMilliseconds(PAUSE_TIME);
   }
}
```

In program `Slider.java`, the **while** loop body performs three additional statements at the start of each iteration.

```
// erase previously rendered circle
g.setColor(BACKGROUND_COLOR);
g.fillOval(x, y, CIRCLE_DIAMETER, CIRCLE_DIAMETER);
g.setColor(FOREGROUND_COLOR);
```

These statements assist the "movement" of the circle. The first two of these statements render a new circle at the position of interest (x, y). Thus, the new circle replaces what previously was displayed. Because the new circle is displayed in the background color, the old circle is effectively gone and the new circle is not distinguishable with the background. The other new statement resets the rendering color to the foreground color.[†]

[†] The three statements are similar in nature to the statements in `SimpleClock.java` that "erased" the previous time display before rendering the new time.

Listing 12.7 Slider.java

```
1.  // simulate a sliding circle
2.
3.  import javax.swing.*;
4.  import java.awt.*;
5.  import ez.Sleep;
6.
7.  public class Slider {
8.      // main(): application entry point
9.      public static void main(String[] args) {
10.         // define animation constants
11.         Color BACKGROUND_COLOR = Color.white;
12.         Color FOREGROUND_COLOR = Color.red;
13.         int PAUSE_TIME = 10;
14.         int CIRCLE_DIAMETER = 10;
15.
16.         // set up display
17.         JFrame window = new JFrame("Sliding");
18.
19.         window.setSize(200, 200);
20.         window.setDefaultCloseOperation(JFrame.EXIT_ON_CLOSE);
21.
22.         window.setBackground(BACKGROUND_COLOR);
23.         window.setVisible(true);
24.
25.         Container c = window.getContentPane();
26.         c.setBackground(BACKGROUND_COLOR);
27.
28.         Graphics g = c.getGraphics();
29.         g.setColor(FOREGROUND_COLOR);
30.
31.         // set up and draw first circle
32.         int x = 0;
33.         int y = c.getHeight()/2;
34.
35.         g.fillOval(x, y, CIRCLE_DIAMETER, CIRCLE_DIAMETER);
36.
37.         // set up generator for subsequent offsets
38.         Step step = new Step (0, 1, -1, 1);
39.
40.         // draw the "sliding" circles
41.         while (x < c.getWidth()) {
42.             // erase previously rendered circle
43.             g.setColor(BACKGROUND_COLOR);
44.             g.fillOval(x, y, CIRCLE_DIAMETFR, CIRCLE_DIAMETER);
45.             g.setColor(FOREGROUND_COLOR);
46.
47.             // draw the circle at its new position
48.             x += step.xShift();
49.             y += step.yShift();
50.             g.fillOval(x, y, CIRCLE_DIAMETER, CIRCLE_DIAMETER);
51.             Sleep.pauseMilliseconds(PAUSE_TIME);
52.         }
53.     }
54. }
```

A new position of interest (x, y) then is calculated and a new circle is rendered at that position in the foreground color.

```
// draw the circle at its new position
x += step.xShift();
y += step.yShift();
g.fillOval(x, y, CIRCLE_DIAMETER, CIRCLE_DIAMETER);
```

The new position is a very slight shifting of the previous position. Because the old and new positions are so close to each other and because the background-colored and foreground-colored circles are rendered in a manner that appears to simultaneous, the visual effect is that of the circle sliding to its new position. The process is depicted in Figure 12.5.

Figure 12.5   Rendering in an iteration of Slider.java.

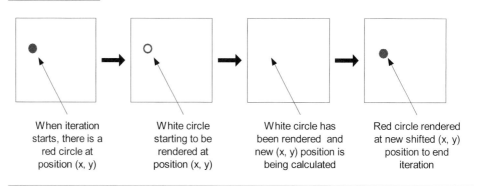

When iteration starts, there is a red circle at position (x, y)

White circle starting to be rendered at position (x, y)

White circle has been rendered and new (x, y) position is being calculated

Red circle rendered at new shifted (x, y) position to end iteration

The short millisecond program pause between circle slides causes the perceived motion to be occurring at a reasonable rate.

```
Sleep.pauseMilliseconds(PAUSE_TIME);
```

As a result, when program Slider.java is run, its display has the appearance of a red ball moving erratically across the window. Listing 12.7 contains the code for Slider.java.

We now our attention to the final example of the chapter—the simulation of three swimming fish.

<table>
<tr><td>**12.4**</td><td># CASE STUDY — SWIMMING FISH</td></tr>
</table>

In order to have three fish swimming, we need an aquarium. For now, our aquarium representation will be quite simple—it will be a window whose background is colored sea green. In the exercises, we consider some alternatives for producing more interesting aquariums. Our aquarium representation is named `Aquarium`.

> The objective of this case study is to practice using threads and animation in the design and implementation of a class

ANALYSIS AND DESIGN

Class `Aquarium` is extended from `JFrame` and it provides a default constructor and two methods. It does not maintain any additional attributes.

> `public Aquarium()`
>> Initializes and displays a sea-green colored window of appropriate size.
> `public Color getWaterColor()`
>> Returns the color of the aquarium water.
> `public Graphics getGraphicsContext()`
>> Returns the graphics context in which the elements (i.e., fish) of the aquarium should be rendered.

The definition of class `Aquarium` is given in Listing 12.8. The constructor and methods are sufficiently simple to not warrant any analysis.

Listing 12.8 Aquarium.java

```
1.  // Represents an aquarium
2.
3.  import java.awt.*;
4.  import javax.swing.*;
5.
6.  class Aquarium extends JFrame {
7.      private static final int AQUARIUM_WIDTH = 400;
8.      private static final int AQUARIUM_HEIGHT = 400;
9.      private static final Color SEA_BLUE = new Color(109,171,177);
10.
11.     public Aquarium() {
12.         super("Fishy swim");
13.         setDefaultCloseOperation(JFrame.EXIT_ON_CLOSE);
14.         getContentPane().setBackground(SEA_BLUE);
15.         setSize(AQUARIUM_WIDTH, AQUARIUM_HEIGHT);
16.         setVisible(true);
17.     }
18.
19.     public Color getWaterColor() {
20.         return SEA_BLUE;
21.     }
22.
23.     public Graphics getGraphicsContext() {
24.         return getContentPane().getGraphics();
25.     }
26. }
```

Listing 12.9 MovingFish.java

```
1.  // Represent a moving fish
2.
3.  import java.awt.*;
4.
5.  public class MovingFish extends Fish {
6.      // movement attribute
7.      private Step stroke;
8.
9.      // MovingFish(): default fish with default movement
10.     public MovingFish() {
11.         super();
12.         stroke = new Step(0, 1, -1, 1);
13.     }
14.
15.     // swim(): move the fish
16.     public void swim() {
17.         int x = getX();
18.         int y = getY();
19.
20.         x += stroke.xShift();
21.         y += stroke.yShift();
22.         setPosition(x, y);
23.     }
24. }
```

The simplest approach to produce a moving fish is to extend class Fish of Listing 9.14. This approach is taken with class MovingFish of Listing 12.9. A MovingFish object has one additional attribute that a plain Fish object does not have—a stroke. The MovingFish instance variable stroke is of type Step and it represents how the fish can change its position in a single swim stroke.

private Step stroke

Describes the possible range of motion for a single swim stroke of the fish.

Class MovingFish should provide constructors that correspond to the Fish constructors and it should provide constructors that allow the swimming stroke to be specified. The MovingFish implementation of Listing 12.9 is a basic one and supplies only a default constructor. Other constructors are left to the exercises.

public MovingFish()

Constructs a pseudorandomly colored fish with swim stroke x-coordinate movement coming from the interval 0 ... 1 and swim stroke y-coordinate movement coming from the interval –1 ... 1.

To implement a default MovingFish constructor is simple. The default superclass constructor is used to configure the Fish attributes of the new MovingFish object. The stroke attribute then is configured by constructing a new Step with appropriate x- and y-axis intervals.

```
// MovingFish(): default fish with default movement
public MovingFish() {
    super();
    stroke = new Step(0, 1, -1, 1));
}
```

Because our implementation is minimal, only one `MovingFish` mutator is defined—
`swim()`. Method `swim()` updates the position of the fish by making a single pseudorandom stroke.

> `public void swim()`
>
> Updates the position of the fish through the generation of x- and y-coordinate
> offsets. The offsets are generated using the `Step` shifting methods. The new
> position of the fish is shifting of its previous position with respect to the offsets.

To implement the behavior required of method `swim()`, the current position (x, y) of
the fish must be determined.

```
// swim(): move the fish
public void swim() {
    int x = getX();
    int y = getY();

    x += stroke.xShift();
    y += stroke.yShift();
    setPosition(x, y);
}
```

The new position then can be determined by incrementing x by `stroke.xShift()` and
incrementing y by `stroke.yShift()`. The new value (x, y) then can be used to update
the position attribute of the fish.

IMPLEMENTATION

We now turn our attention to the actual aquarium simulation. Our approach is again one
of minimality. Our simulation will animate 1000 swim strokes for each of the three fish.
The fish will not "react" to swimming into the sides of the aquarium by changing course.
Instead they will continue their course and disappear. (The exercises consider how to
implement a bumping reaction.) A snapshot of the simulation is depicted in Figure 12.6.

The simulation will have two parts. The first part will set up the aquarium and place
the fish. The second part will simulate the 1000 swim strokes.

To set up the animation, we will need an `Aquarium` representation and three `Mov-
ingFish`.

```
Aquarium aquarium = new Aquarium()
MovingFish[] fish = { new MovingFish(), new MovingFish(),
                      new MovingFish() };
```

For reason of aesthetics, the fish should be positioned in different areas of the aquarium.

```
fish[0].setPosition(   0, 100);
fish[1].setPosition(  50, 200);
fish[2].setPosition(-100, 300);
```

The positioning we prefer starts with only two of the fish being visible initially.

Figure 12.6 **Snapshot of ThreeSwimmingFish.java display.**

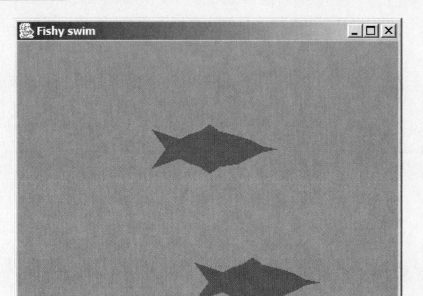

In order to simulate movement, the fish need to be rendered both in their true color and in the background color. Thus, the animation needs access to the graphic context of the aquarium and to the color of its water.

```
Graphics g = aquarium.getGraphicsContext();
Color water = aquarium.getWaterColor();
```

Because one of the rendering operations require a resetting of a fish to its true color, it is appropriate to maintain a `Color` array c of the true fish colors.

```
Color[] c = new Color[fish.length];
for (int i = 0; i < fish.length; ++i) {
   c[i] = fish[i].getColor();
}
```

With the previously described actions in place, fish movement then can be simulated. The animation should follow the form of `SimpleClock.java` and `Slider.java`; that is, for each scene in the animation the following activities should occur.

- Erase the current renderings of the changeable elements (i.e., the fish at their current positions);

- Update the changeable elements (i.e., have each fish swim a stroke);
- Render the changeable elements (i.e., the fish at their new positions).
- Pause the animation to allow the change to be perceived.

Each of the first three activities can be implemented using a **for** loop that iterates once for each fish. For the first activity, the fish need to be rendered in the color of the water.

```
// erase the previous position
for (int j = 0; j < fish.length; ++j) {
    fish[j].setColor(water);
    fish[j].paint(g);
}
```

For the second activity, the fish need to swim a stroke.

```
// have each fish swim a stroke
for (int j = 0; j < fish.length; ++j) {
    fish[j].swim();
}
```

For the third activity, the fish need to be rendered in their true colors.

```
// paint the fish at their new positions
for (int j = 0; j < fish.length; ++j) {
    fish[j].setColor(c[j]);
    fish[j].paint(g);
}
```

The last activity can be accomplished by having the animation sleep for several milliseconds.

```
// pause to allow the movement to be perceived
ez.Sleep.pauseMilliseconds(5);
```

A complete implementation of the preceding animation description is given in program ThreeFishSwimming.java of Listing 12.10.

This analysis completes our introduction to threads.

Listing 12.10 ThreeSwimmingFish.java

```
1.  // Represent three swimming fish
2.
3.  import java.awt.*;
4.
5.  public class ThreeSwimmingFish {
6.     public static void main(String[] args) {
7.        // set up the animation
8.        Aquarium aquarium = new Aquarium();
9.        MovingFish[] fish = { new MovingFish(), new MovingFish(),
10.                              new MovingFish() };
11.
12.        fish[0].setPosition(   0, 100);
13.        fish[1].setPosition(  50, 200);
14.        fish[2].setPosition(-150, 300);
15.
16.        Graphics g = aquarium.getGraphicsContext();
17.        Color water = aquarium.getWaterColor();
18.
19.        Color[] c = new Color[fish.length];
20.        for (int i = 0; i < fish.length; ++i) {
21.           c[i] = fish[i].getColor();
22.        }
23.
24.        // start the animation
25.        for (int i = 0; i < 1000; ++i) {
26.           // erase the previous position
27.           for (int j = 0; j < fish.length; ++j) {
28.              fish[j].setColor(water);
29.              fish[j].paint(g);
30.           }
31.
32.           // have each fish swim a stroke
33.           for (int j = 0; j < fish.length; ++j) {
34.              fish[j].swim();
35.           }
36.
37.           // paint the fish at their new positions
38.           for (int j = 0; j < fish.length; ++j) {
39.              fish[j].setColor(c[j]);
40.              fish[j].paint(g);
41.           }
42.
43.           // pause to allow the movement to be perceived
44.           ez.Sleep.pauseMilliseconds(5);
45.        }
46.     }
47.  }
```

- Programs with single flows of control are known as sequential processes.

- Java supports programs with concurrent flows of control. These independent flows of control are called threads.

- Because threads run within a program and make use of its resources in their execution, threads are also called lightweight processes

- To simulate multiprocessing, uniprocessor computing systems normally practice timesharing. A timesharing computer system repeatedly gives each process a slice of time on the processor to make progress with respect to its action. Because the time slices are so small and occur so frequently, the computing system has the appearance of simultaneous behavior.

- Java has several classes that support the creation and scheduling of threads. Classes `java.util.Timer` and `java.util.TimerTask` are generally the easiest to use. They allow a thread to be created and run either at a time relative to the current time or at some specific time.

- Class `Timer` has methods named `schedule()` for creating threads either after some specified delay or at some specific time.
  ```
  public void schedule(TimerTask task, long m)
  ```
  Runs `task.run()` after waiting m milliseconds.
  ```
  public void schedule(TimerTask task, long m, long n)
  ```
  Runs `task.run()` after waiting m milliseconds. It then repeatedly reruns `task.run()` every **n** milliseconds.
  ```
  public void schedule(TimerTask task, Date y)
  ```
  Runs `task.run()` at time t.

- By extending **abstract** class `TimerTask` and specifying a definition for its **abstract** method `run()`, an application-specific thread can be created.
  ```
  abstract void run()
  ```
  Implements the action to be performed by this task.

- A subclass implementation of `TimerTask`'s **abstract** method `run()` has typically two parts. The first part defines the application-specific action the thread is to perform. The second part ends the thread using its method `cancel()`.

- Class `Date` is Java's principal class for time representation. Some of its constructors and methods include
  ```
  public Date()
  ```
  Creates a date representation reflecting the current time to the millisecond.
  ```
  public String toString()
  ```
  Returns a textual representation of the date.

- Swing class `JOptionPane` provides a rich collection of class methods for displaying dialogs windows of various standard forms. One such method is `showMessageDialog()`.

```
public static void showMessageDialog(Component c, Object s)
  throws HeadlessException
```

Displays an information popup dialog with message s in the frame of component c. If c is **null** or has no associated frame, then a default frame is created for the dialog. A runtime `java.awt.HeadlessException` is thrown if the current environment does not support a keyboard, mouse, and display.

- Class `Calendar` is an **abstract** class that provides several methods named `getInstance()` for creating calendar times. The primary purpose of class `Calendar` is to support the setting and conversion of `Date` information. Some of its methods include

```
static public Calendar getInstance()
```

Returns a new calendar representing the current time using the default time zone and locale.

```
public void set(int f, int v) throws
  ArrayIndexOutOfBoundsException
```

Sets the time field indicated by f to value v. Throws an `ArrayIndexOutOfBoundsException` if f is not a valid time field indicator. The valid time field and associated values are given in Table 12.1.

- Class `java.lang.Thread` has a class method `sleep()` for pausing a flow of control.

```
public static void sleep(long n) throws InterruptedException
```

Pauses execution for n milliseconds. It then throws an `InterruptedException`.

12.6   SELF-TEST

S12.1 Suppose t is a `Timer` and task is a specialized `TimerTask`. Schedule two immediate occurrences of threads that run task.

S12.2 Suppose t is a `Timer` and task is a specialized `TimerTask`. Schedule an immediate occurrence of a thread that runs task. Also schedule an occurrence of a thread that runs task three seconds later.

S12.3 Suppose t is a `Timer` and task is a specialized `TimerTask`. Schedule an immediate occurrence of a thread that runs task two seconds from the current time. Reoccurrences of the thread start every second.

S12.4 Extend class `Sleep` to provide a method `pauseMinutes()` with a single **int** parameter n that pauses execution for n minutes.

12.7   EXERCISES

12.1   What is a thread?

12.2 What happens when a thread runs?

12.3 Do programs with a graphical user interface automatically have more than one thread?

The following definitions are in effect for Exercises 12.4–12.6.

```
DisplayCharSequence c = new DisplayCharSequence("J");
Timer t = new Timer();
```

12.4 When is the thread scheduled in the following statement.

```
t.schedule(c, 2000);
```

12.5 When is the thread scheduled in the following statement.

```
t.schedule(c, -100);
```

12.6 When is the thread scheduled in the following statement.

```
t.schedule(c, 2000, 1500);
```

12.7 Modify `SimpleClock.java` to display the time using a format appropriate to your locale.

12.8 Modify `SimpleClock.java` to support user selection of the display format.

12.9 Add accessor methods to class `Step`.

12.10 Add mutator methods to class `Step`.

12.11 Add `toString()`, `equals()`, and `clone()` methods to class `Step`.

12.12 Develop a program `CalendarAlert.java` that reads from a file `calendar.txt`. The file contains data in the format: *month day hour* : *event*, where month, day, and hour are integers and event is a string. The program should pop up an alert message that warns about the event. The alert should appear 15 minutes before the scheduled time of the event. The following listing represents a possible data file for the program.

```
 1  4  9 : Sing happy birthday to mom
 4 15  5 : Pay taxes
 5 12  9 : Sing happy birthday to dad
10 31 19 : Go trick-or-treating
```

12.13 Create a program `Butterfly.java` based on program `Wiggle.java` that displays a polygon in the shape of a butterfly rather than a circle.

12.14 Develop the following `MovingFish` constructors.

```
public MovingFish(Color c, Polygon p, int x, int y)
```
Creates a fish with color c and shape p at coordinate (x, y). The fish should have the same type of movement as a default-constructed fish.
```
public MovingFish(Step s)
```
Creates a fish with default shape and position, and movement s.
```
public MovingFish(Color c, Polygon p, int x, int y, Step s)
```
Creates a fish with color c, shape p at coordinate (x, y) and movement s.

12.15 Develop the following `MovingFish` facilitator.

> **public void** paint(Color c, Graphics g)
>> Renders the fish in color c in graphics context g.

12.16 How might paint() method of Exercise 12.15 be used to simplify ThreeMovingFish.java.

12.17 Design and implement a class UnderwaterPlant for representing plants. Provide a class method makePlant() that creates a basic underwater plant. The default constructor should make use of the method.

12.18 Design and implement a class Aerator for representing an aquarium air bubbler. Provide a class makeAerator() that creates a basic aerator. The default constructor should make use of the method. An aerator release bubbles in a regular manner that slowly rise to the surface.

12.19 Design and implement a class Sand for representing the gravel surface often found in aquariums. Provide a class method makeSand(). The default constructor should make use of the method.

12.20 Redesign and reimplement class Aquarium so that it supports both different-sized aquariums and the presence of sand, plants, and aerators. The implementation should make use of the classes UnderwaterPlant, Aerator, and Sand from Exercises 12.17–12.19.

12.21 Modify ThreeSwimmingFish.java so that rather erasing the changeable elements, the stationery elements of the aquarium are redrawn. Such a change should allow for a complex background as produced by the modified aquarium representation of Exercise 12.20.

12.8   PROGRAMMING PROJECT — BETTER FISH

Aquarium.java of Listing 12.10 is only a first step at creating an aquarium simulator. For example, Exercises 12.14–12.21 propose changes that enable a more realistic aquarium background to be represented.

> The objective of this case study is to practice using threads and animation in the design and implementation of a class

Our interest here is to develop a more realistic fish that has capability to change course when it reaches the limit of its territory. In support of this development, you will design and implement classes Territory and BoundaryBehavior.

Class Territory supports objects that maintain and give access to four values: a minimum x-coordinate, a maximum x-coordinate, a minimum y-coordinate, and a maximum y-coordinate. In implementing the constructors and methods make use of the following instance variables.

    private int xMin
        Represents the minimum x-coordinate value.
    private int xMax
        Represents maximum x-coordinate value.

`private int` yMin

Represents the minimum y-coordinate value.

`private int` yMax

Represents maximum y-coordinate value.

These instance variables should also be used in implementing the following behaviors.

`public boolean` inside(int x, int y)

Indicates whether location (x, y) lies inside or on the edge of the territory.

`public boolean` outside(int x, int y)

Indicates whether location (x, y) lies neither inside nor on the edge of the territory.

`public boolean` atLimit(int x, int y)

Indicates whether location (x, y) lies on the edge of the territory.

Class `BoundaryBehavior` should provide six **public** class constants of type `BoundaryBehavior`. It should also provide a **protected** default constructor that performs no action. The constants will correspond to common behaviors with regard to an object's continued motion when it reaches a vertical or horizontal boundaries:

- `BoundaryBehavior.Freeze`: When a vertical or horizontal boundary is reached by the object, its motion pauses.
- `BoundaryBehavior.Wraparound`: When a vertical or horizontal boundary is reached by the object, motion continues from the same relative position on the opposite boundary.
- `BoundaryBehavior.Reverse`: When a vertical or horizontal boundary is reached by the object, motion continues in the opposite direction from the current position.
- `BoundaryBehavior.Ignore`: When a vertical or horizontal boundary is reached by the object, it is ignored.
- `BoundaryBehavior.Clockwise`: When a vertical or horizontal boundary is reached by the object, motion continues from the current position in the clockwise direction from the reached boundary.
- `BoundaryBehavior.CounterClockwise`: When a vertical or horizontal boundary is reached by the object, motion continues from the current position in the counterclockwise direction from the reached boundary.

Design and implement a class `BetterFish` that extends `MovingFish`. A `BetterFish` provides two additional fish attributes—a `Territory` and a `BoundaryBehavior`. Class `BetterFish` should at a minimum provide the following constructors.

`public` BetterFish()

Creates a fish with default shape, position, and movement. The territory of the fish should be boundless. Although it does matter, its boundary behavior is reversal.

`public` MovingFish(Step s)

Creates a fish with default shape, position, territory, and boundary behavior. The stroke of the fish should be s.

`public` MovingFish(Territory t, BoundaryBehavior b)

Creates a fish with default shape, position and movement. The territory of the fish should be t and its boundary behavior should be b.

```
public MovingFish(Color c, Polygon p, int x, int y, Step s,
    Territory t, BoundaryBehavior b)
```
Creates a fish with color c, shape p at coordinate (x, y), movement s, territory t, and boundary behavior b.

The class should also provide accessors and mutators for its `Territory` and a `BoundaryBehavior` attributes.

Most importantly, the class should also override `MovingFish` method `swim()`. The new `swim()` method should respond appropriately when a stroke would bring a fish outside of its territory.

```
public void swim()
```
Makes a stroke. If the stroke would leave the bounding box for the fish completely within its territory, the new position is accepted. If the stroke does not allow the bounding box of the fish to remain within its territory, then one or more of the following actions are performed as necessary depending upon the boundary behavior of the fish and which boundary(s) would be crossed.

- Reverse the stroke;
- Update the stroke in a clockwise manner;
- Update the stroke in a counterclockwise manner;
- Shift the position of the fish in a wrap-around manner;
- Flip the outline of the fish right-to-left.

Each of these possible actions should be implemented as a **protected** method.

Lastly, develop a program `ThreeSwimmingBetterFish.java` that demonstrates your fish in action. The loop that runs the animation should be an infinite loop.

12.9	SELF-TEST ANSWERS

S12.1 The following code segment suffices.

```
t.schedule(task, 0);
t.schedule(task, 0);
```

S12.2 The following code segment suffices.

```
t.schedule(task, 0);
t.schedule(task, 3000);
```

S12.3 The following code segment suffices.

```
t.schedule(task, 2000, 1000);
```

S12.4 The following definition suffices.

```
public class Sleep {
    // class constant
    private static final int MILLISECONDS_PER_SECOND = 1000;

    // pauseMilliseconds(): pauses n milliseconds
    public static void pauseMilliseconds(long n) {
        if (n <= 0) {
            return;
```

```
        }
        else {
            try {
                Thread.sleep(n);
            }
            catch (java.lang.InterruptedException e) {
                return;
            }
        }
    }

    // pauseSeconds(): pauses n seconds
    public static void pauseSeconds(long n) {
        pauseMilliseconds(n*MILLISECONDS_PER_SECOND);
    }

    // pauseMinutes(): pauses n minutes
    public static void pauseMinutes(long n) {
        pauseSeconds(n*60);
    }
}
```

13 TESTING AND DEBUGGING

Two important aspects of software development are testing and debugging. The purpose of testing is to identify any problems before the software is put to use. Software testing is a major aspect of producing quality software. For large software projects, testing and debugging are 40 to 50 percent of the overall project costs. For major software projects, a large software company might employ as many as one or two testers for every development programmer. Debugging is the process of locating and repairing a problem identified by testing or reported by a user. Debugging is a two-step process—you locate the problem; and then you fix it. Like testing, debugging, if not done properly, can consume significant time and resources. In this chapter, we discuss the basics of testing software and strategies for debugging once a problem has been recognized.

OBJECTIVES

- Introduce various testing techniques including black-box testing, white-box testing, unit testing, integration testing, and system testing.
- Present and explain the value of inspections and code reviews.
- Introduce techniques for developing effective and efficient test cases such as statement coverage, path coverage, and equivalence partitioning.

13.1   TESTING

We have all encountered bugs or problems in programs we have used. If you have ever had your word processor crash after entering a particularly long passage of text, you know how irritating bugs can be. Some bugs are so costly that they make the newspaper headlines. The crash of the Mars Polar Lander on the surface of Mars in 1999 is a recent example. In this incident, a 165 million dollar mission was lost because of a problem that went undetected despite extensive testing. The story of why the Polar Lander crashed illustrates the difficulties of thorough testing.

The landing was supposed to go like this. As the lander entered the atmosphere of Mars, a parachute would deploy to slow the lander's descent. As it neared the surface, the parachute would be discarded, the lander's three legs would snap into position for landing, and the lander's 12 engines would fire to slow the craft to a speed where it could land safely. Each of the lander's three legs had a sensor that would send a signal to the onboard computer to turn off the spacecraft's landing engines when at least one of the legs touched the surface.

Using a similar lander, investigators determined that when the legs were deployed for landing, vibrations could have caused the leg sensors to send spurious signals. In this scenario, the engines would shut down when the craft was about 130 feet high, and the lander would hit the surface at 50 miles per hour.

So how did this problem go undetected? Various postcrash investigations showed that tests of individual systems would not have exposed the problem. One full-scale system test was conducted that should have revealed the presence of the problem. However, the sensors were improperly wired for that test, and the problem went undetected. After the wiring was corrected, a full-scale test was not repeated because of budgetary constraints and time pressures.

The Mars Polar Lander illustrates why thorough testing is so difficult to do. While all the components work correctly when tested individually (unit testing), the system may not work correctly when tested as a whole (system testing). Thus, one must do both thorough unit testing as well as thorough system testing. Because of budgetary constraints and deadlines, however, all too often we convince ourselves that, even though some aspect of the system has changed, further testing is not warranted. Careful programmers retest before delivering software even after the most trivial changes.

After you have written a program, how do you convince yourself that the program works correctly? The not-so-careful programmer runs the program with a few test inputs and then checks to see if the answers are correct. For the simplest programs, running a few tests may be enough, but this approach is hardly adequate even for a program of moderate complexity, and it surely will not be sufficient for a complex program of more than a 1,000 lines.

In this chapter we discuss some strategies for testing the software that you design and implement. Unfortunately, a thorough discussion of testing is beyond the scope of this book. There are many excellent texts devoted just to the theory, science, and art of testing software. Section 13.4 lists several of the texts that we have found to contain helpful information about testing strategies and procedures.

We note before proceeding that testing is not a panacea for producing high-quality software. There is a well-known quote by the late computer scientist Edgar Dijkstra that gets to the heart of the problem. He observed that "Program testing can be used to show the presence of bugs, but never to show their absence." High-quality software can be achieved only by applying testing along with a number of other software engineering techniques. These techniques include formal and informal reviews of the software specification, the proposed design or architecture of the system, as well as the actual code. Indeed, software engineering studies have shown that a disciplined, systematic review process is more effective at avoiding bugs in shipped software than testing. Another important element is the ability to manage and track evolving software effectively. Source-code control systems and software for tracking bugs are commonly used to help automate these tasks. These subjects are covered in depth in software engineering courses.

13.1.1 TESTING — AN EXAMPLE

The first thing to realize about bugs and testing is that the earlier problems are found, the better. Software engineering studies have shown that the costs of finding and fixing a problem grow logarithmically with time. For example, a bug found early during the specification phase may cost little or nothing to repair. For the sake of argument, let's say it costs a dollar to fix. That same bug, if discovered during the final testing of the software, may cost hundreds or thousands of dollars to fix.

The high cost of fixing bugs discovered late in the software development process means that we should test code as we write it. This approach makes sense from a number of standpoints. Let's say we are designing and coding one particular function that is part of a larger system we are working on. At this point in time, we are enmeshed in the details of the problem. This is a good point to test this module. If a problem is discovered, because of our immediate familiarity of the code, we can most likely fix it quickly. On the other hand, if the problem crops up months later, we will need to refamiliarize ourselves with the code before we can diagnose and fix the problem. Furthermore, it's likely the method or class has grown over time, which again will make finding the bug harder. The process of testing a single module or function is known as *unit testing*.

To illustrate the process of testing, and unit testing in particular, let's begin development of an LED timer for displaying elapsed time. LED clocks are used in many consumer electronic devices such as microwave ovens, digital watches, clock radios, and VCRs to display numbers and time (time of day, elapsed time, etc.). An LED timer could be a handy class for building games that have a time limit, developing a computerized scoreboard, and so forth.

Our initial task is to develop the LED class that we will need to build the clock. As we will see, unit testing of our LED class will help us find any problems before we tackle larger problems, but it will also help us refine the interface to the object early: before it is used in a larger project and modification becomes more costly.

Following our object-oriented design approach, we must determine the attributes and behaviors of an LED. Obviously we need to control the value displayed. Our approach for realizing an LED is to use GIF images of digits to display a number. For example, the image of the GIF for the number three looks like this:

Our website has GIF images for the numerals zero through nine.

The Swing API class `JLabel`, besides being useful for display short text strings, can also be used for displaying images. Class `JLabel` supports display GIF and JPEG images. Because class `JLabel` already has the basic attributes and behaviors we need to realize an abstraction of an LED, we decide it would be smart to extend `JLabel` via inheritance.

For our initial cut at designing class LED, we determine that in addition to all the attributes and behaviors of class `JLabel`, class LED needs the following additional attributes.

- `value`—an integer value that he LED should display.
- `images`—an array that contains a GIF image for each possible digit.

For the public interface, we will need an inspector and mutator for the `value` attribute. Our initial declaration for class LED is given in Listing 13.1.

Our use of inheritance makes the implementation of class LED quite simple. The only interesting part of the implementation is definition of the array `images` to hold the GIF images for each digit. This array is defined to be a **private final static** array. By making the array **static**, we are indicating that the GIF images are to be shared across all instantiations of class LED. This sharing of images between instantiations of LED objects will save space and it is possible since the GIF images will not change—only which image is displayed will change depending on the value of the LED.

Now that we have a preliminary version of class LED, we have a choice. We can continue to develop the code for the clock, or we can stop and test class LED to make sure it works properly by doing unit testing. As we mentioned earlier, it is much easier to test and find problems now, while we are familiar with the code, rather than waiting for problems to crop up down the road. However, how do we test our class given that we haven't written the program yet? We must provide a *test harness* or *test stub* to exercise our code. A test harness is a small piece of code written to test or exercise the code being developed.

Writing test harnesses is a standard subtask of unit testing. It is tempting to discard these code fragments after testing is completed, but the modest time and effort it takes to save these stubs is an investment that will pay off later when a bug is uncovered. You will already have a set of test harnesses available to help locate the bug and then ensure that

Listing 13.1 Class LED

```
1.  // Class LED: simulates an LED for a clock or timer
2.  import javax.swing.*;
3.
4.  public class LED extends JLabel {
5.
6.      // private data members
7.      private int value;
8.
9.      // array holding images of digits
10.     private static final Icon images[] = {
11.       new ImageIcon("digit0.gif"),
12.       new ImageIcon("digit1.gif"),
13.       new ImageIcon("digit2.gif"),
14.       new ImageIcon("digit3.gif"),
15.       new ImageIcon("digit4.gif"),
16.       new ImageIcon("digit5.gif"),
17.       new ImageIcon("digit6.gif"),
18.       new ImageIcon("digit7.gif"),
19.       new ImageIcon("digit8.gif"),
20.       new ImageIcon("digit9.gif")
21.     };
22.
23.     // LED(): default constructor
24.     LED(int i) {
25.         setValue(i);
26.     }
27.
28.     // getValue(): set the LED to a new value
29.     public int getValue() {
30.         return value;
31.     }
32.
33.     // setValue(): set the LED to a new value
34.     public void setValue(int i) {
35.         value = i;
36.         setIcon(images[i]);
37.     }
38. }
```

the fix did not break something else. We often create a test directory where the various test harnesses we have written for a project are kept.

Listing 13.2 contains a test harness code for the LED class. The code creates a JFrame object, creates an LED with value zero, adds it to the frame, and then makes the frame visible. When we compile and run this code, the following window appears.

Listing 13.2 LED test harness — version 1

```
1.  // Test harness for class LED
2.  import java.awt.*;
3.  import javax.swing.*;
4.
5.  public class LEDTest {
6.      // instance constants and variables
7.      private static final int WINDOW_WIDTH = 200;
8.      private static final int WINDOW_HEIGHT = 150;
9.
10.     // main(): application entry point
11.     public static void main(String[] args) {
12.         JFrame w1 = new JFrame("LED Test");
13.         w1.setSize(WINDOW_WIDTH, WINDOW_HEIGHT);
14.
15.         Container c = w1.getContentPane();
16.         c.setLayout(new FlowLayout());
17.
18.         LED digit = new LED(0);
19.         c.add(digit);
20.
21.         w1.setVisible(true);
22.     }
23. }
```

Our code worked! Depending on what we are planning to do, this amount of testing might be enough. However, for code used in a commercial application, we are not even close to being done. To test this code thoroughly, we need to think about how the code will be used and what could possibly go wrong. What we need is a systematic approach to unit testing.

First off, we need test cases that demonstrate that the code satisfies its requirements. What are the requirements of class LED? Unfortunately, we did not formally write these down. In a real software project, the first step is to write down formal specifications of what a class is supposed to do. However, we do have an informal idea of the capabilities class LED should provide because it is to be used to develop clock type objects, calculators, and other objects requiring a numeric display.

- Class LED should be capable of displaying the digits 0 through 9.

- The value that an LED object is displaying can be changed.

Using this informal specification, we can design a more comprehensive set of tests. Basically we need to ensure that class LED satisfies the stated requirements. Our test cases should make sure that class LED supports displaying each digit correctly, and we should also include tests to make sure that we can change the value displayed by an LED object. With a little work, we can write one test harness that does all this in a single run. After some trial and error to get the window sized correctly, we produce the code in Listing 13.3.

Listing 13.3 LED test harness – version 2

```
1.  // GUI test harness for class LED
2.  import java.awt.*;
3.  import javax.swing.*;
4.
5.  public class LEDTest {
6.      // instance constants and variables
7.      private static final int WINDOW_WIDTH = 350;
8.      private static final int WINDOW_HEIGHT = 200;
9.
10.     public static void sleep(int time) {
11.         try {
12.             Thread.sleep(time);
13.         }
14.         catch (Exception e) {}
15.     }
16.
17.     // main(): application entry point
18.     public static void main(String[] args) {
19.         JFrame w1 = new JFrame("LED Test");
20.         w1.setSize(WINDOW_WIDTH, WINDOW_HEIGHT);
21.
22.         Container c = w1.getContentPane();
23.         c.setLayout(new FlowLayout());
24.
25.         LED digit[] = new LED[10];
26.         for (int i = 0; i < 10; ++i) {
27.             digit[i] = new LED(i);
28.             c.add(digit[i]);
29.         }
30.
31.         w1.setVisible(true);
32.
33.         sleep(5000);
34.         for (int i = 0; i < 10; ++i) {
35.             digit[i].setValue(9-i);
36.         }
37.     }
38. }
```

The revised test harness creates a frame to hold the LED objects (lines 19–20), gets a container to hold the LEDs, and indicates that the default layout manager should be used to control the display of the objects in the container.

The next segment of code creates an array to hold 10 LED objects. The **for** loop initializes array element *i* to have an LED that displays value *i* and adds the element to container. The frame is then displayed.

We want this test case to demonstrate that the values displayed by an LED can be changed. To accomplish this aspect of the test, using our knowledge of threads, we create a simple sleep function (lines 10–15 of Listing 13.3) that enables us to suspend execution for some number of milliseconds. We use this function to suspend execution for 5,000 milliseconds (i.e., 5 seconds), then we change the values displayed by the LEDs. After 5 seconds, the frame is updated to the following.

The not-so-careful programmer would be done at this point. However, the careful programmer also tests for what happens when the object is used in a way not permitted by the requirements. One of the benefits of this process is that as you think about unit test cases, bugs are often discovered before you even run the test cases. For example, as we think about test cases to ensure the object behaves appropriately when illegal values are requested, we realize immediately that class LED does not handle this case at all. Class LED will crash if a value less than 0 and greater than 9 is passed to it. We had better fix that. Again, it's much easier to fix it now rather than later.

To address this issue, we modify member function setValue() to indicate that it may throw an ArrayIndexOutOfBoundsException. This indicates that it is up to the users of class LED to decide how they want to handle the error. This approach is more flexible than having method setValue() detect the error and exit. The revised member function is:

```
// setValue(): set the LED to a new value
public void setValue(int i)
 throws ArrayIndexOutOfBoundsException {
    myValue = i;
    setIcon(Images[i]);
}
```

We generate some test cases to make sure that the error detection code works. One test case passes a value less than 0; the other test case passes a value greater than 9. When we test, we run all the tests to make sure that all the test cases, both the new ones and the old ones, still pass.

So far, so good. However, we are still not done. Class LED will be used to build clocks. To test whether class LED will work in this application, we can do a quick prototype of a clock display. Prototyping is a common activity—you build a mock-up of the thing you plan to build to work out how it should look. In this case, we will produce a static clock face—the time will not change. This activity makes us realize that class LED is missing some features. To display a clock time like 12:30 P or 11:00 A, class LED needs the ability to display a colon and the letters *A* and *P* to denote and antimeridian (i.e., A.M.) and postmeridian time (i.e., P.M.), respectively. Again, we revise the implementation of class LED to include these features. The display produced by a possible test harness is shown here. The actual harness is left as an exercise for the reader.

The prototype unit test process makes us realize we have another problem with class LED. How do we display a time like 1:30 P? We need a way to display a blank (i.e., an unlit LED). Again, adding this new capability is easy at this stage as we are very familiar with class LED (maybe too familiar!). Listing 13.4 contains the final implementation of class LED.

Listing 13.4 Class **LED** (final version)

```
1.  // Class LED: simulates an LED for a clock or timer
2.  import javax.swing.*;
3.
4.  public class LED extends JLabel {
5.
6.      // private data members
7.      private int myValue;
```

Listing 13.4 Class **LED** (final version) (Continued)

```
8.         // array holding images of digits
9.         private final static Icon myImages[] = {
10.          new ImageIcon("digit0.gif"),
11.          new ImageIcon("digit1.gif"),
12.          new ImageIcon("digit2.gif"),
13.          new ImageIcon("digit3.gif"),
14.          new ImageIcon("digit4.gif"),
15.          new ImageIcon("digit5.gif"),
16.          new ImageIcon("digit6.gif"),
17.          new ImageIcon("digit7.gif"),
18.          new ImageIcon("digit8.gif"),
19.          new ImageIcon("digit9.gif"),
20.          new ImageIcon("colon.gif"),
21.          new ImageIcon("leta.gif"),
22.          new ImageIcon("letm.gif"),
23.          new ImageIcon("letp.gif"),
24.          new ImageIcon("blank.gif")
25.        };
26.        public final static int COLON = 10;
27.        public final static int LETA  = 11;
28.        public final static int LETM  = 12;
29.        public final static int LETP  = 13;
30.        public final static int BLANK = 14;
31.        // LED(): default constructor
32.        LED(int i) {
33.            myValue = i;
34.            setIcon(myImages[i]);
35.        }
36.        // getValue(): set the LED to a new value
37.        public int getValue() {
38.            return myValue;
39.        }
40.        // setValue(): set the LED to a new value
41.        public void setValue(int i)
42.         throws ArrayIndexOutOfBoundsException {
43.            myValue = i;
44.            setIcon(myImages[i]);
45.        }
46. }
```

After we add the new capability, we add another test program to our growing suite of
programs that test the functioning of the new capability. This test program given in Listing 13.5 produces the following display, which verifies that we can produce a blank.

We should emphasize that each time we make a change to class LED we rerun the entire suite of test programs. This avoids introducing a bug that is discovered only after a series of changes have been made. It is much easier to understand what went wrong when only one set of changes is involved.

Listing 13.5 LED clock face test

```java
1.  // Clock face test harness for class LED
2.  import java.awt.*;
3.  import javax.swing.*;
4.
5.  public class LEDTest {
6.      // instance constants and variables
7.      private static final int WINDOW_WIDTH = 400;
8.      private static final int WINDOW_HEIGHT = 125;
9.
10.     // main(): application entry point
11.     public static void main(String[] args) {
12.         JFrame w1 = new JFrame("Clock LED Test");
13.         w1.setSize(WINDOW_WIDTH, WINDOW_HEIGHT);
14.
15.         Container c = w1.getContentPane();
16.         c.setLayout(new FlowLayout());
17.
18.         LED clock[] = new LED[6];
19.         clock[0] = new LED(LED.BLANK);
20.         clock[1] = new LED(2);
21.         clock[2] = new LED(LED.COLON);
22.         clock[3] = new LED(5);
23.         clock[4] = new LED(8);
24.         clock[5] = new LED(LED.LETA);
25.
26.         for (int i = 0; i < 6; ++i) {
27.             c.add(clock[i]);
28.         }
29.
30.         w1.setVisible(true);
31.     }
32. }
```

After our exercise with testing class LED, you can see why testing is such a time-consuming and expensive part of software development. Running a comprehensive test suite after each change is time-consuming, but there are some things we can do to make it less painful. Programmers typically write "scripts" that automatically run the test suite and report any errors. Using scripts means running the tests is as simple as invoking a command. As new test programs are written, the script is modified so the new test program is included. These scripts, along with documentation on their use, are included with the test programs so that other developers know how to run the test programs. Thus, the script serves as documentation for future developers and testers.

Prototyping

Building a prototype or mock-up is a widely used technique in engineering and design disciplines. Architects build models so customers can see what the building will look like and how it will fit in to its surroundings. Engineers build models of airplanes, automobiles, bridges, etc. so the design can be tested and evaluated before significant resources have been expended building the real artifact. Designers often build mock-ups of products so the utility of the design can be evaluated before the product goes into production.

Prototyping is also an important software development technique. A prototype helps customers and developers understand and refine the requirements for the system. For example, a customer can experiment with a prototype to see if the system will meet their needs. A prototype also helps expose misunderstandings between the users and the developers. In some cases, the prototype can serve as a starting point for building the real system.

Thus, prototyping has many benefits, which include:

- refinement and clarification of system requirements,
- delivered system is more likely to meet users needs,
- missing capabilities can be identified, and
- reduced development time and cost.

13.1.2   TESTING FUNDAMENTALS

As we mentioned earlier, testing is a serious discipline that is a key to producing high-quality, robust software. Thus it should come as no surprise that testing is a well-studied area with its own terminology and research results. As beginning programmers, devoting some time to understanding the fundamentals of testing will pay handsome dividends in the years to come.

As Section 13.1.1 explained, the purpose of testing is to find bugs as early as possible in the development process and to make sure they get fixed before the software is shipped. Exactly what is a bug? Certainly, when a program crashes (e.g., blue-screen of death), that's a bug. However, there are many other types of bugs that are just as serious and not so obvious. For example, suppose the user manual for a document editor says that the way to set a word in boldface type is to highlight it and then click the bold button on the toolbar. Suppose you do this, and the selected word remains unchanged. Is this a bug? The program didn't crash, it just did not perform as advertised. Not performing as specified is also a bug.

If we practice sound software engineering techniques, then we will write a complete and detailed specification of what the software is supposed to do, how it will operate, the features it will and will not support, and its performance requirements. In general, a bug is when the program does not meet the specification. However, testers and most programmers classify bugs into the following four broad categories:

- software crashes or data corruption;
- failure to meet or satisfy the specification;
- poor or unacceptable performance; and
- hard or difficult to use.

A software crash is when a program fails in a noticeable way. Examples of software crashes include when the program exits unexpectedly or it stops responding to commands and has to be manually terminated via operating system commands.

Data corruption occurs when a program writes bad data to a file. Suppose you were editing a file with your favorite word processor or editor, and after you saved the file you discovered the file contained gibberish. This situation is an example of a data corruption bug. Data corruption bugs are particularly insidious because they can go undetected easily. The error can propagate to other data files, and if the error goes undetected for a long period of time, it can be difficult to restore the corrupted files to a correct state.

An important component of a software specification is the features the system will provide. A list of features helps everybody, including the customer, know when the system is complete functionally. For example, the specification for a calculator program may state that the program should provide operations for converting between various number bases. If this feature gets left out or is incomplete (e.g., you can only convert to binary), then there is a bug.

A performance bug is present when the program fails to meet the performance requirements contained in the specification, or the program performs so poorly that it, in effect, does not satisfy the specification. As an example of a performance bug, suppose your e-mail system includes a feature for searching your archive of saved messages. While the feature works, a search takes so long that you never use the feature. In effect, it is as if the e-mail system did not provide the feature.

Modern user interfaces have made software easier to use than ever. However, we also expect software to do more and more. Designing software that is easy for people of various skill levels to use is a very difficult task. Indeed, the area of user interfaces and usability are subdisciplines of computer science. If the design of a program makes accomplishing a task overly difficult, this too is a bug—a bug in the design of the user interface. Note this kind of bug can be very expensive to fix as a project is nearing completion. Consequently, it is very important to do early testing of the user interface to ensure that the program is easy to use or, as some people like to say, user-friendly.

Interestingly, when you are testing a program, crashes and data corruption are the best kind of bugs to encounter. The behavior is clearly an error, and it is often pretty obvious what has gone wrong. On the other hand, bugs where the program has an odd quirk, is slow, or is difficult to use are much more subjective. A developer may argue that the quirk is not a bug, but a feature; that the program is not that slow; or that the program is really not that hard to use.

It is important to understand the limitations of testing. As mentioned in the introduction, testing cannot show or prove a program is bug free. It only can show or expose bugs. Furthermore, for all but the most trivial programs it is impossible to test a program completely. The problem is that the number of inputs to most programs is very large, and the

Types of programming errors

Program errors generally fall into three categories—compilation errors, runtime errors, and logic errors.

Compilation errors. A compilation error is an error detected by the compiler during the compilation process. Compilation errors are easiest type of error to fix. A common type of compilation error is a *syntax error*. A syntax error is when the form of a statement or expression is not constructed according to the rules of the language. Typical syntax errors include forgetting a semicolon at the end of a statement, leaving off a closing curly brace, misspelling a keyword, etc. Another kind of compilation error is a *semantic error*. A semantic error is when the syntax of the statement or expression is correct, but the meaning of the statement is invalid according to the rules of the language. Examples of semantic errors are applying the modulus operator to a floating-point value, using a floating-point value to index an array, and forgetting to define an object before using it.

Runtime errors. As the name indicates, a runtime error is an error that occurs when the program is running. Runtime errors are harder than compilation errors to diagnose and fix. Fortunately, Java's runtime checks and exception mechanism provide information that is useful for identifying and fixing the error. Typical runtime errors include many of the exceptions caught by Java: `NullPointerException`, `IoException`, `IndexOutOfBoundsException`, and `ArithmeticException`.

Logic errors. A logic error is when the program runs (i.e., no runtime errors) but it produces incorrect output or it fails in some other unanticipated way. A logic error is typically the hardest kind of error to find and fix. Logic errors are hard to characterize. Sometimes the error can be caused by a simple typographical error that does not create a compilation error (e.g., typing a constant incorrectly), or it can be because the programmer's algorithm had a flaw (e.g., the algorithm does not handle a case that sometimes arises). Using the scientific method of debugging described in Section 13.2 is the preferred approach for finding logic errors.

number of possible paths through the program is also very large. To simplify the problem, let's just talk about the number of paths in a program. Consider a simple program whose control flow graph is shown in Figure 13.1.

Each circle represents a block of statements. To test this program completely, we must cause the program to execute every possible permutation of statements because any sequence could potentially fail. Disregarding the loop, there are three distinct paths through the program. If the loop executes 20 times, there are 3^{20} different sequences of execution of the statements. That is about 3 billion different test cases! Exhaustively testing all possible executions of a program is impossible.

Clearly, we need some good procedures and strategies for testing so that as many bugs as possible are found before the software is delivered, yet testing is done efficiently.

Figure 13.1   **Program control flow graph.**

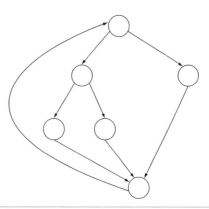

13.1.3   REVIEWS AND INSPECTIONS

Recall our earlier comment that the sooner you find bugs the better. The goal of design and code reviews is to find bugs even before the code is run. Reviews of a design or code can run the spectrum from an informal meeting where one programmer explains the design or code to another programmer to a rigorous formal process. Whether the review is informal or formal the goal is the same—to identify bugs or problems early in the development process. However, reviews, if done and managed properly, can have other benefits.

A review can be a learning process for all involved. During a review, you may see a particularly elegant or effective design or technique for solving a problem. Similarly, you may see bad design or a poor implementation identified along with an explanation of why it is bad. We learn from successes as well as mistakes.

Reviews can help entry-level programmers learn the expectations and coding standards of the company. When working on a large project, it is vital that each programmer adheres to the coding standard that has been chosen. A coding standard specifies how the program is to be laid out (i.e., the indentation to use for the various language constructs, expectations for the form and content of comments, constructs that are not permitted, etc.). Uniform use of a coding standard produces code that is more reliable and easier to maintain.

Reviews are also useful for project management. Reviews help managers assess the skills of the project members. These assessments can be used to determine the assignment of tasks to project members and to form effective teams. Reviews can also help management assess the progress of the project. This information can also be used to take corrective action such as shifting resources, adding more resources, or allocating more time to certain aspects of the project.

Software engineering studies have shown that reviews are very effective at bug detection—more so than other kinds of testing. A study of a large software organization showed that reviews led to a 14 percent increase in productivity and a 90 percent decrease in defects. Another study found that reviews are at least twice as effective as unit testing.

A review process that has been shown to be very effective is the *inspection*. An inspection is a formal process where the personnel involved are assigned specific roles. Inspections were first employed by IBM in 1976. This pioneering work showed that design and code inspections typically remove 60 percent of the bugs in a product.

One characteristic that distinguishes an inspection from other types of reviews is that an inspection is highly structured. Each person involved in the inspection is assigned one of four roles. Furthermore, each participant receives training on how inspections are carried out and what her or his duties are. A participant in an inspection serves in one of four roles: moderator, inspector, author, or scribe.

Moderator. The moderator is in charge of running the inspection. The moderator's most important job is ensuring that the inspection proceeds at a reasonable pace. The inspection should be thorough so that as many problems as possible are identified, but it should not drag out so as to be unproductive. A very important aspect of being moderator is making sure that the inspection participants treat each other with respect and courtesy. In addition to running the inspection, the moderator is also responsible for distributing the code or design being reviewed to the inspection participants, scheduling the time and place of the inspection, reporting the inspection results, and making sure any action items generated as a result of the inspection are completed.

Inspector. An inspector, or reviewer, is someone other than the author who has some interest in the design or code (e.g., using the code to build a component, implementing the design, testing, etc.). The job of the inspector is to carefully scrutinize the design or code to find any potential problems. The inspection of the code is done prior to the inspection meeting.

Author. The author of the code or the design plays a minor role in the inspection. If the author has done her or his job, the code will be well-documented, easy to understand, and bug free. If the reviewers detect problems or the code is unclear in certain areas, an action item is generated directing the author to remedy the situation. Sometimes what may be perceived as an error by an inspector is in fact not an error. In this situation, the author can explain why the code is correct.

Scribe. The role of the scribe is to record all the errors that are detected and keep a list of action items generated.

Interestingly, managers are excluded from inspections. Software inspections are technical reviews with the goal of finding as many problems as possible, as early as possible. The presence of management personnel can change the tenor of the inspection. Inspection participants may become more defensive or less likely to speak up if they feel they are being evaluated.

Another characteristic that distinguishes an inspection from other types of reviews is that it consists of five well-defined phases or steps.

Planning. During the planning step, the portion of code to be inspected is chosen, and the moderator assigns tasks to the inspectors. Inspectors may be assigned different parts of the code to review, or they may be asked to review the code from a certain perspective (e.g., testability, extensibility, performance, etc.). Checklists are created to focus the inspectors' attention on certain areas that are known to be critical or that have caused problems in past projects. The moderator also chooses one of the inspectors to be the presenter. During the inspection step, the presenter will walk through the code, presenting it to the inspection team.

Overview. At the overview the author describes any high-level aspects of the project that may have affected the design or code being reviewed. If all of the project participants are familiar with these aspects of the project, the overview can be skipped.

Preparation. Working alone, each inspector carefully reviews the code using the supplied checklists as a guide. The inspectors note any problems or deficiencies in the code and come to the inspection meeting prepared to present their results. The inspector chosen as presenter uses the preparation plans to present the code or design during the inspection meeting. Studies of the inspection process have shown that this phase should last no more than a couple of hours. Reading code is hard work, and after two hours inspectors become tired and errors can go undetected.

Inspection meeting. At the inspection meeting, the presenter walks through the code line by line, explaining what the code does. As the presenter reads and explains the code, any problems for that portion of code are identified and discussed. The scribe records all the errors detected and the action items associated with them. The moderator makes sure that the inspection proceeds at a reasonable pace and the inspection stays focused. For example, it is tempting to discuss how a problem might be fixed. Fixing problems is not the goal of an inspection. Like the preparation phase, the inspection meeting should not last longer than a couple of hours.

Inspection report. After an inspection meeting, the moderator prepares a written report that identifies the work that needs to be done and who is responsible for each task. Depending on the magnitude of changes, an inspection of the revised code may be scheduled. The inspection report may suggest additions or changes to the checklist based on the results of the inspection. This information can improve the effectiveness of subsequent inspections.

Inspections are effective because they provide a structured environment for having the code read and understood. Left to their own devices, most people find reading code rather boring. As you read code, it is easy to slip into a mode in which you are just skimming the code and not fully understanding what the code is doing. Inspections help people read code in a focused, productive way. Inspections are also effective because they provide feedback about common problems. Integrating this information into checklists for future inspections improves the effectiveness of subsequent inspections.

13.1.4　BLACK-BOX AND WHITE-BOX TESTING

Two other testing strategies for delivering robust, high-quality software are block-box and white-box testing. The testing of class LED at the beginning of this chapter is an example of white-box testing. The term *white-box testing* indicates that we can "see" or examine the code as we devise our test cases. The term *black-box testing* indicates that we cannot examine the code as we devise test cases. The code is hidden in a black-box we cannot see through.

How can you test code when you cannot see it? Why would you want to test code that you cannot see? There are good answers to both these questions. With black-box testing, although you do not know how the code works, the specification tells you what the code is supposed to do. You can create inputs, get output, and check the results for correctness without having access to the source code. The answer to the second question is that white-box testing can bias the testing toward finding errors in the code. If the code does not implement the specification, white-box testing is unlikely to expose that type of bug. The advantage to white-box testing is that knowledge of how the code works can help you test more effectively by avoiding redundant test cases.

Because black-box and white-box testing are complementary, both techniques are used on large software projects. Because this text is about programming, we will focus our discussion on white-box testing. However, the techniques we discuss apply to black-box testing as well.

The key to successful, efficient testing is producing good test cases—test cases that are most likely to expose bugs. This task is hard because the input possibilities accepted by a nontrivial program are, for all practical purposes, infinite. Thus we must find a way to reduce the number of possible test cases into a smaller, more manageable set that is still effective at exposing any potential bugs. The process of weeding out unnecessary or redundant test cases is called *equivalence partitioning*.

The basic idea behind equivalence partitioning is that if two inputs test the same portions of code, you only need one of the inputs in your test set. From a testing standpoint, the two inputs are equivalent. For example, suppose you are developing a calculator program. You have just implemented the addition operation and you are developing test cases to make sure addition works properly before implementing other operations. You try the test cases $1 + 2$, $2 + 1$, $0 + 3$, and $0 + 0$. The calculator produces the correct sums for these test cases. Do you think it will be useful to add the test case $1 + 3$? No, because on any reasonable platform test case $1 + 3$ is in the same equivalence class as $1 + 2$. If test case $1 + 2$ worked, test case $1 + 3$ will work. A good test case to add would be $-1 + 3$. This test case is in a new equivalence class because the first operand is negative. The self-check exercises ask you to develop additional test cases for the calculator program that are in new equivalence classes.

There are several strategies programmers and testers use to generate effective test cases. One of the most common strategies is boundary testing. The motivation for boundary testing is that program bugs occur most often at boundaries. Furthermore, if the code works properly at the boundaries, it probably works correctly elsewhere. One analogy sometimes used is that if you can walk along an edge of a cliff on a plateau without falling off, you can probably walk in the middle of the plateau. There are several types of boundaries depending on the code. There are loop boundaries—does the loop do the right thing at the beginning and the end; data boundaries—does the code do the right thing when handling data that is at the boundary of allowable values; and capacity boundaries—does the code correctly handle the situation when the array is full and empty.

With white-box testing, we can examine the code to look for boundary conditions. For example, Listing 13.6 contains function `binarySearch()` introduced in Chapter 8. Initial inspection of this code suggests that the boundary conditions are when the key value being searched for is located at the beginning of the array or at the end of the array. If the code works for those situations, it will likely work when the key is located somewhere in the middle of array `data`.

Listing 13.6 binarySearch method

```
1.  public static int binarySearch(char[] data, char key) {
2.      int left = 0;
3.      int right = data.length - 1;
4.      while (left <= right) {
5.          int mid = (left + right)/2;
6.          if (data[mid] == key) {
7.              return mid;
8.          }
9.          else if (data[mid] < key) {
10.             left = mid + 1;
11.         }
12.         else {
13.             right = mid - 1;
14.         }
15.     }
16.
17.     return data.length;
18. }
```

An example of a capacity boundary condition is whether the code works when the size of array `data` is one or zero. We should include tests for these two cases. Test cases like these two are testing degenerate situations. *Degenerate situations* are ones that would not arise in typical use of the code, but if they occur the program should work. Because the loop is controlled by the size of the list, these tests also serve as loop boundary tests. If array `data` is empty, the loop will not be executed at all. Does this code work when array `data` has size one? What about when its size is zero?

As another example of boundary testing, consider the code fragment in Listing 13.7 from the Chapter 5 program that computes the days in a given month and year.

Listing 13.7 Code fragment from DaysInMonth.java

```
1.  // validate input
2.  if ((year < CALENDAR_START) || (month < 1) || (month > 12)) {
3.      System.output.println("Bad request: " + year + " "
4.          + month);
5.      return;
6.  }
```

Examination of the code shows that the code checks the validity of the input year and month. The code outputs an error message if the input year is less than CALENDAR_START or the month is not between one and twelve. The error checks immediately suggests the data boundary test cases in Table 13.1.

Table 13.1   Boundary values for DaysInMonth.java.

Input Year	Input Month
1582	2
1583	0
1583	13
1583	1
1583	12

The first test case checks whether the program detects an error when the input year is invalid and the month is valid. The second test case checks whether the program detects an error when the input year is just valid but the month is less than one. The third test is similar, but it checks to make sure an error is detected if the month entered is too large. Finally, the last two tests check the valid ranges of the month given a valid year.

The test cases can be partitioned into two equivalence classes. The first three test cases are invalid inputs, while the last two are valid inputs. Thus, the first three test cases should cause the program to generate an error message. If the program does not generate an error message, then we have exposed a bug. The program should produce correct output for the last two test cases. The tester should make sure that the output produced is indeed correct. In general, it is a good idea to classify all test cases as to whether they are valid inputs and the program should produce valid output, or whether they are invalid inputs and the program should generate an error message.

Another approach for generating test cases is to produce a set of test cases that cause each statement in the program to be executed at least once. This is known as *statement* or *code coverage testing*. The basic idea is that unless you have executed every line of code at least once you have not thoroughly tested the code. Of course, statement coverage testing can miss bugs because you may not execute a particular sequence of statements that exposes a bug. Also, for complicated programs, the number of test cases needed to guarantee complete code coverage can be quite high. Nonetheless, code coverage is a technique that is sometimes used. To support code coverage testing, there are software tools available that instrument the code and produce reports that show which program statements have been executed.

There are other techniques for test set generation. One approach is to generate a test set that causes each edge of the program's controlflow graph to be executed. This technique is called *path coverage* or *path testing*. To illustrate path testing, consider the following code fragment.

```
if (x != y) {
    y = 5;
}
else {
    z = z - z;
}
if (x > 1) {
    z = z / x;
}
else {
```

```
        z = 0;
    }
```

The controlflow graph of this program is shown in Figure 13.2. A set of tests that cause each edge to be traversed is <x = 0, z = 1> and <x = 3, z = 3>. The first test case causes paths A, B, G, H to be executed. The second test case causes paths E, F, C, D to be executed. The problem with this test set is that an important case has been missed. What happens when test case <x = 0, z = 3> is executed? To address this problem, we would need to test every possible path, which we have seen, in general, is infeasible. However, path testing can identify portions of code that may need closer inspection.

Figure 13.2 **Controlflow graph of two if-else statements.**

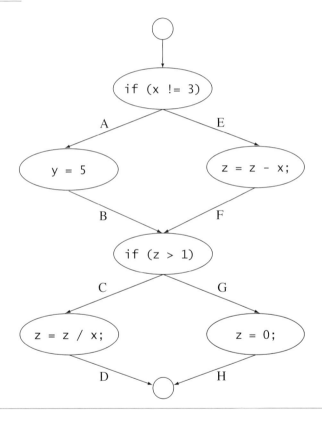

Regardless of the amount of testing and the strategy used to produce the test cases, an important component of testing is automation. As the software is developed, tests will need to be rerun periodically. Thus, it is important to set up an automated procedure for running the tests, capturing the output, and comparing the actual output to the expected output. Developing automated procedures promotes running *regression tests* periodically. A regression test compares the operation of the new version of the software to the operation of a previous version. The idea is that the behavior of the program should not change in unanticipated ways. If something that once worked no longer works, you have a regression. Regression testing ensures that you do not introduce new bugs or resurrect old ones!

The other reason to automate testing is that the testing procedure will serve to document how to run the tests. Taking these steps now is helpful when a bug is reported and fixed several years after the software is released. Without an automated testing procedure, you would have to remember how to run all the tests and which were supposed to pass and which were supposed to fail.

In summary, testing software is an integral and key component of the software development process. The size, complexity, and importance of today's software systems demand the application of effective testing techniques.

Testing tips.

The following are some general tips for effective testing.

Test early. The sooner you find bugs, the easier they are to fix. Also, it is easier and more effective to generate tests cases as you develop the code. Unit tests are an effective way to find bugs early in individual components or modules.

Use inspections. Inspections are extremely effective at exposing bugs and other deficiencies in the software. Even if a formal inspection process is not practical, sitting down and explaining your code to another programmer can be productive.

Test boundaries. Look for boundary conditions in your code and make sure you have test cases that test on the boundary and around the boundary. Off-by-one errors are fairly common, so it pays to test for them specifically.

Test exceptional conditions. Try to think of situations that shouldn't happen, and then add tests for them. Typical situations include empty files, no data entered, invalid data, too little data, and too much data. A robust program should handle all these cases.

Make testing repeatable. Set up an automated procedure for running your tests and comparing the actual output to the expected output. Scripting languages and shell languages are useful tools for this purpose.

13.1.5   INTEGRATION AND SYSTEM TESTING

Unit testing focuses on a single function, module, or component. Testing done as the pieces of the software are put together is called *integration testing*. *System testing* is testing done when the whole system is put together. Good unit testing simplifies integration and system testing. Because we are confident that the pieces work, we can focus our efforts on testing the interfaces between the pieces or components. Furthermore, because we are confident the individual pieces work, when a test fails we can focus our effort to find the problem on the interfaces between the components.

The guidelines for developing good unit tests apply to integration and system testing. The difference is the focus. With integration testing the focus is on testing the interaction between the software components. Thus, the test inputs you develop should focus on exercising that aspect of the system. Similarly with system testing, the test inputs should look to test overall system behavior, not the behavior of an individual component. That was accomplished by unit testing.

Such a modular approach to testing is necessary because as components are assembled to build larger components and the final system, testing the entire system becomes infeasible.

DEBUGGING

Testing is the processing of detecting the existence of a bug. *Debugging* is the processing of revealing what the bug is and removing it. Sometimes when a test case exposes a bug, the reason for the bug is obvious. Those are the easy bugs. Other times discovering why a program does not work correctly can be a tedious and time-consuming task—especially if an undisciplined approach is used. In Section 13.2.1, we describe an approach to debugging based on the scientific method. In Section 13.2.2 we give other advice and tips about debugging that experienced programmers use.

SCIENTIFIC METHOD

Finding that last elusive bug before an assignment is due or the software is shipped can be a frustrating and stressful experience, sometimes so much so that otherwise bright programmers resort to making random changes to their code in hopes that insight into the problem will emerge. Such an approach is not a very productive. In this section we introduce the notion of applying the scientific method to debugging.

The scientific method is a systematic way of reaching a conclusion based on inductive logic. The scientific method uses the following steps.

Gather data. Observe facts and look for patterns in the data.

Develop a hypothesis. Formulate a plausible explanation that accounts for or explains the observed facts. This explanation is the hypothesis.

Predict new facts. Using the hypothesis, predict new facts or new behaviors that have not yet been observed.

Perform experiments. Design experiments to observe the new facts. Run the experiments and collect data.

Prove or disprove the hypothesis. If the predicted facts are observed, the hypothesis is assumed to be true. If observations do not support the hypothesis, the process is repeated by developing an alternative hypothesis. Additional data may need to be collected to formulate an alternative hypothesis.

Here's a simple example to illustrate the application of the scientific method to debugging. A program is throwing an exception because of a division by zero in an arithmetic statement. You observe that the value used as the divisor in the offending statement is computed by a loop that counts the number of nonzero values in an array. Based on this observation, you hypothesize that the array must not contain any nonzero values. Using this hypothesis, you predict that if you insert code to print the array right before the loop the output will contain all zeros. Running the modified code is the experiment. If the output shows the array contained only zeros, your hypothesis is true. If the output has non-zero values, the result of the experiment did not support the original hypothesis, and you need to formulate another hypothesis to explain why the divisor is zero.

This process sounds time-consuming, but it is really not. Often, the experiment to test the hypothesis can be carried out using a debugger. A debugger is a program that allows a programmer to control the execution of another program. Typical debuggers allow programmers to suspend execution of a program at a particular statement in the program. This operation is called setting a *breakpoint*. When the program executes the statement with the breakpoint, control is transferred to the debugger. Debuggers also allow program values to be displayed including the activation record. Sun Microsystems provides a Java debugger called `jdb`.

In the previous example, instead of inserting code and recompiling the program, you could have used a *debugger* to set a breakpoint before the loop and then print the array. The important point is that we need to reason about the code and not go willy-nilly changing statements without some clear idea of what we hope to discover.

Here's a another example to illustrate the power of the scientific method applied to debugging. Sally Code and Chuck Hacker (the names have been changed to protect the innocent) have been asked to create a simple statistical analysis program that processes a list of numbers and produces various statistics such as the mean, median, and mode, etc. They are confidant they can do this task and they produce the code shown in Listing 13.8.

The implementation is partial (it computes only the average) as they plan to add more features after they get this part working. The partial implementation is a sign they are good programmers—they develop their code incrementally.

Another indication that Sally and Chuck are good programmers is that after they created and implemented the initial version of `FileStats`; they developed a test input to make sure the preliminary version of `FileStats` works correctly. If there are any problems with `FileStats`, debugging now will be easier than later when the implementation is more complex. The test input is contained in a file named `test1.dat` and it contains the following list of numbers one per line: 10, 10, 20, 4.

To their surprise, when Sally and Chuck run their program, the behavior shown in the screen snapshot of Figure 13.3 occurs. The program seems to hang and produces no output at all.

It must be a simple error. Sally and Chuck decide to employ the scientific method to find the bug. Chuck comes up with the following hypothesis. He thinks that the program is not executing the loop at all. The program is just exiting without reading any data. Sally points out that even if this was the case, they would see some output. Chuck sees the logic of what Sally says. Even though Sally and Chuck did not run the code, they still did an experiment. In this case, Sally and Chuck ran a "thought experiment." Running thought experiments when appropriate is much faster than setting up experiments and running code.

Listing 13.8 Compute the statistics on a file of numbers

```
1.  // Compute the statistics on a user-specified file of data values
2.
3.  import java.io.*;
4.
5.  public class FileStats {
6.
7.      // main(): application entry point
8.      public static void main(String[] args) throws IOException {
9.          // set up standard input stream
10.         BufferedReader stdin = new BufferedReader(
11.             new InputStreamReader( System.in ) );
12.
13.         // determine filename
14.         System.out.print("Filename: ");
15.         String filename = stdin.readLine();
16.
17.         // open file stream for text processing
18.         FileReader reader = new FileReader(filename);
19.         BufferedReader filein = new BufferedReader(reader);
20.
21.         // initially no values have been processed
22.         int valuesProcessed = 0;
23.         double valueSum = 0;
24.
25.         // process values one by one
26.         String toBeProcessed = filein.readLine(); // get first value
27.         while (toBeProcessed != null) {          // did we get value
28.             // convert string to numeric value
29.             double value = Double.parseDouble(toBeProcessed);
30.             // add value to running total
31.             valueSum += value;
32.             // processed another total
33.             ++valuesProcessed;
34.             // prepare for next iteration
35.             toBeProcessed = stdin.readLine();
36.         }
37.
38.         // ready to compute average
39.         if (valuesProcessed > 0) {
40.             double average = valueSum / valuesProcessed;
41.             System.out.println("Average file data value: " + average);
42.         }
43.         else {
44.             System.err.println(filename + ": no values to average");
45.         }
46.
47.         return;
48.     }
49. }
```

Sally and Chuck need more data to help formulate a plausible hypothesis. Sally suggests printing out the values read inside the loop. They insert the following statement inside the while loop immediately after line 29.

```
System.out.println("value is " + value);
```

Figure 13.3 **Running program FileStats.**

When they run the program, they observe the behavior shown in Figure 13.4. The program is reading one value and then stopping. This observation eliminates the code before the loop that opens the file and reads the first value as the problem. The problem must be with the loop. Careful inspection of the loop shows that the readLine() inside the loop is being invoked for stdin not filein. So that explains it! The program is waiting for input from the console.

Figure 13.4 **Running program FileStats with a debug statement.**

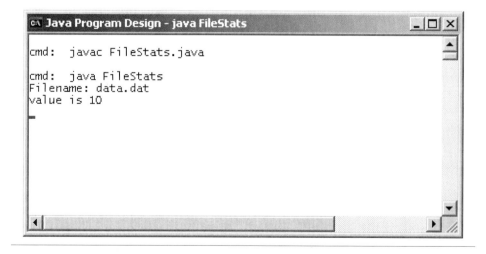

Chuck now remembers that he was doing some testing and he had changed all the readLine() calls to use stdin so he could type in input rather than creating different test files. He must have forgotten to change one back. Fortunately, Sally and Chuck were able to find and fix the error before the code they were developing got too large. After correcting this line of code, Chuck and Sally retest the program and this time it works correctly.

13.2.2   DEBUGGING TIPS AND TECHNIQUES

The most powerful weapon in your arsenal against bugs is your ability to reason. There are also some handy techniques and tips that can reduce the time spent debugging. Many of these techniques help you apply the scientific method more efficiently.

Simplify the problem. Try to come up with the smallest amount of code that still exhibits the error. You can do this by removing calls to methods that are unnecessary and removing statements that should have no bearing on the problem. Anything you can do to reduce the complexity of the code you are debugging can be helpful. As you are removing code, you probably want to periodically run the code to make sure the bug is still there. If it goes away, you have discovered valuable information that you can use to reason about the cause of the bug. As you remove code, be sure and retain a copy of the original code.

Along these same lines, you should produce the smallest input that still causes the bug. If the program is interactive, try to find the shortest sequence of commands that cause the error to occur. Knowing the precise input that causes the problem is useful information.

Stabilize the error. Bugs that occur sporadically are some of the hardest to track down. If the bug does not happen consistently, work to make the bug appear reliably. If the bug is a hard one to track down, you will probably be running the program over and over again. In this case, you want each run to be productive.

How you make the bug appear reliably depends on the program; you will have to be resourceful. Here are some common techniques programmers use, depending on the situation.

Determine the exact sequence of inputs or the precise conditions that cause the bug to occur. If you are using a random number generator, make sure the seed is set to the same value on each run.

If the bug only occurs after the program has been running a long time, figure out ways to simulate that behavior. Perhaps there's a memory leak, and the bug only occurs after many dynamic memory allocations. Simulate this behavior by writing a function that allocates lots of memory. Call the function at the beginning of the program to simulate the effect of the program running a long time.

Dump the state of the program periodically. That is, print out key values and data structures. Use this last "state" information you've collected to initialize the program so it fails quickly and reliably.

Locate the error. Try to determine what function or section of code is causing the problem. To do this, print data values and observe at what point in the execution incorrect values are produced. It also helps to try different input values and observe the effect on the code. Sometimes with the right inputs you can "triangulate" the location of the error in the code. Figure 13.5 illustrates the process of triangulating the location of a bug.

Figure 13.5   Triangulating the location of a bug.

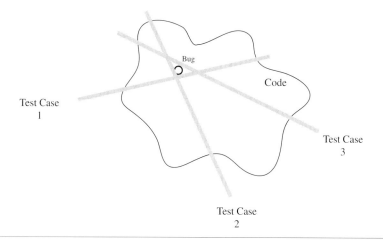

Locating a bug via triangulation often requires running a handful of test cases to narrow the location of the bug down to a region of code small enough to be helpful. The problem is that each test set may identify a large region of code. Consequently, more than two or three test cases are needed to zero in on the location of the bug.

Explain the bug to someone else. In the `FileStats` example, explaining the code to someone else could have caught the error. Hopefully, the person you explain the code to has a different mindset or different mental model of what's going on and will immediately see the problem that you were blind to.

If you have worked at a help desk, you have probably experienced the phenomena known as "confessional debugging." A person is explaining the problem and as they do so, it suddenly dawns on them what the problem is. The act of explaining the code to someone makes you think a little more clearly, not skip steps, and so on. Confessional debugging is surprisingly effective.

Recognize common bugs. Some common bugs have specific symptoms. Knowing the symptoms of commonly occurring bugs can help you identify them quickly.

A common bug is *oversubscripting or undersubscripting an array.* Java throws an `ArrayIndexOutOfBoundsException` if an array is improperly accessed. A common cause of an `ArrayIndexOutOfBoundsException` an off-by-one-error in a loop—the loop iterates one time too many, or the loop starts off with the index initialized improperly.

Dereferencing null is another classic bug. This bug occurs when the program attempts to access an object through a reference variable and the variable has value **null**. Again, Java will throw a `NullPointerException` when a program attempts to dereference **null**. The real issue, however, is why is the pointer null. Sometimes the variable is legitimately null, and you just forgot to guard the statement dereferencing the variable with an if-statement. Other times, you have a live bug that you need to remove. In these cases, using the scientific method of debugging to locate the bug is the best course of action.

Recompile everything. Modern IDEs are extremely useful, but sometimes they can get confused. If you have been making lots of changes to the code looking for a bug and the code is not behaving the way you think it should, or changes you have made do not seem to be having an effect, rebuild the entire project from scratch and rerun the code.

Gather more information. If you are stuck and cannot seem to understand what's going on, generate more data. Some standard actions taken by experienced programmers include running different test cases, using the debugger to observe the program's flow of execution, printing out intermediate results, and displaying data structures. You need to be selective and only print as much as you can reasonably digest. Sifting through mountains of data can be like searching for a needle in a haystack.

Pay attention to the compiler. Modern compilers are very good at detecting certain types of errors. However, they tend to be conservative and sometimes produce warning messages that end up being spurious. When you are searching for a bug, it's a good time to pay attention to all those warning messages you have been ignoring. If the compiler reports an object is used before being set, then that problem is something worth investigating.

Many compilers allow the programmer to control the level at which error and warning messages are issued. Setting the compiler to the strictest level can sometimes yield information that is helpful in searching for a bug.

Fix bugs as you find them. It often happens that when you are looking for a bug, you discover another bug. This bug seems unrelated to the bug you are trying to find. It is tempting to put off doing something about the bug just discovered since you are in the middle of tracking down the original bug. You do not want the trail to go cold.

Generally, it is good practice to fix bugs as you find them. The bug you just found could be related to the one you were originally trying to find. Fixing this bug, could make the other bug go away. This phenomena happens quite often. On the other hand, if you are sure the newly found bug is unrelated to the bug you were originally searching for, then it may be worthwhile to keep searching.

Take a break. Sometimes you get nowhere with a bug despite spending hours trying different strategies to locate it. While perseverance is a valuable programmer trait, knowing when to take a break and get away from a problem is also valuable. Experienced problem solvers know how important it is to get away and do something that lets the mind wander—jog, listen to music, take a walk, stare out the window, and so on. As you relax, the solution to the problem might just come to you.

Most experienced programmers have war stories about bug hunts. A common story is the "debugger's epiphany." The story goes something like this. Sally has been hunting a particularly nasty bug for days. None of the tried-and-true techniques for finding the bug have worked. Sally decides to take a break and hit the hills for some mountain biking action. When Sally is flying down a hill with trees whizzing by, the last thing she is thinking about is the elusive bug in the Web browser. After a great afternoon, Sally heads home for a shower. As she showers, she starts to think about the bug again, and it hits her—the solution to the browser problem suddenly becomes crystal clear. Sally heads to work to run an experiment to validate her hypothesis, but she's confident she's got it.

Stories like Sally's are common. Of course, the best stories always have the programmer doing something unusual when the epiphany occurs!

Think outside the box. It is very easy to get locked into a particular way of looking at or attacking a problem. If you are getting nowhere with a problem, try thinking outside the box. Try something unusual or new that you have not tried before. For example, do the opposite of what you have been doing and see what happens.

Debugging is an important part of the programming process. As you gain experience with programming, you will no doubt develop your own personal style of debugging—favorite techniques, tricks, tools, and so forth. You will also learn to use a source-level debugger. A source-level debugger integrated into a modern IDE is a powerful tool for tracking down bugs. However, the most important point to remember is that the key to effective debugging is to follow a disciplined process. Together, disciplined testing and disciplined debugging ensure that high-quality software is delivered on time and within budget.

13.3 REVIEW

- Testing cannot prove that software has no bugs. It can only show the presence of bugs.
- Bugs fall into four broad categories: software crashes or data corruption, failure to meet or satisfy the specification, poor or unacceptable performance, and difficulty of use.
- Test early in the development process. It is cheaper and easier to fix bugs when they are identified early.
- It is generally impossible to test a program completely.
- Develop prototypes to test functional requirements.
- A code inspection is a rigorous process of reading code to find errors and flaws before testing.
- Testing without knowledge of how the code works is called black-box testing.
- Testing with knowledge of how the code works is called white-box testing.
- Equivalence partitioning helps develop smaller, more effective test suites.
- Good test suites include inputs that test the software's boundary conditions.
- Statement coverage testing creates test inputs so that every statement in the software is executed at least once.
- Path coverage testing creates inputs so that every controlflow edge in the software is executed at least once.
- Set up automated procedures for running and checking the results of your tests. Automating test procedures will make testing go faster, and it also serves to document the testing process for future developers and maintainers.
- Use the scientific method for debugging.
- Take time to fix a bug properly. Resist the temptation to apply a quick fix to get the code running. Time spent fixing a bug properly early in the software development process is an investment that will pay off in the future.
- When debugging, try to produce the simplest input that causes the problem. Be sure to add the input to your set of test cases.
- Work to make the error consistently repeatable. This will help you understand the bug, and it will speed the debugging process.
- Learn to recognize the symptoms of common bugs.

13.4 REFERENCES

There are many excellent texts that discuss testing and debugging. The student interested in learning more about testing can begin with the following texts.

- Brian Kernighan and Rob Pike, *The Practice of Programming,* Reading, MA: Addison-Wesley, 1999.

- Steve McConnell, *Code Complete: A Practical Handbook of Software Construction*, Redmond, WA: Microsoft Press, 1993.
- Glenford Myers, *The Art of Software Testing*, New York: Wiley, 1979.
- Ron Patton, *Software Testing,* Indianapolis: Sams Publishing, 2001.

13.5   SELF-TEST

S13.1 Typically, what percentage of a project is devoted to testing and debugging?

S13.2 Explain the difference between testing and debugging.

S13.3 What is a unit test?

S13.4 What is a test harness?

S13.5 Name the four roles used in an inspection.

S13.6 With many inspection methodologies, the presenter is someone other than the author of the code. Why should someone other than the author be the presenter?

S13.7 Explain the difference between black-box testing and white-box testing.

S13.8 What is statement coverage testing?

S13.9 What is path coverage testing?

S13.10 Devise test cases that cause each statement in the following method to be executed at least once.

```java
public int Euclid(int x, int y) {
    while (x != y) {
        if (x > y)
            x = x - y;
        else
            x = y - x;
    }
    return 0;
}
```

S13.11 Describe the steps of the scientific method.

S13.12 What kind of logic, inductive or deductive, does the scientific method use?

13.6   EXERCISES

13.1 The crash of the Ariane 5 was the result of poor testing practices. Using your library or Internet research facilities, find out about the Ariane 5 crash, and explain how the test procedure was flawed.

13.2 Develop test inputs to test the program of Listing 5.4 Your test inputs should achieve full statement coverage of the program. That is, the test inputs should cause every statement in the program to be executed at least once.

13.3 Revise the test harness for class LED that displayed all the numerals to include the blank, the A, the P, and the colon.

13.4 Test data is often partitioned into inputs that test for error conditions and inputs that test that the program works when given valid data. Examine the program of Listing 5.5. Develop one set of test inputs for error conditions and a separate set of inputs to demonstrate the program works.

13.5 Set up a test harness for the binary search function, and test it thoroughly. Report any errors you found.

13.6 How many unique paths are there in the following controlflow graph?

13.7 Develop a test harness, and test input for the class Box.java given in Listing 10.8.

13.8 With four other classmates, perform an inspection of the ValueReader.java presented in Listing 10.11. Prepare an inspection report that describes any problems that the inspection discovered.

13.9 Explain why it is a good idea to have someone other than the programmer responsible for testing a program.

13.10 Use the Internet to research the Therac-25 accidents. Describe what happened.

13.7 PROGRAMMING PROJECT — GETLIST()

In this programming project, we exercise our testing and debugging skills by testing and debugging a method developed for reading a list of numbers into an array. The code for the method is given in Listing 13.9. Users of this code have reported that the method sometimes does not return the correct list. The users report that the error seems to occur when the method is invoked multiple times on the same file.

> The objective of this case study is to develop and practice testing and debugging skills

ANALYSIS

The first step is to walk through the code and gain an understanding of its operation. An examination of the code shows that the method getList() receives a single **int** param-

---

Listing 13.9 getList() method

```
1.  public static int[] getList(int maxListSize) {
2.     BufferedReader stdin = new BufferedReader(
3.      new InputStreamReader(System.in));
4.     int[] input = new int[maxListSize];
5.     int n = 0;
6.     String currentInput = stdin.readLine();
7.     while ((n < maxListSize) && (!currentInput != null)) {
8.        input[n] = Integer.parseInt(currentInput);
9.        ++n;
10.       currentInput = stdin.readLine();
11.    }
12.    int[] values = new int[n];
13.    for (int i = 0; i < values.length; ++i) {
14.       values[i] = input[i];
15.    }
16.    return values;
17. }
```

---

eter called `maxListSize`. This is the number of numbers to attempt to read. The method then allocates a temporary array, `input`, to hold the values. The method then reads integers until it has read `maxListSize` integers or the call to `stdin.readLine()` returns a **null**.

The method then allocates another array, `values`, and copies the elements from array `input` to array `values`. It returns the array `values`. Overall the code looks straightforward, but there is a bug and we must find it.

IMPLEMENTATION

To locate the bug, we need to do extensive testing. To efficiently test the code, we should develop a test harness. The test harness we develop should invoke method `getList()` and verify that the list returned is correct. To this end, it might be appropriate to have the test harness code accept, as a command line argument, the test file to read. This will facilitate running different test cases.

Implementing the part of the test harness that verifies that the list returned is correct requires careful thought. You should consider how you might accomplish checking the list returned by method `getList()` is correct without having to read a separate list. Devising an efficient scheme now will pay off later when you begin testing the code.

TESTING

Because users have reported errors when method `getList()` is invoked multiple times on the same file, we definitely need to develop test cases that exercise using method `getList()` in this way. After you have developed the necessary test cases, the next step is reproduce the bug.

If your initial set of test cases does not expose the bug, you will need to develop additional test cases. You should develop a hypothesis to explain the erroneous behavior and develop test cases to prove or disprove your hypothesis. You should always use the scientific method as you seek to find and fix bugs.

After you have found the bug, you should fix the bug and rerun all the test cases to ensure they still work properly. Sometimes we fix one bug, but we introduce another, so it is important to always test the code if it has been modified.

13.8   SELF-TEST ANSWERS

S13.1   Typically 40 to 50 percent of a project is devoted to debugging and testing.

S13.2   The purpose of testing is to identify problems or errors in the software prior to delivery. The purpose of debugging is to locate and fix a problems and errors identified by testing or reported by users.

S13.3   A unit test tests a small component in isolation before the component is integrated into the larger system being constructed.

S13.4   A test harness is a small piece of code written to test or exercise the code being developed.

S13.5   The roles during an inspection are: moderator, inspector, author, scribe.

S13.6   Having the presenter be someone other than the author has a neutral person (i.e., someone who does not have ego involved in the code inspection) presenting the code.

S13.7   With black-box testing, the tester creates test cases without having seen the code. With white-box testing, the tester is able to inspect the code and use their knowledge of the internal workings of the code to create test cases.

S13.8   Statement coverage testing creates test inputs so that every statement in the software is executed at least once.

S13.9   Path coverage testing creates inputs so that every controlflow edge in the software is executed at least once.

S13.10 Two test cases suffice: $x = 2$, $y = 3$, and $x = 5$, $y = 2$.

S13.11 The steps of the scientific method are: 1) gather data, 2) develop a hypothesis, 3) predict new facts, 4) perform experiments, and 5) prove or disprove hypothesis.

S13.12 The scientific method uses inductive logic.

A TABLES AND OPERATORS

This appendix presents information on the Unicode character set, reserved words, operators, and their precedence.

| A.I | UNICODE CHARACTER SET |

Most traditional programming languages use the ASCII character set as their base character set. This character set is English-centric, although it does support many diacritical variants on the English alphabet. And even for English, ASCII does not support all of the punctuation marks and technical symbols in use. These limitations arise because ASCII uses a single byte for a character—allowing only 256 characters to be represented. Java uses the Unicode character set, which is the international character set standard. Unicode uses a 2-byte representation. Therefore, it can represent over 65,000 characters. This number is sufficiently large to represent all major written world alphabets and dialects. For example, Unicode includes several Philippine dialects including Tagalog, Hanunoo, Buhid, and Tagbanwa. The following table lists the first 128 characters of the set. For a detailed description of the Unicode character set visit `www.unicode.org`.

Unicode	Char.	Name	Unicode	Char.	Unicode	Char.	Unicode	Char.
0	CTL-@	NUL	32	SP	64	@	96	`
1	CTL-A	SOH	33	!	65	A	97	a
2	CTL-B	STX	34	"	66	B	98	b
3	CTL-C	ETX	35	#	67	C	99	c
4	CTL-D	EOT	36	$	68	D	100	d
5	CTL-E	ENQ	37	%	69	E	101	e
6	CTL-F	ACK	38	&	70	F	102	f
7	CTL-G	BEL	39	'	71	G	103	g
8	CTL-H	BS	40	(	72	H	104	h
9	CTL-I	TAB	41	)	73	I	105	i
10	CTL-J	LF	42	*	74	J	106	j
11	CTL-K	VT	43	+	75	K	107	k
12	CTL-L	FF	44	,	76	L	108	l
13	CTL-M	CR	45	-	77	M	109	m
14	CTL-N	SO	46	.	78	N	110	n
15	CTL-O	SI	47	/	79	O	111	o
16	CTL-P	DLE	48	0	80	P	112	p
17	CTL-Q	DC1	49	1	81	Q	113	q
18	CTL-R	DC2	50	2	82	R	114	r
19	CTL-S	DC3	51	3	83	S	115	s
20	CTL-T	DC4	52	4	84	T	116	t
21	CTL-U	NAK	53	5	85	U	117	u
22	CTL-V	SYN	54	6	86	V	118	v
23	CTL-W	ETB	55	7	87	W	119	w
24	CTL-X	CAN	56	8	88	X	120	x
25	CTL-Y	EM	57	9	89	Y	121	y
26	CTL-Z	SUB	58	:	90	Z	122	z
27	CTL-[	ESC	59	;	91	[	123	{
28	CTL-\	FS	60	<	92	\	124		
29	CTL-]	GS	61	=	93	]	125	}
30	CTL-^	RS	62	>	94	^	126	~
31	CTL-_	US	63	?	95	_	127	DEL

A.2   RESERVED WORDS

The following identifiers are keywords in Java and cannot be used as identifier names.

abstract	double	int	strictfp
boolean	else	interface	super
break	extends	long	switch
byte	final	native	synchronized
case	finally	new	this
catch	float	package	throw
char	for	private	throws
class	goto	protected	transient
const	if	public	try
continue	implements	return	void
default	import	short	volatile
do	instanceof	static	while

Keywords **const** and **goto** are currently unused. Words **false**, **null**, and **true** are also reserved for special meaning and cannot be used as identifier names.

A.3   OPERATORS AND PRECEDENCE

The following table lists the precedence of operators from highest to lowest precedence. Operators of equal precedence are evaluated left to right except for the assignment operators, which are evaluated from right to left.

Operator precedence table	
group	(*op*)
postfix	[] . (*params*) *op*++ *op*--
prefix	++*op* --*op* +*op* -*op* ~ !
creation or casting	**new** (type)*op*
multiplicative	* / %
additive	+ -
shift	<< >> >>>
relational	< > <= >= **instanceof** ==
equality	== !=
bitwise and	&
bitwise exclusive and	^
bitwise inclusive or	|
logical and	&&
logical or	||
conditional	? :
assignment	= += -= *= /= %= &= ^= |= <<= >>= >>>=

The arithmetic operations have the following definitions.

op1 + *op2*

Evaluates to the sum of *op1* and *op2*.

op1 - op2
>Evaluates to the difference of *op2* from *op1*.

*op1 * op2*
>Evaluates to the product of *op1* and *op2*.

op1 / op2
>Evaluates to the quotient of *op1* divided by *op2*.

op1 % op2
>Evaluates to the remainder of dividing *op1* by *op2*.

The rules for binary numeric operands with operand of mixed types is as follows.

- If both of the operands are integer and one operand is of type **long**, then **long** arithmetic is performed by first *widening through numeric promotion* the non-**long** integer operand to the type **long**.

- If both of the operands are integer and neither integer operand is of type **long**, then **int** arithmetic is performed by first widening through numeric promotion any non-**int** operand(s) to the type **int**.

- If one of the operands is of type **double**, then **double** arithmetic is performed by first widening through numeric promotion any non-**double** operand to the type **double**.

- If one operand is of type **float** and the other operand is not of type **double**, then **float** arithmetic is performed by first widening through numeric promotion any non-**float** operand to the type **float**.

The unary arithmetic operators have the following definitions.

+op
>Evaluates to *op*.

-op
>Evaluates to the negation of *op*.

op++
>Increments *op* by 1; evaluates to the value of op before it was incremented.

++op
>Increments *op* by 1; evaluates to the value of op after it was incremented.

op--
>Decrements *op* by 1; evaluates to the value of *op* before it was decremented.

--op
>Decrements *op* by 1; evaluates to the value of *op* after it was decremented.

The relational operators have the following definitions.

op1 > op2
>Tests whether *op1* is greater than *op2*.

op1 >= op2
>Tests whether *op1* is greater than or equal to *op2*.

op1 < op2
>Tests whether *op1* is less than *op2*.

op1 <= op2
>Tests whether *op1* is less than or equal to *op2*.

op1 == op2
>Tests whether *op1* and *op2* are equal.

op1 != op2

> Tests whether *op1* and *op2* are different.

The conditional operators have the following definitions.

op1 && op2

> Tests whether *op1* and *op2* are both true. Only evaluates *op2* if *op1* is true.

op1 || op2

> Tests whether either of *op1* or *op2* is true. Only evaluates *op2* if *op1* is true.

! op

> Tests whether *op* is false.

op1 & op2

> Always evaluates both *op1* and *op2*. If operands are numeric types, then it evaluates to the logical and of the individual bits of *op1* and *op2*. If *op1* and *op2* are boolean, it evaluates to *op1 && op2*.

op1 | op2

> Always evaluates both *op1* and *op2*. If operands are numeric types, then it evaluates to the logical or of the individual bits of *op1* and *op2*. If *op1* and *op2* are boolean, it evaluates to *op1 || op2*.

op1 ^ op2

> If operands are numeric types, then it evaluates to the logical exclusive or of the individual bits of *op1* and *op2*. If *op1* and *op2* are boolean, it evaluates to *op1 != op2*.

The shifting operators have the following definitions.

op1 >> op2

> Evaluates to a rightward shifting of the bits of *op1* by distance *op2*.

op1 << op2

> Evaluates to a leftward shifting of the bits of *op1* by distance *op2*.

op1 >>> op2

> Evaluates to an unsigned rightward shifting of the bits of *op1* by distance *op2*.

The assignment operators have the following definitions.

op1 = op2

> Evaluates *op1* and *op2*. The value of *op1* is now the value of *op2*. Assignment evaluates to the new value of *op1*.

op1 += op2

> Evaluates to *op1 = op1 + op2*. Operator *op1* is evaluated only once.

op1 -= op2

> Evaluates to *op1 = op1 - op2*. Operator *op1* is evaluated only once.

*op1 *= op2*

> Evaluates to *op1 = op1 * op2*. Operator *op1* is evaluated only once.

op1 /= op2

> Evaluates to *op1 = op1 / op2*. Operator *op1* is evaluated only once.

op1 %= op2

> Evaluates to *op1 = op1 % op2*. Operator *op1* is evaluated only once.

op1 &= op2

> Evaluates to *op1 = op1 & op2*. Operator *p1* is evaluated only once.

op1 |= op2

> Evaluates to *op1 = op1 | op2*. Operator *op1* is evaluated only once.

op1 ^= *op2*

Evaluates to *op1* = *op1* ^ *op2*. Operator *op1* is evaluated only once.

op1 <<= *op2*

Evaluates to *op1* = *op1* << *op2*. Operator *op1* is evaluated only once.

op1 >>= *op2*

Evaluates to *op1* = *op1* >> *op2*. Operator *op1* is evaluated only once.

op1 >>>= *op2*

Evaluates to *op1* = *op1* >>> *op2*. Operator *op1* is evaluated only once.

The other operators have the following definitions.

(*op*)

Evaluates to *op*.

op1 ? *op2* : *op3*

If *op1* is **true**, evaluates to *op2*; otherwise, evaluates to *op3*.

new *type*[*op*]

Creates a new array with *op* elements of type *type*.

new *type*

Creates a new object of reference type *type*.

type[]

Declares an array of unknown length, which contains elements of type *type*.

op1[*op2*]

Evaluates to the element with index *op2* in array *op1*.

op1.*op2*

Evaluates to the *op2* member of *op1*.

op1(*params*)

Declares or invokes the method named *op1* with the specified parameter list *params*.

(*type*) *op*

Casts *op* to type *type*.

op1 instanceof *op2*

Tests whether *op1* is an instance of *op2*.

B NUMBER REPRESENTATION

This appendix presents information on the number representation.

BINARY NUMBER REPRESENTATION

Computers use the binary number system to represent data, programs, and messages. The principles underlying the binary number system are the same as those used in the decimal number system. Both the decimal and binary number systems are *positional number systems*, that is, the position of a digit indicates its relative value. For example, in the decimal number 4506, the 5 is in the 100's place and thus indicates a value of 500. Reading the number from the right, each digit represents an increasing power of 10. Thus the value of the 4506 can be expressed as

$$4 \times 10^3 + 5 \times 10^2 + 0 \times 10^1 + 6 \times 10^0$$

We say that the *leading* digit 4 is the *most significant* digit and that the *trailing* digit 6 is the *least significant* digit.

The binary number system works the same way except that we use increasing powers of 2. For example, the binary number 1101 represents the decimal 13.

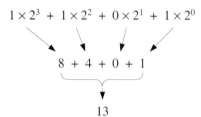

$$1 \times 2^3 + 1 \times 2^2 + 0 \times 2^1 + 1 \times 2^0$$

$$8 + 4 + 0 + 1$$

$$13$$

To indicate that a number is in a base other than decimal, the base is written as a subscript at the end of the number. So 100000_2 is the binary representation of the decimal value 32, whereas 100000_{10} represents the decimal value 100,000.

The *octal* and *hexadecimal* number systems are also used in programming. In the octal system, digits can take on the values 0 through 7. For example, 135_8 is the octal representation of 93_{10} because

$$1 \times 8^2 + 3 \times 8^1 + 5 \times 8^0 = 64 + 24 + 5 = 93.$$

The hexadecimal number system is the base 16 number system. Since a hexadecimal digit can take on 16 possible values, extra symbols are required to represent the digits greater than nine. The convention is to use the letters A through F to represent the digits equivalent to the decimals 10 through 15 (i.e., A represents the decimal 10, B represents the decimal 11, and so on). For example, 59_{16} equals 89_{10} and $1CA_{16}$ equals 450_{10} because

$$5 \times 16^1 + 9 \times 16^0 = 80 + 9 = 89$$

$$1 \times 16^2 + 12 \times 16^1 + 10 \times 16^0 = 256 + 184 + 10 = 450$$

To convert an integer decimal number m to its binary equivalent is tedious but not hard. The following algorithm describes the conversion process.

Step 1.   Let m be the number we want to convert.
Step 2.   Let i have the value 0.
Step 3.   Divide m by 2. Let q be the quotient and let r be the remainder.
Step 4.   Increment i by 1

Step 5. The ith least significant digit is r.
Step 6. Set m equal to q.
Step 7. If m is not 0, go to Step 3 and repeat the process.
Step 8. The conversion is 0 completed.

We will use our algorithm to convert the decimal number 13 into its binary equivalent. We start off in Steps 1 and 2 by initializing m and i to 13 and 0 respectively. Then in Step 3, we divide our number 13 by 2. The result is a quotient q of 6 and a remainder r of 1. In Step 4 we increment i to 1. Therefore, in Step 5 we announce that the least significant digit is 1. Thus, the answer so far is

1

Our number m is now 6 and because 6 is not 0, Step 7 causes us to repeat the process by going back to Step 3. This time we divide 6 by 2. The result is a quotient q of 3 and a remainder r of 0. After incrementing i to 2 in Step 4, we announce in Step 5 that the next most least significant digit is 0. Thus, the answer so far is

01

Our number is now 3 and because 3 is not 0, we again Step 7 causes us to repeat the process by going back to Step 3. This time we divide 3 by 2. The result is a quotient q of 1 and a remainder r of 1. After incrementing i to 3 in Step 4, we announce in Step 5 that the next most least significant digit is 1, Thus, the answer so far is

101

Our number is now 1 and because 1 is not 0, Step 7 causes us yet again to repeat the process by going back to Step 3. This time we divide 1 by 2. The result is a quotient q of 0 and a remainder r of 1. After incrementing i to 4 in Step 4, we announce in Step 5 that the next most least significant digit is 1. Thus, the answer so far is

1101

Our number is now 0 and because it is, Step 7 does not cause us to repeat the process. Instead Step 8 indicates that we have completed the translation. Thus, the binary equivalent of 13 is 1101_2.

B.2   TWO'S-COMPLEMENT REPRESENTATION

A world consisting of just ones and zeros needs to adopt some convention for the representation of negative integer values. All computers use a fixed number of binary digits to represent a value. This basic unit of storage is called a *word*. To keep things simple, we assume that we are dealing with a computer with a 4-bit word rather than the typical 32-bit word size.

With a 4-bit word we can represent the nonnegative integers 0 through 15 ($2^4 - 1$) in this amount of storage. However, if we want to represent negative values and be able to perform subtraction, we have to give up some of the positive values.

Table B.1   **4-bit two's-complement numbers and decimal equivalents.**

Binary	Decimal	Binary	Decimal
0000	0	1000	-8
0001	1	1001	-7
0010	2	1010	-6
0011	3	1011	-5
0100	4	1100	-4
0101	5	1101	-3
0110	6	1110	-2
0111	7	1111	-1

Most modern computers use a system known as *two's complement* to represent integers. In the two's-complement system, nonnegative numbers (i.e., positive numbers and zero) are represented as we described previously. However, negative numbers are represented differently. For a machine with an n-bit word, the two's-complement representation of a negative number x is $2^n - x$ represented in binary.

In the two's-complement system, the most significant bit of the word serves as the sign bit. A one in the most significant bit position indicates a negative value, and a zero indicates a positive value. The range of numbers that can be represented in an 4-bit word is –8 to 7. In general, the range of numbers that can be represented in two's-complement notation in a word of n bits is -2^{n-1} through $2^{n-1} - 1$.

Suppose we add decimals 4 and 5 using a 4-bit two's-complement representation. From Table B.1, we know 4's encoding is 0100 and 5's encoding is 0101. Adding the two numbers in binary produces 1001, which is the encoding of –7. Yet the decimal sum of 4 and 5 is 9. What has happened is that the sum of 4 and 5 is too big for the number of bits—the largest integer that can be stored in 4-bit two's-complement representation is 7. This situation is called *overflow*.

Most computer systems also have a binary representation for *floating-point values* (real number values, e.g., 6.9 and 11.82) that uses one or two words of memory to encode a number. As such, there are limits both on the smallest and largest numbers that can be represented and on the number of places of accuracy. The representation limits mean that some numeric values can only be approximated. For example, the decimal 0.1 does not have a finite representation in the binary system. As a result, care must be taken when doing floating-point computations. Expressions that may be equivalent mathematically may not compute the same result. For example, the expression

```
0.1 + 0.1 + 0.1 + 0.1 + 0.1 + 0.1 + 0.1 + 0.1 + 0.1 + 0.1
```

does not evaluate to 1 in the Java programming language. The result is extremely close to 1.0, but not exactly 1.0.

C APPLETS

This appendix introduces the basics of creating an applet. An applet is a Java program that is embedded in a Web page. Applets enable Web designers to develop pages that accept input, perform computations, and display results. Such pages are said to have active content as opposed to contents that are unchanging or static.

C.1   A SIMPLE APPLET

The Internet has become an extremely valuable resource. Originally, information available on Web pages was static. That is, the information presented on a Web page was constant—there were no facilities that enabled Web pages to compute new values based on inputs from users. An applet is a Java program that has been embedded in a Web page. When a browser visits a Web page containing an applet, the Web server sends the applet code to the browser and the browser arranges for the code to be executed. Consequently, a Java applet enables designers to create Web pages that accept input, compute values, and display the output to the user. Basically, Java's applet mechanism enables Web designers to create pages that can do anything a program can do.

We begin our introduction to applets in a manner similar to our introduction to Java console applications in Chapter 1. We give an applet program and Web page that displays a quotation. Listing C.1 contains the code for DisplayQuote.java.

Listing C.1   DisplayQuote.java

```
1.  // Simple applet that displays a string
2.  import java.awt.*;
3.  import javax.swing.*;
4.  public class DisplayQuote extends JApplet {
5.      public void paint(Graphics g) {
6.          g.drawString("Anyone who spends their life on a computer "
7.                  + "pretty unusual.", 20, 30);
8.          g.drawString("Bill Gates, Chairman of Microsoft", 25, 45);
9.      }
10. }
```

The Web page Quote.html in Listing C.2 contains the following hypertext markup language (HTML) code.

Listing C.2   Quote.htm

```
1.  <html>
2.      <title> Quotation </title>
3.      <applet code="DisplayQuote.class" width=400 height=200>
4.      </applet>
5.  </html>
```

When a user visits Web page Quote.html, the following image is displayed in the browser window.

Let's examine `DisplayQuote.java` and `Quote.html` line by line. Applet `DisplayQuote.java` begins by importing the necessary classes from the `awt` and `swing` packages.

```
import java.awt.*;
import javax.swing.*;
```

As line 4 specifies, our applet is a subclass of `swing` class `JApplet`. In turn, class `JApplet` is a subclass of `Applet`.

```
public class DisplayQuote extends JApplet {
```

Java requires that every applet be a subclass of `Applet`. However, most Java programmers extend it through `JApplet` rather than directly from `Applet` itself. By extending `JApplet`, `DisplayQuote` inherits methods that support menu bar and pane manipulation (see Appendix E). Because `JApplet` is an extension of class `Applet`, `DisplayQuote` also inherits the actual mechanics to run an applet. What must be specified in the definition of class `DisplayQuote` is how this applet differs from a basic applet.

What's different in the `DisplayQuote` applet from the basic applet provided by package `JApplet` is that `DisplayQuote` will display a quotation. To display a quotation, subclass `DisplayQuote` defines a single member method named `paint()`. As we shall discuss shortly, the code is overriding the method `paint()` provided by the superclass `Applet`.

```
public void paint(Graphics g) {
    g.drawString("Anyone who spends their life on a computer "
            + "pretty unusual.", 20, 30);
    g.drawString("Bill Gates, Chairman of Microsoft", 25, 45);
}
```

Method `paint()` is where applet `DisplayQuote` will do its work. `DisplayQuote`'s `paint()` method takes a single parameter of type `Graphics`, which is the applet's onscreen drawing context. The body of `paint()` invokes method `drawString()` to display both the quotation and attribution. Method `drawString()`'s parameters represent the string to display and the x- and y-coordinates of the desired position in the display area of the leftmost character of the string.

Now let's examine the HTML code in `Quote.html`, which runs the `DisplayQuote` applet. The code begins with the tag `<html>`. This tag indicates that the file contains HTML code. Notice that there is a matching tag `</html>` that brackets the HTML code of the applet. This tag signals the end of the HTML code. Most HTML elements are specified in this manner—an opening tag and a corresponding closing tag.

The tag `<title>` indicates the string that follows is to be displayed in the title bar of the window. A closing tag `</title>` then marks end of the title string. For our applet "Quotation" is displayed.

The tag `applet` indicates that this Web page will contain an applet. The applet code to download and execute is specified by setting the attribute `code` to the name of the file containing the class file. It is important that the class file reside in the same directory as the HTML file, otherwise the Web server will not be able to locate it and download it to the browser. The attributes `width` and `height` are used to specify the width and height in pixels of the applet's display area.

Now that we understand our simple Java applet and the HTML file required to embed an applet in a Web page, we can discuss some of the basic capabilities of an applet.

C.2   APPLET METHODS

An applet is run under the control of the browser that downloads the class file. Consequently, an applet must respond to events that occur as the browser prepares the applet for execution, as the applet executes, and as the applet is terminated. There are four major events or milestones in the lifetime of an applet. These milestones are

- initialization—which occurs when the applet is loaded;
- start execution—which occurs after the applet is loaded;
- stop execution—which occurs when the user leaves the Web page containing the applet, or the user terminates the browser; and
- destruction—which occurs before the applet is unloaded.

A basic applet class contains methods that are invoked as each of these events occur. The following code illustrates the basic skeleton of an applet.

```
public class MyApplet extends JApplet {
    ...
    public void init() { ... }
    public void start() { ... }
    public void stop() { ... }
    public void destroy() { ... }
    ...
}
```

A subclass of `JApplet` can override any of these methods as necessary. In the following sections, we describe these methods in more detail.

C.2.1   METHOD INIT()

Method `init()` is invoked by the browser to inform an applet that it has been loaded. It is always invoked before method `start()` is invoked. Generally one can think of method `init()` as the constructor for the applet. Typical uses of the method `init()` would be to construct any objects required, load any images required by the applet, or create any threads that will be used when the applet is run. The method init() inherited from class Applet does nothing. Often a subclass of Applet need not override the superclass init() method.

C.2.2 | **METHOD START()**

Method start() is invoked by the browser to inform an applet that it should start its execution. Generally every applet that does something after initialization (except in direct response to user actions) must override the method start(). Method start() either performs the applet's work or (more likely) starts up one or more threads to perform the work. The method start() inherited from class Applet does nothing.

C.2.3 | **METHOD STOP()**

Method stop() is invoked by the browser to inform an applet to stop its execution. It is invoked when the Web page that contains an applet has been replaced by another page and also just before the applet is to be destroyed. Method stop() should be overridden if the applet has any operation that it should perform each time the Web page containing it is no longer visible. For example, an applet with animation might want to use method start() to resume animation and method stop() to suspend the animation. The method stop() inherited from class Applet does nothing.

C.2.4 | **METHOD DESTROY()**

Method destroy() is invoked by the browser to inform an applet that it is being reclaimed and that it should release any resources that it has allocated. Method stop() will always be invoked before method destroy(). Method destroy() should be overridden if the applet has any operation that it wants to perform before it is destroyed. For example, an applet with threads would use the method init() to create the threads and method destroy() to kill them. The method destroy() inherited from class Applet does nothing.

C.2.5 | **METHOD PAINT()**

The paint() method is responsible for displaying the current state of the applet's graphical interface. The method is invoked automatically after the applet execution has started.

The invocation is a signal to the applet that its graphical interface needs to be displayed. Because different applets have different graphical interfaces, the `paint()` method is normally redefined by an applet subclass.

The definition of `paint()` for `DisplayQuote.java` is:

```
public void paint(Graphics g) {
    g.drawString("Anyone who spends their life on a computer "
        + "pretty unusual.", 20, 30);
    g.drawString("Bill Gates, Chairman of Microsoft", 25, 45);
}
```

The two integer parameters in the `drawString()` invocations are the coordinates to draw the string. In particular, Java applets use a coordinate system that use pixel positions to specify locations. A pixel is the minimal-sized graphical element that can be drawn on the particular monitor doing the display. Figure C.1 illustrates an applet's coordinate system.

Figure C.1   Applet coordinate system.

When a drawing request is made, the location of the drawing is specified relative to the upper-left-hand corner of the object on which the drawing commands are performed. The direction of the x-axis is rightward. Therefore, increasing an x-coordinate value means moving rightward. The direction of the y-axis is downward. Therefore, increasing a y-coordinate value means moving downward.

For method `paint()` to do its job, it requires the graphical context in which the drawing commands issued by `paint()` are to occur. The browser sends the graphical context by invoking method `paint()` with an object of type `Graphics`.

The graphical context includes such information as the current background and foreground colors, the current font, rendering style, and the object on which rendering commands are to be performed. Besides encapsulating such information, `Graphics` objects have a variety of methods for drawing strings, lines, arcs, ovals, rectangles, and other polygons. The available methods are detailed in Appendix E. Applet `DrawDisplay.java` in Listing C.3 demonstrates some of these `Graphics` methods.

The `DrawDisplay paint()` method begins by setting the current color for the graphical context to `Color.BLACK`.

```
g.setColor(Color.BLACK);
```

A drawing request is then made to draw a filled rectangle whose upper-left-hand corner is the origin of applet's window pane.

```
g.fillRect(0, 0, 300, 200);
```

The rectangle is to be 300 pixels wide and 200 pixels high. Because the applet window pane has those same dimensions, the fill request effectively makes the background color of the window pane black.

Listing C.3 DrawDisplay.java

```
1.  // Demonstrate the use of several Graphics methods in paint()
2.  import java.awt.*;
3.  import javax.swing.*;
4.
5.  public class DrawDisplay extends JApplet {
6.
7.      // paint(): issues the drawing and color setting requests
8.      public void paint(Graphics g) {
9.          g.setColor(Color.BLACK);
10.         g.fillRect(0, 0, 300, 200);
11.         g.setColor(Color.BLUE);
12.         g.drawRect(50, 50, 75, 50);
13.         g.setColor(Color.GREEN);
14.         g.fillOval(50, 50, 75, 50);
15.         g.drawLine(200, 25, 250, 125);
16.         g.setColor(Color.YELLOW);
17.         g.drawOval(125, 125, 50, 50);
18.     }
19. }
```

Method `paint()` then sets the current color for the graphical context to `Color.BLUE`.

```
g.setColor(Color.BLUE);
```

Because `Color.BLUE` is now the current color, the next drawing request

```
g.drawRect(50, 50, 75, 50);
```

results in the perimeter of a blue rectangle being displayed. The rectangle is 75 pixels wide and 50 pixels high. Its upper-left-hand corner is at location (50, 50).

Method `paint()` next sets the current color for the graphical context to `Color.GREEN`.

```
g.setColor(Color.GREEN);
```

The next drawing request is for a filled-in oval. Because `Color.GREEN` is the current color, the oval is green.

```
g.fillOval(50, 50, 75, 50);
```

The oval is to be 75 pixels wide and 50 pixels high. The bounding box for this oval is at location (50, 50). Thus, the rectangle that the applet previously drew circumscribes the oval now being drawn.

The next drawing request is for a line to be drawn from location (200, 25) to location (250, 125).

```
g.drawLine(200, 25, 250, 125);
```

Because `Color.GREEN` remains the current color, the line is drawn green.

Method `paint()` next sets the current color for the graphical context to `Color.YELLOW`.

```
g.setColor(Color.YELLOW);
```

A drawing request is then made for an oval whose bounding box is a 50 x 50 square with the upper-left-hand corner of the bounding box at (125, 125).

```
g.drawOval(125, 125, 50, 50);
```

Such an oval is, in fact, a circle. When the browser visits the Web page that references the class file `DrawDisplay.java`, the following image appears in the browser window.

APPLETS AND THREADS

As mentioned in the introduction to this appendix, an applet provides the ability to have dynamic content. A common approach is to use a thread to continually change the information displayed by the applet. This technique can be used to create animations, ticker tapes, and continuously updated displays. To illustrate the use of applets and threads, we present an applet that displays a clock that is continuously updated. The applet program, ClockApplet.java, is based on the program SimpleClock.java presented in Listing 12.2. The applet code is presented in Listing C.4.

ClockApplet extends JApplet and implements the interface Runnable. Because ClockApplet implements the interface Runnable, ClockApplet must provide a method run(). As you examine the body of ClockApplet, notice that the ClockApplet overrides the superclass's init(), start(), and stop() methods. Method init() is invoked when the applet is loaded. It initializes instance variable update-Thread to **null**.

```
updateThread = null;
```

A **null** value for updateThread indicates that the applet is not currently displaying and updating a clock.

Method start() is invoked by the browser to start the action of the applet. Clock-Applet's start() method first tests whether updateThread is **null**.

```
if (updateThread == null) {
    updateThread = new Thread(this);
    updateThread.start();
}
```

If updateThread is non-**null**, no additional action is required by the applet because the clock display is running. If it is **null**, then a new thread is started. This applet's run() method will then be invoked by the thread scheduler. (There must be such a method because ClockApplet implements the interface Runnable.)

Method run() for ClockApplet is

```
public void run() {
        Thread me = Thread.currentThread();
        while (updateThread == me) {
          try {
             me.sleep(1000);
          } catch (InterruptedException e) {
             break;
          }
          repaint();
        }
    }
```

Method run() obtains the currently executing thread. If that thread is the thread initiated by the applet's start() method, then the body of the **while** loop is executed. The loop repeatedly sleeps for 1000 milliseconds and then invokes method repaint(). Method repaint() arranges for the applet's paint() method to be invoked. The loop continues

Listing C.4   ClockApplet.java

```java
1.  // Demonstrate a threaded applet
2.  import java.awt.*;
3.  import java.util.*;
4.  import javax.swing.*;
5.
6.  public class ClockApplet extends JApplet implements Runnable {
7.      private Thread updateThread;
8.      private String clockFace = "";
9.
10.     // init():  perform initialization
11.     public void init() {
12.         updateThread = null;
13.     }
14.
15.     // start():  start up the applet
16.     public void start() {
17.         if (updateThread == null) {
18.             updateThread = new Thread(this);
19.             updateThread.start();
20.         }
21.     }
22.
23.     // run():  thread activity
24.     public void run() {
25.         Thread me = Thread.currentThread();
26.         while (updateThread == me) {
27.             try {
28.                 me.sleep(1000);
29.             }
30.             catch (InterruptedException e) {
31.                 break;
32.             }
33.             repaint();
34.         }
35.     }
36.
37.     // paint(): issues the drawing and color setting requests
38.     public void paint(Graphics g) {
39.         Date time = new Date();
40.         g.setColor(Color.WHITE);
41.         g.drawString(clockFace, 10, 20);
42.         clockFace = time.toString();
43.         g.setColor(Color.BLUE);
44.         g.drawString(clockFace, 10, 20);
45.     }
46.
47.     // stop(): all done
48.     public void stop() {
49.         updateThread = null;
50.     }
51. }
```

as long as updateThread is equal to me (i.e., they reference the same thread). Thus, once started, the loop continues to iterate until method stop() is invoked by the browser. For it is method stop() that resets updateThread to **null**.

Method paint() is largely identical to the code in the method run() of Listing 12.2.

```
public void paint(Graphics g) {
    Date time = new Date();
    g.setColor(Color.WHITE);
    g.drawString(clockFace, 10, 20);
    clockFace = time.toString();
    g.setColor(Color.BLUE);
    g.drawString(clockFace, 10, 20);
}
```

The code gets the date and displays the previous time using the background color (Color.WHITE). This effectively erases the displayed time. The new time is converted to a string and displayed using the color blue.

When the browser moves to a new page or the browser is closed, method stop() is invoked. As previously explained, ClockApplet's stop() method simply sets the updateThread to **null**, which causes the **while** loop in method run() to terminate.

When a Web page with the ClockApplet embedded in it is visited by a browser, the following image appears in the browser window.

The time is continuously updated.

ClockApplet demonstrates the standard design pattern for an applet that implements a simple animation. A thread is created that executes the run() method. The run() method updates the display and then sleeps until it is time to update the display again.

C.4   APPLET SECURITY

Because an applet is downloaded from a server and runs on the user's machine, applets pose a potential security threat to the user's machine. For example, a malicious person could place an applet on a Web page that when downloaded reads private information on the user's machine and sends it back to the malicious person. To avoid such security breaches, browsers impose the following restrictions on any applet that is loaded over the network.

- An applet cannot load libraries or define native methods.
- An applet cannot ordinarily read or write files on the host that's executing it.
- An applet cannot make network connections except to the host that it came from.
- An applet cannot start any program on the client that is executing it.
- An applet cannot read certain system properties.
- Windows that an applet brings up look different than windows that an application brings up.

C.5   SUMMARY

Java applets provide a powerful tool to Web designers. Applets enable Web designers to embed a Java program in a Web page. This ability enables Web pages to have active content—Web pages can accept input, perform computations, and display outputs based on the results of the computations.

D STANDARD JAVA PACKAGES

We describe most of the classes and interfaces from standard packages java.io, java.lang, java.math, java.text, and java.util.

D.1	JAVA.IO

io	**class** BufferedReader **extends** Reader

PURPOSE

Represents a buffered input stream with functionality for character, array, and line extraction.

CONSTRUCTOR SUMMARY

BufferedReader(Reader r)

Constructs a new buffered input stream using stream r.

BufferedReader(Reader r, **int** n)

Constructs a new buffered input stream using stream r with a buffer size of length n.

INSTANCE METHOD SUMMARY

void close()

Closes this BufferedReader.

void mark(**int** n)

Marks the current position in this BufferedReader stream as a reset point. Parameter n indicates a limit on the number of characters that can be read while still preserving this reset point.

boolean markSupported()

Returns **true**; that is, that a BufferedReader stream does support marking.

int read()

Returns the next character from this BufferedReader stream.

abstract int read(**char**[] c, **int** i, **int** n)

Attempts to read the next n characters from this Reader stream and store them in c starting at index i. Returns the number of characters that have been read (–1 if end of file occurs).

String readLine()

Returns the next line of text from this BufferedReader stream.

boolean ready()

Returns whether this BufferedReader stream is ready for reading.

void reset()

Reset this BufferedReader stream.

long skip(**long** n)

Ignore the next n characters in this Reader stream.

io	**class** BufferedWriter **extends** Writer

PURPOSE

Represents a buffered output stream with functionality for character, array, and string insertion.

CONSTRUCTOR SUMMARY

`BufferedWriter(Writer w)`

> Constructs a new buffered input stream using stream w.

`BufferedWriter(Writer w, int n)`

> Constructs a new buffered output stream using stream w with a buffer size of length n.

INSTANCE METHOD SUMMARY

`void close()`

> Closes this `OutputStreamWriter`.

`void flush()`

> Flushes this `OutputStreamWriter`.

`void newLine()`

> Writes a line separator to this `OutputStreamWriter`.

`void write(char[] c, int i, int n)`

> Inserts n characters from array c to this `OutputStreamWriter`. The first character to be displayed is c[i].

`void write(int c)`

> Inserts character c to this `OutputStreamWriter`.

`void write(String s, int i, int n)`

> Inserts an n character substring from string s to this `OutputStreamWriter`. The first character in the substring to be displayed has index i.

---

io	`class` File `implements` Serializable, Comparable

PURPOSE

Represents file and directory path names.

FIELD SUMMARY

`static final String pathSeparator`

> Separator character symbol used by the operator system for path lists (e.g., ":" and ";").

`static final char pathSeparatorChar`

> Separator character symbol used by the operator system for path lists (e.g., ":" and ";").

`static final String separator`

> Name separator character symbol used by the operator system (e.g., "\" or "/").

`static final char separatorChar`

> Name separator character symbol used by the operator system (e.g., "\" or "/").

CLASS METHOD SUMMARY

`static File createTempFile(String s, String t)`

> Creates an empty file in the operating-system dependent, default temporary-file folder. The name of the empty file is s and the suffix of the file is t. The method returns a `File` instance for the new file.

`static File createTempFile(String s, String t, File d)`

> Creates an empty file in folder d. The name of the empty file is s and the suffix of the file is t. The method returns a `File` instance for the new file.

```
static File[] listRoots()
```
Returns a File array of root file system folders.

```
File(File d, String f)
```
Constructs a new File instance using file path f relative to folder d.
```
File(String f)
```
Constructs a new File instance using file path f.
```
File(String d, String f)
```
Constructs a new File instance using file path f relative to folder d.
```
File(URI u)
```
Constructs a new File instance using Universal Resource Identifier u.

```
boolean canRead()
```
Returns whether the path name of this File instance refers to an application readable file.
```
boolean canWrite()
```
Returns whether the path name of this File instance refers to an application writable file.
```
int compareTo(File f)
```
Returns a negative value, zero, or a positive value depending respectively on whether the File value represented by this object is lexicographically less than, equal to, or greater than f.
```
int compareTo(Object v)
```
Returns a negative value, zero, or a positive value depending respectively on whether the File value represented by this object is lexicographically less than, equal to, or greater than v.
```
boolean createNewFile()
```
Attempts to create a new empty file or folder with the path name indicated by this File. The method returns whether the creation request was successful.
```
boolean delete()
```
Attempts to delete the file or empty folder indicated by this File. The method returns whether the deletion request was successful.
```
void deleteOnExit()
```
Attempts to delete the file or empty folder indicated by this File when the application terminates normally.
```
boolean equals(Object v)
```
Returns **true** if and only if v is an instance of File representing the same file or folder that this object represents.
```
boolean exists()
```
Returns whether the path name of this File instance refers to an existing file or folder.
```
File getAbsoluteFile()
```
Returns a new File instance representing the absolute path name for the path name of this File.
```
String getAbsolutePath()
```
Returns a String representing the absolute path name for the path name of this File.

`File getCanonicalFile()`

Returns a new `File` instance representing the canonical path name for the path name of this `File`. A *canonical* name is an absolute name with no symbolic links or redundant folder entries (e.g., `\.` or `/.`).

`String getCanonicalPath()`

Returns a `String` representing the canonical path name for the path name of this `File`. A *canonical* name is an absolute name with no symbolic links or redundant folder entries (e.g., `\.` or `/.`).

`String getName()`

Returns the name of the file or folder represented by this `File`.

`String getParent()`

Returns the path name to the folder containing the file or folder represented by this `File`. If there is no such folder, then the method returns **null**.

`File getParentFile()`

Returns a new `File` representing the folder containing the file or folder represented by this `File`. If there is no such folder, then the method returns **null**.

`String getPath()`

Return the path name to the file or folder represented by this `File`.

`int hashCode()`

Returns the hash code of this object.

`boolean isAbsolute()`

Returns whether the path name of this `File` instance is an absolute path.

`boolean isDirectory()`

Returns whether the path name of this `File` instance is directory.

`boolean isFile()`

Returns whether this `File` instance is the path name to a file.

`boolean isHidden()`

Returns whether this `File` instance refers to a hidden file.

`long lastModified()`

Returns the most recent modification time of the file or folder represented by this `File`.

`long length()`

Returns the length of the file represented by this `File`.

`String[] list()`

Returns a `String` array of the files and folders in the folder represented by this `File`.

`String[] list(FilenameFilter p)`

Returns a `String` array of the files and folders in the folder represented by this `File` that match filter pattern p.

`File[] listFiles()`

Returns a `File` array of the files and folders in the folder represented by this `File`.

`File[] listFiles(FileFilter p)`

Returns a `File` array of the files and folders in the folder represented by this `File` that match filter pattern p.

```
File[] listFiles(FilenameFilter p)
```

Returns a `File` array of the files and folders in the folder represented by this `File` that match filter pattern **p**.

```
boolean mkdir()
```

Attempts to create the folder named by this `File`. Returns whether the folder was created.

```
boolean mkdirs()
```

Attempts to create the folder and any necessary parent folders named by this `File`. Returns whether the folder was created.

```
boolean renameTo(File f)
```

Attempts to rename the file or folder represented by this `File` to the name indicated by **f**. Returns whether the file or folder was created.

```
boolean setLastModified(long t)
```

Attempts to set most recent modification time of the file or folder represented by this `File`. Returns whether the last-modified time of the file was updated.

```
boolean setReadOnly()
```

Attempts to set the status of the file or folder represented by this `File` as read only.

```
String toString()
```

Returns a `String` representing the path name of this `File`.

```
URI toURI()
```

Returns a Universal Resource Indicator representing the path name of this `File`.

```
URL toURL()
```

Returns a Universal Resource Locator representing the path name of this `File`.

---

io   **class** FileReader **extends** InputStreamReader

PURPOSE

Represents an output stream with file reading functionality.

CONSTRUCTOR SUMMARY

```
FileReader(File f)
```

Constructs a new `FileReader` using **f**.

```
FileReader(FileDescriptor f)
```

Constructs a new `FileReader` using **f**.

```
FileReader(String f)
```

Constructs a new `FileReader` using **f**.

---

io   **class** FileWriter **extends** OutputStreamWriter

PURPOSE

Represents an output stream with file writing functionality.

    FileWriter(File f)
        Constructs a new FileWriter using f in nonappend mode.
    FileWriter(File file, **boolean** b)
        Constructs a new FileWriter using f with an append mode based on b.
    FileWriter(FileDescriptor f)
        Constructs a new FileWriter using f in nonappend mode.
    FileWriter(String f)
        Constructs a new FileWriter using f in nonappend mode.
    FileWriter(String f, **boolean** b)
        Constructs a new FileWriter using f with an append mode based on b.

---

io	**class** IOException **extends** Exception

PURPOSE
Represents the occurrence of an input or output exception.
CONSTRUCTOR SUMMARY
    IOException()
        Constructs a new IOException with a **null** message.
    IOException(String s)
        Constructs a new IOException with a message s.

---

io	**class** OutputStreamWriter **extends** Writer

PURPOSE
Represents a character output stream view.
CONSTRUCTOR SUMMARY
    OutputStreamWriter(OutputStream o)
        Constructs a new OutputStreamWriter from stream o using the default char-
        acter set encoding.
    OutputStreamWriter(OutputStream o, Charset c)
        Constructs an OutputStreamWriter from stream o using the character set c.
    OutputStreamWriter(OutputStream o, CharsetEncoder c)
        Constructs a new OutputStreamWriter from stream o using the character set
        encoding c.
    OutputStreamWriter(OutputStream o, String s)
        Constructs a new OutputStreamWriter from stream o using the character set
        with name s.
INSTANCE METHOD SUMMARY
    void close()
        Closes this OutputStreamWriter.
    void flush()
        Flush this OutputStreamWriter.

```
String getEncoding()
```
Returns the name of the character set encoding used by this OutputStream-Writer.
```
void write(char[] c, int i, int n)
```
Inserts n characters from array c to this OutputStreamWriter. The first character to be displayed is c[i].
```
void write(int c)
```
Inserts character c to this OutputStreamWriter.
```
void write(String s, int i, int n)
```
Inserts an n character substring from string s to this OutputStreamWriter. The first character in the substring to be displayed has index i.

---

io   **class** PrintStream **extends** FilterOutputStream

PURPOSE
Represents an output stream with expanded functionality.

CONSTRUCTOR SUMMARY
```
PrintStream(OutputStream o)
```
Constructs a new PrintStream from stream o using the default character set encoding. The stream is not automatically flushed.
```
PrintStream(OutputStream o, boolean b)
```
Constructs a new PrintStream from stream o using the default character set encoding. The stream is automatically flushed depending on b.
```
PrintStream(OutputStream out, boolean b, String s)
```
Constructs a new PrintStream from stream o using the character set encoding with name s. The stream is automatically flushed depending on b.

INSTANCE METHOD SUMMARY
```
boolean checkError()
```
Flushes this PrintStream and returns its error state.
```
void close()
```
Closes this PrintStream.
```
void flush()
```
Flushes this PrintStream.
```
void print(boolean b)
```
Prints b to this PrintStream.
```
void print(char c)
```
Prints c to this PrintStream.
```
void print(char[] c)
```
Prints each character in array c to this PrintStream.
```
void print(double n)
```
Prints n to this PrintStream.
```
void print(float n)
```
Prints n to this PrintStream.
```
void print(int n)
```
Prints n to this PrintStream.

```
void print(long n)
```
Prints n to this PrintStream.
```
void print(Object v)
```
Prints v.toString() to this PrintStream.
```
void print(String s)
```
Prints s to this PrintStream.
```
void println()
```
Equivalent to print("\n").
```
void println(boolean b)
```
Equivalent to print(b + "\n").
```
void println(char c)
```
Equivalent to print(c + "\n").
```
void println(char[] c)
```
Equivalent to print(c + "\n").
```
void println(double n)
```
Equivalent to print(n + "\n").
```
void println(float n)
```
Equivalent to print(n + "\n").
```
void println(int n)
```
Equivalent to print(n + "\n").
```
void println(long n)
```
Equivalent to print(n + "\n").
```
void println(Object v)
```
Equivalent to print(v + "\n").
```
void println(String s)
```
Equivalent to print(s + "\n").
```
protected void setError()
```
Set the error state of this PrintStream to **true**.
```
void write(byte[] b, int i, int n)
```
Prints n bytes from array b to this PrintStream, where the index of the first element to be printed is i.
```
void write(int b)
```
Prints byte b to this PrintStream.

---

io	**abstract class** Reader **extends** FilterOutputStream

PURPOSE
Represents basic input stream functionality.
FIELD SUMMARY
```
protected Object lock
```
Represents the operation synchronization object of this Reader.
CONSTRUCTOR SUMMARY
```
protected Reader()
```
Constructs a new Reader with synchronized operations.

```
protected Reader(Object v)
```

Constructs a new Reader whose synchronized operations use lock v.

INSTANCE METHOD SUMMARY

```
abstract void close()
```

Closes this Reader stream.

```
void mark(int n)
```

Marks the current position in this Reader stream as a reset point. Parameter n indicates a limit on the number of characters that can be read while still preserving this reset point.

```
boolean markSupported()
```

Returns whether this Reader stream supports marking.

```
int read()
```

Returns the next character from this Reader stream.

```
int read(char[] c)
```

Reads the remaining characters from this Reader stream and stores them in c. Returns the number of characters that have been read (–1 if end of file occurs).

```
abstract int read(char[] c, int i, int n)
```

Attempts to read the next n characters from this Reader stream and store them in c starting at index i. Returns the number of characters that have been read (–1 if end of file occurs).

```
boolean ready()
```

Returns whether this Reader stream is ready for reading.

```
void reset()
```

Reset this Reader stream.

```
long skip(long n)
```

Ignore the next n characters in this Reader stream.

---

io   **abstract class** Writer **extends** FilterOutputStream

PURPOSE

Represents basic output stream functionality.

FIELD SUMMARY

```
protected Object lock
```

Represents the operation synchronization object of this Writer.

CONSTRUCTOR SUMMARY

```
protected Writer()
```

Constructs a new Writer with synchronized operations.

```
protected Writer(Object v)
```

Constructs a new Writer whose synchronized operations use lock v.

INSTANCE METHOD SUMMARY

```
abstract void close()
```

Flushes and closes this Writer stream.

```
abstract void flush()
```

Flushes this Writer stream.

> **void** write(**char**[] c)
>> Writes array c to this Writer stream.
>
> **abstract void** write(**char**[] c, **int** i, **int** n)
>> Writes n characters of array c to this Writer stream. The first character to be written has index i.
>
> **void** write(**int** c)
>> Writes character c to this Writer stream.
>
> **void** write(String s)
>> Writes string s to this Writer stream.
>
> **void** write(String s, **int** i, **int** n)
>> Writes n characters of string s to this Writer stream. The first character to be written has index i.

D.2   JAVA.LANG

lang | **class** ArithmeticException **extends** RuntimeException

PURPOSE
Represent an unexpected arithmetic event.

CONSTRUCTOR SUMMARY

> ArithmeticException()
>> Constructs a new ArithmeticException with a **null** message.
>
> ArithmeticException(String s)
>> Constructs a new ArithmeticException with message s.

lang | **class** ArrayIndexOutOfBoundsException **extends** IndexOutOfBoundsException

PURPOSE
Represent an illegal array indexing event.

CONSTRUCTOR SUMMARY

> ArrayIndexOutOfBoundsException()
>> Constructs a new ArrayIndexOutOfBoundsException with a **null** message.

ArrayIndexOutOfBoundsException(**int** i)

> Constructs a new ArrayIndexOutOfBoundsException with a message that i is an illegal index.

ArrayIndexOutOfBoundsException(String s)

> Constructs a new ArrayIndexOutOfBoundsException with message s.

`lang` **class** ArrayStoreException **extends** RuntimeException

PURPOSE

Represent an illegal array element assignment event.

CONSTRUCTOR SUMMARY

ArrayStoreException()

> Constructs a new ArrayStoreException with a **null** message.

ArrayStoreException(String s)

> Constructs a new ArrayStoreException with message s.

`lang` **class** AssertionError **extends** Error

PURPOSE

Represent a failed assertion event.

CONSTRUCTOR SUMMARY

AssertionError()

> Constructs a new AssertionError with a **null** message.

AssertionError(**boolean** b)

> Constructs a new AssertionError with a message indicating the value of b.

AssertionError(**char** c)

> Constructs a new AssertionError with a message indicating the value of c.

AssertionError(**double** n)

> Constructs a new AssertionError with a message indicating the value of n.

AssertionError(**float** n)

> Constructs a new AssertionError with a message indicating the value of n.

AssertionError(**int** n)

> Constructs a new AssertionError with a message indicating the value of n.

AssertionError(**long** n)

> Constructs a new AssertionError with a message indicating the value of n.

AssertionError(Object v)

> Constructs a new AssertionError with a message indicating the value of v.

| lang | **final class** Boolean **implements** Serializable |

PURPOSE

Represent a **boolean** value within a class wrapper.

FIELD SUMMARY

    static final Boolean FALSE

        Boolean constant representing the **boolean** value **false**.

    final Boolean TRUE

        Boolean constant representing the **boolean** value **true**.

    static final Class TYPE

        Represents the type **boolean**.

CLASS METHOD SUMMARY

    static boolean getBoolean(String s)

        Returns **true** if and only if the system property named s exists and equals "true".

    static String toString(**boolean** b)

        Returns a String object representing **boolean** value b.

    static Boolean valueOf(**boolean** b)

        Returns a Boolean object representing **boolean** value b.

    static Boolean valueOf(String s)

        Returns a Boolean representing **boolean** value **true** if s is non-**null** and s.toLowerCase() equals "true"; otherwise, it constructs a Boolean object representing **boolean** value **false**.

CONSTRUCTOR SUMMARY

    Boolean(**boolean** b)

        Constructs a Boolean object representing **boolean** value b.

    Boolean(String s)

        Constructs a Boolean object representing **boolean** value **true** if s is non-**null** and s.toLowerCase() equals "true"; otherwise, it constructs a Boolean object representing **boolean** value **false**.

INSTANCE METHOD SUMMARY

    boolean booleanValue()

        Returns the **boolean** value represented by this object.

    boolean equals(Object v)

        Returns **true** if and only if v is an instance of Boolean representing the same **boolean** value that this object represents.

    int hashCode()

        Returns the hash code of this object.

    String toString()

        Returns a String representation of the value of this object.

| lang | **final class** Byte **extends** Number **implements** Comparable |

PURPOSE
Represent a **byte** value within a class wrapper.

FIELD SUMMARY

static final byte MAX_VALUE
Represents the maximum value of type **byte** (i.e., $2^7 - 1$).

static final byte MIN_VALUE
Represents the minimum value of type **byte** (i.e., -2^7).

static final Class TYPE
Represents the type **byte**.

CLASS METHOD SUMMARY

static Byte decode(String s)
Constructs a new Byte object representing Byte.parseByte(s, n), where n is 8, 10, or 16 depending on whether s is respectively a numeric string in octal, decimal, or hexadecimal format.

static byte parseByte(String s)
Returns Byte.parseByte(s, 10).

static byte parseByte(String s, int n)
Returns the **byte** value represented by parsing string s as an optionally signed **byte** value in radix n.

static String toString(**byte** n)
Returns a new String object representing **byte** value n.

static Byte valueOf(String s)
Returns Byte.valueOf(s, 10).

static Byte valueOf(String s, int n)
Returns a new Byte object representing Byte.parseByte(s, n).

CONSTRUCTOR SUMMARY

Byte(**byte** n)
Constructs a new Byte object representing value n.

Byte(String s)
Constructs a new Byte object representing Byte.parseByte(s).

INSTANCE METHOD SUMMARY

byte byteValue()
Returns the **byte** value represented by this object.

int compareTo(Byte n)
Returns a negative value, zero, or a positive value depending respectively on whether the **byte** value represented by this object is less than, equal to, or greater than n.

int compareTo(Object v)
Returns a negative value, zero, or a positive value depending respectively on whether the **byte** value represented by this object is less than, equal to, or greater than v.

double doubleValue()
Returns the **byte** value represented by this object as a **double**.

`boolean` equals(Object v)

Returns **true** if and only if v is an instance of Byte representing the same Byte value that this object represents.

`float` floatValue()

Returns the **byte** value represented by this object as a **float**.

`int` hashCode()

Returns the hash code of this object.

`int` intValue()

Returns the **byte** value represented by this object as a **int**.

`long` longValue()

Returns the **byte** value represented by this object as a **long**.

`short` shortValue()

Returns the **byte** value represented by this object as a **short**.

`String` toString()

Returns a String representation of the value of this object.

`lang`	`interface` CharSequence

PURPOSE

Describe a representation for supplying read-only access to sequence of characters.

INSTANCE METHOD SUMMARY

`char` charAt(int i)

Returns the character at index i of the sequence.

`int` length()

Returns the length of this character sequence.

`CharSequence` subSequence(int i, int j)

Returns a new CharSequence representing the elements with indices i ... j − 1 from the character sequence of this CharSequence.

`String` toString()

Returns a String representing the characters of the sequence in index order.

`lang`	`final class` Character `implements` Serializable, Comparable

PURPOSE

Represent a **char** value within a class wrapper.

NESTED CLASS SUMMARY

`static class` Character.Subset

Represent a subset of the Unicode character set.

`static class` Character.UnicodeBlock

Represent a disjoint collection of Unicode character blocks.

FIELD SUMMARY

`static final byte` COMBINING_SPACING_MARK

Represents Unicode general category *Mc*.

```
static final byte CONNECTOR_PUNCTUATION
```
Represents Unicode general category *Pc*.
```
static final byte CONTROL
```
Represents Unicode general category *Cc*.
```
static final byte CURRENCY_SYMBOL
```
Represents Unicode general category *Sc*.
```
static final byte DASH_PUNCTUATION
```
Represents Unicode general category *Pd*.
```
static final byte DECIMAL_DIGIT_NUMBER
```
Represents Unicode general category *Nd*.
```
static final byte DIRECTIONALITY_ARABIC_NUMBER
```
Represents Unicode weak bidirectional character type *AN*.
```
static final byte DIRECTIONALITY_BOUNDARY_NEUTRAL
```
Represents Unicode weak bidirectional character type *BN*.
```
static final byte DIRECTIONALITY_COMMON_NUMBER_SEPARATOR
```
Represents Unicode weak bidirectional character type *CS*.
```
static final byte DIRECTIONALITY_EUROPEAN_NUMBER
```
Represents Unicode weak bidirectional character type *EN*.
```
static final byte DIRECTIONALITY_EUROPEAN_NUMBER_SEPARATOR
```
Represents Unicode weak bidirectional character type *ES*.
```
static final byte DIRECTIONALITY_EUROPEAN_NUMBER_TERMINATOR
```
Represents Unicode weak bidirectional character type *ET*.
```
static final byte DIRECTIONALITY_LEFT_TO_RIGHT
```
Represents Unicode strong bidirectional character type *L*.
```
static final byte DIRECTIONALITY_LEFT_TO_RIGHT_EMBEDDING
```
Represents Unicode strong bidirectional character type *LRE*.
```
static final byte DIRECTIONALITY_LEFT_TO_RIGHT_OVERRIDE
```
Represents Unicode strong bidirectional character type *LRO*.
```
static final byte DIRECTIONALITY_NONSPACING_MARK
```
Represents Unicode weak bidirectional character type *NSM*.
```
static final byte DIRECTIONALITY_OTHER_NEUTRALS
```
Represents Unicode neutral bidirectional character type *ON*.
```
static final byte DIRECTIONALITY_PARAGRAPH_SEPARATOR
```
Represents Unicode neutral bidirectional character type *B*.
```
static final byte DIRECTIONALITY_POP_DIRECTIONAL_FORMAT
```
Represents Unicode weak bidirectional character type *PDF*.
```
static final byte DIRECTIONALITY_RIGHT_TO_LEFT
```
Represents Unicode strong bidirectional character type *R*.
```
static final byte DIRECTIONALITY_RIGHT_TO_LEFT_ARABIC
```
Represents Unicode strong bidirectional character type *AL*.
```
static final byte DIRECTIONALITY_RIGHT_TO_LEFT_EMBEDDING
```
Represents Unicode strong bidirectional character type *RLE*.
```
static final byte DIRECTIONALITY_RIGHT_TO_LEFT_OVERRIDE
```
Represents Unicode strong bidirectional character type *RLO*.
```
static final byte DIRECTIONALITY_SEGMENT_SEPARATOR
```
Represents Unicode neutral bidirectional character type *S*.

```
static final byte DIRECTIONALITY_UNDEFINED
```
Represents Unicode undefined bidirectional character type.
```
static final byte DIRECTIONALITY_WHITESPACE
```
Represents Unicode neutral bidirectional character type *WS*.
```
static final byte ENCLOSING_MARK
```
Represents Unicode general category *Me*.
```
static final byte END_PUNCTUATION
```
Represents Unicode general category *Pe*.
```
static final byte FINAL_QUOTE_PUNCTUATION
```
Represents Unicode general category *Pf*.
```
static final byte FORMAT
```
Represents Unicode general category *Cf*.
```
static final byte INITIAL_QUOTE_PUNCTUATION
```
Represents Unicode general category *Pi*.
```
static final byte LETTER_NUMBER
```
Represents Unicode general category *Nl*.
```
static final byte LINE_SEPARATOR
```
Represents Unicode general category *Zl*.
```
static final byte LOWERCASE_LETTER
```
Represents Unicode general category *Ll*.
```
static final byte MATH_SYMBOL
```
Represents Unicode general category *Sm*.
```
static final int MAX_RADIX
```
Represents the maximum allowable radix value in converting to and from strings.
```
static final char MAX_VALUE
```
Represents the largest value of type **char** (i.e., `'\uFFFF'`).
```
static final int MIN_RADIX
```
Represents the minimum radix allowable radix in converting to and from strings.
```
static final char MIN_VALUE
```
Represents the smallest value of type **char** (i.e., `'\u0000'`).
```
static final byte MODIFIER_LETTER
```
Represents Unicode general category *Lm*.
```
static final byte MODIFIER_SYMBOL
```
Represents Unicode general category *Sk*.
```
static final byte NON_SPACING_MARK
```
Represents Unicode general category *Mn*.
```
static final byte OTHER_LETTER
```
Represents Unicode general category *Lo*.
```
static final byte OTHER_NUMBER
```
Represents Unicode general category *No*.
```
static final byte OTHER_PUNCTUATION
```
Represents Unicode general category *Po*.
```
static final byte OTHER_SYMBOL
```
Represents Unicode general category *So*.
```
static final byte PARAGRAPH_SEPARATOR
```
Represents Unicode general category *Zp*.

```
static final byte PRIVATE_USE
```
Represents Unicode general category *Co*.
```
static final byte SPACE_SEPARATOR
```
Represents Unicode general category *Zs*.
```
static final byte START_PUNCTUATION
```
Represents Unicode general category *Ps*.
```
static final byte SURROGATE
```
Represents Unicode general category *Cs*.
```
static final byte TITLECASE_LETTER
```
Represents Unicode general category *Lt*.
```
static final Class TYPE
```
Represents the type **char**.
```
static final byte UNASSIGNED
```
Represents Unicode general category *Cn*.
```
static final byte UPPERCASE_LETTER
```
Represents Unicode general category *Lu*.

CLASS METHOD SUMMARY

```
static int digit(char c, int n)
```
Returns the numeric value of the character c in radix n.
```
static char forDigit(int m, int n)
```
Returns the **char** representation of digit m in the radix n.
```
static byte getDirectionality(char c)
```
Returns the Unicode directionality property for **char** value c.
```
static int getNumericValue(char c)
```
Returns the **int** value that the specified Unicode character represents.
```
static int getType(char c)
```
Returns a value indicating **char** value c's Unicode general category.
```
static boolean isDefined(char c)
```
Returns whether **char** value c is a defined Unicode character.
```
static boolean isDigit(char c)
```
Returns whether **char** value c is a digit.
```
static boolean isIdentifierIgnorable(char c)
```
Returns whether **char** value c is an ignorable identifier character.
```
static boolean isISOControl(char c)
```
Returns whether **char** value c is an ISO control character.
```
static boolean isJavaIdentifierPart(char c)
```
Returns whether **char** value c may be part of a Java identifier.
```
static boolean isJavaIdentifierStart(char c)
```
Returns whether **char** value c can be the first character in a Java identifier.
```
static boolean isLetter(char c)
```
Returns whether **char** value c is a letter.
```
static boolean isLetterOrDigit(char c)
```
Returns whether **char** value c is a letter or digit.
```
static boolean isLowerCase(char c)
```
Returns whether **char** value c is a lowercase character.

`static boolean` isMirrored(`char` c)

Returns whether **char** value c is mirrored according to the Unicode simple mirroring property (see www.unicode.org).

`static boolean` isSpaceChar(`char` c)

Returns whether **char** value c is a space character.

`static boolean` isTitleCase(`char` c)

Returns whether **char** value c is a title-case character.

`static boolean` isUnicodeIdentifierPart(`char` c)

Returns whether **char** value c may be part of a Unicode identifier.

`static boolean` isUnicodeIdentifierStart(`char` c)

Returns whether **char** value c may be the first character in a Unicode identifier.

`static boolean` isUpperCase(`char` c)

Returns whether **char** value c is an uppercase character.

`static boolean` isWhitespace(`char` c)

Returns whether **char** value c is whitespace.

`static char` toLowerCase(`char` c)

Converts **char** value c to lowercase using case mapping information from the UnicodeData file of the Unicode Character databases (see www.unicode.org).

`static String` toString(`char` c)

Returns a `String` representation of **char** value c.

`static char` toTitleCase(`char` c)

Converts the character argument to title-case using case mapping information from the UnicodeData file of the Unicode Character databases (see www.unicode.org).

`static char` toUpperCase(`char` c)

Converts the character argument to uppercase using case mapping information from the UnicodeData file of the Unicode Character databases (see www.unicode.org).

CONSTRUCTOR SUMMARY

Character(`char` c)

Constructs a new `Character` object representing value c.

INSTANCE METHOD SUMMARY

`char` charValue()

Returns the **char** value represented by this object.

`int` compareTo(Character c)

Returns a negative value, zero, or a positive value depending respectively on whether this object is less than, equal to, or greater than c.

`int` compareTo(Object v)

Returns a negative value, zero, or a positive value depending respectively on whether this object is less than, equal to, or greater than v.

`boolean` equals(Object v)

Returns **true** if and only if v is an instance of `Character` representing the same `Character` value that this object represents.

`int` hashCode()

Returns the hash code of this object.

`String` toString()

Returns a `String` representation of the value of this object.

---

lang | **static class** Character.Subset

PURPOSE
Represent a subset of the Unicode character set.
CONSTRUCTOR SUMMARY
    protected Character.Subset(String s)
        Constructs a new Subset with name s.
INSTANCE METHOD SUMMARY
    boolean equals(Object v)
        Returns **true** if and only if v is an instance of Character.Subset representing the same Character.Subset value that this object represents.
    int hashCode()
        Returns the hash code of this object.
    String toString()
        Returns a String representation of the value of this object (i.e., its name),

---

lang | **static final class** Character.UnicodeBlock **extends** Character.Subset

PURPOSE
Represent a disjoint collection of Unicode character blocks.
FIELD SUMMARY
    static final Character.UnicodeBlock
    ALPHABETIC_PRESENTATION_FORMS
        Represents the Unicode block of the same name.
    static final Character.UnicodeBlock ARABIC
        Represents the Unicode block of the same name.
    static final Character.UnicodeBlock ARABIC_PRESENTATION_FORMS_A
        Represents the Unicode block of the same name.
    static final Character.UnicodeBlock ARABIC_PRESENTATION_FORMS_B
        Represents the Unicode block of the same name.
    static final Character.UnicodeBlock ARMENIAN
        Represents the Unicode block of the same name.
    static final Character.UnicodeBlock ARROWS
        Represents the Unicode block of the same name.
    static final Character.UnicodeBlock BASIC_LATIN
        Represents the Unicode block of the same name.
    static final Character.UnicodeBlock BENGALI
        Represents the Unicode block of the same name.
    static final Character.UnicodeBlock BLOCK_ELEMENTS
        Represents the Unicode block of the same name.
    static final Character.UnicodeBlock BOPOMOFO
        Represents the Unicode block of the same name.

`static final` Character.UnicodeBlock BOPOMOFO_EXTENDED

    Represents the Unicode block of the same name.

`static final` Character.UnicodeBlock BOX_DRAWING

    Represents the Unicode block of the same name.

`static final` Character.UnicodeBlock BRAILLE_PATTERNS

    Represents the Unicode block of the same name.

`static final` Character.UnicodeBlock CHEROKEE

    Represents the Unicode block of the same name.

`static final` Character.UnicodeBlock CJK_COMPATIBILITY

    Represents the Unicode block of the same name.

`static final` Character.UnicodeBlock CJK_COMPATIBILITY_FORMS

    Represents the Unicode block of the same name.

`static final` Character.UnicodeBlock
  CJK_COMPATIBILITY_IDEOGRAPHS

    Represents the Unicode block of the same name.

`static final` Character.UnicodeBlock CJK_RADICALS_SUPPLEMENT

    Represents the Unicode block of the same name.

`static final` Character.UnicodeBlock CJK_SYMBOLS_AND_PUNCTUATION

    Represents the Unicode block of the same name.

`static final` Character.UnicodeBlock CJK_UNIFIED_IDEOGRAPHS

    Represents the Unicode block of the same name.

`static final` Character.UnicodeBlock
  CJK_UNIFIED_IDEOGRAPHS_EXTENSION_A

    Represents the Unicode block of the same name.

`static final` Character.UnicodeBlock COMBINING_DIACRITICAL_MARKS

    Represents the Unicode block of the same name.

`static final` Character.UnicodeBlock COMBINING_HALF_MARKS

    Represents the Unicode block of the same name.

`static final` Character.UnicodeBlock COMBINING_MARKS_FOR_SYMBOLS

    Represents the Unicode block of the same name.

`static final` Character.UnicodeBlock CONTROL_PICTURES

    Represents the Unicode block of the same name.

`static final` Character.UnicodeBlock CURRENCY_SYMBOLS

    Represents the Unicode block of the same name.

`static final` Character.UnicodeBlock CYRILLIC

    Represents the Unicode block of the same name.

`static final` Character.UnicodeBlock DEVANAGARI

    Represents the Unicode block of the same name.

`static final` Character.UnicodeBlock DINGBATS

    Represents the Unicode block of the same name.

`static final` Character.UnicodeBlock ENCLOSED_ALPHANUMERICS

    Represents the Unicode block of the same name.

`static final` Character.UnicodeBlock
  ENCLOSED_CJK_LETTERS_AND_MONTHS

    Represents the Unicode block of the same name.

`static final` Character.UnicodeBlock ETHIOPIC

    Represents the Unicode block of the same name.

```
static final Character.UnicodeBlock GENERAL_PUNCTUATION
```
Represents the Unicode block of the same name.
```
static final Character.UnicodeBlock GEOMETRIC_SHAPES
```
Represents the Unicode block of the same name.
```
static final Character.UnicodeBlock GEORGIAN
```
Represents the Unicode block of the same name.
```
static final Character.UnicodeBlock GREEK
```
Represents the Unicode block of the same name.
```
static final Character.UnicodeBlock GREEK_EXTENDED
```
Represents the Unicode block of the same name.
```
static final Character.UnicodeBlock GUJARATI
```
Represents the Unicode block of the same name.
```
static final Character.UnicodeBlock GURMUKHI
```
Represents the Unicode block of the same name.
```
static final Character.UnicodeBlock
  HALFWIDTH_AND_FULLWIDTH_FORMS
```
Represents the Unicode block of the same name.
```
static final Character.UnicodeBlock HANGUL_COMPATIBILITY_JAMO
```
Represents the Unicode block of the same name.
```
static final Character.UnicodeBlock HANGUL_JAMO
```
Represents the Unicode block of the same name.
```
static final Character.UnicodeBlock HANGUL_SYLLABLES
```
Represents the Unicode block of the same name.
```
static final Character.UnicodeBlock HEBREW
```
Represents the Unicode block of the same name.
```
static final Character.UnicodeBlock HIRAGANA
```
Represents the Unicode block of the same name.
```
static final Character.UnicodeBlock
  IDEOGRAPHIC_DESCRIPTION_CHARACTERS
```
Represents the Unicode block of the same name.
```
static final Character.UnicodeBlock IPA_EXTENSIONS
```
Represents the Unicode block of the same name.
```
static final Character.UnicodeBlock KANBUN
```
Represents the Unicode block of the same name.
```
static final Character.UnicodeBlock KANGXI_RADICALS
```
Represents the Unicode block of the same name.
```
static final Character.UnicodeBlock KANNADA
```
Represents the Unicode block of the same name.
```
static final Character.UnicodeBlock KATAKANA
```
Represents the Unicode block of the same name.
```
static final Character.UnicodeBlock KHMER
```
Represents the Unicode block of the same name.
```
static final Character.UnicodeBlock LAO
```
Represents the Unicode block of the same name.
```
static final Character.UnicodeBlock LATIN_1_SUPPLEMENT
```
Represents the Unicode block of the same name.

static final Character.UnicodeBlock LATIN_EXTENDED_A
    Represents the Unicode block of the same name.
static final Character.UnicodeBlock LATIN_EXTENDED_ADDITIONAL
    Represents the Unicode block of the same name.
static final Character.UnicodeBlock LATIN_EXTENDED_B
    Represents the Unicode block of the same name.
static final Character.UnicodeBlock LETTERLIKE_SYMBOLS
    Represents the Unicode block of the same name.
static final Character.UnicodeBlock MALAYALAM
    Represents the Unicode block of the same name.
static final Character.UnicodeBlock MATHEMATICAL_OPERATORS
    Represents the Unicode block of the same name.
static final Character.UnicodeBlock MISCELLANEOUS_SYMBOLS
    Represents the Unicode block of the same name.
static final Character.UnicodeBlock MISCELLANEOUS_TECHNICAL
    Represents the Unicode block of the same name.
static final Character.UnicodeBlock MONGOLIAN
    Represents the Unicode block of the same name.
static final Character.UnicodeBlock MYANMAR
    Represents the Unicode block of the same name.
static final Character.UnicodeBlock NUMBER_FORMS
    Represents the Unicode block of the same name.
static final Character.UnicodeBlock OGHAM
    Represents the Unicode block of the same name.
static final Character.UnicodeBlock
  OPTICAL_CHARACTER_RECOGNITION
    Represents the Unicode block of the same name.
static final Character.UnicodeBlock ORIYA
    Represents the Unicode block of the same name.
static final Character.UnicodeBlock PRIVATE_USE_AREA
    Represents the Unicode block of the same name.
static final Character.UnicodeBlock RUNIC
    Represents the Unicode block of the same name.
static final Character.UnicodeBlock SINHALA
    Represents the Unicode block of the same name.
static final Character.UnicodeBlock SMALL_FORM_VARIANTS
    Represents the Unicode block of the same name.
static final Character.UnicodeBlock SPACING_MODIFIER_LETTERS
    Represents the Unicode block of the same name.
static final Character.UnicodeBlock SPECIALS
    Represents the Unicode block of the same name.
static final Character.UnicodeBlock SUPERSCRIPTS_AND_SUBSCRIPTS
    Represents the Unicode block of the same name.
static final Character.UnicodeBlock SURROGATES_AREA
    Represents the Unicode block of the same name.
static final Character.UnicodeBlock SYRIAC
    Represents the Unicode block of the same name.

static final Character.UnicodeBlock TAMIL

Represents the Unicode block of the same name.

static final Character.UnicodeBlock TELUGU

Represents the Unicode block of the same name.

static final Character.UnicodeBlock THAANA

Represents the Unicode block of the same name.

static final Character.UnicodeBlock THAI

Represents the Unicode block of the same name.

static final Character.UnicodeBlock TIBETAN

Represents the Unicode block of the same name.

static final Character.UnicodeBlock
  UNIFIED_CANADIAN_ABORIGINAL_SYLLABICS

Represents the Unicode block of the same name.

static final Character.UnicodeBlock YI_RADICALS

Represents the Unicode block of the same name.

static final Character.UnicodeBlock YI_SYLLABLES

Represents the Unicode block of the same name.

INSTANCE METHOD SUMMARY

static Character.UnicodeBlock of(**char** c)

Returns the Character.UnicodeBlock containing c. If there is no such block, **null** is returned.

| **lang** | final class Class implements Serializable |

PURPOSE

Represent a Java type or interface. Class objects are constructed automatically by Java.

CLASS METHOD SUMMARY

static Class forName(String s)

Returns forName(s, **true**, **this**.getClass().getClassLoader()).

static Class forName(String s, **boolean** b, ClassLoader c)

Returns the Class object named s and loads the class as part of the application using loader c. The class is initialized, if and only if b is **true** and the class has not been previously initialized.

INSTANCE METHOD SUMMARY

boolean desiredAssertionStatus()

Returns whether this class is processing its assertions.

Class[] getClasses()

Returns a Class array whose elements represent the **public** classes and interfaces that are members of the class represented by this Class object.

ClassLoader getClassLoader()

Returns the class loader for this Class.

Class getComponentType()

If this Class is an array type, the method returns the component type of the array; otherwise, the method returns **null**.

Constructor getConstructor(Class[] c)

Returns a Constructor for the class represented by this Class whose **public** constructor parameter signature is described by c.

```
Constructor[] getConstructors()
```
Returns a `Constructor` array representing all of the **public** constructors of the class represented by this `Class`.

```
Class[] getDeclaredClasses()
```
Returns a `Class` array whose elements represent the classes and interfaces that are noninherited members of the class represented by this `Class` object.

```
Constructor getDeclaredConstructor(Class[] c)
```
Returns a `Constructor` for the class represented by this `Class` whose constructor parameter signature is described by `c`.

```
Constructor[] getDeclaredConstructors()
```
Returns a `Constructor` array whose elements represent the constructors of the class represented by this `Class`.

```
Field getDeclaredField(String s)
```
Returns a `Field` that represents the field with name `s` of the class or interface represented by this `Class` object.

```
Field[] getDeclaredFields()
```
Returns a `Field` array whose elements represent the noninherited fields declared by the class or interface represented by this `Class`.

```
Method getDeclaredMethod(String s, Class[] c)
```
Returns a `Method` that represents the method with name `s` and whose parameter signature is described by `c` from the class or interface represented by this `Class`.

```
Method[] getDeclaredMethods()
```
Returns a `Method` array whose elements represent the noninherited methods of the class or interface represented by this `Class`.

```
Class getDeclaringClass()
```
Returns the `Class` representing the class whose definition specifies the class represented by this `Class`.

```
Field getField(String s)
```
Returns a `Field` that represents the **public** field with name `s` of the class or interface represented by this `Class` object.

```
Field[] getFields()
```
Returns a `Field` array whose elements represent the **public** fields declared by the class or interface represented by this `Class`.

```
Class[] getInterfaces()
```
Returns a `Class` array whose elements represent the interfaces implemented by the class represented by this `Class` object.

```
Method getMethod(String name, Class[] c)
```
Returns a `Method` that represents the **public** method with name `s` and whose parameter signature is described by `c` from the class or interface represented by this `Class`.

```
Method[] getMethods()
```
Returns a `Method` array whose elements represent the **public** methods of the class or interface represented by this `Class`.

```
int getModifiers()
```
Returns an integer representing the modifiers for the class or interface represented by this `Class`. Decoding of the integer value is accomplished via class `Modifier`.

```
String getName()
```
Returns the name of the type represented by this `Class`.
```
Package getPackage()
```
Returns the `Package` that represents the package specifying the definition of the type represented by this `Class`.
```
ProtectionDomain getProtectionDomain()
```
Returns the `ProtectionDomain` of this `Class`.
```
URL getResource(String s)
```
Returns a URL resource from the Web with address s.
```
InputStream getResourceAsStream(String s)
```
Returns an `InputStream` representation of a URL resource from the Web with address s.
```
Object[] getSigners()
```
Returns an array whose elements reference the signers of this `Class`.
```
Class getSuperclass()
```
Returns a `Class` representing the superclass of the type represented by this `Class`.
```
boolean isArray()
```
Returns **true** if and only if the type represented by this `Class` is an array type.
```
boolean isAssignableFrom(Class c)
```
Returns **true** if and only if an object of the class or interface represented by c is assignable to an object of the class or interface represented by this `Class`.
```
boolean isInstance(Object v)
```
Returns **true** if and only if v is assignable to an object of the class or interface represented by this `Class`.
```
boolean isInterface()
```
Returns **true** if and only if the type represented by this `Class` object is an interface type.
```
boolean isPrimitive()
```
Returns **true** if and only if the type represented by this `Class` object is a primitive type
```
Object newInstance()
```
Returns a default-constructed instance of the class represented by this `Class`.
```
String toString()
```
Returns a `String` representation of this `Class`.

`lang`   **interface** `Comparable`

PURPOSE
Describe a representation that has a total ordering of its objects. The ordering is commonly referred to as the natural ordering.

A `Comparable` implementation is expected to fulfill the following contract for all `Comparable` objects x, y, and z, where in the contract *sign(n)* evaluates to −1, 0, 1 depending on whether *n* is respectively negative, zero, or positive.

- *sign*(x.`compareTo`(y)) equals −*sign*(y.`compareTo`(x)).

- If ((x.compareTo(y) > 0) && (y.compareTo(z) > 0)) evaluates to **true**, then x.compareTo(z) is greater than zero.
- If x.compareTo(y) evaluates to 0, then *sign*(x.compareTo(z)) equals *sign*(y.compareTo(z)).
- x.compareTo(**null**) throws a NullPointerException.

It is strongly expected that the following property also holds.

- If x.compareTo(y) evaluates to 0, then x.equals(y) evaluates to **true**.

INSTANCE METHOD SUMMARY

int compareTo(Object v)

Returns a negative value, zero, or a positive value depending respectively on whether this object is less than, equal to, or greater than v.

---

lang final class Double extends Number implements Comparable

PURPOSE

Represent a **double** value within a class wrapper.

FIELD SUMMARY

static final double MAX_VALUE

Represents the maximum finite value of type **double** (i.e., $(2 - 2^{-52})2^{1023}$).

static final double MIN_VALUE

Represents the minimum positive nonzero value of type **double** (i.e., 2^{-1074}).

static final double NaN

Represents the Not-a-Number value (NaN) for type **double**.

static final double NEGATIVE_INFINITY

Represents negative infinity for type **double**.

static final double POSITIVE_INFINITY

Represents positive infinity for type **double**.

static final Class TYPE

Represents the type **double**.

CLASS METHOD SUMMARY

static int compare(double m, double n)

Returns a negative value, zero, or a positive value depending respectively on whether m is less than, equal to, or greater than n.

static long doubleToLongBits(double n)

Returns a representation of **double** value n using the *IEEE 754 floating-point double-format bit layout* standard.

static long doubleToRawLongBits(double n)

Returns a representation of **double** value n using the *IEEE 754 floating-point double-format bit layout* standard while preserving not-a-number values.

static boolean isInfinite(double n)

Returns **true** if and only if n is equal to Double.NEGATIVE_INFINITY or to Double.POSITIVE_INFINITY.

static boolean isNaN(double n)

Returns **true** if and only if the **double** value n is equal to Double.NaN.

static **double** longBitsToDouble(**long** n)

> Returns the **double** value corresponding to the bit representation of value n.

static **double** parseDouble(String s)

> Returns the **double** value represented by parsing string s as an optionally signed floating-point value.

static String toString(**double** n)

> Returns a string representation of **double** value n.

static Double valueOf(String s)

> Returns a new Double object representing Double.parseDouble(s).

Double(**double** n)

> Constructs a new Double object representing value n.

Double(String s)

> Constructs a new Double object representing Double.parseDouble(s).

INSTANCE METHOD SUMMARY

byte byteValue()

> Returns the **double** value of this Double as a **byte**.

int compareTo(Double n)

> Returns a negative value, zero, or a positive value depending respectively on whether the **double** value represented by this object is less than, equal to, or greater than n.

int compareTo(Object v)

> Returns a negative value, zero, or a positive value depending respectively on whether the **double** value represented by this object is less than, equal to, or greater than v.

double doubleValue()

> Returns the **double** value of this Double.

boolean equals(Object v)

> Returns **true** if and only if v is an instance of Boolean representing the same **boolean** value that this object represents.

float floatValue()

> Returns the **double** value of this Double as a **float**.

int hashCode()

> Returns the hash code of this object.

int intValue()

> Returns the **double** value of this Double as an **int**.

boolean isInfinite()

> Returns **true** if and only if the **double** value of this object is equal to Double.NEGATIVE_INFINITY or to Double.POSITIVE_INFINITY.

boolean isNaN()

> Returns **true** if and only if the **double** value of this object is equal to Double.NaN.

long longValue()

> Returns the **double** value of this Double as a **long**.

short shortValue()

> Returns the **double** value of this Double as a **short**.

```
String toString()
```
Returns a String representation of the value of this object.

---

lang	**class** Error **extends** Throwable

PURPOSE

Represent an abnormal event that should never occur.

CONSTRUCTOR SUMMARY

```
Error()
```
Equivalent to Error(**null, null**).
```
Error(String s)
```
Equivalent to Error(s, **null**).
```
Error(String s, Throwable t)
```
Constructs a new Error with message s and cause t.
```
Error(Throwable t)
```
Equivalent to Error(s, t), where s equals **null** if t equals **null**; otherwise s equals t.toString().

---

lang	**class** Exception **extends** Throwable

PURPOSE

Represents an unexpected event that is catchable.

CONSTRUCTOR SUMMARY

```
Exception()
```
Constructs a new Exception with a **null** message and cause.
```
Exception(String s)
```
Constructs a new Exception with message s and a **null** cause.
```
Exception(String s, Throwable t)
```
Constructs a new Exception with message s and cause t.
```
Exception(Throwable t)
```
Constructs a new Exception with cause t. If t is non-**null**, then the exception message is t,toString(); otherwise, the exception message is **null**.

---

lang	**final class** Float **extends** Number **implements** Comparable

PURPOSE

Represent a **float** value within a class wrapper.

FIELD SUMMARY

```
static final float MAX_VALUE
```
Represents the maximum finite value of type **float** (i.e., $(2 - 2^{-23})2^{127}$).
```
static final float MIN_VALUE
```
Represents the minimum positive nonzero value of type **float** (i.e., 2^{-149}).

```
static final float NaN
```
Represents Not-a-Number value (NaN) for type **double**.
```
static final float NEGATIVE_INFINITY
```
A constant holding the negative infinity of type float.
```
static final float POSITIVE_INFINITY
```
A constant holding the positive infinity of type float.
```
static final Class TYPE
```
Represents the type **float**.

CLASS METHOD SUMMARY
```
static int compare(float m, float n)
```
Returns a negative value, zero, or a positive value depending respectively on whether m is less than, equal to, or greater than n.
```
static int floatToIntBits(float n)
```
Returns a representation of **float** value n using the *IEEE 754 floating-point single-format bit layout* standard.
```
static int floatToRawIntBits(float n)
```
Returns a representation of **float** value n using the *IEEE 754 floating-point single-format bit layout* standard while preserving not-a-number values.
```
static boolean isInfinite(float n)
```
Returns **true** if and only if n is equal to Double.NEGATIVE_INFINITY or to Double.POSITIVE_INFINITY.
```
static boolean isNaN(float n)
```
Returns **true** if and only if the **float** value n is equal to Float.NaN.
```
static float intBitsToFloat(int n)
```
Returns the **float** value corresponding to the bit representation of value n.
```
static float parseFloat(String s)
```
Returns the **float** value represented by parsing string s as an optionally signed floating-point value.
```
static String toString(float n)
```
Returns a string representation of **float** value n.
```
static Float valueOf(String s)
```
Returns a new Float object representing Float.parseFloat(s).

CONSTRUCTOR SUMMARY
```
Float(double n)
```
Constructs a new Float object representing value n.
```
Float(float n)
```
Constructs a new Float object representing value n.
```
Float(String s)
```
Constructs a new Float object representing Float.parseFloat(s).

INSTANCE METHOD SUMMARY
```
byte byteValue()
```
Returns the **float** value of this Float as a **byte**.
```
int compareTo(Float n)
```
Returns a negative value, zero, or a positive value depending respectively on whether the **float** value represented by this object is less than, equal to, or greater than n.

```
int compareTo(Object v)
```
Returns a negative value, zero, or a positive value depending respectively on whether the **float** value represented by this object is less than, equal to, or greater than v.
```
double doubleValue()
```
Returns the **double** value of this Float as a **float**.
```
boolean equals(Object v)
```
Returns **true** if and only if v is an instance of Boolean representing the same **boolean** value that this object represents.
```
float floatValue()
```
Returns the **float** value of this Float.
```
int hashCode()
```
Returns the hash code of this object.
```
int intValue()
```
Returns the **float** value of this Float as an **int**.
```
boolean isInfinite()
```
Returns **true** if and only if the **float** value of this object is equal to Float.NEGATIVE_INFINITY or equal to Float.POSITIVE_INFINITY.
```
boolean isNaN()
```
Returns **true** if and only if the **float** value of this object is equal to Float.NaN.
```
long longValue()
```
Returns the **float** value of this Float as a **long**.
```
short shortValue()
```
Returns the **float** value of this Float as a **short**.
```
String toString()
```
Returns a String representation of the value of this object.

---

lang   **class** IllegalAccessException **extends** Exception

PURPOSE
Represent an unexpected event in which an illegal access of some constructor or member field or method was attempted.

CONSTRUCTOR SUMMARY
```
IllegalAccessException()
```
Constructs an IllegalAccessException without a default message.
```
IllegalAccessException(String s)
```
Constructs an IllegalAccessException with message s.

---

lang   **class** IndexOutOfBoundsException **extends** RuntimeException

PURPOSE
Represent an illegal element indexing event.

CONSTRUCTOR SUMMARY
```
IndexOutOfBoundsException()
```
Constructs a new IndexOutOfBoundsException with a default message.

IndexOutOfBoundsException(String s)

>   Constructs an IndexOutOfBoundsException with message s.

| `lang` | **final class** Integer **extends** Number **implements** Comparable |

PURPOSE

Represent an **int** value within a class wrapper.

FIELD SUMMARY

static int MAX_VALUE

>   Represents the maximum value of type **int** (i.e., $2^{31} - 1$).

static int MIN_VALUE

>   Represents the minimum value of type **int** (i.e., -2^{31}.)

static Class TYPE

>   Represents the type **int**.

CLASS METHOD SUMMARY

static Integer decode(String s)

>   Constructs a new Integer object representing Integer.parseInt(s, n), where n is 8, 10, or 16 depending on whether s is respectively a numeric string in octal, decimal, or hexadecimal format.

static Integer getInteger(String s)

>   Returns Integer.getInteger(s, **null**).

static Integer getInteger(String s, **int** n)

>   Returns Integer.getInteger(s, **new** Integer(n)).

static Integer getInteger(String s, Integer n)

>   Returns the value of the system property named s if it exists; otherwise, it returns n.

static int parseInt(String s)

>   Returns Integer.parseInt(s, 10).

static int parseInt(String s, **int** n)

>   Returns the **int** value represented by parsing string s as an optionally signed integer value in radix n.

static String toBinaryString(**int** m)

>   Returns Integer.toString(m, 2).

static String toHexString(**int** m)

>   Returns Integer.toString(m, 16).

static String toOctalString(**int** m)

>   Returns Integer.toString(m, 8).

static String toString(**int** m)

>   Returns Integer.toString(m, 10).

static String toString(**int** m, **int** n)

>   Returns a new String object representing the value of m in base n.

static Integer valueOf(String s)

>   Returns Integer.valueOf(s, 10)).

static Integer valueOf(String s, **int** n)

>   Returns a new Integer object representing Integer.parseInt(s, n).

CONSTRUCTOR SUMMARY

`Integer(int n)`

Constructs a new `Integer` object representing value n.

`Integer(String s)`

Constructs a new `Integer` object representing `Integer.parseInt(s)`.

INSTANCE METHOD SUMMARY

`byte byteValue()`

Returns the **int** value of this `Integer` as a **byte**.

`int compareTo(Integer n)`

Returns a negative value, zero, or a positive value depending respectively on whether the **int** value represented by this object is less than, equal to, or greater than n.

`int compareTo(Object v)`

Returns a negative value, zero, or a positive value depending respectively on whether the **float** value represented by this object is less than, equal to, or greater than v.

`double doubleValue()`

Returns the **int** value of this `Integer` as a **double**.

`boolean equals(Object v)`

Returns **true** if and only if v is an instance of `Integer` representing the same **int** value that this object represents.

`float floatValue()`

Returns the **int** value of this `Integer` as a **float**.

`int hashCode()`

Returns the hash code of this object.

`int intValue()`

Returns the **int** value of this `Integer`.

`long longValue()`

Returns the **int** value of this `Integer` as a **long**.

`short shortValue()`

Returns the **int** value of this `Integer` as a **short**.

`String toString()`

Returns a `String` representation of the value of this object.

`lang`   `final class Long extends Number implements Comparable`

PURPOSE

Represent a **long** value within a class wrapper.

FIELD SUMMARY

`static long MAX_VALUE`

Represents the maximum value of type **long** (i.e., $2^{63} - 1$).

`static long MIN_VALUE`

Represents the minimum value of type **long** (i.e., -2^{63}.)

`static Class TYPE`

Represents the type **long**.

CLASS METHOD SUMMARY

static Long decode(String s)

Constructs a new Long object representing Integer.parseLong(s, n), where n is 8, 10, or 16 depending on whether s is respectively a numeric string in octal, decimal, or hexadecimal format.

static Long getLong(String s)

Returns Long.getLong(s, **null**).

static Long getLong(String s, **long** n)

Returns Long.getLong(s, **new** Long(n)).

static Long getLong(String s, Long n)

Returns the value of the system property named s if it exists; otherwise, it returns n.

static long parseLong(String s)

Returns Long.parseLong(s, 10).

static long parseLong(String s, int n)

Returns the **long** value represented by parsing string s as an optionally signed integer value in radix n.

static String toBinaryString(long m)

Returns Long.toString(m, 2).

static String toHexString(long m)

Returns Long.toString(m, 16).

static String toOctalString(long m)

Returns Long.toString(m, 8).

static String toString(long m)

Returns Long.toString(m, 10).

static String toString(long m, int n)

Returns a new String object representing the value of m in base n.

static Long valueOf(String s)

Returns Long.valueOf(s, 10).

static Long valueOf(String s, int n)

Returns a new Long representing Long.parseLong(s, n).

CONSTRUCTOR SUMMARY

Long(long n)

Constructs a new Long object representing value n.

Long(String s)

Constructs a new Long object representing Long.parseLong(s).

INSTANCE METHOD SUMMARY

byte byteValue()

Returns the **long** value of this Long as a **byte**.

int compareTo(Long n)

Returns a negative value, zero, or a positive value depending respectively on whether the **long** value represented by this object is less than, equal to, or greater than n.

int compareTo(Object v)

Returns a negative value, zero, or a positive value depending respectively on whether the **long** value represented by this object is less than, equal to, or greater than v.

double doubleValue()

Returns the **long** value of this Long as a **double**.

boolean equals(Object v)

Returns **true** if and only if v is an instance of Long representing the same **int** value that this object represents.

float floatValue()

Returns the **long** value of this Long as a **float**.

int hashCode()

Returns the hash code of this object.

int intValue()

Returns the **long** value of this Long as an **int**.

long longValue()

Returns the **long** value of this Long.

short shortValue()

Returns the **long** value of this Long as a **short**.

String toString()

Returns a String representation of the value of this object.

| lang | **final class** Math |

PURPOSE

Defines two class constants for representing *e* and π, and a collection of class methods for computing common exponential, logarithm, square root, and trigonometric functions.

FIELD SUMMARY

static double E

Represents the **double** approximation to *e*.

static double PI

Represents the **double** approximation to π.

CLASS METHOD SUMMARY

static double abs(**double** n)

Returns the absolute value of **double** value n.

static float abs(**float** n)

Returns the absolute value of **float** value n.

static int abs(**int** n)

Returns the absolute value of **int** value n.

static long abs(**long** n)

Returns the absolute value of **long** value n.

static double acos(**double** n)

Returns the angle in the interval 0 ... MATH.PI whose cosine is n.

static double asin(**double** n)

Returns the angle in the interval –MATH.PI/2 ... MATH.PI/2 whose sine is n.

static double atan(**double** a)

Returns the angle in the interval –MATH.PI/2 ... MATH.PI/2 whose tangent is n.

```
static double atan2(double y, double x)
```
Returns $\tan(y/x)$.
```
static double ceil(double n)
```
Returns the smallest integral **double** value that is not less than n.
```
static double cos(double n)
```
Returns the cosine of angle n.
```
static double exp(double n)
```
Returns $MATH.E^n$.
```
static double floor(double n)
```
Returns the largest integral **double** value that is not greater than n.
```
static double IEEEremainder(double m, double n)
```
Returns the remainder of m divided by n as specified by the *IEEE 754 standard*.
```
static double log(double n)
```
Returns $\log_e$ n.
```
static double max(double m, double n)
```
Returns the maximum of the **double** values m and n.
```
static float max(float m, float n)
```
Returns the maximum of the **float** values m and n.
```
static int max(int m, int n)
```
Returns the maximum of the **int** values m and n.
```
static long max(long m, long n)
```
Returns the maximum of the **long** values m and n.
```
static double min(double m, double n)
```
Returns the minimum of the **double** values m and n.
```
static float min(float m, float n)
```
Returns the minimum of the **float** values m and n.
```
static int min(int m, int n)
```
Returns the minimum of the **int** values m and n.
```
static long min(long m, long n)
```
Returns the minimum of the **long** values m and n.
```
static double pow(double m, double n)
```
Returns m^n.
```
static double random()
```
Returns a positive pseudorandom uniform **double** value from the interval [0, 1) (i.e., the return value is greater than or equal to 0 and less than 1).
```
static double rint(double n)
```
Returns the integral **double** value closest to n.
```
static long round(double n)
```
Returns the **long** value closest to n.
```
static int round(float n)
```
Returns the **int** value closest to n.
```
static double sin(double n)
```
Returns the sine of angle n.
```
static double sqrt(double n)
```
Returns the positive-valued $\sqrt{n}$.
```
static double tan(double n)
```
Returns the tangent of angle n.

static double toDegrees(double n)
> Returns the radian equivalent to n degrees.

static double toRadians(double n)
> Converts the degrees equivalent to n radians.

---

lang class NoClassDefFoundError extends LinkageError

PURPOSE
Represent an unexpected event where the definition of a needed class could not be found.

CONSTRUCTOR SUMMARY
NoClassDefFoundError()
> Constructs a new NoClassDefFoundError with a default message.

NoClassDefFoundError(String s)
> Constructs a new NoClassDefFoundError with message s.

---

lang class NullPointerException extends RuntimeException

PURPOSE
Represent an unexpected event where a reference to an object was needed and instead the **null** value was supplied.

CONSTRUCTOR SUMMARY
NullPointerException()
> Constructs a NullPointerException with a default message.

NullPointerException(String s)
> Constructs a NullPointerException with message s.

---

lang abstract class Number implements Serializable

PURPOSE
Represent a numeric value within a class wrapper.

CONSTRUCTOR SUMMARY
Number()
> Constructs a number representation.

INSTANCE METHOD SUMMARY
byte byteValue()
> Returns the value of this Number as a **byte**.

abstract double doubleValue()
> Returns the value of this Number as a **double**.

abstract float floatValue()
> Returns the value of this Number as a **float**.

abstract int intValue()
> Returns the value of this Number as an **int**.

abstract long longValue()
> Returns the value of this Number as a **long**.

short shortValue()

>Returns the value of this Number as a **short**.

---

class Object

PURPOSE

Represent the basic characteristics and behaviors of an object in Java. Class Object is the root superclass of all Java arrays and classes.

CONSTRUCTOR SUMMARY

Object()

>Constructs an object representation.

INSTANCE METHOD SUMMARY

protected Object clone()

>Returns a new clone of this object. By convention, classes that override this method should define a **public** clone() method that makes a deep copy.

boolean equals(Object v)

>Returns **true** if and only if v is the same object as this object. By convention, classes that override this method should fulfill the following contract.
>
>- Reflexivity: For any object x, x.equals(x) should be true.
>- Symmetry: For any objects x and y, if x.equals(y), then y.equals(s);
>- Transitivity: For any objects x, y, and z, if x.equals(y) and y.equals(z), then x.equals(z);
>- Consistency: For any unchanging objects x and y, repeated evaluations of x.equals(y) should return the same value.
>- Physicality: For any object x, x.equals(**null**) should return **false**.

protected void finalize()

>Invoked by the garbage collector when Java has determined there are no more references to this object.

final Class getClass()

>Returns the runtime class of this object.

int hashCode()

>Returns the hash code of this object.

final void notify()

>Wakes up one of the thread(s) that is waiting on the monitor for this object.

final void notifyAll()

>Wakes up all of the threads that are waiting on the monitor for this object.

String toString()

>Returns a String representation of the value of this object.

final void wait()

>Returns **this**.wait(0, 0).

final void wait(long m)

>Returns **this**.wait(m, 0).

final void wait(long m, int n)

>Causes current thread to wait until one of the following conditions is true: a thread invokes notify() or notifyAll() of this object; some other thread

interrupts the current thread; 1,000,000 · m + n nanoseconds have passed.

| lang | **interface** Runnable |

PURPOSE
Describe the method needed for objects to be executed as threads.
INSTANCE METHOD SUMMARY
    void run()
        The method to be executed when a Runnable object-based thread is started.

| lang | **class** Runtime |

PURPOSE
Represent an interface to the Java runtime environment.
CLASS METHOD SUMMARY
    static Runtime getRuntime()
        Returns the object that is runtime interface for the current application.
INSTANCE METHOD SUMMARY
    void addShutdownHook(Thread t)
        Registers thread t to be run during the Java virtual machine shutdown process.
    int availableProcessors()
        Returns the number of processors available to the Java virtual machine for executing threads.
    Process exec(String s)
        Runs the command s as a separate process. Returns a Process for managing that process. Equivalent to exec(**new** String[] = {s}, **null**, **null**).
    Process exec(String[] s)
        Returns exec(s, **null**, **null**).
    Process exec(String[] s, String[] t)
        Returns exec(s, t, **null**).
    Process exec(String[] s, String[] t, File d)
        Runs command s[0] as a separate process with s[1] through s[s.length-1] as the parameters to the process. The elements of t are operating system variable settings that are evaluated before s[0] is run. If d is non-**null**, then the working folder of the process is d; otherwise, the working folder is the working folder of the current thread. Returns a Process for managing that process.
    Process exec(String s, String[] t)
        Returns exec(**new** String[] = {s}, t, **null**).
    Process exec(String s, String[] t, File d)
        Returns exec(**new** String[] = {s}, t, d).
    void exit(**int** n)
        Initiates the shutdown process of the Java virtual machine. The return value given to the operating system is n, where a nonzero value indicates abnormal termination.
    long freeMemory()
        Returns the number of nonallocated memory bytes available to Java.

void gc()

> Invokes System.gc().

void halt(int n)

> Terminates the Java virtual machine without running any shutdown hooks. The return value given to the operating system is n, where a nonzero value indicates abnormal termination.

void load(String s)

> Loads the file with name s as a dynamic library.

void loadLibrary(String s)

> Loads the dynamic library with name s.

long maxMemory()

> Returns the maximum number of bytes that Java will attempt to use.

boolean removeShutdownHook(Thread t)

> Removes thread t from Java virtual machine shutdown process.

void runFinalization()

> Invokes System.runFinalization().

long totalMemory()

> Returns the number of bytes available to Java.

void traceInstructions(boolean b)

> Sets whether Java should display debugging output for each executed bytecode.

void traceMethodCalls(boolean b)

> Sets whether Java should display debugging output for each method invocation.

| lang | **final class** Short **extends** Number **implements** Comparable |

PURPOSE

Represent a **short** value within a class wrapper.

FIELD SUMMARY

static short MAX_VALUE

> Represents the maximum value of type **short** (i.e., $2^{15} - 1$).

static short MIN_VALUE

> Represents the minimum value of type **short** (i.e., -2^{15}).

static Class TYPE

> Represents the type **int**.

CLASS METHOD SUMMARY

static Short decode(String n)

> Constructs a new Short object representing Integer.parseShort(s, n), where n is 8, 10, or 16 depending on whether s is respectively a numeric string in octal, decimal, or hexadecimal format.

static short parseShort(String s)

> Returns Short.parseShort(s, 10).

static short parseShort(String s, int n)

> Returns the **short** value represented by parsing string s as an optionally signed integer value in radix n.

```
static String toString(short n)
```
Returns a new `String` object equal to the value of n.
```
static Short valueOf(String s)
```
Returns `Short.parseShort(s, 10)`.
```
static Short valueOf(String s, int n)
```
Returns a new `Short` representing `Short.parseShort(s, n)`.

CONSTRUCTOR SUMMARY
```
Short(short n)
```
Constructs a new `Short` object representing value n.
```
Short(String s)
```
Constructs a new `Short` object representing `Integer.parseShort(s)`.

INSTANCE METHOD SUMMARY
```
byte byteValue()
```
Returns the **short** value of this `Short` as a **byte**.
```
int compareTo(Object v)
```
Returns a negative value, zero, or a positive value depending respectively on whether this object is less than, equal to, or greater than v.
```
int compareTo(Short n)
```
Returns a negative value, zero, or a positive value depending respectively on whether this object is less than, equal to, or greater than n.
```
double doubleValue()
```
Returns the **short** value of this `Short` as a **double**.
```
boolean equals(Object v)
```
Returns **true** if and only if v is an instance of `Integer` representing the same **int** value that this object represents.
```
float floatValue()
```
Returns the **short** value of this `Short` as a **float**.
```
int hashCode()
```
Returns the hash code of this object.
```
int intValue()
```
Returns the **short** value of this `Short` as an **int**.
```
long longValue()
```
Returns the **short** value of this `Short` as a **long**.
```
short shortValue()
```
Returns the **short** value of this `Short`.
```
String toString()
```
Returns a `String` representation of the value of this object.

---

lang

```
final class String implements Serializable, Comparable,
    CharSequence
```

PURPOSE
Represent a sequence of characters using methods that provide inspection but not mutation of the sequence.

Field summary

static final Comparator CASE_INSENSITIVE_ORDER

Represents a string Comparator that orders strings using method compareTo-IgnoreCase().

Class method summary

static String copyValueOf(char[] c)

Returns **new** String(c, 0, c.length).

static String copyValueOf(char[] c, int i, int n)

Returns **new** String(c, i, n).

static String valueOf(**boolean** b)

Returns the string representation of **boolean** value b.

static String valueOf(**char** c)

Returns the string representation of **char** value c.

static String valueOf(**char**[] c)

Returns **new** String(c, 0, c.length).

static String valueOf(**char**[] c, int i, int n)

Returns **new** String(c, i, n).

static String valueOf(**double** n)

Returns the string representation of the **double** value n.

static String valueOf(**float** n)

Returns the string representation of the **float** value n.

static String valueOf(**int** n)

Returns the string representation of the **int** value n.

static String valueOf(**long** n)

Returns the String representation of the **long** value n.

static String valueOf(Object v)

Returns v.toString().

Constructor summary

String()

Constructs a new String object representing the empty character string.

String(**byte**[] b)

Invokes String(b, 0, b.length, s), where s is the name of the default character set.

String(**byte**[] b, int i, int n)

Invokes String(b, i, n, s), where s is the name of the default character set.

String(**byte**[] b, int i, int n, String s)

Constructs a new String by decoding a length n subarray of b starting with the element with i using the character set with name s.

String(**byte**[] bytes, String s)

Invokes String(b, 0, b.length, s).

String(**char**[] c)

Invokes String(c, 0, c.length).

String(**char**[] value, int i, int n)

Constructs a new String of length n from the subarray of c starting with the element with i.

```
String(String s)
```
Constructs a new `String` that is a copy of the character sequence represented by s.
```
String(StringBuffer b)
```
Returns `String(b.toString())`.

INSTANCE METHOD SUMMARY
```
char charAt(int i)
```
Returns the character at index i in the character sequence represented by this `String`.
```
int compareTo(Object v)
```
Lexicographically compares this `String` to v by returning a negative value, zero, or a positive value depending respectively on whether this object is less than, equal to, or greater than v.
```
int compareTo(String s)
```
Lexicographically compares this `String` to s by returning a negative value, zero, or a positive value depending respectively on whether this object is less than, equal to, or greater than s.
```
int compareToIgnoreCase(String s)
```
Lexicographically compares this `String` to s by returning a negative value, zero, or a positive value depending respectively on whether this `String` is less than, equal to, or greater than s while ignoring case differences.
```
String concat(String s)
```
Returns a `String` that is concatenation of this `String` with s.
```
boolean contentEquals(StringBuffer b)
```
Returns `equals(b.toString())`.
```
boolean endsWith(String s)
```
Returns **true** if and only if the last n characters in the character sequence represented by this `String` equal the character string sequence represented by s.
```
boolean equals(Object v)
```
Returns **true** if and only if v is an instance of `String` representing the same character sequence that this `String` represents.
```
boolean equalsIgnoreCase(String s)
```
Returns **true** if and only if s represents the same character sequence that this `String` represents while ignoring case differences.
```
byte[] getBytes()
```
Returns a new **byte** array that encodes the character sequence represented by this `String` using the default character set.
```
byte[] getBytes(String s)
```
Returns a new **byte** array that encodes the character sequence represented by this `String` using the character set with name s.
```
void getChars(int i, int j, char[] c, int k)
```
Copies the character subsequence of this `String` with indices i through j into array c starting at its element with index k.
```
int hashCode()
```
Returns the hash code of this `String`.
```
int indexOf(int c)
```
Returns `indexOf(c, 0)`.

int indexOf(int c, int i)

If character c occurs in character sequence of this String starting from index i on, then the method returns the index of the first such occurrence; otherwise, the method returns –1.

int indexOf(String s)

Returns indexOf(s, 0).

int indexOf(String s, int i)

If the character sequence of s occurs as a subsequence of this String starting somewhere from index i on, then the method returns the index of the first such occurrence; otherwise, the method returns –1.

String intern()

Returns a String that is a duplicate of this String such that Java considers the returned string to be the canonical representation of the character sequence represented by this String.

int lastIndexOf(int c)

Returns lastIndexOf(c, length() - 1).

int lastIndexOf(int c, int i)

If character c occurs in character sequence of this String prior to index i+1, then the method returns the index of the last such occurrence; otherwise, the method returns –1.

int lastIndexOf(String s)

Returns lastIndexOf(s, length() - 1).

int lastIndexOf(String s, int i)

If the character sequence of s occurs as a subsequence of this String starting somewhere prior to index i+1, then the method returns the index of the last such occurrence; otherwise, the method returns –1.

int length()

Returns the length of the character sequence of this String.

boolean matches(String r)

Returns whether this String is an element of the set represented by regular expression r.

boolean regionMatches(boolean b, int i, String s, int j, int k)

Returns whether the length k character subsequence of this String starting at index i equals length k character subsequence of s starting at index j are equal. If and only if b is **true** does testing for equality ignore character case.

boolean regionMatches(int i, String s, int j, int k)

Returns regionMatches(**false**, i, s, j, k).

String replace(**char** c, **char** d)

Returns a new String whose character sequence is a pseudo-duplicate of the character sequence of this String. In creating the character sequence of the new String from this String, each occurrence of character c is replaced with character d.

String replaceAll(String r, String s)

Returns a new String whose character sequence is a pseudo-duplicate of the character sequence of this String. In creating the character sequence of the new String from this String, each occurrence of regular expression r is replaced with s.

String replaceFirst(String r, String s)

> Returns a new String whose character sequence is a pseudo-duplicate of the character sequence of this String. In creating the character sequence of the new String from this String, the first occurrence of regular expression r is replaced with s.

String[] split(String r)

> Returns split(r, 0).

String[] split(String r, int n)

> Returns a new String array whose elements are (possibly empty) substrings of this String such that the substring represented by each element of the array is followed with this String by an occurrence of regular expression r or is the substring that ends this String. If n is negative, then the regular expression is matched as many times as possible. If instead, n has the value 0, then the regular expression is also matched as many times as possible; however, any trailing elements representing the empty string are removed. If instead, n is positive, then the regular expression is matched at most n-1 times and the last element of the new array represents the substring of this String following the last matched occurence of regular expression r.

boolean startsWith(String s)

> Returns startsWith(s, 0).

boolean startsWith(String s, int i)

> Returns whether the character sequence of s occurs as a subsequence of this String starting at index i.

CharSequence subSequence(int i, int j)

> Returns a new CharSequence representing the elements with indices i ... j - 1 from the character sequence of this String.

String substring(int i)

> Returns substring(i, length()).

String substring(int i, int j)

> Returns a new String representing the elements with indices i ... j - 1 from the character sequence of this String.

char[] toCharArray()

> Returns a new **char** array representing the character sequence of this String.

String toLowerCase()

> Returns toLowerCase(l), where l is the default locale for this system,

String toLowerCase(Locale l)

> Returns a new String that is a duplicate of this String such that all characters in the new String are the lowercase equivalents with respect to locale l of the corresponding characters in this String.

String toString()

> Returns **this**.

String toUpperCase()

> Returns toUpperCase(l), where l is the default locale for this system,

String toUpperCase(Locale l)

> Returns a new String that is a duplicate of this String such that all characters in the new String are the uppercase equivalents with respect to locale l of the corresponding characters in this String.

String trim()

> Returns a new String that is a duplicate of this String such that no leading or trailing whitespace of this String is duplicated.

---

lang   **final class** StringBuffer **implements** Serializable, CharSequence

PURPOSE

Represent a mutable sequence of characters. Thus, unlike a String, a StringBuffer can be modified.

CONSTRUCTOR SUMMARY

StringBuffer()

> Invokes StringBuffer(16).

StringBuffer(**int** n)

> Constructs a new StringBuffer object representing the empty character string with an initial capacity of representing character sequences of length n or less.

StringBuffer(String s)

> Constructs a new StringBuffer object representing the same character sequence that string s represents with an initial capacity of representing character sequences of length n+16 or less.

INSTANCE METHOD SUMMARY

StringBuffer append(**boolean** b)

> Returns append(String.valueOf(b)).

StringBuffer append(**char** c)

> Returns append(String.valueOf(c)).

StringBuffer append(**char**[] c)

> Returns append(String.valueOf(c)).

StringBuffer append(**char**[] c, **int** i, **int** n)

> Returns append(String.valueOf(c, i, n)).

StringBuffer append(**double** n)

> Returns append(String.valueOf(n)).

StringBuffer append(**float** n)

> Returns append(String.valueOf(n)).

StringBuffer append(**int** n)

> Returns append(String.valueOf(n)).

StringBuffer append(**long** n)

> Returns append(String.valueOf(n)).

StringBuffer append(Object v)

> Returns append(String.valueOf(n)).

StringBuffer append(String s)

> Returns this StringBuffer after appending the character sequence represented by s to the character sequence represented by this StringBuffer.

StringBuffer append(StringBuffer s)

> Returns this StringBuffer after appending the character sequence represented by s to the character sequence represented by this StringBuffer.

int capacity()

Returns the current capacity of this StringBuffer.

char charAt(int i)

Returns the character at index i in the character sequence represented by this StringBuffer.

StringBuffer delete(int i, int j)

Returns this StringBuffer after removing the elements with indices i … j – 1 from the character sequence of this StringBuffer.

StringBuffer deleteCharAt(int i)

Invokes delete(i, i+1).

void ensureCapacity(int n)

If capacity() < n, then the method increases the capacity of this String-Buffer to n.

void getChars(int i, int j, char[] c, int k)

Copies the elements with indices i … j – 1 from the character sequence represented by this StringBuffer into array c starting with its element with subscript j.

int indexOf(String s)

Invokes indexOf(s, 0).

int indexOf(String s, int i)

If the character sequence of s occurs as a subsequence of this StringBuffer starting somewhere from index i on, then the method returns the index of the first such occurrence; otherwise, the method returns –1.

StringBuffer insert(int i, boolean b)

Returns insert(i, String.valueOf(b)).

StringBuffer insert(int i, char c)

Returns insert(i, String.valueOf(c)).

StringBuffer insert(int i, char[] c)

Returns insert(i, String.valueOf(c)).

StringBuffer insert(int i, char[] s, int j, int n)

Returns insert(i, new String(c, j, n)).

StringBuffer insert(int i, double n)

Returns insert(i, String.valueOf(n)).

StringBuffer insert(int i, float n)

Returns insert(i, String.valueOf(n)).

StringBuffer insert(int i, int n)

Returns insert(i, String.valueOf(n)).

StringBuffer insert(int i, long n)

Returns insert(i, String.valueOf(n)).

StringBuffer insert(int i, Object v)

Returns insert(i, v.toString(n)).

StringBuffer insert(int i, String s)

If s is **null**, then the method returns insert(i, "null"). If instead, s is non-**null**, then the method returns this StringBuffer after inserting the character sequence represented by s into the character sequence represented by this StringBuffer. The insertion occurs immediately before the element with index i in the character sequence represented by this StringBuffer.

int lastIndexOf(String s)

Returns lastIndexOf(s, length() - 1).

int lastIndexOf(String s, int i)

If the character sequence of s occurs as a subsequence of this String starting somewhere prior to index i+1, then the method returns the index of the last such occurrence; otherwise, the method returns –1.

int length()

Returns the length of the character sequence represented by this StringBuffer.

StringBuffer replace(int i, int j, String s)

Returns this StringBuffer after invoking delete(i, j) and then insert(i, s).

StringBuffer reverse()

Returns this StringBuffer after reversing the elements of its character sequence.

void setCharAt(int i, char c)

Sets to c the element at index i in the character sequence represented by this StringBuffer.

void setLength(int n)

If n < length(), then the method invokes delete(n, length()). If instead n equals length(), then the method does nothing. If instead n > length, then the length of the character sequence represented by this StringBuffer is increased to n by appending a sufficient number of the null characters ('\u0000') to it.

CharSequence subSequence(int i, int j)

Returns a new CharSequence representing the elements with indices i ... j – 1 from the character sequence of this StringBuffer.

String substring(int i)

Returns substring(i, length()).

String substring(int i, int j)

Returns a new String representing the elements with indices i ... j – 1 from the character sequence of this StringBuffer.

String toString()

Returns a String representation of the value of this StringBuffer.

| lang |

class StringIndexOutOfBoundsException extends IndexOutOfBoundsException

PURPOSE

Represent an illegal element indexing event with a String method.

CONSTRUCTOR SUMMARY

StringIndexOutOfBoundsException()

Constructs a new StringIndexOutOfBoundsException with a default message.

StringIndexOutOfBoundsException(int i)

Constructs a new StringIndexOutOfBoundsException class with a message indicating i is an illegal index value.

StringIndexOutOfBoundsException(String s)

Constructs a StringIndexOutOfBoundsException with message s.

| lang | **final class** System **extends** Object |

PURPOSE

Define three standard streams and several common, miscellaneous class methods.

FIELD SUMMARY

static PrintStream err

Represents the standard error stream. By default, standard error output stream is associated with the console window.

static InputStream in

Represents the standard input stream. By default, standard input stream is gotten from the keyboard's interface with the console window.

static PrintStream out

Represents the standard output stream. By default, standard output stream is associated with the console window

INSTANCE METHOD SUMMARY

static void arraycopy(Object u, **int** i, Object v, **int** j, **int** k)

Sets k elements of array u starting with the element with index j to the corresponding values of k elements of array u starting with the element with index i.

static long currentTimeMillis()

Returns the current time in milliseconds.

static void exit(**int** n)

Ends the current program with status n, where a nonzero value for n indicates abnormal termination.

static void gc()

Invokes the Java garbage collector.

static Properties getProperties()

Returns the current system properties.

static String getProperty(String s)

Returns getProperty(s, **null**).

static String getProperty(String s, String t)

Returns the value of the system property named s if it exists; otherwise, it returns t.

static SecurityManager getSecurityManager()

Returns the system security manager.

static int identityHashCode(Object v)

Returns the hash code that method hashCode() of class Object would return for object v (i.e., the value is not necessarily returned by v.hashCode()).

static void load(String s)

Loads the file with name s as a dynamic library.

static void loadLibrary(String s)

Loads the system library with name s as a dynamic library.

static String mapLibraryName(String s)

Returns a platform-specific string associated with the library with name s.

static void runFinalization()

Causes Java to invoke the finalize() methods for any unreferenced objects whose finalize() methods have not yet been run.

```
static void setErr(PrintStream s)
```
Sets the standard error stream to s.
```
static void setIn(InputStream s)
```
Sets the standard input stream to s.
```
static void setOut(PrintStream s)
```
Sets the standard output stream to s.
```
static void setProperties(Properties s)
```
Sets the system properties to s.
```
static String setProperty(String s, String t)
```
Sets system property s by to value t.
```
static void setSecurityManager(SecurityManager s)
```
Sets the system security manager to s.

---

lang   **class** Thread **extends** Object **implements** Runnable

PURPOSE

Represent a prioritized thread of execution (a flow of control) in a program.

FIELD SUMMARY
```
static int MAX_PRIORITY
```
Represents the maximum possible thread priority.
```
static int MIN_PRIORITY
```
Represents the minimum possible thread priority.
```
static int NORM_PRIORITY
```
Represents the default thread priority.

CLASS METHOD SUMMARY
```
static int activeCount()
```
Returns the number of active threads in the thread group of the thread that is currently executing.
```
static Thread currentThread()
```
Returns a reference to the thread that is currently executing.
```
static void dumpStack()
```
Prints to the standard error stream a stack trace of the thread that is currently executing.
```
static int enumerate(Thread[] a)
```
Copies into array a all of the active threads in the thread group of the thread that is currently executing.
```
static boolean interrupted()
```
Tests whether the thread that is currently executing has been interrupted since a prior invocation of this method.
```
static void sleep(long n)
```
Causes the currently executing thread to pause its execution for n milliseconds.
```
static void sleep(long m, int n)
```
Causes the thread that is currently executing to pause its execution for 1,000,000 · m + n nanoseconds.

```
static void yield()
```
Causes the thread that is currently executing to temporarily pause if there exists other threads.

CONSTRUCTOR SUMMARY

```
Thread()
```
Invokes Thread(**null**, **null**, s), where s is a new name of the form "Thread-" + n, where n is an integer.

```
Thread(Runnable r)
```
Invokes Thread(**null**, r, s), where s is a new name of the form "Thread-" + n, where n is an integer.

```
Thread(Runnable r, String s)
```
Invokes Thread(**null**, r, s).

```
Thread(String s)
```
Invokes Thread(**null**, **null**, s).

```
Thread(ThreadGroup g, Runnable r)
```
Invokes Thread(t, r, s), where s is a new name of the form "Thread-" + n, where n is an integer.

```
Thread(ThreadGroup g, Runnable r, String s)
```
Constructs a new Thread object belonging to thread group g with run object r, and name s.

```
Thread(ThreadGroup g, Runnable r, String s, long n)
```
Constructs a new Thread belonging to thread group g with run object r, name s, and a requested stack size of n. The stack size is the number of bytes of memory to reserve for this object's execution. Whether and how the stack size request is handled is system dependent.

```
Thread(ThreadGroup g, String s)
```
Invokes Thread(g, **null**, s).

INSTANCE METHOD SUMMARY

```
void checkAccess()
```
Throws a SecurityException if the thread that is currently executing does not have permission to modify this Thread.

```
void destroy()
```
Destroys this Thread.

```
ClassLoader getContextClassLoader()
```
Returns the ClassLoader for this Thread.

```
String getName()
```
Returns the name of this Thread.

```
int getPriority()
```
Returns the priority of this Thread.

```
ThreadGroup getThreadGroup()
```
Returns the group of this Thread.

```
static boolean holdsLock(Object v)
```
Returns **true** if and only if this Thread holds the monitor lock on object v.

```
void interrupt()
```
Interrupts this Thread.

```
boolean isAlive()
```
Tests whether this Thread is alive.

boolean isDaemon()

> Tests whether this Thread is a daemon.

boolean isInterrupted()

> Tests whether this Thread has ever been interrupted.

void join()

> Returns join(0).

void join(long m)

> If m is nonzero, then Java waits at most m milliseconds for this thread to die; otherwise it waits forever.

void join(long m, int n)

> Waits at most 1,000,000 · m + n nanoseconds for this thread to die.

void run()

> If this Thread has a non-**null** Runnable object then the run() method of that object is run; otherwise, the method returns immediately.

void setContextClassLoader(ClassLoader c)

> Sets the ClassLoader for this Thread to c.

void setDaemon(**boolean** b)

> If b is **true**, then this Thread is a daemon thread; otherwise it is a user thread.

void setName(String s)

> Sets the name of this Thread to name s.

void setPriority(int n)

> Sets the priority of this Thread to n.

void start()

> Causes this Thread to start executing.

String toString()

> Returns a String representation of this Thread, which includes it name, priority, and thread group.

| lang | **class** ThreadGroup |

PURPOSE

Represent a set of thread and thread groups.

CONSTRUCTOR SUMMARY

ThreadGroup(String s)

> Equivalent to ThreadGroup(g, s), where g is the ThreadGroup of the thread currently running.

ThreadGroup(ThreadGroup g, String s)

> Constructs a new ThreadGroup with name s and with g the parent Thread-Group of the new ThreadGroup.

INSTANCE METHOD SUMMARY

int activeCount()

> Returns the number of active threads in this ThreadGroup or its subgroups.

int activeGroupCount()

> Returns the number of active groups in this ThreadGroup or its subgroups.

void checkAccess()

> Throws a SecurityException if the currently running thread does not have permission to modify this ThreadGroup.

void destroy()

> Throws an IllegalThreadStateException if this ThreadGroup is either not empty or has already been destroyed; otherwise, this ThreadGroup is destroyed. Note, a daemon ThreadGroup is destroyed automatically when either its last thread has been stopped or its last subgroup has been destroyed.

int enumerate(Thread[] t)

> Returns enumerate(t, **true**).

int enumerate(Thread[] t, **boolean** b)

> Returns the number of references copied to t, where if b is **true**, then references to active threads belonging to this ThreadGroup or its subgroups are copied to t; otherwise, only references to active threads belonging to this ThreadGroup are copied to t.

int enumerate(ThreadGroup[] g)

> Returns enumerate(g, **true**).

int enumerate(ThreadGroup[] t, **boolean** b)

> Returns the number of references copied to t, where if b is **true**, then references to active subgroups belonging to this ThreadGroup or its subgroups are copied to t; otherwise, only references to active subgroups belonging to this Thread-Group are copied to t.

int getMaxPriority()

> Returns the maximum priority to which a thread in this ThreadGroup can be set.

String getName()

> Returns the name of this ThreadGroup.

ThreadGroup getParent()

> Returns the parent ThreadGroup of this ThreadGroup.

void interrupt()

> Invokes t.interrupt() for any thread t belonging to this ThreadGroup or its subgroups.

boolean isDaemon()

> Returns **true** if and only if this ThreadGroup is a daemon ThreadGroup.

boolean isDestroyed()

> Returns **true** if and only if this ThreadGroup has been destroyed.

void list()

> Displays debugging information to standard output regarding this Thread-Group.

boolean parentOf(ThreadGroup g)

> Returns **true** if and only if this ThreadGroup is g or if an ancestor Thread-Group is g.

void setDaemon(**boolean** b)

> If b is **true**, then this ThreadGroup is made a daemon ThreadGroup; otherwise, this ThreadGroup is made a normal ThreadGroup.

void setMaxPriority(**int** n)

> Sets the maximal assignable priority of this ThreadGroup to n.

String toString()

> Returns a String representation of this ThreadGroup.

> void uncaughtException(Thread t, Throwable e)
>> Invoked by Java when thread t from this ThreadGroup is stopped because of uncaught exception e.

---

lang   **class** Throwable **implements** Serializable

PURPOSE

Represent an exception or error in Java. In particular, Throwable is the superclass of all other exception and error classes.

CONSTRUCTOR SUMMARY

> Throwable()
>> Equivalent to Throwable(**null, null**).

> Throwable(String s)
>> Equivalent to Throwable(s, **null**).

> Throwable(String s, Throwable t)
>> Constructs a new Throwable with message s and cause t.

> Throwable(Throwable t)
>> Equivalent to Throwable(s, t), where s equals **null** if t equals **null**; otherwise s equals t.toString().

INSTANCE METHOD SUMMARY

> Throwable fillInStackTrace()
>> Updates this Throwable with information regarding the execution sequence of the current thread.

> Throwable getCause()
>> Returns the cause of this Throwable.

> String getLocalizedMessage()
>> Creates a Locale-specific representation of the message of this Throwable.

> String getMessage()
>> Returns the message of this Throwable.

> StackTraceElement[] getStackTrace()
>> Returns an array of stack frame elements that trace the execution of the current thread.

> Throwable initCause(Throwable t)
>> Sets the cause of this Throwable to t.

> void printStackTrace()
>> Invokes printStackTrace(System.err).

> void printStackTrace(PrintStream s)
>> Displays to s both this Throwable and a string representation of the getStackTrace().

> void printStackTrace(PrintWriter s)
>> Displays to s both this Throwable and a string representation of the getStackTrace().

> void setStackTrace(StackTraceElement[] s)
>> Sets to s the stack trace elements to be returned by the method getStackTrace() of this Throwable.

> String toString()
>> Returns a String representation of this Throwable.

| **lang** | **final class** Void |

PURPOSE

Represent a **void** value within a class wrapper. Because there are no **void** values, class Void class cannot be instantiated.

FIELD SUMMARY

    static Class TYPE

        Represents the type **void**.

| **D.3** | **JAVA.MATH** |

| **math** | **class** BigDecimal **extends** Number **implements** Comparable |

PURPOSE

Represent immutable decimal numbers of arbitrary precision. In particular, a decimal number is represented using a BigInteger and a scaling factor. If the BigInteger in a BigDecimal representation is n and the scaling factor is d, then the decimal number being represented is $n / 10^d$.

FIELD SUMMARY

    static int ROUND_CEILING

        Represents rounding toward positive infinity.

    static int ROUND_DOWN

        Represents rounding toward zero.

    static int ROUND_FLOOR

        Represents rounding toward negative infinity.

    static int ROUND_HALF_DOWN

        Represents rounding toward nearest integer with ties broken by rounding down.

    static int ROUND_HALF_EVEN

        Represents rounding mode with ties broken by rounding to the even number.

    static int ROUND_HALF_UP

        Represents rounding nearest integer with ties broken by rounding up.

    static int ROUND_UNNECESSARY

        Represents rounding is unnecessary as operation is exact.

    static int ROUND_UP

        Represents rounding away from zero.

CLASS METHOD SUMMARY

CLASS METHOD SUMMARY

> **static** BigDecimal valueOf(**long** n)
>> Returns valueOf(n, 0) equal to n. The scaling factor in the result is equal to zero.
>
> **static** BigDecimal valueOf(**long** n, **int** d)
>> Returns a BigDecimal equal to n. The scaling factor in the result is equal to d.

CONSTRUCTOR SUMMARY

> BigDecimal(BigInteger n)
>> Invokes **this**(n, 0).
>
> BigDecimal(BigInteger n, **int** d)
>> Constructs a new BigDecimal using n as a basis with d digits of accuracy after the decimal point.
>
> BigDecimal(**double** n)
>> Constructs a new BigDecimal using n as a basis with the scaling factor equal to the number of digits in the fractional part of n.
>
> BigDecimal(String s)
>> Constructs a new BigDecimal using s as a text-based representation of a number. The scaling factor is equal to the number of digits in the fractional part of s.

INSTANCE METHOD SUMMARY

> BigDecimal abs()
>> Returns a BigDecimal equal to the absolute value of this BigDecimal. The scaling factor in the result is equal to **this**.scale().
>
> BigDecimal add(BigDecimal n)
>> Returns a BigDecimal equal to the sum of n and this BigDecimal. The scaling factor in the result is equal to max(n, **this**.scale()).
>
> **int** compareTo(BigDecimal n)
>> Returns a negative value, zero, or a positive value depending respectively on whether the BigDecimal value represented by this object is less than, equal to, or greater than n.
>
> **int** compareTo(Object v)
>> Returns a negative value, zero, or a positive value depending respectively on whether the BigDecimal value represented by this object is less than, equal to, or greater than v.
>
> BigDecimal divide(BigDecimal n, **int** m)
>> Returns a BigDecimal equal to the division of this BigDecimal by n with any rounding of using rounding mode m. The scaling factor in the result is equal to **this**.scale().
>
> BigDecimal divide(BigDecimal n, **int** d, **int** m)
>> Returns a BigDecimal equal to the division of this BigDecimal by n with any rounding using rounding mode m. The scaling factor in the result is equal to d.
>
> **double** doubleValue()
>> Returns a **double** representation of this BigDecimal.
>
> **boolean** equals(Object x)
>> Returns **true** if and only if v is an instance of BigDecimal representing the same numeric value with the same scaling factor that this object represents.
>
> **float** floatValue()
>> Returns a **float** representation of this BigDecimal.

```
int hashCode()
```

Returns the hash code of this `BigDecimal`.

```
int intValue()
```

Returns an **int** representation of this `BigDecimal`.

```
long longValue()
```

Returns a **long** representation of this `BigDecimal`.

```
BigDecimal max(BigDecimal n)
```

Returns the maximum of n and this `BigDecimal`.

```
BigDecimal min(BigDecimal n)
```

Returns the minimum of n and this `BigDecimal`.

```
BigDecimal movePointLeft(int n)
```

Returns a `BigDecimal` equal to product of this `BigDecimal` and 10^{-n}.

```
BigDecimal movePointRight(int n)
```

Returns a `BigDecimal` equal to product of this `BigDecimal` and 10^{n}.

```
BigDecimal multiply(BigDecimal n)
```

Returns a `BigDecimal` equal to the product of n and this `BigDecimal`. The scaling factor in the result is equal to n.`scale()` + **this**.`scale()`.

```
BigDecimal negate()
```

Returns a `BigDecimal` equal to the additive inverse of this `BigDecimal`. The scaling factor in the result is equal to **this**.`scale()`.

```
int scale()
```

Returns the scaling factor maintained by this `BigDecimal`.

```
BigDecimal setScale(int d)
```

Returns a `BigDecimal` equal to `unscaledValue()` * 10^{-d} with a scaling factor of d.

```
BigDecimal setScale(int d, int m)
```

Returns a `BigDecimal` equal to `unscaledValue()` * 10^{-d} with a scaling factor of d. If rounding is required to produce the value then the rounding mode is m.

```
int signum()
```

Returns –1, 0, or 1 depending on whether this `BigDecimal` is respectively negative, zero, or positive.

```
BigDecimal subtract(BigDecimal n)
```

Returns a `BigDecimal` equal to the difference this `BigDecimal` and n. The number of digits of accuracy in the result is equal to max(n, **this**.`scale()`).

```
BigInteger toBigInteger()
```

Returns a `BigInteger` representation of this `BigDecimal`.

```
String toString()
```

Returns a `String` representation of the value of this `BigDecimal`.

```
BigInteger unscaledValue()
```

Returns a `BigInteger` representation of the product of this `BigDecimal` and $10^{scale()}$.

| math | **class BigInteger extends** Number **implements** Comparable |

PURPOSE

Represent immutable integer numbers of arbitrary precision. The integer is represented in two's complement form.

FIELD SUMMARY

> **static** BigInteger ONE
>> Represents the BigInteger corresponding to 1.
> **static** BigInteger ZERO
>> Represents the BigInteger corresponding to 0.

CLASS METHOD SUMMARY V

> **static** BigInteger probablePrime(**int** n, Random r)
>> Returns an n-bit pseudorandomly generated positive BigInteger using r.
> **static** BigInteger valueOf(**long** n)
>> Returns a BigInteger whose value is equal to n.

CONSTRUCTOR SUMMARY

> BigInteger(**byte**[] a)
>> Constructs a new BigInteger corresponding to the two's-complement binary representation represented by array **a**.
> BigInteger(**int** s, **byte**[] a)
>> Constructs a BigInteger corresponding to the two's-complement binary representation represented by array **a**. The sign of the number is determined by s. If s is 1, then the number is positive; if s is 0, then the number is 0; and if s is –1, then the number is negative.
> BigInteger(**int** n, **int** m, Random r)
>> Constructs using r an n-bit pseudorandomly generated positive BigInteger whose probability of being composite is at most $1 / 2^m$.
> BigInteger(**int** n, Random r)
>> Constructs a new n-bit pseudorandomly generated positive BigInteger using r.
> BigInteger(String s)
>> Constructs a new BigInteger using s as a text-based representation of a number.
> BigInteger(String s, **int** r)
>> Constructs a new BigInteger using s as a text-based, radix r representation of a number.

INSTANCE METHOD SUMMARY V

> BigInteger abs()
>> Returns a BigInteger equal to the absolute value of this BigInteger. The scaling factor in the result is equal to **this**.scale().
> BigInteger add(BigInteger n)
>> Returns a BigInteger equal to the sum of n and this BigInteger. The scaling factor in the result is equal to max(n, **this**.scale()).
> BigInteger and(BigInteger n)
>> Returns a BigInteger whose value is the bitwise logical and of this BigInteger and n.

`BigInteger andNot(BigInteger n)`

Returns a `BigInteger` whose value is the logical and of this `BigInteger` and the complement of n.

`int bitCount()`

Returns the number of bits in the two's-complement representation of this `BigInteger` that are equal to the complement of its sign bit.

`int bitLength()`

Returns $n-1$, where n equals number of bits in the minimal two's-complement representation of this `BigInteger`.

`BigInteger clearBit(int i)`

Returns a `BigInteger` whose value is equal to this `BigInteger` with the ith bit cleared.

`int compareTo(BigInteger n)`

Returns a negative value, zero, or a positive value depending respectively on whether the `BigInteger` value represented by this object is less than, equal to, or greater than n.

`int compareTo(Object v)`

Returns a negative value, zero, or a positive value depending respectively on whether the `BigInteger` value represented by this object is less than, equal to, or greater than v.

`BigInteger divide(BigInteger n, int m)`

Returns a `BigInteger` equal to the integer division of this `BigInteger` by n.

`BigInteger divide(BigInteger n, int d, int m)`

Returns a `BigInteger` equal to this `BigInteger` divided by n.

`BigInteger[] divideAndRemainder(BigInteger n)`

Returns a two-element `BigInteger` array with the first element equal to the quotient of this `BigInteger` divided by n and the element equal to the remainder of this `BigInteger` divided by n.

`double doubleValue()`

Returns a **double** representation of this `BigInteger`.

`boolean equals(Object x)`

Returns **true** if and only if v is an instance of `BigInteger` representing the same numeric value with the same scaling factor that this object represents.

`BigInteger flipBit(int i)`

Returns a `BigInteger` whose value is equal to this `BigInteger` with the ith bit flipped.

`float floatValue()`

Returns a **float** representation of this `BigInteger`.

`BigInteger gcd(BigInteger n)`

Returns a `BigInteger` whose value is the greatest common divisor of this `BigInteger` and n.

`int getLowestSetBit()`

Returns the index of the least significant one-bit in this `BigInteger`.

`int hashCode()`

Returns the hash code of this `BigInteger`.

`int intValue()`

Returns an **int** representation of this `BigInteger`.

```
boolean isProbablePrime(int m)
```

Returns **true** if the probability that this `BigInteger` is composite is at most $1 / 2^m$.

```
long longValue()
```

Returns a **long** representation of this `BigInteger`.

```
BigInteger max(BigInteger n)
```

Returns the maximum of n and this `BigInteger`.

```
BigInteger min(BigInteger n)
```

Returns the minimum of n and this `BigInteger`.

```
BigInteger mod(BigInteger n)
```

Returns a `BigInteger` whose value is the remainder of this `BigInteger` divided by n.

```
BigInteger modInverse(BigInteger n)
```

Returns a `BigInteger` whose value is the remainder of k by n, where k is one less than this `BigInteger`.

```
BigInteger modPow(BigInteger m, BigInteger n)
```

Returns a `BigInteger` whose value is the remainder of k by n, where k is this `BigInteger` raised to the power m.

```
BigInteger multiply(BigInteger n)
```

Returns a `BigInteger` equal to the product of n and this `BigInteger`.

```
BigInteger negate()
```

Returns a `BigInteger` equal to the additive inverse of this `BigInteger`.

```
BigInteger not()
```

Returns a `BigInteger` equal to the bitwise complement of this `BigInteger`.

```
BigInteger or(BigInteger n)
```

Returns a `BigInteger` equal to the bitwise logical or of n and this `BigInteger`.

```
BigInteger pow(int n)
```

Returns a `BigInteger` equal to this `BigInteger` raised to the power n.

```
BigInteger remainder(BigInteger n)
```

Returns a BigInteger equal to the remainder of this `BigInteger` divided by n.

```
BigInteger setBit(int i)
```

Returns a `BigInteger` equal to this `BigInteger` with the ith bit set.

```
BigInteger shiftLeft(int n)
```

Returns a `BigInteger` equal to this `BigInteger` multiplied by 2^n.

```
BigInteger shiftRight(int n)
```

Returns a `BigInteger` equal to this `BigInteger` divided by 2^n.

```
int signum()
```

Returns -1, 0, or 1 depending on whether this `BigInteger` is respectively negative, zero, or positive.

```
BigInteger subtract(BigInteger n)
```

Returns a `BigInteger` equal to the difference this `BigInteger` and n.

```
boolean testBit(int i)
```

Returns **true** if this `BigInteger` has its ith bit set; otherwise, returns **false**.

```
byte[] toByteArray()
```

Returns the two's-complement representation of this `BigInteger` as a **byte** array.

```
String toString()
```
Returns a `String` representation of the value of this `BigInteger`.
```
String toString(int r)
```
Returns a `String` representation of the value of this `BigInteger` in radix r.
```
BigInteger xor(BigInteger n)
```
Returns a `BigInteger` equal to the bitwise exclusive or of n and this `BigInteger`.

net   `final class` URL `implements` Serializable

PURPOSE

Represent a Universal Resource Locator (i.e., a Web resource).

CLASS METHOD SUMMARY
```
static void setURLStreamHandlerFactory(URLStreamHandlerFactory
  f)
```
Sets the `URLStreamHandlerFactory` of the program to f.

CONSTRUCTOR SUMMARY
```
URL(String s)
```
Constructs a new URL object using s.
```
URL(String p, String h, int n, String f)
```
Constructs a new URL object using protocol p, host h, port number n, and file f.
```
URL(String p, String h, int n, String f, URLStreamHandler u)
```
Constructs a new URL object using protocol p, host h, port number n, file f, and handler u.
```
URL(String p, String h, String f)
```
Constructs a new URL object using protocol p, host h, and file f.
```
URL(URL u, String s)
```
Constructs a new URL object by using s within URL context u.
```
URL(URL u, String s, URLStreamHandler h)
```
Constructs a new URL object by using s with handler h within URL context u.

INSTANCE METHOD SUMMARY
```
boolean equals(Object v)
```
Returns **true** if and only if v is an instance of URL specifying the same Web resource.

```
String getAuthority()
```
Returns the authority of this URL.
```
Object getContent()
```
Returns the contents of this URL.
```
Object getContent(Class[] t)
```
Returns the first contents of this URL that matches a type in t.
```
int getDefaultPort()
```
Returns the default port number of the protocol associated with this URL.
```
String getFile()
```
Returns the file name of this URL.
```
String getHost()
```
Return the host name of this URL.
```
String getPath()
```
Returns the path of this URL.
```
int getPort()
```
Returns the port number of this URL.
```
String getProtocol()
```
Returns the protocol of this URL.
```
String getQuery()
```
Returns the query part of this URL.
```
String getRef()
```
Returns the anchor of this URL.
```
String getUserInfo()
```
Returns the user information of this URL.
```
int hashCode()
```
Returns the hash code of this URL.
```
URLConnection openConnection()
```
Returns a URLConnection representing a connection to the Web resource repre-
sented by this URL.
```
InputStream openStream()
```
Returns an **InputStream** for reading the opened connection to this URL.
```
boolean sameFhile(URL u)
```
Returns **true** if this URL is the same as u excluding their fragment components;
otherwise, returns **false**.
```
protected void set(String p, String h, int n, String f, String
  r)
```
Sets the protocol, host, port number, file, and internal reference fields of this URL
to respectively p, h, n, f, and r.
```
protected void set(String p, String h, int n, String a, String
  u, String path, String q, String r)
```
Sets the protocol, host, port number, authority, user information, file, query, and
internal reference fields of this URL to respectively p, h, n, a, u, f, q, and r.
```
String toExternalForm()
```
Returns a String representation of the value of this URL.
```
String toString()
```
Returns a String representation of the value of this URL.

net	**class** URLEncoder

PURPOSE

Provides a method for converting a String to HTML.

CLASS METHOD SUMMARY

static String encode(String s, String e)
  throws UnsupportedEncodingException

> Returns a String representing s in application/x-www-form-urlencoded format using encoding scheme e for unsafe characters.

D.5	**JAVA.TEXT**

---

text	**abstract class** DateFormat **extends** Format

PURPOSE

Provides methods for formatting and parsing dates and times and serves as an abstract superclass for date and time formatting.

FIELD SUMMARY

static int AM_PM_FIELD

> Represents the AM_PM alignment field.

protected Calendar calendar

> Represents the calendar that produces the time field values.

static int DATE_FIELD

> Represents the DATE alignment field.

static int DAY_OF_WEEK_FIELD

> Represents the DAY_OF_WEEK alignment field.

static int DAY_OF_WEEK_IN_MONTH_FIELD

> Represents the DAY_OF_WEEK_IN_MONTH alignment field.

static int DAY_OF_YEAR_FIELD

> Represents the DAY_OF_YEAR alignment field.

static int DEFAULT

> Represents default style pattern.

static int ERA_FIELD

> Represents the ERA alignment field.

static int FULL

> Represents full style pattern.

```
static int HOUR_OF_DAY0_FIELD
```
Represents the zero-based HOUR_OF_DAY alignment field.
```
static int HOUR_OF_DAY1_FIELD
```
Represents the one-based HOUR_OF_DAY alignment field.
```
static int HOUR0_FIELD
```
Represents the zero-based HOUR alignment field.
```
static int HOUR1_FIELD
```
Represents the one-based HOUR alignment field.
```
static int LONG
```
Represents long style pattern.
```
static int MEDIUM
```
Represents medium style pattern.
```
static int MILLISECOND_FIELD
```
Represents the MILLISECOND alignment field.
```
static int MINUTE_FIELD
```
Represents the MINUTE alignment field.
```
static int MONTH_FIELD
```
Represents the MONTH alignment field.
```
protected NumberFormat numberFormat
```
Represents the NumberFormat that formats date and time numbers.
```
static int SECOND_FIELD
```
Represents the SECOND alignment field.
```
static int SHORT
```
Represents short style pattern.
```
static int TIMEZONE_FIELD
```
Represents the TIMEZONE alignment field.
```
static int WEEK_OF_MONTH_FIELD
```
Represents the WEEK_OF_MONTH alignment field.
```
static int WEEK_OF_YEAR_FIELD
```
Represents the WEEK_OF_YEAR alignment field.
```
static int YEAR_FIELD
```
Represents the YEAR alignment field.

CLASS METHOD SUMMARY
```
static Locale[] getAvailableLocales()
```
Returns an array of possible DateFormat locales.
```
static DateFormat getDateInstance()
```
Returns a DateFormat using the default date formatting style for the default locale.
```
static DateFormat getDateInstance(int d)
```
Returns a DateFormat using date formatting style d for the default locale.
```
static DateFormat getDateInstance(int d, Locale l)
```
Returns a DateFormat using date formatting style d for locale l.
```
static DateFormat getDateTimeInstance()
```
Returns a DateFormat using the default date and time formatting style for the default locale.

`static` `DateFormat getDateTimeInstance(`**`int`**` d, `**`int`**` t)`

Returns the `DateFormat` using date formatting style d and time formatting style t for the default locale.

`static` `DateFormat getDateTimeInstance(`**`int`**` d, `**`int`**` t, Locale l)`

Returns a `DateFormat` using date formatting style d and time formatting style t for locale l.

`static` `DateFormat getInstance()`

Returns a `DateFormat` using the date and time SHORT formatting style for the default locale.

`static` `DateFormat getTimeInstance()`

Returns a `DateFormat` using the default time formatting style for the default locale.

`static` `DateFormat getTimeInstance(`**`int`**` t)`

Returns a `DateFormat` using time formatting style t for the default locale.

`static` `DateFormat getTimeInstance(`**`int`**` t, Locale l)`

Returns a `DateFormat` using time formatting style t for locale l.

CONSTRUCTOR SUMMARY

`protected` `DateFormat()`

Constructs a new date format.

INSTANCE METHOD SUMMARY

`Object clone()`

Returns a new clone of this `DateFormat`.

`boolean` `equals(Object v)`

Returns **true** if and only if v is an instance of `DateFormat` representing the same date format value that this object represents.

`String format(Date d)`

Formats date d into a date and time string using this `DateFormat`.

`abstract` `StringBuffer format(Date d, StringBuffer s, FieldPosition f)`

Returns s after formatting date d into a date and time string into s using this `DateFormat`. If f indicates a field, then its indices are updated to reflect the position of the field within s.

`final` `StringBuffer format(Object d, StringBuffer s, FieldPosition f)`

Returns s after formatting date d into a date and time string into s using this `DateFormat`. If f indicates a field, then its indices are updated to reflect the position of the field within s.

`Calendar getCalendar()`

Returns the calendar of this `DateFormat`.

`NumberFormat getNumberFormat()`

Returns the number formatter of this `DateFormat`.

`TimeZone getTimeZone()`

Returns the time zone of this `DateFormat`.

`int` `hashCode()`

Returns the hash code of this `DateFormat`.

```
boolean isLenient()
```

Returns whether this `DateFormat` parses dates and times leniently (i.e., whether strings need not absolutely follow the date and time specification).

```
Date parse(String s)
```

Parses `s` to produce a date using this `DateFormat`.

```
abstract Date parse(String s, ParsePosition i)
```

Parses `s` to produce a date using this `DateFormat`. The parsing starts with the parse position indicated by `i`. Upon completion of parsing, `i` reflects the last parsed position.

```
Object parseObject(String s, ParsePosition i)
```

Parses `s` to produce a date using this `DateFormat`. The parsing starts with the parse position indicated by `i`. Upon completion of parsing, `i` reflects the last parsed position.

```
void setCalendar(Calendar c)
```

Sets to `c` the calendar used by this `DateFormat`.

```
void setLenient(boolean b)
```

Sets whether date and time parsing is to be lenient by this `DateFormat` (i.e., whether strings need not absolutely follow the date and time specification).

```
void setNumberFormat(NumberFormat n)
```

Sets to `n` the number formatter used by this `DateFormat`.

```
void setTimeZone(TimeZone t)
```

Sets to `t` the time zone for the calendar used by this `DateFormat`.

| text | **static class** DateFormat.Field **extends** Format.Field |

PURPOSE

Represents `DateFormat` field positions.

FIELD SUMMARY

```
static DateFormat.Field AM_PM
```

Represents the time of day indicator field in the formatting of a date and format.

```
static DateFormat.Field DAY_OF_MONTH
```

Represents the day of month field in the formatting of a date and format.

```
static DateFormat.Field DAY_OF_WEEK
```

Represents the day of week field in the formatting of a date and format.

```
static DateFormat.Field DAY_OF_WEEK_IN_MONTH
```

Represents the day of week in month field in the formatting of a date and format.

```
static DateFormat.Field DAY_OF_YEAR
```

Represents the day of year field in the formatting of a date and format.

```
static DateFormat.Field ERA
```

Represents the era field in the formatting of a date and format.

```
static DateFormat.Field HOUR_OF_DAY0
```

Represents the hour of day field in the zero-based formatting of a date and time format (i.e., the legal values are 0 to 23).

`static` DateFormat.Field HOUR_OF_DAY1

Represents the hour of day field in the one-based formatting of a date and time format (i.e., the legal values are 1 to 24).

`static` DateFormat.Field HOUR0

Represents the hour field in the zero-based formatting of a date and time format (i.e., the legal values are 0 to 11).

`static` DateFormat.Field HOUR1

Represents the hour field in the one-based formatting of a date and time format (i.e., the legal values are 1 to 12).

`static` DateFormat.Field MILLISECOND

Represents the millisecond field in the formatting of a date and format.

`static` DateFormat.Field MINUTE

Represents the minute field in the formatting of a date and format.

`static` DateFormat.Field MONTH

Represents the month field in the formatting of a date and format.

`static` DateFormat.Field SECOND

Represents the second field in the formatting of a date and format.

`static` DateFormat.Field TIME_ZONE

Represents the time zone field in the formatting of a date and format.

`static` DateFormat.Field WEEK_OF_MONTH

Represents the week of month field in the formatting of a date and format.

`static` DateFormat.Field WEEK_OF_YEAR

Represents the week of year field in the formatting of a date and format.

`static` DateFormat.Field YEAR

represents the year field in the formatting of a date and format.

CONSTRUCTOR SUMMARY

`protected` DateFormat.Field(String s, `int` n)

Constructs a new `DateFormat.Field` with the name s for field n.

INSTANCE METHOD SUMMARY

`int` getCalendarField()

Returns the `Calendar` field of this `DateFormat.Field`.

`static` DateFormat.Field ofCalendarField(`int` f)

Returns the `DateFormat.Field` constant corresponding to the `Calendar` field f.

`protected` Object readResolve()

Returns a resolved field.

---

text | **abstract class** NumberFormat **extends** Format

PURPOSE

Provides methods for formatting and parsing numbers and serves as an abstract superclass for number formatting.

FIELD SUMMARY

`static int` FRACTION_FIELD

Indicates the fraction field of a `FieldPosition`.

```
static int INTEGER_FIELD
```
Indicates the integer field of a `FieldPosition`.

CLASS METHOD SUMMARY

```
static Locale[] getAvailableLocales()
```
Returns the array of possible `NumberFormat` locales.

```
static NumberFormat getCurrencyInstance()
```
Returns a default currency `NumberFormat` for the default locale.

```
static NumberFormat getCurrencyInstance(Locale l)
```
Returns a default currency `NumberFormat` for the locale l.

```
static NumberFormat getInstance()
```
Returns a default `NumberFormat` for the default locale.

```
static NumberFormat getInstance(Locale l)
```
Returns a default `NumberFormat` for locale l.

```
static NumberFormat getIntegerInstance()
```
Returns a default integer `NumberFormat` for the default locale.

```
static NumberFormat getIntegerInstance(Locale l)
```
Returns a default integer `NumberFormat` for locale l.

```
static NumberFormatgetNumberInstance()
```
Returns a default number `NumberFormat` for the default locale.

```
static NumberFormat getNumberInstance(Locale l)
```
Returns a default number `NumberFormat` for locale l.

```
static NumberFormat getPercentInstance()
```
Returns a default percentage `NumberFormat` for the default locale.

```
static NumberFormat getPercentInstance(Locale l)
```
Returns a default percentage `NumberFormat` for locale l.

CONSTRUCTOR SUMMARY

```
NumberFormat()
```
Constructs a new `NumberFormat` number formatter.

INSTANCE METHOD SUMMARY

```
Object clone()
```
Returns a clone of this `NumberFormat`.

```
boolean equals(Object v)
```
Returns **true** if and only if v is an instance of `NumberFormat` representing the same format value that this object represents.

```
String format(double n)
```
Formats number n into a string using this `NumberFormat`.

```
abstract StringBuffer format(double n, StringBuffer s,
   FieldPosition f)
```
Returns s after formatting number n into string s using this `NumberFormat`. If f indicates a field, then its indices are updated to reflect the position of the field within s.

```
String format(long n)
```
Formats number n into a string using this `NumberFormat`.

```
abstract StringBuffer format(long n, StringBuffer s,
  FieldPosition f)
```

Returns s after formatting number n into string s using this NumberFormat. If f indicates a field, then its indices are updated to reflect the position of the field within s.

```
StringBuffer format(Object n, StringBuffer s, FieldPosition f)
```

Returns s after formatting the number represented by n into string s using this NumberFormat. If f indicates a field, then its indices are updated to reflect the position of the field within s.

```
Currency getCurrency()
```

Returns the currency format used by this NumberFormat.

```
int getMaximumFractionDigits()
```

Returns the maximum number of digits used in formatting the fractional part of a number by this NumberFormat.

```
int getMaximumIntegerDigits()
```

Returns the maximum number of digits used in formatting the integer part of a number by this NumberFormat.

```
int getMinimumFractionDigits()
```

Returns the minimum number of digits used in formatting the fractional part of a number by this NumberFormat.

```
int getMinimumIntegerDigits()
```

Returns the minimum number of digits used in formatting the integer part of a number by this NumberFormat.

```
int hashCode()
```

Returns the hash code of this NumberFormat.

```
boolean isGroupingUsed()
```

Returns whether this NumberFormat uses grouping.

```
boolean isParseIntegerOnly()
```

Returns whether this NumberFormat only parses numbers as integers.

```
Number parse(String s)
```

Parses s to produce a number using this DateFormat.

```
abstract Number parse(String s, ParsePosition i)
```

Parses s to produce a Number using this NumberFormat. The parsing starts with the parse position indicated by i. Upon completion of parsing, i reflects the last parsed position. The preferred actual type is Long. If Long is unsuitable, then Double is used.

```
Object parseObject(String s, ParsePosition i)
```

Parses s to produce a Number using this NumberFormat. The parsing starts with the parse position indicated by i. Upon completion of parsing, i reflects the last parsed position.

```
void setCurrency(Currency c)
```

Sets to c the Currency used by this NumberFormat.

```
void setGroupingUsed(boolean b)
```

Sets whether this NumberFormat uses grouping.

```
void setMaximumFractionDigits(int n)
```

Sets to n the maximum number of digits used in formatting the fractional part of a number by this NumberFormat.

```
void setMaximumIntegerDigits(int n)
```
Sets to n the maximum number of digits used in formatting the integer part of a number by this `NumberFormat`.
```
void setMinimumFractionDigits(int n)
```
Sets to n the minimum number of digits used in formatting the fractional part of a number by this `NumberFormat`.
```
void setMinimumIntegerDigits(int n)
```
Sets to n the minimum number of digits used in formatting the integer part of a number by this `NumberFormat`.
```
void setParseIntegerOnly(boolean b)
```
Sets whether this `NumberFormat` parses numbers only as integers.

---

text   `static class NumberFormat.Field extends Format.Field`

PURPOSE
Provide field constants for number formatting.

FIELD SUMMARY
```
static NumberFormat.Field CURRENCY
```
Represents the currency field in the formatting of a number.
```
static NumberFormat.Field DECIMAL_SEPARATOR
```
Represents the decimal separator field in the formatting of a number.
```
static NumberFormat.Field EXPONENT
```
Represents the exponent field in the formatting of a number.
```
static NumberFormat.Field EXPONENT_SIGN
```
Represents the exponent sign field in the formatting of a number.
```
static NumberFormat.Field EXPONENT_SYMBOL
```
Represents the exponent symbol field in the formatting of a number.
```
static NumberFormat.Field FRACTION
```
Represents the fraction field in the formatting of a number.
```
static NumberFormat.Field GROUPING_SEPARATOR
```
Represents the grouping separator field in the formatting of a number.
```
static NumberFormat.Field INTEGER
```
Represents the integer field in the formatting of a number.
```
static NumberFormat.Field PERCENT
```
Represents the percent field in the formatting of a number.
```
static NumberFormat.Field PERMILLE
```
Represents the permille field in the formatting of a number.
```
static NumberFormat.Field SIGN
```
Represents the sign field in the formatting of a number.

CONSTRUCTOR SUMMARY
```
protected NumberFormat.Field(String s)
```
Constructs a new `NumberFormat.Field` with name s.

INSTANCE METHOD SUMMARY
```
protected Object readResolve()
```
Returns a resolved field.

D.6	**JAVA.UTIL**

util	**class** ArrayList **extends** AbstractList **implements** List, Cloneable, RandomAccess, Serializable

PURPOSE

Represents a resizable array with complete List functionality. An ArrayList has been designed so that its element accessor and mutator methods are guaranteed to be very efficient. Its element accessor and mutator methods run in *constant time*. Adding (*appending*) an element to the end of the list is guaranteed to be fast on average (i.e., an append operation operates in constant time on average). The class also provides a number of other methods for inserting and deleting elements to the list. These other methods can require time proportional to the number of elements in the list to perform their tasks (i.e., these methods run in *linear time*). Associated with each ArrayList is a *capacity*, which is the maximum number of elements that the list can currently store without growing.

CONSTRUCTOR SUMMARY

ArrayList()

Constructs an empty list with initial capacity to represent 10 elements.

add(Collection c)

Constructs a list containing the elements of c.

ArrayList(**int** n)

Constructs an empty list with an initial capacity to represent n elements.

INSTANCE METHOD SUMMARY

void add(**int** i, Object v)

Inserts value v into the list such that v has index i. Any preexisting elements with indices i or greater are shifted backward by one element position.

boolean add(Object v)

Appends the list with a new element with value v and returns **true**.

boolean addAll(Collection c)

Appends the list with all of the elements in c and returns **true** if the list has changed.

boolean addAll(**int** i, Collection c)

Inserts the elements of c into this list and returns **true** if the list has changed. Any preexisting elements with indices i or greater are shifted backward by one element position.

void clear()

Removes all elements from the list.

Object clone()

Returns a shallow copy of this list.

boolean contains(Object v)

Returns whether the list has an element with value v.

void ensureCapacity(**int** n)

Ensures that the list has the capacity to represent n elements.

Object get(**int** i)

If i is a valid index, it returns the ith element; otherwise an exception is generated.

int indexOf(Object v)

Returns the index of the first occurrence of v in the list. If v is not in the list, then −1 is returned.

boolean isEmpty()

Returns **true** if there are no elements; otherwise, it returns **false**.

int lastIndexOf(Object v)

Returns the index of the last occurrence of v in the list. If v is not in the list, then −1 is returned.

Object remove(**int** i)

If i is a valid index, it removes the ith element from the list by shifting forward elements i+1 and on. In addition, the removed value is returned. Otherwise, an exception is generated.

Object removeRange(**int** i, **int** j)

Removes elements from list whose indices are in the interval i … j-1. Elements with indices j+1 and on are shifted forward to replace the removed elements. With this definition, if j ≤ i, then no elements are removed.

Object set(**int** i, Object v)

If i is a valid index, then the ith element is set to v and the previous value of the element is returned. Otherwise, an exception is thrown.

int size()

Returns the numbers of elements in the list.

Object[] toArray()

Returns an array whose elements correspond to the elements of this list.

Object[] toArray(Object[] a)

Returns an array of the same type as array a whose elements correspond to the elements of this list. The returned array is a if a is big enough.

void trimToSize()

Sets the capacity of this list to size().

---

util		**class** Arrays

PURPOSE

Provide basic array manipulation functionality.

INSTANCE METHOD SUMMARY

static List asList(Object[] a)

Returns a fixed-size List backed by array a.

static int binarySearch(**byte**[] a, **byte** v)

Returns the index of v in sorted array a. If v is not in a, then it returns i-1, where i is the minimal index such that v < a[i].

static int binarySearch(**char**[] a, **char** v)

Returns the index of v in sorted array a. If v is not in a, then it returns i-1, where i is the minimal index such that v < a[i].

```
static int binarySearch(double[] a, double v)
```
Returns the index of v in sorted array a. If v is not in a, then it returns i-1, where i is the minimal index such that v < a[i].
```
static int binarySearch(float[] a, float v)
```
Returns the index of v in sorted array a. If v is not in a, then it returns i-1, where i is the minimal index such that v < a[i].
```
static int binarySearch(int[] a, int v)
```
Returns the index of v in sorted array a. If v is not in a, then it returns i-1, where i is the minimal index such that v < a[i].
```
static int binarySearch(long[] a, long v)
```
Returns the index of v in sorted array a. If v is not in a, then it returns i-1, where i is the minimal index such that v < a[i].
```
static int binarySearch(Object[] a, Object v)
```
Returns the index of v in naturally sorted array a using a binary search algorithm. If v is not in a, then it returns i-1, where i is the minimal index such that v < a[i].
```
static int binarySearch(Object[] a, Object v, Comparator c)
```
Returns the index of v in sorted array a with respect to comparator c using a binary search algorithm. If v is not in a, then it returns i-1, where i is the minimal index such that v < a[i].
```
static int binarySearch(short[] a, short v)
```
Returns the index of v in sorted array a. If v is not in a, then it returns i-1, where i is the minimal index such that v < a[i].
```
static boolean equals(boolean[] a1, boolean[] a2)
```
Returns whether the elements of a1 and a2 are all pairwise equal.
```
static boolean equals(byte[] a1, byte[] a2)
```
Returns whether the elements of a1 and a2 are all pairwise equal.
```
static boolean equals(char[] a1, char[] a2)
```
Returns whether the elements of a1 and a2 are all pairwise equal.
```
static boolean equals(double[] a1, double[] a2)
```
Returns whether the elements of a1 and a2 are all pairwise equal.
```
static boolean equals(float[] a1, float[] a2)
```
Returns whether the elements of a1 and a2 are all pairwise equal.
```
static boolean equals(int[] a1, int[] a2)
```
Returns whether the elements of a1 and a2 are all pairwise equal.
```
static boolean equals(long[] a1, long[] a2)
```
Returns whether the elements of a1 and a2 are all pairwise equal.
```
static boolean equals(Object[] a1, Object[] a2)
```
Returns whether the elements of a1 and a2 are all pairwise equal.
```
static boolean equals(short[] a1, short[] a2)
```
Returns whether the elements of a1 and a2 are all pairwise equal.
```
static void fill(boolean[] a, boolean v)
```
Assigns value v to the elements of array a.
```
static void fill(boolean[] a, int i, int j, boolean v)
```
Assigns value v to elements i through j-1 of array a.
```
static void fill(byte[] a, byte v)
```
Assigns value v to the elements of array a.

```
static void fill(byte[] a, int i, int j, byte v)
```
Assigns value v to elements i through j-1 of array a.
```
static void fill(char[] a, char v)
```
Assigns value v to the elements of array a.
```
static void fill(char[] a, int i, int j, char v)
```
Assigns value v to elements i through j-1 of array a.
```
static void fill(double[] a, int i, int j, double v)
```
Assigns value v to elements i through j-1 of array a.
```
static void fill(double[] a, double v)
```
Assigns value v to the elements of array a.
```
static void fill(float[] a, int i, int j, float v)
```
Assigns value v to elements i through j-1 of array a.
```
static void fill(float[] a, float v)
```
Assigns value v to the elements of array a.
```
static void fill(int[] a, int i, int j, int v)
```
Assigns value v to elements i through j-1 of array a.
```
static void fill(int[] a, int v)
```
Assigns value v to the elements of array a.
```
static void fill(long[] a, int i, int j, long v)
```
Assigns value v to elements i through j-1 of array a.
```
static void fill(long[] a, long v)
```
Assigns value v to the elements of array a.
```
static void fill(Object[] a, int i, int j, Object v)
```
Assigns value v to elements i through j-1 of array a.
```
static void fill(Object[] a, Object v)
```
Assigns value v to the elements of array a.
```
static void fill(short[] a, int i, int j, short v)
```
Assigns value v to elements i through j-1 of array a.
```
static void fill(short[] a, short v)
```
Assigns value v to the elements of array a.
```
static void sort(byte[] a)
```
Sorts array a into nondescending order.
```
static void sort(byte[] a, int i, int j)
```
Sorts elements i through j-1 of array a into nondescending order.
```
static void sort(char[] a)
```
Sorts array a into nondescending order.
```
static void sort(char[] a, int i, int j)
```
Sorts elements i through j-1 of array a into nondescending order.
```
static void sort(double[] a)
```
Sorts array a into nondescending order.
```
static void sort(double[] a, int i, int j)
```
Sorts elements i through j-1 of array a into nondescending order.
```
static void sort(float[] a)
```
Sorts array a into nondescending order.
```
static void sort(float[] a, int i, int j)
```
Sorts elements i through j-1 of array a into nondescending order.

```
static void sort(int[] a)
```
Sorts array a into nondescending order.
```
static void sort(int[] a, int i, int j)
```
Sorts elements i through j-1 of array a into nondescending order.
```
static void sort(long[] a)
```
Sorts array a into nondescending order.
```
static void sort(long[] a, int i, int j)
```
Sorts elements i through j-1 of array a into nondescending order.
```
static void sort(Object[] a)
```
Sorts array a into nondescending order using the natural ordering.
```
static void sort(Object[] a, Comparator c)
```
Sorts array a into nondescending order using comparator c.
```
static void sort(Object[] a, int i, int j)
```
Sorts elements i through j-1 of array a into nondescending order using the natural ordering.
```
static void sort(Object[] a, int i, int j, Comparator c)
```
Sorts elements i through j-1 of array a into nondescending order using comparator c.
```
static void sort(short[] a)
```
Sorts array a into nondescending order.
```
static void sort(short[] a, int i, int j)
```
Sorts elements i through j-1 of array a into nondescending order.

| util | **abstract class** Calendar **implements** Cloneable, Serializable |

PURPOSE

Represent a calendar and provide conversion methods for dates

FIELD SUMMARY

```
static int AM
```
Represents the period from midnight to just before noon for the AM_PM field.
```
static int AM_PM
```
Represents the field for whether the hours is before or after noon.
```
static int APRIL
```
Represents the fourth month of the year for the MONTH field.
```
protected boolean areFieldsSet
```
Indicates whether the fields of this Calendar agree with the currently set time.
```
static int AUGUST
```
Represents the eighth month of the year for the MONTH field.
```
static int DATE
```
Represents the field for the day of the month.
```
static int DAY_OF_MONTH
```
Represents the field for the day of the week within the day of the month.
```
static int DAY_OF_WEEK
```
Represents the field for the day of the week.

```
static int DAY_OF_WEEK_IN_MONTH
```
Represents the field for the day of the week within the current month.
```
static int DAY_OF_YEAR
```
Represents the field for the day number within the current year.
```
static int DECEMBER
```
Represents the twelfth month of the year for the MONTH field.
```
static int DST_OFFSET
```
Represents the field for the daylight savings milliseconds offset.
```
static int ERA
```
Represents the field for the era in the Julian calendar.
```
static int FEBRUARY
```
Represents the second month of the year for the MONTH field.
```
static int FIELD_COUNT
```
Represents the number of distinct `Calendar` fields.
```
protected int[] fields
```
The field values for this `Calendar`.
```
static int FRIDAY
```
Represents the Friday for the DAY_OF_WEEK field.
```
static int HOUR
```
Represents the field for the hour in the morning or the afternoon.
```
static int HOUR_OF_DAY
```
Represents the field for the hour in the day.
```
protected boolean[] isSet
```
Indicates which fields of this `Calendar` are set.
```
protected boolean isTimeSet
```
Indicates whether the time has been set.
```
static int JANUARY
```
Represents the first month of the year for the MONTH field.
```
static int JULY
```
Represents the seventh month of the year for the MONTH field.
```
static int JUNE
```
Represents the sixth month of the year for the MONTH field.
```
static int MARCH
```
Represents the third month of the year for the MONTH field.
```
static int MAY
```
Represents the fifth of the year for the MONTH field.
```
static int MILLISECOND
```
Represents the field for the millisecond within the second.
```
static int MINUTE
```
Represents the field for the minute within the hour.
```
static int MONDAY
```
Represents the Monday for the DAY_OF_WEEK field.
```
static int MONTH
```
Represents the field for the month.
```
static int NOVEMBER
```
Represents the eleventh month of the year for the MONTH field.

`static int` OCTOBER

Represents the tenth month of the year for the MONTH field.

`static int` PM

Represents the period from noon to just before midnight for the AM_PM field.

`static int` SATURDAY

Represents the Saturday for the DAY_OF_WEEK field.

`static int` SECOND

Represents the field for the second within the minute.

`static int` SEPTEMBER

Represents the ninth month of the year for the MONTH field.

`static int` SUNDAY

Represents the Sunday for the DAY_OF_WEEK field.

`static int` THURSDAY

Represents the Thursday for the DAY_OF_WEEK field.

`protected long` time

Represents the currently set time for this `Calendar`. The value is expressed as the number of milliseconds since January 1, 1970, 0:00:00 GMT.

`static int` TUESDAY

Represents the Tuesday for the DAY_OF_WEEK field.

`static int` UNDECIMBER

Represents the thirteenth month of the year for the MONTH field.

`static int` WEDNESDAY

Represents the Wednesday for the DAY_OF_WEEK field.

`static int` WEEK_OF_MONTH

Represents the field for the week number within the current month.

`static int` WEEK_OF_YEAR

Represents the field for the week number within the current year.

`static int` YEAR

Represents the field for the year.

`static int` ZONE_OFFSET

Represents the field for the raw milliseconds offset from GMT.

CLASS METHOD SUMMARY

`static Locale[]` getAvailableLocales()

Returns an array of available locales.

`static Calendar` getInstance()

Returns a `Calendar` for the default time zone and locale

`static Calendar` getInstance(Locale l)

Returns a `Calendar` for the default time zone for locale l.

`static Calendar` getInstance(TimeZone t)

Returns a `Calendar` for the default locale for time zone t.

`static Calendar` getInstance(TimeZone t, Locale l)

Returns a `Calendar` for time zone t and locale l.

CONSTRUCTOR SUMMARY

`protected Calendar`()

Constructs a new `Calendar` for the default time zone and locale.

`protected Calendar`(TimeZone t, Locale l

Constructs a new `Calendar` for time zone t and locale l.

INSTANCE METHOD SUMMARY

abstract void add(int f, int n)

Increments field f of this Calendar by amount n.

boolean after(Object t)

Returns whether the time t occurs before the time of this Calendar.

boolean before(Object t)

Returns whether the time t occurs after the time of this Calendar.

void clear()

Clears the time fields of this Calendar.

void clear(int f)

Clears time field f of this Calendar.

Object clone()

Returns a clone of this Calendar.

protected void complete()

Sets any unset fields of this Calendar.

protected abstract void computeFields()

Sets the fields of this Calendar based on the currently set time.

protected abstract void computeTime()

Sets the current time of this Calendar based its field values.

boolean equals(Object v)

Returns **true** if and only if v is an instance of Calendar representing the same calendar time as this Calendar.

int get(int f)

Returns the value of field f for this Calendar.

int getActualMaximum(int f)

Returns the maximum value of field f for this Calendar.

int getActualMinimum(int f)

Returns the minimum value of field f for this Calendar.

int getFirstDayOfWeek()

Returns the first day of the week for the default locale.

abstract int getGreatestMinimum(int f)

Returns the highest minimum value for field f of this Calendar.

abstract int getLeastMaximum(int f)

Returns the lowest maximum value for field f of this Calendar.

abstract int getMaximum(int f)

Returns the maximum value for field f of this Calendar.

int getMinimalDaysInFirstWeek()

Returns the minimal number of days required in the first week of the year for this Calendar.

abstract int getMinimum(int f)

Returns the minimum value for field f for this Calendar.

Date getTime()

Returns the current time for this Calendar.

long getTimeInMillis()

Returns the current time for this Calendar.

TimeZone getTimeZone()

Returns the time zone for this Calendar.

`int` hashCode()

Returns the hash code of this object.

`protected int` internalGet(`int` f)

Returns the value of field f for this `Calendar`.

`boolean` isLenient()

Returns whether date and time parsing is lenient for this `Calendar`.

`boolean` isSet(`int` f)

Returns whether field f of this `Calendar` is set.

`abstract void` roll(`int` f, `boolean` increment)

Increments or decrements field f of this `Calendar` depending on **boolean** value increment.

`void` roll(`int` f, `int` n)

Increments field f of this `Calendar` by n units.

`void` set(`int` f, `int` n)

Sets the field f to n for this `Calendar`.

`void` set(`int` y, `int` m, `int` d)

Sets the year, month, and day respectively to y, m, and d for this `Calendar`.

`void` set(`int` y, `int` m, `int` d, `int` h, `int` n)

Sets the year, month, day, hour, and minute respectively to y, m, d, h, and n for this `Calendar`.

`void` set(`int` y, `int` m, `int` d, `int` h, `int` n, `int` s)

Sets the year, month, day, hour, minute, and second respectively to y, m, d, h, n, and s for this `Calendar`.

`void` setFirstDayOfWeek(`int` d)

Sets the first day of the week to d for this `Calendar`.

`void` setLenient(`boolean` b)

Sets to b whether date and time parsing for this `Calendar` is to be lenient.

`void` setMinimalDaysInFirstWeek(`int` n)

Sets to n the minimal days required in the first week of the year for this `Calendar`.

`void` setTime(`Date` d)

Sets the current time to d this `Calendar`.

`void` setTimeInMillis(`long` n)

Sets current time to n for this `Calendar`.

`void` setTimeZone(`TimeZone` t)

Sets the time zone to t for this `Calendar`.

`String` toString()

Returns a `String` representation of the value of this object.

---

util   **interface** Collection

PURPOSE

Describe a view of a list as a group of elements.

INSTANCE METHOD SUMMARY

`boolean` `add(Object v)`

Ensures that this `Collection` has an element with value v and returns **true** if the collection changes by the addition.

`boolean` `addAll(Collection c)`

Ensures that this `Collection` has all of the element values in c and returns **true** if the collection has changed.

`void` `clear()`

Removes all elements from this `Collection`.

`boolean` `contains(Object v)`

Returns whether this `Collection` has an element with value v.

`boolean` `containsAll(Collection c)`

Returns whether this `Collection` contains all of the values in the collection c.

`boolean` `equals(Object v)`

Returns **true** if and only if v is an instance of `Collection` representing the same collection as this `Collection`.

`int` `hashCode()`

Returns the hash code of this object.

`boolean` `isEmpty()`

Returns whether this `Collection` has any elements.

`Iterator` `iterator()`

Returns an iterator for the elements in this `Collection`.

`boolean` `remove(Object v)`

Attempts to remove an element with value v this `Collection`. Returns whether a value was removed. The operation is optional.

`boolean` `removeAll(Collection c)`

Attempts to remove each of the values in c from this `Collection`. Returns whether a value was removed. The operation is optional.

`boolean` `retainAll(Collection c)`

Attempts to remove from this `Collection` all of the values not in c. Returns whether a value was removed. The operation is optional.

`int` `size()`

Returns the number of elements in this `Collection`.

`Object[]` `toArray()`

Returns an array containing all elements of this `Collection`.

`Object[]` `toArray(Object[] a)`

Returns an array of the same type as array a whose elements correspond to the elements of this `Collection`. The returned array is a if a is big enough.

---

util	**class** Collections

PURPOSE

Provide basic list and collection manipulation functionality.

FIELD SUMMARY

static List EMPTY_LIST

Represents the empty list.

static Map EMPTY_MAP

Represents the empty map.

static Set EMPTY_SET

Represents the empty set.

CLASS METHOD SUMMARY

static int binarySearch(List[] a, Object v)

Returns the index of v in naturally sorted list a using a binary search algorithm. If v is not in a, then it returns i-1, where i is the minimal index such that v < a[i].

static int binarySearch(List[] a, Object v, Comparator c)

Returns the index of v in sorted list a with respect to comparator c using a binary search algorithm. If v is not in a, then it returns i-1, where i is the minimal index such that v < a[i].

static void copy(List t, List s)

Copies the elements from list s to list t.

static Enumeration enumeration(Collection c)

Returns an enumeration of collection c.

static void fill(List a, Object v)

Replaces the elements of the list a with value v.

static int indexOfSubList(List s, List t)

Returns the starting index of the first occurrence of list t within list s. If t is not a sublist of s, then −1 is returned.

static int lastIndexOfSubList(List s, List t)

Returns the starting index of the last occurrence of list t within list s. If t is not a sublist of s, then −1 is returned.

static ArrayList list(Enumeration e)

Returns an **ArrayList** containing the elements of enumeration e.

static Object max(Collection c)

Returns the maximum element of collection c with respect to its natural ordering.

static Object max(Collection a, Comparator c)

Returns the maximum element of collection a with respect to comparator c.

static Object min(Collection c)

Returns the minimum element of collection c with respect to its natural ordering.

static Object min(Collection a, Comparator c)

Returns the minimum element of collection a with respect to comparator c.

static List nCopies(**int** n, Object v)

Returns an n-element immutable list with each element having value v.

static **boolean** replaceAll(List a, Object x, Object y)

Replaces all occurrences of value x with value y in list a. Returns whether list a has changed.

static void reverse(List a)

Reverses the order of the elements in list a.

```
static Comparator reverseOrder()
```
Returns a comparator that is the reverse of the natural ordering on a collection that implements `Comparable`.
```
static void rotate(List a, int n)
```
Performs the equivalent of `n` circular shifts of the elements in list `a`.
```
static void shuffle(List a)
```
Pseudorandomly permutes list `a`.
```
static void shuffle(List a, Random r)
```
Pseudorandomly permutes list `a` using `r`.
```
static Set singleton(Object v)
```
Returns an immutable singleton set containing `v`.
```
static List singletonList(Object v)
```
Returns an immutable single-element list containing `v`.
```
static Map singletonMap(Object v1, Object v2)
```
Returns an immutable single-element map associating `v1` with `v2`.
```
static void sort(List a)
```
Sorts list `a` into nondescending order using the natural ordering.
```
static void sort(List a, Comparator c)
```
Sorts list `a` into nondescending order using comparator `c`.
```
static void swap(List a, int i, int j)
```
Swaps the `i`th and `j`th elements in list `a`.
```
static Collection synchronizedCollection(Collection c)
```
Returns a synchronized collection using collection `c`.
```
static List synchronizedList(List a)
```
Returns a synchronized list using list `a`.
```
static Map synchronizedMap(Map m)
```
Returns a synchronized map using map `m`.
```
static Set synchronizedSet(Set s)
```
Returns a synchronized set using set `s`.
```
static SortedMap synchronizedSortedMap(SortedMap m)
```
Returns a synchronized sorted map using sorted map `m`.
```
static SortedSet synchronizedSortedSet(SortedSet s)
```
Returns a synchronized list sorted set sorted set `s`.
```
static Collection unmodifiableCollection(Collection c)
```
Returns an unmodifiable view of collection `c`.
```
static List unmodifiableList(List a)
```
Returns an unmodifiable view of list `a`.
```
static Map unmodifiableMap(Map m)
```
Returns an unmodifiable view of map `m`.
```
static Set unmodifiableSet(Set s)
```
Returns an unmodifiable view of set `s`.
```
static SortedMap unmodifiableSortedMap(SortedMap m)
```
Returns an unmodifiable view of sorted map `m`.
```
static SortedSet unmodifiableSortedSet(SortedSet s)
```
Returns an unmodifiable view of sorted set `s`.

util	**interface** Comparator

PURPOSE

Describe total ordering comparison functionality.

INSTANCE METHOD SUMMARY

`int` compare(Object v1, Object v2)

Returns a negative integer, zero, or positive integer depending on whether v1 is respectively less than, equal to, or greater than v2.

By convention, class that override this method should fulfill the following contract.

- Symmetry: For any objects x and y, the sign of compare(x, y) should equal – the sign of compare(x, y);
- Transitivity: For any objects x, y, and z, if compare(x, y) and compare(y, z) are both positive, then compare(x, z) is positive;
- Consistency: For any objects x, y, and z, if compare(x, y) is 0, then the signs of compare(x, z) and compare(y, z) are equal.

`boolean` equals(Object v)

Returns whether v is equal to this Comparator.

util	**class** Date **implements** Serializable, Cloneable, Comparable

PURPOSE

Represents time with millisecond precision.

CONSTRUCTOR SUMMARY

Date()

Constructs a Date object that represents the time of its construction.

Date(**long** t)

Constructs a Date object that represents the time corresponding to n milliseconds after January 1, 1970, 00:00:00 GMT.

INSTANCE METHOD SUMMARY

`boolean` after(Date d)

Returns whether the time d occurs before the time of this Date.

`boolean` before(Date d)

Returns whether the time d occurs after the time of this Date.

Object clone()

Returns a clone of this Date.

`int` compareTo(Date d)

Returns a negative value, zero, or a positive value depending respectively on whether the Date value represented by this object is less than, equal to, or greater than d.

`int` compareTo(Object v)

Returns a negative value, zero, or a positive value depending respectively on whether the Date value represented by this object is less than, equal to, or greater than v.

```
boolean equals(Object v)
```
> Returns whether v is equal to this Date.

```
long getTime()
```
> Returns the number of milliseconds since January 1, 1970, 00:00:00 GMT for the time represented by this Date.

```
int hashCode()
```
> Returns the hash code of this object.

```
void setTime(long n)
```
> Sets this Date object that to n milliseconds after January 1, 1970, 00:00:00 GMT.

```
String toString()
```
> Returns a String representation of the value of this object.

---

util	**interface** Enumeration

PURPOSE

Describes list enumeration functionality. This interface is not preferred to Iterator for new implementations.

INSTANCE METHOD SUMMARY

```
boolean hasMoreElements()
```
> Returns whether this Enumeration has more elements to return.

```
Object nextElement()
```
> Returns next element of this Enumeration. If there is no next element, then it throws a NoSuchElementException.

---

util	**class** HashTable **extends** Dictionary **implements** Map, Cloneable, Serializable

PURPOSE

Provides hash table functionality that maps keys to values.

CONSTRUCTOR SUMMARY

```
Hashtable()
```
> Constructs a new HashTable with a default capacity of eleven mappings and a 75% load factor.

```
Hashtable(int n)
```
> Constructs a new HashTable with a capacity of n mappings and a 75% load factor.

```
Hashtable(int n, float x)
```
> Constructs a new HashTable with a capacity of n mappings and an x% load factor.

```
Hashtable(Map m)
```
> Constructs a new HashTable with the same mappings as m.

INSTANCE METHOD SUMMARY

void clear()

Clears this HashTable of keys.

Object clone()

Returns a shallow copy of this HashTable.

boolean contains(Object v)

Returns whether some key of this HashTable maps to value of v.

boolean containsKey(Object v)

Returns whether value v is a key in this HashTable.

boolean containsValue(Object v)

Returns whether some key of this HashTable maps to value v.

Enumeration elements()

Returns an enumeration of this HashTable.

Set entrySet()

Returns a Set view of this HashTable.

boolean equals(Object v)

Returns whether v is equal to this HashTable.

Object get(Object v)

Returns the value to key v maps in this HashTable.

int hashCode()

Returns the hash code of this object.

boolean isEmpty()

Returns whether this HashTable has any mappings.

Enumeration keys()

Returns an enumeration of the keys of this HashTable.

Set keySet()

Returns a Set view of the keys in this HashTable.

Object put(Object v1, Object v2)

Maps the key v1 to value v2 in this HashTable. Returns the previous value to which v1 maps. If there was no previous value, then **null** is returned.

void putAll(Map m)

Copies the mappings of m to this HashTable.

protected void rehash()

Resets the capacity and loading factor of this HashTable for purposes of efficieny.

Object remove(Object v)

Removes key v and its corresponding value from this HashTable.

int size()

Removes the number of keys in this HashTable.

String toString()

Returns a String representation of the value of this object.

Collection values()

Returns a Collection view of the values in this HashTable.

util	**interface** Iterator

PURPOSE

Provides an enumeration view of a collection.

INSTANCE METHOD SUMMARY

boolean hasNext()

> Returns whether this Collection has more elements to return.

Object next()

> Returns next element of this Collection. If there is no next element, then it throws a NoSuchElementException.

void remove()

> Removes from this Collection the last element returned by the iterator. The operation is optional.

util	**class** LinkedList **extends** AbstractSequentialList **implements** List, Cloneable, Serializable

PURPOSE

Provides a linked list view of a collection.

CONSTRUCTOR SUMMARY

LinkedList()

> Constructs a new empty LinkedList.

LinkedList(Collection c)

> Constructs a new LinkedList using the elements of collection c as a basis.

INSTANCE METHOD SUMMARY

void add(**int** i, Object v)

> Inserts value v into the list such that v has index i. Any preexisting elements with indices i or greater are shifted backward by one element position.

boolean add(Object v)

> Appends the list with a new element with value v and returns **true**.

boolean addAll(Collection c)

> Appends the list with all of the elements in c and returns **true** if the list has changed.

boolean addAll(**int** i, Collection c)

> Inserts the elements of c into this list and returns **true** if the list has changed. Any preexisting elements with indices i or greater are shifted backward by one element position.

void addFirst(Object v)

> Inserts a new element with value v at the beginning of this list.

void addLast(Object v)

> Adds a new element with value v at the end of this list.

void clear()

> Removes all elements from the list.

`Object clone()`

Returns a shallow copy of this list.

`boolean contains(Object v)`

Returns whether the list has an element with value v.

`Object get(int i)`

Returns the ith element in this list. Throws a NoSuchElementException if the list is empty.

`Object getFirst()`

Returns the first element in this list. Throws a NoSuchElementException if the list is empty.

`Object getLast()`

Returns the last element in this list. Throws a NoSuchElementException if the list is empty.

`int indexOf(Object v)`

Returns the index of the first occurrence of v in the list. If v is not in the list, then −1 is returned.

`int lastIndexOf(Object v)`

Returns the index of the last occurrence of v in the list. If v is not in the list, then −1 is returned.

`ListIterator listIterator(int i)`

Returns a list iterator of the elements in this list starting with the ith element.

`int lastIndexOf(Object v)`

Returns the index of the last occurrence of v in the list. If v is not in the list, then −1 is returned.

`Object remove(int i)`

If i is a valid index, it removes the ith element from the list by shifting forward elements i+1 and on. In addition, the removed value is returned. Otherwise, an exception is generated.

`boolean remove(Object v)`

Attempts to remove the first element with value v in this list. Returns whether a value was removed.

`Object removeFirst()`

Removes and returns the initial element in this list. Throws a NoSuchElement-Exception if the list is empty.

`Object removeLast()`

Removes and returns the last element in this list. Throws a NoSuchElementEx-ception if the list is empty.

`Object set(int i, Object v)`

If i is a valid index, then ith element is set to v and the previous value of the element is returned. Otherwise, an exception is thrown.

`int size()`

Returns the numbers of elements in the list.

`Object[] toArray()`

Returns an array whose elements correspond to the elements of this list.

`Object[] toArray(Object[] a)`

Returns an array of the same type as array a whose elements correspond to the elements of this list. The returned array is a if a is big enough.

> int hashCode()
>> Returns the hash code of this object.
>
> String toString()
>> Returns a `String` representation of the value of this object.

---

util	interface List extends Collection

PURPOSE

Describes an ordered list view of a collection. The view supports a bidirectional iterator `ListIterator` allowing element insertion and replacement.

INSTANCE METHOD SUMMARY

> void add(int i, Object v)
>> Inserts value v into the list such that v has index i. Any preexisting elements with indices i or greater are shifted backward by one element position. This operation is optional.
>
> boolean add(Object v)
>> Appends the list with a new element with value v and returns **true**. This operation is optional.
>
> boolean addAll(Collection c)
>> Appends the list with all of the elements in c and returns **true** if the list has changed. This operation is optional.
>
> boolean addAll(int i, Collection c)
>> Inserts the elements of c into this list and returns **true** if the list has changed. Any preexisting elements with indices i or greater are shifted backward by one element position. This operation is optional.
>
> void clear()
>> Removes all elements from the list. This operation is optional.
>
> boolean contains(Object v)
>> Returns whether the list has an element with value v.
>
> boolean containsAll(Collection c)
>> Returns whether this `Collection` contains all of the values in the collection c.
>
> boolean equals(Object v)
>> Returns **true** if and only if v is an instance of `List` representing the same list as this `List`.
>
> Object get(int i)
>> Returns the ith element in this list. Throws a `NoSuchElementException` if the list is empty.
>
> int hashCode()
>> Returns the hash code of this object.
>
> int indexOf(Object v)
>> Returns the index of the first occurrence of v in the list. If v is not in the list, then −1 is returned.
>
> boolean isEmpty()
>> Returns whether this list has any elements.

```
Iterator iterator()
```
Returns an iterator over the elements in this list.
```
int lastIndexOf(Object v)
```
Returns the index of the last occurrence of v in the list. If v is not in the list, then −1 is returned.
```
ListIterator listIterator()
```
Returns a list iterator of the elements in this list starting with the first element.
```
ListIterator listIterator(int i)
```
Returns a list iterator of the elements in this list starting with the ith element.
```
int lastIndexOf(Object v)
```
Returns the index of the last occurrence of v in the list. If v is not in the list, then −1 is returned.
```
Object remove(int i)
```
If i is a valid index, it removes the ith element from the list by shifting forward elements i+1 and on. In addition, the removed value is returned. Otherwise, an exception is generated.
```
boolean remove(Object v)
```
Attempts to remove the first element with value v in this list. Returns whether a value was removed.
```
boolean removeAll(Collection c)
```
Attempts to remove each of the values in c from this List. Returns whether a value was removed. The operation is optional.
```
boolean retainAll(Collection c)
```
Attempts to remove from this List all of the values not in c. Returns whether a value was removed. The operation is optional.
```
Object set(int i, Object v)
```
If i is a valid index, then ith element is set to v and the previous value of the element is returned. Otherwise, an exception is thrown.
```
int size()
```
Returns the numbers of elements in the list.
```
List subList(int i, int j)
```
Returns a sublist of this list using the elements with indices from the interval i ... j-1.
```
Object[] toArray()
```
Returns an array whose elements correspond to the elements of this list.
```
Object[] toArray(Object[] a)
```
Returns an array of the same type as array a whose elements correspond to the elements of this list. The returned array is a if a is big enough.

---

util   **interface** ListIterator **extends** Iterator

PURPOSE

Provides an enumeration view of a collection where the iterator position is always between elements of the list.

INSTANCE METHOD SUMMARY

void add(Object v)

Inserts a new element into the list at the current position. The operation is optional.

boolean hasNext()

Returns whether the list has more elements to return in the forward direction.

boolean hasPrevious()

Returns whether the list has more elements to return in the reverse direction.

Object next()

Returns next element of the list in the forward direction. If there is no next element, then it throws a NoSuchElementException.

int nextIndex()

Returns the index of the element of the list that would be returned next().

Object previous()

Returns next element of the list in the reverse direction. If there is no next element, then it throws a NoSuchElementException.

int previousIndex()

Returns the index of the element of the list that would be returned previous().

void remove()

Removes from the list the last element returned by the iterator. The operation is optional.

void set(Object v)

Replaces with v the last element returned by the iterator of the list. The operation is optional.

| util |

final class Locale **implements** Cloneable, Serializable

PURPOSE

Represents a specific geographical, political, or cultural region.

FIELD SUMMARY

static Locale CANADA

Represents a political unit.

static Locale CANADA_FRENCH

Represents a cultural unit.

static Locale CHINA

Represents a political unit.

static Locale CHINESE

Represents a language.

static Locale ENGLISH

Represents a language.

static Locale FRANCE

Represents a political unit.

static Locale FRENCH

Represents a language.

static Locale GERMAN

 Represents a language.

static Locale GERMANY

 Represents a political unit.

static Locale ITALIAN

 Represents a language.

static Locale ITALY

 Represents a political unit.

static Locale JAPAN

 Represents a political unit.

static Locale JAPANESE

 Represents a language.

static Locale KOREA

 Represents a cultural unit.

static Locale KOREAN

 Represents a language.

static Locale PRC

 Represents a political unit.

static Locale SIMPLIFIED_CHINESE

 Represents a language.

static Locale TAIWAN

 Represents a political unit.

static Locale TRADITIONAL_CHINESE

 Represents a language.

static Locale UK

 Represents a political unit.

static Locale US

 Represents a political unit.

CLASS METHOD SUMMARY

static Locale[] getAvailableLocales()

 Returns a list of possible locales.

static Locale getDefault()

 Returns the default locale.

static String[] getISOCountries()

 Returns a list of ISO country codes.

static String[] getISOLanguages()

 Returns a list of ISO language codes.

static void setDefault(Locale l)

 Sets the default locale to l.

CONSTRUCTOR SUMMARY

Locale(String s)

 Constructs the default Locale for country code s.

Locale(String s, String c)

 Construct the default Locale for language code s and country code c.

Locale(String s, String c, String v)

 Construct a Locale from language code s, country code c, and variant v.

INSTANCE METHOD SUMMARY

String getCountry()

Returns the country/region code for this Locale.

Object clone()

Returns a copy of this Locale.

boolean equals(Object v)

Returns whether v is equal to this Locale.

String getDisplayCountry()

Returns the name of the country for this Locale.

String getDisplayCountry(Locale l)

Returns the name of the country for locale l.

String getDisplayLanguage()

Returns the name of the language for this Locale.

String getDisplayLanguage(Locale l)

Returns the name of the language for locale l.

String getDisplayName()

Returns the name of this Locale.

String getDisplayName(Locale l)

Returns the name for locale l.

String getDisplayVariant()

Returns the name of the variant for this Local.

String getDisplayVariant(Locale l)

Returns the name of locale l for this Local.

String getISO3Country()

Returns the country code for this Locale.

String getISO3Language()

Returns the language for this Locale.

String getLanguage()

Returns the language code for this Locale.

String getVariant()

Returns the variant code of this Locale.

int hashCode()

Returns the hash code of this object. Returns the name of locale l for this Local.

String getISO3Country()

Returns the country code for this Locale.

String getISO3Language()

Returns the language for this Locale.

String getLanguage()

Returns the language code for this Locale.

String getVariant()

Returns the variant code of this Locale.

int hashCode()

Returns the hash code of this object.

String toString()

Returns a String representation of the value of this object.

util

interface Map

PURPOSE

Represent mappings of keys to values.

INSTANCE METHOD SUMMARY

void clear()

Removes all mappings in this Map. The operation is optional.

boolean containsKey(Object v)

Returns whether this Map contains a mapping for the key v.

boolean containsValue(Object v)

Returns whether this Map has a key that maps to value v.

Set entrySet()

Returns a Set view of this Map.

boolean equals(Object v)

Returns **true** if and only if v is an instance of List representing the same list as this List.

Object get(Object v)

Returns the value to which key v maps in this Map.

int hashCode()

Returns the hash code of this object.

boolean isEmpty()

Returns whether this Map has any mappings.

Set keySet()

Returns a Set view of the keys in this Map.

Object put(Object v1, Object v2)

Associates key v1 with value v2 in this Map. Returns the previous value associated with v2. The operation is optional.

void putAll(Map m)

Copies the mappings of map m to this Map. The operation is optional.

Object remove(Object v)

Removes the mapping of key v this Map. Returns the previous value associated with v. The operation is optional.

int size()

Returns the number of mappings in this Map.

Collection values()

Returns a Collection view of the values in this Map.

util.
regex

class Pattern **implements** Serializable

PURPOSE

Represents a regular expression.

FIELD SUMMARY

static int CANON_EQ

Represents canonical equivalence.

static int CASE_INSENSITIVE

Represents case-insensitive matching.

static int COMMENTS

Represents the allowing of whitespace and comments in pattern.

static int DOTALL

Represents dotall mode.

static int MULTILINE

Represents multiline mode.

static int UNICODE_CASE

Represents case folding.

static int UNIX_LINES

Represents Unix lines mode.

CLASS METHOD SUMMARY

static Pattern compile(String s)

Returns the regular expression Pattern as denoted by string s.

static Pattern compile(String s, **int** f)

Returns the regular expression Pattern as denoted by string s with respect to flags f.

static boolean matches(String s, CharSequence t)

Returns whether the regular expression Pattern denoted by string s matches input t.

INSTANCE METHOD SUMMARY

int flags()

Returns the match flags of this Pattern.

Matcher matcher(CharSequence s)

Returns a new Matcher that will match input s using this Pattern.

String pattern()

Returns the regular expression for this Pattern.

String[] split(CharSequence s)

Returns a String array that splits the input sequence s around matches of this Pattern.

String[] split(CharSequence s, **int** n)

Returns a String array that splits the input sequence s around matches of this Pattern. If n > 0, then this Pattern is applied at most n-1 times and the last array element is a copy of all input in s beyond the last matched delimiter. If n < 0, then this Pattern is applied as many times as possible. If n = 0, then this Pattern is applied as many times as possible with the discarding of any trailing empty strings.

| util | **class** Random **implements** Serializable |

PURPOSE

Represent a pseudorandom number generator.

CONSTRUCTOR SUMMARY

Random()

> Constructs a new random number generator Random whose seed is based on the current time.

Random(**long** n)

> Constructs a new random number generator Random using a seed n.

INSTANCE METHOD SUMMARY

protected int next(**int** n)

> Used by other methods for generating the next pseudorandom number. The method contract requires that an override return an **int** value with the n low-order bits being independent pseudorandom binary values.

boolean nextBoolean()

> Returns the next pseudorandom, uniformly distributed value from this Random.

void nextBytes(byte[] a)

> Fills array a with random bytes using this Random.

double nextDouble()

> Returns the next pseudorandom, uniformly distributed value between 0.0 and 1.0 from this Random.

float nextFloat()

> Returns the next pseudorandom, uniformly distributed value between 0.0 and 1.0 from this Random.

double nextGaussian()

> Returns the next pseudorandom, normally distributed value mean 0 and standard deviation 1 from this Random.

int nextInt()

> Returns the next pseudorandom, uniformly distributed value from this Random.

int nextInt(**int** n)

> Returns from interval 0 … n-1 the next pseudorandom, uniformly distributed value of this Random.

long nextLong()

> Returns the next pseudorandom, uniformly distributed value from this Random.

void setSeed(**long** n)

> Sets to n the seed of this Random.

| util | **interface** Set **extends** Collection |

PURPOSE

Describe a set view of a collection; i.e., different elements have different values.

INSTANCE METHOD SUMMARY

`boolean add(Object v)`

Attempts to add a new element to this Set with value v and returns **true** if the value v was not previously there. This operation is optional.

`boolean addAll(Collection c)`

Adds to this Set all of the elements in c and returns **true** if the set has changed. This operation is optional.

`void clear()`

Removes all elements from this Set. This operation is optional.

`boolean contains(Object v)`

Returns whether this Set has an element with value v.

`boolean containsAll(Collection c)`

Returns whether this Set contains all of the values in set c.

`boolean equals(Object v)`

Returns **true** if and only if v is an instance of Set representing the same list as this Set.

`int hashCode()`

Returns the hash code of this object.

`boolean isEmpty()`

Returns whether this Set has any elements.

`Iterator iterator()`

Returns an iterator over the elements in this Set.

`boolean remove(Object v)`

Attempts to remove value v from this Set and returns whether this Set has changed. The operation is optional.

`boolean removeAll(Collection c)`

Attempts to remove elements of c from this Set and returns whether this Set has changed. The operation is optional.

`boolean retainAll(Collection c)`

Attempts to remove from this Set all of the values not in c. Returns whether a value was removed. The operation is optional.

`int size()`

Returns the number of elements in this Set.

`Object[] toArray()`

Returns an array whose elements correspond to the elements of this Set.

`Object[] toArray(Object[] a)`

Returns an array of the same type as array a whose elements correspond to the elements of this Set. The returned array is a if a is big enough.

---

util	**interface** SortedMap **extends** Map

PURPOSE

Describe a map with the added functionality that keys are arranged in sorted order.

INSTANCE METHOD SUMMARY

INSTANCE METHOD SUMMARY

Comparator comparator()

Returns the comparator of this sorted map, with **null** indicating the natural ordering.

Object firstKey()

Returns the first key of this sorted map.

SortedMap headMap(Object v)

Returns the subportion of this sorted map whose keys are strictly less than value v.

Object lastKey()

Returns the last key of this sorted map.

SortedMap subMap(Object v1, Object v2)

Returns the subportion of this sorted map whose keys are greater than or equal to value v and strictly less than value v2.

---

util   **class** Stack **extends** Vector

PURPOSE

Provides a stack view of a vector; i.e., last-in-first-out behavior.

CONSTRUCTOR SUMMARY

Stack()

Constructs a new empty Stack.

INSTANCE METHOD SUMMARY

boolean empty()

Returns whether this Stack is empty.

Object peek()

Returns the next value that **pop**() would return for this Stack.

Object pop()

Removes and returns the top element of this Stack.

Object push(Object v)

Pushes value v onto the top of this Stack.

int search(Object v)

Returns the position of value v onto the top of this Stack, where position is 1-based; i.e., the top element has position1, and so on. If the value is not there, the method returns −1.

---

util   **class** StringTokenizer **implements** Enumeration

PURPOSE

Provides a token view of a string.

CONSTRUCTOR SUMMARY

StringTokenizer(String s)

> Constructs a new StringTokenizer for string s using whitespace as token delimiters. Delimiters are not returned as tokens.

StringTokenizer(String s, String t)

> Constructs a new StringTokenizer for string s with the characters in t as the token delimiters.

StringTokenizer(String s, String t, **boolean** b)

> Constructs a new StringTokenizer for string s with the characters in t as the token delimiters. Delimiters are returned as tokens depending on b.

INSTANCE METHOD SUMMARY

int countTokens()

> Returns the number of times that nextToken() can invoked for this String-Tokenizer without generating an exception.

boolean hasMoreElements()

> Returns whether this StringTokenizer has any more tokens to return.

hasMoreTokens()

> Returns whether this StringTokenizer has any more tokens to return.

Object nextElement()

> Returns the next token of this StringTokenizer. Throws a NoSuchElement-Exception if there is no next token.

String nextToken()

> Returns the next token of this StringTokenizer. Throws a NoSuchElement-Exception if there is no next token.

String nextToken(String t)

> Returns the next token of this StringTokenizer with the characters in t now being its token delimiters. Throws a NoSuchElementException if there is no next token.

---

util   **class** Timer

PURPOSE

Provides a mechanism for generating threads.

CONSTRUCTOR SUMMARY

Timer()

> Constructs a new Timer whose thread may not run as a daemon.

Timer(**boolean** b)

> Constructs a new Timer whose thread may run as a daemon depending on b.

INSTANCE METHOD SUMMARY

void cancel()

> Terminates any scheduled threads of this Timer.

void schedule(TimerTask t, Date d)

> Schedules task t for execution at the time d using this Timer.

void schedule(TimerTask t, Date d, **long** n)

Schedules task t for execution at the time d using this Timer. The task is repeatedly rescheduled to run every n milliseconds from the time previous run started.

void schedule(TimerTask t, **long** n)

Schedules task t for execution after a delay of n milliseconds using this Timer.

void schedule(TimerTask t, **long** n1, **long** n2)

Schedules task t for execution after a delay of n1 milliseconds using this Timer. The task is also repeatedly rescheduled to run n2 milliseconds from the time previous run started.

void scheduleAtFixedRate(TimerTask t, Date d, **long** n)

Schedules task t for execution at time d using this Timer. The task is also repeatedly rescheduled to run every n milliseconds after time d.

void scheduleAtFixedRate(TimerTask t, **long** n1, **long** n2)

Schedules task t for execution after a delay of n1 milliseconds using this Timer. The task is also repeatedly rescheduled to run every n2 milliseconds from that delay time.

---

util   **class** TimerTask **implements** Runnable

PURPOSE
Represents a schedulable action for a Timer.

CONSTRUCTOR SUMMARY
protected TimerTask()

Constructs a new TimerTask.

INSTANCE METHOD SUMMARY
boolean cancel()

Terminates any scheduled threads of this TimerTask.
Cancels this timer task.

abstract void run()

The action performed by this TimerTask.

long scheduledExecutionTime()

Returns the scheduled time of the most recent execution of this TimerTask.

---

util   **class** Vector **extends** AbstractList **implements** List, RandomAccess, Cloneable, Serializable

PURPOSE
Provides a dynamic list representation.

FIELD SUMMARY
protected int capacityIncrement

Represents the amount by which this Vector grows when its size exceeds its capacity.

```
protected int elementCount
```
Represents the number of elements in this `Vector`.
```
protected Object[] elementData
```
Represents the internal buffer that maintains the elements of this `Vector`.

CONSTRUCTOR SUMMARY
```
Vector()
```
Invokes **this**(10, 0).
```
Vector(Collection c)
```
Constructs a new `Vector` whose elements are the elements of the collection `c`.
```
Vector(int n)
```
Invokes **this**(n, 0).
```
Vector(int n1, int n2)
```
Constructs a new `Vector` with no elements and with a capacity for `n1` elements and a capacity increment of `n2`.

INSTANCE METHOD SUMMARY
```
void add(int i, Object v)
```
Inserts value `v` into the list such that `v` has index `i`. Any preexisting elements with indices `i` or greater are shifted backward by one element position. This operation is optional.
```
boolean add(Object v)
```
Appends this `Vector` with a new element with value `v` and returns **true**.
```
boolean addAll(Collection c)
```
Appends this `Vector` with all of the elements in `c` and returns **true** if this `Vector` has changed.
```
boolean addAll(int i, Collection c)
```
Inserts the elements of `c` into this list and returns **true** if the list has changed. Any preexisting elements with indices `i` or greater are shifted backward by one element position.
```
void addElement(Object v)
```
Appends this `Vector` with a new element with value `v`.
```
int capacity()
```
Returns the capacity of this `Vector`.
```
void clear()
```
Removes all elements from this `Vector`.
```
Object clone()
```
Returns a shallow copy of this `Vector`.
```
boolean contains(Object v)
```
Returns whether this `Vector` has an element with value `v`.
```
boolean containsAll(Collection c)
```
Returns whether this `Vector` contains all of the elements in the collection `c`.
```
void copyInto(Object[] a)
```
Pairwise copies the elements of array `a` to this `Vector`. If the capacity of this `Vector` is insufficient, then an `ArrayIndexOutOfBoundsException` is thrown.
```
Object elementAt(int i)
```
If `i` is a valid index in this `Vector`, it returns the `i`th element; otherwise an `ArrayIndexOutOfBoundsException` is thrown.

`Enumeration elements()`

Returns a new `Enumeration` of the elements of this `Vector`.

`void ensureCapacity(int n)`

Ensures this `Vector` has the capacity to represent n elements.

`boolean equals(Object v)`

Returns **true** if and only if v is an instance of `Vector` representing the same list as this `Vector`.

`Object firstElement()`

Returns the first element of this `Vector`.

`int hashCode()`

Returns the hash code of this object.

`Object get(int i)`

If i is a valid index in this `Vector`, it returns the ith element; otherwise an `ArrayIndexOutOfBoundsException` is thrown.

`int indexOf(Object v)`

Returns the index of the first occurrence of v in this `Vector`. If v is not in this `Vector`, then −1 is returned.

`int indexOf(Object v, int i)`

Returns the index of the first occurrence of v in this `Vector` from element i on. If v is not in the list, then −1 is returned.

`void insertElementAt(Object v, int i)`

Inserts value v into this `Vector` such that v has index i. Any preexisting elements with indices i or greater are shifted backward by one element position.

`boolean isEmpty()`

Returns **true** if there are no elements in this `Vector`; otherwise, it returns **false**.

`Object lastElement()`

Returns the last element of this `Vector`.

`int lastIndexOf(Object v)`

Returns the index of the last occurrence of v in this `Vector`. If v is not in the list, then −1 is returned.

`int lastIndexOf(Object v, int i)`

Returns the index of the last occurrence of v in this `Vector` occurring not after the ith element. If v is not in the `Vector`, then −1 is returned.

`Object remove(int i)`

If i is a valid index, it removes the ith element from the list by shifting forward elements i+1 and on. In addition, the removed value is returned. Otherwise, an exception is generated.

`boolean remove(Object v)`

Attempts to remove value v from this `Vector` and returns whether this `Vector` has changed.

`boolean removeAll(Collection c)`

Attempts to remove elements of c from this `Vector` and returns whether this `Vector` has changed.

`void removeAllElements()`

Removes all elements from this `Vector`; i.e., its size becomes zero.

```
boolean removeElement(Object v)
```

Removes the first occurrence of value v this `Vector`. Returns whether a value was removed. Trailing elements are shifted forward.

```
void removeElementAt(int i)
```

Removes the element with index i from this `Vector`. Trailing elements are shifted forward.

```
Object removeRange(int i, int j)
```

Removes elements from this `Vector` whose indices are in the interval i ... j-1. Trailing elements are shifted forward. With this definition, if j ≤ i, then no elements are removed.

```
boolean retainAll(Collection c)
```

Remove from this `Vector` all of the values not in c. Returns whether a value was removed.

```
Object set(int i, Object v)
```

If i is a valid index in this `Vector`, then ith element is set to v and the previous value of the element is returned. Otherwise, an `ArrayIndexOutOfBoundsException` is thrown.

```
void setElementAt(Object v, int i)
```

If i is a valid index in this `Vector`, then ith element is set to v. Otherwise, an `ArrayIndexOutOfBoundsException` is thrown.

```
void setSize(int n)
```

Sets the size of this `Vector`.

```
int size()
```

Returns the numbers of elements in this `Vector`.

```
Object[] toArray()
```

Returns an array whose elements correspond to the elements of this `Vector`.

```
Object[] toArray(Object[] a)
```

Returns an array of the same type as array a whose elements correspond to the elements of this `Vector`. The returned array is a if a is big enough.

```
String toString()
```

Returns a `String` representation of the value of this object.

```
void trimToSize()
```

Sets the capacity of this `Vector` to `size()`.

E STANDARD JAVA GRAPHICAL PACKAGES

We describe many of the classes and interfaces from standard graphical packages `java.applet`, `java.awt`, and `javax.swing`.

E.1 JAVA.APPLET

applet class Applet extends Panel

PURPOSE
Represents a program that is run within another program such as Web browser.

CLASS METHOD SUMMARY

static AudioClip newAudioClip(URL u)

Returns the audio clip at Web location u.

CONSTRUCTOR SUMMARY

Applet()

Creates a new Applet.

INSTANCE METHOD SUMMARY

void destroy()

Signals this Applet that it is about to be terminated.

AccessibleContext getAccessibleContext()

Returns the accessibility context of this Applet.

AppletContext getAppletContext()

Returns the environmental context of this Applet.

String getAppletInfo()

Returns identifying information for this Applet.

AudioClip getAudioClip(URL u)

Returns the audio clip at location u for this Applet.

AudioClip getAudioClip(URL u, String s)

Returns the audio clip with name s at location u for this Applet.

URL getCodeBase()

Returns the base location of this Applet.

URL getDocumentBase()

Returns the location of the document containing this Applet.

Image getImage(URL u)

Returns the image at location u for this Applet.

Image getImage(URL u, String s)

Returns the image with name s at location u for this Applet.

Locale getLocale()

Returns the locale of this Applet.

String getParameter(String s)

Returns the value of parameter s in the HTML tag for this Applet.

String[][] getParameterInfo()

Returns the parameter values for this Applet.

void init()

Signals this Applet that it has been loaded.

boolean isActive()

Returns whether this Applet active.

void play(URL u)

Plays the audio clip at location u for this Applet.

```
void play(URL u, String s)
```
Plays the audio clip with name s at location u for this Applet.
```
void resize(Dimension d)
```
Requests this Applet resized itself to dimension d.
```
void resize(int w, int h)
```
Requests this Applet resized itself to width w and height *h*.
```
void setStub(AppletStub a)
```
Sets a as the stub of this Applet.
```
void showStatus(String s)
```
Requests this Applet to displayed message s in the status window.
```
void start()
```
Signals this Applet to start its execution.
```
void stop()
```
Signals this Applet to stop its execution.

E.2   JAVA.AWT

awt.event   **class** ActionEvent **extends** AWTEvent

PURPOSE
Represents events for which application-specific responses are appropriate.
FIELD SUMMARY
```
static int ACTION_FIRST
```
Represents the minimal action event indicator.
```
static int ACTION_LAST
```
Represents the maximal action event indicator.
```
static int ACTION_PERFORMED
```
Represents a meaningful action indicator.
```
static int ALT_MASK
```
Represents the alt modifier.
```
static int CTRL_MASK
```
Represents the control modifier.
```
static int META_MASK
```
Represents the meta modifier.
```
static int SHIFT_MASK
```
Represents the shift modifier.
CONSTRUCTOR SUMMARY
```
ActionEvent(Object v, int n, String s)
```
Constructs a new ActionEvent whose source is v. The kind of the Action-Event is n and its message is s.

ActionEvent(Object v, **int** n, String s, **int** m)

> Constructs a new `ActionEvent` with modifier m whose source is v. The kind of the `ActionEvent` is n and its message is s.

ActionEvent(Object v, **int** n, String s, **long** t, **int** m)

> Constructs a new `ActionEvent` with modifier m and time stamp t whose source is v. The kind of the `ActionEvent` is n and its message is s.

INSTANCE METHOD SUMMARY

String getActionCommand()

> Returns the command string of this `ActionEvent`.

int getModifiers()

> Returns the modifier keys of this `ActionEvent`.

long getWhen()

> Returns the time stamp of this `ActionEvent`.

String paramString()

> Returns a representation of this `ActionEvent`.

`awt.event`   **interface** ActionListener **extends** EventListener

PURPOSE

Describes the necessary method of a responder to an `ActionEvent`.

INSTANCE METHOD SUMMARY

void actionPerformed(ActionEvent e)

> Processes action event e for this action listener.

`awt.event`   **class** BorderLayout **implements** LayoutManager2, Serializable

PURPOSE

Represent a layout manager that arranges its components with five regions north, south, east, west, and center.

FIELD SUMMARY

static String AFTER_LAST_LINE

> Equivalent to PAGE_END.

static String AFTER_LINE_ENDS

> Equivalent to LINE_END.

static String BEFORE_FIRST_LINE

> Equivalent to PAGE_START.

static String BEFORE_LINE_BEGINS

> Equivalent to LINE_START.

static String CENTER

> Represents a middle of the container constraint.

static String EAST

> Represents a right side of the container constraint.

static String LINE_END

> Represents component placed at the end of the line constraint.

```
static String LINE_START
```
Represents component placed at the start of the line constraint.
```
static String NORTH
```
Represents a top side of the container constraint.
```
static String PAGE_END
```
Represents component placed at the end of the page constraint.
```
static String PAGE_START
```
Represents component placed at the start of the page constraint.
```
static String SOUTH
```
Represents a bottom side of the container constraint.
```
static String WEST
```
Represents a left side of the container constraint.

CONSTRUCTOR SUMMARY
```
BorderLayout()
```
Constructs a new **BorderLayout** with no gaps.
```
BorderLayout(int h, int v)
```
Constructs a new **BorderLayout** with no gaps. The inter-row horizontal gap is h and the interelement vertical gap is v.

INSTANCE METHOD SUMMARY
```
void addLayoutComponent(Component c, Object v)
```
Adds component c using constraint v to the layout of this layout manager.
```
void addLayoutComponent(String s, Component c)
```
Adds component c using constraint s to the layout of this layout manager.
```
int getHgap()
```
Returns the intercomponent horizontal gap used by this layout manager.
```
float getLayoutAlignmentX(Container c)
```
Returns the x-axis alignment policy with regard to container c.
```
float getLayoutAlignmentY(Container c)
```
Returns the y-axis alignment policy with regard to container c.
```
int getVgap()
```
Returns the intercomponent vertical gap used by this layout manager.
```
void invalidateLayout(Container c)
```
Invalidates the layout with regard to container c.
```
void layoutContainer(Container c)
```
Arranges the components of container c using this layout manager.
```
Dimension maximumLayoutSize(Container c)
```
Returns the maximum size of container c using this layout manager.
```
Dimension minimumLayoutSize(Container c)
```
Returns the minimum size of container c using this layout manager.
```
Dimension preferredLayoutSize(Container c)
```
Returns the preferred size of container c using this layout manager.
```
void removeLayoutComponent(Component c)
```
Removes component c from the arrangement of this layout manager.
```
void setHgap(int h)
```
Sets h as the horizontal gap between components by this layout manager.
```
void setVgap(int v)
```
Sets v as the vertical gap between components by this layout manager.

```
String toString()
```
Returns a representation of this layout manager.

---

class Canvas **extends** Component **implements** Accessible

PURPOSE
Represent a rectangular region for drawing and trapping input events.
CONSTRUCTOR SUMMARY
```
Canvas()
```
Constructs a new Canvas.
```
Canvas(GraphicsConfiguration g)
```
Constructs a new Canvas for graphics configuration g.
INSTANCE METHOD SUMMARY
```
void addNotify()
```
Creates the peer of this Canvas.
```
void createBufferStrategy(int n)
```
Creates a new buffering strategy for this Canvas using n buffers.
```
void createBufferStrategy(int n, BufferCapabilities c)
```
Creates a new buffering strategy for this Canvas using n buffers and capabilities
c.
```
AccessibleContext getAccessibleContext()
```
Returns the accessibility context of this Canvas.
```
BufferStrategy getBufferStrategy()
```
Returns the buffer strategy of this Canvas.
```
void paint(Graphics g)
```
Paints this Canvas using graphical context g.
```
void update(Graphics g)
```
Updates the display of this Canvas using graphical context g.

---

class Color **implements** Paint, Serializable

PURPOSE
Represents colors from a color space. Associated with each color is an *alpha* attribute
specifying its visibility (the range corresponds to transparency to opaqueness).
FIELD SUMMARY
```
static Color black, static Color BLACK
```
Represent black.
```
static Color blue, static Color BLUE
```
Represents blue.
```
static Color cyan, static Color CYAN
```
Represent cyan.
```
static Color darkGray, static Color DARK_GRAY
```
Represent dark gray.

static Color gray, static Color GRAY

Represent gray.

static Color green, static Color GREEN

Represent green.

static Color lightGray, static Color LIGHT_GRAY

Represent light gray.

static Color magenta, static Color MAGENTA

Represent magenta.

static Color orange, static Color ORANGE

Represent orange.

static Color pink, static Color PINK

Represents pink.

static Color red, static Color RED

Represents red.

static Color white, static Color WHITE

Represents white.

static Color yellow, static Color YELLOW

Represents yellow.

CLASS METHOD SUMMARY

static Color getColor(String s)

Returns a new Color based on the value of system property s.

static Color getColor(String s, Color c)

Attempts to return a new Color based on the value of system property s. If the attempt fails, then it returns color c.

static Color getColor(String s, int c)

Attempts to return a new Color based on the value of system property s. If the attempt fails, then it returns color based on RGB value c.

static Color getHSBColor(float h, float s, float b)

Returns a new Color based on values h, s, and b using the HSB color model.

static int HSBtoRGB(float h, float s, float b)

Returns the RGB representation for the color based on values h, s, and b using the HSB color model.

static float[] RGBtoHSB(int r, int g, int b, float[] a)

Returns an HSB color representation using array a for the RGB color based on r, b, and g.

CONSTRUCTOR SUMMARY

Color(ColorSpace s, float[] c, float a)

Creates a new Color with alpha level a in color space s using the elements of c to specify its red, green, and blue levels.

Color(float r, float g, float b)

Creates a new opaque Color in the standard color space using r, b, and g to specify respectively its red, green, and blue levels as percentages.

Color(float r, float g, float b, float a)

Creates a new Color with alpha level a in the standard color space using r, b, and g to specify respectively its red, green, and blue levels as percentages.

```
Color(int n)
```
Creates a new opaque `Color` in the standard color space using the bits of n to specify respectively its red, green, and blue levels relative to the interval 0 ... 255.
```
Color(int n, boolean b)
```
Creates a new opaque `Color` in the standard color space using the bits of n to specify respectively its alpha (depending on b), red, green, and blue levels relative to the interval 0 ... 255.
```
Color(int r, int g, int b)
```
Creates a new opaque `Color` in the standard color space using r, b, and g to specify respectively its red, green, and blue levels relative to the interval 0 ... 255.
```
Color(int r, int g, int b, int a)
```
Creates a new `Color` with alpha a in the standard color space using r, b, and g to specify respectively its red, green, and blue levels relative to the interval 0 ... 255.

INSTANCE METHOD SUMMARY
```
Color brighter()
```
Returns a new brighter version of this `Color`.
```
PaintContext createContext(ColorModel c, Rectangle r1,
  Rectangle2D r2, AffineTransform t, RenderingHints h)
```
Returns a new painting context generate a solid color pattern according to the parameter description.
```
Color darker()
```
Returns a new darker version of this `Color`.
```
static Color decode(String s)
```
Returns **new** `Color(Integer.parseInt(s)`.
```
boolean equals(Object v)
```
Returns whether v is a `Color` is equal to this `Color`.
```
int getAlpha()
```
Returns the alpha level of this `Color`.
```
int getBlue()
```
Returns the blue level of this `Color`.
```
float[] getColorComponents(ColorSpace c, float[] a)
```
Returns the color components of this `Color` with respect to color space c using array a as the return value.
```
float[] getColorComponents(float[] a)
```
Returns the color components of this `Color` using array a as the return value.
```
ColorSpace getColorSpace()
```
Returns the color space of this `Color`.
```
float[] getComponents(ColorSpace c, float[] a)
```
Returns the color and alpha components of this `Color` with respect to color space c.
```
float[] getComponents(float[] a)
```
Returns the color and alpha components of this `Color` using array a as the return value.

```
int getGreen()
```
Returns the green level of this Color.
```
int getRed()
```
Returns the red level of this Color.
```
int getRGB()
```
Returns the RGB value of this Color.
```
float[] getRGBColorComponents(float[] a)
```
Returns the color components of this Color using array a as the return value.
```
float[] getRGBComponents(float[] a)
```
Returns the color and alpha components of this Color using array a as the return value.
```
int getTransparency()
```
Returns the transparency mode of this Color.
```
int hashCode()
```
Returns the hash code of this Color.
```
String toString()
```
Returns a representation of this Color.

---

awt	**class** Container **implements** Component

PURPOSE
Represents a container for other GUI components.

CONSTRUCTOR SUMMARY
```
Container()
```
Creates a new container.

INSTANCE METHOD SUMMARY
```
Component add(Component a)
```
Appends component c to the component list of this Container.
```
Component add(Component c, int i)
```
Inserts component c at position i in the component list of this Container.
```
void add(Component c, Object v)
```
Appends component c in the component list of this Container with the layout manager using constraints v.
```
void add(Component c, Object v, int i)
```
Inserts component c at position i in the component list of this Container with the layout manager using constraints v.
```
void addContainerListener(ContainerListener l)
```
Adds l as a listener of the container events of this Container.
```
protected void addImpl(Component c, Object v, int i)
```
Inserts component c at position i in the component list of this Container with the layout manager using constraints v.
```
void addNotify()
```
Makes this Container displayable.
```
void addPropertyChangeListener(PropertyChangeListener l)
```
Adds l as a property change listener for this Container.

```
void addPropertyChangeListener(String s, PropertyChangeListener
  l)
```
Adds l as a type s property change listener for this Container.
```
void applyComponentOrientation(ComponentOrientation o)
```
Sets c as the component orientation property of this Container.
```
boolean areFocusTraversalKeysSet(int n)
```
Returns whether the type n focus traversal has been defined for this Container.
```
void doLayout()
```
Signals this Container to lay out its components.
```
Component findComponentAt(int x, int y)
```
Returns the visible child component at location (x, y) in this Container.
```
Component findComponentAt(Point p)
```
Returns the visible child component at location p in this Container.
```
float getAlignmentX()
```
Returns the x-axis alignment of this Container.
```
float getAlignmentY()
```
Returns the y-axis alignment of this Container.
```
Component getComponent(int i)
```
Returns the ith component in this Container.
```
Component getComponentAt(int x, int y)
```
Returns the component at location (x, y) in this Container.
```
Component getComponentAt(Point p)
```
Returns the component at location p in this Container.
```
int getComponentCount()
```
Returns the number of components in this Container.
```
Component[] getComponents()
```
Returns the components in this Container.
```
ContainerListener[] getContainerListeners()
```
Returns the container listeners of this Container.
```
Set getFocusTraversalKeys(int n)
```
Returns the type n traversal keys for this Container.
```
FocusTraversalPolicy getFocusTraversalPolicy()
```
Returns the focus traversal policy for this Container.
```
Insets getInsets()
```
Returns the insets of this Container.
```
LayoutManager getLayout()
```
Returns the layout manager for this Container.
```
EventListener[] getListeners(Class t)
```
Returns the type t listeners of this Container.
```
Dimension getMaximumSize()
```
Returns the maximum size of this Container.
```
Dimension getMinimumSize()
```
Returns the minimum size of this Container.
```
Dimension getPreferredSize()
```
Returns the preferred size of this Container.
```
void invalidate()
```
Invalidates this Container.

boolean isAncestorOf(Component c)

    Returns whether component c is logically in this Container.

boolean isFocusCycleRoot()

    Returns whether this Container is the root of its focus cycle.

boolean isFocusCycleRoot(Container c)

    Returns whether the container c is the focus cycle root of this Container.

boolean isFocusTraversalPolicySet()

    Returns whether this Container has a focus traversal policy.

void list(PrintStream s, **int** n)

    Prints a listing of the components of this Container to stream s with each line indented n characters.

void list(PrintWriter s, **int** n)

    Prints a listing of the components of this Container to stream s with each line indented n characters.

void paint(Graphics g)

    Renders this Container in graphical context g.

void paintComponents(Graphics g)

    Renders the components of this Container in graphical context g.

protected String paramString()

    Returns a representation of this Container.

void print(Graphics g)

    Prints this Container in graphical context g.

void printComponents(Graphics g)

    Prints the components of this Container in graphical context g.

protected void processContainerEvent(ContainerEvent e)

    Invokes the performer method of the container event listeners of this Container.

protected void processEvent(AWTEvent e)

    Invokes the container event listeners for this Container if e is a container event; otherwise, invokes **super**.processEvent(e).

void remove(Component c)

    Removes the component c from this Container.

void remove(**int** i)

    Removes the ith component from this Container.

void removeAll()

    Removes all components from this Container.

void removeContainerListener(ContainerListener l)

    Removes l from the container listener list of this Container.

void removeNotify()

    Makes this Container nondisplayable.

void setFocusCycleRoot(**boolean** b)

    Sets based on b whether this Container is the root of its focus traversal cycle.

void setFocusTraversalKeys(**int** n, Set s)

    Sets s as the focus traversal keys for a type n traversal of this Container.

void setFocusTraversalPolicy(FocusTraversalPolicy f)

    Sets f as the focus traversal policy of this Container.

void setFont(Font f)

Sets f as the font of this Container.

void setLayout(LayoutManager l)

Sets l as the layout manager of this Container.

void transferFocusBackward()

Transfers focus to the previous component.

void transferFocusDownCycle()

Transfers the focus down one cycle for this Container.

void update(Graphics g)

Updates the display of this Container using graphical context g.

void validate()

Validates this Container and its subcomponents with respect to needing display.

protected void validateTree()

Recursively recomputes the layout of invalid components of this Container.

---

awt	**class** FlowLayout **implements** LayoutManager, Serializable

PURPOSE

Represents layout manager that arranges components in a left-to-right, top-to-bottom flow.

FIELD SUMMARY

static int CENTER

Represents a row-centering layout policy.

static int LEADING

Represents a leading edge justification layout policy.

static int LEFT

Represents a left justification layout policy.

static int RIGHT

Represents a right justification layout policy.

static int TRAILING

Represents a trailing edge justification layout policy.

CONSTRUCTOR SUMMARY

FlowLayout()

Constructs a new FlowLayout with a centering layout policy.

FlowLayout(**int** p)

Constructs a new FlowLayout with layout policy p.

FlowLayout(**int** p, **int** h, **int** v)

Constructs a new FlowLayout with layout policy p. The inter-row horizontal gap is h and the interelement vertical gap is v.

INSTANCE METHOD SUMMARY

void addLayoutComponent(String s, Component c)

Adds component c with name s to the layout of this layout manager.

int getAlignment()

Returns the alignment policy of this layout manager.

int getHgap()

Returns the intercomponent horizontal gap used by this layout manager.

`int` getVgap()

Returns the intercomponent vertical gap used by this layout manager.

`void` layoutContainer(Container c)

Arranges the components of container c using this layout manager.

`Dimension` minimumLayoutSize(Container c)

Returns the minimum size of container c using this layout manager.

`Dimension` preferredLayoutSize(Container c)

Returns the preferred size of container c using this layout manager.

`void` removeLayoutComponent(Component c)

Removes component c from the arrangement of this layout manager.

`void` setAlignment(`int` p)

Sets p as the alignment policy of this layout manager.

`void` setHgap(`int` h)

Sets h as the horizontal gap between components by this layout manager.

`void` setVgap(`int` v)

Sets v as the vertical gap between components by this layout manager.

`String` toString()

Returns a representation of this layout manager.

| awt | `class` Font `implements` Serializable |

PURPOSE
Represents the logical font information needed for rendering characters and glyphs.

FIELD SUMMARY

`static int` BOLD

Represents the bold style.

`static int` CENTER_BASELINE

Represents the baseline for ideographic scripts.

`static int` HANGING_BASELINE

Represents the baseline in Devanigiri-like scripts.

`static int` ITALIC

Represents the italic style.

`static int` LAYOUT_LEFT_TO_RIGHT

Represents left to right layout of text and glyphs.

`static int` LAYOUT_NO_LIMIT_CONTEXT

Represents that text beyond the specified length should not be considered.

`static int` LAYOUT_NO_START_CONTEXT

Represents that text before the specified start should not be considered.

`static int` LAYOUT_RIGHT_TO_LEFT

Represents left to right layout of text and glyphs.

`protected` String name

Represents the logical name of this Font.

`static int` PLAIN

Represents the plain style.

`protected float` pointSize

Represents the point size of this Font.

```
static int ROMAN_BASELINE
```
Represents the baseline for Latin scripts.
```
protected int size
```
Represents the point size of this Font.
```
protected int style
```
Represents the style of this Font.
```
static int TRUETYPE_FONT
```
Represents the TrueType font style.

CLASS METHOD SUMMARY
```
static Font createFont(int f, InputStream s)
```
Returns a new Font of type f using the font data in stream s.
```
static Font decode(String s)
```
Returns the Font of type s.
```
static Font getFont(Map m)
```
Returns the Font of type m.
```
static Font getFont(String s)
```
Returns the Font of type s.
```
static Font getFont(String s, Font f)
```
Returns the font of system property s using f as the return value.

CONSTRUCTOR SUMMARY
```
Font(Map m)
```
Creates a new Font of type m.
```
Font(String s, int n1, int n2)
```
Creates a new Font of type n1 and point size n2 and name s.

INSTANCE METHOD SUMMARY
```
boolean canDisplay(char c)
```
Returns whether this Font has a glyph for character c.
```
int canDisplayUpTo(char[] c, int i, int n)
```
Returns whether this Font can display the substring of the n characters denoted by array c starting with its ith character.
```
int canDisplayUpTo(CharacterIterator c, int i, int n)
```
Returns whether this Font can display the substring of the n characters denoted by iterator c starting with its ith character.
```
int canDisplayUpTo(String s)
```
Returns whether this Font can display string s.
```
GlyphVector createGlyphVector(FontRenderContext f, char[] c)
```
Returns a characters to glyphs GlyphVector for this Font using font-rendering context f.
```
GlyphVector createGlyphVector(FontRenderContext f,
  CharacterIterator c)
```
Returns a characters to glyphs GlyphVector for this Font using font-rendering context f.
```
GlyphVector createGlyphVector(FontRenderContext f, int[] g)
```
Returns a characters to glyphs GlyphVector for this Font using font-rendering context f.

GlyphVector createGlyphVector(FontRenderContext f, String s)

> Returns a new GlyphVector for string s in this Font using font-rendering context f.

Font deriveFont(AffineTransform a)

> Returns a new Font based on affine transformation a on this Font.

Font deriveFont(**float** n)

> Returns a new Font of point size n based on this Font.

Font deriveFont(**int** n)

> Returns a new Font of style n based on this Font.

Font deriveFont(**int** n, AffineTransform a)

> Returns a new Font of point size n based on affine transformation a on this Font.

Font deriveFont(**int** n1, **float** n2)

> Returns a new Font of style n1 and point size n2 based on this Font.

Font deriveFont(Map m)

> Returns a new Font with attributes m based on this Font.

boolean equals(Object v)

> Returns whether v is a Font equal to this Font.

protected void finalize()

> Disposes the native font associated with this Font.

Map getAttributes()

> Returns the font attributes of this Font.

AttributedCharacterIterator.Attribute[] getAvailableAttributes()

> Returns the keys for the attributes of this Font.

byte getBaselineFor(**char** c)

> Returns the base line of character in this Font.

String getFamily()

> Returns the family name of this Font.

String getFamily(Locale l)

> Returns the family name with respect to locale l of this Font.

String getFontName()

> Returns the name of this Font.

String getFontName(Locale l)

> Returns the locale l name of this Font.

float getItalicAngle()

> Returns the italic angle of this Font.

LineMetrics getLineMetrics(**char**[] c, **int** i, **int** n, FontRenderContext f)

> Returns, with respect to context f, the line metrics of the length n sequence of characters denoted by list c starting with its ith element in this Font.

LineMetrics getLineMetrics(CharacterIterator c, **int** i, **int** n, FontRenderContext f)

> Returns, with respect to context f, the line metrics of the substring of the n characters denoted by iterator c starting with its ith character in this Font.

LineMetrics getLineMetrics(String s, FontRenderContext f)

> Returns the line metrics of string s in this context f.

```
LineMetrics getLineMetrics(String s, int i, int n,
  FontRenderContext f)
Rectangle2D getMaxCharBounds(FontRenderContext f)
```
Returns, with respect to context f, the bounding box of the character in the font of this Font with a maximum bounding box.

```
int getMissingGlyphCode()
```
Returns the glyph code used by this Font for a non-Unicode glyph.

```
String getName()
```
Returns the logical font name of this Font.

```
int getNumGlyphs()
```
Returns the number of glyphs in this Font.

```
String getPSName()
```
Returns the PostScript name of this Font.

```
int getSize()
```
Returns the point size of this Font.

```
float getSize2D()
```
Returns the point size of this Font.

```
LineMetrics getLineMetrics(CharacterIterator c, int i, int n,
  Graphics g)
```
Returns, with respect to context f, the line metrics of the substring of the sequence characters denoted by iterator c starting with its ith character in this Font.

```
Rectangle2D getStringBounds(char[] c, int i, int n,
  FontRenderContext f)
```
Returns, with respect to context f, the bounding box of the substring of the n characters denoted by list c starting with its ith element in this Font.

```
Rectangle2D getStringBounds(CharacterIterator c, int i, int n,
  FontRenderContext f)
```
Returns, with respect to context f, the bounding box of the substring of n characters denoted by iterator c starting with its ith character in this Font.

```
Rectangle2D getStringBounds(String s, FontRenderContext f)
```
Returns the bounding box of string of s with respect to context f.

```
Rectangle2D getStringBounds(String s, int i, int n,
  FontRenderContext f)
```
Returns, with respect to context f, the bounding box of a substring of s starting with the ith character.

```
int getStyle()
```
Returns the style of this Font.

```
AffineTransform getTransform()
```
Returns a clone of the affine transform of this Font.

```
int hashCode()
```
Returns a hash code for this Font.

```
boolean hasUniformLineMetrics()
```
Returns whether this Font has uniform line metrics.

```
boolean isBold()
```
Returns whether the style of this Font is bold.

boolean isItalic()

Returns whether the style of this Font is italic.

boolean isPlain()

Returns whether the style of this Font is plain.

boolean isTransformed()

Returns whether this Font has a transform that affects its size.

GlyphVector layoutGlyphVector(FontRenderContext f1, char[] c,
  int i, int n, int f2)

Returns a new GlyphVector for the sequence of characters denoted by list c starting with its ith element with respect font rendering context f1 and flags f2.

String toString()

Returns a representation of this Font.

| awt | **abstract class** FontMetrics **implements** Serializable |

PURPOSE

Represents rendering information for individual characters and strings with respect to a font and a graphical context.

FIELD SUMMARY

protected Font font

Represents the font in question for this FontMetrics.

CONSTRUCTOR SUMMARY

protected FontMetrics(Font f)

Constructs a new FontMetrics for font f.

INSTANCE METHOD SUMMARY

int bytesWidth(byte[] c, int i, int n)

Returns the advance width of the substring of the n characters denoted by list c starting with its ith element in this FontMetrics.

int charsWidth(char[] c, int i, int n)

Returns the advance width of the substring of the n characters denoted by list c starting with its ith element in this FontMetrics.

int charWidth(char c)

Returns the advance width of character c in the font of this FontMetrics.

int charWidth(int c)

Returns the advance width of character c in the font of this FontMetrics.

int getAscent()

Returns the ascent of the font of this FontMetrics.

int getDescent()

Returns the descent of the font of this FontMetrics.

Font getFont()

Returns the font of this FontMetrics.

int getHeight()

Returns the standard height in the font of this FontMetrics.

int getLeading()

Returns the standard leading in the font of this FontMetrics.

LineMetrics getLineMetrics(**char**[] c, **int** i, **int** n, Graphics g)

> Returns, with respect to graphics g, the line metrics of the sequence of characters denoted by list c starting with its ith element in this FontMetrics.

LineMetrics getLineMetrics(CharacterIterator c, **int** i, **int** n, Graphics g)

> Returns, with respect to graphics g, the line metrics of the substring of the n characters denoted by iterator c starting with its ith character in this FontMetrics.

LineMetrics getLineMetrics(String s, Graphics g)

> Returns the line metrics of string s in this Graphics.

LineMetrics getLineMetrics(String s, **int** i, **int** n, Graphics g)

> Returns, with respect to graphics g, the line metrics of a substring of the length n string s starting with the ith character in this Graphics.

int getMaxAdvance()

> Returns the maximum advance of any character in the font of this FontMetrics.

int getMaxAscent()

> Returns the maximum ascent in the font of this FontMetrics.

Rectangle2D getMaxCharBounds(Graphics g)

> Returns, with respect to graphics g, the bounding box of the character in the font of this FontMetrics with a maximum bounding box.

int getMaxDescent()

> Returns the maximum descent in the font of this FontMetrics.

Rectangle2D getStringBounds(**char**[] c, **int** i, **int** n, Graphics g)

> Returns, with respect to graphics g, the bounding box of the sequence of characters denoted by list c starting with its ith element in this FontMetrics.

Rectangle2D getStringBounds(CharacterIterator c, **int** i, **int** n, Graphics g)

> Returns, with respect to graphics g, the bounding box of the substring of the n characters denoted by iterator c starting with its ith character in this FontMetrics.

Rectangle2D getStringBounds(String s, Graphics g)

> Returns the bounding box of the string s in this Graphics.

Rectangle2D getStringBounds(String s, **int** i, **int** n, Graphics g)

> Returns, with respect to graphics g, the bounding box of a substring of s starting with the ith character in this Graphics.

int[] getWidths()

> Returns the advance widths of the first 256 characters in the font of this FontMetrics.

boolean hasUniformLineMetrics()

> Returns whether the font of this FontMetrics has uniform line metrics.

int stringWidth(String s)

> Returns the advance width of string s in the font of this FontMetrics.

String toString()

> Returns a representation of this FontMetrics.

awt	**abstract class** Graphics

PURPOSE

Represents the information needed for a rendering operation.

CONSTRUCTOR SUMMARY

protected Graphics()

Constructs a new Graphics object.

INSTANCE METHOD SUMMARY

abstract void clearRect(**int** x, **int** y, **int** w, **int** w)

Fills the rectangular region with origin (x, y) and width w and height h in this Graphics with the background color.

abstract void clipRect(**int** x, **int** y, **int** w, **int** h)

Sets the clipping rectangle of this Graphics as the intersection of the current clipping rectangle and the rectangular region with origin (x, y) and width w and height h.

abstract Graphics copyArea(**int** x, **int** y, **int** w, **int** h, **int** dx, **int** dy)

Copies the rectangular region of this Graphics with origin (x, y) and width w and height h at location (x+dx, y+dy).

abstract Graphics create()

Returns a new clone of this Graphics.

Graphics create(**int** x, **int** y, **int** w, **int** h)

Creates a new Graphics based on this Graphics, where the new graphical context translates this Graphics by (x, y) and has clipping rectangle with width w and height h.

abstract void dispose()

Disposes of this Graphics.

void draw3DRect(**int** x, **int** y, **int** w, **int** h, **boolean** b)

Renders, using this Graphics, a three-dimensional outline of the rectangular region with origin (x, y) and width w and height h, where the rectangular appears raised depends on b.

abstract void drawArc(**int** x, **int** y, **int** w, **int** h, **int** a1, **int** a2)

Renders, using this Graphics, an elliptical arc with origin (x, y) and width w and height h and starting and ending angles a1 and a2.

void drawBytes(**byte**[] b, **int** i, **int** n, **int** x, **int** y)

Renders, using this Graphics, n bytes of array a starting with a[i], where the text baseline is (x, y).

void drawChars(**char**[] a, **int** i, **int** n, **int** x, **int** y)

Renders, using this Graphics, n characters of array a starting with a[i], where the text baseline is (x, y).

abstract boolean drawImage(Image i, **int** x, **int** y, Color c, ImageObserver o)

Renders, using this Graphics, image i at location (x, y) using image observer o. Returns whether the image was completed loaded prior to rendering.

`abstract boolean` `drawImage(Image i, int x, int y, ImageObserver o)`

Renders, using this `Graphics`, image i at location (x, y) with background color c using image observer o. Returns whether the image was completed loaded prior to rendering.

`abstract boolean` `drawImage(Image i, int x, int y, int w, int h, Color c, ImageObserver o)`

Renders a scaled version of image i with width w and height h using this `Graphics`, at location (x, y) with background color c using image observer o. Returns whether the image was completed loaded prior to rendering. Returns whether the image was completed loaded prior to rendering.

`abstract boolean` `drawImage(Image i, int x, int y, int w, int h, ImageObserver o)`

Renders a scaled version of image i with width w and height h using this `Graphics`, at location (x, y) using image observer o. Returns whether the image was completed loaded prior to rendering. Returns whether the image was completed loaded prior to rendering.

`abstract boolean` `drawImage(Image i, int dx1, int dy1, int dx2, int dy2, int sx1, int sy1, int sx2, int sy2, Color c, ImageObserver o)`

Renders a scaled version of the rectangular subregion specified by source locations (sx1, sy1) and (sx2, sy2) of image i in the destination rectangular subregion specified by locations (dx1, dy1) and (dx2, dy2) using this `Graphics` with background color c using image observer o. Returns whether the image was completed loaded prior to rendering.

`abstract boolean` `drawImage(Image i, int dx1, int dy1, int dx2, int dy2, int sx1, int sy1, int sx2, int sy2, ImageObserver o)`

Renders a scaled version of the rectangular subregion specified by source locations (sx1, sy1) and (sx2, sy2) of image i in the destination rectangular subregion specified by locations (dx1, dy1) and (dx2, dy2) using this `Graphics` using image observer o. Returns whether the image was completed loaded prior to rendering.

`abstract void` `drawLine(int x1, int y1, int x2, int y2)`

Renders a line in the current color with endpoints (x1, y1) and (x2, y2) using this `Graphics`.

`abstract void` `drawOval(int x, int y, int w, int h)`

Renders the outline of an oval in the current color with origin (x, y), width w, and height h using this `Graphics`.

`abstract void` `drawPolygon(int[] x, int[] y, int n)`

Invokes `drawPolygon(new Polygon(x, y, n))`.

`void` `drawPolygon(Polygon p)`

Renders the outline of a closed polygon in the current color using this `Graphics`.

`abstract void` `drawPolyline(int[] x, int[] y, int n)`

Renders an open polygon in the current color based on x, y, and n in the current color using this `Graphics`.

void drawRect(int x, int y, int w, int h)

    Renders the outline of a rectangle in the current color with width w and height h using this Graphics, at location (x, y).

abstract void drawRoundRect(int x, int y, int w1, int h2, int w2, int h2)

    Renders the outline of a rounded rectangle in the current color with width w1 and height h1 using this Graphics, at location (x, y), where the corners are elliptical with width w2 and height h2.

abstract void drawString(AttributedCharacterIterator i, int x, int y)

    Renders the text represented by iterator i at baseline (x, y) using this Graphics.

abstract void drawString(String s, int x, int y)

    Renders the text represented by string s at baseline (x, y) using this Graphics.

void fill3DRect(int x, int y, int w, int h, boolean b)

    Renders, using this Graphics, a three-dimensional filled rectangular region with origin (x, y) and width w and height h, where the rectangular appears raised depends on b.

abstract void fillArc(int x, int y, int w, int h, int a1, int a2)

    Renders, in the current color using this Graphics, a filled elliptical arc with origin (x, y) and width w and height h and starting and ending angles a1 and a2.

abstract void fillOval(int x, int y, int w, int h)

    Renders a filled oval in the current color with origin (x, y), width w, and height h using this Graphics.

abstract void fillPolygon(int[] x, int[] y, int n)

    Invokes fillPolygon(**new** Polygon(x, y, n)).

void fillPolygon(Polygon p)

    Renders a filled closed polygon in the current color using this Graphics.

abstract void fillRect(int x, int y, int w, int h)

    Renders a filled rectangle in the current color with width w and height h using this Graphics, at location (x, y).

abstract void fillRoundRect(int x, int y, int w1, int h1, int w2, int h2)

    Renders a filled rounded rectangle in the current color with width w1 and height h1 using this Graphics, at location (x, y), where the corners are elliptical with width w2 and height h2.

void finalize()

    Disposes of this Graphics when it does not have any references.

abstract Shape getClip()

    Returns the clipping area of this Graphics.

abstract Rectangle getClipBounds()

    Returns the bounding rectangle of the clipping area of this Graphics.

Rectangle getClipBounds(Rectangle r)

    Returns using r the bounding rectangle of the clipping area of this Graphics.

abstract Color getColor()

    Returns the color of this Graphics.

abstract Font getFont()

Returns the font of this Graphics.

FontMetrics getFontMetrics()

Returns the font metrics of this Graphics.

abstract FontMetrics getFontMetrics(Font f)

Returns the font metrics for font f with this Graphics.

boolean hitClip(int x, int y, int w, int h)

Returns whether the rectangle with width w and height h at location (x, y) intersects the clipping area of this Graphics.

abstract void setClip(int x, int y, int w, int h)

Sets the clipping area of this Graphics to the rectangle with width w and height h at location (x, y).

abstract void setClip(Shape s)

Sets s as the clipping area of this Graphics.

abstract void setColor(Color c)

Sets c as the color of this Graphics.

abstract void setFont(Font f)

Sets f as the font of this Graphics.

abstract void setPaintMode()

Sets the paint mode of this Graphics to alternate between the current color and the color of destination.

abstract void setXORMode(Color c)

Sets the paint mode of this Graphics to alternate between the current color and color c.

String toString()

Returns a representation of this Graphics.

abstract void translate(int dx, int dy)

Translates the origin of this Graphics by distances dx and dy respectively on the x- and y-axes.

| awt | **class** GridLayout **implements** LayoutManager, Serializable |

PURPOSE

Represents a layout manager that arranges its components in a rectangular grid.

CONSTRUCTOR SUMMARY

GridLayout()

Constructs a new GridLayout for managing a single component.

GridLayout(int r, int c)

Constructs a new GridLayout for managing r rows of components with c components per row.

GridLayout(int r, int c, int h, int v)

Constructs a new GridLayout for managing r rows of components with c components per row. The inter-row horizontal gap is h and the intercolumn vertical gap is v.

    void addLayoutComponent(String s, Component c)

Adds component c with name s to the layout of this layout manager.
    int getColumns()

Returns the number of columns used by this layout manager.
    int getHgap()

Returns the intercomponent horizontal gap used by this layout manager.
    int getRows()

Returns the number of rows used by this layout manager.
    int getVgap()

Returns the intercomponent vertical gap used by this layout manager.
    void layoutContainer(Container c)

Arranges the components of container c using this layout manager.
    Dimension minimumLayoutSize(Container c)

Returns the minimum size of container c using this layout manager.
    Dimension preferredLayoutSize(Container c)

Returns the preferred size of container c using this layout manager.
    void removeLayoutComponent(Component c)

Removes component c from the arrangement of this layout manager.
    void setColumns(**int** n)

Sets n as the number of columns used by this layout manager.
    void setHgap(**int** h)

Sets h as the horizontal gap between components by this layout manager.
    void setRows(**int** r)

Sets n as the number of rows used by this layout manager.
    void setVgap(**int** v)

Sets v as the vertical gap between components used by this layout manager.
    String toString()

Returns a representation of this layout manager.

---

awt   **abstract class** Image

PURPOSE
Serves as a superclass for image representations.
FIELD SUMMARY
    static int SCALE_AREA_AVERAGING

Represents a scaling algorithm that performs area averaging.
    static int SCALE_DEFAULT

Represents the default scaling algorithm.
    static int SCALE_FAST

Represents a scaling algorithm that gives precedence to scaling speed.
    static int SCALE_REPLICATE

Represents a scaling algorithm of class ReplicateScaleFilter.
    static int SCALE_SMOOTH

Represents a scaling algorithm that gives precedence to image smoothness.

`static` `Object` `UndefinedProperty`

Represents that the requested property value is not defined.

CONSTRUCTOR SUMMARY

`Image()`

Creates a new `Image`.

INSTANCE METHOD SUMMARY

`abstract void flush()`

Flushes the resources of this `Image`.

`abstract Graphics getGraphics()`

Returns a new graphics context for rendering this `Image`.

`abstract int getHeight(ImageObserver i)`

Returns the height of this `Image`.

`abstract Object getProperty(String s, ImageObserver i)`

Returns the value of property `s` of this `Image`.

`Image getScaledInstance(int w, int h, int a)`

Returns a scaled version of this `Image` with width w and height h, where the requested scaling algorithm is a.

`abstract ImageProducer getSource()`

Returns a pixel producer for this `Image`.

`abstract int getWidth(ImageObserver i)`

Returns the width of this `Image`.

`awt.event`	`abstract class` `KeyAdapter` `implements` `KeyListener`

PURPOSE

A convenience class for handling keyboard events. Its methods perform no actions. A specialized class overrides them as needed.

CONSTRUCTOR SUMMARY

`KeyAdapter()`

Constructs a new `KeyAdapter`.

INSTANCE METHOD SUMMARY

`void keyPressed(KeyEvent e)`

Ignores a key pressing event.

`void keyReleased(KeyEvent e)`

Ignores a key release event.

`void keyTyped(KeyEvent e)`

Ignores a key typing event.

`awt.event`	`class` `KeyEvent` `implements` `InputEvent`

PURPOSE

Represents a keystroke event.

FIELD SUMMARY

`static char` CHAR_UNDEFINED

Represents key events whose key character is not a Unicode character.

`static int` KEY_FIRST

Represents the minimal index of a key event type.

`static int` KEY_LAST

Represents the maximal index of a key event type.

`static int` KEY_LOCATION_LEFT

Represents that the key character for a key event is left-positioned.

`static int` KEY_LOCATION_NUMPAD

Represents that the key character for a key event is part of the numerical keypad.

`static int` KEY_LOCATION_RIGHT

Represents that the key character for a key event is right-positioned.

`static int` KEY_LOCATION_STANDARD

Represents that the key character for a key event is neither a left nor a right distinguishing key character nor a numeric pay key character.

`static int` KEY_LOCATION_UNKNOWN

Represents that the key character for a key event is of unknown position.

`static int` KEY_PRESSED

Represents a key pressing event.

`static int` KEY_RELEASED

Represents a key released event.

`static int` KEY_TYPED

Represents a key typed event.

`static int` VK_UNDEFINED

Represents that the key code is unknown.

The following class constants are identified with keys with the indicated names. Not all keys are available on all keyboards.

VK_0	VK_1
VK_2	VK_3
VK_4	VK_5
VK_6	VK_7
VK_8	VK_9
VK_A	VK_ACCEPT
VK_ADD	VK_AGAIN
VK_ALL_CANDIDATES	VK_ALPHANUMERIC
VK_ALT	VK_ALT_GRAPH
VK_AMPERSAND	VK_ASTERISK
VK_AT	VK_B
VK_BACK_QUOTE	VK_BACK_SLASH
VK_BACK_SPACE	VK_BRACELEFT
VK_BRACERIGHT	VK_C
VK_CANCEL	VK_CAPS_LOCK
VK_CIRCUMFLEX	VK_CLEAR
VK_CLOSE_BRACKET	VK_CODE_INPUT
VK_COLON	VK_COMMA
VK_COMPOSE	VK_CONTROL
VK_CONVERT	VK_COPY
VK_CUT	VK_D
VK_DEAD_ABOVEDOT	VK_DEAD_ABOVERING
VK_DEAD_ACUTE	VK_DEAD_BREVE
VK_DEAD_CARON	VK_DEAD_CEDILLA
VK_DEAD_CIRCUMFLEX	VK_DEAD_DIAERESIS

VK_DEAD_DOUBLEACUTE	VK_DEAD_GRAVE
VK_DEAD_IOTA	VK_DEAD_MACRON
VK_DEAD_OGONEK	VK_DEAD_SEMIVOICED_SOUND
VK_DEAD_TILDE	VK_DEAD_VOICED_SOUND
VK_DECIMAL	VK_DELETE
VK_DIVIDE	VK_DOLLAR
VK_DOWN	VK_E
VK_END	VK_ENTER
VK_EQUALS	VK_ESCAPE
VK_EURO_SIGN	VK_EXCLAMATION_MARK
VK_F	VK_F1
VK_F10	VK_F11
VK_F12	VK_F13
VK_F14	VK_F15
VK_F16	VK_F17
VK_F18	VK_F19
VK_F2	VK_F20
VK_F21	VK_F22
VK_F23	VK_F24
VK_F3	VK_F4
VK_F5	VK_F6
VK_F7	VK_F8
VK_F9	VK_FINAL
VK_FIND	VK_FULL_WIDTH
VK_G	VK_GREATER
VK_H	VK_HALF_WIDTH
VK_HELP	VK_HIRAGANA
VK_HOME	VK_I
VK_INPUT_METHOD_ON_OFF	VK_INSERT
VK_INVERTED_EXCLAMATION_MARK	VK_J
VK_JAPANESE_HIRAGANA	VK_JAPANESE_KATAKANA
VK_JAPANESE_ROMAN	VK_K
VK_KANA	VK_KANA_LOCK
VK_KANJI	VK_KATAKANA
VK_KP_DOWN	VK_KP_LEFT
VK_KP_RIGHT	VK_KP_UP
VK_L	VK_LEFT
VK_LEFT_PARENTHESIS	VK_LESS
VK_M	VK_META
VK_MINUS	VK_MODECHANGE
VK_MULTIPLY	VK_N
VK_NONCONVERT	VK_NUM_LOCK
VK_NUMBER_SIGN	VK_NUMPAD0
VK_NUMPAD1	VK_NUMPAD2
VK_NUMPAD3	VK_NUMPAD4
VK_NUMPAD5	VK_NUMPAD6
VK_NUMPAD7	VK_NUMPAD8
VK_NUMPAD9	VK_O
VK_OPEN_BRACKET	VK_P
VK_PAGE_DOWN	VK_PAGE_UP
VK_PASTE	VK_PAUSE
VK_PERIOD	VK_PLUS
VK_PREVIOUS_CANDIDATE	VK_PRINTSCREEN
VK_PROPS	VK_Q
VK_QUOTE	VK_QUOTEDBL
VK_R	VK_RIGHT
VK_RIGHT_PARENTHESIS	VK_ROMAN_CHARACTERS
VK_S	VK_SCROLL_LOCK
VK_SEMICOLON	VK_SEPARATOR
VK_SHIFT	VK_SLASH
VK_SPACE	VK_STOP
VK_SUBTRACT	VK_T
VK_TAB	VK_U

VK_UNDERSCORE	VK_UNDO
VK_UP	VK_V
VK_W	VK_X
VK_Y	VK_Z

CLASS METHOD SUMMARY

`static String getKeyModifiersText(int m)`

Returns a representation of key modifier m.

`static String getKeyText(int n)`

Returns a representation of key code n.

CONSTRUCTOR SUMMARY

`KeyEvent(Component v, int n, long t, int m, int k, char c)`

Constructs a new KeyEvent of type n occurring at time t in component v using key modifiers m, where k is key code of the typed character and c is its Unicode encoding.

`KeyEvent(Component v, int n, long t, int m, int k, char c, int l)`

Constructs a new KeyEvent of type n occurring at time t in component v using key modifiers m, where k is key code of the typed character, c is its Unicode encoding, and l is its location.

INSTANCE METHOD SUMMARY

`char getKeyChar()`

Returns the character associated with this KeyEvent.

`int getKeyCode()`

Returns the key code of this KeyEvent.

`int getKeyLocation()`

Returns the location of the key associated with this KeyEvent.

`boolean isActionKey()`

Returns whether the key of this KeyEvent is an action key.

`String paramString()`

Returns a representation of this KeyEvent.

`void setKeyChar(char c)`

Sets c as the character associated with this KeyEvent.

`void setKeyCode(int n)`

Sets n as the key code of this KeyEvent.

---

awt.event   `class KeyListener implements EventListener`

PURPOSE

Describes the methods a key listener must perform.

INSTANCE METHOD SUMMARY

`void keyPressed(KeyEvent e)`

Handles a key pressing event.

`void keyReleased(KeyEvent e)`

Handles a key released event.

`void keyTyped(KeyEvent e)`

Handles a key typing event.

`class MouseEvent` **implements** `InputEvent`

PURPOSE
Represents a mouse interaction event.

FIELD SUMMARY

`static int BUTTON1`
Represents the first mouse button.

`static int BUTTON2`
Represents the second mouse button.

`static int BUTTON3`
Represents the third mouse button.

`static int MOUSE_CLICKED`
Represents a mouse clicking event.

`static int MOUSE_DRAGGED`
Represents a mouse dragging event.

`static int MOUSE_ENTERED`
Represents a mouse component-entering event.

`static int MOUSE_EXITED`
Represents a mouse component-exiting event.

`static int MOUSE_FIRST`
Represents the minimal index of a mouse event.

`static int MOUSE_LAST`
Represents the maximal index of a mouse event.

`static int MOUSE_MOVED`
Represents a mouse movement event.

`static int MOUSE_PRESSED`
Represents a mouse button-pressing event.

`static int MOUSE_RELEASED`
Represents a mouse button-release event.

`static int MOUSE_WHEEL`
Represents a mouse wheel event.

`static int NOBUTTON`
Represents no mouse button.

CLASS METHOD

`static String getMouseModifiersText(int m)`
Returns a description of key modifier m.

CONSTRUCTOR SUMMARY

`MouseEvent(Component v, int n, long t, int m, int x, int y, int c, boolean b)`
Constructs a new `MouseEvent` of type n at location (x, y) occurring at time t in component v using key modifiers m and click count c, where b indicates this event triggers a popup menu.

`MouseEvent(Component v, int n, long t, int m, int x, int y, int c, boolean b, int b)`
Constructs a new `MouseEvent` involving button b of type n at location (x, y) occurring at time t in component v using key modifiers m and click count c, where b indicates this event triggers a popup menu.

INSTANCE METHOD SUMMARY

int getButton()

Returns which button triggered this MouseEvent.

int getClickCount()

Returns the number of button clicks with this MouseEvent.

Point getPoint()

Returns the location of this MouseEvent.

int getX()

Returns the x-coordinate position of this MouseEvent.

int getY()

Returns the y-coordinate position of this MouseEvent.

boolean isPopupTrigger()

Returns whether this MouseEvent is a popup menu trigger event.

String paramString()

Returns a representation of this MouseEvent.

void translatePoint(int dx, int dy)

Shifts the location of this MouseEvent by distances dx and dy respectively on the x- and y-axes.

`awt.event`   abstract class MouseAdapter implements MouseListener

PURPOSE

A convenience class for handling mouse events. Its methods perform no actions. A specialized class overrides them as needed.

CONSTRUCTOR SUMMARY

MouseAdapter()

Constructs a new MouseAdapter.

INSTANCE METHOD SUMMARY

void mouseClicked(MouseEvent e)

Ignores a mouse clicking event.

void mouseEntered(MouseEvent e)

Ignores a mouse component-entering event.

void mouseExited(MouseEvent e)

Ignores a mouse component-exiting event.

void mousePressed(MouseEvent e)

Ignores a mouse button-pressing event.

void mouseReleased(MouseEvent e)

Ignores a mouse button-release event.

`awt.event`   interface MouseListener extends EventListener

PURPOSE

Describes the actions a mouse listener must perform.

INSTANCE METHOD SUMMARY
   void mouseClicked(MouseEvent e)
      Handles a mouse clicking event.
   void mouseEntered(MouseEvent e)
      Handles a mouse component-entering event.
   void mouseExited(MouseEvent e)
      Handles a mouse component-exiting event.
   void mousePressed(MouseEvent e)
      Handles a mouse button-pressing event.
   void mouseReleased(MouseEvent e)
      Handles a mouse button-release event.

---

awt   **class** Point **extends** Point2D **implements** Serializable

PURPOSE
Represents a point in two-dimensional space.
FIELD SUMMARY
   int x
      Represents the x-coordinate of this Point.
   int y
      Represents the y-coordinate of this Point.
CONSTRUCTOR SUMMARY
   Point()
      Constructs a new Point representing the origin (0, 0).
   Point(**int** x, **int** y)
      Constructs a new Point representing the location (x, y).
   Point(Point p)
      Constructs a new Point that is a clone of point p.
INSTANCE METHOD SUMMARY
   boolean equals(Object v)
      Returns whether v is a point equal to this Point.
   Point getLocation()
      Returns a clone of this Point.
   double getX()
      Returns the x-coordinate of this Point.
   double getY()
      Returns the y-coordinate of this Point.
   void move(**int** x, **int** y)
      Resets this Point to represent the location (x, y).
   void setLocation(**double** x, **double** y)
      Resets this Point to represent the location (x, y).
   void setLocation(**int** x, **int** y)
      Resets this Point to represent the location (x, y).
   void setLocation(Point p)
      Resets this Point to be a clone of point p.

```
String toString()
```
Returns a representation of this `Point`.
```
void translate(int dx, int dy)
```
Shifts this `Point` by distances `dx` and `dy` respectively on the x- and y-axes.

---

class `Polygon` **implements** `Shape, Serializable`

PURPOSE
Represents a polygon in two-dimensional coordinate space.

FIELD SUMMARY
```
protected Rectangle
```
Represents the bounding box of this `Polygon`.
```
int npoints
```
Represents the number of endpoints describing this `Polygon`.
```
int[] xpoints
```
Represents the x-coordinates of this `Polygon`.
```
int[] ypoints
```
Represents the x-coordinates of this `Polygon`.

CONSTRUCTOR SUMMARY
```
Polygon()
```
Creates a new `Polygon` with no segments.
```
Polygon(int[] x, int[] y, int n)
```
Creates a new `Polygon` composed of `n` points, where the `i`th point is (`x[i]`, `y[i]`).

INSTANCE METHOD SUMMARY
```
void addPoint(int x, int y)
```
Appends point (`x`, `y`) to the list of points represented by this `Polygon`.
```
boolean contains(double x, double y)
```
Returns whether this `Polygon` contains point (`x`, `y`).
```
boolean contains(double x, double y, double w, double h)
```
Returns whether this `Polygon` contains the rectangle with origin (`x`, `y`) with width `w` and height `h`.
```
boolean contains(int x, int y)
```
Returns whether this `Polygon` contains point (`x`, `y`).
```
boolean contains(Point p)
```
Returns whether this `Polygon` contains point `p`.
```
boolean contains(Point2D p)
```
Returns whether this `Polygon` contains point `p`.
```
boolean contains(Rectangle2D r)
```
Returns whether this `Polygon` contains rectangle `r`.
```
Rectangle getBounds()
```
Returns the bounding box of this `Polygon`.
```
Rectangle2D getBounds2D()
```
Returns the bounding box of this `Polygon`.

PathIterator getPathIterator(AffineTransform a)

Returns an iterator that iterates over a list of segments approximating the boundary of this Polygon, where segment endpoints are modified with respect to transform a.

PathIterator getPathIterator(AffineTransform a, **double** v)

Returns an iterator that iterates over a list of segments approximating the boundary of this Polygon, where segment endpoints are modified with respect to transform a and where value v is a limit on the distance of a segment point from its true position on the shape outline.

boolean intersects(**double** x, **double** y, **double** w, **double** h)

Returns whether this Polygon intersects the rectangle with origin (x, y), width w, and height h.

boolean intersects(Rectangle2D r)

Returns whether this Polygon intersects rectangle r.

void invalidate()

Signals the invalidity of any objects that use this Polygon.

void reset()

Resets this Polygon to represent an empty polygon.

void translate(**int** dx, **int** dx)

Translates the origin of this Polygon by distances dx and dy respectively on the x- and y-axes.

Returns the intersection of this Rectangle with rectangle r.

<table>
<tr><td>awt</td><td>**class** Rectangle **extends** Rectangle2D **implements** Shape, Serializable</td></tr>
</table>

PURPOSE

Represents a rectangle in two-dimensional coordinate space.

FIELD SUMMARY

int height

Represents the height of this Rectangle.

int width

Represents the width of this Rectangle.

int x

Represents the x-coordinate of this Rectangle.

int y

Represents the y-coordinate of this Rectangle.

CONSTRUCTOR SUMMARY

Rectangle()

Constructs a new Rectangle with origin (0, 0) with a zero width and height.

Rectangle(Dimension d)

Constructs a new Rectangle with origin (0, 0) and dimensions d.

Rectangle(**int** w, **int** h)

Constructs a new Rectangle with origin (0, 0) with width w and height h.

Rectangle(**int** x, **int** y, **int** w, **int** h)

Constructs a new Rectangle with origin (x, y) with width w and height h.

Rectangle(Point p)

    Constructs a new Rectangle with origin p with a zero width and height.

Rectangle(Point p, Dimension d)

    Constructs a new Rectangle with origin p and dimension d.

Rectangle(Rectangle r)

    Constructs a clone of rectangle r.

INSTANCE METHOD SUMMARY

void add(**int** x, **int** y)

    Returns the union of this Rectangle with point (x, y).

void add(Point p)

    Returns the union of this Rectangle with point p.

void add(Rectangle r)

    Returns the union of this Rectangle with rectangle r.

boolean contains(**int** x, **int** y)

    Returns whether this Rectangle contains point p.

boolean contains(**int** x, **int** y, **int** w, **int** h)

    Returns whether this Rectangle contains the rectangle with origin (x, y), width w, and height h.

boolean contains(Point p)

    Returns whether this Rectangle contains point p.

boolean contains(Rectangle r)

    Returns whether this Rectangle contains rectangle r.

Rectangle2D createIntersection(Rectangle2D r)

    Returns the intersection of rectangle r and this Rectangle.

Rectangle2D createUnion(Rectangle2D r)

    Returns the union of rectangle r and this Rectangle.

boolean equals(Object v)

    Returns whether v is a rectangle equal to this Rectangle.

Rectangle getBounds()

    Return the bounding box of this Rectangle.

Rectangle2D getBounds2D()

    Return the bounding box of this Rectangle.

double getHeight()

    Returns the height of this Rectangle.

Point getLocation()

    Returns the origin of this Rectangle.

Dimension getSize()

    Returns the dimensions of this Rectangle.

double getWidth()

    Returns the width of this Rectangle.

double getX()

    Returns the x-coordinate of the origin of this Rectangle.

double getY()

    Returns the y-coordinate of the origin of this Rectangle.

void grow(**int** dw, **int** dh)

    Increases the width and height of this Rectangle respectively by dw and dh.

Rectangle intersection(Rectangle r)

Returns the intersection of this Rectangle with rectangle r.

boolean intersects(Rectangle r)

Returns whether this Rectangle intersects rectangle r.

boolean isEmpty()

Returns whether this Rectangle is empty.

int outcode(**double** x, **double** y)

Returns where the (x, y) lies with respect to this Rectangle.

void setBounds(**int** x, **int** y, **int** w, **int** h)

Sets the bounding rectangle of this Rectangle equal to a rectangle with (x, y) as its origin and with width w and height h.

void setBounds(Rectangle r)

Sets the bounding rectangle of this Rectangle equal to rectangle r.

void setLocation(**int** x, **int** y)

Sets (x, y) as the origin of this Rectangle.

void setLocation(Point p)

Sets p as the origin of this Rectangle.

void setRect(**double** x, **double** y, **double** w, **double** h)

Sets the origin to (x, y) and size to width w and height h for this Rectangle.

void setSize(Dimension d)

Sets the size of this Rectangle to that of dimension d.

void setSize(**int** w, **int** h)

Sets the size of this Rectangle to width w and height h.

String toString()

Returns a representation of this Rectangle.

void translate(**int** dx, **int** dy)

Translates the origin of this Rectangle by distances dx and dy respectively on the x- and y-axes.

Rectangle union(Rectangle r)

Returns the union of this Rectangle with rectangle r.

---

awt	**interface** Shape

PURPOSE

Describes the methods necessary for representing a shape described by a path iterator that specifies both the outline and the means for identifying how the shapes divides a plane into interior and external regions.

INSTANCE METHOD SUMMARY

boolean contains(**double** x, **double** y)

Returns whether (x, y) lies within the boundary of this Shape.

boolean contains(**double** x, **double** y, **double** w, **double** h)

Returns whether the interior of this Shape contains the rectangular region originating at (x, y) with width w and height h.

boolean contains(Point2D p)

Returns whether p lies within the boundary of this Shape.

> **boolean** contains(Rectangle2D r)
>
>> Returns whether the interior of this Shape contains the rectangular region represented by r.
>
> Rectangle getBounds()
>
>> Returns the bounding rectangle of this Shape.
>
> Rectangle2D getBounds2D()
>
>> Returns the bounding rectangle of this Shape.
>
> PathIterator getPathIterator(AffineTransform a)
>
>> Returns an iterator that iterates over a list of segments approximating the boundary of this Shape, where segment endpoints are modified with respect to transform a.
>
> PathIterator getPathIterator(AffineTransform a, **double** v)
>
>> Returns an iterator that iterates over a list of segments approximating the boundary of this Shape, where segment endpoints are modified with respect to transform a and where value v is a limit on the distance of a segment point from its true position on the shape outline.
>
> **boolean** intersects(**double** x, **double** y, **double** w, **double** h)
>
>> Returns whether the interior of this Shape intersects the rectangular region originating at (x, y) with width w and height h.
>
> **boolean** intersects(Rectangle2D r)
>
>> Returns whether the interior of this Shape intersects the rectangular region represented by r.

---

awt.event   **class** TextEvent **extends** AWTEvent

PURPOSE

Represents a text-changing event.

FIELD SUMMARY

> **static int** TEXT_FIRST
>
>> Represents the minimal index of a text event.
>
> **static int** TEXT_LAST
>
>> Represents the maximal index of a text event.
>
> **static int** TEXT_VALUE_CHANGED
>
>> Represents a text change event.

CONSTRUCTOR SUMMARY

> TextEvent(Object v, **int** n)
>
>> Constructs a new TextEvent of type n for originating object v.

INSTANCE METHOD SUMMARY

> String paramString()
>
>> Returns a representation of this TextEvent.

---

awt.event	**interface** TextListener **extends** EventListener

PURPOSE
Describes the action a text listener must perform.
INSTANCE METHOD SUMMARY
    void textValueChanged(TextEvent e)
        Handles change in text event e.

---

awt.event	**class** WindowEvent **extends** ComponentEvent

PURPOSE
Represents a change in window status.
FIELD SUMMARY
    static int WINDOW_ACTIVATED
        Represents an activation event.
    static int WINDOW_CLOSED
        Represents a window closed event.
    static int WINDOW_CLOSING
        Represents a closing event.
    static int WINDOW_DEACTIVATED
        Represents a deactivation event.
    static int WINDOW_DEICONIFIED
        Represents a deiconifying event.
    static int WINDOW_FIRST
        Represents the minimal index of a windowing event.
    static int WINDOW_GAINED_FOCUS
        Represents a gaining focus event.
    static int WINDOW_ICONIFIED
        Represents an iconifying event.
    static int WINDOW_LAST
        Represents the maximal index of a windowing event.
    static int WINDOW_LOST_FOCUS
        Represents a losing focus event.
    static int WIND OW_OPENED
        Represents an opening event.
    static int WINDOW_STATE_CHANGED
        Represents a change in state event.
CONSTRUCTOR SUMMARY
    WindowEvent(Window w, **int** n)
        Constructs a new WindowEvent of type n for originating window w.
    WindowEvent(Window w, **int** n, **int** s1, **int** s2)
        Constructs a new WindowEvent of type n for originating window w, where s1
        and s2 are respectively the old and new window states.

WindowEvent(Window w1, **int** n, Window w2)

> Constructs a new WindowEvent of type n for originating window w1 and other window w2.

WindowEvent(Window w1, **int** n, Window w2, **int** s1, **int** s2)

> Constructs a new WindowEvent of type n for originating window w1 and other window w2, where s1 and s2 are respectively the old and new window states.

INSTANCE METHOD SUMMARY

int getNewState()

> Returns the state of the originating window of this WindowEvent.

int getOldState()

> Returns the previous state of the originating window for this WindowEvent.

Window getOppositeWindow()

> Returns the other window involved in this WindowEvent.

Window getWindow()

> Returns the originating window of this WindowEvent.

String paramString()

> Returns a representation of this WindowEvent.

---

awt.event   **interface** WindowListener **extends** EventListener

PURPOSE

Describes the actions required of a window listener.

INSTANCE METHOD SUMMARY

void windowActivated(WindowEvent e)

> Handles the window becoming active.

void windowClosed(WindowEvent e)

> Handles the closing of the window.

void windowClosing(WindowEvent e)

> Handles a signaling that the window is to close.

void windowDeactivated(WindowEvent e)

> Handles when a window becoming inactive.

void windowDeiconified(WindowEvent e)

> Handles a window becoming normal.

void windowIconified(WindowEvent e)

> Handles a window becoming minimized.

void windowOpened(WindowEvent e) of

> Handles the initial opening of the window.

E.3   JAVAX.SWING

---

swing   **class** ButtonGroup **implements** Serializable

PURPOSE
Represent a set of mutually exclusive buttons.

FIELD SUMMARY
    protected Vector buttons
        Represents the buttons in this ButtonGroup.

CONSTRUCTOR SUMMARY
    ButtonGroup()
        Constructs a new empty ButtonGroup.

INSTANCE METHOD SUMMARY
    void add(AbstractButton b)
        Adds button b to this ButtonGroup.
    int getButtonCount()
        Returns the number of buttons in this ButtonGroup.
    Enumeration getElements()
        Returns an enumeration of the buttons in this ButtonGroup.
    ButtonModel getSelection()
        Returns the model of the currently selected button in this ButtonGroup.
    boolean isSelected(ButtonModel b)
        Returns whether button model b is selected for this ButtonGroup.
    void remove(AbstractButton b)
        Removes button b from this ButtonGroup.
    void setSelected(ButtonModel b, **boolean** s)
        Sets s as the state of button model b for this ButtonGroup.

---

swing   **interface** Icon

PURPOSE
Describe functionality of a small static image.

INSTANCE METHOD SUMMARY
    int getIconHeight()
        Returns the height of this Icon.
    int getIconWidth()
        Returns the width of this Icon.
    void paintIcon(Component c, Graphics g, **int** x, **int** y)
        Paints this Icon at location (x, y) in graphics context g with component c provides rendering characteristics.

| swing | **class** ImageIcon **implements** Icon, Serializable, Accessible |

PURPOSE

Represents a small static image. Images based on a Web resource or a file are preloaded using a media tracker that monitors the image.

CONSTRUCTOR SUMMARY

ImageIcon()

Constructs a new ImageIcon with no display image.

ImageIcon(byte[] b)

Constructs a new ImageIcon using the bytes in array b as the display image.

ImageIcon(byte[] b, String s)

Constructs a new ImageIcon with description s using the bytes in array b as the display image.

ImageIcon(Image i)

Constructs a new ImageIcon using i as the display image.

ImageIcon(Image i, String s)

Constructs a new ImageIcon with description s using image i as the display image.

ImageIcon(String f)

Constructs a new ImageIcon using the image in the file named f as the display image.

ImageIcon(String f, String s)

Constructs a new ImageIcon with description s using the image in the file named f as the display image.

ImageIcon(URL u)

Constructs a new ImageIcon using the image at Web location u as the display image.

ImageIcon(URL u, String s)

Constructs a new ImageIcon with description s using the image at Web location u as the display image.

INSTANCE METHOD SUMMARY

AccessibleContext getAccessibleContext()

Returns the AccessibleContext of this ImageIcon.

String getDescription()

Returns the description of this ImageIcon.

int getIconHeight()

Returns the height of this ImageIcon.

int getIconWidth()

Returns the width of this ImageIcon.

Image getImage()

Returns the image of this ImageIcon.

int getImageLoadStatus()

Returns the status of the last image-loading operation of this ImageIcon.

ImageObserver getImageObserver()

Returns the image observer of this ImageIcon.

protected void loadImage(Image i)

Loads image i for this ImageIcon.

> **void** paintIcon(Component c, Graphics g, **int** x, **int** y)
>
> Paints this Icon at location (x, y) in graphics context g using observer c if this ImageIcon has no image observer.
>
> **void** setDescription(String s)
>
> Sets s as the description of this ImageIcon.
>
> **void** setImage(Image i)
>
> Sets i as the image displayed by this ImageIcon.
>
> **void** setImageObserver(ImageObserver i)
>
> Sets i as the image observer of this ImageIcon.
>
> String toString()
>
> Returns a representation of this ImageIcon.

---

swing

class JApplet **extends** Applet **implements** Accessible, RootPaneContainer

PURPOSE

Provides a swing-compatible version of an applet. An applet is a program that is run within another program such as Web browser. A JApplet contains a *root pane* to which other graphical components can be added. Components should not be added to the JApplet itself nor should a layout manager be set for JApplet. Instead components should be added to the root pane and the root pane should have a manager.

FIELD SUMMARY

> **protected** AccessibleContext accessibleContext
>
> Represents the accessibility context of this JApplet.
>
> **protected** JRootPane rootPane
>
> Represents the root pane this JApplet.
>
> **protected boolean** rootPaneCheckingEnabled
>
> Represents whether improper additions to this JApplet should generate exceptions.

CONSTRUCTOR SUMMARY

> JApplet()
>
> Constructs a new JApplet.

INSTANCE METHOD SUMMARY

> **protected void** addImpl(Component c, Object v, **int** i)
>
> Attempts to insert component c as the ith component of this JApplet using constraints v. An exception is thrown if root pane checking is enabled for this JApplet.
>
> **protected** JRootPane createRootPane()
>
> Invoked by constructors to create the root pane for this JApplet.
>
> AccessibleContext getAccessibleContext()
>
> Returns the accessibility context of this JApplet.
>
> Container getContentPane()
>
> Returns the content pane object of this JApplet.
>
> Component getGlassPane()
>
> Returns the glass pane of this JApplet.

JMenuBar getJMenuBar()

Returns the menu bar of this JApplet.

JLayeredPane getLayeredPane()

Returns the layered pane of this JApplet.

JRootPane getRootPane()

Returns the root pane of this JApplet.

protected boolean isRootPaneCheckingEnabled()

Returns whether invocations of add() and setLayout() to this JApplet generate exceptions.

protected String paramString()

Returns a representation of this JApplet.

void remove(Component c)

Removes the component c from this JApplet.

void setContentPane(Container c)

Sets c as the content pane of this JApplet.

void setGlassPane(Component g)

Sets g as the glass pane of this JApplet.

void setJMenuBar(JMenuBar m)

Sets m as the menu of this JApplet.

void setLayeredPane(JLayeredPane p)

Sets p as the layered pane of this JApplet.

void setLayout(LayoutManager m)

Attempts to sets the layout manager of this JApplet to m. An exception is thrown if root pane checking is enabled for this JApplet.

protected void setRootPane(JRootPane r)

Sets r as the root pane of this JApplet.

protected void setRootPaneCheckingEnabled(boolean b)

Returns whether invocations of add() and setLayout() by this JApplet generate exceptions.

void update(Graphics g)

Invokes paint(g).

---

swing   class JButton extends AbstractButton implements Accessible

PURPOSE

Represents a push button.

CONSTRUCTOR SUMMARY

JButton()

Constructs a new JButton with no label or icon.

JButton(Action a)

Constructs a new JButton with action a.

JButton(Icon i)

Constructs a new JButton with label image i.

JButton(String s)

Constructs a new JButton with label text s.

JButton(String s, Icon i)

Constructs a new JButton with label text s and image i.

INSTANCE METHOD SUMMARY

protected void configurePropertiesFromAction(Action a)

Sets a as the action properties of this JButton.

AccessibleContext getAccessibleContext()

Returns the accessibility context of this JButton.

String getUIClassID()

Returns a string that specifies the look and feel rendering this JButton.

boolean isDefaultButton()

Returns whether this JButton is the default button for its root pane.

boolean isDefaultCapable()

Returns whether this JButton is default capable.

protected String paramString()

Returns a representation of this JButton.

void removeNotify()

If this JButton was the default button for its root pane, then it is no longer the default button.

void setDefaultCapable(boolean b)

Sets whether this JButton can be the default button for its root pane.

void updateUI()

Resets the UI attribute of this object to the current look and feel.

---

swing

abstract class JComponent extends Container implements Serializable

PURPOSE

Represents a swing GUI component that is placeable in a top-level swing container.

FIELD SUMMARY

protected AccessibleContext accessibleContext

Represents the accessibility context of this JComponent.

protected EventListenerList listenerList

Represents the list of event listeners for this JComponent.

static String TO OL_TIP_TEXT_KEY

Represents the cursor fly over display comment.

protected ComponentUI u

Represents the look and feel delegate for this JComponent.

static int UNDEFINED_CONDITION

Represents that no condition is defined.

static int WHEN_ANCESTOR_OF_FOCUSED_COMPONENT

Indicates the registerKeyboardAction should be invoked when the receiver is either the focused component or an ancestor of the focused component.

static int WHEN_FOCUSED

Indicates the registerKeyboardAction should be invoked when the component has the focus.

static int WHEN_IN_FOCUSED_WINDOW

Indicates the registerKeyboardAction should be invoked when the receiver is either the focused component or is in the window that has the focus.

CLASS METHOD SUMMARY

static Locale getDefaultLocale()

Returns the default locale.

static void setDefaultLocale(Locale l)

Sets l as the default locale for a JComponent.

CONSTRUCTOR SUMMARY

JComponent()

Creates a new JComponent.

INSTANCE METHOD SUMMARY

void addAncestorListener(AncestorListener a)

Registers a as an ancestor event listener for this JComponent.

void addNotify()

Notifies this JComponent that it a parent component.

void addPropertyChangeListener(PropertyChangeListener p)

Registers p as property change listener for this JComponent.

void addPropertyChangeListener(String s, PropertyChangeListener p)

Registers p as property change listener for property s for this JComponent.

void addVetoableChangeListener(VetoableChangeListener v)

Registers p as vetoable change listener for this JComponent.

void computeVisibleRect(Rectangle r)

Sets the attributes of r to the intersection of the visible rectangles for this JComponent and its ancestors.

boolean contains(int x, int y)

Returns whether this JComponent contains logical point (x, y).

JToolTip createToolTip()

Returns the tool tip for this JComponent.

void firePropertyChange(String s, boolean v1, boolean v2)

Reports a change in bound property s from v1 to v2 for each property change listener for this JComponent.

void firePropertyChange(String s, byte v1, byte v2)

Reports a change in bound property s from v1 to v2 for each property change listener for this JComponent.

void firePropertyChange(String s, char v1, char v2)

Reports a change in bound property s from v1 to v2 for each property change listener for this JComponent.

void firePropertyChange(String s, double v1, double v2)

Reports a change in bound property s from v1 to v2 for each property change listener for this JComponent.

void firePropertyChange(String s, float v1, float v2)

Reports a change in bound property s from v1 to v2 for each property change listener for this JComponent.

void firePropertyChange(String s, **int** v1, **int** v2)

> Reports a change in bound property s from v1 to v2 for each property change listener for this JComponent.

void firePropertyChange(String s, **long** v1, **long** v2)

> Reports a change in bound property s from v1 to v2 for each property change listener for this JComponent.

protected void firePropertyChange(String s, Object v1, Object v2)

> Reports a change in bound property s from v1 to v2 for each property change listener for this JComponent.

void firePropertyChange(String s, **short** v1, **short** v2)

> Reports a change in bound property s from v1 to v2 for each vetoable change listener for this JComponent.

protected void fireVetoableChange(String s, Object v1, Object v2)

> Reports a vetoable change in constrained property s from v1 to v2 for each property change listener for this JComponent.

AccessibleContext getAccessibleContext()

> Returns the accessibility context for this JComponent.

ActionListener getActionForKeyStroke(KeyStroke c)

> Returns the action listener for this JComponent associated with keystroke character c.

ActionMap getActionMap()

> Returns the action mapper that maps action listeners to keystroke characters for this JComponent.

float getAlignmentX()

> Returns the vertical alignment for this JComponent.

float getAlignmentY()

> Returns the horizontal alignment for this JComponent.

AncestorListener[] getAncestorListeners()

> Returns the ancestor listeners for this JComponent.

boolean getAutoscrolls()

> Returns the autoscroll policy for this JComponent.

Border getBorder()

> Returns the border for this JComponent.

Rectangle getBounds(Rectangle r)

> Both sets the attributes of r to the bounding box of this JComponent and returns r.

Object getClientProperty(Object v)

> Returns the value of property v for this JComponent.

protected Graphics getComponentGraphics(Graphics g)

> Returns the graphics context for rendering this JComponent based on graphics context g.

int getConditionForKeyStroke(KeyStroke a)

> Returns the condition that determines whether the keystroke action listener for keystroke character a is invoked for this JComponent.

`int getDebugGraphicsOptions()`

Returns the graphics debugging information for this JComponent.

`Graphics getGraphics()`

Returns the graphics context for rendering this JComponent.

`int getHeight()`

Returns the height of this JComponent.

`InputMap getInputMap()`

Returns the input mapper that maps input focus listeners for this JComponent.

`InputMap getInputMap(int i)`

Returns the input mapper that maps input listeners for condition i for this JComponent.

`InputVerifier getInputVerifier()`

Returns the input verifier for this JComponent.

`Insets getInsets()`

Returns the border insets for this JComponent.

`Insets getInsets(Insets i)`

Returns the border insets for this JComponent using i if possible.

`EventListener[] getListeners(Class a)`

Returns the listeners for listener type event a for this JComponent.

`Point getLocation(Point p)`

Returns the origin for this JComponent using p.

`Dimension getMaximumSize()`

Returns the maximum size for this JComponent.

`Dimension getMinimumSize()`

Returns the minimum size for this JComponent.

`Dimension getPreferredSize()`

Returns the preferred size for this JComponent.

`PropertyChangeListener[] getPropertyChangeListeners()`

Returns the property change listeners for this JComponent.

`PropertyChangeListener[] getPropertyChangeListeners(String s)`

Returns the property change listeners of property s for this JComponent.

`KeyStroke[] getRegisteredKeyStrokes()`

Returns the keystrokes that have listeners for this JComponent.

`JRootPane getRootPane()`

Returns the root pane ancestor for this JComponent.

`Dimension getSize(Dimension d)`

Returns the dimensions for this JComponent using d.

`Point getToolTipLocation(MouseEvent e)`

Returns the logical location of the tool tip for this JComponent.

`String getToolTipText()`

Returns the tool tip for this JComponent.

`String getToolTipText(MouseEvent e)`

Returns the tool tip for event e for this JComponent.

`Container getTopLevelAncestor()`

Returns the top-level ancestor for this JComponent.

`TransferHandler getTransferHandler()`

Returns the transfer handler policy for this JComponent.

`String getUIClassID()`

Returns the name of the look and feel for this JComponent.

`boolean getVerifyInputWhenFocusTarget()`

Returns whether the focus owner is notified before this JComponent gets focus.

`VetoableChangeListener[] getVetoableChangeListeners()`

Returns the vetoable change listeners for this JComponent.

`Rectangle getVisibleRect()`

Returns the visibility bounding box for this JComponent.

`int getWidth()`

Returns the width of this JComponent.

`int getX()`

Returns the x-coordinate of the origin of this JComponent.

`int getY()`

Returns the y-coordinate of the origin of this JComponent.

`void grabFocus()`

Indicates that this JComponent wants the input focus.

`boolean isDoubleBuffered()`

Returns a buffer should be used to paint this JComponent.

`static boolean isLightweightComponent(Component c)`

Returns whether this JComponent is lightweight.

`boolean isMaximumSizeSet()`

Returns whether the maximum size for this JComponent has been set.

`boolean isMinimumSizeSet()`

Returns whether the minimum size for this JComponent has been set.

`boolean isOpaque()`

Returns whether this JComponent is opaque (i.e., it hides completely component that lies under it).

`boolean isOptimizedDrawingEnabled()`

Returns whether this JComponent has tiled its children.

`boolean isPaintingTile()`

Returns whether this JComponent is painting.

`boolean isPreferredSizeSet()`

Returns whether the preferred size for this JComponent has been set.

`boolean isRequestFocusEnabled()`

Returns whether this JComponent should get the focus.

`boolean isValidateRoot()`

Indicates whether a validation request of an ancestor requires the tree rooted by this JComponent be validated.

`void paint(Graphics g)`

Paints this JComponent using graphical context g.

`protected void paintBorder(Graphics g)`

Paints the border of this JComponent using graphical context g.

`protected void paintChildren(Graphics g)`

Paints the children of this JComponent using graphical g.

`protected void paintComponent(Graphics g)`

Invokes the user interface delegate paint method of this JComponent with graphical context parameter g.

void paintImmediately(int x, int y, int w, int h)

Paints the rectangular region with origin (x, y) and dimensions w and h for this JComponent and its region overlapping descendants.

void paintImmediately(Rectangle r)

Paints rectangular region r of this JComponent.

protected String paramString()

Returns a representation of this JComponent.

void print(Graphics g)

Invokes printBorder(), printChildren(), and printComponent() for this JComponent using graphical context g.

void printAll(Graphics g)

Printing method for this JComponent.

protected void printBorder(Graphics g)

Prints the border of this JComponent using graphical context g. Override this method, if special printing behavior is needed.

protected void printChildren(Graphics g)

Prints the children of this JComponent using graphical context g. Override this method, if special printing behavior is needed.

protected void printComponent(Graphics g)

Prints this JComponent using this JComponent. Override this method, if special printing behavior is needed.

protected void processComponentKeyEvent(KeyEvent e)

Override this method, if this JComponent must also process a key event.

protected boolean processKeyBinding(KeyStroke c, KeyEvent e, int i, boolean b)

Processes key event e for key stroke character c subject to condition i and pressing indicator b. Returns whether there was a registered listener.

protected void processKeyEvent(KeyEvent e)

Process key event e for this JComponent.

protected void processMouseMotionEvent(MouseEvent e)

Processes mouse event e for this JComponent.

void putClientProperty(Object v1, Object v2)

Adds a property v1 with value v2 for this JComponent.

void removeAncestorListener(AncestorListener a)

Removes ancestor event listener p as a listener for this JComponent.

void removeNotify()

Signals this JComponent that it not a parent component.

void removePropertyChangeListener(PropertyChangeListener p)

Removes property listener p as a listener for this JComponent.

void removePropertyChangeListener(String s, PropertyChangeListener p)

Removes property listener p as a listener for property s for this JComponent.

void removeVetoableChangeListener(VetoableChangeListener l)

Removes vetoable change listener p for this JComponent.

void repaint(long i, int x, int y, int w, int h)

Indicates that the rectangular region with origin (x, y) and dimensions w and h for this JComponent needs repainting, after the current painting completes.

void repaint(Rectangle r)

> Indicates that rectangular region r for this JComponent needs repainting, after this painting completes.

void requestFocus()

> Indicates that this JComponent should get the focus.

boolean requestFocusInWindow()

> Indicates that this JComponent should get the focus if its ancestor window has the focus. Returns whether the request is expected to be satisfied.

void resetKeyboardActions()

> Removes the registered input and action mappers of this JComponent.

void reshape(int x, int y, int w, int h)

> Moves this JComponent to location (x, y) and sets its dimensions to w and h.

void revalidate()

> Supports automatic relayout when an attribute of this JComponent changes.

void scrollRectToVisible(Rectangle r)

> Invokes with parameter r the scrollRectToVisible() method of the parent of this JComponent.

void setActionMap(ActionMap a)

> Uses a as the action mapper of this JComponent.

void setAlignmentX(float n)

> Makes n the vertical alignment of this JComponent.

void setAlignmentY(float n)

> Makes n the horizontal alignment of this JComponent.

void setAutoscrolls(boolean b)

> Uses b to set whether this JComponent autoscrolls.

void setBackground(Color c)

> Sets c as the color of this JComponent.

void setBorder(Border b)

> Sets b as the border of this JComponent.

void setDebugGraphicsOptions(int i)

> Sets how diagnostics should be displayed regarding this JComponent and its children depending on condition i.

void setDoubleBuffered(boolean b)

> Uses b to set whether this JComponent should use a paint buffer.

void setEnabled(boolean b)

> Uses b to set whether this JComponent is enabled.

void setFont(Font f)

> Sets f as the font for this JComponent.

void setForeground(Color c)

> Sets c as the foreground color for this JComponent.

void setInputMap(int i, InputMap m)

> Sets m the input map to use under condition i for this JComponent.

void setInputVerifier(InputVerifier i)

> Sets i as the input verifier of this JComponent.

void setMaximumSize(Dimension d)

> Sets d as the maximum size of this JComponent.

void setMinimumSize(Dimension d)

Sets d as the minimum size of this JComponent.

void setOpaque(**boolean** b)

Uses b to indicate whether this JComponent paints all its pixels.

void setPreferredSize(Dimension d)

Sets d as the preferred size of this JComponent.

void setRequestFocusEnabled(**boolean** b)

Uses b to hint whether JComponent should get focus.

void setToolTipText(String s)

Sets s as the tool tip text display for this JComponent.

void setTransferHandler(TransferHandler h)

Sets h as the transfer handler policy for this JComponent.

protected void setUI(ComponentUI c)

Sets c as the look and feel delegate for this JComponent.

void setVerifyInputWhenFocusTarget(**boolean** b)

Uses b to set whether the input verifier for the focus owner takes precedence over this JComponent.

void setVisible(**boolean** b)

Uses b to set whether JComponent is to be visible.

void update(Graphics g)

Invokes paint(g) for this JComponent.

void updateUI()

Resets the UI attribute of this object to the current look and feel.

| **swing** | **class** JFileChooser **extends** JComponent **implements** Accessible |

PURPOSE

Represent a file and folder selection mechanism.

FIELD SUMMARY

static String ACCEPT_ALL_FILE_FILTER_USED_CHANGED_PROPERTY

Indicates a change in the accept all file filter use.

protected AccessibleContext accessibleContext

Represents the accessibility context of this JFileChooser.

static String ACCESSORY_CHANGED_PROPERTY

Indicates the use of a different accessory component.

static String APPROVE_BUTTON_MNEMONIC_CHANGED_PROPERTY

Indicates a change in the approve button tool mnemonic.

static String APPROVE_BUTTON_TEXT_CHANGED_PROPERTY

Indicates a change in the approve button text.

static String APPROVE_BUTTON_TOOL_TIP_TEXT_CHANGED_PROPERTY

Indicates a change in the approve button tool tip text.

static int APPROVE_OPTION

Represents an approval selection.

static String APPROVE_SELECTION

Indicates to approve the selection.

`static int` CANCEL_OPTION

Represents a cancel selection.

`static String` CANCEL_SELECTION

Indicates to cancel the selection.

`static String` CHOOSABLE_FILE_FILTER_CHANGED_PROPERTY

Indicates a change the predefined file filters.

`static String` CONTROL_BUTTONS_ARE_SHOWN_CHANGED_PROPERTY

Indicates the display of control buttons.

`static int` CUSTOM_DIALOG

Indicates that the custom file operation dialog should be used.

`static String` DIALOG_TITLE_CHANGED_PROPERTY

Indicates a change in the dialog title.

`static String` DIALOG_TYPE_CHANGED_PROPERTY

Identifies a change in whether files or folders or both should be displayed.

`static int` DIRECTORIES_ONLY

Indicates the JFileChooser should display only folders.

`static String` DIRECTORY_CHANGED_PROPERTY

Indicates a change in the current folder.

`static int` ERROR_OPTION

Represents an error.

`static String` FILE_FILTER_CHANGED_PROPERTY

Indicates a change in the file filter.

`static String` FILE_HIDING_CHANGED_PROPERTY

Indicates a change in the display of hidden files.

`static String` FILE_SELECTION_MODE_CHANGED_PROPERTY

Indicates a change in file selection mode.

`static String` FILE_SYSTEM_VIEW_CHANGED_PROPERTY

Indicates a change in the detector of available drives.

`static String` FILE_VIEW_CHANGED_PROPERTY

Indicates a change in the file view.

`static int` FILES_AND_DIRECTORIES

Indicates the JFileChooser should display both files and folders.

`static int` FILES_ONLY

Indicates the JFileChooser should display only files.

`static String` MULTI_SELECTION_ENABLED_CHANGED_PROPERTY

Indicates the JFileChooser supports multiple file selection.

`static int` OPEN_DIALOG

Indicates the JFileChooser supports a file open operation.

`static int` SAVE_DIALOG

Indicates the JFileChooser supports a file save operation.

`static String` SELECTED_FILE_CHANGED_PROPERTY

Indicates a change in the selected file.

`static String` SELECTED_FILES_CHANGED_PROPERTY

Indicates a change in selected files.

CONSTRUCTOR SUMMARY

JFileChooser()

Constructs a new JFileChooser with the default folder as the current folder.

```
JFileChooser(File f)
```
Constructs a new JFileChooser with file f indicating the current folder.
```
JFileChooser(File f, FileSystemView v)
```
Constructs a new JFileChooser with f as the current folder and v as the file system view.
```
JFileChooser(FileSystemView v)
```
Constructs a new JFileChooser with v as the file system view.
```
JFileChooser(String s)
```
Constructs a new JFileChooser with s indicating the current folder.
```
JFileChooser(String s, FileSystemView v)
```
Constructs a new JFileChooser with s indicating the current folder and v as the file system view.

INSTANCE METHOD SUMMARY

boolean accept(File f)

Returns whether file f should be displayed by this JFileChooser.

void addActionListener(ActionListener l)

Adds listener l to the action listeners for this JFileChooser.

void addChoosableFileFilter(FileFilter f)

Adds filter f to choosable file filters for this JFileChooser.

void approveSelection()

Initiates an approve selection event for this JFileChooser.

void cancelSelection()

Initiates a cancel selection event for this JFileChooser.

void changeToParentDirectory()

Changes the current folder for this JFileChooser to the parent folder of the current folder.

protected JDialog createDialog(Component c)

Returns a new JDialog for this JFileChooser centered on component c.

void ensureFileIsVisible(File f)

Sets f as viewable file for this JFileChooser.

protected void fireActionPerformed(String s)

Invokes all event type s listeners for this JFileChooser.

FileFilter getAcceptAllFileFilter()

Returns the accept all file filter of this JFileChooser.

AccessibleContext getAccessibleContext()

Returns the accessibility context of this JFileChooser.

JComponent getAccessory()

Returns the accessory component of this JFileChooser.

ActionListener[] getActionListeners()

Returns the action listeners of this JFileChooser.

int getApproveButtonMnemonic()

Returns the approve button mnemonic of this JFileChooser.

String getApproveButtonText()

Returns the approve button of this JFileChooser.

String getApproveButtonToolTipText()

Returns the approve button tool tip text of this JFileChooser.

FileFilter[] getChoosableFileFilters()

Returns user choosable file filters of this JFileChooser.

boolean getControlButtonsAreShown()

Returns whether control buttons are shown by this JFileChooser.

File getCurrentDirectory()

Returns the current folder of this JFileChooser.

String getDescription(File f)

Returns the description for f for this JFileChooser.

String getDialogTitle()

Returns the title of this JFileChooser.

int getDialogType()

Returns the dialog type of this JFileChooser.

boolean getDragEnabled()

Returns whether drop and drag is supported by this JFileChooser.

FileFilter getFileFilter()

Returns the current file filter for this JFileChooser.

int getFileSelectionMode()

Returns the file selection mode for this JFileChooser.

FileSystemView getFileSystemView()

Returns the file system view of this JFileChooser.

FileView getFileView()

Returns the current file view for this JFileChooser.

Icon getIcon(File f)

Returns the icon for file f for this JFileChooser.

String getName(File f)

Returns the name of file f for this JFileChooser.

File getSelectedFile()

Returns the file selected by this JFileChooser.

File[] getSelectedFiles()

Returns the files selected by this JFileChooser.

String getTypeDescription(File f)

Returns the type of file f for this JFileChooser.

FileChooserUI getUI()

Returns the look and feel that renders this component.

String getUIClassID()

Returns the name of the look and feel that renders this object.

boolean isAcceptAllFileFilterUsed()

Sets whether accept all is a filter choice for this JFileChooser.

boolean isDirectorySelectionEnabled()

Returns whether directories are selectable with this JFileChooser.

boolean isFileHidingEnabled()

Returns whether file hiding is in effect for this JFileChooser.

boolean isFileSelectionEnabled()

Returns whether file selection is enabled for this JFileChooser.

boolean isMultiSelectionEnabled()

Returns whether multiple files can be selected by this JFileChooser.

`boolean` `isTraversable(File f)`

Returns whether folder f can be visited by this `JFileChooser`.

`protected` `String paramString()`

Returns a representation of this object.

`void` `removeActionListener(ActionListener l)`

Removes l as an action listener for this `JFileChooser`.

`boolean` `removeChoosableFileFilter(FileFilter f)`

Removes f as a possible file filter for this `JFileChooser`.

`void` `rescanCurrentDirectory()`

Causes a refresh of the current directory for this `JFileChooser`.

`void` `resetChoosableFileFilters()`

Resets the choosable file filter list for this `JFileChooser`.

`void` `setAcceptAllFileFilterUsed(boolean b)`

Sets using b whether accept all is a filter choice for this `JFileChooser`.

`void` `setAccessory(JComponent c)`

Sets c as the accessory component for this `JFileChooser`.

`void` `setApproveButtonMnemonic(char c)`

Sets c as the approve button mnemonic for this `JFileChooser`.

`void` `setApproveButtonMnemonic(int m)`

Sets n as the approve button mnemonic for this `JFileChooser`.

`void` `setApproveButtonText(String s)`

Sets s as the text used by the approve button for this `JFileChooser`.

`void` `setApproveButtonToolTipText(String s)`

Sets s as the tool tip text used by the approve button for this `JFileChooser`.

`void` `setControlButtonsAreShown(boolean b)`

Sets using b whether this `JFileChooser` displays approve and cancel control buttons.

`void` `setCurrentDirectory(File d)`

Sets d as the current directory for this `JFileChooser`.

`void` `setDialogTitle(String s)`

Sets s as the window title for this `JFileChooser`.

`void` `setDialogType(int n)`

Sets n as the dialog type of this `JFileChooser`.

`void` `setDragEnabled(boolean b)`

Sets whether this `JFileChooser` supports drop and drag using b.

`void` `setFileFilter(FileFilter f)`

Sets f as the current file filter for this `JFileChooser`.

`void` `setFileHidingEnabled(boolean b)`

Sets whether file hiding is in effect for this `JFileChooser` using b.

`void` `setFileSelectionMode(int m)`

Sets m as the policy whether a file, folder, or both are selectable with this `JFile-Chooser`.

`void` `setFileSystemView(FileSystemView f)`

Sets f as the file system view used by this `JFileChooser`.

`void` `setFileView(FileView f)`

Sets f as the file view used by this `JFileChooser`.

> void setMultiSelectionEnabled(**boolean** b)
>
> > Sets using b whether multiple selection is in effect for this JFileChooser.
>
> void setSelectedFile(File f)
>
> > Sets f as the selected file to f for this JFileChooser.
>
> void setSelectedFiles(File[] f)
>
> > Sets f as the selected files for this JFileChooser.

---

swing	**class** JFrame **extends** Frame **implements** WindowConstants, Accessible, RootPaneContainer

PURPOSE
Provides a representation of a window.

FIELD SUMMARY

> **protected** AccessibleContext accessibleContext
>
> > Represents the accessibility context of this JFrame.
>
> **static int** EXIT_ON_CLOSE
>
> > Represents the terminate application on window closing policy.
>
> **protected** JRootPane rootPane
>
> > Represents the JRootPane instance that manages the various components of the window (e.g., content pane, border, and title bar).
>
> **protected boolean** rootPaneCheckingEnabled
>
> > Represents whether improper additions or layout management to this JFrame should generate exceptions.

CLASS METHOD SUMMARY

> **static boolean** isDefaultLookAndFeelDecorated()
>
> > Returns whether a new JFrame should have its window decorations provided by the current look and feel.
>
> **static void** setDefaultLookAndFeelDecorated(**boolean** b)
>
> > Uses b to set whether a new JFrame should have its window decorations provided by the current look and feel.

CONSTRUCTOR SUMMARY

> JFrame()
>
> > Constructs a new invisible JFrame.
>
> JFrame(GraphicsConfiguration g)
>
> > Constructs a new invisible JFrame for screen device g.
>
> JFrame(String s)
>
> > Constructs a new invisible JFrame with title s.
>
> JFrame(String s, GraphicsConfiguration g)
>
> > Constructs a new invisible JFrame with title s for screen device g.

INSTANCE METHOD SUMMARY

> **protected void** addImpl(Component c, Object v, **int** i)
>
> > Attempts to insert component c as the ith component of this JFrame using constraints v. An exception is thrown if root pane checking is enabled for this JFrame.

protected JRootPane createRootPane()

Creates the default root pane for this JFrame.

protected void frameInit()

Initializes this JFrame.

AccessibleContext getAccessibleContext()

Returns the accessibility context of this object.

Container getContentPane()

Returns the content pane for this JFrame.

int getDefaultCloseOperation()

Returns the operation that occurs when the user closes this JFrame.

Component getGlassPane()

Returns the glass pane for this JFrame.

JMenuBar getJMenuBar()

Returns the menu bar for this JFrame.

JLayeredPane getLayeredPane()

Returns the layered pane for this JFrame.

JRootPane getRootPane()

Returns the root pane for this JFrame.

protected boolean isRootPaneCheckingEnabled()

Returns whether invocations of add() and setLayout() to this JFrame generate exceptions.

protected String paramString()

Returns a representation of this object.

protected void processWindowEvent(WindowEvent e)

Processes window event e on this JFrame.

void remove(Component c)

Removes the component c from this JFrame.

void setContentPane(Container c)

Sets c as the content pane for this JFrame.

void setDefaultCloseOperation(**int** n)

Sets n as the operation that occurs when the user closes this JFrame.

void setGlassPane(Component c)

Sets c as the glass pane for this JFrame.

void setJMenuBar(JMenuBar m)

Sets m as the menu bar for this JFrame.

void setLayeredPane(JLayeredPane l)

Sets l as the layered pane this JFrame.

void setLayout(LayoutManager m)

Attempts to sets the layout manager of this JFrame to m. An exception is thrown if root pane checking is enabled for this JFrame.

protected void setRootPane(JRootPane r)

Sets r as the root pane for this JFrame.

protected void setRootPaneCheckingEnabled(**boolean** b)

Uses b to set whether invocations of add() and setLayout() to this JFrame generate exceptions.

void update(Graphics g)

Invokes paint(g).

swing	**class** JLabel **extends** JComponent **implements** SwingConstants, Accessible

PURPOSE

Represents a label with text and image. The horizontal alignment policy of the label is controlled by using constants: SwingConstants.LEFT, SwingConstants.CENTER, RIGHT, SwingConstants.LEADING or SwingConstants.TRAILING.

FIELD SUMMARY

    protected Component labelFor

        Represents the component being labeled.

CONSTRUCTOR SUMMARY

    JLabel()

        Constructs a new JLabel instance with no image or title.

    JLabel(Icon i)

        Constructs a new JLabel instance with image i.

    JLabel(Icon i, **int** h)

        Constructs a new JLabel instance with image i and horizontal alignment policy h.

    JLabel(String s)

        Constructs a new JLabel with text s.

    JLabel(String s, Icon i, **int** h)

        Constructs a new JLabel with text s, image i, and horizontal alignment policy h.

    JLabel(String s, **int** h)

        Constructs a new JLabel with the text s and horizontal alignment policy h.

INSTANCE METHOD SUMMARY

    protected int checkHorizontalKey(**int** n, String s)

        Throws an exception with message s if n is not a horizontal alignment policy.

    protected int checkVerticalKey(**int** n, String s)

        Throws an exception with message s if n is not a vertical alignment policy.

    AccessibleContext getAccessibleContext()

        Returns the accessibility context of this object.

    Icon getDisabledIcon()

        Returns the value of the disabled icon property for this JLabel. If the value had not been previously produced, then the disable icon is computed.

    int getDisplayedMnemonic()

        Return the key code for this JLabel.

    int getDisplayedMnemonicIndex()

        Returns the index into the label text that the look and feel should use as the mnemonic character for this JLabel.

    int getHorizontalAlignment()

        Returns the horizontal alignment policy for this JLabel.

    int getHorizontalTextPosition()

        Returns the horizontal alignment policy of the text relative to the image for this JLabel.

    Icon getIcon()

        Returns the graphic image of this JLabel.

`int getIconTextGap()`

Returns the number of pixels separating the text and the icon of this JLabel.

`Component getLabelFor()`

Returns the component this JLabel is identifying.

`String getText()`

Returns the text of this JLabel.

`LabelUI getUI()`

Returns the look and feel that renders this component.

`String getUIClassID()`

Returns the name of the look and feel that renders this object.

`int getVerticalAlignment()`

Returns the vertical alignment policy for this JLabel.

`int getVerticalTextPosition()`

Returns the vertical alignment policy of the text relative to the image for this JLabel.

`boolean imageUpdate(Image i, int n, int x, int y, int w, int h)`

Returns whether image i with width w and height h using loading parameter n has been completely loaded at location (x, y).

`protected String paramString()`

Returns a representation of this object.

`void setDisabledIcon(Icon i)`

Set the disabled icon to i for this JLabel.

`void setDisplayedMnemonic(char c)`

Sets c as the mnemonic display character for this JLabel.

`void setDisplayedMnemonic(int n)`

Sets n as the key code for this JLabel.

`void setDisplayedMnemonicIndex(int n)`

Indicates n should be the character used as the mnemonic for this JLabel.

`void setHorizontalAlignment(int h)`

Sets h as the horizontal alignment policy for this JLabel.

`void setHorizontalTextPosition(int h)`

Sets h as the horizontal alignment policy of the text relative to the image for this JLabel.

`void setIcon(Icon i)`

Sets i as the icon this JLabel displays.

`void setIconTextGap(int n)`

Sets n as the number of pixels separating the icon and text for this JLabel.

`void setLabelFor(Component c)`

Set c as the component this JLabel is identifying.

`void setText(String s)`

Sets s as the text for this JLabel.

`void setUI(LabelUI u)`

Sets u as the look and feel for this JLabel.

`void setVerticalAlignment(int v)`

Sets v as the vertical alignment policy for this JLabel.

> void setVerticalTextPosition(int n)
>> Sets v as the vertical alignment policy of the text relative to the image for this JLabel.
>
> void updateUI()
>> Resets the UI attribute of this object to the current look and feel.

---

swing **class** JOptionPane **extends** JComponent **implements** Accessible

PURPOSE

Represents a standard dialog box.

FIELD SUMMARY

> static int CANCEL_OPTION
>> Represents that the user-selected cancel option of the JOptionPane.
>
> static int CLOSED_OPTION
>> Represents that the user closed the JOptionPane without any selection.
>
> static int DEFAULT_OPTION
>> Represents an option for a show and confirm dialog.
>
> static int ERROR_MESSAGE
>> Represents an error message.
>
> protected Icon icon
>> Represents the icon used in this JOptionPane.
>
> static String ICON_PROPERTY
>> Represents the bound name for member icon.
>
> static int INFORMATION_MESSAGE
>> Represents an information message.
>
> static String INITIAL_SELECTION_VALUE_PROPERTY
>> Represents the bound name for member initialSelectionValue.
>
> static String INITIAL_VALUE_PROPERTY
>> Represents the bound name for member initialValue.
>
> protected Object initialSelectionValue
>> Represents the initial selectable value in this JOptionPane.
>
> protected Object initialValue
>> Represents the initial option in this JOptionPane.
>
> static String INPUT_VALUE_PROPERTY
>> Represents the bound property name for member inputValue.
>
> protected Object inputValue
>> Represents the value the user has entered.
>
> protected Object message
>> Represents the message to display in this JOptionPane.
>
> static String MESSAGE_PROPERTY
>> Represents the bound property name for member message.
>
> static String MESSAGE_TYPE_PROPERTY
>> Represents the bound property name for member type.
>
> protected int messageType
>> Represents the message type of this JOptionPane.

static int NO_OPTION

Represents that the user selected no from the JOptionPane.

static int OK_CANCEL_OPTION

Represents an option for a *showConfirmDialog*.

static int OK_OPTION

Represents that the user selected ok from the JOptionPane.

static String OPTION_TYPE_PROPERTY

Represents the bound property name for member optionType.

protected Object[] options

Represents the list of options displayed by this JOptionPane.

static String OPTIONS_PROPERTY

Represents the bound property name for member option.

protected int optionType

Represents the option type of this JOptionPane. The legal values are OK_CANCEL_OPTION, YES_NO_OPTION, YES_NO_CANCEL_OPTION, and DEFAULT_OPTION.

static int PLAIN_MESSAGE

Represents a message with no icon.

static int QUESTION_MESSAGE

Represents a question message.

static String SELECTION_VALUES_PROPERTY

Represents the bound property name for member selectionValues.

protected Object[] selectionValues

Represents the values from which the user can choose in this JOptionPane.

static Object UNINITIALIZED_VALUE

Represents that the user has not yet selected a value.

protected Object value

Represents the currently selected value of this JOptionPane.

static String VALUE_PROPERTY

Represents the bound property name for member value.

static String WANTS_INPUT_PROPERTY

Represents the bound property name for member wantsInput.

protected boolean wantsInput

Represents whether an input-providing component is provided in this JOption-Pane.

static int WARNING_MESSAGE

Represents a warning message.

static int YES_NO_CANCEL_OPTION

Represents an option for a *showConfirmDialog*.

static int YES_NO_OPTION

Represents an option for a *showConfirmDialog*.

static int YES_OPTION

Represents that the user selected yes from the JOptionPane.

CLASS METHOD SUMMARY

static Frame getRootFrame()

Returns the frame used by JOptionPane class methods that do not supply their own frame.

static JDesktopPane getDesktopPaneForComponent(Component c)

Returns the desktop pane for parent component c of this JOptionPane.

static Frame getFrameForComponent(Component c)

Returns the frame for parent component c of this JOptionPane.

static void setRootFrame(Frame f)

Makes f the frame used by JOptionPane class methods that do not supply their own frame.

static int showConfirmDialog(Component p, Object m)

Displays a confirmation dialog with message m within frame p. The return value is the selection option.

static int showConfirmDialog(Component p, Object m, String s, int n)

Displays a confirmation dialog of option type n1 with message m and title s within frame p. The return value is the selection option.

static int showConfirmDialog(Component p, Object m, String s, int n1, int n2)

Displays a confirmation dialog of message type n2, option type n1 with title s, message m, in the frame of parent component p. The return value is the selection option.

static int showConfirmDialog(Component p, Object m, String s, int n1, int n2, Icon i)

Displays a dialog of message type n2, option type n1 with title s, message m, in the frame of parent component p. Brings up a dialog where the number of choices is determined by the optionType parameter. The return value is the selection option.

static String showInputDialog(Object m)

Displays a question dialog with message m. The return value is the user input.

static String showInputDialog(Component p, Object m)

Displays a question dialog with message m within frame p. The return value is the user input.

static String showInputDialog(Component p, Object m, String s, int n1)

Displays a dialog of message type n1 with message m within frame p. The return value is the user input.

static Object showInputDialog(Component p, Object m, String s, int n1, Icon i, Object[] a, Object v)

Displays a blocking dialog of message type n1 with message m and icon i within frame p. The list of possible selection values is list a; and the initial selection is v. The return value is the user selection.

static int showInternalConfirmDialog(Component p, Object m)

Displays an internal dialog panel with default options and title with message m within frame p. The return value is the selection option.

static int showInternalConfirmDialog(Component p, Object m, String s, int n1)

Displays an internal dialog panel with title s and options determined by option type n1 with message m within frame p. The return value is the selection option.

```
static int showInternalConfirmDialog(Component p, Object m,
  String s, int n1, int n2)
```

Displays an internal dialog panel of message type n2, option type n1 with title s, message m, in the frame of parent component p. The return value is the selection option.

```
static int showInternalConfirmDialog(Component p, Object m,
  String s, int n', int n2, Icon i)
```

Displays an internal dialog panel using icon i of message type n2, option type n1 with title s, message m, in the frame of parent component p. The return value is the selection option.

```
static String showInternalInputDialog(Component p, Object m)
```

Displays an internal question dialog with message m within frame p. The return value is the user input.

```
static String showInternalInputDialog(Component p, Object m,
  String s, int n1)
```

Displays an internal dialog of message type n1 with message m within frame p. The return value is the user input.

```
static Object showInternalInputDialog(Component p, Object m,
  String s, int n1, Icon i, Object[] a, Object v)
```

Displays a blocking internal dialog of message type n1 with message m and icon i within frame p. The list of possible selection values is list a; and the initial selection is v. The return value is the user selection.

```
static void showInternalMessageDialog(Component p, Object m)
```

Displays an internal confirmation dialog panel with message m within frame p.

```
static void showInternalMessageDialog(Component p, Object m,
  String s, int n1)
```

Displays an internal confirmation dialog panel of message type n1 with message m within frame p. The return value is the user input.

```
static void showInternalMessageDialog(Component p, Object m,
  String s, int n1, Icon i)
```

Displays an internal confirmation dialog panel using icon i of message type n1 with message m within frame p. The return value is the user input.

```
static int showInternalOptionDialog(Component p, Object m,
  String s, int n1, int n2, Icon i, Object[] a, Object v)
```

Displays an internal dialog panel using icon i of message type n2, option type n1 with title s, message m, in the frame of parent component p. The return value is the selection option. The list of possible selection values is list a; and the initial selection is v. The return value is the user selection.

```
static void showMessageDialog(Component p, Object m)
```

Displays an information message dialog with message m within frame p.

```
static void showMessageDialog(Component p, Object m, String s,
  int n1)
```

Displays a message dialog of message type n1 with message m and title s within frame p.

```
static void showMessageDialog(Component p, Object m, String s,
    int n1, Icon i)
```

Displays a message dialog using icon i of message type n1 with message m and title s within frame p.

```
static int showOptionDialog(Component p, Object m, String s, int
    n1, int n2, Icon i, Object[] a, Object v)
```

Displays an option dialog using icon i of message type n2, option type n1 with title s, message m, in the frame of parent component p. The return value is the selection option. The list of possible selection values is list a; and the initial selection is v. The return value is the user selection.

CONSTRUCTOR SUMMARY

```
JOptionPane()
```

Constructs a new JOptionPane with a test message.

```
JOptionPane(Object v)
```

Constructs a new plain-message JOptionPane that displays message v.

```
JOptionPane(Object v, int n)
```

Constructs a new JOptionPane of message type n that displays message v.

```
JOptionPane(Object v, int n1, int n2)
```

Constructs a new JOptionPane of message type n1 using option type n2 that displays message v.

```
JOptionPane(Object v, int n1, int n2, Icon i)
```

Constructs a new JOptionPane of message type n1 using option type n2 that displays message v and icon i.

```
JOptionPane(Object v, int n1, int n2, Icon i, Object[] a)
```

Constructs a new JOptionPane of message type n1 using option type n2 that displays message v, icon i, and options a.

```
JOptionPane(Object v, int n1, int n2, Icon i, Object[] a, Object
    j)
```

Constructs a new JOptionPane of message type n1 using option type n2 that displays message v, icon i, and options a with initially selected option j.

INSTANCE METHOD SUMMARY

```
JDialog createDialog(Component p, String s)
```

Returns a new JDialog with title s centering this JOptionPane on parent component p.

```
JInternalFrame createInternalFrame(Component c, String s)
```

Returns a new JInternalFrame with title s centering this JOptionPane on parent component c.

```
AccessibleContext getAccessibleContext()
```

Returns the accessibility context of this object.

```
Icon getIcon()
```

Returns the icon of this JOptionPane.

```
Object getInitialSelectionValue()
```

Returns the initial selected input value that is displayed to the user of this JOptionPane.

```
Object getInitialValue()
```

Returns the initial value of this JOptionPane.

`Object getInputValue()`

Returns the value the user has input in this JOptionPane.

`int getMaxCharactersPerLineCount()`

Returns the maximum number of characters per message line this JOption-Pane.

`Object getMessage()`

Returns the message displayed by this JOptionPane.

`int getMessageType()`

Returns the message type of this JOptionPane.

`Object[] getOptions()`

Returns the choices of this JOptionPane.

`int getOptionType()`

Returns the type of options of this JOptionPane.

`Object[] getSelectionValues()`

Returns the input selection values of this JOptionPane.

`OptionPaneUI getUI()`

Returns the look and feel that renders this component.

`String getUIClassID()`

Returns the name of the look and feel that renders this object.

`Object getValue()`

Returns the value the user has selected in this JOptionPane.

`boolean getWantsInput()`

Returns the value of the wantsInput property of this JOptionPane.

`protected String paramString()`

Returns a representation of this object.

`void selectInitialValue()`

Sets and gives focus to the initial value of this JOptionPane.

`void setIcon(Icon i)`

Sets i as the icon for this JOptionPane.

`void setInitialSelectionValue(Object v)`

Sets v as the initially selected input value of this JOptionPane.

`void setInitialValue(Object v)`

Sets v as the initial input value of this JOptionPane.

`void setInputValue(Object v)`

Sets v as the input value of this JOptionPane.

`void setMessage(Object m)`

Sets m as the message of the option pane of this JOptionPane.

`void setMessageType(int n)`

Sets n as the message type for this JOptionPane.

`void setOptions(Object[] a)`

Sets a as the options array for this JOptionPane.

`void setOptionType(int n)`

Sets n as the option type for this JOptionPane.

`void setSelectionValues(Object[] a)`

Sets a as the input selection values array for this JOptionPane.

`void setUI(PanelUI u)`

Sets u as the look and feel provider for this JOptionPane.

```
void setValue(Object v)
```
Sets v as the chosen value for this JOptionPane.
```
void setWantsInput(boolean b)
```
Sets b as the wants input policy of this JOptionPane.
```
void updateUI()
```
Resets the UI attribute of this object to the current look and feel.

---

swing	**class** JPanel **extends** JComponent **implements** Accessible

PURPOSE

Represents a container.

CONSTRUCTOR SUMMARY
```
JPanel()
```
Constructs a new JPanel with double buffering and flow layout.
```
JPanel(boolean b)
```
Constructs a new JPanel with flow layout. Double buffering depends on b.
```
JPanel(LayoutManager l)
```
Constructs a new JPanel with double buffering and with layout manager l.
```
JPanel(LayoutManager l, boolean b)
```
Constructs a new JPanel with layout manager l. Double buffering depends on b.

INSTANCE METHOD SUMMARY
```
AccessibleContext getAccessibleContext()
```
Returns the accessibility context of this object.
```
PanelUI getUI()
```
Returns the look and feel that renders this component.
```
String getUIClassID()
```
Returns the name of the look and feel that renders this object.
```
protected String paramString()
```
Returns a representation of this object.
```
void setUI(PanelUI u)
```
Sets u as the look and feel provider for this JPanel.
```
void updateUI()
```
Resets the UI attribute of this object to the current look and feel.
```
protected void configurePropertiesFromAction(Action a)
```
Sets a as the action properties of this JPanel.

---

swing	**class** JRadioButton **extends** JToggleButton **implements** Accessible

PURPOSE

Represents a radio button.

CONSTRUCTOR SUMMARY

`JRadioButton()`

Constructs an new unset `JRadioButton` with no text or image.

`JRadioButton(Action a)`

Constructs a new unset `JRadioButton`. The settings of the button depends on `a`.

`JRadioButton(Icon i)`

Constructs a new unset `JRadioButton` with no text but image `i`.

`JRadioButton(Icon i, boolean b)`

Constructs a new `JRadioButton` with no text and image `i`. The setting of the button depends on `b`.

`JRadioButton(String s)`

Constructs a new unset `JRadioButton` with text `s` and no image.

`JRadioButton(String s, boolean b)`

Constructs a new `JRadioButton` with text `s` and no image. The setting of the button depends on `b`.

`JRadioButton(String s, Icon i)`

Constructs a new unset `JRadioButton` with text `s` and image `i`.

`JRadioButton(String s, Icon i, boolean b)`

Constructs a new `JRadioButton` with text `s` and image `i`. The setting of the button depends on `b`.

INSTANCE METHOD SUMMARY

`protected void configurePropertiesFromAction(Action a)`

Sets `a` as the action properties for this `JRadioButton`.

`protected PropertyChangeListener createActionPropertyChangeListener(Action a)`

Creates and returns the property change listener that updates the `ActionEvent` source as action properties change for this `JRadioButton`.

`AccessibleContext getAccessibleContext()`

Returns the accessibility context of this object.

`String getUIClassID()`

Returns the name of the look and feel that renders this object.

`protected String paramString()`

Returns a representation of this object.

`void updateUI()`

Resets the UI attribute of this object to the current look and feel.

---

swing | `class JScrollPane extends JComponent implements Accessible, ScrollPaneConstants`

PURPOSE

Represents a scrollable view of a component.

FIELD SUMMARY

`protected JViewport columnHeader`

Represents the column header of this `JScrollPane`.

protected JScrollBar horizontalScrollBar

Represents the horizontal scroll bar of this JScrollPane.

protected int horizontalScrollBarPolicy

Represents the horizontal scroll bar display policy of this JScrollPane.

protected Component lowerLeft

Represents the component to display in the lower-left corner of this JScroll-Pane.

protected Component lowerRight

Represents the component to display in the lower-right corner of this JScroll-Pane.

protected JViewport rowHeader

Represents the row header of this JScrollPane.

protected Component upperLeft

Represents the component to display in the upper-left corner of this JScroll-Pane.

protected Component upperRight

Represents the component to display in the upper-right corner of this JScroll-Pane.

protected JScrollBar verticalScrollBar

Represents the vertical scroll bar of this JScrollPane.

protected int verticalScrollBarPolicy

Represents the vertical scroll bar display policy of this JScrollPane.

protected JViewport viewport

Represents the viewport of this JScrollPane.

CONSTRUCTOR SUMMARY

JScrollPane()

Constructs a new empty JScrollPane in a viewport with default horizontal and vertical scroll bar policies.

JScrollPane(Component c)

Constructs a new JScrollPane displaying component c in a viewport with default horizontal and vertical scroll bar policies.

JScrollPane(Component c, int v, int h)

Constructs a new JScrollPane displaying component c in a viewport with horizontal and vertical scroll bar policies specified respectively by v and h.

JScrollPane(int v, int h)

Constructs a new empty JScrollPane with horizontal and vertical scroll bar policies specified respectively by v and h.

INSTANCE METHOD SUMMARY

JScrollBar createHorizontalScrollBar()

If this JScrollPane does not have a horizontal scroll bar, then one is created. Returns the horizontal scroll bar of this JScrollPane.

JScrollBar createVerticalScrollBar()

If this JScrollPane does not have a vertical scroll bar, then one is created. Returns the vertical scroll bar of this JScrollPane.

protected JViewport createViewport()

If this JScrollPane does not have a viewport, then one is created. Returns the viewport of this JScrollPane.

AccessibleContext getAccessibleContext()

Returns the accessibility context of this object.

JViewport getColumnHeader()

Returns the column header viewport of this JScrollPane.

Component getCorner(String s)

Returns the component at the corner s of this JScrollPane.

JScrollBar getHorizontalScrollBar()

Returns the vertical scroll bar of this JScrollPane.

int getHorizontalScrollBarPolicy()

Returns the horizontal scroll bar policy of this JScrollPane.

JViewport getRowHeader()

Returns the row header viewport of this JScrollPane.

ScrollPaneUI getUI()

Returns the look and feel that renders this component.

String getUIClassID()

Returns the name of the look and feel that renders this object.

JScrollBar getVerticalScrollBar()

Returns the vertical scroll bar of this JScrollPane.

int getVerticalScrollBarPolicy()

Returns the vertical scroll bar policy of this JScrollPane.

JViewport getViewport()

Returns the viewport of this JScrollPane.

Border getViewportBorder()

Returns the border that surrounds the viewport of this JScrollPane.

Rectangle getViewportBorderBounds()

Returns the bounds of the viewport border for this JScrollPane.

boolean isValidateRoot()

Invokes method revalidate() on any descendant of this JScrollPane.

boolean isWheelScrollingEnabled()

Returns whether scrolling take place in response to mouse wheel movement in this JScrollPane.

protected String paramString()

Returns a representation of this object.

void setColumnHeader(JViewport c)

Makes c the column header for this JScrollPane.

void setColumnHeaderView(Component c)

If this JScrollPane does not have a column header viewport, then one is created. The view of this viewport for this JScrollPane is set to c.

void setComponentOrientation(ComponentOrientation c)

Sets c as the vertical and horizontal scroll bar orientation for this JScrollPane.

void setCorner(String s, Component c)

Sets c as the component that should appear in a scroll pane corner s of this JScrollPane when there is sufficient room.

void setHorizontalScrollBar(JScrollBar h)

Sets v as the horizontal scroll bar for the viewport of this JScrollPane.

void setHorizontalScrollBarPolicy(int p)

Sets p as the horizontal scroll bar appearance policy for this JScrollPane.

```
void setLayout(LayoutManager l)
```
Sets l as the layout manager for this JScrollPane.
```
void setRowHeader(JViewport r)
```
Sets r as the row header for this JScrollPane.
```
void setRowHeaderView(Component c)
```
If this JScrollPane does not have a row header viewport, then one is created. The view of this viewport for this JScrollPane is set to c.
```
void setUI(ScrollPaneUI u)
```
Sets u as the look and feel provider for this JScrollPane.
```
void setVerticalScrollBar(JScrollBar v)
```
Sets v as the vertical scroll bar for the viewport of this JScrollPane.
```
void setVerticalScrollBarPolicy(int i)
```
Sets i as the vertical scroll bar appearance policy of this JScrollPane.
```
void setViewport(JViewport v)
```
Sets v as the viewport of this JScrollPane.
```
void setViewportBorder(Border b)
```
Adds a border b around the viewport of this JScrollPane.
```
void setViewportView(Component c)
```
If this JScrollPane does not have a viewport, then one is created. The view of the viewport for this JScrollPane is set to c.
```
void setWheelScrollingEnabled(boolean b)
```
Sets whether scrolling should occur in response to mouse wheel movement in this JScrollPane.
```
void updateUI()
```
Resets the UI attribute of this object to the current look and feel.

| swing | **class** JTextArea **extends** JTextComponent |

PURPOSE

Represents a multiline text area.

CONSTRUCTOR SUMMARY

```
JTextArea()
```
Constructs a new JTextArea with zero rows and columns using a default document model.
```
JTextArea(Document d)
```
Constructs a new empty JTextArea using zero rows and columns and document model d.
```
JTextArea(Document d, String s, int r, int c)
```
Constructs a new JTextArea with text s using r rows, c columns, and document model d.
```
JTextArea(int r, int c)
```
Constructs a new empty JTextArea using r rows, c columns, and a default document model.

JTextArea(String s)

Constructs a new **JTextArea** with text **s** using zero rows and columns and a default document model.

JTextArea(String s, int r, int c)

Constructs a new **JTextArea** with text **s** using **r** rows, **c** columns, and a default document model.

INSTANCE METHOD SUMMARY

void append(String s)

Appends text **s** to the end of the document in this **JTextArea**.

protected Document createDefaultModel()

Returns and creates (if necessary) the default document model for this **JText-Area**.

AccessibleContext getAccessibleContext()

Returns the accessibility context of this object.

int getColumns()

Returns the number of columns in this **JTextArea**.

protected int getColumnWidth()

Returns column width of this **JTextArea**.

int getLineCount()

Returns the number of lines contained in this **JTextArea**.

int getLineEndOffset(**int** n)

Returns the offset of the end of the line **n** in this **JTextArea**.

int getLineOfOffset(**int** n)

Returns the line whose text contains offset **n** into this **JTextArea**.

int getLineStartOffset(**int** n)

Returns the offset of the start of the line **n** in this **JTextArea**.

boolean getLineWrap()

Returns the line wrapping policy of this **JTextArea**.

Dimension getPreferredScrollableViewportSize()

Returns the preferred size of a viewport for this **JTextArea**.

Dimension getPreferredSize()

Returns the preferred size of this **JTextArea**.

protected int getRowHeight()

Returns the height of a row for this **JTextArea**.

int getRows()

Returns the number of rows in this **JTextArea**.

boolean getScrollableTracksViewportWidth()

Returns whether a viewport should force the width of this **JTextArea** to match the width of the viewport.

int getScrollableUnitIncrement(Rectangle r, **int** n, **int** d)

Returns the increment for unit scrolling in this **JTextArea** in the direction indicated by **n** and **d**. If **n** is **SwingConstant.VERTICAL**, the orientation is vertical, and if **n** is **SwingConstant.HORIZONTAL**, the orientation is horizontal. Depending on the orientation, the direction is either left or up if **d** is negative and it is either right or down if **d** is positive. For the purpose of the calculation, the size of the viewable area is **r**.

int getTabSize()

> Returns the number of characters in a tab expansion in this JTextArea.

String getUIClassID()

> Returns the name of the look and feel that renders this object.

boolean getWrapStyleWord()

> Returns whether word wrapping is used by this JTextArea.

void insert(String s, int i)

> Inserts text s starting at position i of this JTextArea.

protected String paramString()

> Returns a representation of this object.

void replaceRange(String s, int n1, int n2)

> Replaces with s the text at positions n1 ... n2 of this JTextArea.

void setColumns(int c)

> Sets c as the number of columns for this JTextArea.

void setFont(Font f)

> Sets f as the font for this JTextArea.

void setLineWrap(boolean b)

> Sets using b whether this JTextArea performs line wrapping.

void setRows(int r)

> Sets r as the number of rows for this JTextArea.

void setTabSize(int n)

> Sets n as the number of characters to which tabs expand in this JTextArea.

void setWrapStyleWord(boolean b)

> Sets using b whether this JTextArea performs word wrapping.

---

swing

class JTextField extends JTextComponent implements
   SwingConstants

PURPOSE

Represents an editable line of text.

FIELD SUMMARY

static String notifyAction

> Represents the action (i.e., carriage return) causing notification that the contents of the field have been accepted.

CONSTRUCTOR SUMMARY

JTextField()

> Constructs a new empty JTextField.

JTextField(Document d, String s, int n)

> Constructs a new JTextField composed of text s using n columns using text model d.

JTextField(int n)

> Constructs a new empty JTextField composed of n columns.

JTextField(String s)

> Constructs a new JTextField composed of text s with a default number of columns.

JTextField(String s, **int** n)

Constructs a new JTextField composed of text s using n columns.

void addActionListener(ActionListener l)

Makes listener l one the action listeners of this JTextField.

protected void configurePropertiesFromAction(Action a)

Sets a as the action event properties for this JTextField.

protected PropertyChangeListener
  createActionPropertyChangeListener(Action a)

Creates and returns the property change listener that updates the ActionEvent source as action properties change for this JTextField.

protected Document createDefaultModel()

Creates (if necessary) and returns the default document model for this JText-Field.

protected void fireActionPerformed()

Invokes the actionPerformed() method of all listeners of this JTextField.

AccessibleContext getAccessibleContext()

Returns the accessibility context of this object.

Action getAction()

Returns the currently set action for the ActionEvent source for this JText-Field.

ActionListener[] getActionListeners()

Returns the action listeners of this JTextField.

Action[] getActions()

Returns the command list for the editor of this JTextField.

int getColumns()

Returns the number of columns in this JTextField.

protected int getColumnWidth()

Returns the column width of this JTextField.

int getHorizontalAlignment()

Returns the horizontal alignment policy of this JTextField.

BoundedRangeModel getHorizontalVisibility()

Returns the visibility of this JTextField.

Dimension getPreferredSize()

Returns the preferred size of this JTextField.

int getScrollOffset()

Returns the pixel scroll offset of this JTextField.

String getUIClassID()

Returns the name of the look and feel that renders this object.

boolean isValidateRoot()

If this JTextField is within a JViewport, the method returns **false**; otherwise, the method returns **true**.

protected String paramString()

Returns a representation of this object.

void postActionEvent()

Invokes the action listeners of this JTextField.

```
void removeActionListener(ActionListener a)
```
Removes listener l as action listener of this JTextField.
```
void scrollRectToVisible(Rectangle r)
```
Scrolls rectangular region r of this JTextField.
```
void setAction(Action a)
```
Sets a as the action for the ActionEvent source of this JTextField.
```
void setActionCommand(String s)
```
Sets s as the action command string for this JTextField.
```
void setColumns(int c)
```
Sets c as the number of columns in this JTextField.
```
void setDocument(Document d)
```
Sets d as the document editor of for this JTextField.
```
void setFont(Font f)
```
Sets f as the current font for this JTextField.
```
void setHorizontalAlignment(int i)
```
Sets h as the horizontal alignment policy for this JTextField.
```
void setScrollOffset(int i)
```
Sets i as the scroll pixel offset of this JTextField.

| swing | **class** JTextPane **extends** JEditorPane |

PURPOSE

Represent a text component that can be marked up graphically.

CONSTRUCTOR SUMMARY
```
JTextPane()
```
Constructs a new of default document style.
```
JTextPane(StyledDocument s)
```
Constructs a new JTextPane of document type s.

INSTANCE METHOD SUMMARY
```
Style addStyle(String s, Style p)
```
Adds style s into the document hierarchy of this JTextPane with p as its parent.
```
protected EditorKit createDefaultEditorKit()
```
Creates and returns the default editor kit of this JTextPane.
```
AttributeSet getCharacterAttributes()
```
Returns the character attributes in effect at the current location of the caret in this JTextPane.
```
MutableAttributeSet getInputAttributes()
```
Returns the input attributes of this JTextPane.
```
Style getLogicalStyle()
```
Returns the style in effect at the current caret position of this JTextPane.
```
AttributeSet getParagraphAttributes()
```
Returns the attributes in effect at the current caret position of this JTextPane.
```
Style getStyle(String s)
```
Returns the style with name s for this JTextPane.

StyledDocument getStyledDocument()

Returns the editor model of this JTextPane.

protected StyledEditorKit getStyledEditorKit()

Returns the editor kit for this JTextPane.

String getUIClassID()

Returns the class ID for the UI for this JTextPane.

void insertComponent(Component c)

Replaces the currently selected content with component c in this JTextPane.

void insertIcon(Icon i)

Replaces the currently selected content with icon i in this JTextPane.

protected String paramString()

Returns a representation of this object.

void removeStyle(String s)

Removes the style with name s for this JTextPane.

void replaceSelection(String s)

Replaces the currently selected content with s in this JTextPane.

void setCharacterAttributes(AttributeSet a, **boolean** b)

Applies attribute set a to the currently selected text. If b is **true**, then existing attributes are reset first.

void setDocument(Document d)

Sets d as the document editor of this JTextPane.

void setEditorKit(EditorKit e)

Sets e as the editor kit for this JTextPane.

void setLogicalStyle(Style s)

Sets s as the logical style at the current caret position for this JTextPane.

void setParagraphAttributes(AttributeSet a, **boolean** b)

Applies attribute set a to the currently selected paragraphs. If b is **true**, then existing attributes are reset first.

void setStyledDocument(StyledDocument d)

Sets d as the document editor of this JTextPane.

---

swing   **class** JToggleButton **extends** AbstractButton **implements** Accessible

PURPOSE

Represents a two-state button whose label can consist of text and an image.

CONSTRUCTOR SUMMARY

JToggleButton()

Constructs a new unset JToggleButton with no text or image.

JToggleButton(Action a)

Constructs a new unset JToggleButton. The settings of the button depends on a.

JToggleButton(Icon i)

Constructs a new unset JToggleButton with no text but image i.

JToggleButton(Icon i, **boolean** b)

> Constructs a new JToggleButton with no text and image i. The setting of the button depends on b.

JToggleButton(String s)

> Constructs a new unset JToggleButton with text s and no image.

JToggleButton(String s, **boolean** b)

> Constructs a new JToggleButton with text s and no image. The setting of the button depends on b.

JToggleButton(String s, Icon i)

> Constructs a new unset JToggleButton with text s and image i.

JToggleButton(String s, Icon i, **boolean** b)

> Constructs a new JToggleButton with text s and image i. The setting of the button depends on b

INSTANCE METHOD SUMMARY

AccessibleContext getAccessibleContext()

> Returns the accessibility context of this object.

String getUIClassID()

> Returns the name of the look and feel that renders this object.

protected String paramString()

> Returns a representation of this object.

void updateUI()

> Resets the UI attribute of this object to the current look and feel.

Index